The Global Trading System

Kym Anderson is Professor of Economics and Executive Director of the Centre for International Economic Studies at the University of Adelaide, Australia. He was a WTO Dispute Settlement Panelist during 1996–2000.

Bernard Hoekman leads the International Trade Group at the World Bank in Washington, DC.

The editors worked together in the Economic Research and Analysis Division of the GATT Secretariat in Geneva during the latter years of the Uruguay Round. Both have authored and edited several books on trade policy and the global trading system.

Tauris Guides to Global Economic Issues

International Debt
S.E. Corbridge
ISBN 1 86064 274 8

The Global Trading System
K. Anderson and B. Hoekman
ISBN 1 86064 058 3

Global Transport Issues
R. Tolley and B. Turton
ISBN 1 86064 564 X

The Global Trading System

Edited by

Kym Anderson

Professor of Economics and Director, Centre for International Economic Studies, University of Adelaide

and

Bernard Hoekman

Senior Economist, International Trade Group, World Bank

Volume 4:
'New' issues for the WTO

I.B.Tauris *Publishers*

LONDON • NEW YORK

Published in 2002 by I.B.Tauris & Co. Ltd
6 Salem Road, London W2 4BU
175 Fifth Avenue, New York NY 10010

In the United States of America and in Canada distributed by
St Martin's Press, 175 Fifth Avenue, New York NY 10010

A full CIP record for this book is available from the British Library
A full CIP record for this book is available from the Library of Congress

ISBN 1 86064 058 3

Library of Congress catalog card number: available

Typeset by I.T.S., Edinburgh
Printed and bound in Great Britain by MPG Books Ltd, Bodmin, Cornwall

Contents

INTRODUCTION TO VOLUME 4: 'NEW' ISSUES FOR THE WTO

Kym Anderson and Bernard Hoekman

Trading has been going on ever since humankind began seeking to improve well-being. It involves exchanging either endowments or the goods and services produced with them, including through specialization in production: between individuals within households or tribes, between households or tribes located within walking distance of each other, between rural and urban areas within nation states, between nation states and, for more than half a millennium, between continents. The Silk Road provided the first major inter-continental trade link, between Europe and Asia, but it was not until the expeditions of European mariners to the Americas, the Far East and Australasia from the middle of the past millennium that truly global trade began.

Anyone familiar with the history of international trade prior to the mid-twentieth century is acutely aware of its unruliness. Indeed it often took a war between nations before leaders would get together to develop a trade agreement. Even then it would typically be a limited bilateral agreement which, if it hurt other economies, could exacerbate tensions elsewhere. The recent popular history of the spice trade from 1553 to 1667 by Milton (1999) is a reminder of the brutal lawlessness with which international trade was conducted in centuries past. Certainly trade relations were relatively tranquil in the five decades to World War I, but they became unruly again in the interwar period.

When viewed from this historical perspective, the development of the modern global trading system since World War II has been both extremely rapid and far more successful than its planners dared hope for. The modern, legally binding, rules-based global trading system originated with the 1947 General Agreement on Tariffs and Trade (GATT). This was encapsulated in the World Trade Organization (WTO) that came into being in 1995 following the successful completion of the Uruguay Round of multilateral trade negotiations. Over that half-century international trade rose rapidly: more than one-fifth of global output is now exported, double the proportion of the 1950s. The GATT was a major contributor to that growth, as it proved to be a powerful vehicle through which nations were able to overcome domestic resistance to trade liberalization. GATT rules outlawing quantitative restrictions on trade, and successive GATT rounds of negotiations that resulted in cuts in bound tariffs on imports of manufactures by industrial countries led to tariffs coming down to 'nuisance' levels for many products. Manufacturing tariffs of OECD countries now average less than 4 per cent, compared with more than 40 per cent when the GATT was first signed in

1947 by the original 23 contracting parties (who at that time accounted for four-fifths of world trade). That membership, incidentally, has since grown to more than 140, with another 30 in the process of joining. Once the largest traders in that latter group accede, which include China and Taiwan (whose accession is imminent), as well as Russia, the WTO membership will account for more than 95 per cent of global international trade.

Appreciating the differences between the trading environment pre-GATT and today's system is an essential precursor to evaluating the latter. The GATT and now the WTO provide not only a set of multilateral rules and disciplines but also a forum to negotiate tariff reductions and rules changes, plus a legal mechanism to settle trade disputes that is recognized as an integral part of the world's body of international law. The WTO has added three other contributions to those of the earlier GATT: to monitor and report on trade and trade-related policy developments on a regular basis, thereby adding to policy transparency; to facilitate the fuller integration of developing and transition economies into the global trading system; and to improve cohesion between the WTO and other international economic agencies such as the World Bank and International Monetary Fund.

Superior though it is, the current system nonetheless still has plenty of room for improvement. Indeed much attention has been directed in recent years at its shortcomings. Among the issues that have focused attention are globalization, regional integration, noisy trade disputes across the North Atlantic and elsewhere, a perception by some that the system is unfair to developing countries, linkages between trade and other policy areas such as foreign investment or competition policy, and concerns about possible adverse impacts of trade on such things as inequality, poverty, the environment, labour standards, and food safety and security. These concerns were voiced loudly at the third WTO trade ministerial meeting in Seattle in late 1999, contributing to the postponing of the first comprehensive round of multilateral trade negotiations under WTO auspices.

There is thus a need for more-accessible information, knowledge and understanding of what the global trading system is about, how it evolved, how it works, why the world needs it, and what more it can, should, or should not try to do to make the world a more peaceful and prosperous place. These needs were accentuated at Seattle (and subsequently at other economic meetings of world leaders) where it was clear that many of the protesting groups knew little about the WTO and the workings of the rules-based global trading system, nor about what the world might be like without that institution and its rules and procedures.

There are a number of books on the GATT/WTO rules-based global trading system that are readily available.[1] The present set of readings is designed to complement those books with less-readily available journal articles and chapters from edited volumes. They come from the core trade disciplines of economics, law, and political science, but with an emphasis on the editors' profession of economics.[2] Our objective was to collect papers that have been cited often, provide a pertinent historical perspective, and/or address current and future issues that confront the trading system. Because of space constraints, quantitative ex ante and ex post assessments of the economic effects of trade reforms are explicitly excluded.[3] The selection is based on responses to a survey of around one hundred of our colleagues, whom we sincerely thank (with apologies for not being able to include more of their papers!). We also thank the original publishers of the included papers for permission to reproduce them in this collection. A list of the full set of papers in the four volumes, together with their original source, is provided in the Acknowledgements.

The present four-volume set has been prepared around the following topics: the genesis of the GATT; the rules and procedures embodied in the GATT (and, since its inception in 1995, the General Agreement on Trade in Services, or GATS); the exceptions to those rules; and the 'new' issues that confront the WTO membership in the twenty-first century as internationalization progresses further (the lowering of the transactions costs of doing business across national borders). Within each of the four volumes the readings appear in alphabetical order, since that makes them easier to find than if they were ordered chronologically or by sub-topics.

The rest of this chapter provides an introduction to the readings in the current volume, which cover 'new' issues for the WTO. The word new is in inverted commas because several of the issues discussed here have been around for some time. (Also, trade in services is a new addition to GATT but it is included in Volume 3 as one of the product-coverage exceptions to the GATT.) All of these are more 'trade-related' than direct trade issues. Foreign investment laws and competition policies clearly affect trade and the international competitiveness of firms in major ways. Laws concerning intellectual property rights may not appear to be closely tied to trade but they are becoming increasingly important as the digital revolution transforms the information and R&D (especially biotechnology) industries. And there is a whole swathe of other 'trade and . . .' issues that have to do with the fairness of trade, national sovereignty and international externalities. The most prominent of these have to do with environmental and labour standards but the list includes food safety and animal welfare standards and even human rights. The readings in this volume touch on the most prominent of these as of the start of the twenty-first century.

FOREIGN INVESTMENT

For a range of reasons, trade in capital (for that is what foreign investment is) attracts much more attention by governments than does trade in goods and services. For most of the post-war period, capital flows have tended to be subject to considerable government control. Consistent with that, attempts to bring multilateral rules-based disciplines to foreign investment have faced severe difficulties. Yet because trade in products, protection policies, and foreign investment flows are co-determinants of the international location of production, restricting the latter nonetheless impacts on product trade and thereby factor prices. Reading 9 by McCulloch and Owen, which was written in the early 1980s before the rash of unilateral liberalization of foreign investment (both direct and portfolio) and of markets for currencies and securities, remains pertinent. It looks at how and why countries regulate foreign direct investment (FDI). Much of the justification for government regulation of multinationals ostensibly has to do with perceived externalities. However, protectionism and nationalism are also part of the reason for intervention, and in so far as the externality arguments apply to any large firm, regardless of whether it is foreign owned, they belong in the competition policy box (see next section).

Reading 9 also provides a post-Tokyo Round perspective on foreign investment issues and the GATT. It begins by pointing out that multilateral negotiations over investment principles differ from those over trade rules because all countries export and import products whereas only a subset of countries export capital and the non-exporters tend to be mostly developing countries. Thus even though investment rules may be justified on efficiency grounds, they have been perceived by some developing countries as potentially eroding part of their hard-won national sovereignty. Indeed developed countries also have expressed that concern in the past. The US Senate's dissatisfaction with the investment provision in the original charter for the International Trade Organization played an important part in the Senate's failure to ratify the ITO charter.

The extent of foreign investment both absolutely and relative to the extent of product trade was far greater in the late 1990s than in the early 1980s. As well, bilateral investment treaties have proliferated, with a four-fold increase over the 1990s to no less than 1,600. Yet government regulation of foreign investment has far from disappeared, so the question remains as to whether a multilateral agreement on foreign investment is worth pursuing and, if so, whether the WTO is the appropriate forum to pursue it.

At first sight there seems to be a compelling case for the WTO to take this issue on board. However, numerous authors (e.g. Hoekman and Saggi, 2000) argue against such a course at this time. They would prefer instead that such negotiating effort be concentrated on liberalizing the FDI mode of supply of services that is built in already to the WTO's General Agreement on Trade in Services (GATS) where enormous scope for liberalization remains. That, together with reductions in barriers to product trade that induce globally inefficient FDI (including through regional integrations agreements), would bring much of the gains that could come from a multilateral investment agreement. And it would do so without involving the huge negotiating effort (witness the failure of OECD countries to come to a plurilateral agreement on investment in the mid-1990s) that would be needed to add this issue to the agenda of the next comprehensive round of WTO negotiations. Moreover, the bringing of FDI into the WTO may only be possible by bringing with it such issues as environmental and labour standards that – as discussed below – could open a Pandora's box of 'fair trade' concerns that undermine the WTO's prime purpose of liberalizing trade.

COMPETITION POLICIES

Competition policies, as with investment, were part of the charter of the still-born ITO. The issue did not go away, however, as it was taken up in the early 1950s by an ad hoc committee under the UN's Economic and Social Council. That too failed in its attempt to provide an international body for the control of restrictive business practices (RBPs). The issue was revived by developing countries via UNCTAD in its 1972 planning conference, where RBPs (including in the international transfer of technology) were linked explicitly with the activities of multinational corporations. That linkage complicated the matter, but by 1980 a set of global anti-trust principles was at least endorsed by the UN General Assembly. Reading 5 by Davidow examines the texts that were negotiated and concludes that while they were not expected to be codified into international law, the mere existence of the principles serves at least as a deterrent to the most anti-competitive of practices.

Likewise, the OECD over many years developed 'codes of conduct' concerning restrictive business practices but they too are not legally enforceable. The relevant question in the post-Uruguay Round is similar to that relating to foreign investment, namely, is there a case for seeking to negotiate a multilateral agreement on trade-related anti-trust principles (TRAPs) and, if so, is the WTO the best forum for that negotiation?

Reading 8 by Hoekman examines this question. It evaluates the various options that have been put forward and discusses their feasibility. It points out that there is no clear North-South divide on any of the possible TRAPs options considered, and that the scope for agreement on common substantive norms for competition law is quite limited. The one option that in principle should simultaneously improve market access, enhance economic welfare and strengthen the global trading system is the introduction of anti-trust criteria into anti-dumping (assuming anti-dumping cannot be outlawed in the foreseeable future). As with the investment issue though, much can be done to improve competition simply by pursuing the WTO's traditional goal of reducing governmental barriers to product trade, especially of services.

INTELLECTUAL PROPERTY RIGHTS

The issue of trade-related intellectual property rights is not 'new', in the sense that it is already part of the WTO mainstream as a consequence of the TRIPs agreement that was negotiated during the Uruguay Round. Its 'newness' relates to the fact that it is at odds with the rest of the WTO's activities in that it sanctions monopolistic activities. Specifically, the TRIPs agreement seeks to extend intellectual property rights beyond the country of origin of the IP to the rest of the world. Since intellectual property is produced mostly in developed countries, and yet it can be of great value to developing countries, this issue has a clear North-South dimension. Those producing it believe it is only fair that they be able to capture some of the rewards of their creative endeavour (without which there would be less incentive for technology to advance), while those wishing to make use of the IP would like to be charged little more than the marginal cost of access to it, which may be close to zero.

The readings included in this volume focus on just one type of intellectual property, namely patents, but the principles involved are similar for other forms of industrial property rights such as trademarks, registered designs and lay-outs of integrated circuits. TRIPs also covers copyright and, in agriculture, plant variety rights, geographical indications, and traditional expressions. Reading 6 by Deardorff exposes the contentious economic welfare implications of the patent issue from the viewpoint of economic theory, while reading 10 by Nogues focuses on how this applies in the case of pharmaceutical drugs – a case that upsets those concerned for the health of the world's poorer people in developing countries. Nogues shows that, over time, three forces have combined to encourage pharmaceutical drug companies to seek (and, through the TRIPs agreement, obtain) improved conditions of access to developing countries' markets. One is the erosion of effective patent protection in industrial countries because of increasing government regulations. The second is the growth in competition from generic drug companies. And the third is the rapid growth in the potential market in developing countries.

Deardorff's analysis is important because it shows that extending patent protection globally not only transfers welfare from importing to producing countries (relative to a situation where that IP is being used without payment of royalties) but may also reduce global economic welfare. This could happen if the gains to the IP producers are more than outweighed by the consumer losses as the number of consuming countries now having to pay royalties is enlarged. It needs to be kept in mind that this result depends on two important empirical matters. One is the extent to which the extension of patent protection stimulates the generation of more IP: the greater this dynamic effect on R&D activities, the more likely TRIPs will boost global welfare. The other empirical issue is the extent to which developing countries had access to the IP prior to the TRIPs agreement: if they were to otherwise have no such access, then they have nothing to lose (and potentially a lot to gain) from the extension of patent protection to their shores. Moreover, the improvement of IP law in developing countries, as required under the TRIPs agreement, also has the potential to boost domestic IP generation, adding further to their potential welfare gains from that agreement.

FAIR TRADE, RECIPROCITY AND HARMONIZATION OF STANDARDS

Perhaps the greatest challenge for the WTO in the new millennium is the resurgence of popular belief that liberal trade is not 'fair'. Import-competing producers make this claim whenever they perceive conditions of competition abroad to be laxer than at home. For example, if environmental or labour standards are lower abroad, the costs of production of foreign competitors will be lower than if those producers were required to meet the stricter standards of the home country. Yet requiring other countries to meet the home country's high standards would be considered by those other countries as an infringement of their national sovereignty. These competitiveness and sovereignty concerns, which are opposite sides of the same coin, are growing in importance as traditional barriers to trade fall. The declines in transactions costs of doing business across national borders include cuts to not just import tariffs but also costs of transport and especially communications, thanks to the digital revolution.

In reading 2 Bhagwati puts this fair 'trade' issue in historical perspective. He suggests there have been seven episodes over the past two centuries when the doctrine of free trade has been challenged. The first six all relate to market failure, whereas the seventh and current challenge poses a novel and more complex threat. It focuses not so much on other countries' trade barriers (for the WTO already has the main framework in place to discipline them), but rather on their domestic government policies that affect producer incentives abroad. That implies deeper economic integration which, in the absence of the WTO delivering to date, is something that has been sought within regional economic integration agreements during the 1990s. That is an easier task not least because there are typically more similarities between countries in a small group than in the much broader WTO membership. The question is: to what extent should the WTO move down this deeper integration track and, if so, how?

In reading 13 Tussie points to the two obvious choices in terms of how: harmonization of domestic policies and standards (but which ones?), or mutual recognition of existing measures notwithstanding their differences. Upward harmonization has already begun to creep into the trading system from the viewpoint of many developing countries, for example in the form of Uruguay Round's TRIPs agreement and in its two standards agreements (on technical barriers to trade, and on sanitary and phytosanitary (SPS) measures affecting farm products). That upward creep is often considered an affront on the national sovereignty of developing countries.

National sovereignty concerns are also raised by high-standards countries. The European Union, for example, has been fighting for years for the right to continue to uphold a higher standard than the United States in the food safety area. Its insistence on banning sales of beef from cattle that were fed growth hormones has not yet been able to be justified on scientific grounds as being necessary for human health, as required under the WTO's SPS agreement. Believing that the measure was more to protect European farmers from import competition than consumers' health, the case was brought by the USA and Canada to the WTO dispute settlement body, which ruled against the EU. The EU has sought time to come up with additional scientific evidence but meanwhile has had trade sanctions applied on an equivalent value of EU exports to North America. Sykes makes the argument in reading 12 that the WTO rules outlawing regulatory protectionism make sense from a political economy viewpoint. Yet scientific uncertainty surrounding emotional issues such as food safety raise golden opportunities for vested interests to seek regulatory protection under cover of the precautionary principle – and if/when a dispute settlement panel rules against it, WTO is accused of eroding national sovereignty.

National sovereignty concerns also arise over the fair trade/harmonization issue. In countries such as the USA, environmental groups feel that competition from lower-standards countries reduces the willingness of domestic producers to support high standards at home. The latter therefore are willing to go along with the former groups' demands for maintaining or raising domestic standards only if the measures are designed in ways that increase the local firms' competitiveness vis-à-vis foreign firms. The case studies examined in reading 14 by Vogel show that such manipulation can lead to measures that are both inefficient in terms of meeting environmental objectives and trade-restricting. Indeed they were so discriminatory that they led to complaints being filed against the USA in the GATT/WTO dispute settlement body. When those panel reports ruled against the USA, the environmental movement was incensed that an international body could interfere in national policy making in that way – notwithstanding the fact that both the economy and the environment in the USA would have been better off if less trade-restrictive measures that were GATT consistent had been used to address those environmental concerns.

Reading 11 by Palmeter also considers some contentious environmental cases plus a human rights case, all of which involved the WTO dispute settlement body. Palmeter challenges the notion that the WTO is interfering with US national sovereignty in such cases. On the contrary, he sees the USA as having several options under WTO law and it simply chooses the option that maximizes its long-term interests. He also points out that by agreeing, along with all other WTO members, to limit the exercise of its national sovereignty it has contributed significantly to diminishing trade frictions globally and thereby – to return to the theme of the opening paragraph of this Introduction — promoted peace.

The entwining of environmental issues with trade is not only because of competitiveness concerns. Reading 1 by Anderson stresses that there are also genuine concerns about international environmental externalities. The most obvious are physical spillovers that are perceived to be contributing to global environmental problems such as ozone depletion and global warming. Greenhouse gases contribute to climate change regardless of which country they are emitted from. There is thus a concern that if one set of countries seeks to tax or otherwise induce less of these emissions by firms located in their region, the environmental benefits of those measures will be offset insofar as the activities responsible relocate to countries with lower environmental standards. The freer are international trade and investment flows, the less effective will be sub-global regulation and hence the greater the need for international cooperation or coercion. Since countries differ in both their contribution to the environmental problem and in their willingness or capacity to contribute towards its solution, frictions between countries are inevitable.

Is there a parallel claim with respect to labour standards? Many would say no, because there is no physical spillover involved of the global-warming kind. But some people claim to be affected emotionally by and have ethical or humanitarian concerns for activities abroad such as poor working conditions just as much as they do for the felling of tropical forests or the catching of dolphin in tuna fishing nets. Even so, it is argued in reading 1 that neither these nor physical spillovers are reason to entwine the WTO in finding solutions to such environmental or labour problems. Three reasons are given: first, trade policy instruments are not first-best instruments for achieving non-trade objectives (as demonstrated in reading 3); second, civil society groups are likely to be captured by protectionist producer groups; and therefore third, insofar as this leads to an escalation in trade disputes, the global trading system would be undermined. Rather than involving the WTO, attention should turn to multilateral environmental or labour agreements.

Reading 3 by Bhagwati and Srinivasan goes into the issue of ethical preferences in some depth. They believe WTO sanctioning of the use of unilateral government actions to suspend other countries' trading rights unless those other countries adopted the same environment standards would be inappropriate for several reasons: such values are more a result of culture or income level than basic or universal; the larger/more powerful traders could more easily impose their values on smaller/weaker nations; there would be nothing to stop this action proliferating to a wider range of issues beyond environmental or labour standards; and there are alternative, more equitable ways to spread one's values.

Reading 4 by Brown, Deardorff and Stern points out that both ethical and competitiveness concerns with diverse labour standards date back nearly two centuries. In the mid-nineteenth century it was taken as given that liberal trade should not be interfered with and moral suasion and international agreements were seen as the appropriate way to deal with differences in labour standards. The creation of the International Labour Office following World War I made this potentially possible. However, the problem remains that it lacks significant enforcement power (as do multilateral environmental agreements often), which is partly why protagonists for higher standards want these issues integrated into the WTO: to enable the use of trade sanctions.

Brown, Deardorff and Stern also explore whether it is in a country's economic interest to adopt common labour standards internationally. They demonstrate that if labour standards are desired to overcome some domestic market failure, they should be introduced unilaterally. Insofar as those market failures differ across countries we would not expect identical standards, and harmonization of them internationally would be welfare-reducing. Nor is it reasonable to characterize as 'unfair' the trade that results from those differences as long as they are consistent with efficient resource use in the course of correcting for differing market failures (and do not introduce inequities such as slave labour). Finally, they show reasonable conditions under which the imposition of high standards on developing countries could worsen economic welfare in rich countries and raise economic welfare in developing countries, contrary to what one might assume from the stances taken by the two country groups in international fora.

If people in the advanced economies really do care about the poor labour conditions in developing countries, a much more effective solution than seeking higher labour standards there is to allow workers from such countries to migrate to higher-standard countries. Economic history shows that this is a powerful force for convergence in living standards (see reading 15 by Williamson). Reading 7 by Hamilton and Whalley shows that liberalization of movement of labor would raise global economic welfare enormously. In the context of the WTO, labor movement discussions are part and parcel of the GATS, since the movement of service suppliers is a major mode of supplying services internationally. Barriers to liberalization of such movement, even if temporary, are great. History also warns us that large movements of labor can generate serious backlashes, and may increase opposition to globalization, although Williamson downplays the relevance of the experience at the turn of the previous century for today. Nonetheless, the point has not gone unnoticed by developing country members of the WTO, who are seeking to place liberalization of the movement of service providers ('natural persons') high on the agenda of the second round of GATS negotiations, which were launched in early 2000. That pressure will be greater the less developed countries open their markets to the goods such workers can best supply from their developing country base, most notably farm and textile products.

NOTES

1. See, for example, Diebold (1952), Curzon (1965), Jackson (1969, 1997), Dam (1970), Hudec (1975, 1987, 1993), Tumlir (1985), Winham (1992), Davey, Jackson and Sykes (1995), Hoekman and Kostecki (2001), and Trebilcock and Howse (1999). A new one by economic theorists is due shortly (Bagwell and Staiger, 2002). The legal texts of the GATT/WTO rules are collected in WTO (1995a), while GATT legal case history is summarized in WTO (1995b). Detailed negotiating histories of the Uruguay Round can be found in Stewart (1993, 1999) and Croome (1998).
2. A lawyer's collection is available in Howse (1997).
3. See, for example, Deardorff and Stern (1981) on the Tokyo Round and Martin and Winters (1996) on the Uruguay Round of GATT negotiations.

REFERENCES

BAGWELL, KYLE AND ROBERT W. STAIGER (2002), *The Economics of the World Trading System*, Cambridge, Massachussetts: MIT Press (forthcoming).

CROOME, JOHN (1998), *Reshaping the World Trading System: A History of the Uruguay Round* (revised edition), Geneva: World Trade Organization.

CURZON, GERARD (1965), *Multilateral Commercial Diplomacy*, London: Michael Joseph.

DAM, KENNETH W. (1970), *The GATT: Law and International Economic Relations*, Chicago: University of Chicago Press.

DAVEY, WILLIAM, JOHN H. JACKSON AND ALAN SYKES (1995), *Legal Problems of International Economic Relations*, St. Paul: West Publishing Co.

DEARDORFF, ALLAN V. AND ROBERT STERN (1981), 'A Disaggregated Model of World Production and Trade: An Estimate of the Impact of the Tokyo Round', *Journal of Policy Modeling* 3(2): 127–52.

HOEKMAN, BERNARD AND KAMAL SAGGI (2000), 'Assessing the Case for Extending WTO Disciplines on Investment-Related Policies', *Journal of Economic Integration* 15(4): 629–53.

HOEKMAN, BERNARD AND MICHEL KOSTECKI (2001), *The Political Economy of the World Trading System: The WTO and Beyond*, London and New York: Oxford University Press.

HOWSE, ROBERT (ed.) (1997), *The World Trading System* (4 vols of readings), London: Routledge.

HUDEC, ROBERT E. (1975), *The GATT Legal System and World Trade Diplomacy (2nd edition)*, Salem, New Hampshire: Butterworth.

HUDEC, ROBERT E. (1987), *GATT and the Developing Countries*, Aldershot: Gower for the Trade Policy Research Centre.

HUDEC, ROBERT E. (1993), *Enforcing International Trade Law: The Evolution of the Modern GATT Legal System*, Salem, New Hampshire: Butterworth.

JACKSON, JOHN H. (1969), *World Trade and the Law of GATT*, Indianapolis, Indiana: Bobbs-Merrill.

JACKSON, JOHN H. (1997), *The World Trading System: Law and Policy of International Economic Relations (2nd edition)*, Cambridge, Massachussetts: MIT Press.

MARTIN, WILL AND L. ALAN WINTERS (eds.) (1996), *The Uruguay Round and the Developing Countries*, Cambridge and New York: Cambridge University Press.

MILTON, GILES (1999), *Nathaniel's Nutmeg*, London: Sceptre (Hodder and Stoughton).

STEWART, TERENCE (1993), *The GATT Uruguay Round, A Negotiating History (1986–1992)*, Volumes I to III.

STEWART, TERENCE (1999), *The GATT Uruguay Round, A Negotiating History (1986–1992)*, Volume IV.

TREBILCOCK, MICHAEL J. AND ROBERT HOWSE (1999), *The Regulation of International Trade (2nd edition)*, London and New York: Routledge.
TUMLIR, JAN (1985), *Protectionism: Trade Policy in Democratic Societies*, Washington D.C.: American Enterprise Institute.
WINHAM, GILBERT R. (1992), *The Evolution of International Trade Agreements*, Toronto: University of Toronto Press.
WTO (1995a), *The Results of the Uruguay Round of Multilateral Trade Negotiations: The Legal Texts*, Geneva: World Trade Organization.
WTO (1995b), *Analytical Index: Guide to GATT Law and Practice*, Vols. I and II, Geneva: World Trade Organization.

Acknowledgements

The publishers and editors are grateful for permission to use copyright material.

VOLUME 1: GENESIS OF THE GATT

1. Bagwell, Kyle and Robert W. Staiger (1999), 'An Economic Theory of GATT', *American Economic Review* 89(1): 215–48, March. Nashville, Tennessee: American Economic Association
2. Corden, W. Max (1987), 'On Making Rules for the International Trading System', Ch. 10 in Robert Stern (ed.), *U.S. Trade Policies in a Changing World Economy*, pp. 413–26. Cambridge, Massachusetts: MIT Press.
3. Deardorff, Alan V. (1996), 'An Economist's Overview of the World Trade Organization', in Gordon Flake and Florence Myeong-Hwa Lowe-Lee (eds), *The Emerging WTO System and Perspectives From East Asia*, Washington, D.C.: Korea Economic Institute of America.
4. Diebold, William, Jr. (1952), *The End of the ITO*, Essays in International Finance No. 16, pp.1–37. Princeton, New Jersey: International Finance Section, Department of Economics and Social Institutions, Princeton University Press.
5. Eichengreen, Barry and Marc Uzan (1993), 'The 1933 World Economic Conference as an Instance of Failed International Cooperation', Ch. 6 in Peter Evans, Harold Jacobson and Robert Putnam (eds), *Double-Edged Diplomacy: International Bargaining and Domestic Politics,* pp. 171–206. Berkeley: University of California Press.
6. Finger, J. Michael (1991), 'The GATT as an International Discipline Over Trade Restrictions: A Public Choice Approach', Ch. 7 in Roland Vaubel and Thomas Willett (eds), *The Political Economy of International Organizations: A Public Choice Approach*, pp. 125–41. Boulder, Colorado: Westview Press.
7. Goldstein, Judith (1993), 'Creating the GATT Rules: Politics, Institutions and American Policy', Ch. 6 in J. Ruggie (ed.), *Multilateralism Matters: The Theory and Praxis of an Institutional Form*, pp.201–32. New York: Columbia University Press.
8. Hungerford, Thomas L. (1991), 'GATT: A Cooperative Equilibrium in a Noncooperative Trading Regime?' *Journal of International Economics* 31: 357–69. Elsevier Science Publishers.

9. Irwin, Douglas A. (1993), 'Multilateral and Bilateral Trade Policies in the World Trading System: An Historical Perspective', Ch. 4 in Jaime De Melo and Arvind Panagariya (eds), *New Dimensions in Regional Integration*, pp.90–119. Cambridge and New York: Cambridge University Press.
10. Irwin, Douglas A. (1995), 'The GATT in Historical Perspective', *American Economic Review* 85(2): 323–8, May. Nashville, Tennessee: American Economic Association.
11. Johnson, Harry G. (1965), 'An Economic Theory of Protectionism, Tariff Bargaining and the Formation of Customs Unions', *Journal of Political Economy* 73(3): 256–83, June. Chicago: University of Chicago Press.
12. Kindleberger, Charles P. (1951), 'Group Behaviour and International Trade', *Journal of Political Economy* 59(1): 30–46, February. Chicago: University of Chicago Press.
13. Kindleberger, Charles P. (1989), 'Commercial Policy Between the Wars', Ch. 2 in Peter Mathias and Sidney Pollard (eds), *The Cambridge Economic History of Europe, Vol. 8*, pp. 161–96. Cambridge: Cambridge University Press.
14. Meade, James (1942), 'A Proposal for an International Commercial Union', British War Cabinet paper reproduced in *The World Economy* 10: 399–407, 1987, and in Susan Meade (ed.), *The Collected Papers of James Meade, Volume III: International Economics*, London: Unwin Hyman, 1988.
15. Staiger, Robert and Guido Tabellini (1999), 'Do GATT Rules Help Governments Make Domestic Commitments?' *Economics and Politics* 11(2): 109–44, July. Oxford: Blackwell.
16. United States Tariff Commission (1919), *Reciprocity and Commercial Treaties*, pp.17–48 & 9–14. Washington, D.C.: Government Printing Office.
17. Viner, Jacob (1924), "The Most-Favored-Nation Clause in American Commercial Treaties', *Journal of Political Economy* 32(1), February, pp.17–39. University of Chicago Press. (Reprinted as Ch. 1 in his *International Economics: Studies by Jacob Viner*, Glencoe, Illinois: The Free Press.)

VOLUME 2: CORE RULES AND PROCEDURES

1. Baldwin, Robert (1986), 'Toward More Efficient Procedures for Multilateral Trade Negotiations', *Aussenwirtschaft* 41: 379–94. *The Swiss Review of International Economic Relations.* Swiss Institute for Research in International Economics, University of St Gallen, Switzerland.
2. Baldwin, Robert E. and Richard N. Clarke (1988), 'Game-Modeling Multilateral Trade Negotiations', *Journal of Policy Modeling* 9: 257–84. Elsevier.© Society for Policy Modeling 1987.
3. Caplin, A. and Karla Krishna (1988), 'Tariffs and the Most-Favored-Nation Clause: A Game Theoretic Approach', *Seoul Journal of Economics* 1(3): 267–89.
4. Conybeare, H.A.C. (1988), 'Managing International Trade Conflicts: Explanations and Prescription', *Journal of International Affairs* 42(1): 75–91.© Trustees of Columbia University in the City of New York.

5. Finger, J. Michael (1974), 'GATT Tariff Concessions and the Exports of Developing Countries – United States Concessions at the Dillon Round', *Economic Journal* 84(335): 566–75, September. Oxford: Blackwell.
6. Hillman, Arye and Peter Moser (1995), 'Trade Liberalization as Politically Optimal Exchange of Market Access', in M. Canzoneri, Wilfred Ethier and Vittorio Grilli (eds), *The New Transatlantic Economy*, Cambridge and New York: Cambridge University Press.
7. Jackson, John H. (1998), 'Designing and Implementing Effective Dispute Settlement Procedures: WTO Dispute Settlement, Appraisal and Prospects', Ch. 5 in Anne O. Krueger (ed.), *The WTO as an International Organization*, pp.161–80. Chicago: University of Chicago Press.
8. Kovenock, Dan and Marie Thursby (1992), 'GATT, Dispute Settlement and Cooperation', *Economics and Politics* 4(2): 151–70, July. Oxford: Blackwell.
9. Laird, Sam (1999), 'The WTO's Trade Policy Review Mechanism – From Through the Looking Glass', *The World Economy* 22(6): 741–64, August. Oxford: Blackwell.
10. Ludema, Rodney D. (1991), 'International Trade Bargaining and the Most-Favored-Nation Clause', *Economics and Politics* 3(1): 1–20, March. Oxford: Blackwell.
11. McMillan, John (1989), 'A Game-Theoretic View of International Trade Negotiations: Implications for the Developing Countries', Ch. 2 in John Whalley (ed.), *Rules, Power and Credibility*, pp. 26–44. London: University of Western Ontario.
12. Rhodes, Carolyn (1989), 'Reciprocity in Trade: The Utility of a Bargaining Strategy', *International Organization* 43(2): 273–99. ©1989 World Peace Foundation and the Massachusetts Institute of Technology.
13. Schwartz, Warren F. and Alan O. Sykes (1996), 'Toward a Positive Theory of the Most-Favored-Nation Obligation and Its Exceptions in the WTO/GATT System', *International Review of Law and Economics* 16(1): 27–51, March. Elsevier Science.
14. Stern, Robert M. (1976), 'Evaluating Alternative Formulae for Reducing Industrial Tariffs', *Journal of World Trade Law* 10(1): 50–64.
15. Viner, Jacob (1931), 'The Most-Favored-Nation Clause', *Index 6*, pp.94–108. Stockholm: Svenska Handelsbanken, January. (Reprinted as Ch. 5 in his *International Economics: Studies by Jacob Viner*, Glencoe IL: The Free Press.)
16. Winters, L. Alan (1987), 'Negotiating the Abolition of Non-Tariff Barriers', *Oxford Economic Papers* 39: 465–80. Oxford: Oxford University Press.
17. Winters, L. Alan (1987), 'Reciprocity', Ch. 7 in J. Michael Finger, and Andrzej Olechowski (eds), *The Uruguay Round: A Handbook on the Multilateral Trade Negotiations*, pp. 45–51. Washington, D.C.: The World Bank.
18. Wolf, Martin (1984), 'Two-Edged Sword: Demands of Developing Countries and the Trading System', Ch. 9 in Jagdish Bhagwati and John Gerard Ruggie (eds), *Power, Passions, and Purpose: Prospects for North-South Negotiations*, pp. 201–29. Cambridge, Massachussetts: MIT Press.

VOLUME 3: EXCEPTIONS TO THE CORE RULES

1. Anderson, Kym (2001), 'Bringing Discipline to Agricultural Policy via WTO', Ch. 3 in Bernard Hoekman and Will Martin (eds), *Developing Countries and the WTO: A Pro-active Agenda*, Oxford: Blackwell.
2. Finger, J. Michael (1991), 'Development Economics and the General Agreement on Tariffs and Trade', Ch. 13 in Jaime De Melo and Andre Sapir (eds), *Trade Theory and Economic Reform: North, South, and East: Essays in Honor of Bela Balassa*, pp. 203–23. Oxford: Blackwell.
3. Finger, J. Michael, H. Keith Hall and Douglas R. Nelson (1982), 'The Political Economy of Administered Protection', *American Economic Review* 72(3): 452–66, June. Nashville, Tennessee: American Economic Association.
4. Finger, J. Michael and L. Alan Winters (1998), 'What Can the WTO Do for Developing Countries?' Ch. 14 in Anne O. Krueger (ed.), *The WTO as an International Organization*, pp. 365–93. Chicago: University of Chicago Press.
5. Higgott, Richard A. and Andrew F. Cooper (1990), 'Middle Power Leadership and Coalition Building: Australia, the Cairns Group and the Uruguay Round of Trade Negotiations', *International Organization* 44(4): 589–632, Autumn. ©1990 World Peace Foundation and the Massachusetts Institute of Technology.
6. Hoekman, Bernard (1996), 'Assessing the General Agreement on Trade in Services', Ch. 4 in Will Martin and L. Alan Winters (eds), *The Uruguay Round and the Developing Countries*, pp. 88–123. Cambridge and New York: Cambridge University Press.
7. Ingco, Merlinda D. (1996), 'Tariffication in the Uruguay Round: How Much Liberalisation?' *The World Economy* 19(4): 425–46, July. Oxford: Blackwell.
8. Kahler, Miles and John Odell (1988), 'Developing Country Coalition-Building and International Trade Negotiations', Ch. 8 in John Whalley (ed.), *Rules, Power and Credibility*, pp.149–67. London: University of Western Ontario.
9. Messerlin, Patrick A. (1989), 'The EC Antidumping Regulations: A First Economic Appraisal, 1980–85', *Weltwirtschaftliches Archiv*, 125(3): 563–87.
10. Michalopoulos, Constantine (1999), 'The Developing Countries' Participation in the WTO', *The World Economy*, 22(1): 117–43, January. Oxford: Blackwell.
11. Sampson, Gary and Richard H. Snape (1985), 'Identifying the Issues in Trade in Services', *The World Economy*, 8: 171–81. Oxford: Blackwell.
12. Snape, Richard H. (1991), 'International Regulation of Subsidies', *The World Economy,* 14: 139–64. Oxford: Blackwell.
13. Snape, Richard H. (1992), 'History and Economics of GATT's Article XXIV', Ch. 12 in Kym Anderson and Richard Blackhurst (eds), *Regional Integration and the Global Trading System*, pp.273–91. London: Harvester Wheatsheaf and New York: St Martin's Press.
14. Winters, L. Alan (1998), 'Regionalism versus Multilateralism', in Richard

Baldwin, David Cole, Andre Sapir and Anthony Venables (eds), *Regional Integration*, pp. 1–39. Cambridge and New York: Cambridge University Press.

15. Wolf, Martin (1990), 'How to Cut the Textile Knot: Alternative Paths to Liberalization of the MFA', Ch. 9 in Carl Hamilton (ed.), *Textiles Trade and the Developing Countries: Elimination of the MFA in the 1990s*, pp. 215–37. Washington, D.C.: World Bank.

VOLUME 4: 'NEW' ISSUES FOR THE WTO

1. Anderson, Kym (1998), 'Environmental and Labor Standards: What Role for the WTO?' Ch. 8 in Anne O. Krueger (ed.), *The WTO as an International Organization*, pp. 231–55. Chicago: University of Chicago Press.
2. Bhagwati, Jagdish N. (1994), 'Fair Trade, Reciprocity and Harmonization: The New Challenge to the Theory and Policy of Free Trade', Ch. 13 in Alan V. Deardorff and Robert M. Stern (eds), *Analytical and Negotiating Issues in the Global Trading System*, pp.547–61. Ann Arbor: University of Michigan Press.
3. Bhagwati, Jagdish N. and T.N. Srinivasan (1996), 'Trade and the Environment: Does Environmental Diversity Detract from the Case for Free Trade?' Ch. 4 in Jagdish N. Bhagwati and Robert E. Hudec (eds), *Fair Trade and Harmonization: Prerequisites for Free Trade? Vol. 1: Economic Analysis*, pp. 159–99. Cambridge, Massachusetts: MIT Press.
4. Brown, Drusilla K., Alan V. Deardorff and Robert M. Stern (1996), 'International Labor Standards and Trade: A Theoretical Analysis', Ch. 5 in Jagdish N. Bhagwati and Robert E. Hudec (eds), *Fair Trade and Harmonization: Prerequisites for Free Trade? Vol. 1: Economic Analysis*, pp. 227–80. Cambridge, Massachusetts: MIT Press.
5. Davidow, Joel (1981), 'The Seeking of a World Competition Code: Quixotic Quest?' pp. 361–403 in Oscar Schachter and Robert Hellawell (eds), *Competition in International Business*, New York: Columbia University Press.
6. Deardorff, Alan V. (1992), 'Welfare Effects of Global Patent Protection', *Economica* 59: 35–51, February. Oxford: Blackwell.
7. Hamilton, Bob and John Whalley (1984), 'Efficiency and Distributional Implications of Global Restrictions on Labour Mobility', *Journal of Development Economics* 14: 61–75. Elsevier Science Publishers.
8. Hoekman, Bernard (1997), 'Competition Policy and the Global Trading System', *The World Economy* 20(4): 383–406, July. Oxford: Blackwell.
9. McCulloch, Rachel and Robert Owen (1983), 'Linking Negotiations on Trade and Foreign Direct Investment', Ch. 14 in Charles Kindleberger and David Audretsch (eds), *The Multinational Corporation in the 1980s*, pp. 334–58. Cambridge, Massachusetts: MIT Press.
10. Nogues, Julio (1990), 'Patents and Pharmaceutical Drugs: Understanding the Pressures on Developing Countries', *Journal of World Trade* 24(6): 81–104.

11. PALMETER, DAVID (1999), 'National Sovereignty and the World Trade Organization', *Journal of World Intellectual Property* 2(1): 77–91. Geneva, Switzerland: Werner Publishing Company.
12. SYKES, ALAN O. (1999), 'Regulatory Protectionism and the Law of International Trade', *University of Chicago Law Review* 66(1): 1–46, Winter. ©1999 University of Chicago.
13. TUSSIE, DIANA (1994), 'The Policy Harmonization Debate: What Can Developing Countries Gain From Multilateral Negotiations?' *UNCTAD Review* 5: 1–8. Geneva and New York: United Nations.
14. VOGEL, DAVID (1997), 'Trouble for Us and Trouble for Them: Social Regulations as Trade Barriers', Ch. 3 in Pietro Nivola (ed.), *Comparative Disadvantages: Social Regulations and the Global Economy*, pp. 98–145. Washington, D.C.: Brookings Institution.
15. WILLIAMSON, JEFFREY G. (1998), 'Globalization, Labor Markets and Policy Backlash', *Journal of Economic Perspectives* 12(4): 51–72, Fall. Nashville, Tennessee: American Economic Association.

1. Environmental and Labor Standards: What Role for WTO?

K. Anderson

During the past decade there has been a resurgence of interest in the links between trade and environmental and labor standards. Social standards in poor countries are being questioned by groups in richer countries concerned about resource depletion, environmental degradation, and abuses of human rights in the workplace. Many in developing countries perceive the entwining of these social issues with trade policy as a threat to both their sovereignty and their economies, while significant groups in richer countries consider it unfair, ecologically unsound, even immoral to trade with countries adopting much lower social standards than theirs.

After first summarizing the issues involved, this paper examines why these issues are becoming more prominent, why they are being entwined with trade policy, why this is a concern to liberal traders, and what roles if any the World Trade Organization (as compared with other multilateral fora) should play in providing international rules and other institutional support needed for ensuring adequate environmental and labor standards.

8.1 WHAT ARE THE ISSUES?

Two separable but related sets of issues are involved. One is the concern in high-standard countries that some of their firms suffer a competitive disadvantage because of lower environmental and labor standards abroad. The other has to do with international externalities.

8.1.1 Competitiveness Concerns

We should not be surprised that there are vast differences across countries in environmental policies and labor standards. These policy differences in part are a natural consequence of differences in national incomes: as communities become richer, they increase their demands for all normal goods, including higher environmental and labor standards. Environmental and labor policies differ also because of international differences in tastes and preferences. Indeed, one of the defining historical features of many countries was the bringing together of a group of people whose preferences were more similar to each other than to those of neighboring groups (Alesina and Spolare 1995).

As international economic integration proceeds, pressure increases to reduce differences in domestic policies that have significant trade consequences. This pressure is driven not just by the desire to reduce administrative and conformance costs. More important are concerns in countries with high standards that costs of production for their pollution- or labor-intensive firms are higher than those in countries with lower standards, causing them to be less competitive. Such differences become ever more important as traditional barriers to trade and investment between countries fall (Bhagwati 1996). They lead to claims in the North of eco- or social dumping, and fears in the South of reduced access to their export markets in high-income countries.

In high-standard countries some groups fear a "race to the bottom" as governments compete to attract and keep investments in their territory by lowering standards. In poor countries, on the other hand, people fear being forced to raise standards at an earlier stage of development than they would otherwise choose, thereby reducing their comparative advantage in products whose production is intensive in the use of natural resources or unskilled labor.

8.1.2 International Spillovers

The issues are made more complicated by the fact that they also can involve some externalities that spill over national boundaries. The most obvious examples are physical spillovers associated with global environmental problems such as global warming and ozone depletion. Greenhouse gases contribute to climate change, and chlorofluorocarbons (CFCs) deplete the ozone layer, regardless of which country they are emitted from. Hence there is a concern that if one set of countries seeks to tax or otherwise induce less of these emissions by firms located in their region, the environmental benefits from those measures will be offset insofar as the activities responsible relocate to countries with lower standards. The freer are international trade and investment flows, the less effective will be subglobal regulation and hence the greater the need will be for international cooperation or coercion.

There are at least three difficulties that need to be addressed in coping with global environmental issues. One is the problem of free riding on the efforts of other countries in a many-country world without global governance. Another is that countries contribute to these problems unequally, with the richer countries tending in the past at least to have contributed most. And third, countries differ in the importance they place on reducing global environmental problems, depending on income, preferences, information as to causes, and so on. Hence a North–South divide also exists in seeking solutions to these global environmental problems.

To what extent is there a parallel claim with respect to labor standards? Many economists would say there is none, because they perceive no physical labor spillovers of the global-warming or ozone-depleting kind.[1] In addition to physical spillovers, though, people can be affected emotionally by and have humanitarian concerns for activities abroad. An example is that people may grieve if another country's activities threaten a particular animal or plant species in its jurisdiction, or involve abuse of worker rights or poor working conditions. Or they may grieve if they believe that the desires of another country's citizens for higher environmental or labor standards in their country are not being recognized sufficiently by their national government (a political market failure).

Some would argue that such emotional/humanitarian concerns are less worthy of consideration than physical spillovers, not least because they are less measurable, less objective, and hence offer more scope for "capture" by traditional protectionists. Others would counter that there is so much uncertainty about the extent and effects of physical spillovers that they too are subjective and hence are qualitatively no different from emotional/humanitarian concerns. Nor is there any reason a priori to presume that the latter are less important than physical spillovers in some "willingness-to-pay" sense. Again, though, richer people are able to afford to place a larger value on such emotional/humanitarian concerns than poorer people, adding to the gap between North and South in terms of perceptions about the need for international mechanisms to deal with these problems.

8.2 WHY ENVIRONMENTAL AND LABOR STANDARDS HAVE GROWN IN PROMINENCE

Fluctuate though they might with the business cycle (positively in the case of environmental issues, negatively in the case of labor standards), these concerns are likely to keep growing. In the case of the environment, one reason is that, even though uncertainties remain, the scientific basis for many of the concerns is perceived as becoming ever more solid. Another reason is that both the world's population and its real per capita income continue to increase at very high rates by historical standards, adding to demands on the environment. Unfortunately, though, the supplies of most natural resources and environmental services are limited, and markets for many of them are incomplete or absent (because of disputed, ambiguous, or nonexistent property rights, and/or because of the high cost of enforcing those rights).

It is true that the more advanced economies have established national institutional structures to help handle the tasks of arriving at a social consensus on what are appropriate environmental or sustainable development policies of allocating property rights, and of enforcing policies. The same is true in some traditional societies, before they begin to modernize and their resources come under pressure because of declining mortality rates. But these institutions are less common in the newly modernizing economies, where growth in the world's population and consumption is expected to be concentrated during the next few decades. And at the multilateral level, cooperative intergovernmental mechanisms for environmental policy have only recently begun to be formed and will take some time to become effective, especially where free-rider problems are rife.

Income growth and expanding knowledge also are factors in the case of labor standards: as people become more affluent, they can afford to demand both better working conditions for themselves and, should it concern them, more information on worker rights and conditions abroad (the cost of which is dropping as travel and communication costs fall).

In addition to these general trends, three other economic developments have heightened the prominence of these issues recently. One is the rapid spread of export-oriented industrialization to a growing number of developing countries. That has expanded the demand for natural resources and environmental services in general and the use of fuels in particular, which is adding to greenhouse gases. It has also expanded the supply of labor-intensive manufactures, depressing their relative price and hence eroding the demand for workers and capital in unskilled labor-intensive industries in high-income countries. That has contributed to other forces there that have resulted in high unemployment levels and/or a growing wage differential between skilled and unskilled workers in rich countries. These has been a tendency for trade from developing countries to be blamed disproportionately for the poor performance of labor markets in advanced economies, and for relatively low labor standards to be seen as part of the reason for low production costs in the newly industrializing countries.

The second economic development of significance is the accelerating economic integration of national economies regionally and globally. With the internationalization of the world economy, the decline in traditional trade barriers has ensured that any given cost-raising social standard is becoming *relatively* more important as a determinant of international competitiveness, and the deregulation of foreign direct investment abroad has increased the possibilities for firms to relocate their factories from high- to lower-standard countries.

And the third reason why environmental and labor issues have become more prominent at the global level is because they succeeded recently in penetrating regional integration agreements. Specifically, there is the Protocol on Social Policy annexed to the Treaty of Maastricht signed by European Union member governments in February 1992 (Sapir 1996). As well, these issues became the subject of side agreements to the North American Free Trade Agreement (NAFTA) in 1993 – a price President Clinton paid to buy off opposition from environmental and labor groups to NAFTA's passage through the U.S. Congress. Having been encouraged by their success in those regional economic integration settings, and before that in some minor trade and investment agreements in the 1980s (see Lawrence 1995 for details), the advocates for those side agreements are now seeking to influence the multilateral trade system. In both situations, the desires of the GATT's contracting parties to conclude, ratify, and implement the Uruguay Round agreements on trade liberalization and to create the World Trade Organization (WTO) are simply being used opportunistically by these groups to further their own causes, despite the tenuous connection of those causes with trade. Their relative success to date is in large part because their causes have superficial popular appeal, while the downside in terms of the potential risk to the global trading system is far from obvious to the layperson.

8.3 WHY IS TRADE POLICY BEING ENTWINED WITH SOCIAL STANDARDS?

In response to the above concerns, both North America and Western Europe sought successfully to have a Committee on Trade and Environment set up at the outset of the WTO's establishment, and they have since been actively seeking a WTO working party on trade and labor standards. In the latter case, the concern in high-standard countries ostensibly is not so much the lower wage level in developing countries but rather such things as poor occupational health and safety standards, worker rights to form unions and seek a minimum wage level and other improved conditions of employment, the use of child or prison or forced labor, and the derogation from national labor laws in export-processing zones. For example, the United States, the European Union (EU), and Norway have been seeking the universal adoption of what they see as "core" labor standards: freedom of association and collective bargaining, elimination of exploitative forms of child labor, prohibition of forced labor, and nondiscrimination in employment. The United States and France were at pains to make clear at Marrakesh that their push for the WTO to consider trade/labor issues was very much focused on differences in labor standards other than wages. Like "green" groups pushing for tougher environmental regulations, human rights activities and development nongovernmental organizations (NGOs) often add support to union calls for higher labor standards in developing countries, believing that would improve the quality of life there.

To more fully understand why concerns about environmental and labor standards are being entwined with international trade and investment policy, it is helpful first to ask what economic theory suggests might link them and then to look for empirical evidence that might support that theory.

8.3.1 What Does Economic Theory Suggest?

The standard theory of changing comparative advantages in a growing world economy has been developed without consideration of environmental concerns, but it can readily be modified to incorporate at least some of those concerns. As espoused by Krueger (1977) and Leamer (1987), this theory suggests that, when a developing country opens up to international trade, its exports initially will be specialized in primary products. This is because its stocks of produced capital relative to natural resources are comparatively low. Should those nonnatural capital stocks per worker (including human skills) expand more of this country than globally, the country's comparative advantage will tend gradually to shift to more capital- and skill-intensive activities (particularly manufactures and services). If such countries are relatively land-abundant, some of that produced capital and new or newly imported capital-intensive technology may be employed profitably to extract minerals or farm the land. But in most such countries the new capital will encourage the expansion of nonprimary sectors and shift these countries' comparative advantage away from primary products. Thus countries that are relatively lightly endowed with natural resources or that are densely populated will tend to industrialize at an earlier stage of economic development, and their nonprimary exports will tend to be more intensive in the use of unskilled labor initially. In the case of manufactures, the gradual process of upgrading to more capital-intensive production leaves room in international markets for later-industrializing, resource-poor countries to also begin with labor-intensive, export-oriented manufacturing.

If national boundaries were such that there were no international environmental spillovers and no global commons, the above determinants of comparative advantage need be complicated only slightly to incorporate labor standards and nonmarketed environmental services and pollution by-products. The complication required is simply to allow for the fact that, as a country's per capital income and industrial output grow, the values its citizens place on the environment and on labor conditions increase and with it their demands for proper valuation of resource depletion and environmental degradation, for the assigning and better policing of property rights, and for the implementation of costly domestic pollution abatement and labor policies – at least after certain threshold levels of income or pollution are reached. Beyond those threshold points the severity of abatement policies is likely to be positively correlated with per capita income, population density, and the degree of urbanization.

If all economies were growing equally rapidly but from different bases, the progressive introduction of national environmental taxes and regulations would tend to cause pollution-intensive production processes to gradually relocate from wealthier or more densely populated countries to developing or more sparsely populated countries. Those environmental policies would also slow or reverse the growth in demand for products whose consumption is pollutive, especially in wealthier or more densely populated countries, where taxes on such products would tend to become high. If more-advanced economies are net importers or products whose production is pollutive, as is likely, the imposition of these countries' optimal environmental policies would worsen their terms of trade to the benefit of poorer economies. Such policies would also worsen the terms of trade of more-advanced economies if they were net exporters of products whose consumption is pollutive (Siebert et al. 1980; Anderson 1992c). The extent of the benefit to developing countries would be greater the more their terms of trade improved as a result of rising standards in advanced economies.

In the case of labor standards, such things as shorter working weeks, higher overtime pay, longer annual leave, and safer and healthier working conditions may (but need not) ultimately raise worker welfare. They presumably raise the cost of employing labor though, otherwise they would have been adopted voluntarily and there would be no need for government or union action.[2] They are therefore similar to other taxes on production that differ across industries in that their *indirect* effects need to be considered as well (Ehrenberg 1994). Specifically, they effectively make (particularly low-skilled) labor scarcer. Their gradual introduction as living standards rise contributes to ensuring that the cost of production in labor-intensive industries rises even faster than it otherwise would in relatively rapidly growing economies, thereby reducing the capacity of those industries to compete with producers in low-standard countries while enhancing the capacity of other industries in high-standard countries to so compete, along Rybczynski (1959) lines.

Thus even countries without (or with unchanged) environmental and labor standards are affected through foreign trade and investment by the development of environmental and labor policies that accompany growth in *other* countries. Hence one country's environmental or labor policy choice is not independent of the choice of standards of other countries. The imposition of higher standards at home alters the international competitiveness of industries, in particular by harming the more pollution-intensive (or labor-intensive) industries in countries with higher standards. Unless they had been developing new, environmentally friendlier (or laborsaving) technologies, such industries would tend to lobby against the imposition of higher standards at home, particularly if their competitors abroad were not being subjected to similar cost-raising policies and/or were equally able to access new technologies. Producers in the less-polluting (or less capital-intensive) industries at home, on the other hand, could benefit from the raising of a particular environmental (or labor) standard.

Environmental and labor groups in rich countries perceive that, since the loss of competitiveness of pollution- and labor-intensive industries could be offset by restrictions on imports from lower-standard countries, such restrictions could at the same time reduce such industries' opposition to higher standards at home and increase the incentive for foreign firms and their governments to adopt higher standards abroad to avoid being labeled a pollution or cheap-labor haven and subjected to duties aimed at preventing eco- or social "dumping." Not surprisingly, those features make trade policy very attractive to environmentalists and unionists. But because such uses of trade policy are discriminatory and protectionist, they are equally unattractive to supporters of liberal world trade. For those concerned about the welfare of unskilled laborers in poor countries, it should be kept in mind that import restrictions in rich countries simply reduce the demand for such workers. So too would the raising of labor standards in the formal sector of poor countries: it simply drives employment into the informal sector (where labor standards are even lower), and/or lengthens the queues of unemployed people seeking high-paid, high-standard formal sector jobs.[3] In the case of young women displaced from their jobs by higher labor standards, they may to have to marry and bear children earlier than otherwise, or even to enter prostitution, in order to survive.[4]

As already mentioned, the demand for unilateral use of trade policy for the above reasons has grown with the internationalization of the global economy, in two ways. One is that the decline in traditional trade barriers (tariffs, transport and communications costs, and so on) is making any given environmental charge or labor and standard relatively more important as a determinant of international competitiveness, ceteris paribus. The other is that, with the deregulation of financial markets and foreign direct investment during the 1980s, the possibilities for firms to disinvest in countries with high standards and relocate their factories in countries with lower standards have increased markedly. Environmental and labor groups fear this development will result in governments delaying the introduction or enforcement of stricter environmental policies or labor standards – in their attempts to attract or retain investments and hence jobs (Wilson 1996). They also worry that greater relocation opportunities will reduce the incentive for firms to develop more environmentally friendly technologies.[5]

The story becomes more complicated when important international environmental or labor spillovers are taken into account, be they physical or psychological. Controversial though they may be, many people perceive a need for multilateral action to reduce these spillover problems – and that is where trade policy again enters the debate. Trade measures are seen by environmentalists and unionists as providing powerful carrots and sticks for attracting signatories to multilateral environmental or labor agreements and for penalizing nonsignatories, as well as for encouraging other countries to adopt higher national standards for the sake of their own citizens and environment. Just the threat of trade sanctions (particularly if broadened to include unrelated products) may have a rapid and persuasive effect on raising national standards or encouraging a country to join an international environmental or labor agreement and subsequently to abide by its rules.

We know from the standard theory of distortions and welfare that if there is only one distortion in the global economy (for example, trade restrictions), then reducing the extent of that distortion will be welfare enhancing for the world as a whole. Not all groups need gain, but the extent of gain to those who benefit is more than enough to compensate all those who lose. That theory also tells us that if the world has more than that one distortion (for example, also environmental externalities that have not been addressed by optimal policies from a global viewpoint), then reducing only one distortion (trade restrictions) may not increase global welfare. For example, liberalizing trade between industrial and developing countries could led to excessive felling of tropical forests if there were inadequate protection of forest property rights in the developing countries (Chichilnisky 1994). In such cases all other divergences must be reduced at the same time as trade is being liberalized in order to achieve unequivocal global welfare improvement. Even then, theory tells us that some countries may be made worse off and the environment may still be harmed (Copland and Taylor 1995). Thus it should be acknowledged by liberal traders that it is not possible to claim with certainty that trade liberalization will improve the environment and welfare for different groups of countries in the presence of significant environmental externalities without appropriately offsetting environmental policies in place.[6] But equally it should be acknowledged by environmental groups that in many situations trade liberalization may actually help not only the economy but also the environment.

As with environmental standards, traditional protectionist forces in high-income countries are prompt to support goods from lower-standard countries. They sometimes bolster their case by quoting simple trade theory (the factor-price equalization and Stolper-Samuelson theorems) in support of their argument that liberal trade can lead to factor-price convergence and in particular to a drop in low-skill wages in high-wage countries (Brown, Deardorff, and Stern 1996) – even though those theorems have been shown to be not very robust when more than two countries, goods, and factors are involved.[7] As with the environment, it is an empirical question as to what extent if any trade has contributed to the poor labor-market performance of countries in the Organization for Economic Cooperation and Development (OECD) during the past couple of decades.

8.3.2 What Does the Empirical Evidence Show?

The reasons often give by environmental groups for their opposition to trade and investment liberalization tend to be based on one or more of the following grounds: freer trade means more output and income, which they presume would mean more resource depletion and degradation of the natural environment; freer trade and investment encourages the relocation of environmentally degrading industries to countries with lower environmental-protection standards or more fragile natural environments, and leads to greater transport activity, which contributes further environmental damage; and freer foreign investment reduces the incentive to develop environmentally friendlier technologies.

However, none of these assertions is unambiguously supported by empirical evidence. The first, that income increases mean greater damage to the natural environment, may be true initially for some developing countries (in which case any additional environmental damage has to be weighted against the marginal economic benefits of higher incomes for poor people). But once middle-income status is reached, people tend to alter their behavior in ways that reduce the rate of environmental degradation due to population pressures in developing countries. In rural areas it means fewer people felling trees and denuding hillsides to eke out a subsistence income, while in urban areas it means fewer unemployed or underemployed squatters in shanty towns with poor water and sanitation services. This no doubt is one reason for the empirical finding that many forms of pollution first increase and then decrease as per capita income rises (Grossman 1995; Grossman and Krueger 1993, 1995; Hettige, Lucas, and Wheeler 1992; Radetzki 1992; Seldon and Song 1994; Shafi and Bandyopadhyay 1992). That evidence suggests the demand for implementing and enforcing pollution-abatement policies is income-elastic, and that an inverted U-shaped environmental transition may be commonplace as stricter environmental policies are implemented and less-pollutive technologies are introduced.[8]

Another common behavioral change as economies open up and incomes rise is that the demand for education expands, and with more income and education comes more skillful management of all resources, including the environment, and more forceful demands on governments to improve the establishment policies (as indicated by the inverted U-shaped or environmental transition curve mentioned above). As well, the political cost of implementing such policy reforms is reduced because of increased opportunities for business to meet stricter standards by acquiring more and cheaper environmentally benign production processes and products from abroad. One might therefore expect that, as trade and investment liberalization leads to upward convergence in incomes around the world, there would be an upward harmonization of environmental standards as well (Casella 1996).

As to the assertion by some groups that the relocation of production following trade and investment liberalization necessarily harms the global environment, we know from the law of comparative advantage that not all industries will relocate from rich to poor economies when trade barriers in rich economies are lowered: some industries will expand at the expense of industries in developing countries, and conversely. Recent preliminary examinations of the likely environmental effects of reducing government assistance to two of the most protected industries in industrial countries – coal and food – reveal that in both cases the global environment may benefit from trade liberalization, especially if complementary environmental policies are in place. That outcome is possible partly because production of those goods tends to have a higher environmental cost in industrial countries than elsewhere. Moreover, reducing coal-producer subsidies in Europe would raise the international price of coal, thereby discouraging its use elsewhere and so lowering global carbon emissions (Anderson 1992a, 1992b; Anderson and McKibbin 1997).[9]

The extent of international relocation of productive activities due to the raising and enforcing of environmental or labor standards should not be exaggerated. Recent studies suggest that the effects of such policies on comparative costs may be quite small (Leonard 1988; Low 1992; Jaffe et al. 1995; OECD 1996; Levinson 1996). They also indicate that multinational corporations tend to use cleaner technology than local firms in developing countries (Harrison and Esekeland 1996), and tend to provide higher labor standards than local firms. Japanese multinational corporations are in fact required to adopt the same environmental standards abroad as operate in Japan. Moreover, Tobey (1990) finds little evidence of actual changes in patterns of trade specialization in response to the imposition of environmental regulations since the 1960s – although as Hoekman and Leidy (1992) note, the absence of observed changes in trade patterns may be the result of import barriers that were raised to offset any decline in the competitiveness of affected industries. Technological changes induced by the raising of standards, and environmental and labor standards raised by the availability of new technologies also would reduce the likelihood of observing a correlation between rising standards and the international relocation of production.

Nor need the risk of environmental damage from transport activity increase with trade reform. The lowering of import barriers to processed primary products, for example, would allow more raw materials to be processed in resource-rich countries, reducing the bulkiness of shipments. And if there are negative externalities associated with shipping itself (such as the risk of oil spills), a more efficient course of action rather than reducing trade generally would be to ensure shippers pay more of the full cost of their activity (say, through an international agreement requiring a minimum standard of double hulls on oil tankers).

What of the argument that the opportunity for capital outflow breeds pollution havens abroad and thereby reduces the development of environmentally friendlier production technologies in countries with higher environmental standards? Some observers have argued that the opportunities for such innovations are so great that raising environmental standards could boost rather than retard a country's economy (Porter and van der Linde 1996). But that argument begs the question of why such investments would not have been made in an open economy without the imposition of stricter standards (Palmer, Oates, and Portney 1996). In any case, there is little empirical evidence to suggest that raising standards stimulates innovation, just as there is little theoretical or empirical support for the notion that raising standards has a significant impact on the competitiveness of firms in industrial countries or on their decisions to invest in developing countries (Jaffe et al. 1995; Wilson 1996).[10]

What evidence is there that trade liberalization and/or differences in labor standards between rich and poor countries contribute, through trade's effects on factor markets, to the poor performance of labor markets in rich countries? At the outset it should be noted that, once allowance is made for differences in labor productivity, labor is not much cheaper in developing countries than in high-income countries (Trefler 1993). Also, in their recent simulation work. Francois, McDonald, and Nordstrom (1996) found real wages in all country groups are projected to increase as a result of implementing the Uruguay Round. Using a similar global computable general equilibrium (CGE) model, Tyers and Yang (1995) found through both backcasting and forecasting that increased imports from Asia do contribute to unskilled-skilled wage dispersion and possibly lower real wages and/or unemployment in the United States and EU, but only to a minor extent. Significantly, they also found that restricting imports from Asia would be an inefficient response since its impact through contracting the global economy would be to lower real rewards to *all* types of labor in industrial countries. Lawrence (1994) and Burtless (1995) also found that imports are at most only a minor contributor to poor labor-market performance in the United States, while the Commission of the European Communities (1996) found that the unemployment problems in the EU were mostly attributable to structural distortions within the union. Other contributors of much more importance to the changing demand for unskilled relative to skilled workers than trade with newly industrializing countries are the computer and information technology revolutions and the growth of the service sector (Wood 1994). The survey by the OECD (1996) concurred. Moreover, the OECD found little evidence that economies with low labor standards performed better than high-standard economies, or that economies with low labor standards attracted more foreign direct investment. It also found a positive correlation over time between sustained trade reform and improvements in labor standards.

8.4 WHY WORRY ABOUT THE ENTWINING OF TRADE POLICY AND SOCIAL STANDARDS?

The use of trade policy as a stick (or possibly a carrot) to influence unilaterally the social policies of other countries, and/or to increase the workability of multilateral environmental or labor agreements, raise potential conflicts of interest between rich and poorer economies. There is even dispute over what constitutes national sovereignty and the global commons. Some would argue, for example, that a country or region should not have to bow to international pressure to preserve endangered species in their territory (or at least not without adequate compensation), while others would argue that such countries are merely the custodians of those resources for the benefit of humankind generally.

Such uses of trade policy should concern the world at large, and developing countries in particular. The reason is not so much because the latter may be required to impose higher environmental or labor standards in order to avoid seeing trade barriers raised against their exports. In fact, the competitiveness of some industries in middle-income countries with midlevel standards might well be enhanced if low-income countries with low standards were required to raise their standards more than them to reach minimum acceptable levels. Even the negative direct effect for low-income economies of having to raise their standards could be offset somewhat by a terms-of-trade improvement if many such countries were to raise their standards simultaneously. And such benefits would be greater the more developing countries taxed or otherwise restricted the export (or better still the production or consumption) of environmentally sensitive products rather than left the developed countries to tax imports of such products (the lesson from the Organization of Petroleum Exporting Countries). Still, people in developing countries are suspicious of the motives of high-income countries, and object to what they perceive as social imperialism and a denial of their national sovereignty.

While developing countries are not being singled out per se, the fact is that environmental and labor standards tend to be lower in developing countries simply because they are poorer. That, together with the fact that their comparative advantages often are in natural resource-intensive and labor-intensive industries, means those countries are vulnerable either to being pressured to enforce stricter standards or to facing less market access for their exports to countries with stricter standards and/or less foreign investment from such countries.

In addition, there are at least three other reasons why the world should worry about the entwining of trade policy with social standards. First, trade policy measures usually are not the best instruments for achieving social objectives. This is because trade sanctions do not directly affect the root cause of environmental or labor-market problems. Their use in place of more efficient instruments increases the use of global resources[11] and reduces unnecessarily the level and growth of global economic welfare as conventionally measured – and may even add to rather than reduce global environmental degradation.[12]

The second reason for concern is that producer interest groups and some environmental groups are finding it mutually advantageous to use environmental and worker rights arguments to support their claim for unilateral import restrictions, particularly following the costly imposition of stricter standards on domestic producers (Hillman and Ursprung 1992; Hoekman and Leidy 1992). In this sense environmental and labor concerns can provide a convenient additional excuse for raising trade barriers – and one that is socially respectable (Steil 1994). However, such protectionist actions reduce real incomes not just at home but elsewhere, especially in developing and natural resource-abundant countries.

Third, insofar as this activity can lead to an escalation in trade disputes – as is almost inevitable, especially given the North–South dimension involved and the fact that environmental or labor uses of trade policy are inherently discriminatory – they could be followed by retaliatory and counterretaliatory action, the result of which would be an undermining of the global trading system.

8.5 WHAT ROLES FOR THE WTO?

The demands for greater harmonization across countries of domestic policies, for competitiveness reasons, coupled with the greening of world politics and the growing interest in worker rights and conditions beyond national borders, are likely to put the WTO and trade policy under pressure to perform tasks for which they were not designed and are not well suited – and at a time when the WTO needs first to consolidate its role in the world and ensure the completion of unfinished business and implementation of the Uruguay Round.[13] Supporters of the WTO are therefore tempted to say the institution should resist all attempts to become involved in these issues.

That strategy is risky, however. While many developing countries might support it, reflect for a moment on its possible consequences. One is that we might see more aggressive unilateral use of trade measures against countries with lower social standards (as with the United States against Mexico regarding tuna fishing). Another might be a lesser willingness of advanced economies to maintain liberal trade policies and to participate in future multilateral trade negotiations.[14] A third possible consequence is that we might see more regional integration agreements with side agreements on these issues (as with NAFTA).

Hence some engagement in the debate by the WTO may be wise. At the very least, that could involve reminding the world of some of the nontrade measures and actions available. One is to encourage private actions by firms and consumers (eco- and social labeling, consumer boycotts, corporate codes of conduct).[15] Another is for nations to use unilateral aid as a carrot (greater Generalized System of Preferences (GSP) preferences, more development assistance in return for enforcing higher social standards).[16] Multilateral aid and World Bank structural adjustment loans also could be geared to reward developing countries that raise their standards. The WTO could participate in studies aimed at showing the extent to which trade and investment liberalization is accompanied or followed by a rise in social standards (i.e., showing that reform is part of the solution, not the problem). Studies identifying more appropriate measures for addressing these issues also would be helpful.

How "green" are the GATT's rules at present, how have they been adapted over time, and should they be altered further? From the outset it could be claimed that the GATT has been a conservationist institution in the sense that its purpose is to reduce trade barriers and thereby the inefficiency in the use of the world's resources. The heart of the GATT, agreed to by twenty-three original contracting parties in 1947 and since then by another hundred or so countries, is the nondiscrimination requirements of articles I and III. These articles obligate parties to treat imports from any GATT contracting party/WTO member no less favorably than other imports (the most-favored-nation requirement) and no less favorably, after border taxes are paid, than similar domestic products (the national-treatment requirements). That is, they preclude any country's using trade measures as sticks to penalize other countries for having, for example, lower environmental or labor standards.

Article XX provides exceptions to these general rules, however, including provisions for some environmental and labor regulations. Specifically, parts b, e, and g of article XX allow trade restrictions "necessary to protect human, animal, or plant life or health," "relating to the products of prison labour," and "relating to the conservation of exhaustible natural resources if such measures are made effective in conjunction with restrictions on domestic production or consumption," subject to the requirement that such restrictions "are not applied in a manner which would constitute a means of arbitrary or unjustifiable discrimination between countries where the same conditions prevail, or a disguised restriction on international trade." The environmental parts of this article have been interpreted to mean that the measure be *primarily* for a conservation purpose (rather than for a mixture of motives) and must be *necessary* in the sense of being the *least GATT-inconsistent* measure available. These provisos have ensured that the article has been rather narrowly interpreted, which is partly why some environmental groups have felt that further greening of the GATT is required (Charnovitz 1991; Esty 1994). But there is nothing in the GATT that prevents a country from adopting the most efficient measures to offset environmental externalities, which typically are associated with production, consumption, or disposal activities. Nor is a country precluded from using a trade measure so long as it is prepared to compensate any trading partner harmed by that measure. But since trade itself is almost never claimed to be the root cause of an environmental problem, GATT supporters traditionally have seen little need to consider trade measures as part of the solution to environmental problems not involving international spillovers.

Trade policy actions are more likely to occur – and to be more difficult to dismiss as inappropriate – when there *are* international spillovers. Consider, for example, the U.S.–Mexico dispute over the use of dolphin-unfriendly nets for tuna fishing. In that case the GATT dispute panel ruled against the U.S. ban on imports of tuna from Mexico, partly because the ban did not discriminate according to which type of net was used. That kind of discrimination is difficult to achieve efficiently because what is considered objectionable is an aspect of the production process rather than the final traded product itself. Had the GATT panel ruled in favor of the tuna import ban by the United States, it would have set a major precedent. It would have opened a potentially huge loophole in the GATT for any country unilaterally to apply trade restrictions as a means of imposing its environmental standards on other countries. Such a loophole would work against the main objective of the multilateral trading system, which is to provide stable and predictable nondiscriminatory market-access opportunities through agreed rules and disciplines and bound tariffs on imports. This is why calls to amend article XX of the GATT to include environmental protection as an acceptable exception to the nondiscrimination principles of articles I and II should be resisted.

Environmental and labor groups perceive trade policy as useful not only as a means of raising national environmental or labor standards at home and abroad but also of inducing countries to become signatories to and to abide by international environmental and labor agreements where free-rider problems arise. One of the more obvious and possibly more cost-effective ways to reduce the free-rider problem is to write trade provisions into the agreements, as was done in the 1987 Montreal protocol on reducing the use of CFCs and halons to slow ozone depletion. To date no GATT contracting party has formally objected to that use of trade policy. Nor have they objected to the bans on trade in ivory, rhino horn, and tiger products that are part of the Convention on International Trade in Endangered Species, or to the trade provisions in the Basel convention on trade in hazardous wastes. Conflicts may well arise in the future, however, if trade provisions are drafted into more contentious multilateral agreements (say, an attempt to impose a global carbon tax or higher labor standards).

In assessing the appropriate role for trade policy in multilateral environmental or labor agreements, it is helpful to recall that supporters of trade liberalization and of environmental or labor standards share a common goal: to improve social welfare. They also share a common problem: the need to foster multilateral cooperation to fully achieve that objective, because in each sphere (the economy, the environment, and, indirectly, the labor market) there is considerable and increasing interdependence among countries. But the groups differ in the important respect that supporters of liberal world trade have understood its virtues for two centuries and have been active for more than fifty years in building institutions such as the GATT and the WTO to help achieve their goal. Widespread concerns about the environment, on the other hand, are relatively new, and supporters of environmental protection only recently became significant players in international policy arenas.

Understandably, supporters of liberal trade and the WTO resent the encroachment of these special-interest groups onto what they perceive as their hard-won territory, especially when they believe that reducing trade barriers is likely to be environmentally friendly and consistent with sustainable development and improved labor outcomes in the long run because it allows the world to use its resources more efficiently. But advocates of greater environmental protection are equally frustrated that international agreements as important as those resulting from the Uruguay Round can be implemented without being subject to environmental impact assessments or environmental safeguards.

Clearly there is scope for greater understanding and altered strategies on both sides. More than that, there is the distinct possibility that, by working together, all groups' objectives will be further enhanced – a win-win outcome. Some observers believe that it may ultimately require a world environment organization to set rules, incorporate existing international environmental agreements and negotiate new ones, monitor compliance, and settle disputes over environmental policies – in the same way that the GATT has presided over trade rules and policies for the past five decades (Esty 1994). And just as the GATT/WTO strengthens the capacity of governments to resist the demands of domestic vested-interest groups seeking higher import taxes, so a world environment organization may help governments resist interest-group demands to set low environmental standards (Deardorff 1995).

The advantage of a world environment organization for liberal traders, Esty argues, is that such an organization could reflect environmentalists' attention away from the use of trade measures and toward ensuring the implementation of more appropriate policy instruments for achieving environmental objectives, allowing both sets of policies to more effectively contribute, in mutually supportive ways, to the common goals of sustainable development and improvement in the quality of life.

However, a world environment organization is unlikely to be created in the near future, partly because governments in many countries are under pressure to downsize and some have a growing mistrust and even hostility toward international bureaucracies. In any case a world environment organization, like the International Labor Organization and other standards-setting international organizations, would lack the teeth to ensure enforcement of agreements.[17] Moreover, the issue of whether the rules of the WTO or a world environment organization would have precedence would need to be resolved. We know from theory that, where the objectives of the two groups are in conflict, achieving the optimal welfare-maximizing outcome requires both to compromise somewhat (Corden 1997), but managing that tension would be difficult.

Thus the trade policy community needs to be involved in the negotiating of multilateral environmental agreements that are likely to include trade provisions, and to develop criteria by which WTO members can assess in advance the extent to which trade restrictions within such agreements are acceptable. The relevant criteria, some of which were enunciated clearly at the United Nations Conference on Environment and Development in Brazil, include the following: First, it is important to ensure that trade provisions are strictly necessary, in the sense that there are no alternative, more effective instruments than trade restrictions, and they need to be effective in achieving the environmental objectives involved. Second, where trade instruments are required in the absence of less costly policy measures, they should be used only in proportion to the size of the associated environmental problem. Finally, the measures ought to be transparent and not protectionist in impact, and where possible be consistent with both the GATT principles of nondiscrimination (most favored nation and national treatment) and key environmental principles such as the polluter pays and the precautionary principles. If those conditions were met, WTO members would be unlikely to object to the use of trade measures in multilateral environmental agreements. Hence even the possible need to use trade provisions in multilateral environmental agreements does not provide sufficient reason to amend GATT article XX to allow in the list of exceptions the use of trade measures for environmental protection.

Since the entwining of environmental and labor issues with trade and investment policy is more likely to tighten than to disentangle in the foreseeable future, the question arises as to how developing countries ought to respond. One response is to point out that industrial countries had lower standards at earlier stages of their development and still have sweatshops operating illegally. Another is that, since developing countries have contributed a disproportionately small amount per capita to global environmental problems such as the greenhouse effect, they should be compensated for contributing to their solutions rather than have that contribution demanded of them under threats of trade sanctions. Compensation would be even more justified in cases where industrial countries are demanding responses by other countries to reduce the emotional/humanitarian concerns mentioned earlier. As Srinivasan (1996) notes, those in rich countries genuinely concerned about low labor standards in developing countries can always transfer income to such groups or lobby to allow such workers to migrate to the more-advanced economies.

Another response by developing countries could be to disseminate more widely the sound arguments for not using trade-restrictive measures to achieve environmental and labor objectives and hence for not amending article XX of the GATT to allow trade discrimination for those purposes. Those arguments are that

* differences in standards are a legitimate source of comparative advantage insofar as they reflect differences in resource endowments and societies' preferences and ability to afford the good things in life;

* standards rise with per capita income, and liberal trade promotes income growth;
* theory and empirical evidence provide little reason to expect that the raising of standards in industrial countries will contribute significantly to costs of production and hence to trade and investment patterns, nor that downward harmonization of standards (a "race to the bottom") is occurring;
* if freer trade were to worsen welfare because of inappropriate environmental or labor policies in some countries, nontrade measures such as ecolabeling and income transfers would be more cost-effective than trade policies because they allow consumers to exercise their preferences through the market;
* the GATT rules-based multilateral trading system is threatened by the risk of environmental and worker-rights groups being captured by traditional protectionist groups in countries with high standards, and will be at further risk if GATT article XX is amended to allow in its list of exceptions the use of unilateral trade measures for environmental or labor purposes; and
* if such an amendment were made for environmental and labor standards, there would be pressure to add ever more domestic-policy items to the list of exceptions, including health, education, and taxation.

More empirical analyses to support some of these arguments are sorely needed. The experiences of the Uruguay Round and of the Intergovernmental Panel on Climate Change made clear that empirical studies are far more powerful than abstract arguments in focusing attention on the need for policy reform and the shape it should take. Those quantitative exercises have provided the world with a suite of multisector, multicountry models that are capable of being modified to estimate the linkages between trade, labor standards, resource depletion, and environmental degradation. Modeling efforts are now being made in that direction, but there is great scope for further, high-payoff research in this area.

Such forward-looking modeling requires the inclusion of endogenous behavioral relationships not only for private households and firms but also for governments, so as to capture not just the demographic transition but also the transitions in trade, labor, and environmental policies that typically accompany per capita income growth. Government behavior needs to be included in the base case not to suggest that policy choices are inevitable but rather to represent what would happen if no further action is taken. Against that base case various alternative cases can be compared, with a view to using the results to convince governments of the wisdom of choosing a more appropriate set of policies. In particular, empirical estimates could be given of the contribution that trade liberalization in industrial countries in farm products, labor-intensive manufactures, and coal could make to raising wages and reducing environmental damage at the same time as improving the global economy.

Helpful though such argumentation and analysis could be, more dialogue and compromise between high-income and developing countries is likely to be needed. For example, if developing countries were to commit themselves to enforcing minimum standards and to raising those standards over time according to a specified schedule, in return for gradual improvements in access to developed-country markets, vocal interest groups in social standards are positively related to income and trade growth. That would be using trade policy as a carrot rather than a stick. Likewise, if developing countries were seen to be enforcing reasonable standards especially effectively on their foreign investors, concerns about capital outflows to "pollution havens" or "cheap-labour havens" and the consequent loss of jobs in high-standard countries would be less justifiable. Alternatively or additionally, developing countries could transfer the onus back to high-standard countries to insist their firms accede to the same high standards when they invest in developing countries as in more advanced economies. And anxiety over deforestation could be reduced if developing countries were able to demonstrate they can police restrictions on felling and are prepared to do so in return for adequate compensation in the form of greater access to OECD markets and/or aid (e.g., via the UNDP/UNEP/World Bank Global Environment Facility administered by the World Bank).

To conclude, it is instructive to examine the progress of labor policies in the subglobal arena of the EU. A recent assessment by Sapir (1996) concludes that in Europe there have always been the optimists who believe economic integration breeds greater economic growth and equality of social policies (led by the Ohlin report to the International Labor Office [1956] at the time of the formation of the European Economic Community), and the pessimists who believe upward harmonization needs to be imposed on lower-standard countries to improve citizens' conditions there and avoid "social dumping" through trade. In practice, relatively little has been imposed effectively on the poorer member countries of the EU; the most that has been agreed to is the adoption of some minimum standards and mutual recognition. Yet standards have risen rapidly with the acceleration of income growth in the poorer EU countries.

NOTES

This paper draws on the author's earlier papers for the World Bank and the National Bureau of Economic Research. Thanks are due to Jagdish Bhagwati, Richard Blackhurst, Maureen Cooper, Jane Drake-Brockman, Bernard Hoekman, Robert Hudec, Takatoshi Ito, Anne Krueger, Deepak Lal, Will Martin, Rodrigo Prudencio, David Richardson, Dani Rodrik, and T. N. Srinvasan for helpful comments on this and those earlier papers, and to the World Bank, NBER, and the Australian Research Council for financial support.

1 At least one minor spillover may be present in some times and places, though. It is the effect of high standards for low-skilled workers in attracting unwanted migrants from less-developed economies across borders that may be difficult to police. My thanks go to David Richardson for offering this suggestion. The first-best response to such a possibility may simply be to adopt measures to reduce illegal immigration.

2 So-called neoinstitutionalists argue that higher labor standards would raise worker productivity (see, e.g., Hanson 1983, 53–63), but it is reasonable to assume firms have already recognized any such possibilities and incorporated them in their work practices. If not, the first-best role for government is to subsidize the provision of information about those opportunities.

3 This could easily be shown using a Harris-Todaro type of model as modified, for example, by Corden and Findlay (1975). The consequences of raising labor standards in a multigood, multicountry world can be quite complex and sometimes counter-intuitive, depending on the assumptions adopted. See the theoretical analysis of several possibilities by Brown, Deardorff, and Stern (1996).

4 I am grateful to Anne Krueger for suggesting this possibility.

5 Where the environmental damage caused by production is purely local, the calls by disadvantaged firms for trade restrictions or subsidies to offset the decline in their international competitiveness because of standards being raised has no economic logic: such assistance would tend to offset the desired effect of limiting by-product pollution. See, for example, Baumol (1971) and Siebert (1974). Such protection from import competition cannot be justified on economic efficiency grounds (or for that matter on environmental grounds) because the environmental policy is aiming to eliminate an unjustifiable (implicit) subsidy arising through undervaluation of environmental resources, rather than to add an unjustifiable tax (Snape 1992). Nor is it reasonable to conclude that other countries are engaging in "ecodumping" if the imports that they are able to supply are produced with laxer environmental standards, if those lower standards are consistent with the preferences and natural resource endowments of the exporting countries (for example, because those countries are poorer, less densely populated, or less urbanized).

6 Even so, the first-best action is to overcome that political market failure so that trade reform *can* contribute to boosting welfare (Bhagwati and Strinvasan 1996).

7 See Falvey (1995). Markusen and Venables (1996) develop a model in which, while multinationals can increase the skilled-unskilled wage gap in rich countries, imposing import barriers does not protect their unskilled labor.

8 See also Deacon and Shapiro (1975) on the correlation between income levels and voter attitudes toward environmental priorities. Studies aimed at explaining this transition (sometimes called an environmental Kuznets curve) are now beginning to emerge. Beltratti (1995) seeks to explain in terms of transitional dynamics of endogenous growth models, while Jones and Manuelli (1995) provide a positive political-economy model. See also Dean (1996) for an econometrically testable simultaneous-equations model to measure the effect of trade liberalization on the environment, taking into account the income growth from liberalization.

9 The question of whether it is environmentally friendly to pursue broadly based liberalizations such as the Uruguay Round, as distinct from liberalization in individual product markets, requires large-scale formal global modeling analysis that as yet has barely begun to be attempted. Even if quantitative estimates of the various key environmental effects were available, a formidable task would remain in valuing those pluses and minuses and comparing the net value with the conventionally measured economic welfare gain from trade liberalization.

10 That does not mean, however, that developing-country firms would find it inexpensive to conform to the high environmental standards of industrial countries. The reason is that local firms in developing countries may be using older, less environmentally friendly technology that would be more costly to adapt. Indeed, the cost of conformance in industrial countries may be relatively low simply because the raising of legislated standards to some extent follows rather than precedes the development of cleaner technologies. That has been cited as one reason for the relative ease with which agreement was reached on reducing the use of ozone-depleting substances under the Montreal protocol (see Enders and Porges 1992).

11 Even the *threat* of trade restrictions can be environmentally counterproductive. The talk of European import bans on tropical hardwood logs (together with tariff escalation on timber-product imports) has encouraged Indonesia to obtain log exports. But since felling and timber-product exports have been allowed to continue, this policy has lowered the domestic price of logs and thereby raised effective assistance to Indonesia's furniture and other timber-using industries to extremely high levels (GATT 1991, 127). With lower log prices and lower-quality saw-milling techniques than in importing countries, it is not surprising that less of each tree is now used and little reduction in logging has been observed since the log export ban was introduced.

12 The ban on ivory trade provides a case in point. By lowering the value of elephant products, the ban reduces the incentive for rural Africans to tolerate elephants trampling their crops and so ultimately could result in more rather than less culling of elephants in some cases. In other cases with poor meat storage and transport facilities, the ivory-trade ban has reduced the value of the animal so much that it is no longer profitable to cull the herd. An unfortunate environmental consequence is that brushland in national parks is being decimated by the increased number of elephants, which is endangering other species (Barbier et al. 1990).

13 The suggestion has been made, for example, that the WTO become active in monitoring and enforcing agreed minimum social standards. That presumably would involve environmental and labor standards being reviewed as part of the WTO's Trade Policy Mechanism. Since that mechanism is already stretched to its limit in covering even the major trade policies of contracting parties, such an addition to its workload would require a substantial boost to its resources – not to mention the extra burden on those employed in national capitals when the reviews are under way. An even greater potential increase in workload would result for the WTO's dispute settlement mechanism.

14 Williamson (1996) warns of this possibility after examining the growth in wage inequality following the globalization of the latter nineteenth century.

15 Such codes have been suggested by multilateral institutions, such as the International Labor Office (ILO) in 1977 in its Declaration of Principles concerning Multinational Enterprise and Social Policy, and more recently the OECD in its Code on Multinational Enterprises.

16 Woolcock (1996) notes that the EU decided in 1995 that it will consider in 1998 ways to offer additional GSP preferences to those developing countries that meet the requirements of ILO conventions on forced labor, freedom of association and collective bargaining, and the minimum working age. He also notes that the U.S. 1984 Trade and Tariff Act provides for GSP preferences to be withdrawn (a stick rather than carrot approach) if similar labor standards are not met. Likewise, benefits are to be withdrawn (1) under the Caribbean Basin Initiative if the United States deems a country is not complying with those minimum labor standards, and (2) under section 301 of the 1974 and 1988 trade acts. The *threat* of withdrawal of benefits has in most cases been sufficient to induce changes satisfying the United States without its resorting to actual trade sanctions. Nonetheless, a carrot rather than stick approach would be more WTO-consistent.

17 The ILO has been operating for more than seventy-five years, but has had little success in dealing with disputes (Charnovitz 1987; Woolcock 1996).

REFERENCES

Alesina, A., and E. Spolaore. 1995. On the Number and Size of Nations. NBER Working Paper no. 5050. Cambridge, MA: National Bureau of Economic Research, March.

Anderson, K. 1992a. Agricultural Trade Liberalization and the Environment: A Global Perspective. *World Economy* 15, no. 1: 153–71.

——. 1992b. Effects on the Environment and Welfare of Liberalizing World Trade: The Cases of Coal and Food. In *The Greening of World Trade Issues*, ed. K. Anderson and R. Blackhurst, chap. 8. Ann Arbor: University of Michigan Press; London: Harvester Wheatsheaf.

——. 1992c. The Standard Welfare Economics of Policies Affecting Trade and the Environment. In *The Greening of World Trade Issues*, ed. K. Anderson and R. Blackhurst, chap. 2. Ann Arbor: University of Michigan Press; London: Harvester Wheatsheaf.

Anderson, K. and W. McKibbin. 1997. Reducing Coal Subsidies and Trade Barriers; Their Contribution to Greenhouse Gas Abatement. CIES Seminar Paper no. 97–07, University of Adelaide, July.

Barbier, E. B., J. C. Burgess, T. M. Swanson, and D. W. Pearce. 1990. *Elephants, Economics, and Ivory*. London: Earthscan.

Baumol, W. 1971. *Environmental Protection, International Spillovers, and Trade*. Stockholm: Almqvist and Wiksell.

Beltratti, A. 1995. Can a Growth Model with Defensive Expenditures Generate an Environmental Kuznets Curve? Paper for a workshop, "Designing Economic Policy for Management of Natural Resources and the Environment," Venice, 12–13 May.

Bhagwati, J. N. 1996. The Demands to Reduce Domestic Diversity among Trading Nations. In *Fair Trade and Harmonization: Prerequisites for Free Trade?* vol. 1, ed. J. N. Bhagwati and R. E. Hudec, chap. 1. Cambridge: MIT Press.

Bhagwati, J. N., and T. N. Srinivasan. 1996. Trade and the Environment: Does Environmental Diversity Detract from the Case for Free Trade? In *Fair Trade and Harmonization: Prerequisites for Free Trade?* vol. 1, ed. J. N. Bhatwai and R. E. Hudec, chap. 4. Cambridge: MIT Press.

Brown, D. K., A. V. Deardorff, and R. M. Stern. 1966. International Labor Standards and Trade: A Theoretical Analysis. In *Fair Trade and Harmonization: Prerequisites for Free Trade?* vol. 1, ed. J. N. Bhatwati and R. E. Hudec, chap. 5. Cambridge: MIT Press.

Burtless, G. 1995. International Trade and the Rise of Earnings Inequality. *Journal of Economic Literature*, 33, no. 2: 800–816.

Casella, A. 1996. Free Trade and Evolving Standards. In *Fair Trade and Harmonization: Prerequisites for Free Trade?* vol. 1, ed. J. N. Bhagwati and R. E. Hudec, chap. 3. Cambridge: MIT Press.

Charnovitz, S. 1987. The Influence of International Labour Standards on the World Trading Regime: A Historical Review. *International Labour Review*, 126, no. 5: 565–84.

——. 1991. Exploring the Environmental Exceptions in GATT Article XX. *Journal of World Trade*, 25, no. 5.

Chichlinisky, G. 1994. North–South Trade and the Global Environment. *American Economic Review* 84, no. 4: 851–74.

Commission of the European Communities. 1996. *Growth, Competitiveness, Employment: The Challenges and Way Forward into the 21st Century*. Brussels: Commission of the European Communities.

Copland, B. R., and M. S. Taylor. 1995. Trade and Transboundary Pollution. *American Economic Review* 85, no. 4: 716–37.

Corden, W. M. 1997. The Environment and Trade Policy. In *Trade Policy and Economic Welfare*, 2d. edn, chap. 13. Oxford: Clarendon Press.

Corden, W. M. and R. Findlay. 1975. Urban Employment, Intersectoral Capital Mobility, and Development Policy. *Economica* 42: 59–78.

Deacon, R. and P. Shapiro. 1975. Private Preference for Collective Goods Revealed through Voting on Referenda. *American Economic Review* 65: 943–55.

Dean, J. 1996. Testing the Impact of Trade Liberalization on the Environment. CIES Seminar Paper no. 96–11, University of Adelaide, September.

Deardorff, A. V. 1995. International Externalities in the Use of Pollution Policies. Discussion Paper no. 383, School of Public Policy. Ann Arbor: University of Michigan, November.

Ehrenberg, R. 1994. *Labour Markets and Integrating National Economies*. Washington, DC: Brookings Institution.

Enders, A., and A. Porges. 1992. Successful Conventions and Conventional Success: Saving the Ozone Layer. In *The Greening of World Trade Issues*, ed. K. Anderson and R. Blackhurst, chap. 7. Ann Arbor: University of Michigan Press; London: Harvester Wheatsheaf.

Esty, D. C. 1994. *Greening the GATT: Trade, Environment, and the Future*. Washington, DC: Institute for International Economics.
Falvey, R. 1995. International Trade and Factor Price Convergence. Working Paper no. 290. Canberra: Australian National University, August.
Francois, J. F., B. McDonald, and H. Nordstrom. 1996. The Uruguay Round: A Numerically Based Qualitative Assessment. In *The Uruguay Round and the Developing Countries*, ed. W. Martin and L. A. Winters, chap. 9. Cambridge: Cambridge University Press.
General Agreement on Tariffs and Trade. 1991. *Trade Policy Review: Indonesia*. Geneva: GATT Secretariat.
Grossman, G. M. 1995. Pollution and Growth: What Do We Know? In *The Economics of Sustainable Development*, ed. I. Goldin and L. A. Winters. Cambridge: Cambridge University Press.
Grossman, G. M. and A. B. Krueger. 1993. Environmental Impacts of a North American Free Trade Agreement. In *The Mexico–U.S. Free Trade Agreement*, ed. P. M. Garber, 13–56. Cambridge: MIT Press.
——. 1995. Economic Growth and the Environment. *Quarterly Journal of Economics* 110, no. 2: 353–78.
Hanson, G. 1983. *Social Clauses and International Trade: An Economic Analysis of Labour Standards in Trade Policy*. New York: St Martin's Press.
Harrison, A. E., and G. S. Eskeland. 1996. Playing Dirty? Multinationals and the Pollution Haven Hypothesis. Columbia University, New York, February. Mimeo.
Hettige, H., R. E. B. Lucas, and D. Wheeler. 1992. The Toxic Intensity of Industrial Production: Global Patterns, Trends, and Trade Policy. *American Economic Review* 82, no. 2: 478–81.
Hillman, A. L., and H. N. Ursprung, 1992. The Influence of Environmental Concerns on the Political Determination of Trade Policy. In *The Greening of World Trade Issues*, ed. K. Anderson and R. Blackhurst, chap. 10. Ann Arbor: University of Michigan Press; London: Harvester Wheatsheaf.
Hoekman, B., and M. Leidy, 1992. Environmental Policy Formation in a Trading Economy: A Public Choice Perspective. In *The Greening of World Trade Issues*, ed. K. Anderson and R. Blackhurst, chap. 11. Ann Arbor: University of Michigan Press; London: Harvester Wheatsheaf.
International Labor Office. 1956. *Social Aspects of European Economic Cooperation*. Report by a Group of Experts (the Ohlin report). Geneva: ILO.
Jaffe, A. B., S. R. Peterson, P. R. Portney, and R. N. Stavins. 1995. Environmental Regulation and the Competitiveness of U.S. Manufacturing: What Does the Evidence Tell Us? *Journal of Economic Literature* 33, no. 1: 132–63.
Jones, L. A. and R. E. Manuelli. 1995. A Positive Model of Growth and Pollution Controls. NBER Working Paper no. 5205. Cambridge, MA: National Bureau of Economic Research. August.
Krueger, A. 1977. *Growth, Distortions, and Patterns of Trade among Many Countries*. Princeton, NJ: International Finance Section.
Lawrence, R. Z. 1994. Trade, Multinationals, and Labour. In *International Integration of the Australian Economy*, ed. P. Lowe and J. Dwyer, 233–65. Sydney: Reserve Bank of Australia.
——. 1995. *Regionalism, Multilateralism, and Deeper Integration*. Washington, DC: Brookings Institution.
Leamer, E. E. 1987. Paths of Development in the Three Factor, n-Good General Equilibrium Model. *Journal of Political Economy* 95, no. 5:961–99.
Leonard, N. J. 1988. *Pollution and the Struggle for World Product: Multinational Corporations, Environment, and International Comparative Advantage*. Cambridge: Cambridge University Press.

Levinson, A. 1996. Environmental Regulation and Industry Location: International and Domestic Evidence. In *Fair Trade and Harmonization: Prerequisites for Free Trade?* vol. 1, ed. J. N. Bhagwati and R. E. Hudec, chap. 11. Cambridge: MIT Press.

Low, P. 1992. Trade Measures and Environmental Quality: The Implications for Mexico's exports. In *International Trade and the Environment*, Discussion Paper 159, ed. P. Low, chap. 7. Washington, DC: World Bank.

Markusen, J. R. and A. J. Venables. 1996. Multinational Production, Skilled Labor, and Real Wages. NBER Working Paper no. 5483. Cambridge, MA: National Bureau of Economic Research, March.

Organization for Economic Cooperation and Development. 1996. *Report to the Council at Ministerial Level on Trade, Employment, and Labour Standards*. Paris: OECD.

Palmer, K., W. E. Oates, and P. R. Portney. 1996. Tightening Environmental Standards: The Benefit-Cost or the No-Cost Paradigm? *Journal of Economic Perspectives* 9, no. 4: 119–32.

Porter, M. E. and C. van der Linde. 1996. Towards a New Conception of the Environment-Competitiveness Relationship. *Journal of Economic: Perspectives* 9, no. 4: 119–32.

Porter, M. E., and C. van der Linde. 1996. Towards a New Conception of the Environment-Competitiveness Relationship. *Journal of Economic Perspectives* 9, no. 4: 97–118.

Radetzki, M. 1992. Economic Growth and Environment. In *International Trade and the Environment*, Discussion Paper no. 159, ed. P. Low, chap. 8. Washington, DC: World Bank.

Rybczynski, T. M. 1959. Factor Endowment and Relative Commodity Prices. *Economica* 22, no. 84: 336–41.

Sapir, A. 1996. Trade Liberalization and the Harmonization of Social Policies: Lessons from European Integration. In *Fair Trade and Harmonization: Prerequisites for Free Trade?* vol. 1, ed. J. N. Bhagwati and R. E. Hudec, chap. 15. Cambridge: MIT Press.

Seldon, T. M., and D. Song, 1994. Environmental Quality and Development: Is There a Kuznets Curve for Air Pollution Emissions? *Journal of Environmental Economics and Management* 27, no. 2: 147–62.

Shafi, N., and S. Bandyopadhyay. 1992. Economic Growth and Environmental Quality: Time Series and Cross-Country Evidence. World Bank Policy Research Paper WPS 904. Washington, DC.

Siebert, H. 1974. Environmental Protection and International Specialization. *Weltwirtschaftliches Archiv* 110:494–508.

Siebert, H., J. Eichberger, R. Gronych, and R. Pethig. 1980. *Trade and Environment: A Theoretical Enquiry*. Amsterdam: Elsevier.

Snape, R. H. 1992. The Environment, International Trade, and Competitiveness. In *The Greening of World Trade Issues*, ed. K. Anderson and R. Blackhurst, chap. 4. Ann Arbor: University of Michigan Press; London: Harvester Wheatsheaf.

Srinivasan, T. N. 1996. International Trade and Labour Standards from an Economic Perspective. In *Challenges to the New World Trade Organization*, ed. P. Van Dijck and G. Faber, chap. 11. Dordrecht: Kluwer Law International.

Steil, B. 1994. "Social Correctness" Is the New Protectionism. *Foreign Affairs* 73, no. 1:14–20.

Tobey, J. A. 1990. The Effects of Domestic Environmental Policies on Patterns of World Trade: An Empirical Test. *kyklos* 43, no. 2: 191–209.

Trefler, D. 1993. International Factor Price Differences: Leontief Was Right! *Journal of Political Economy* 101, no. 6:961–87.

Tyers, R., and Y. Yang 1995. Trade with Asia and Skill Upgrading: Effects on Factor Markets in the Older Industrial Countries. Australian National University, Canberra, October. Mimeo.

Williamson, J. G. 1996. Globalization and Inequality Then and Now: The Late 19th and Late 20th Centuries Compared. NBER Working Paper no. 5491. Cambridge, MA: National Bureau of Economic Research, March.

Wilson, J. D. 1996. Capital Mobility and Environmental Standards: Is There a Theoretical Basis for a Race to the Bottom? In *Fair Trade and Harmonization: Prerequisites for Free Trade?* vol. 1, ed. J. N. Bhagwati and R. E. Hudec, chap. 10. Cambridge: MIT Press.

Wood, A. 1994. *North–South Trade, Employment, and Inequality: Changing Fortunes in a Skill-Driven World*. Oxford: Clarendon Press.

Woolcock, S. 1996. An Agenda for the WTO: Strengthening or Overburdening the System. Global Economic Institutions Working Paper no. 4 London School of Economics, October.

2. Fair Trade, Reciprocity and Harmonization: The New Challenge to the Theory and Policy of Free Trade

J. Bhagwati

1. INTRODUCTION

Trade theorists of my generation, who spearheaded the modern theory of commercial policy from the 1950s through the 1970s, exploring several types of market failure and the appropriate nature of governmental intervention (including the use of trade tariffs, quotas and subsidies) in each such instance, have found it puzzling that some economists today suggest that economic theory was believed until the 1980s to imply that free trade was "always right".[1] The writings of younger trade theorists who have used imperfectly competitive models recently and made seminal contributions to the theory of commercial policy have expressed such sentiment from time to time. But their arguments are hard to accept.

To begin with, the view that the case for Free Trade is currently in maximal jeopardy since 1817, largely due to the theoretical developments in the 1980s in the theory of trade under product market imperfections, does not appear to be consistent with historical facts. As I argue below, a backward glance shows that earlier crises, some of equal and others of greater significance, have occurred in regard to the policy presumption in favor of free trade: all reflecting different blends of current economic circumstance and theoretical reflections.

Moreover, and this is a theme that I develop principally here, the true and greater crisis that we face in regard to the theory and policy of Free Trade today comes, *not* from the theoretical modelling of imperfect competition and other conventional market failures, but from the growth of demands for "level playing fields", "harmonization," "fair trade," etc. These demands undermine insidiously the legitimacy and feasibility of Free Trade since it is virtually impossible to harmonize everything so that playing fields are truly level in every way. There will always be something that an opponent of Free Trade will be able to find that is *different* in the country of one's successful rival and hence can be argued to make Free Trade unfair and therefore illegitimate and unacceptable.

I intend here to explore this problem, which I consider to be the truly greatest threat since the early 1930s when (as reviewed below) Keynes was driven to abandon Free Trade in the face of massive unemployment and many followed in his footsteps. But first, I consider the different ways in which the intellectual presumption that Free Trade was the policy to follow has been shaken repeatedly over the period since 1817.

Free Trade: National Versus Cosmopolitan Formulations

Unfortunately, in the popular as also in the professional discussion of Free Trade, the critical distinction between the *national* and the *cosmopolitan* formulations of Free Trade is blurred. They share common foundations; but they also have different implications for matters that have become contentious from time to present time.

The *national* formulation of the case for Free Trade is the one that predominantly shapes the policy debate. It posits national welfare as the objective of policy and proceeds to demonstrate that Free Trade will maximize national welfare.

In essence, the case depends of course on the set of assumptions that ensure that market prices reflect social costs, to use the old and apt Pigovian way of saying things. While the case, if we must make it rigorously, requires the usual theoretical armor, the simplest and most intuitive way to state it is to say that, if there are any domestic or foreign market "distortions," Free Trade ceases to be optimal (and indeed even its superiority over autarky no longer follows as necessity). Of course, these distortions imply market failures, including (in the cases where external prices of goods and services can be influenced by firms or governments, requiring us therefore to distinguish between average market prices and marginal revenues in trade) the failure of the market prices in trade to reflect the true social costs and benefits of trade. Note, however, that Free Trade ceases to be optimal only as long as the market failure is not addressed through appropriate policy intervention. But, as the theoretical developments in the 1950s through the 1970s shows, Free Trade remains the optimal policy in those many cases where the market failure arises *domestically* and is, therefore, appropriately corrected through domestic policy intervention targeted at the source of the failure.

These postwar analytical developments in the theory of commercial policy, especially during the 1950s through the 1970s, have set out the basic principles. They constitute a substantial body of scientific analysis of several market failures, typically in the shape of *factor* market imperfections such as monopsony, generalized sticky wages, sector-specific sticky wages, and different varieties of wage differentials among sectors. The 1980s witnessed the extension of the theoretical analysis to *product* market imperfections, of both the large-group and the small-group varieties, completing the architecture of this theory.

An important component of this theory, developed mainly during the 1960s, has also been the analysis of the implications for commercial policy where the conventional objective function that the economist maximizes becomes inappropriate. When "non-economic" objectives (such as the valuation in themselves of specific outputs such as manufactures or high-tech industry so that a dollar worth of output is valued at four, for instance) are admitted into the analysis, Free Trade will generally cease to be the optimal solution.[2] Trade theorists have then analyzed, for diverse non-economic objectives (which are abundantly in evidence and ceaselessly impose themselves on the political and policy scene), the optimal first-best and second-best ways of departing from Free Trade. Once again, in heuristic duality to the principal of targeting for market failures, it has been shown that Free Trade remains the appropriate policy, and domestic policy is the appropriate intervention, when non-economic objectives arise in the domestic arena.

While the study of commercial policy by economists has focused on national advantage and hence on the national formulation of the case for Free Trade, there is also the *cosmopolitan* formulation of the case for costs, the cosmopolitan argument simply elevates to the world level what the national argument did at the nation-state level. World efficiency follows Free Trade.

But there is one overriding difference that follows for policy. If the case for national Free Trade holds (i.e., the premises underlying it are broadly reflected in the reality that the nation in question faces), then it really is irrelevant whether *other* nations follow Free Trade or not. "Fair trade" and "reciprocity," defined as the requirement that others follow Free Trade if one's own Free Trade is to make economic sense, are incompatible with this "essential" case for Free Trade. The prescription that emerges then is for *unilateral* Free Trade.[3]

Not so, however, under the cosmopolitan case. World efficiency requires that *everyone* follow Free Trade. It is simply not enough that one or more do so. The prescription now is: *universal* Free Trade.

The contrast between the two cases for Free Trade, one implying that reciprocity does not matter and the other giving it central place, has however been less stark in practice. Unilateral Free Trade as the ideal trade policy has been argued to be possibly deficient on theoretical grounds since Adam Smith and has also been the subject of considerable debate among eminent economists since the end of the 19th century.

Since Free Trade has not been widely practiced at most times, the demands for reciprocity have also implied threats to the pursuit of Free Trade for oneself, transmitting the issue therefore into one of Free Trade versus protection. At the same time, the appeal of reciprocity is such that it has spilled over in recent years into parallel demands for reciprocity and "level playing fields" in a variety of other ways, taking the form of objections to the diversity of the myriad governmental policies and national institutions of trading nations.

It is necessary therefore to probe the issue of reciprocity further, prior to considering below the old and new challenges to Free Trade.

Reciprocity and the National Case for Free Trade

Foreign Barriers Subject to Change:

At the outset, it should be obvious that if the trade barriers of others can be regarded as changeable by the closure of one's markets, then a case can be made for departing from unilateral Free Trade in pursuit of national advantage.[4] In fact, this *was* evident even to Adam Smith 1776 pp. 434–435:

> "The case in which it may sometimes be a matter of deliberation how far it is proper to continue the free importation of certain foreign goods, is, when some foreign nation restrains by high duties or prohibition the importation of some of our manufactures into their country. Revenge in this case naturally dictates

retaliation, and that we should impose the like duties and prohibitions upon the importation of some or all of their manufactures into ours. Nations accordingly seldom fail to retaliate in the manner.

There may be good policy in retaliations of this kind, when there is a probability that they will procure the repeal of the high duties or prohibitions complained of. The recovery of a great foreign market will generally more than compensate the transitory inconvenience of paying dearer during a short time for some sorts of goods. To judge whether such retaliations are likely to produce such an effect, does not, perhaps belong so much to the science of a legislator, whose deliberations ought to be governed by general principles which are always the same, as to the skill of that insidious and crafty animal, vulgarly called a statesman or politician, whose councils are directed by the momentary fluctuations of affairs. When there is no probability that any such repeal can be procured, it seems a bad method of compensating the injury done to certain classes of our people, to do another injury ourselves, not only to those classes, but to almost all the other classes of them."

The case for the use of one's trade barriers to remove those of others raises, of course, several questions that have recurred in the debates on reciprocity through the last century:

(*i*) Does one really have the power to effectively pry open others' markets; could this power not be overestimated, partly because of the self-interest-induced optimism of the lobbies that provide the political drive for such aggressive policies, leading to confrontational situations that create an ethos of mutual recriminations within which protectionist interests thrive?

(*ii*) Will not the use of trade barriers for this purpose be "captured" by one's own protectionists for their purpose, leaving one saddled with tariffs?

(*iii*) Could the power of example, rather than sanction, not suffice to induce others to follow Free Trade since one's own Free Trade should lead to prosperity at home whereas others' reliance on protection should undermine it abroad, making unilateral Free Trade a more efficacious and less dangerous path to reciprocity in Free Trade?

As argued below, the answers to these questions in end-of-19th century Britain and in end-of-20th century United States have tended to be altogether different. In the former case, unilateralism survived the discord and debate. In the latter case, the use of muscle via threats to close markets in the absence of concessions on unilateral demands made under the Section 301 provisions of the 1988 Omnibus Trade and Competitiveness Act has emerged as U.S. trade policy.[5] Yet another contrast, as noted in Bhagwati and Irwin 1987, of course, is that whereas Britain was indeed a unilateral Free Trader, with its new rivals Germany and the United States explicitly resorting to protection, the United States can make no claim to being a unilateral Free Trader, nor are its tariff and non-tariff trade barriers in the 1980s significantly less than those of her rivals, the European Community and Japan.

But while the questions posed above were predicated on the narrow question as to whether *national* advantage can be enhanced by the renunciation of unilateral Free Trade, the key questions (raised by the use of threats and actions to close one's markets to pry open other') take one inevitably into the *cosmopolitan* arena. That is, one must ask questions such as:

(1) Will not the use of power to extract unilateral concessions threaten the rule of law under which a trading regime should function, by legitimating the use of force and spreading such methods to other trading nations?

(2) would it not also lead to concessions being granted to the powerful, diverting trade from the less powerful, replacing economic competitiveness by political clout as the guiding force behind trade, thus undermining world efficiency?

(3) Would not such use of power deteriorate also into unilateral (and therefore self-serving and biased) determination of the closedness of others' markets – a danger that is manifestly great when one is dealing with allegations of "invisible and inscrutable" trade barriers that can be flung freely at all and sundry but be forced to stick only for the benefit of the strong?

(4) Should we not regret the impact on world efficiency that would follow also if the strong can fully indulge their own interest and browbeat the weak into removing protection or promotion (i.e., production subsidies) when in fact these may be correcting market failure rather than creating it?[6]

In fact, one could argue that if these adverse *systemic* (and hence cosmopolitan-efficiency-focused) implications of the pursuit of national advantage through the use of muscle to extract trade concessions are indeed likely to transpire, then the immediate gain in national welfare could well yield (in a reverse-J-curve outcome) to ultimate loss of welfare as the world trading system gets impaired.

Foreign Barriers Unchangeable

But what if the prospect of getting others to reduce their trade barriers is negligible? Then, the case of unilateral Free Trade stands intact, quite unambiguously. To recall Joan Robinson's 1937 famous observation, you don't throw rocks into your own harbor just because others have done so in theirs.

Of course, if there are any distortions to contend with, Free Trade ceases to be the optimal policy. And this applies equally to all market failures whether, for instance, in factor markets or in product markets.

But there is an important implication for the question of reciprocity in trade which must be grasped since it is precisely the opposite of what is generally believed to be the theoretical consequence of market failures. This implication is that when trade occurs with market failures such as imperfect competition (uncorrected by appropriate intervention), it is no longer possible to assert with Adam Smith that the successful removal of others' tariffs (and indeed other barriers and interventions) adds to the benefits from one's own Free Trade.

In short, in the presence of market failure, it no longer follows that my Free Trade in the absence of yours necessarily makes me worse off than if we both had Free Trade (because, say, my insistence on reciprocity had led to the embrace of Free Trade by you as well). But reciprocity does offer added benefits to unilateral Free Trade when there are no distortions. Nonetheless, the popular belief, certainly in policy circles, is that the recent theoretical analyses of product-market imperfections imply that, *because* there are imperfect markets everywhere, we must insist on reciprocity in Free Trade. That is, that the presence of oligopoly, for example, strengthens, instead of weakening, the case for reciprocity!

TABLE 13.1 *Reciprocity of Free Trade Under Alternative Regimes: No-Distortions and Oligopoly*

Policy Choices by Home Country	Foreign Country	Utility of Home Country
	I. NO DISTORTIONS	
Unilateral FT (Free Trade)	Trade Barriers Given	$U_{FT(U)}$
Reciprocity in FT	FT imposed or induced	$U_{FT(R)} > U_{FT(U)}$
	II. OLIGOPOLY	
Unilateral FT	Trade Barriers Given	$U_{FT(U)}$
Reciprocity in FT	FT imposed or induced	$U_{FT(R)} >< U_{FT(U)}$
Appropriate Intervention: Departure from FT and/or Domestic Instruments*	Trade Barriers Given	$U_{INT} > U_{FT(U)}$

*Eaton and Grossman 1986.

Notation: U stands for the home country's utility; and the subscripts FT(R), FT(U) and INT for the cases where there is reciprocity in Free Trade, unilateral Free Trade, and appropriate intervention by Home Country, respectively.

Table 13.1 summarizes what we can say about this question, for the two contrasting cases: no-distortions (and therefore also perfect competition) and oligopoly (drawing on the recent analyses by Brander and Spencer 1981 and Eaton and Grossman 1986). It states that, in the former case, one can safely share Adam Smith's presumption that reciprocal Free Trade supplements the national gains from unilateral Free Trade. In the case of oligopoly, however, this is no longer so. That, in some *specific* parametric cases one can show that reciprocal Free Trade is welfare improving over unilateral Free Trade is, of course, compatible with the general proposition that it is not always or necessarily the case.[7]

Fairness and Prudence

The arguments so far presumed that the question of unilateral Free Trade versus reciprocity for national advantage could be assessed without reference to the role of emotions. But the policy question cannot be decided together in this fashion.

Adam Smith, in the quote above, spoke of revenge as motivating the demand for reciprocity and compromising the ability to pursue a policy of unilateral Free Trade. But the sense that reciprocity is required by *fairness* is more pertinent today. Lack of reciprocity in Free Trade is generally considered, regardless of its impact on national welfare, as simply unfair.

In consequence, there can follow a *prudential* argument for seeking reciprocity in Free Trade. The option of unilateral Free Trade may be impractical and attempts at keeping markets open unilaterally without attempting to extend Free Trade to one's trading partners and rivals may turn out in pluralistic countries to be a recipe for politically losing one's own Free Trade.[8]

Reciprocity and the Cosmopolitan Case for Free Trade

But the demands for reciprocity come perfectly naturally, as I have already indicated, if one approaches the question from the detached position of a *custodian* of world efficiency or, somewhat distinctly, from a *systemic* viewpoint.

Cosmopolitan Efficiency. World efficient allocation of resources requires that no members of the world economy depart from Free Trade: the sin of one visits on all by compromising world efficiency (just as a monopolist is known to affect the Pareto-optimality of the economic equilibrium for all). It is necessary then to insist on *all* adhering to Free Trade. That is, reciprocal embrace of Free Trade follows. To return to Joan Robinson's 1937 telling example, if any nation insists on throwing rocks in its harbor, we must throw rocks at it until it dredges them up.

Systemic Rationale. But there is also the distinct argument that, if one is creating a trading regime, such as the GATT, to establish a rules-based system, it is inevitable that it will impose symmetric or uniform rights and obligations on members. This is, of course, compatible with differences in obligations defined by accepted functional categories: for example, developed and developing countries, the latter enjoying asymmetry of obligations (i.e., Special and Differential Treatment in GATT language). But, outside such functionally-sanctioned discrimination, it is hard to imagine a regime that will tolerate asymmetries of Free Trade obligations.

Reciprocity then belongs with the regime approach: it thus finds itself *naturally* embedded in the GATT. In fact, the GATT also generally practices what I have called (Bhagwati 1988) *first difference* reciprocity, i.e., matching reductions in trade barriers, as distinct from "zero option" or *full* reciprocity.[9]

II. THE THREATS TO FREE TRADE: FROM THEN TO NOW

Now that I have distinguished among the alternative formulations, national and cosmopolitan, of the Free Trade doctrine, and analyzed the question of unilateralism verses reciprocity, it is possible to review with analytical clarity the manifold challenges to Free Trade since 1776 when Adam Smith invented both Economics and International Economics, grounding them in the principle of the division of labor.[10]

Several "episodes" of challenges to Free Trade can be distinguished over these two centuries and more. Of these, six (ending in the 1980s) fall broadly into one common pattern: they relate, in one way or another, to market failure. The seventh, now emerging, is radically different in nature and poses a novel, and more complex, type of threat. The six market-failure-related threats are now considered; the seventh, the principal subject of this paper, is addressed in the next section. All are summarized and listed in Table 13.2.

Episode I: Free Trade with Some Theoretical Exceptions: 19th Century

The repeal of the Corn Laws in 1846 ushered in Free Trade. It followed the shift from mercantilist thinking in Adam Smith and David Ricardo. The division of labor, and the gains from Free Trade, were in an essential way flip sides of the same coin. The relative importance of the roles played by the new economic doctrines and the industrial interests that would profit from cheap imports of corn have been the object of extensive debate; and the precise nature of the conversion by Prime Minister Sir Robert Peel has been analyzed with acute insight by Irwin 1987.

In the rest of the 19th century, until near the end thereof, unilateral Free Trade was Britain's policy. There was no serious threat to British dominance as a producer of manufactures during this period. The economic circumstance was therefore propitious for the continued embrace of Free Trade: strength makes it easier for politicians and industry to believe that the Darwinian process of survival of the fittest will serve one's interests well in competition.

The economic theory of Free Trade, however, was not left unchanged and unqualified during this period. It is only a mild caricature to say that, ever since Adam Smith invented the case for the Invisible Hand (and hence also for Free Trade), economists have made their reputation by inventing reasons why the Invisible Hand fails.

John Stuart Mill, in that respect no exception, produced the "infant industry" argument (1848, p. 922):[11]

> "The only case in which, on mere principle of political economy, protecting duties can be defensible, is when they are imposed temporarily (especially in a young and rising nation) in hopes of naturalizing a foreign industry, in itself perfectly suitable to the circumstances of the country. The superiority of one country over another in a branch of production often arises only from having begun it sooner. There may be no inherent advantage on one part, or disadvantage on the other, but only a present superiority of acquired skill and experience. A country which has this skill and experience yet to acquire, may in other respects be better adapted to the production than those which were earlier in the field. . . . A protecting duty, continued for a reasonable time, will sometimes be the least convenient mode in which the nation can tax itself for the support of such an experiment. But the protection should be confined to cases in which there is good ground of assurance

> that the industry which it fosters will after a time be able to dispense with it; nor should the domestic producers ever be allowed to expect that it will be continued to them beyond the time necessary for a fair trial of what they were accomplishing."

Mill started an argument whose theoretical formulation has undergone considerable refinement over the last century. And while it has proved to be of great influence in subsequent periods and in the latecoming nations, with the British Free Traders forecasting accurately its potency in practice – John Bright, Cobden's great ally in the movement to repeal the Corn Laws, remarked that Mill's one paragraph justifying infant industry protection "would cause hereafter more injury to the world than all his writings would do good"[12] – it did little to influence British policy, of course, and remained a theoretical curiosum there.

So did the argument for the use of tariffs to extract greater gains from trade by improving the terms of trade, originally produced by Robert Torrens in 1844. Widely debated, by Mill, Bickerdike, Marshall, and Edgeworth, it has now become the celebrated argument for an Optimal Tariff. But again, it found no place in British policy, a policy judgment supported by most of the eminent economists of the time but a folly according to McCloskey 1980.[13]

I would also be remiss not to recall that the case for Free Trade was debated almost exclusively from the viewpoint of national advantage. And that it took a unilateral form, though it was seen from the time of Adam Smith himself that the unilateralism assumed that the trade barriers of others were immutable.

All in all, therefore, the period until the rise of the United States and Germany by the last quarter of the 19th century was characterized by the dominance of (unilateral) Free Trade in Britain, by the development of two remarkable theoretical exceptions to the case for Free Trade, and by lively academic debate over the policy merits of these exceptions and over the further issue that Britain's embrace of unilateral Free Trade raised concerning the efficacy and the wisdom of British attempts at turning instead to reciprocity in Free Trade. Since Britain remained wedded to unilateral Free Trade throughout this period, and there was little sentiment among the leading economists of the time to change this policy despite the theoretical debates outlined here, the threat to Free Trade during this period can be dismissed as negligible. It was indeed the heyday of this doctrine.

Episode II: Reciprocity and Fair Trade; Infant Industry Protection: Last Quarter of the 19th Century

By the end of the 19th century, however, the relative decline of Britain and the rise of the United States and Germany in the world economy had produced in Britain the "diminished giant" syndrome (that would recur in the United States a century later as it confronted the rise of Japan and the Far East).[14]

The consensus in Britain over its policy of unilateral Free Trade was now to be shaken. "Fair Trade" and "reciprocity" became the common words of discourse. They also became the focus of organized lobbying: during the 1870s and 1880s, fair trade organizations such as the National Fair Trade League, the National Society for the Defense of British Industry, and the Reciprocity Free Trade Association arose on the British scene. The Conservative Party was deeply

TABLE 13.2 *The Threats to Free Trade since Adam Smith and David Ricardo*

	EPISODE	ECONOMIC CIRCUMSTANCES	ECONOMIC THEORY	THREAT LEVEL
1.	*19th Century:* *Free Trade with some Theoretical Exceptions*	British Dominance during prosperous century. No serious threat to British competitiveness since the repeal of the Corn Laws in 1846.	The case for Free Trade was qualified in three ways; 1. Infant Industry Argument in John Stuart Mill; 2. Monopoly Power in Trade Argument in Robert Torrens and John Stuart Mill; 3. Possible use of Tariffs to pry open Others' Tariffs: Argument Adam Smith	* The conjunction of happy economic circumstance and the perceived inapplicability of the theoretical exceptions (to Free Trade) to British circumstances meant that these theoretical exceptions, of great potency in later periods, had very little impact on the embrace of unilateral Free Trade by Britain
II.	*End of 19th Century:* *Reciprocity and Fair Trade Infant Industry Protection*	1. Britain's *relative* decline as Germany and the United States rose: the *Diminished Giant Syndrome* (Bhagwati and Irwin 1987) gripped Britain. "Fairness" and "Reciprocity" became fashionable demands. The belief in unilateral Free Trade was seriously challenged. 2. The flip side of the coin was that both Germany and United States were "coming from behind" and willing to use protection to industrialize, making the "infant industry" argument finally most potent.	No major theoretical developments transpired.	*** The threat to Free Trade was very real in the case of Britain, though it finally receded. The "latecomers", Germany and United States, practiced protection.

EPISODE	ECONOMIC CIRCUMSTANCES	ECONOMIC THEORY	THREAT LEVEL
III. *1930s* *Macroeconomic Failure*	The onset of the Great Depression and the massive macroeconomic distress during and thereafter in the 1930s provided a compelling economic environment for protectionist demands to arise and flourish.	Keynes' change of mind away from Free Trade in the early 1930s foreshadowed the macroeconomic revolution that would effectively introduce the notion that tariffs could switch expenditure from foreign to domestic goods and thereby increase employment and national income. Later developments would include Joan Robinson's classic *caveat* about beggar-my-neighbour policies and, later still, the analysis of policies to maintain both external and internal under the adjustable peg system.	**** The threat to Free Trade was not merely acute, reflecting both economic circumstance and new economic doctrine, but it also translated into reality through the 1930s.
IV. *1930s and Thereafter* *Imperfect Competition*	The economic circumstance propelling protectionist forces was the Depression and its aftermath: it occupied center stage, to the exclusion of other forces. Nothing in the economic situation lent itself to demands for protection on grounds related to imperfect competition, in any event.	The pathbreaking developments in the theory of imperfect competition by Edward Chamberlin and Joan Robinson undermined the basic premise of the theory of Free Trade that prices would reflect social costs. However, unlike in the 1980s, this was not accompanied by significant developments in the trade-theoretic applications of imperfect competition. This reduced the overall forcefulness of this threat to Free Trade.	** The lack of correspondence between economic circumstance and the new theory of imperfect competition, and the competing presence of the more powerful macroeconomic threat to Free Trade, made the force of this threat to Free Trade pretty limited.

EPISODE	ECONOMIC CIRCUMSTANCES	ECONOMIC THEORY	THREAT LEVEL
V. *1950s through 1970s:* *Imperfect Competition in Factor Markets and Non-Economic Objectives*	The demand for protection during this period, came essentially from the developing countries. The presence of market imperfections, especially in their factor (rather than product) markets, was considered a legitimate reason for protecting their nascent industrialization. Equally, "non-economic" objectives such as industrialization for modernization were considered to be valid reasons for departing from Free Trade. By contrast, the developed countries were committed to trade liberalization under GATT auspices. They enjoyed economic prosperity which reinforced, in a virtuous circle, the pro-trade policies.	Economic theory also developed, in tandem, to explore alternative factor market imperfections and to rank-order different trade and domestic policy interventions to improve welfare. Equally, the economic theory of policy was extended to rank-order policy interventions, not to fix market failure, but to accommodate "non-economic" objectives. By granting legitimacy to such objectives, trade theorists developed new arguments for policy interventions, including departures from Free Trade. Both for factor market imperfections and for non-economic objectives, trade theory made gigantic strides in developing theoretical arguments for the first-best and second-best uses of tariffs, export duties and trade subsidies to improve on Free Trade.	*** The developing countries did resort to protectionism generally. They successfully sought Special & Differential treatment at the GATT in order to do so. At the theoretical level, however, the developments in the theory of commercial policy could be, and were, interpreted as *narrowing down* the scope for departures from Free Trade by showing that the first-best case for trade interventions was limited to cases where the market failures arose in the external markets whereas the best way to deal with other ("domestic") market failures ("distortions") was through domestic policy interventions instead. Equally, the use of trade instruments was optimal only when the non-economic objective was in the external sector.
VI. *1980s:* *Renewed Imperfect Competition in Product Markets: Renewed Diminished Giant Syndrome: and DUP and Rent-seeking Activities*	The economic situation was precisely the opposite of that in the 1950s through 1970s: The developing countries turned increasingly to trade liberalization (having seen the success of the Far East), whereas the developed countries started flirting actively with protectionism. The Diminished Giant Syndrome that characterized Britain in Episode II returned to center stage, now in the United States, driving again both	The demands for protection and for fair trade and reciprocity coincided with theoretical advances in the analysis of imperfect competition in product markets, and the resulting application thereof to international trade theory in significant ways. These developments underlined sharply the message of the 1930s, in Episode IV which had dealt with Imperfect Competition (in *both* product and factor markets), by specifically working out the	*** The coincidence of the demand for protection and reciprocity (resulting from the Diminished Giant Syndrome) with the theoretical developments that could produce renewed demonstrations of the *possibly* beneficial effects of indulging these demands (in specific parametric situations) led to a significant threat to Free Trade, greater than during Episode IV and closer to that under Episode II.

EPISODE	ECONOMIC CIRCUMSTANCES	ECONOMIC THEORY	THREAT LEVEL
	protectionist demands and arguments for "fair trade" and for "reciprocity."	economics of welfare-improving intervention through trade instruments under imperfect competition (of both the large and the small group variety) in product markets. The theory of Directly-unproductive Profit seeking (DUP) and rent-seeking activities, and of political economy generally, was another equally dramatic development in the analysis of international trade. It served to countervail the anti-Free Trade message of imperfect-competition-in-product-markets developments by formalizing new sources of protectionist losses.	
VII. *Late 1980s and 1990s:* *Fair Trade, Reciprocity, and Harmonization*	Increased competitiveness due to several structural changes in the world economy has led to enhanced sensitivity to any foreign governmental policies and institutions (whose continuation in existing forms is itself taken as implying policy intolerance and therefore by implication as an act of policy) that may confer competitive advantage on one's rivals. This leads to impossible demands for harmonization, failing which there follow demands for managed trade, protection from unfair trade and from the absence of level playing fields.	Economic analysis of these new threats to Free Trade is only just beginning; it is different from all earlier threats (which reflected market failure). It should dominate theoretical international economics during the 1990s. It will intersect, in turn, with the major new developments in the theory of political economy and international trade during the 1980s.	**** The threat to Free Trade from the rising tide of demands for "level playing fields" and the ensuing demands for managed trade has gathered strength. It has the potential to become far more serious than most of the earlier, market-failure-variety threats.

Note: Seven threats to Free Trade since Adam Smith and David Ricardo are tabulated here. They are tabulated chronologically, with stars awarded under the column, THREAT LEVEL, to rank-order them in terms of their efficacy in affecting Free Trade as the preferred policy.

split on the issue. Academic opinion, however, remained united behind the doctrine of unilateral Free Trade and the wisdom of continuing adherence to it by Britain despite manifest protection by its new and successful rivals.[15]

While unilateral Free Trade survived in Britain into the 20th century, protection was embraced by the new economic powers, Germany and the United States. The appeal of the doctrine of Free Trade was less compelling for the latecomers. Instead, the argument for infant industry protection, propounded ably by John Stuart Mill, had a greater resonance in these countries, just as it would after World War II in the newly-independent developing countries.

Thus, this episode during the last quarter of the 19th century, was marked by a serious, if eventually unsuccessful, challenge to the doctrine of (unilateral) Free Trade in the country that had embraced it in 1846 in a pioneering departure from the protectionism of the past, and by the explicit practice of the protection by the newly-emerging industrial powers. Both in terms of threat, to itself, and actual breach of its tenets, Free Trade must then be regarded as having been subjected to a serious challenge during this period.

Episode III: Macroeconomic Failure: 1930s

The most dramatic episode in the life of the (national) Free Trade doctrine, however, was to come with the onset of the Great Depression. The massive macroeconomic distress during the 1930s and thereafter provided a compelling economic environment for protectionist demands to arise and to flourish.

Writing in 1951, Hicks recounted how the unemployment of these years had seriously undermined the belief in the doctrine of Free Trade:[16]

> "The main thing which caused so much liberal opinion in England to lose its faith in Free Trade was the helplessness of the older liberalism in the face of massive unemployment, and the possibility of using import restriction as an element in an active programme fighting unemployment. One is, of course, obliged to associate this line of thought with the name of Keynes. It was this, almost alone, which led Keynes to abandon his early belief in Free Trade." (1959, p. 48)

Keynes's apostasy on Free Trade had been suggested in *A Treatise on Money* (1930) and in this evidence before the MacMillan Committee in February 1930 where he offered the view that tariffs, while unwise as a long-term policy, could immediately alleviate the slump.[17] This viewpoint however becomes more pronounced in Keynes's thinking and writings through 1931, resulting in a celebrated controversy with Lionel Robbins and the Beveridge-led 1931 riposte by Robbins, Hicks et al. to Keynes in *Tariffs: The Case Examined.*

Interestingly, Keynes seems to have anticipated the later objection that the superior intervention to achieve full employment was domestic reflation rather than expenditure-switching protection: "If nations can learn to provide themselves with full employment by their domestic policy . . . there would no longer be a pressing motive why one country need force its wares on another or repulse the offerings of it neighbors."[18]

Later theoretical analysis would then show how, under fixed exchange rates, the reflation would cause external imbalance and therefore the two policies, reflation and devaluation, would be generally necessary to attain the two targets of external and internal balance. Tariffs would then appear to be inferior to the optimal combination of devaluation and reflation as the policy solution to unemployment.

But these insights came later. During the 1930s, Keynes' renunciation of the doctrine of Free Trade remained a potent source of disbelief in the doctrine. Combined with the massive unemployment unleashed by the Great Depression and the lingering aftermath of its distress, this apostasy turned the 1930s into the most deadly episode among the challenges to the (national) doctrine of Free Trade.

Episode IV: Imperfect Competition: 1930s and Thereafter

The 1930s also witnessed the emergence of a threat to Free Trade from an altogether different direction. It came, not from economic circumstance as the earlier threats had partly or wholly done, but entirely from theoretical progress: and that too in a curiously tangential way.

As the 1920s ended, Chamberlin 1929 and Robinson 1931 independently came up with important theoretical analyses of imperfect competition, opening up to systematic exploration and middle ground between perfect competition and pure monopoly.[19] The result was to undermine seriously the notion that market prices reflected social costs, calling into question, more widely, the virtue of laissez faire, and, more narrowly with it, the merit of Free Trade as well.

The economists of the Chicago School correctly saw this as a threat that would legitimise interventionism. Therefore, they proceeded to counter the threat by taking to econometrics to demonstrate that, although markets seemed imperfect to the naked eye, in reality there was "as if" or "working" competition and that the imperfections did not amount to a hill of beans.[20] Today, we talk, not of "as if" competition but of "contestable markets." But, by and large, the key thought is the same.

Despite Chicago's riposte, however, the skepticism about prices not reflecting social costs due to imperfect competition remained a potent source of erosion in the belief that Free Trade was a desirable policy. In his earlier-cited essay of 1951, analyzing the different reasons why the doctrine of Free Trade had lost "much of its strength" and "been called into question,"[21] John Hicks captured this reality well;[22]

> ". . . the Monopoly-Competition argument . . . is of much less practical importance than the others, but it deserves at least a passing mention, because of the undoubted influence which it undoubtedly exercises – in a negative sort of way – upon the minds of economics students . . . If apparent costs only equal true costs under conditions of perfect competition, and competition hardly ever is perfect, the bottom seems to drop out of the Free Trade argument. This is in fact a fair description of the state of mind which quite a number of economic students seem to have reached." (1959, p. 46)

But the damage that the theory of imperfect competition did to the policy of Free Trade cannot be argued, as Hicks also suggests, to have been serious. There were two reasons. First, there was nothing in economic circumstance that led to the demand for protection, citing this kind of theory: the attack on Free Trade was of the nihilistic variety, hard to tap by specific interest groups. Besides, Free Trade was already imperilled far more seriously by Keynes's desertion, by the economic circumstance of massive unemployment, and by the new macroeconomic ideas that I discussed as Episode III. When economists returned to imperfect competition in the 1980s, the threat would become more serious: economic circumstance would have changed, with more compelling craving for protection, and the idiom and substance of the new work on imperfect competition would be more readily accessible for capture by the protectionist interests.

Episode V: Renewed Imperfect Competition in Factor Markets; Non-Economic Objectives: 1950s Through 1970s

The postwar period, at the outset, was characterized by the emergence of the General Agreement on Tariffs and Trade (GATT) with initial ratification by twenty-three nations. It was the first multilateral trade institution, establishing the legitimacy of a liberal trading regime embodying a common set of rules for member nations.[23] Among these rules, possibly central among them, was the most-favored-nation (MFN) obligation (with well-defined exceptions, in the main for customs unions and free trade areas in Article XXIV).

The 1950s through 1970s were the decades of increasingly freer trade in the developed countries. Successive GATT Rounds of negotiations brought tariffs down to low levels. Trade expansion and income growth interacted virtuously to make these two decades the Golden Age that the later, more troubled years in the 1970s would contrast unhappily with. In this respect, this was again the heyday of Free Trade.

But the increasing trade liberalization of the developed countries contrasted with the turn to import substitution and protectionist policies in much of the underdeveloped world. The newly-independent developing countries were determined to use the "infant industry" argument freely to support nascent industries. Equally, they considered these industries to be necessary features of a modern economy and society, implying what international economists in the 1960s would call a "non-economic" preference. Besides, it was widely believed that the developing countries were characterized by a number of market imperfections, the principal ones being in factor markets: distorting intersectoral wage differentials, sticky wages such that the market wage exceeded the shadow wage, sector-specific minimum wages, and monopsony. All these implied market failure which would seem to require protection.

Interestingly, therefore, since theory often responds to reality, the major developments in the theory of commercial policy during this period came from, not the developed-country liberalization (though, the growth of the European Common Market did stimulate the new theory of customs unions and preferential trade liberalization),[24] but rather from the developing-country concerns and policies of protection.

Thus, the theory of optimal policy intervention in the presence of non-economic objectives was fuelled by these concerns: its major contours were established in contributions by Corden 1957, Johnson 1965, Bhagwati and Srinivasan 1969 and many others.[25] But, much more so, there was an explosion of theoretical developments concerning the optimal, and second-best, policies to remedy the distorting effects of several different factor market imperfections.

However, these developments led to a most important twist in favor of Free Trade. Instead of underlining the need for protection to fix these market failures, these analyses led to the conclusion that the best way to address *domestic distortions* (such as most factor market imperfections) was through *domestic policy interventions*, and that in these cases protection was at best a second-best measure. This principle was established independently by James Meade 1952 and by Bhagwati and Ramaswami 1963, and its numerous ramifications were explored in countless theoretical contributions in the two decades since the latter article was published.

The net effect of this central insight was to *narrow*, not widen the case for protection, since until then it was commonly believed that protection was the appropriate way to handle all kinds of market failure. Now, protection was seen to be the first-best policy only when the distortion was foreign, not domestic.[26]

This insight applied equally to the important question of non-economic objectives. Symmetrically, the trade theorists showed that only when the non-economic objective was in the foreign sector (e.g., one wanted to reduce imports in the pursuit of "self-sufficiency") would optimal intervention be in the shape of protection; in other cases, it required domestic policy intervention.[27]

Thus, this episode was characterized by contrasting phenomena:

* a *substantial* threat to Free Trade from the demands for protection from the many developing countries which, in fact, embraced extensive protection as part of their developmental strategy of import substitution; and a *reduced* threat to Free Trade from the developed countries which pursued trade liberalization instead; and

* a *substantial* concern with the market failure (through factor markets) and non-economic objectives, both stemming from developing-county concerns, which implied increased legitimacy for intervention and presumably therefore for protection; and a *reduced* threat of protection because theoretical analysis, stimulated by these questions, showed that the appropriate intervention required was mostly in domestic markets, not in the form of trade protection.

Episode VI: Renewed Imperfect Competition in Product Markets; Renewed Diminished Giant Syndrome; Directly Unproductive Profit-Seeking (DUP) and Rent-Seeking Theory: 1980s

The 1980s shared with the 1950s–1970s the distinction of having the theory of Free Trade extended in the realm of imperfect competition. But whereas the earlier period was concerned with *factor* market imperfections, the latter period was concerned with *product* market imperfections.

In turn, this reflected a shift from preoccupation with protectionism in the developing countries to preoccupation with protectionism in the developed countries. In fact, by the end of the 1970s, the combination of economic writings and far-ranging research into the costs of import substitution and the benefits of export promotion, conditionality imposed by the World Bank on the basis of these ideas and findings, and the example provided by the successful export-promoting nations of the Far East, had led to growing trade liberalization among the developing countries.

By contrast, the developed countries had lapsed into resorting to non-tariff barriers (NTBs) in lieu of the reduced tariffs "bound" at the GATT. In fact, the rise of these NTBs, in shape of Voluntary Export Restraints (VERs) and "administered protection" in shape of the unfair use of fair trade mechanisms such as anti-dumping (AD) actions and (subsidy-) countervailing duties (CVD), got quite out of hand, including in the United States, during the early 1980s.

The growth of protectionist outcomes reflected increases in both the *demand for*, and the *supply of*, protection. The demand for protection had escalated to unmanageable levels owing to the Volcker-led recession. In addition, the United States suffered from serious dollar overvaluation during the first Reagan administration. The United States was also succumbing to a return of the "diminished giant syndrome" (Bhagwati and Irwin 1987). The developments in the theory of imperfect competition in product markets thus turned out to be ripe for capture, legitimating protectionism and therefore facilitating the supply of protection by Congress and the administration. The intense competition among the firms of the developed countries, and the desire to protect against inroads by foreign rivals, provided the context within which these developments were set. They caught the protectionist fancy, met the protectionist needs, and therefore immediately got into the center stage of public policy debate.

From the protectionist viewpoint, therefore, the imperfect-competition models of the 1950s through 1970s were popular in the developing countries as legitimating (to the uncritical eye) their protectionism. The imperfect-competition models of the 1980s were equally popular in the developed countries as legitimating (to the uncritical eye) *their* protectionism.

One rather important difference in the interaction of theory with the demand for protection in the two cases, however, appears to have been the greater capture of the theorists by the protectionists during the 1980s. This reflects perhaps the occasional tendency of the 1980s theorists of imperfect competition (to product markets) to present their important scientific work as also revolutionary in regard to its implications for Free Trade, in the shape of claims that *finally a theoretical* case for departure from Free Trade had been made.[28] Such claims were freely used by the popular press, the politicians and the protectionist lobbies to delegitimate the arguments for Free Trade as a broadly desirable policy.[29] This process of capture was facilitated by the vast expansion of the business media[30] looking for "news" of interest to their business readers with an evident stake in protectionism and often writing without the nuances required by their subject matter.

In the end, the theorists of the imperfect-competition-in-product-markets have returned to the fold of Free Trade in one of two ways.

(*i*) Either they have followed the Chicago School approach of saying that the market imperfections do not amount to a hill of beans and should therefore be ignored by policymakers. This is the view embraced, in varying degrees, by economists such as Grossman 1986 who argue, for instance, that rent-shifting towards oneself by using trade policy in oligopolistic industries, scientifically shown to be a good policy intervention, requires that there be significant rents to shift; but that arguably there are few such rents in reality.

(*ii*) Else, they have followed the *Public Choice School* approach, which essentially argues that the visible hand will strangulate: intervention will produce worse outcomes than the imperfect markets that we seek to fix. This can happen if you have a predatory view of government, which should not be surprising. But it comes from the public-choice-theoretic view that special-interest lobbying will distort the outcome. Krugman 1987 takes this view which, in my judgment, is a more conservative option to return to Free Trade than the Chicago School route.

The theoretical developments in the 1980s, however, were not one-sided. The case for Free Trade was strengthened indirectly by the new interest in political-economy-theoretic modelling that has by now become a compelling trend in economic theorizing more generally. In particular, the notion that the cost of protection was low and therefore unworthy of policy attention simply because the deadweight losses measured were a small fraction of the national income, was seen as naive when the induced rent-seeking (Krueger 1974) or revenue-seeking (Bhagwati and Srinvasan 1980) was taken into account. The general theory of DUP (directly unproductive profit-seeking) activities (Bhagwati 1982) considers alternative ways in which resource-using but zero-output-producing (and income-earning) activities can result from lobbying for policy change to redistribute income towards oneself (as with tariffs) or through lobbying to share in the rents or revenues from existing policies (as when lobbies compete for rent-fetching import quotas already in place). Such DUP activities could add significantly to the deadweight cost of protection.[31]

While therefore the 1980s began by marrying the rising protectionist demand in the developed countries to the theoretical developments in the theory of imperfect competition in product markets, and protectionism did break out, making the period one of high threat to Free Trade, it ended with the proponents of the theory backing off into Free Trade and with the new developments in the political-economy theory of DUP and rent-seeking activities strengthening the case against protection.[32]

Episode VII: Fair Trade, Reciprocity, and Harmonization: Late 1980s and 1990s

Until now, therefore, the challenges to the doctrine of Free Trade were concentrated on its national version. In turn, they reflected varying combinations of economic circumstance (fuelling the demand for protection) and economic theory (fuelling the supply of protection).[33]

The latter again reflected different varieties of market failure that undermined the basic premise of the Free Trade doctrine: that market prices should reflect social costs. But, even if there was no evident market failure, the question raised by Adam Smith had to be addressed: would one renounce Free Trade for oneself if others did not embrace it too? this issue of unilateralism versus reciprocity was never wholly dormant; but it turned to center stage during the two episodes

(II and VI), a century apart, when Great Britain and the United States, both Free Traders in actual policy and self-perception, confronted the rise of new and successful trading rivals, either avowedly protectionist or accused of being deviously so, and were engulfed in demands for Reciprocity in trade. "Free Trade by oneself' would have to confront "Free Trade for all or Free Trade for None."

Indeed the emphasis on Reciprocity and its kin, Fair Trade, is a natural outgrowth of economic weakness or, more accurately, of *perceived* economic weakness. The shifted focus onto what others are doing that may aid their producers vis-à-vis ours is an inevitable consequence of the "competitiveness" concerns that attend the rise of new and fiercely successful rivals abroad.

In the earlier episode relating to the affliction by many in Britain by the diminished giant syndrome and for much of the 1980s in the parallel case of American affliction, the concerns were focussed largely on whether others had trade barriers as well. Doubtless, tariffs by others reduce one's gains from trade. This is a matter that strong countries with commensurate faith in their strength would not however elevate to a policy concern. But not so, when the strong, feeling diminished, face the weak. The giants, diminished relative to erstwhile Lilliputians, were still giants in both the end-of-19th-century Britain and end-of-20th-century American episodes. So the academic (and policy) debate that ensued was mainly about the empirical relevance, and the wider systemic consequences, of Adam Smith's old "strategic" argument. In Randolph Churchill's class phrase, the question became: "should Free Trade be renounced in favor of protection as an instrument for opening foreign markets, the way one pried open oysters with a clasp knife?"[34]

But, in the recent replay, the Reciprocitarians and Fair Traders have gone considerably further than seeking a mutuality of trade barrier levels and reductions thereof, raising an altogether different and more dangerous kind of threat to Free Trade. Let me explain.

The Fair Trade notion now extends to *any* foreign governmental policy or institution that is different from one's own. Such differences, myriad in principle, are assumed to create an unfair advantage of one kind or another in favor of foreign producers, implying the absence of "level playing fields." This results in demands for getting these policies harmonized (in practice, to what the diminished giant prefers, reflecting of course its own political and ideological constraints and objectives), or (failing harmonization) for getting the alleged trade consequences of these different policies neutralized through countervailing duties, subsidies, etc. The latter set of policies, of course, amounts to protectionist intervention on behalf of one's industries.

The proponents of managed trade, i.e., a fix-quantity as against a fix-rule engine, also draw comfort from the widespread notion that, if level playing fields are absent, Free Trade does not make sense. The delegitimation of Free Trade makes the case for managing trade through bureaucratically-set market shares, and allocations of production and trade targets, seem like the solution that is both natural and desirable when trading countries have different policies and institutions.

Reasons for the Rise of Fair Trade. The demands for Fair Trade are not altogether

TABLE 13.3 *Theoretical Arguments Against Free Trade for Oneself (i.e., Unilateralism)*

Episodes	Free Trade: Essential Case	Unilateralism Versus Reciprocity
Episode I	Doctrine was accepted but with *theoretical* exceptions for (1) *infant industry* and (2) *variable terms of trade*, by John Stuart Mill, Robert Torrens, et al.	Unilateralism was accepted but a *theoretical* case was made for tariffs to pry open foreign markets, and hence for reciprocity, by Adam Smith.
Episode II	Same as in Episode I	No new theoretical case of substance was developed for reciprocity, but several arguments for unilateralism emerged in the great debate over fair trade and reciprocity that marked the British scene as Britain was afflicted by the Diminished Giant Syndrome.
Episode III	Doctrine was frontally rejected by Keynes: macro *unemployment* was the source of market failure now.	Unilateralism was not an issue.
Episode IV	Doctrine was undermined because of the new theories of imperfect and monopolistic competition: (1) *Imperfect Competition in product markets*: monopoly, oligopoly and the large-group case; and (2) *Imperfect Competition in factor markets*: monopsony (Joan Robinson).	Unilateralism was not an issue.
Episode V	During this period, there was focus on two sets of market failure: (1) *Imperfect Competition in factor markets*: monopsony, wage differentials between sectors, sticky or minimum wages, etc., and (2) *Non-Economic Objectives*: the failure of markets to reflect non-economic objectives.	Unilateralism was not an issue.
Episode VI	The market failure was that arising from *imperfect competition in product markets*: oligopoly; and the large-group case.	Unilateralism again became an issue, reflecting both the renewal of the Diminished Giant Syndrome (now in the United States) and demonstration that lack of reciprocity may produce loss, rather than gains, vis-à-vis autarky.

novel. They have been more or less confined traditionally to foreign subsidies and predatory dumping, both of which have long been countervailed, both before the GATT arrived on the world stage and certainly under GATT auspices. But today the demands have grown out of hand.[35]

They have been extended, in the case of the Structural Impediments Initiative (SII) with Japan by the United States, to nearly 240 items including Japan's savings rate, its working hours, its retail distribution system, its *keiretsus*, etc. The 1988 Omnibus Trade and Competitiveness Act now defines as unreasonable, and hence actionable, a variety of foreign policies and institutions such as labor standards and export targeting. Differences in environmental policies have also come under the fair trade rubric: Senators Baucus and Danforth have recently introduced legislation in Congress to countervail differentially-smaller pollution abatement costs of production in foreign countries. Believe it or not, there have even been proposals to equalize similarly, through countervailing duties, the differentially-higher legal costs imposed on domestic producers by the "extortionary" tort system that American lawyers have gifted to their nation.

Many of my examples come from the United States where the diminished giant syndrome has prompted an acute search for unfair trade by others. The payments deficit and the special chord that fairness plays in the American political psyche have further fuelled this search. But I suspect that there are also broader forces at work which will make this a continuing phenomenon that should further diffuse internationally:

* since it is easier to get protection if one alleges unfair trade by others than if one simply pleads for assistance citing the difficulty of one's situation, the unfair trade route will be well traveled once it is discovered;

* given the decline of transparent tariffs and the rise of NTBs, of varying degrees of transparency, it is somewhat easier to charge others with unfair trade: thus, for instance, the tendency has become manifest to "construct" what imports "should" be and are not, just as in anti-dumping actions it has become customary to "construct" fair value (and win through exploiting the scope for chicanery that this procedure opens up);

* the slide to unfair trade allegations has also been facilitated by the fact that the main newly-emergent trading nation has been Japan with its manifest differences of culture and economic organization, and with its long history of being regarded since the 1930s by its fearful rivals as an unfair trader;

* the continuing globalization of the world economy, with its spider's web of criss-crossing investments and rising shares of trade to GNP, has increasingly made the force of international competition more palpable to many, making producers ever more sensitive to whether, in one way or another, their rivals gain an unjustified, unreasonable, unfair advantage in the lethal struggle for markets and survival; and

* the volatility of exchange rates, a fact of life despite "managed floats" since 1971, may have contributed to this sensitivity, though there is little econometric support for the thesis that trade volumes have been adversely affected in any significant fashion by the arrival of flexible exchange rates.

For these reasons, the concern over whether others are fairly trading, whether in our markets or in theirs or in third markets, has intensified. It will grow, rather than diminish. It can overwhelm the fix-rule, open trading system unless it is confronted: for, in principle and in revealed practice, the scope for unfair trade allegations is open-ended. A Pandora's box is open.

Confronting Fair Trade. How does one cope with the serious consequences of Fair Trade, ever looming larger, for the doctrine and regime of Free Trade?

A pragmatic response would simply be to get nations to agree to a set of constraints beyond which the absence of level playing fields cannot be a ground for suspending Free Trade. This certainly should help; but it does not get to grips with the underlying theoretical problem that the issue of Fair Trade creates and which requires us to reconsider the way we think of Free Trade.

This theoretical question arises because for over two centuries we have deduced Free Trade essentially as a mutual-gain trade arrangement among nations with private agents differentially endowed with taste, technology and resources, but with governments that exist only to implement our recommendations on trade policy. Free Trade, and letting market-determined comparative advantage work, are thus two sides of the same coin: for, in our basic models of commercial policy where Free Trade and the gains from trade are analyzed, governments play no independent role.

But as soon as one lets governments in, with their own myriad policies, they will wittingly or unwittingly affect comparative advantage: i.e., few policies are "neutral" in their impact on resource allocation. Thus, as soon as governmental policies are taken from the back burner and put onto the table, as the Fair Traders are now doing, there is no way that we can pretend that there is a (wholly) market-determined comparative advantage. Comparative advantage is inevitably "distorted," "created," in fact "shaped" by myriad governmental policies, wittingly or unwittingly.

Therefore, if Fair Traders are to be confronted, we need a revolution in the way we think about the theory of commercial policy and gains from trade, divorcing it altogether from (untenable) notions of "market-determined" comparative advantage. In short, having discarded this baggage of market-determined comparative advantage, we need to ask questions such as:

* Can Free Trade produce mutual gains from trade even if two nations have different policies on, say, retail distribution or minimum wages or working hours or abatement of pollution entirely affecting one's own citizens? Or do such differences cause predation by one at the expense of the others under Free Trade (relative to autarky or other forms of intervention)?

* Would different types of harmonization in one's image, or the others' or in an altogether different fashion, produce more overall gains from trade? If so, how would it affect the distribution of the gains from trade?

* When can one expect that non-harmonization will imply greater gains from trade for each nation, just as greater differences in private tastes between countries generally would increase trade gains?

But before I consider these and other ways of getting at the way we must now address the question of Free Trade, putting governments and their actions squarely into our models, let me turn to the pragmatic agenda for containing the fallout from the growing flood of Fair Trade.

Pragmatic Solutions. A slight reflection, if not familiarity with the way in which the traditional fair trade mechanisms in shape of CVD and AD processes have evolved, shows at least four pragmatic forms of containment:

1. *Principle of Proportionality:* For any specific policy where the absence of level playing fields becomes contentious, the principle of proportionality can be applied. That is, we can accept procedures which eliminate complaints that do not amount to much. In essence, the application of an injury test is precisely a test of proportionality. Whereas it deals with proportionality of consequences, proportionality could equally be applied to the gradient on the level playing field: for example, an anti-dumping margin of less than 20% may be declared inadmissible as a ground for action.[36]

2. *Principle of Intentionality:* Yet another way to contain the Fair Traders would be to ask whether any particular playing field is intentionally fixed in favor of the home team or whether one is dealing with unwitting consequences. Thus, a nation subsidizing its higher education is shifting the endowment of skilled labor and therefore indirectly favoring those activities that use skilled labor. But the specific trade effect is unintended. So this range of governmental policies should be excluded from the Fair Traders' grasp.

3. *Principle of Selectivity:* Again, one may agree to exclude policies that are not selectively designed in their impact. Thus, a general R&D credit, not confined to a specific industry or set of (say high-tech) industries, may be accepted as admissible even though it may have non-neutral effects on resource allocation. Equally, accelerated tax credit for investment amounts to an interest-free loan that can affect the choice of technique and also differentially impact on different sectors with different capital intensities. Yet, because it is applied non-selectively, it may be accepted as a policy that should be exempt from Fair Traders' attention.

4. *Principle of Proximity:* Finally, one may delimit Fair Trade concerns to include only policies that proximately, rather than indirectly, affect comparative advantage. Thus, agricultural export subsidies are offensive but not income support payments that keep farmers alive and may indirectly therefore lead to more production and exports.

Principled Solution: Reworking the Theory of Free Trade. But these ways of containment of the Fair Traders, while helpful, do not get at the basic problem that Fair Traders find with Free Trade: that, in the absence of level playing fields, Free Trade is illegitimate since it distorts in one way or another the market-determined comparative advantage.

Since governments will not self-destruct to oblige either Bakunin or Friedman, since politicians get elected or seize power to do myriad things, and since harmonizing everything is generally impossible, a theory of Free Trade and the gains from trade that does not squarely put governmental policies (other than the trade policies which we seek to rank order for benign governments to consider) into the specification of the model and its analysis will fail to address the concern that agitates the Fair Traders and undermines Free Trade.

It is no longer enough, as in the classic welfare-theoretic analysis of Samuelson 1939, 1962, Kemp 1972, Kenen 1957, Grandmont and McFadden 1972 and others to argue that, in conventional economic models that postulate absent governments, we can prove well-known theorems such as that Free Trade dominates No Trade (FT>NT) for national welfare and for world welfare, and that Free Trade is a mutual-gain policy for trading nations.

We need to rewrite our models to allow for governments explicitly to have other policies, harmonized or otherwise. That is, we must build the theory of Free Trade on the foundations of the theory of political economy that has been developing through the 1980s, but with different sets of questions. Equally, since these other policies may be driven (as in the case of environmental and labor-standards policies) by considerations which suggest that they define "non-economic objectives" (Corden 1957, Johnson 1965, Bhagwati and Srinivasan 1969), and others, it may be necessary in the case of some of these policies to augment the social objective function to include considerations such as: despite mutual gains from trade, will FT (relative to NT) not lead to more pollution or to harm to child labor?"

Thus, in the analysis required to address the concerns of Fair Traders and nonetheless argue for Free Trade, it would sometimes be necessary to combine two great traditions in the theory of commercial policy: the incorporation of non-economic objectives into the analysis, which is part of the early postwar development of the theory of commercial policy, and the explicit treatment of government, which is part of the recent (political-economy) developments in the theory of commercial policy.

Again, while the analysis so sketched would treat these other policies as exogenous to the choice of trade policy, so that comparisons such as FT versus NT are carried out subject to these policies pre-set in the analysis, we must also allow for the fact that some of these policies are *endogenous* to the choice of trade policy itself. For example, if my labor standards are more stringent than yours, or my pollution abatement requirements are more drastic than yours, the competitive pressures that this builds on my industry in Free Trade may lead to political lobbying to reduce environmental and labor standards at my end, in which case those of us who value environmental and labor standards would have good reason to object to Free Trade if harmonization of these standards to their own preference is not obtained.

Thus, we need, in the following analysis of Fair-Trade-prompted refashioning of the theory of commercial policy, to distinguish among three main classes of possibilities:

(*i*) Other Policies Exogenous; Conventional Objective Function;
(*ii*) Other Policies Exogenous; Non-economic Objectives Considered; and
(*iii*) Other Policies Endogenous; Non-economic Objectives Considered

Let me indicate each type of analysis, in turn, setting out the way we need to develop the theory rather than taking any particular policy and undertaking the theoretical analysis I argue to be necessary now.

(*i*) Exogenous Other Policies: Conventional Objective Function

This is the most "natural" case to consider, for a variety of policies where demands for harmonization (i.e., for level playing fields) have been raised. What questions should we ask here?

Where we traditionally drive theorems that state that, for two countries I and II, FT > NT such that $U_I^{FT} > U_I^{NT}$ and $U_{II}^{FT} > U_{II}^{NT}$, we must now ask the following questions for the cases where there is harmonization (H) and non-harmonization (NH) and the countries then go from NT to FT. Where harmonization occurs at country I's policy, denote it by H(I); at country II's level, it is denoted by H(II).

Question 1. The most important question which we must ask then, and which is the natural counterpart of the earlier Free Trade doctrine in the absence of governments, is: *will Free Trade, without harmonization, still lead to mutual gain?* That is, can we still find that:

$$U_I^{NH,FT} > U_I^{NH,NT}; \tag{1}$$

and

$$U_{II}^{NH,FT} > U_{II}^{NH,NT}; \tag{2}$$

This is a key question since most Fair Traders seem to imply that predation, rather than mutual gains, will follow from Free Trade in the absence of harmonization.

From the theory of immiserizing growth (Bhagwati 1968), we know immediately that, as long as there are no market failures in either country, Free Trade will indeed benefit both. The question of non-harmonization of policies leading to predation, i.e., immiserization, being visited on a trading country is then pertinent only insofar as there is market failure, with prices not reflecting true social costs.

Thus, the problem allegedly raised by non-harmonization of "other" (non-trade) policies for the case for mutually-beneficial Free Trade is theoretically nonexistent unless these policies fail to address, or they create, market failure. Evidently, then, competition policy in a world of imperfect competition can be an example where lack of harmonization (as also its presence) is compatible with predation and therefore becomes a serious question for theoretical analysis and clarification.

Question 2. Harmonization: Them Like Us: But the Fair Traders may well be interested in a different question as well. That is, *will Free Trade with harmonization imposed on the other country in one's image produce more gains than Free Trade without harmonization?*

I suspect that, in the case of the SII policy of the United States towards Japan where attempts are being made to remold Japan's retail distribution system, her *keiretsus*, etc. so that Japan gets closer on these policies to the United States, the motivation is as much the fear that otherwise there will be predation (i.e., Question I will be answered in the negative for the United States) as the chagrin that the gains from trade are being *diminished* for the United States by Japan's differential policies.

This then leads to the comparison and question whether:

$$U_I^{H(I),FT} > U_I^{NH,FT}; \tag{3}$$

Question 3. Harmonization: Us Like Them: The question can then be turned around to ask if one's welfare would increase, relative to non-harmonization, if one changed one's policies in the image of the other.

This has been suggested, for instance, by admirers of the Japanese system (as imagined by them), in regard to institutions and policies such as the *keiretsus* and industrial policy. In this case, the assumption to be examined, for any policy in question is, whether:

$$U_I^{H(II),FT} > U_I^{NH,FT} ; \tag{4}$$

An important observation to make here is that there is no presumption that, in these harmonization versus non-harmonization comparisons, the former will win. If anything, policy differences between countries may act like private taste differences and lead to greater, rather than less, gains from trade. But this is precisely the issue that awaits former analysis for different kinds of policies.

Question 4. In case of both forms of harmonization, we should also ask the world-welfare or cosmopolitan-efficiency questions as to whether harmonization at one or other policy improves world efficiency over the case where non-harmonization prevails. We should contrast:[38]

$$\{U_I^{H(I),FT}, U_{II}^{H(I),FT} \textit{ versus } U_I^{NH,FT}, U_{II}^{NH,FT}\} \tag{5}$$
$$\{U_I^{H(II),FT}, U_{II}^{H(II),FT} \textit{ versus } U_I^{NH,FT}, U_{II}^{NH,FT}\} \tag{6}$$

and

$$\{U_I^{H(I),FT}, U_{II}^{H(I),FT} \textit{ versus } U_I^{H(II),FT}, U_{II}^{H(II),FT}\} \tag{7}$$

(*ii*) Exogenous Other Policies; Non-economic Objectives Considered

Consider now that the "other" governmental policies (e.g., on environment or labor standards) are aimed at outcomes which are valued alongside income, so that (as in the theory of policy in the presence of "non-economic" objectives) one must consider an augmented social utility function that is not confined conventionally to goods and services.

All questions posed above when only economic objectives were considered would still need to be considered. It should be noted in particular that, in regard to Question 1, we can again deduce the absence of predation as long as prices now reflect social costs defined so as to include impact also on the non-economic objectives specified as the target of the "other" governmental policies. That is, these policies must be assumed to be optimally set by the government, given the underlying preferences over economic and non-economic outcomes, resources, technology and trade opportunity.

But it may not be possible to have governmental policies set optimally. Since one's government has no jurisdiction over the other, there could be impacts under Free Trade that could immiserize one's (augmented) welfare. The example that acid rain from abroad may increase as a result of acid-rain-creating activity increasing abroad thanks to Free Trade and its disutility through endangering of the health of one's citizens could outweigh the conventional gains from trade. Or dolphin-killing tuna fishing may increase abroad with Free Trade, its disutility to one's outraged citizens again outweighing the conventional gains from trade.

(*iii*) Endogenous Other Policies; Non-economic Objectives Considered

The theoretical analysis changes further when, in matters such as environment and labor standards, the policies designed to ensure a targeted fulfilment of such objectives become endogenous to the trade policy chosen.

There is, in political-economy-theoretic modelling of these questions, an interesting interplay between trade policy and, say, environmental policy. The environmentalists fear that Free Trade will, by putting competitive pressure on their industries that bear differentially higher abatement costs, trigger demands to reduce the environmental standards. So they ask for harmonization by others up to their own domestic standards or else they oppose Free Trade. The industry interests seek harmonization, given the stringent domestic standards, on competitiveness grounds. The two groups then unite in their demands for Fair Trade and harmonization up by others to the more stringent standards at home, failing which Free Trade is to be rejected.

Where such harmonization is rejected by others, *either* as incompatible with their optimal choice given their own constraints and objectives *or* as impossible to enforce effectively (as with, say, child labor laws), this becomes a surefire recipe for protectionism. By asking for harmonization that is impossible to get, one can then get the protection that is otherwise beyond reach.

In fact, there is also the possibility then that protectionist lobbies may *strategically* set (socially sub-optimal) high domestic environmental standards, joining with environmental groups to make demands for harmonization up to these higher standards which are then calculated to be impossible to meet by foreign rivals, and then ensuring the grant of protection because of lack of level playing fields.[39]

III. CONCLUDING REMARKS

I have only been able to sketch here the kinds of questions that must now be explored by the theorists of commercial policy during the 1990s. Only if we rework the theory in these new ways can we hope to contain the slide towards Fair Trade and its consequences. Else, we will simply not be equipped to respond to the growing demands for level playing fields.

In short, the agenda for fundamental thinking on the theory of commercial policy, or what James Meade aptly christened Trade and Welfare, in the 1990s will have to build squarely on foundations laid in the 1980s and earlier in the theory of optimal intervention in the presence of non-economic objectives, in the theory of political economy in open societies that explicitly treats governments in the formal analysis, and in the evolving theory of the design of institutions.[40]

NOTES

1 Thus, writing in the new *Journal of Economic Perspectives* in 1987, my distinguished pupil and successor to my chair at MIT, Paul Krugman, declared:

> ". . . the case for free trade is currently more in doubt than at any time since the 1817 publication of Ricardo's *Principles of Political Economy*. . . . In the last ten years the traditional constant returns, perfect competition models of international trade have been supplemented and to some extent supplanted by a new breed of models that emphasizes increasing returns and imperfect competition. These new models . . . open the possibility that government intervention in trade via import trade restrictions, export subsidies, and so on may under some circumstances be in the national interest after all. . . . Free trade is not passé, but it is an idea that has irretrievably lost its innocence. Its status has shifted from optimum to reasonable rule of thumb. There is still a case for free trade as a good policy, and as a useful target in the world of politics, but it can never again be asserted as the policy that economic theory tells us is always right."

But nearly 150 years ago, even John Stuart Mill 1848 and Robert Torrens 1844 had developed the two celebrated theoretical exceptions to the case for free trade: the infant-industry and the monopoly-power-in-trade arguments, so that no student of international economics or informed policymaker should have believed that economic theory could not generate arguments for departure from free trade. See, for instance, Bhagwati 1989, Corden 1990, and Srinivasan 1988.

2 Strictly speaking, market failure will arise now in the sense that the true social costs, reflecting the costs and benefits as *redefined* by the inclusion of the non-economic objectives, will not equal the market prices.

3 I argue below that this case for unilateral Free Trade has been modified, since Adam Smith himself, to allow theoretically for departures from Free Trade when Free Trade does not obtain elsewhere and one may be able to influence other nations' tariffs by varying one's own. Technically, this implies, of course, that foreign prices do not reflect true social costs.

4 Strictly speaking, one would need to distinguish between the cases where the threat to close one's markets suffices to pry open others' markets and where the threat must be made credible by actually implementing it. In the latter case, one must at least set off the current or "first-period" losses from one's protection against the "later-periods" gains from reduced barriers abroad. The optimal policy choice should then reflect the usual considerations such as the intertemporal function of the nation.

5 For an extended analysis, see Bhagwati and Irwin 1987 and Bhagwati and Patrick 1990. The relevant Sections of the 1988 Act are 301–310 but are popularly subsumed under the rubric "301."

6 Alfred Marshall's 1926 objection to the use of British protection to remove the protection in latecoming nations was based in part on the notion that these foreign nations were justified in using "infant industry" tariffs. Cf. Bhagwati and Irwin 1987. Of course, Marshall, assuming that he could get past the staff to testify in the U.S. Congress with these opinions, would risk the prospect of denunciation as a Free Trade "ideologue," somewhat senile and downright demented, for holding such views.

7 The effect of the demonstration of such a possibility of welfare improvement in Krugman's 1984 classic article on import restrictions leading to export promotion appears to have been precisely to mislead many into deducing erroneously that

imperfect competition in product markets implies a strengthening, rather than weakening, of the case for reciprocal Free Trade.

8 Under imperfect competition, as noted in Table 13.1 for the case of oligopoly, reciprocal Free Trade need not be a desirable policy (for national advantage) compared to imposing appropriate intervention in the presence of exogenously-specified foreign trade barriers.

9 I have discussed several economic rationales for *first difference* reciprocity in my 1990 Harry Johnson Lecture (Bhagwati 1991).

10 One can correctly say that Economics and International Economics were born simultaneously in Adam Smith's *The Wealth of Nations.*

11 Quoted by Irwin 1991a.

12 Cf. Irwin 1991a, p. 203.

13 Also see Irwin 1987 who argues, based on econometric estimates of the relevant elasticities, that the optimal tariff could not have been large and that the maximal estimate of the lsos from adopting Free Trade may have been of the order of 0.5% of GNP.

14 Bhagwati and Irwin 1987 compare the two historical phenomena, drawing both parallels and contrasts.

15 The academic defense of unilateral Free Trade by the best economists of the time, including the celebrated Alfred Marshall of Cambridge and F. Y. Edgeworth of Oxford, was richly textured and nuanced. It is reviewed in Bhagwati and Irwin 1987 and Bhagwati 1988.

16 Hicks's 1959 essay on "Free Trade and Modern Economics" was read to the Manchester Statistical Society in March 1951.

17 I am indebted to Eichengreen 1984, Wolf and Smook 1988 and Irwin 1991b, who offer a richly textured analysis of Keynes' views on Free Trade.

18 Cited in Irwin 1991b. Robinson 1937 and Kaldor 1950–51 analyzed further the argument that expenditure-switching policies to deflect expenditure onto oneself were "beggar-thy-neighbor" policies.

19 There were differences between the two pioneers. In particular, Chamberlin's analysis was deeper on product differentiation whereas Mrs Robinson's analysis of monopsony and price discrimination would prove seminal. Chamberlin insisted on differentiating his analysis of "monopolistic" from Mrs Robinson's analysis of "imperfect" competition. Among those innocent of the resulting acrimony was H. D. Henderson (the Drummond Professor of Political Economy at Oxford at the time). Presiding over Chamberlin's lecture at All Souls College, Henderson introduced him, with unintended double entendre, as the "father of the theory of imperfect competition."

20 I have discussed this response by Chicago at length in my obituary (1977) of Harry Johnson whose views, on migrating to Chicago from England, had progressively changed towards those of the Chicago school. An alternative response to the assertion that markets are imperfect and therefore, say, Free Trade must yield to welfare-improving intervention, would be to argue along with the Public Choice school that intervention will, in practice, make things worse rather than better. I turn to this alternative method of returning to Free Trade corner when I discuss Threat VI, during the 1980s, when the question of imperfect competition returned to center stage.

21 Hicks writes: "Free Trade is no longer accepted by economists, even as an ideal, in the way it used to be. Economics has not lost authority, but the preponderance of economic opinion is no longer so certainly as it was on the Free Trade sale." (1959, pp. 41–42). Doubtless, the readers will want to juxtapose Hick's forthright statements on the challenges to Free Trade, and indeed his masterly analysis thereof, with the Krugman quote I started with in this paper.

22 Interestingly, Hicks does not explicitly cite the theory of imperfect competition or Mrs Robinson, preferring to talk of the Monopoly-Competition argument instead. Was this due to the lack of sentiment between the two great English economists? Or

did Hicks harbor theoretical reservations about the foundations of the new theory, sensing the kinds of problems that later developments in the theory of industrial organization would begin to address meaningfully only in the latter 1970s and 1980s?

23 A "Protocol Provisional Application" brought the GATT into force on January 1, 1948 whereas the International Trade Organization, intended to complement the IMF and the World Bank, did not get off the ground.

24 Starting with Viner 1950, who pioneered the distinction between trade diversion and trade creation, there were important contributions by Lipsey and Lancaster 1956–57, Lipsey 1957, 1960, Meade 1955, Johnson 1958a, 1958b and many others.

25 The influence of developing-country concerns is most evident in many other contributions to this literature, especially by Johnson 1965, Bhagwati 1968 and Cooper and Massell 1965a, 1965b.

26 I might add that this was fully understood only by sophisticated economists. In the last 1970s, when the U.S. auto industry was looking for protection, my phone at MIT rang. A senior executive at one of the Big Three Detroit firms wanted to get me to write a paper for them, arguing for protectionist relief to the auto industry. He claimed that he had heard that I had developed arguments for protection in the scientific literature. Evidently, his economist informant was confusing my many analyses of market imperfections with protectionist conclusions, if not sympathies.

27 Cf. Bhagwati 1971 and Corden 1974.

28 Recall the extended quote in footnote 1.

29 Some readers have questioned this. But anyone familiar with the writings of influential journalists such as Robert Kuttner and James Fallows, and their frequent citation of the "new" trade-theory in support of their arguments for protection should have no doubts on this score.

30 Leaving magazines aside, we now have daily Business sections in major newspapers such as *The New York Times* and *The Washington Post*.

31 Cf. Varian 1989 for measurement problems and Hillman and Riley 1988 on the analysis as to whether a dollar worth of rents would lead to a dollar worth of resource loss due to rent-seeking.

32 The 1980s also witnessed the return of demands for Reciprocity and Fair Trade, a matter which I deal with in Episode VII.

33 In Table 13.3, I divide the theoretical arguments into two broad classes: those that pertain to Free Trade per se, reflecting market failures of one kind or another, and those that pertain to unilateralism versus reciprocity.

34 This would not be the way the policy issue of reciprocity would arise for a weak country. Whereas the strong who feel weak can try to force *others* to reciprocate, the weak can only force reciprocity on *themselves*. I do not go into the theoretical and policy analysis of 301 actions of the US administration here, referring the reader instead to Bhagwati and Patrick 1990.

35 A proper history would trace the beginning of this breakout to the early 1970s in the United States, in the wake of the dollar crisis that forced the United States off gold convertibility, and on to the 1974 Trade Act.

36 In practice, however, there are documented instances of apparently minuscule margins being countervailed. Proportionality of cause is distinctly less evident in practice as against proportionality of consequences.

37 One's non-economic objective function may incorporate such effects even when they operate abroad rather than at home.

38 These would be "situation" comparisons of utility possibilities, of course, under each policy set.

39 Some of these questions have been discussed in the 1991 GATT Annual Report on *Trade and the Environment*.

40 Political-economy-oriented trade theorists have been analyzing the question recently of the design of institutions. For example, Panagariya and Rodrik 1991 have recently developed political-economy-theoretic rationales for uniform tariffs even though traditional theory shows that nonuniform tariffs will generally be optimal. For instance, if tariffs are endogenous, and produced by lobbying, the free rider problem will work to *reduce* tariff protection under uniform tariffs because any lobbying will increase others' tariffs (and additionally reduce the value of any protection) as well.

REFERENCES

Beveridge, W. (ed.). 1932. *Tariffs: The Case Examined.* New York: Longmans, Green and Co.

Bhagwati, Jagdish. 1968. "Distortions and Immiserizing Growth: A Generalization." *Review of Economic Studies* 35:481–485.

Bhagwati, Jagdish. 1971. "The Generalised Theory of Distortions and Welfare," in J. Bhagwati et al. (ed.), *Trade, Balance of Payments, and Growth: Papers in International Economics in Honor of Charles P. Kindleberger.* Amsterdam: Elsevier Publishing Company.

Bhagwati, Jagdish. 1977. "Harry G. Johnson," *Journal of International Economics* 7:221–230.

Bhagwati, Jagdish. 1982. "Directly-unproductive Prof-seeking (DUP) Activities," *Journal of Political Economy* 90:988–1002.

Bhagwati, Jagdish. 1988. *Protectionism.* Cambridge: MIT Press.

Bhagwati, Jagdish. 1989. "Is Free Trade Passé After All?" *Weltwirtschaftliches Archiv* 125(1):17–44; reprinted in Jagdish Bhagwati, *Political Economy and International Economics*, Douglas Irwin (ed.). Cambridge: MIT Press, 1991.

Bhagwati, Jagdish. 1991. *The World Trading System at Risk.* Princeton: Princeton University Press.

Bhagwati, Jagdish and Douglas Irwin. 1987. "The Return of the Reciprocitarians: U.S. Trade Policy Today," *The World Economy* 10:109–130; reprinted in Jagdish Bhagwati, *Political Economy and International Economics*, Douglas Irwin (ed.). Cambridge: MIT Press, 1991.

Bhagwati, Jagdish and Hugh Patrick (eds.). 1991. *Aggressive Unilateralism.* Ann Arbor: University of Michigan Press.

Bhagwati, Jagdish and V. K. Ramaswami. 1963. "Domestic Distortions, Tariffs and the Theory of Optimum Subsidy," *Journal of Political Economy* 71:44–50.

Bhagwati, Jagdish and T. N. Srinivasan. 1969. "Optimal Intervention to Achieve Non-economic Objectives," *Review of Economic Studies* 36:27–38.

Bhagwati, Jagdish and T. N. Srinivasan. 1980. "Revenue Seeking: A Generalization of the Theory of Tariffs," *Journal of Political Economy* 88:1069–1087.

Brander, James and Barbara Spencer. 1981. "Tariffs and the Extraction of Foreign Monopoly Rents under Potential Entry," *Canadian Journal of Economics* 14:371–389.

Chamberlin, Edward. 1929. *The Theory of Monopolistic Competition.* Cambridge: Harvard University Press.

Cooper, Charles A. and Benton F. Massell. 1965a. "A New Look at Customs Union Theory," *Economic Journal* 75:742–747.

Cooper, Charles A. and Benton F. Massell. 1965b. "Toward a General Theory of Customs Unions for Developing Countries," *Journal of Political Economy* 73:461–476.

Corden, W. Max. 1957. "Tariffs, Subsidies and the Terms of Trade," *Economica* 24:235–242.

Corden, W. Max. 1974. *Trade Policy and Economic Welfare.* Oxford: Oxford University Press.

Corden, W. Max. 1990. "Strategic Trade Policy: How New? How Sensible?" *World Bank Working Paper No. 396.* Washington, D.C.: World Bank.

Eaton, Jonathan and Gene Grossman. 1986. "Optimal Trade and Industrial Policy under Oligopoly," *Quarterly Journal of Economics* 2:383–406.
Eichengreen, Barry. 1984. "Keynes and Protection," *Journal of Economic History* 44:363–373.
General Agreement on Tariffs and Trade (GATT). 1991. *Annual Report on Trade and the Environment*. Geneva: GATT.
Grandmont, J. M. and Daniel McFadden. 1972. "A Technical Note on Classical Gains from Trade," *Journal of International Economics* 2:109–125.
Grossman, Gene. 1986. "Strategic Export Promotion: A Critique," in Paul R. Krugman (ed.), *Strategic Trade Policy and the New International Economics*. Cambridge: MIT Press.
Hicks, John R. 1951. "Free Trade and Modern Economics," in Hicks, 1959, *Essays in World Economics*. Oxford: Clarendon Press.
Hicks, John R. 1959. *Essays in World Economics*. Oxford: Clarendon Press.
Hillman, Ayre and John Riley. 1989. "Politically Contestable Rents and Transfers," *Economics and Politics* 1:17–40.
Irwin, Douglas. 1987. "Welfare Effects of British Free Trade: Debate and Evidence from the 1840's." Presented to Mid-West International Economics Meetings. Ann Arbor.
Irwin, Douglas. 1991a. "Challenges to Free Trade," *Journal of Economic Perspectives* 5:201–208.
Irwin, Douglas. 1991b. "Keynes and the Macroeconomics of Protection," University of Chicago Business School, in process.
Johnson, Harry G. 1958a. "The Gains from Free Trade with Europe: An Estimate," *Manchester School of Economics and Social Studies* 26:247–255.
Johnson, Harry G. 1958b. 'The Economic Gains from Free Trade with Europe," *Three Banks Review* 39:3–19.
Johnson, Harry G. 1965. "An Economic Theory of Protectionism Tariff Bargaining, and the Formation of Customs Unions," *Journal of Political Economy* 73:256–283.
Kaldor, Nicholas. 1950–51. "Employment Policies and the Problem of International Imbalance," *Review of Economic Studies* 19:42–49.
Kemp, Murray C. 1972. "The Gains From International Trade," *Economic Journal* 72:803–819.
Kemp, Murray C. and Henry Wan, Jr. 1976. "An Elementary Proposition Concerning the Formation of Customs Unions," *Journal of International Economics* 6:95–97.
Kenen, Peter B. 1957. "On the Geometry of Welfare Economics," *Quarterly Journal of Economics* 71:426–447.
Krueger, Anne O. 1974. "The Political Economy of the Rent-seeking Society," *American Economic Review* 69:291–303.
Krugman, Paul. 1984. "Import Protection as Export Promotion," in Henryk Kierzkowski (ed.), *Monopolistic Competition and International Trade*. Oxford: Basil Blackwell.
Krugman, Paul (ed.). 1986. *Strategic Trade Policy and the New International Economics*. Cambridge: MIT Press.
Krugman, Paul. 1987. "Is Free Trade Passé," *Journal of Economic Perspectives* 1:133–144.
Lipsey, Richard G. 1957. "The Theory of Customs Unions: Trade Diversion and Welfare," *Economica* 24:40–46.
Lipsey, Richard G. 1960. "The Theory of Customs Unions: A General Survey," *Economic Journal* 70:496–513.
Lipsey, Richard and Kelvin J. Lancaster. 1956–57. 'The General Theory of Second Best," *Review of Economic Studies* 24:11–32.
Marshall, Alfred. 1926. "Memorandum on the Fiscal Policy of International Trade (1903)," in J. M. Keynes (ed.), *Official Papers of Alfred Marshall*. London: Macmillan.

McCloskey, Donald N. 1980. "Magnanimous Albion: Free Trade and British National Income, 1841–1881," *Explorations in Economic History* 17:303–320.
Meade, James E. 1952. *Trade and Welfare*. London: Oxford University Press.
Meade, James E. 1955. *The Theory of Customs Unions*. Amsterdam: North-Holland.
Mill, John Stuart. 1848. *Principles of Political Economy*. London: Longmans, Green, and Co.
Panagariya, Arvind and Dani Rodrik. 1991. "Political-Economy Arguments for a Uniform Tariff," *International Economic Review*, forthcoming.
Robinson, Joan. 1931. *The Economics of Imperfect Competition*. London: Macmillan.
Robinson, Japan. 1937. "Begger-my-neighbour Remedies for Unemployment," in *Essays in the Theory of Unemployment*. New York: Macmillan.
Samuelson, Paul A. 1939. "The Gains from International Trade," *Canadian Journal of Economics and Political Science* 5:195–205.
Samuelson, Paul A. 1962. "The Gains from International Trade Once Again," *Economic Journal* 62:820–829.
Smith, Adam. 1776. *The Wealth of Nations*, Cannan Edition. New York: Modern Library, 1937.
Srinivasan, T. N. 1989. "Recent Theories of Imperfect Competition and International Trade: Any Implications for Development Strategies? *Indian Economic Review* 24:1–24.
Torrens, Robert. 1844. *The Budget: On Commercial and Colonial Policy*. London: Smith, Elder.
Varian, Hal. 1989. "Measuring the Deadweight Costs of DUP and Rent-Seeking Activities," *Economics & Politics* 1:81–95.
Viner, Jacob. 1950. *The Customs Union Issue*. New York: Carnegie Endowment for International Peace.
Wolf, Bernard and N. Smook. 1988. "Keynes and the Question of Tariffs," in O. F. Hamouda and J. N. Smithin (eds), *Keynes and Public Policy After Fifty Years*, Vol II. New York: New York University Press.

COMMENTS ON INITIAL DRAFT OF BHAGWATI CHAPTER

John H. Jackson

My comments will touch upon some issues raised in Bhagwati's paper, but I would like as well to range more broadly and, in particular, to discuss: techniques for managing interdependence; institutional aspects of the GATT system; and a brief outline inventory of the kinds of issues that will face the GATT after the Uruguay Round.

1. MANAGING INTERDEPENDENCE

A great deal of what has been discussed in the conference is designed to address the very perplexing question of how to manage the rapidly growing interdependence of international economic activity. To some degree, the actual economic relations and activities have outrun the capacity of the existing institutions to handle the problems being generated. Various economic characteristics can rapidly flow from one nation and continent to another, with very significant impacts. This can be very frustrating to political leaders who are trying to deliver satisfactory policies and government actions to their constituents, but find that it is increasingly difficult to do so in a world when influences from far away have such a great impact. Indeed, the whole notion of "sovereign state" is under reconsideration, partly for this reason.

In this paper, Bhagwati has rightly pointed to some of these aspects, as have other papers in this conference. However, Bhagwati has focused on "harmonization" as a primary technique for managing some of these problems. I would like to suggest that in fact there are a number of potential techniques for managing increasing interdependence. It is important that policy makers as well as scholars understand the advantages and disadvantages of these various techniques, and be able to rely upon a menu of such techniques, rather than focusing entirely on one or another. Let me briefly review some of these.[41]

Harmonization

Harmonization is clearly an important technique, particularly in such areas as product standards and certain types of government regulation that relate to products or services. Nevertheless, harmonization can probably only be pushed to a limited degree, at least at the broader worldwide level (as compared to regional, or federal-state systems). No one expects the world to become totally uniform, or stamped out of one mold, and indeed it is unlikely that such a world would be particularly desirable to inhabit. Instead, any system must recognize and accommodate a very large degree of diversity, based in some cases on cultural differences, in other cases on differences in level of economic attainment, or government systems, etc., as well as on different rich historical backgrounds.

The European Community (EC) has been experimenting and proceeding further along harmonization lines, but even it has ameliorated the notion of harmonization. Rather than assuming that there must always be a complete similarity or identify of product standards, for example, the EC is experimenting with a notion of certain minimal levels of product standards, accompanied by requirements upon member states to "recognize" satisfactory product standards imposed by other states, even though they differ in certain resects. Harmonization clearly will be an important driving force, but it also clearly has certain important limitations.

Reciprocity

Another technique for managing interdependence is the "reciprocity" notion. Under this concept, there developed a system of *swaps*, or reciprocal *deals*, by which different countries agree to different obligations, but try to match up their effect so that each country feels it is receiving as much benefit as it is giving. To some degree the concept of reciprocity, well known in GATT, is a fallacy. Unilateral trade liberalization measures, for example, can in certain circumstances enhance the welfare of the acting nation. Nevertheless, reciprocity has been an important political driving force for trade liberalization throughout the history of tariff reduction agreements, particularly since the 1934 U.S. Reciprocal Trade Agreements Act.

It should be noted that the most successful achievement of GATT has been the reduction of tariffs on industrial products imported into industrial countries. Yet, the approach of GATT on tariffs was not harmonization. Rather, each country developed a list of tariff buildings, often quite different from those of other countries. One country would bind a tariff on bicycles, another on radios, another on tractors. Over time, the system provided for extensive tariff liberalization, which in a sense drives tariffs towards a *harmonized zero level*, but the notion was not based on a theory of harmonization.

Today of course, the real challenge facing international trade is less focused on tariffs, and more focused on nontariff barriers (NTBs). Nevertheless, there may be ways to utilize the reciprocity notion in connection with NTBs, although often it becomes much more difficult because negotiators tend to want some kind of quantitative standard by which to evaluate the fairness of tradeoffs. Such quantification can be difficult, if not impossible, in connection with rule-oriented code structures. For example, how can negotiators predict what will be the trade advantage of a customs valuation code, even in the first year, and much less for five or ten years in advance?

The Interface Concept

Another technique for managing interdependence, I have termed the *interface concept*.[42] These differences can generate both economic and political problems, that is, a sense of *unfairness* among political constituencies. Thus, these differences, which may be as *simple* as different debt-equity ratios in the capitalization of firms, sometimes need to be ameliorated by some kind of international buffering mechanism so as to soften their impacts, or minimize the tension-creating political if not economic effects. The GATT is an important interface mechanism. However, one also can focus on such well-known structures of international trade as *safeguards* (unfortunately not too successful) as an interface mechanism. I have even written elsewhere (Jackson 1989) that the anti-dumping duties may be performing such a buffering interface mechanism in certain kinds of contexts, although never originally intended to be for that purpose.

Bhagwati has mentioned the importance of the injury test as a moderating factor in a variety of trade policy procedures, and I would suggest that again the injury test becomes an interface mechanism.

The basic idea is that even radically different economic structures (such as nonmarket economies compared to market economies) should be facilitated in trading with each other, but some kind of an interface mechanism will be necessary to prevent one side or the other having the impression of being taken advantage of.

The above three broad categories of techniques for managing interdependence undoubtedly do not exhaust the possibilities. But they illustrate the importance of the system accommodating a variety of approaches, and not just one single approach. Needless to say, a variety of approaches requires a more sophisticated international institutional structure in order appropriately to supervise these techniques.

2. INSTITUTIONAL PROBLEMS OF THE GATT AND POTENTIAL FOR REFORM

There are two important institutional elements of the GATT system being discussed at various levels during the Uruguay Round. The most obvious area is the dispute settlement procedure. Less known but nevertheless discussed in some depth, sometimes termed an MTO (Multilateral Trade Organization), or WTO (World Trade Organization). Again, I have addressed these questions in somewhat more detail in Jackson 1990, but let me make a few points here.

Dispute Settlement

I have already commented during the course of this conference on the growing recognition of the importance of a *rule based system* for international trade as a way to facilitate that trade, provide a measure of predictability/stability to millions of entrepreneurs (particularly relevant for market-oriented systems), and thus to reduce the *risk premium* of a number of such decisions, facilitating exchange, and therefore world welfare. These are subjects and policies that need considerably more attention both by economists and legal and political scholars.

The GATT dispute settlement system has gone through a remarkable period during the last ten years, and is now much more greatly looked to for some of the policy goals mentioned. The number of cases reflects this.[43] The jurisprudence of the GATT dispute settlement system is perhaps the richest of any broad-based multilateral international dispute settlement procedure so far in the history of mankind. The number of cases far exceeds those of the World Court during comparable periods, and at least in some circumstances have considerably more impact than decisions of such court or other tribunals.

It is thus not surprising that the negotiators in the Uruguay Round have been giving considerable attention to the enhancement of this dispute settlement system, even proposing an *appellate tribunal* as part of the process. Hopefully, the end of the Uruguay Round will see some sort of enhancement and the framework for further continued evolution of the dispute settlement procedures.

Legal/Institutional Framework

The GATT was never intended to be an international organization or to be the central international institutional system for trade. But when the Havana Charter (ITO-International Trade Organization) failed to come into being in the late 1940s, the GATT was forced to fill the vacuum and it has done so with remarkable success considering its birth defects.[44] Nevertheless, these defects are many and thus (much more quietly), key negotiating countries in the Uruguay Round have been considering some type of simple institutional charter to replace the GATT and provide a broader and more elastic framework for future evolution of the world trading system, embracing new subjects such as services and intellectual property. Time is too short for me to go into this in detail, but it should be noted that a number of perplexing *end game* issues at the finish of the Uruguay Round will require consideration of such institutional measures. For example, if a unified dispute settlement system is set up (as many delegations desire), to cover not only trade in goods but also services and intellectual property, some type of an institutional structure to supervise and facilitate that dispute settlement procedure will be necessary. Likewise, a framework should be open ended enough for the GATT system to accommodate some future subjects, such as those to be mentioned below.

One new institutional measure that the GATT has already taken is the TPRM-Trade Policy Review Mechanism, and this also may have some potential and could be built into a new institutional structure so that it applies not only to goods, but to services, etc.

As we move towards an evolving institutional structure to help *manage interdependence* and facilitate international trade, for the enhancement of world welfare, the system will have to explore a variety of institutional measures and will need to look towards models and historical experiences. Two prominent models exist. The United States, as a federal system, has been a remarkably successful 'customs union," with 200 years of evolving experience. Likewise, the EC has been influenced by the GATT, but now is moving into subject matter area that will inevitably face the GATT over the next decade or two. Neither of these models can be accepted in their entirety for the broader based world institutional system, but both (as well as others) offer important experiences, from which can be *selected* particular examples of potential structures that could be effective at the broader worldwide level. The development of further regional blocs may also provide us with further experience along this line. Such activities as the U.S.–Japan SII discussions (Structural Impediments Initiative) provide us insights into problems that are further down the road for the GATT as a whole.

One of the problems with the existing GATT system is the extraordinary meagreness of research and analysis resources that it embraces. This too must be changed.

3. THE GATT SYSTEM FUTURE AGENDA

Finally, let me present very briefly and therefore almost in outline form, some thoughts about the types of issues facing the GATT after the Uruguay Round, including a series of new issues, or issues that have not been very much explored.[45] Some of these subjects have been admirably addressed in some papers from this conference.

For convenience and comprehension, I can group the post-Uruguay Round issues facing the GATT into several categories, as follows:

a. Continuation of Uruguay Round Issues

A number of the issues more or less extensively addressed in the Uruguay Round will undoubtedly continue to require important negotiation and consideration. Agriculture is obvious, and it is very likely that such subjects as subsidies, antidumping duties, safeguards, textiles, gray area measures and voluntary restraint agreements will be just a few among a longer list of subjects that will demand further attention.

b. New Substantive Issues

There is a group of issues that are more or less new to the GATT and will be causing increasing difficulty and demanding greater attention. A few can be mentioned:

(1) *Competition (Antimonopoly Policy).* The general area of competition (or antimonopoly) policy is one that has been increasingly noticed as a prime candidate for further attention. The original ITO Charter contained an elaborate title addressing these issues. But when the charter failed, this subject largely dropped to the wayside of international trade policy for 40 years. It is now becoming increasingly apparent that it can no longer be a wayside matter. The general objectives of facilitating world trade demand attention to the attributes of competition in that trading system. The issue is that monopolies can undo the trade liberalization effect of reduced tariffs and NTBs.

(2) *State trading and nonmarket economies.* The GATT has unsuccessfully struggled with the problems of *state trading* and *non-market economies* for many decades. This problem will continue, although in the light of the dramatic developments in East Europe, and a general worldwide trend towards market oriented, or privatized economies, it may become less severe than had been contemplated even two or three years ago.

(3) *Science, product standards, and harmonization.* Product development has been accelerated, and products themselves have become increasingly complex. Thus standards for products have become a very important issue for international trade. When standards are very diverse in a random and unthoughtful way, trade is inhibited and economies of scale become more difficult to attain. This is the lesson that the EC has learned with a vengeance and is trying with considerable vigor to overcome. This lesson is now becoming a part of the deliberations at the broader multilateral scale of the GATT system, as some of the specific cases (e.g., such as beef hormones) have demonstrated full well.

(4) *Cultural impacts on the flow of trade.* We have begun to realize that trade can be importantly influenced by relatively subtle cultural or systemic societal attributes in different countries. Much attention has been given to Japan in this regard, but there are similar issues in the other major trading countries, if not all countries. Canada, the EC, and the United States each have a variety of cultural attitudes and society institutions that can in some circumstances inhibit trade. Japan and the United States have had a series of discussions about these issues under the Structural Impediments Initiative–SII, and these discussions have

clearly demonstrated that there will be increasing future importance given to cultural impediments to international trade. Clearly, there are a number of dilemmas of competing but appropriate governmental objectives imbedded in this subject. No one wants the world to be stamped into uniformity, and cultural diversity is often a desirable attribute for a variety of reasons, including recognition of freedom of individuals and small groups.

c. Links Issues

Another major group of issues facing the post-Uruguay Round GATT system are what I term the link issues. These are issues that involve linking international trade policy to important alternative considerations and governmental international policies, often not traditionally viewed as appropriate for trade policy. Nevertheless, the world and its citizens are demanding linkages, and it is increasingly clear that linkages are indeed appropriate and must be studied and understood. Examples include the following:

(1) *Environmental protection.* Most significantly, there is the question of environmental protection and trade policy. This has been raised in several of the GATT panel dispute cases already, and there has been much discussion about the possibility that trade policy can influence, for better or worse, potentials for environmental protection. In the national debate concerning the Mexico–U.S.–Canada free trade negotiations, these issues have come very prominently to the fore.

(2) *Human rights.* Countries have long exercised the right to undertake certain trade actions such as embargoes or trade sanctions, with a purpose of influencing the actions and attitudes of foreign governments regarding human rights. This trend will undoubtedly continue, and will demand some attention from the trade policy community with respect to appropriate limits and criteria in such cases.

(3) *Monetary and financial policies.* The relations involving international trade and financial need to be included in any list of link issues.

(4) *Arms control.* Governments have long taken actions to restrain arms races and to limit the sale abroad of strategic items deemed potentially dangerous to national security. The GATT has a few clauses that arguably address this question, but there has been much ambiguity about many actions, including various kinds of export controls, in their relationship to the GATT. The Gulf War demonstrated poignantly the importance of these issues, and there is no way that the GATT will be able to escape them.

d. Rethinking Traditional Rules

There are a series of general policies/concepts/rules in the GATT that are considered by many to be central to the whole GATT structure, and yet have caused considerable problems to the more complex and rapidly changing questions of international trade policy. It will be necessary, I believe, to rethink some of these old concepts, even though many practitioners already have manifested a resistance to such rethinking because they fear encroachments on some of the basic pillars of a GATT system. The following illustrate some of these issues:

(1) *Most-Favored-Nation Treatment (MFN).* The MFN clause has often been considered the central rule of the GATT system, and yet when the system includes a very large number of countries such as more than 100 now participating in the GATT, MFN may make it difficult to develop new rules, and affords a particular privilege to the "free rider".[46]

(2) *Reciprocity.* This has been a central driving principle in many of the GATT negotiations. It worked better when negotiations centered on tariffs, and countries could be seen to *swap* concessions, which then made it easier for governments to *sell the resulting agreement* to their home constituencies. However, as the issues have moved away from tariffs and towards NTBs with the resulting complex needs for rule structures, reciprocity often becomes relatively meaningless. Instead, there needs to be an emphasis on the policy of the rules, and presumably virtually all countries will benefit over time if those rules are applied effectively. In any event, it becomes virtually impossible at the time the rule is made to be able to predict with much accuracy which particular countries will be favored and which not.

(3) *National treatment.* Another nondiscrimination principle of GATT that is quite central to that system is the national treatment rules (particularly Article III of GATT). These rules are basically structured to require nondiscrimination as between imported goods and domestically produced goods, but they do not particularly require any minimum standard of rationality or scientific support. Thus a government can argue that its foolish measure is perfectly appropriate provided that it applies it equally to the imported goods as well as to its domestic goods. We have already seen a number of cases, especially in the agriculture and product standards area (so-called phytosanitary rules) where negotiators do not feel that the existing GATT approach is adequate. There must be instead, it is argued, some requirement that governments show a rationale for the rules and product affecting regulations that they adopt.

(4) *Regionalism.* The problem of the relationship of regional preferential arrangements (such as the EC or the U.S.–Canada Free Trade Agreement) to the GATT has been a sore point in the GATT from its beginning. Clearly the original GATT contemplates some measure of deference to groups of nations that wish to bind together in a trading arrangement that can provide for a deeper measure of liberalization of the trade in goods, services, or other matters. How that can be done while giving some recognition to the GATT MFN (non-discrimination) clause, is the troublesome point. The GATT rules (Article XXIV) have been utilized but are deemed by many to be inadequate. As we seem to be moving into a world with even greater importance given to regional trading arrangements (the EC expanding and deepening its relationship; the North American continent developing a new NAFTA; potentially a Pacific basin arrangement, etc.), clearly the GATT will have to face the issue of the relationship of these blocs to the broader multilateral system, and the GATT should play a *traffic cop* role in preventing these blocs from damaging each other.

4. CONCLUSION

As Bhagwati has so ably noted, the task ahead of us is formidable indeed. There is developing a broad political sense of disillusionment in the current institutional and policy structure of the international trading system, and it will be very important for the policy apparatus of the major leading trading countries, which apparatus includes not only the governmental structure but academic and advocacy institutions, to formulate appropriate new structures and policies which can accommodate the extraordinarily fast-paced change and evolution of international economic activities.

NOTES

41 For more detailed discussion, see Jackson 1989 Ch. 14.
42 See Jackson 1989 Ch. 10.1.
43 See, for example, *GATT: Draft Final Act Embodying the Result of the Uruguay Round of Multilateral Trade Negotiations*, NTN:TNC/W/35 (26 November 1990). As of November, 1991 there were sixteen pending cases before the GATT. This includes panels established or formally requested under the various GATT dispute settlement procedures.
44 See Jackson 1969, 1989, for further discussion.
45 The discussion here draws on Jackson 1991.

REFERENCES

Jackson, John H. 1969. *World Trade and the Law of GATT*. Indianapolis: Bobbs-Merrill Company.

Jackson, John H. 1985. "Economic Law, International," in *Encyclopaedia of Public International Law*, published under the auspices of the Max Planck Institute for Comparative Public Law and International Law, Vol. 8. New York: Oxford University Press.

Jackson, John H. 1989. *The World Trading System: Law and Policy of International Economic Relations*. Cambridge: MIT Press.

Jackson, John H. 1991. "GATT and the Future of International Trade Institutions," *Brooklyn Journal of International Law* 18:11–31.

3. Trade and the Environment: Does Environmental Diversity Detract from the Case for Free Trade?

J. Bhagwati and T. N. Srinivasan

THE POTENCY OF THE contention that fair trade or level playing fields constitute a precondition for free trade and that, therefore, harmonization of domestic policies across trading countries is necessary before free trade can be embraced to one's advantage, should not be underestimated today. It is nowhere more manifest or more compelling in its policy appeal than in the area of environmental standards.

Both the *general* view that cross-country intra-industry (CCII) harmonization of environmental standards is required if free trade is to be implemented and the *specific* proposals currently in vogue to implement this view are therefore in need of analytical scrutiny.[1] This is the task that we undertake primarily in the present chapter.

Section 4.1 briefly reviews the factors that drive the demands for cross-country intra-industry harmonization of environmental standards and the specific proposals, in particular the countervailing of so-called "social dumping" when harmonization does not obtain but free trade does. Its main purpose, however, is to categorize the (four) main issues that arise as the "high-standard" and "low-standard" countries engage in freer trade and contemplate consequences of the differences in their environmental standards when the pollution involved is purely domestic.

Section 4.2 sets forth several basic theoretical propositions (derived from the theoretical Appendix), concerning optimal commercial and environmental policies under different circumstances when the environmental problem is purely domestic. In light thereof, the basic legitimacy and desirability of free trade with diversity of domestic environmental standards is established. Also, a detailed examination of two (of the four) issues distinguished in section 4.1 is offered: relating to the objections to diversity under free trade, reflecting fears of unfair trade and the loss of one's high standards.

Section 4.3 considers the related but distinct problems raised by concerns with ethical preferences or "values" that result in objections to free trade with diverse standards.

Section 4.4 addresses the concern that current institutional mechanisms for overseeing free trade, chiefly the GATT and its successor the World Trade Organization (WTO), threaten high standards by permitting successful challenges by low-standard countries on diverse grounds reflecting mainly their market-disruption potential.

While these analyses concern the issues arising from purely domestic environmental problems, section 4.5 concludes by sketching the trade problems that differentially arise when the environmental problems are international (or "global"), that is, when they involve transborder externalities.

4.1 DEMANDS FOR CROSS-COUNTRY INTRA-INDUSTRY HARMONIZATION OF ENVIRONMENTAL STANDARDS: CATEGORIZING THE ISSUES FOR PURELY DOMESTIC ENVIRONMENTAL PROBLEMS

In reviewing and assessing the demands for CCII harmonization of environmental standards, it is customary now to make a distinction of analytical importance between (1) environmental problems that are intrinsically *domestic* in nature (though they may be "internationalized" for reasons we will discuss); and (2) those that are intrinsically *international* in nature because they inherently involve "physical" spillovers across national borders.

Thus, if India pollutes a lake that is wholly within its borders, the pollution is an intrinsically domestic question. If, however, India pollutes a river that flows into Bangladesh, the pollution is an intrinsically international question. So are the well-known problems of acid rain, ozone-layer depletion, and global warming. These intrinsically international problems of the environment raise questions that interface with the trade questions both in common and in different ways from the intrinsically domestic problems.

It has become commonplace among some environmentalists to assert that this distinction is of no consequence because the intrinsically domestic environmental problems are increasingly seen to have transnational impacts. Science has shown, for instance, that aerosol sprays are not just an environmental nuisance where used; they endanger the planet! But the fact that science seems occasionally to turn local (and partial-equilibrium) environmental impacts into transnational (and general-equilibrium) impacts is no proof that the former are an empty set. We should not be deterred, therefore, from using this important conceptual distinction.

4.1.1 Objections to Diversity of Standards

It would seem, at first glance, that at least the intrinsically domestic environmental problems should be matters best left by governments to domestic solutions and within domestic jurisdiction (although transnational, global "educational", and lobbying activities by environmental nongovernmental organizations, the NGOs, are compatible with this solution). Why should anyone object to the conduct of free trade with any country on the ground that its preferred environmental choices and solutions (by way of setting pollution standards and taxes) to intrinsically domestic questions are unacceptable because they are incompatible with the case for (gains from) free trade? Yet, the fact is that they do.

And the objections are directed, not merely at free trade, but also at the institutional safeguards and practices, as at the GATT, which are designed to ensure the proper functioning of an open, multilateral trading system that embodies the principles of free trade. These objections take mainly four forms:

1. *Unfair Trade.* If you do something different, and especially if you do what appears to be less, concerning environment than I do in the same industry or sector, this difference is considered to be tantamount to lack of "level playing fields" and therefore amounts to "unfair trade" by you. Free trade, according to this doctrine, is then unacceptable because it requires, as a precondition, "fair trade."[2]

2. *Losing Higher Standards.* Then again, the flip side of the "fair trade" argument is the environmentalists' fear that if free trade occurs with countries having "lower" environmental standards, no matter what the justification for this situation, the effect will be to lower their own standards. This will follow from the political pressure brought to bear on governments to lower standards to ensure the survival of their industry.

An associated argument is that capital will move to countries with lower standards, so that countries will engage in a "race to the bottom," each winding up with lower standards than desired because standards are lowered to attract capital from each other.

3. *Conflicting Ethical Preferences.* Environmentalists also often worry about the compatibility of ethical preferences and free trade among trading nations who do not share the same ethical preferences. Free trade in products that offend one's moral sense (either in themselves, or because of the way in which they are produced, as in the use of purse seines in catching tuna or leghold traps in hunting for fur) is then considered objectionable because *either* trade in such products should be withheld so as to induce or coerce acceptable of such preferences *or* such trade should be abandoned, even if it has no effective consequence and might even hurt only oneself, simply because "one should have no truck with the devil,"[3] *or* one's labor or industry "should not have to compete" with others who do not uphold the ethical standards that one considers important.

The first argument presumes higher morality in one's behalf, which should be spread to other nations with lower morality (and with corresponding lack of standards/laws therefore to reflect the higher morality). The other arguments seek no such morally imperial outreach; one simply wants no part in complicity with lower morality elsewhere via participating in gainful free trade with nations guilty of tolerating such lower morality while the other rejects these gains from trade somewhat differently as imposing an "unfair" burden on one's producers who conform to the higher ethical standards. In each case, the diversity of standards is considered then to be incompatible with the pursuit of free trade.

4. *Institutional Vulnerability of High Standards to Countries with Low Standards Fearing Protectionism.* Then, finally, the environmentalists fear that they will lose their high standards, not because market forces under free trade bias the *domestic* political equilibrium in favor of lower standards or generate a race to the bottom,[4] but because the current "institutional" arrangements, at the GATT in particular, enable the low-standards countries to object to, and threaten, the high standards in other countries by claiming protectionist intent or consequences, for instance.[5]

4.1.2 The Political Salience of These Objections

Thus, just consider why the first argument concerning the *unfair trade* of lower

CCII standards elsewhere has become such a politically salient issue today. Though we will turn to this argument in greater depth in section 4.2, it should suffice to note here that the fear is that competition will be greater if a rival abroad faces lower burdens of environmental regulations, and hence the argument follows that this competitive advantage enjoyed by one's foreign rivals is *illegitimate* and must be countervailed, much as dumping or subsidization is, or must be eliminated at the source.

Thus, Senator David Boren, who introduced legislation in the U.S. Congress to countervail the "social dumping" allegedly resulting from lower standards abroad, proposed such a measure on the ground that[6] "we can no longer stand idly by while some US manufacturers, such as the US carbon and steel alloy industry, spend as much as 250 percent more on environmental controls as a percentage of gross domestic product than do other countries. . . . I see the *unfair advantage enjoyed by other nations exploiting the environment* and public health for economic gain when I look at many industries important to my own state of Oklahoma."

We will argue, in section 4.2, that environmental diversity is, contrary to these statements, perfectly legitimate, that it can arise not merely because the utility function defined on income and pollution is not identical and homothetic, but also because of differences in endowments and technology across countries. Hence, the common presumption driving harmonization and (alternatively) "social-dumping"-countervailing demands, that others with different CCII standards are illegitimately and unfairly reducing their costs, is untenable.[7]

Nonetheless, these demands are part of a general shift to demands to harmonize a great, and possibly increasing, number of domestic policies: in labor standards, in technology policy, and so on. Why?[8]

With industries everywhere increasingly open to competition, thanks precisely to our postwar success in dismantling trade barriers, with multinationals spreading technology freely across countries through direct investments, and with capital more free than ever to move across countries, producers face now the prospect that their competitive advantage is fragile and that more industries than ever before are "footloose." There is, therefore, much more sensitivity to *an* advantage that one's rivals abroad may enjoy in world competition, and a propensity for the rivals to look over their shoulders to find reasons why their advantage is "unfair."

The notion of unfairness is also attractive to those who seek relief from international competition. If you go to your congresswoman and ask for protection because the competition is tough, it is going to be difficult to get it. After all, many of them have been sufficiently educated, or perhaps brainwashed (depending on your point of view), into thinking that protection, while not a four-letter word, is not something you want to embrace if you aspire to anything like statesmanship. But if you go to her and say that your successful rival is playing by "unfair" rules, you are going to do better. In the United States, in particular, the "unfairness" notion can take you really far, since the economic and social ethos reflects notions of fairness and equality of access (rather than success) more than anywhere else.

The fact that the United States also went through the "diminished giant" syndrome vis-à-vis the Pacific nations, which fed its fear of consequent deindustrialization, also made the American politicians more susceptible during the 1980s to those "unfair trade" arguments from interested lobbies. The continuing dominance of the United States in setting the world's trading agenda powerfully reinforces, in turn, the trend toward "fair trade" and "level playing fields."

While the "unfair trade" argument for rejecting free trade with countries with different environmental standards is therefore part of the generic and more general demands for harmonization and level playing fields in world trade, environment (whose protection is legitimately a virtue in itself) brings to this trend yet added arguments with perhaps even more powerful appeal. Chief among them is the fear, leading to the second argument in the list, that competition with the imports and exports in third markets from countries with lower standards will put pressure on domestic industries, triggering political action by them to lower standards *down* to the levels abroad.

Believing (possibly with justification) that U.S. Vice President Dan Quayle's Competitiveness Council was doing precisely this under the administration of President George Bush, the environmental NGOs in the United States, and their friends in the European Community and elsewhere, came to see this lowering of standards as a real threat to their goals if free trade were embraced and if harmonization *up* were not imposed simultaneously by coercion on foreign countries, especially the poor ones. As Walter Russell Mead put it in a much cited article in *Harper's Magazine*:[9]

> Either the progressive systems of the advanced industrial countries will spread into the developing world or the Third World will move north. Either Mexican wages will move up or American wages will move down. Environmentalists, labor unions, consumer groups, and human-rights groups must go global – just as corporations have done.

This concern reflects at the global level the debate within the EC: the fear that the Common Market's free trade and free capital flows will lead to harmonization *down* of standards "from below" and the efforts by many in consequence to impose harmonization at a *higher* level of standards "from the top."

Finally, the demands for CCII harmonization are fed also by the feared adverse effects of free trade and capital flows on the real wages of workers: an issue that became important in the 1992 presidential election in the United States. The Bill Clinton campaign did not just focus on the failure of the Bush administration to revive the economy. It also made much of the so-called structural problem that is defined by the stagnation of real wages of the unskilled workers during the 1980s. At least one of the candidates for explaining this phenomenon has been the integration of the world economy and the competition in consequence with poor countries with abundant unskilled labor.

We doubt the importance of this explanation,[10] but it has powerful appeal. The attempts at globalizing the higher environmental and labor standards, with the latter coming uncomfortably close to attempts at also raising wages in the industrial sectors of the poor countries on human-rights and labor-rights grounds, can be seen in fact as indirect ways of trying to reduce the perceived threat to real wages of the unskilled in rich countries from free trade with (and capital outflows to) the poor countries.

We may remark that, if the argument about the adverse effect of trade on wages of the unskilled is really bought, we are back to the old concerns that free trade with the poor countries will truly act like free immigration from them: the immigration would directly depress workers' wages; free trade would indirectly do so. Interestingly, in the animated British debate prior to the passage of the 1905 Immigration Act, the free traders were also free immigrationists, and the protectionists were also for restrictions on immigration. Immigration was even described as free trade in paupers![11]

Hence, the growing sentiment that free trade with the poor countries will increasingly depress rich countries' real wages should eventually lead to, not just palliatives like the imposition of environmental and labor standards that are harmonized upward, and attempts at restricting capital outflows (synonymous in politics with "losing jobs") to them by way of direct foreign investment. We predict that we will also witness increasing attempts at encouraging population control in these countries.[12]

4.2 THE CASE FOR FREE TRADE WITH DIVERSITY OF ENVIRONMENTAL STANDARDS

We now argue (based on the theoretical analysis in the Appendix) that the case for free trade, with diversity of environmental standards across countries, is essentially robust. We then proceed to address specifically the two issues distinguished at the beginning of this chapter: unfair trade and fear of loss of higher standards.

At the outset, note that "standards" may refer to general principles such as the "polluter pays" principle, or they may be defined as the precise tax rates that are levied on the polluter. In the political debate over differential standards, along with demands for CCII harmonization or for "ecodumping" duties when harmonization does not obtain, the complaints are evidently against lower pollution tax rates or charges – for example, that widget manufacturers are taxed, for the effluents that they discharge, at lower rates in Mexico than in the United States. These definitions, therefore, indicate the sense in which we will discuss. CCII harmonization in this chapter, unless otherwise specified.

4.2.1 The Basic Theoretical Presumptions

Distinguish again between the two major cases: where the pollution is domestic and where it is global (and spills over across national borders). Then the following basic theoretical conclusions follow (Appendix), defining welfare in the conventional economic sense.

Domestic Pollution

1. For a small country (with no influence on its terms of trade), free trade remains the best policy, with its own pollution being taxed as required and

regardless of whether the other country fixes its own pollution.[13] Where abatement is feasible with spending, there is no case for a subsidy.[14]

2. For a small country, if its own pollution is not taxed optimally, free trade will generally cease to be optimal. Also, it follows equally from the postwar theory of commercial policy under distortions that free trade, with domestic distortions, can immiserize.[15]

3. For a large country, free trade is not an optimal policy, but an optimal tariff is (on the assumption that there is no retaliation), while its domestic pollution is directly fixed through a pollution tax. As is well known, such an optimal solution for the large country is not Pareto optimal for the world economy.[16]

4. With free trade between two countries (small or large) and optimal pollution taxes within each country, global Pareto optimality will follow.

5. However, generally speaking, the optimal pollution taxes (in a globally Pareto optimal solution) will *not* be equal across the countries: *diversity in these tax rates will be both natural and appropriate, hence also "legitimate."*

6. Imposing one country's pollution tax rates on another will then create an *inefficient*, globally Pareto suboptimal solution.

7. Such harmonization, or "straitjacketing" to be more accurate, of the other country's standards toward one's own will also necessarily harm the other country. Thus a lower-standard country, forced to "harmonize up," will be harmed.

8. Whether such "harmonization up" will benefit the higher-standard country is, however, problematic: it may help or harm.[17] The presumption that it will necessarily help is false.

Global Pollution

1. When global pollution occurs, the globally Pareto optimal solution will be characterized by free trade and by pollution taxes in each country producing the pollution, these taxes being different except in singular circumstances.[18]

2. The globally Pareto optimal solution is not necessarily equitable. To be equitable as well, the market solution must be generally supplemented by (lump-sum) transfers.[19]

3. A small country, taking the foreign terms of trade, tariffs, and pollution abatement as given, will continue to find free trade to be its optimal policy. It will combine this with optimal pollution taxes and abatement addressed to its own pollution.[20] But such Cournot behavior makes little sense: it is more likely that each small country will "free ride" on pollution taxes and abatement and reproduce the "tragedy of the commons" in the use of the common property resource (i.e., the target of the pollution).

4. A large country, indulging in Cournot behavior with respect to the foreign tariffs and pollution abatement expenditures, will use an optimal tariff, not free trade, to maximize its welfare. The Cournot behavior, however, will yield a Nash equilibrium that is not Pareto optimal.[21]

4.2.2 Examining the Objections: Unfair Trade and Feared Loss of High Standards

In light of these propositions, we can now proceed to examine the four issues distinguished in section 4.1, especially the first one relating to "unfair trade" and the associated agitation for countervailing duties against "eco-dumping" in the absence of CCII harmonization.

Does Diversity of Environmental Standards Imply that Low-Standard Countries are Indulging in "Unfair Trade"?

The theoretical analysis clearly shows that the basic presumption is that different countries will have *legitimate diversity of CCII environmental taxes and standards.* This diversity will arise even if they share the same "utility function" with associated trade-offs between income and different types of pollution: the diverse tax rates can come from differences in technology and in endowments in the broadest sense (so as to include weather, demography, geography, inherited abatement policies, etc.).[22]

As it happens, there is also no compelling reason to think that every society must share the same utility function. It is perfectly appropriate, and not an indulgence of wilful "sovereignty," for Mexico to value clean water higher than clean air, compared to the United States, because a dollar expended on the former instead of the latter will produce greater health gains for Mexicans, whereas the situation would be the reverse for the United States.

The overall trade-off between income and (some generalized index of) pollution will also be different between societies: income may be more valuable at the margin when societies are poor and poverty takes people close to manipulation than when societies are rich and malnutrition results from overindulgence rather than deprivation. A clear example again is the emphasis on saving dolphins rather than increasing productivity in tuna fishing in the United States and the contrasting emphasis on ameliorating poverty instead in Mexico by using purse seines that kill dolphins while fishing for tuna.

The notion, therefore, that the diversity of CCII pollution standards and taxes is illegitimate and constitutes "unfair trade" or "unfair competition" is itself illegitimate. So is the consequent demand, following from this notion, that CCII harmonization is necessary for "free and fair trade,"[23] in the absence of which CCII differences must be treated as eco-dumping and be countervailed.

In fact, since the effect of such policies would be to force (at least some) countries to harmonize up their preferred lower CCII standards, the consequence would equally be to inflict a welfare loss on them. We might even argue that, while we advocate free trade traditionally, with diversity of domestic standards, on the presumption that voluntary trade is beneficial (relative to autarky) for every trading nation, and hence it is a mutual-gain policy prescription, the opposite is true for CCII harmonization to be superimposed on free trade:[24] it will amount to immiserization of the trading nation whose standards are being "distorted" up.

This basic case against CCII harmonization can be challenged on grounds that we now examine and mainly find unpersuasive.

Objection 1; Competing with Foreign Firms that do not bear Equal Burdens is Unfair. This competitiveness argument is common, especially on the part of some business groups and also some unions. As notions of unfairness are expressed by them, and as implied by proposed legislation to equalize burdens, this is certainly a strongly felt belief. Underlying it is the sense of outrage that one's ability to hold on to an industry is compromised by the fact that one's rivals abroad do not carry the same burdens.

The contrary arguments, which reject this competitiveness argument, are as follows:

(a) The fact that others abroad do not carry the same burdens is symmetric with the fact that these countries have different wages, capital costs, skills, infrastructure, weather, and what have you: all of which lead to differential advantages of production and trade competitiveness. Diversity of environmental tax burdens is thus no ground for complaints of unfairness.

(b) Losing competitive advantage because we put a larger negative value on a certain kind of pollution than others do is simply the flip side of the differential valuations. To object to that implication of the differential valuation is to object to the differential valuation itself, and hence to our own larger negative valuation. To see this clearly, think only of a closed economy without trade. If we were to tax pollution by an industry in such an economy, its implication would be precisely that this industry would shrink: it loses competitive advantage vis-à-vis other industries in our own country. To object to that shrinking is to object to the negative valuation being put on the pollution. there is, therefore, nothing "unfair" from this perspective, if our industry shrinks because we put higher standards on our industry and others, who mind the pollution less, choose lower standards.

(c) Besides, attributing competitive disadvantage to differential pollution tax burdens in the fashion of CCII comparisons for individual industries confuses absolute with comparative advantage. Thus, for example, in a two-industry world, if both industries abroad have lower pollution tax rates than at home, both will not contract at home. Rather, the industry with the *comparatively* higher tax rate will.

Objection 2: Others' Lower Standards do not Reflect their Citizens' Preferences Correctly. In turn, some environmentalist critics argue that the foreign governments do not reflect their citizens' "true preferences," and therefore in relation to these true preferences that would lead to higher valuation of pollution, the governments have unduly low standards, implying "unfair" competition.

There are counterarguments, in turn:

(a) Similar arguments, about failure of "political markets," apply to most countries, including high-standard countries, and to many areas of governmental regulation. It is commonly argued that the earliest legislations mandated "too-high" environmental standards that went beyond the "optimal" levels because costs were ignored and virtually limitless gains were assumed from the regulations. Now, in the United States for sure, cost-benefit considerations are steadily being introduced into the legislative process; and even the judiciary seems to have turned increasingly to this type of analysis, which then tends to weaken the bite of the standards legislatively laid down.[25]

Since arguments can be made persuasively that all legislation strays from the optimal because of political market failures endemic to any political system, however democratic, objecting only to lower environmental standards as reflecting such political market failure is to be arbitrary. It is also to open a Pandora's box, in favor of the more powerful countries that can then throw stones at others' glass houses while building a fortress around their own.

(b) Again, even if one argues that the decisions made undemocratically by a dictatorship or an oligarchy are vitiated, there is no reason to believe that the higher standards being pursued by a foreign country representing the competitive interests of a foreign industry or labor union in an industry are what a more democratic process would yield. The correct approach should rather be to encourage a shift to more democratic procedures in arriving at social and economic legislation, including environmental policy. Process, not outcomes (especially outcomes sought by self-serving groups elsewhere), is what we should aim at in countries that lack democratic ways.[26]

Should High-Standards Countries Force Low-Standards Countries into Upward Harmonization to Preserve their High Standards? In political-economy theory there are two forms of argument for CCII harmonization that take the high standards themselves to be at risk under free trade. Consider each, in turn.

(1) The less common argument is simply that, under pressure of competition from the low-standard countries, the political equilibrium will shift in favor of those who oppose high standards.

But this argument suffers from the fallacy of misplaced concreteness. Intensified international competition, *no matter why it arises*, will put such pressure on governments to reduce business costs. Why pick on lower standards elsewhere, even assuming that they are contributing to the problem?

(2) Far more worrisome to environmentalists than the simple effects of trade competition are the fears that "capital and jobs" will move to countries with lower standards, triggering a "race to the bottom" (or, as John Wilson has remarked, more accurately a race *toward* the bottom) where countries lower their standards in an interjurisdictional context, below a level that some or all would like, in order to attract capital and jobs. So, a cooperative solution that would *coordinate* the setting of standards would, generally speaking, be a better solution. This coordinated solution, however, need not be characterized by harmonization at the level of the standards in the high-standard country or, in fact, by harmonization at all.

What we have here is a valid theoretical argument.[27] It is stated with analytical rigor as follows: independent governments (or jurisdictions), setting public policy for environmental protection (via taxes and abatement) and competing for investment by reducing environmental standards in a world of mobile and scarce capital, will set these standards at levels that are "too low," that is, that are inefficient for the world economy (composed of the nations whose governments compete in this way). The inefficiency is to be construed as usual: alternative policies exist that make at least one jurisdiction better off and no other jurisdiction worse off. In short, we have nonPareto-optimal Cournot-Nash equilibria (as we have already stated in earlier analysis in this chapter), characterized by lower environmental standards than in the cooperative equilibrium.

To see the matter more clearly, consider the following analysis based on arbitrarily specified, conventional payoff matrices reflecting the incomes yielded (in brackets) when different pollution abatement expenditures are undertaken at levels O and *A* (i.e., zero and a finite amount) by the two countries, home and foreign. The abatement expenditures are assumed to be a monotonic and increasing function of environmental standards.

There are thus four possible combinations of home and foreign expenditures on abatement. The payoffs associated with each combination with the first (resp. second) component being the payoff of the home (resp. foreign) jurisdiction are given by the following payoff matrix:

		Foreign expenditure	
		O	*A*
Home expenditure	0	(–2, –2)	(2, –3)
	A	(–3, 2)	(1, 1)

It is easily seen that each jurisdiction has a *dominant* strategy, namely, to spend nothing, because by doing so it maximizes its payoff whether the other jurisdiction spends nothing or *A*. Yet, compared to this *individually* rational dominant-strategy Nash equilibrium which both jurisdictions spending nothing on abatement, the *collectively* rational strategy of each spending *A* will yield a *higher* payoff for *both*.

Of course jurisdictional competition need not necessarily lead to such a "prisoner's dilemma" type of Nash equilibrium. For example, if the payoff matrix is as follows,

(–4, –4)	(2, –3)
(–3, 2)	(1, 1)

so that one jurisdiction spends nothing while the other spends *A*, (0, *A*) and (*A*, 0) are "pure strategy" Nash equilibria.

In both these cases the Nash equilibrium is characterized by a "race to the bottom" in the sense that the pollution abatement expenditure is zero for at least one jurisdiction. But this result need not occur, as consideration of the following payoff matrix shows. Thus, consider

(–2, –2)	(2, –3)
(–3, 2)	(3, 3)

and it is readily seen that we have a unique Nash equilibrium where each jurisdiction spends *A* on abatement.

Of course, these are arbitrarily constructed payoff matrices, and we need to ground them in underlying models of economies to see whether such outcomes are sensible within them. As argued by John Wilson, this can indeed be done to show that the "race to the bottom" need not occur, and that even a "race to the top" might.[28]

The question that now arises is whether this theoretical possibility of the "race to the bottom" is an empirical possibility of any significance. Leaving out the question as to whether the parametric evidence shows that the noncooperative Nash equilibrium, including the special case for the prisoner's dilemma, will be characterized by significantly lower environmental standards relative to the cooperative equilibrium, we may ask whether there is any empirical support anyway for the propositions that (1) capital is in fact responsive to the differences in environmental standards and (2) different countries and jurisdictions actually play the game then of competitive lowering of standards to attract capital. Without both these phenomena holding in a significant fashion in reality, the "race to the bottom" could be a theoretical curiosity.

As it happens, systematic evidence is available for the former proposition alone, but the finding is that the proposition is not supported by the studies to date: at best, there is very weak evidence in favor of interjurisdictional mobility in response to CCII differences in environmental standards. Arik Levinson, who has reviewed the available evidence thoroughly, concludes:[29]

> The conclusion of the literature on domestic location decisions, like that on international locations, is that there is not a lot of evidence that environmental regulations deter investment. In fact, most authors are careful to note the limitations of their research, and to place caveats on their counterintuitive conclusions that stringent regulations do not deter plants nor do lax regulations attract them. But the literature as a whole presents fairly compelling evidence that this is true.

Of course, there are many ways to interpret this finding of an extremely weak effect of CCII differences in environmental standards on industry location. There are three classes of explanation for the finding: (1) that the differences in standards are not significant and are outweighed by other factors that affect locational decisions; (2) that exploiting differences in standards is not a good strategy relative to not exploiting them; and (3) that lower standards may paradoxically even repel, instead of attracting, direct foreign investment.

Explanation 1

a. The obvious, and most cited, explanation is that the standards differences are a small factor in the location decision because they are dominated by other more important factors such as tax breaks, infrastructure facilities, and proximity to markets.[30]

b. Industry location may be seen to be more sensitive to CCII differences in standards if executive enforcement and voters-cum-NGO activism are taken into account as well. The de facto differences in standards may then be more acute than assumed in many studies.[31]

Explanation 2

c. Another (static) explanation is that when multiplant firms, such as most multinationals, invest in different locations, they tend to work uniformly with the most stringent standards they face among these locations, to reduce the transaction costs involved in making diverse choices.[32]

d. Another (dynamic) explanation is that, faced with divergent standards, firms extrapolate that all countries are on an escalator to similar higher standards and therefore decide that it is best to be "ahead of the curve" in the countries that currently have lower standards and to conform to higher standards even though not required. In this case, again, convergence of standards adhered to will emerge, as in the preceding (static) argument, and differences in (required) standards across different jurisdictions will become moot, showing little relationship in practice between such differences and industry-location choices.[33]

e. Another (dynamic) explanation is that firms may argue that the higher-standard countries are the ones that innovate, that many innovations lead to embodied technical change, that such innovations are likely to be embodied (only) in recent vintages of capital goods that already meet the higher standards, and therefore the important benefit of significant technical change will accrue to a firm only insofar as processes and capital goods using higher-standard technology at present are being used by it.

Explanation 3

f. An ingenious explanation of a different analytical variety is that multinationals are discouraged from investing in low-standard countries because local firms have comparative advantage in using pollution-intensive technology that conforms to lower standards. Hence, direct foreign investment (DFI) is likely to be less, not more, when CCII differences in standards are greater between countries![34]

A possible underlying explanation is that firms in the higher-standard countries are likely to scrap their earlier-vintage lower-standard equipment and sell it to the lower-standard countries for the local firms to use, instead of undertaking DFI themselves with such discontinued technology. In short, arm's-length sale of lower-standard equipment to local manufacturers may be preferred to DFI with such equipment, because the local firms are more likely to be able to work with this technology than the multinationals that have moved on to higher-standard, newer-vintage technology – engineering and maintenance know-how tend to be specific to the technology one is working with.

Most of these suggested explanations only reinforce the view that CCII differences in standards, as a factor prompting a "race to the bottom," should not be a source of concern.[35] And this conclusion is further reinforced when one contemplates the fact that there is almost no evidence for the proposition that, regardless of the capital-sensitivity to CCII differences in environmental standards, different countries and jurisdictions nonetheless actually compete for capital by sacrificing environmental standards[36] (as against doing so via tax breaks, infrastructure construction, tariff policy, preferential trading arrangements such as NAFTA where Mexico sought DFI-diversion toward itself through preferential access to the U.S. market, etc.).

The fuss that is made nonetheless over the "race to the bottom" in the political arena, as happened in the NAFTA negotiations, may then be explained either as a reaction to ill-founded fears or as a cynical ploy to advance environmental or protectionist lobbying interests.

Other Arguments and an Alternative Proposal. Therefore, neither the concern with "unfair trade" nor the concern with "threats to high standards," as the reason to push for CCII harmonization as a precondition for free trade or alternatively to invoke eco-dumping duties to countervail CCII differences in pollution tax burdens, is compelling. It is best to take, as a general policy, the option of *mutual recognition* of standards, recognizing the fact that diversity of CCII standards is basically a natural and appropriate phenomenon, consistent with free trade and the consequent gains from trade for all.

Protectionist Capture. The wisdom of the policy conclusion of the preceding paragraph is reinforced by contemplating the certain protectionist consequences of doing otherwise. Thus, consider what an eco-dumping procedure, supplementing our normal antidumping (AD) procedure, would do. We presume that the eco-dumping procedure would calculate the subsidy implied by lower standards and proceed to levy a countervailing duty unless the foreign costs were raised by the estimated amount, with the option that the duty would be lifted when foreign standards were suitably raised and the costs of foreign firms demonstrably raised by the calculated amount.

It is well known that AD actions have become the favored policy instrument of protectionists today. Their desirability from the viewpoint of protectionists derives from the fact that, unlike safeguard actions (under Section 201 of the U.S. law and Article XIX of the GATT), AD actions are *selective*: they can target down to the level of the firm, not just a specific foreign country! Besides, compared to preset tariffs, they are also *elastic*: the duties will be set at rates that are decided during litigation and therefore are a function of litigation expenditure, impartiality of the procedures governing the litigation, and the bilateral game played between the complainants and their targets.

Furthermore, in playing the game, the rules are set in favor of litigants, relative to what the rules would be if the objective of AD actions were truly to avoid economically defined predation. In particular, the usual game of reconstructing true costs, against which prices charged are compared to determine dumping margins, has been played to the hilt to get these margins to be as high as possible in litigation. But, as was the case with the former centrally planned economies whose own prices and costs were dismissed as illegitimate, these reconstructed "true" costs can be arbitrary, leading the procedure to effective protectionist capture.

Such capture would surely be the case also with eco-dumping duties, since the eco-dumping margins would have to be *necessarily* estimated on the basis of reconstructed costs of meeting the pollution standards of the complainant country. The U.S. Environmental Protection Agency, for example, would be estimating the cost of implementing U.S. standards in Rio or in Jakarta, so as to arrive at the implicit (*not* actual and observable) subsidy that must be countervailed through an eco-dumping duty by the United States, just as the Department of Commerce does for conventional dumping. There is no reason to doubt that the inherently arbitrary outcomes would be similarly obliging to local lobbies.[37]

Infinite Shadow Prices? Thus we conclude that the demands for eco-dumping duties to countervail CCII differences in environmental standards and pollution tax and abatement burdens are both illogical (in denying the legitimacy of such diversity) and unwise (in being inherently susceptible to protectionist capture). We have considered, at different stages of our analysis, several reasons why these demands nonetheless appear reasonable and why they have political salience. We must conclude, however, by adding one more reason, which probably has a counterpart also in the case of labor standards and which springs from the nature of our basic argument for the legitimacy of diversity in CCII standards.

Recall our argument that the different shadow prices for pollution that can, and generally will, emerge among different countries, implying differential rather than harmonized environmental taxes and standards, are "natural" for us to contemplate and accept. But suppose that we were putting an infinite price on any and every specific pollution, regardless of its level, small or large. Then these differences would disappear. We believe that many environmentalists have tended to approach their specific environmental concerns with an implicit infinite shadow price, thus leading to demands for harmonization, though this tendency is declining. This fact is well-illustrated by the following remarks in Cropper and Oates' excellent recent review of environmental economics:[38]

> The economists' view had – to the dismay of the profession – little impact on the initial stage of legislation for the control of pollution. In fact, the cornerstones of federal environmental policy in the United States, the Amendments to the Clean Air Act in 1970 and to the Clean Water Act in 1972, explicitly prohibited the weighing of benefits against costs in the setting of environmental standards. The former directed the Environmental Protection Agency to set maximum limitations on pollutant concentrations in the atmosphere "to protect the public health": the latter set as an objective the "elimination of the discharge of *all* [our emphasis] pollutants into the navigable waters by 1985." [Although standards were to be set solely on the basis of health criteria, the 1970 Amendments to the Clean Air Act did include economic feasibility among its guidelines for setting source-specific standards. Roger Noll has suggested that the later 1977 Amendments were, in fact, more "antieconomic" than any that went before. See Matthew McCubbins, Roger Noll, and Barry Weingast (1989) for a careful analysis of this legislation.]
>
> The evolution of environmental policy, both in the U.S. and elsewhere, has inevitably brought economic issues to the fore: environmental regulation has necessarily involved costs – and the question of how far and how fast to push for pollution control in light of these costs has entered into the public debate. Under Executive Order 11291 issued in 1981, many proposed environmental measures have been subject to a benefit-cost test. In addition, some more recent pieces of environmental legislation, notably the Toxic Substances Control Act (TSCA) and the Federal Insecticide, Fungicide, and Rodenticide Act (FIU–FRA), call for weighing benefits against costs in the setting of standards.

Once, therefore, we get away from the limited, perhaps almost empty, set of infinite-shadow-price environmental objectives, we are then back also to the legitimacy of diversity of standards among trading nations as the natural and reasonable way to look at the issue.[39]

An Alternative Proposal. We should thus reject the calls for "CCII harmonization or countervailing duties on eco-dumping." But the political salience of such calls remains a major problem. One may well ask then, Are there any "second-best" approaches, short of the eco-dumping and CCII harmonization proposals, that may address some of the political concerns at least economic cost? In that spirit, we would suggest the following proposal for consideration.

Proposal: Extend the Domestic Standards of High-Standard Countries to their Firms in Low-Standard Countries, Unilaterally or through an OECD Code. In our view, the political salience of the harmful demands for eco-dumping duties and CCII harmonization is greatest when plants are closed by one's own multinationals and shifted to other countries. The actual shifting of location, and the associated loss of jobs in that plant, magnify greatly the fear of the "race to the bottom" and of the "impossibility" of competing against low-standard countries. Similarly, when investment by one's own firms is seen to go to specific countries that happen to have lower standards, resentment is readily focused against those countries and their standards. However, when jobs are lost simply because of *trade* competition, it is much harder to locate one's resentment and fear on one specific foreign country and its policies as a source of unfair competition.[40] Hence, a second-best proposal could well be to address this particular fear, however unfounded and often illogical, of outmigration of plants and investment by one's firms abroad in low-standard countries.

The proposal is to adapt the Sullivan Principles approach to the problem at hand. Under Sullivan, U.S. firms in South Africa were urged to adopt U.S. practices, not the South African apartheid ways, in their operations. If this principle that U.S. firms in Mexico be subject to U.S. environmental policies (choosing the desired ones from the many that obtain across different states in the federal United States) were adopted by U.S. legislation, it would automatically remove whatever incentive there was to move because of environmental burden differences.[41]

This proposal that one's firms abroad behave as if they were at home – do in Rome as you do in New York, not as Romans do – can be either legislated unilaterally by one high-standard country or by a multilateral binding treaty among different high-standard countries. Again, it may be reduced to an exhortation, just as the Sullivan Principles were, by single countries in isolation or by several as through a nonbinding but ethos-defining and policy-encouraging OECD Code.

The disadvantage of this proposal, of course, is that it does violate the diversity-is-legitimate rule whose desirability was discussed earlier. Investment flows, like investment of one's own funds and production and trade therefrom, should reflect this diversity. The proposal, therefore, reduces the efficiency gains from a freer flow of cross-country investments today. But if environmental tax burdens are not very different or do not figure prominently in firms' locational decisions, as the empirical literature seems to stress,[42] the efficiency costs of this proposal could also be minimal while the gains in allaying fears and therefore moderating the demand for bad proposals could be very large indeed.

Yet another objection may focus on intra-OECD differences in high standards. Since there are differences among the OECD countries in CCII environmental tax burdens in specific industries for specific pollution, this proposal would lead to "horizontal inequity" among the OECD firms in third countries. If the British burden is higher than the French, British firms would face a bigger burden in Mexico than the French firms. But then such differences already exist among firms abroad, since tax practices among the OECD countries on taxation of firms abroad are not harmonized in many respects.[43] Interestingly, the problem of horizontal equity has come up in relation also to the demands of the poor countries (which often find it difficult to enforce import restrictions effectively) that the domestic restrictions on hazardous products be automatically extended to exports by every country. Such a practice would put firms in the countries with greater restrictions at an economic disadvantage. But agreement has now been reached to disregard the problem.

Other problems may arise: (1) monitoring of one's firms in a foreign country may be difficult; and (2) the countries with lower standards may object on grounds of "national sovereignty." Neither argument may be compelling. It is unlikely that a developing country would object to foreign firms doing better by its citizens in regard to environmental standards (which it cannot afford to impose, given its own priorities, on its own firms). Equally, it would then assist in monitoring the foreign firms.

4.3 THE QUESTION OF ETHICAL PREFERENCES

So far, we have considered only those demands for harmonization of cross-country intra-industry standards that arise because of considerations centered on "unfair trade" and the fear that one's standards would be endangered if competitiveness were reduced because of lower standards abroad.

However, we must recognize that, for some environmentalists, the desire to spread one's ethical values to others also leads to demands for harmonization, especially of production processes. Thus, opponents in the United States of purse-seine fishing of tuna, which cruelly kills dolphins along with the tuna, would like to see the suspension of trade in Mexican tuna so as to get the Mexicans to accept the U.S. restrictions on such fishing. Of course, some of the agitation proceeds from environmentalists who would find it morally reprehensible to trade in products whose harvesting has cruelly abused nature or a preferred species. But a main impulse is simply the old, morality-driven desire to spread the values to which one subscribes, suspension of access to one's market being justified by a consequentialist ethic rather than a categorical imperative. Consider these two arguments in reverse order.

4.3.1 Spreading Ethical Preferences to Others

We think that GATT sanctioning of the use of unilateral *state* action to suspend other countries' trade access, or (in GATT-defined parlance) their trading rights under the GATT "treaty," unless one's choice of ethical concerns is adopted by others through implicit harmonization in one's direction, is inappropriate for several reasons.[44]

(1) The values sought to be imposed are often not at the level of "human rights" violations such as the massacres perpetuated on one's population or apartheid. They are "lesser" values and are idiosyncratic in the sense of being closely culture-bound rather than reflective of basic and universal aspects of human nature. Thus Americans are particularly touched by dolphins being caught cruelly in purse seines in tuna fishing. But we wonder when we see on television an interview with the man who brought this practice to national attention by filming the dolphins in distress: he is, we think, eating fish in the wilds. If Americans have their dolphins, the Indians have their sacred cows. Animal-rights activists object to slaughterhouses. Others may see the fishing scenes in Robert Redford's *A River Runs Through It*, not as magical moments of rapport with nature, but as violation of it with cruelty to a fish that twists and turns, writhing in agony.

The culture specificity of these values, and hence their lack of salience to other economically weaker nations on whom they are sought to be imposed, creates then the inevitable sense that the use of trade sanctions to impose them is simply an act of unjustified moral militancy that is itself ethically offensive. This view gains further credibility when the "values" being pushed on others are actually at the expense of more fundamental values. For example, Americans would prefer to protect dolphins at the expense of Mexican prosperity. The use of purse seines, which are more productive than other nets, would reduce Mexican poverty, but Americans put dolphins ahead of Mexicans. The Mexican reaction may then well be similar to the way American liberals would react if they had to confront the moral militancy of Pat Robertson allied with Genghis Khan.

(2) And then there is the objection that comes from the lack of symmetry in imposing one's idiosyncratic moral preferences on others, as between the strong and the weak nations. Thus, even some NGOs in poor countries whose natural tendency would be to ally with NGOs in rich countries, have expressed resentment and opposition to the "eco-imperialism" implied when the strong nations use trade power to force their preferred values on the weaker nations but the equally autonomous values of the weaker nations cannot be forced upon the stronger nations in the same way.[45] These NGOs deny that the NGOs of the strong nations have a monopoly on virtue.

Thus we may quote the most radical of today's proenvironment NGOs in India on this issue, in an editorial, "Trade Control is not a Fair Instrument," in the country's leading environmental magazine, *Down to Earth*:[46]

> In the current world reality trade is used as an instrument entirely by northern countries to discipline environmentally errant nations. Surely, if India or Kenya were to threaten to stop trade with USA, it would hardly affect the latter. But the fact of the matter is that it is the northern countries that have the greatest impact on the world's environment and yet, their past record in their own countries . . . is nothing to be proud of . . . the instruments that need to be devised for . . . a system of global discipline must be fair and equally accessible to all. Reinforcing [through unilateral muscle-flexing by rich-country NGOs and their governments via trade sanctions] the power that already flows in a northern direction cannot improve the world.

(3) The 1991 GATT report *Trade and the Environment* drew attention, not to

this disturbing asymmetry of effective enforceability of the "values" of the North versus the equally autonomous "values" of the South owing to differential power. Rather, eschewing the problem of asymmetric power and instead assuming that each nation can play the same game with equal effectiveness, it advanced the "slippery slope" scenario: if any country could suspend another's trading access in products produced in an "unacceptable" fashion (when no international physical spillovers could be cited as a possible justification and only "values" were at stake), the result was likely to be a proliferation of trade restrictions without any discipline or restraint:[47]

> It is difficult to think of a way to effectively contain the cross-border assertion of priorities. If governments suspend the trading rights of other nations because they unilaterally assert that their environmental priorities [i.e., "values"] are superior to those of others, then the same approach can be employed on any number of grounds. Protectionists would welcome such unilateralism. They could exploit it to create embargoes, special import duties and quotas against rivals by enacting national legislation that unilaterally defines environmental agendas that other countries [with different "values"] are likely to find unacceptable.
>
> Changing the world trading rules so as to permit the suspension of trading rights of others by individual contracting parties, based simply on the unilateral and extra-territorial assertion of their environmental priorities, undoubtedly would be difficult because many countries would consider such a change to be a big step down a slippery slope.

(4) These views concerning unilateralism to impose one's values on others acquire yet greater cogency when we recognize that there are alternative ways in which one's values can be indulged and propagated.

(a) Most important, if your values are good, as with human rights values that are now widely shared, they will spread far and wide, not because India had economic power to force it on others or because Western NGOs urged trade sanctions against their own nations to canvas its adoption. The Spanish Inquisition should not be necessary to spread Christianity; quite appropriately, the pope has no troops.

Thus consider the following argument, advanced by one of the ablest advocates of environmentalist causes, Steve Charnovitz, in defense of biodiversity:

> There are important medical reasons to preserve biodiversity. But there are also important moral reasons. Geopolitical boundaries should not override the world of God who directed Noah to take two of every living creature into the Ark "to keep them alive with you."[48]

We must confess that, as two Hindus among nearly 900 million on this planet, we find this moral argument culture-specific rather than universal in its appeal. It is unlikely that it can spread because of its intrinsic moral merit; should it then be forced on others anyway?

(b) Moreover, alternative private options are often available to propagate your particular ethical preferences if greater activism is desired. Nothing today proscribes NGOs in United States, for example, from financing NGOs in Mexico that bring pressure on *their* government to change its attitude on purse seines, thus changing the balance of forces in Mexico away from more productive tuna fishing that benefits Mexico economically and toward "dolphin-safe" fishing that benefits the dolphins in the Eastern Pacific instead.

(c) Then again, voluntary private boycotts can be a potent instrument as well. A long-standing tradition permits such private boycotts in pluralistic democracies. Provided that labelling requirements provide an opportunity for consumers to make choices in the marketplace between, say, "dolphin-safe" and "dolphin-unsafe" tuna, these boycotts will provide an option to "dolphin-agitated" activists.[49]

This option is not the same as proscription, of course. Environmentalists will thus note that labeling may be ineffective because "consumers may act *rationally* in calculating that their individual purchase of environmentally unfriendly products . . . would have only a negligible effect" and that "consumers may act *irrationally*" by not appreciating the ecological importance of avoiding the consumption of the offending product.[50]

Then again, there are bound to be substantive disagreements about the nature and extent of labeling: "dolphin-unsafe" may be considered too weak. The problems that have plagued the labeling issue for a variety of reasons within the United States itself, both in terms of its design and its uniformity versus diversity among the different states of the union, will not go away at the international level: if anything, they will be more fiercely debated.[51]

But, against these factors that weaken the efficacy of the voluntary-boycott prescription, we must put contrary arguments. Indeed, one might argue that, if enough people desire to attach opprobrium to "dolphin-unsafe" tuna, then "dolphin-safe" tuna producers can use their own "dolphin-safe" labels, requiring only state monitoring and prosecution of false labeling by the dolphin-unsafe tuna producers: After all, the Body Shop has done pretty well in this way.

Moreover, boycotts in rich countries with big markets, even when leaky, can carry disproportionate clout, and the funds at the disposal of some of the environmental NGOs and certainly in their aggregate (as demonstrated when they carry enormously expensive full-page ads simultaneously in newspapers such as the *New York Times*, *Washington Post*, and *The Financial Times*) are evidently large relative to what the poor countries they occasionally target can muster in defense of their own practices and preferences.[52]

One might also add that the passionate zeal with which these boycotts have advocated and the occasional willingness to portray those that disapproved morally defective, add to their potency as weapons.

A critic may well suggest that we contradict ourselves if we allow private boycotts but would disallow governmental prohibitions, since governments are only "agents" of the citizens. Strictly speaking, this criticism is not true: there is considerable debate in the social science literature on the "principal-agent" relationship and on how poor an agent the government can be. But, that complexity aside, we do distinguish all the time in democracies between state and private actions, permitting far greater latitude to the latter. Thus, when the Harvard lawyer Alan Dershowitz agitated successfully to have the Boston

Symphony Orchestra cancel Vanessa Redgrave's appearance because of her politically incorrect views, he was considered well within his rights to disgrace himself; but the U.S. government proscribing her appearance would have been a disgrace to the nation and in violation of national tradition and would surely have been struck down by our courts. And this asymmetry between what private parties and public governments may do is likely to be accepted by most democratic governments today.

(5) So far, we have proceeded on the assumption that unilateral suspension of trade access to spread one's ethical preferences is effective and have argued essentially that it is unwise and undesirable. But a legitimate critique may well be that such action is likely to be ineffective in its objective, thus disrupting trade to no advantage.

It is hard to settle this question on theoretical grounds alone. The cost imposed on the nation whose offending trade is suspended may or may not be significant enough to matter in its calculation; the cost itself will reflect the importance of the embargoed market relative to others, ability to evade, and so on. But it is surely improbable that this cost in any specific instance will be compelling.[53]

The matter becomes less problematic if the cost is greatly increased by other punishments and inducements: Mexican compliance with nonuse of purse seines, despite the favorable Tuna-Dolphin Panel ruling, was secured by convincing President Carlos Salinas de Gortari that it would be hard to pass NAFTA in Congress otherwise. These added instruments, however, will be available only to large and powerful nations, chiefly the United States, making the argument's relevance fairly negligible for most nations.

The sanctioning, as WTO-consistent, of unilateral, governmental withdrawal of market access from other nations for their offending products simply with a view to coercing them into accepting one's idiosyncratic "value" preferences seems, therefore, to be undesirable on several grounds, chiefly these:

* It is essentially intransitive, with each nation able to say its specific values are better than another's; it thus creates the potential for chaotic spread of trade restrictions based on self-righteousness, compounded by a likely encouragement of the process by protectionists.

* In its reliance on force rather than persuasion, it is inherently asymmetric toward poor nations with less economic clout, implying that the economically strong nations are also morally superior and their governments must not be constrained by multilateral rules from coercing others into conversion.

* There are alternative private options that can be used to create a multilateral consensus of shared valued based not on the sword but on precept, example, and even pressure through boycotts.[54]

Even though some of the environmental NCOs in the United States, in particular, and perhaps elsewhere too, are skeptical or scornful of them, it is noteworthy that these arguments are spreading within the international community. Thus, Steve Charnovitz has recently complained:[55]

> The GATT's campaign against unilateralism is having some impact. Earlier this year, the UN Conference on Trade and Development adopted a resolution stating that "Unilateral actions to deal with environmental challenges outside the jurisdiction of the importing country should be avoided." The Rio Declaration repeats this statement.

We have little doubt, however, that unilateral actions designed simply to spread "lesser values" to others through the use of suspension of trading access are unwise. We are, therefore, only delighted that this view is gaining ground.

4.3.2 Rejecting Trade in "Defiled" Products

Suppose, however, that your intention in unilaterally denying Mexico access to the U.S. market is not to change Mexican fishing of tuna in a "dolphin-safe" direction, but simply to avoid eating a "defiled" product that offends your moral values.[56] Should you then be forced into consuming Mexican tuna? That would seem a tall order to many.

But there is an answer to this objection. Nothing in current or prospective GATT rules forces you (quite correctly) into this offensive option. For, you could certainly compensate the country whose trading rights (i.e., access to your market) are being denied or suspended by *either* offering other concessions, *or* (in the odd manner of GATT procedures) having the other country withdraw some "equivalent" concessions of its own to you.

Confronted by this argument, some environmentalists are offended: why should we have to pay for our principles? The answer is that it is a small price to pay if the alternative (of unilateralism) has the many drawbacks that we have noted already. If it is right in the Christian tradition to buy indulgences to pay for one's vice, perhaps one should not object to a proposal to pay for one's virtue: at least, the former is for personal gain, the latter (if you accept our arguments) for social gain.[57] Besides, the "payment" is not in cash but in compensation in the form of reductions of other trade barriers against the foreign country to offset the enactment of the trade barrier against its offending export (or retaliatory raising of trade barriers by the foreign country). Such payment, in fact, should work in the direction of moving resources away from the offending foreign activity, thus reinforcing the case for using such a policy option.

Charnovitz also appeals to "original intent" to argue that the original signatories to the GATT, and earlier practice in some cases, permitted exceptions to market access based on extrajurisdictional exercise of "values" in cases such as the prohibited U.S. landing and sale of U.S. sponges from the Gulf of Mexico gathered by "certain harmful methods [such as] diving or using a diving apparatus."[58] We are assured by academic legal exports on the GATT, however, that the GATTs "original intent" is not unambiguously inferred in this as in many other instances.

John Jackson, one of the leading authorities on GATT law, has thus argued:[59]

> It has been argued [by Charnovitz] that the drafting history of the GATT would lead to an interpretation of Article XX that would permit governments to take a variety of environmental measures and justify them under the general exceptions of GATT. While this view is interesting, and the research is apparently thorough, it is not entirely persuasive and overlooks important issues of treaty interpretation. Under typical international law, elaborated by the Vienna Convention on the Law of Treaties, preparatory work history is an ancillary means of interpreting treaties. In the context of interpreting the GATT, we have more than forty years of practice

> since the origin of GATT, and we also have some very important policy questions . . . Thus, unlike certain schools of thought concerning United States Supreme Court interpretation of the United States Constitution, it is this author's view that one cannot rely too heavily on the original drafting history.

In any event, the liberal environmentalists who would ordinarily oppose the appointments of "original intent" judges on the Supreme Court should not endorse this juridical approach in seeking to prevent the GATT from pursuing (what we have argued are) sensible interpretations of its laws on environmental issues.

4.3.3 Dealing with Ethical Preferences

Where does this analysis leave us? Based on it, as also on arguments in the discussion that follows immediately concerning the way GATT deals with objections by contracting parties to processes of production (as distinct from products themselves) used by other contracting parties, we think that the following recommendations have merit in case of ethics-based objections to providing market access:

Unilateralism

* Unilateral suspension of trading access for reasons based on ethical preference should not be sanctioned by the WTO.

* Such unilateral suspensions, where desired, should be "paid for" by other, equivalent trade concessions.

Plurilateralism and Multilateralism

Where the ethical preference is embodied in a plurilateral (i.e, multination) treaty signed by many nations, we need to distinguish between two major cases:

1. Plurilateral treaties concerning an ethical preference, as on preventing the production of chickens in batteries or injecting cattle with hormones, for instance, may be signed by enough nations to enable a WTO waiver; in this case, the compatibility of the plurilateral treaty and the WTO is assured.

2. When the number of nations signing the ethical-preference-embodying treaty falls short of the required WTO waiver majority, then the conflict can lead to problems. In particular:

* *Products:* Where the plurilateral treaty simply provides for *suspension of trade access* for the offending products – such as ivory or tigers or whales – there is no difficulty in enforcing such a ban as long, of course, as the ban extends in a nondiscriminatory fashion to both foreign and domestic supply.[60]

Where, however, the signatory nations seek to impose *trade sanctions* (i.e., trade disruption of products other than the one in dispute), as a punishment aimed at securing compliance, the consensus appears to be that such sanctions would be GATT-inconsistent.[61] In that case, our solution would be to treat these sanctions as indeed so and instead to encourage nations to use other instrumentalities (of the kind discussed earlier, e.g. suasion, NGO activities) to secure the necessary acceptance of the ideas by a plurality of WTO contracting parties sufficient to obtain a waiver. This is indeed the procedure that has been used to undertake trade embargoes in matters such as apartheid where South Africa, despite being a GATT member, was embargoed under multilateralism-based UN procedures that would equally have procured a GATT waiver.

* *Processes:* The GATT would appear to proscribe the suspension of market access to other contracting parties in products whose manufacture or production is objected to by the importing contracting party. In our view, as developed in the next section, this is a desirable proscription. If, therefore, it is desired that such suspension of market access be undertaken in any event – as was the case with the proscription of hormone-fed beef by the EC – then we would recommend that the suspension be "paid for" by compensatory trade concessions elsewhere, exactly as in the case of unilateral trade access suspensions discussed previously.

4.4 INSTITUTIONAL VULNERABILITY OF HIGH STANDARDS TO OBJECTIONS BY LOW-STANDARD COUNTRIES: GATT'S THREAT TO ENVIRONMENTAL AUTONOMY

We turn finally to the question of the threats seen by many environmentalists to their high standards (aimed at domestic regulation) by GATT procedures that enable low-standards. We must ask, Are the environmentalists legitimately worried about the roadblocks that current and prospective GATT rules can pose for environmental regulations and standards aimed entirely at domestic production and consumption, matters that are conventionally and properly within domestic jurisdiction?

Now, as long as these rules are applied without discrimination between domestic and foreign suppliers and among different foreign suppliers, there is really little that GATT rules can do to prevent a country from doing anything that it wants to do. For domestic conservation, safety, and health reasons, a contracting party of the GATT can even undertake discriminatory, selectively targeted trade-restraining action, subject to safeguards, under Articles XX(b) and XX(g).[62]

Thus, if you insist on safety belts or air bags in cars, you can impose them on cars as long as both imports from all sources and domestic production are symmetrically treated. So also for requiring catalytic converters to reduce environmentally harmful emissions.

4.4.1 The Problem of Processes

The most significant and contentious conceptual question arises when you have a rule that says that consumption (from both domestic and foreign sources) of a product will be restricted if the product is produced, *using a process you disapprove of*. Objecting to a process used in a foreign (or, strictly nondomestic) jurisdiction is, under GATT rulings, not acceptable. There are two types of such process-related problems that we might distinguish.

1. Where the process used is objected to because of "values": e.g. purse seines or leghold traps.

2. Where the process used is objected to because it creates cross-border physical spillovers and hence a global pollution problem: e.g., acid rain or global warming.[63]

GATT law, as currently interpreted, forbids the use of trade restrictions for *both* classes of objections. For the first class of actions, this proscription seems to us justified, in light of our discussion in section 4.3.

The presence of cross-border physical spillovers, whose analysis we sketch only briefly in section 4.5, raises more legitimate worries about altogether ruling out process-related trade restraints, and appropriate changes in GATT law will be necessary in this class of cases where it seems evidently inappropriate to prevent nations from *any* use of trade restraints to limit the physical harm being imposed on them by other nations whose trade accentuates this harm. Such use must, however, be regulated in a way that ensures symmetry of rights, equity, and efficiency. Devising appropriate procedures and rules to regulate the use of such trade restraints in the context of global environmental problems is a challenge for the architects of the new GATT system.

4.4.2 Products

It would appear, however, that the GATT rules should cause no problems for the environmentalists (except for the process-related issues) when only purely domestic environmental problems are at issue. Thus, the GATT report argues:[64]

> Under GATT's rules, governments can employ many different measures to protect and improve the local environment. Thus, sales taxes on products that can create pollution (those containing chlorofluorocarbons, for example), deposit refund schemes for recyclable waste (bottles, scrap cars), or favourable tax treatment of environmentally friendly products (lead-free gasoline, solar panels for home heating) and other non-discriminatory measures ensuring a pattern of domestic consumption that minimizes pollution would not normally be open to challenge.
>
> There is also nothing in the GATT that prevents contracting parties from taxing or regulating domestic producers who engage in polluting activities – even to the extent of prohibiting the production and sale of particular goods. For instance, ceilings on air pollution levels, and levies on companies that discharge pollutants into lakes and rivers, are fully consistent with GATT rules.
>
> In certain cases, even a measure taken for environmental protection purposes which would otherwise violate GATT obligations not to discriminate may be permitted under Article XX of the GATT. The narrowly-defined exceptions in Article XX permit a contracting party to place health, safety or domestic resource conservation goals ahead of non-discrimination, but only when certain conditions are fulfilled. In general, these conditions ensure that a trade measure is necessary for the achievement of such goals – and that these goals are not used as a pretext for reducing competition from imports.
>
> GATT rules, therefore, place essentially no constraints on a country's right to protect its own environment against damage from either domestic production or the consumption of domestically produced or imported products. Generally speaking, a country can do anything to imports or exports that it does to its own products, and it can do anything it considers necessary to its own production processes.

Alas, that is not the end of the matter for the environmentalists. For, as the GATT report suggests, even if a regulation or a standard were set in an apparently nondiscriminatory fashion, it is perfectly possible that

* in reality, its intention is to discriminate against imports rather than to reach the stated (environmental or other) objective; and
* in practice, even if the intention is truly to reach the stated goal, the choice from different ways to reach that goal may have been in favor of a regulation or standard that effectively discriminates most, rather than least, against imports.

Then again, especially when safety and health standards are set (as with phytosanitary standards), there have been increasing demands for "scientific tests" as a precondition for the imposition of such standards, so as again to make these palatable to other trading nations who might see their resulting loss of markets as otherwise reasonable.

These are perhaps the most contentious issues today where the trading interests see the reasonableness of current and prospective GATT procedures designed to ensure as much freedom of access to markets as possible, whereas the environmental interests see in the same procedures an unreasonable bias against themselves. In all these areas, the GATT permits challenges to be mounted by contracting parties to be mediated by dispute settlement panels and for codes and rules that define how the panels might adjudicate these disputes. We will say a little about each of these issues.[65]

The Intention Issue

Economists have long recognized the intention issue. Thus the classic instance we regale our students with relates to Gottfried Haberler's example of the provision in the German tariff, dating from 1902 and valid decades later, which was clearly meant to apply to Switzerland and Austria, relating to "brown or dappled cows reared at a level of at least 300 meters above the sea and passing at least one month in every summer at a height of at least 800 meters."[66]

Within the environmental field, a fine example where the United States was the aggrieved party is provided by the Canadian province Ontario's 10 percent tax on beer cans but not bottles, on environmental grounds. Even if the United States authorities did not challenge the objective of restricting the use of cans,[67] they could legitimately note that the law was likely to have been motivated by the desire to discriminate against foreign beer supplies who (unlike local rivals) predominantly used cans rather than bottles, combined tellingly with the fact that the use of cans for other products such as soups and juices (where Ontario producers would have been affected) was not proscribed.[68]

It is hard to see how a good, open trading system cannot permit member countries to examine the bona fides of environmental (and other) regulations in this way. Surely, given the ease with which regulations and standards can be misused for protectionist purposes, *some* mechanism must exist for grievances to be aired and adjudicated. The GATT dispute settlement mechanism, improved after the Uruguay Round and further changed in the direction of greater transparency, is sufficiently objective and neutral between contracting parties to provide a better method for dealing with the problem than national procedures that would always be suspect as having been influenced by national political considerations.

The Alternative-Measures Issue

There are more difficult issues, however, when the question of the use of alternative ways of reaching an environmental objective is raised.

It seems totally sensible that, if alternative ways of meeting an environmental objective exist, a contracting party should be asked to choose one that infringes least on another's trading rights. In fact, this view seems embodied in GATT's Article XX(b), which allows even discriminatory trade restrictions against another contracting party if the measures are deemed "necessary" to protect human, animal, or plant life or health .

Two different views of the matter, however, can be taken in interpreting what is "necessary.' Thus, in the case of Thailand's restrictions on importation and internal taxes on cigarettes, the GATT panel decided that Thailand should use the "least GATT-inconsistent" measure to achieve its domestic objective. Then again, one could consider a "least-trade-restrictiveness" test which, of course, will not necessarily coincide with the "least-GATT-inconsistency" test.[69]

Aside from the greater difficulty of determining ordinally what greater and lesser GATT-consistency means, the economic superiority of the test that requires least damage to trade is manifest. In fact, the December 1991 Dunkel Draft of the proposed Uruguay Round treaty adopted the latter test: it is built into the Standards Code and also into the Sanitary and Phytosanitary Decision. It is also the test used in the GATT panel decision in 1992 on the alcoholic beverages case where the United States lost. The laws in five states that required a common carrier to enforce their tax and alcohol policies were held to be unacceptable because

> the United States has not demonstrated that the common carrier requirement is the least trade restrictive enforcement measure available to the various states and that less restrictive measures, e.g. record-keeping requirements of retailers and importers, are not sufficient for tax adminstration purposes.[70]

This test seems reasonable, of course. The objections to it amount mainly to objections to the methods by which the Beverage Panel arrived at the judgment that less-trade-restrictive measures to achieve the same objectives were available in that instance. But there are indeed inherent difficulties in defining the set of alternative policies that, with differential trade impact, would achieve identical environmental (or other domestic) objectives. It is hard to imagine *identical* results on these objectives from alternative policies, though *similar* results can sometimes be deemed possible (though, here too, judgments will differ in many cases).

In the end, any practical enforcement of the "least-trade-restrictive" test for evaluating the acceptability of an environmental regulation or standard will likely force the adjudicating panel into evaluating, implicitly or explicitly, *trade-offs* between the cost in trade disruption and the cost in reaching the environmental objective: a phenomenon and a problem that economists, who accept free lunches but do not believe in them, have no difficulty recognizing.

The jurisprudence, by necessity if not by choice, will have to move in the direction of evaluating and deciding upon the solution to such trade-offs. Thus, in the case of EC law, in the case involving Denmark's laws concerning disposable beer cans, the European Court of Justice seems to have explicitly considered such a trade-off between the interests of "free movement of goods" (and consequent trade benefits) and "environmental protection."[71]

It is natural, therefore, that environmentalists and trade experts who seem occasionally to attach opposing weights to the environmental and the trade benefits of any regulation or standard will worry about what weights the adjudicating panels would choose in reaching their decisions. If, therefore, disputes are to arise between nations, and tests of "necessity" that imply weighting alternative policies leading to different trade-offs are to be utilized, it is certainly proper for the environmentalists to seek improvements in the dispute settlement process that would give them greater access in terms of the ability to file written friend-of-the-court briefs and also make the panel procedures more transparent than hitherto at the GATT.

A complementary policy of prevention rather than cure would also be useful as we move increasingly into this difficult and contentious area. The input of "principally affected" trading countries into the setting of domestic environmental and other regulatory standards, such that the policy alternatives are discussed and adopted in light of such input, would help to reduce conflict to an irreducible minimum that the judicial process must address and resolve. Instances of such international input into domestic setting of standards are not lacking: the United States, worried by the trade-restrictive implications of EC standards-setting procedures, has indeed gained some access to the EC processes. But clearly more institutionalized and satisfactory procedures for doing so, available to weak and not just to strong nations, would appear to be a most useful innovation.

The Scientific-Test Issue

The use of economic tests to determine whether a product can be proscribed, even on a nondiscriminatory basis between imports and domestic production, creates yet another important source of disagreement. Suppose that the United States uses Alar to spray apples and that the EC does not. Suppose then that, faced with agitation from consumers who consider Alar-sprayed apples to be a hazard to their health, the EC bans their sale. the U.S. industry and government can then be expected to demand that the EC justify, through the use of scientific test, its fear that Alar-sprayed apples are a hazard.

Although this case is hypothetical, the EC–U.S. conflict on the EC's proscription of hormone-fed beef is not. In this instance, the U.S. beef producers that used hormones and the biotech industry that invented and produced the hormones were pitted against what they considered to be a wholly unscientific fear of hormone-fed beef. The United States went to the length of trade retaliation under Section 301; the EC in the end did not countrretaliate; and the matter was not taken to the GATT dispute settlement process for adjudication, with both the EC ban and the U.S. retaliation continuing the place. Given the high probability that a scientific test criterion would have been required by a GATT dispute settlement panel, it is likely that the EC would have lost the case.

But the case was an early warning sign of the tension between commercial and environmental interests on this issue. Admittedly, even hard science is not hard enough most of the time. The many who are convinced of a hazard to their health, no matter what the *current* preponderance of scientific opinion, might well turn out to be right after all. Then again, even if scientists were agreed on measuring the risk from any event or act of consumption or production, the subjective reaction of different people to the objective risk may vary greatly and, in fact, does.

It is tempting then to say, Let any regulation pass, regardless of the scientific test, no matter that it reduces another's access to one's market. But we are back then to the "slippery slope" scenario. Without the restraining hand of current science, the itch to indulge one's fears could be overwhelming.

The solution may then well be to institutionalize what in effect happened with the hormone-fed beef case: have the scientific test; if you lose, "pay up" (as the EC did) if you do not wish to change your regulation or standard; or settle by shifting your regulation or standard so as to broadly move in the direction of achieving your objective by alternative policies (e.g., by labeling hormone-fed beef rather than proscribing it altogether, and then undertaking education, propaganda, and boycotts against its use).

Again, if the notion of "paying up" appears offensive to the environmentalists because science should not stand in the way of our deeply held concerns, we would just urge them to undertake one thought experiment. We all know from science today that AIDS does not spread through simple contact. Suppose that our immigration policy nonetheless rules out HIV-infected immigrants, even when refugees and family reunification are involved, because large numbers of Americans are sure (unscientifically) that such admissions will spread AIDS to them. Would a typically liberal, activist environmentalist agree to such a policy?

The Circumventing-Democracy Issue

We would be remiss if we did not also note the increasing appeal to some environmentalists of the notion that "the process of negotiating international agreements [like the GATT's Uruguay Round] is less subject to public scrutiny, and therefore a threat to democratic accountability,"[72] and that "faceless" and unelected bureaucrats at the GATT will overrule democratically enacted environmental and other social regulations. Leaving aside the question whether such regulations will be overturned – an issue that we just discussed at length – the question regarding democratic process is far more complex than the simplistic denunciations that find their way into anti-GATT propaganda. In particular, we would argue the following:

1. It is inconsistent to hold simultaneously, as many do, that the low standards of other countries should be countervailed by foreign NGOs and governments that are "unelected" and "faceless" as far as these low-standard countries are concerned, while condemning the GATT panel members, chosen by democratic procedures multilaterally agreed among the contracting parties, as "faceless' and "unelected."

2. It is really correct to hold that one level of governance is more "democratic" than another? After all, it is the contracting parties that have chosen the GATT panel procedures democratically.

3. Moreover, it is not necessarily correct to argue that the closer the level of governance to the ground, the better the decision. If local governance were

dominant, Al Capone could flourish without the Feds, capital punishment would thrive, land reforms in developing countries (legislated and enforced from the top when grassroots activism is frustrated by the local power structure) might go slower, and so on.

4. There is no reason to think that the GATT works any worse than the national or local legislatures in these matters. Contrast the contribution of the GATT, including its panels, with the gift that the U.S. Congress gave to the world in 1934 with the Smoot-Hawley Tariff and is currently giving us with its 301 and Super 301–style championing of aggressive unilateralism.

5. The current U.S. position, opposed effectively by other contracting parties, that environmental NGOs be allowed to participate in GATT Council deliberations on panel rulings is couched in terms of transparency and democracy. But it raises compelling objections that presumably emerged during this debate:

a. The NGOs should be able to participate through their own governments, which represent them *and* other constituents in democratic governments; there is no reason to think that their added participation is any more desirable than that of consumer groups, protectionist lobbies, unions, and the like, all of whom can and do compete for influence in national politics and hence on international policy deliberations.

b. The environmental NGOs are not necessarily handicapped financially vis-à-vis the other groups, and their organization and clout are disproportionately greater than their finances, since they can often successfully claim the higher moral ground (e.g., we are "rescuing the dolphins" from the rapacious multinationals; we are "saving the planet"), so they certainly do not need a "second voice," when others are denied it, at the GATT Council.

c. While there are indeed NGOs in the developing countries, the heavily financed ones are in the rich countries and will reflect *their* concerns, priorities, and views (e.g., protecting dolphins rather than aiding Mexico's tuna industry to help Mexico's development and removal of poverty); the rich countries would then have a double voice, when they can often drown out the voice of the poor countries with just one voice, thus undermining the notion of democracy at the *international* level.

4.5 CONCLUDING OBSERVATIONS: ENVIRONMENTAL PROBLEMS WITH TRANSBORDER EXTERNALITIES AND TRADE QUESTIONS

We conclude our exhaustive analysis of the case of purely domestic environmental problems, and the associated demands for CCII harmonization and eco-dumping countervailing duties and so on, with a sketch of the policy problems that arise in the context of transborder externalities. These are generally more complex in character than the ones that arise with purely domestic pollution[73] and more compelling as well. It may be useful, from a policy viewpoint, to distinguish between two cases: (1) a special case where the problem is simplified by assuming a single country that pollutes the other, raising questions of response such as the use of trade barriers by the other; and (2) a general case where the problem is truly global in character. A good example of the former is U.S. transmission of acid rain to Canada; an excellent example of the latter is global warming, to which many countries contribute while all are affected by it (though each in a different degree, and not all negatively).

4.5.1 One-Way Transmission of Pollution and Two Countries

The case of pollution transmitted from one country to another is helpful because it illustrates in a simple way the problem raised by transborder externalities concerning the use of second-best trade instruments by the injured country when the offending country does not implement a first-best solution and uses its jurisdictional autonomy in the spirit of malign neglect. The principal question, then, is whether a country that is being damaged by pollution from another has the right to impose a trade restraint to affect the exports, and hence production, and hence the pollution, of the other country that comes into one's area.[74]

Thus, suppose that the United States is transmitting acid rain to Canada, thanks to its CO_2-producing processes used in producing electricity in a CO_2-intensive way, since U.S. generation of electricity uses fossil fuel (whereas the Canadian industry uses cleaner, hydroelectric processes). If the United States refuses to tax its electricity producers for the SO_2 pollution they generate, or refuses to compensate Canada for the damage that is inflicted by the acid rain that is transmitted to Canada by wind drift, then should Canada have the right to tax its import of U.S. electricity (and even of other U.S. exports that are produced using the electricity that produces the acid rain and then transmits a fraction of it to Canada)?

Modifying the GATT rules to explicitly allow for such a possibility would make sense as a "second-best" solution, since the offending party (the United States in the example) refuses to undertake a "first-best" solution. That also seemed to be, as Charnowitz has noted, the position taken in some early and unofficial thinking by the GATT Secretariat. Of course, the usual caveats about satisfying scientific tests and the like would have to be noted and codified.[75]

The problem, of course, is that this type of trade remedy is generally likely to be so weak for problems like acid rain that one may ask, Is it worth modifying the GATT/WTO to legitimate such trade actions? Thus, take the example of acid rain itself. The generation of acid rain in the United States, a fraction of which comes across to Canada, is geographically concentrated, of course, at the border whereas the import tariff would affect all electricity generation in the United States; moreover, the effect on SO_2 generation would be indirect, not direct through tax on the process itself; then again, only a fraction of the acid rain generation effect would get into the transmission. The tariff instrument would then be extremely weak, and the Canadian gain from its use in reducing the loss from the acid rain would be outweighed by the reduced gains from trade, that is, the gains from importing cheaper electricity from the United States.[76]

4.5.2 Global Transborder Externalities

The chief policy questions concerning trade when global pollution problems are involved, as with ozone-layer depletion and global warming, take a different turn related to the cooperative-solution-oriented multilateral treaties that are sought to address them.[77] They are essentially tied into noncompliance ("defection") by members and "free riding" by nonmembers. Because any action by a member of a treaty relates to targeted actions (such as reducing CFCs or CO_2 emissions) that are public good (in particular, that the benefits are nonexcludable, so that if I incur the cost and do something, I cannot exclude you from benefiting from it), the use of trade sanctions to secure and enforce compliance automatically turns up on the agenda.

At the same time, the problem is compounded because the agreement itself has to be *legitimate* in the eyes of those accused of free riding or noncompliance. Before those pejorative epithets are applied and punishment prescribed in the form of trade sanctions legitimated at the GATT/WTO, these nations have to be satisfied that the agreement being pressed on them is efficient and, especially, that it is equitable in burden sharing.[78] Otherwise, nothing prevents the politically powerful (i.e., the rich nations) from devising a treaty that puts an inequitable burden on the politically weak (i.e., the poor nations) and then using the cloak of a "multilateral" agreement and a new GATT/WTO legitimacy to impose that burden with the aid of trade sanctions with a clear conscience, invoking the "white man's burden" to secure the "white man's gain".

As a result, the policy demand, often made, to alter the GATT/WTO to legitimate trade sanctions on contracting parties who remain outside of a treaty, whenever a plurilateral treaty on a global environmental problem dictates it, is unlikely to be accepted by the poor nations without safeguards to prevent unjust impositions. The spokesmen of the poor countries have been more or less explicit on this issue, with justification. These concerns have been recognized by the rich nations.

Thus, at the Rio Conference in 1992, the Framework Convention on Climate Change set explicit goals under which several rich nations agreed to emission-level-reduction targets (returning, more or less, to 1990 levels), whereas the commitments of the poor countries were contingent on the rich nations footing the bill.

Ultimately, burden sharing by different formulas related to emissions, current income, current population, and so on is inherently arbitrary; such formulas also distribute burdens without regard to efficiency. Economists will argue for burden sharing dictated by cost minimization across countries, for the earth as a whole: if Brazilian rain forests must be saved to minimize the cost of a targeted reduction in CO_2 emissions in the world, while the United States keeps guzzling gas because it is too expensive to cut down, then so be it. But then this efficient "cooperative" solution must not leave Brazil footing the bill! Efficient solutions, with compensation and equitable distribution of the gains from the efficient solution, make economic sense.

A step toward them is the idea of having a market in permits again, at the world level: no country may emit CO_2 without having bought the necessary permit from a worldwide quota. That system would ensure efficiency,[79] whereas the distribution of the proceeds from the sold permits would require a decision reflecting multilaterally agreed ethical or equity criteria (e.g., the proceeds may be used for refugee resettlement, UN peacekeeping operations, and dispensed to poor nations by UNDP, the WHO fight against AIDS, and so on). This type of agreement would have the legitimacy that could then provide the legitimacy in turn for a GATT/WTO rule that permits the use of trade sanctions against free riders.

APPENDIX

We consider a sequence of models to illustrate the trade policy implications of bringing environmental considerations into contexts that differ with respect to (1) the nature of pollution (e.g., purely domestic versus global), (2) whether or not the economy is a price taker in world markets, (3) whether or not pollution can be abated through expenditure of resources, and (4) whether global welfare or national welfare is the policy objective. In much of the analysis pollution is modeled as a production externality that affects welfare. In the last section we relate our analysis to that in the literature.

A4.1 PURELY DOMESTIC POLLUTION

A4.1.1 Small Country, Purely Domestic Pollution, No Abatement Possible

For simplicity consider a two-commodity model with the production transformation function $X_1 = F(X_2)$ where X_i is the output of good i. Pollution $P = P(X_1, X_2) \equiv P(F, X_2)$. Clearly for any given production choice (X_1, X_2) where $X_1 = F(X_2)$, pollution P is determined regardless of trade. As such, since the economy has no market power, free trade is optimal from a consumer perspective.

This model implies in particular that, if the given production choice is fixed at the production vector associated with the autarky optimum, opening the economy to free trade in consumption cannot reduce welfare. As such, as long as appropriate policy instruments are available to ensure the separation of consumption from production, trading cannot hurt.

Now, allow instead a production response to trading opportunities. Writing $Y = X_1 + \pi X_2 = F + \pi X_2$ for income where π is the world relative price of good 2 in terms of good 1, $V(\pi, Y, P)$ for the indirect utility function, the first-order condition for the optimal choice of production is given by[80]

$$V_2(F_1 + \pi) + V_3(P_1F_1 + P_2) = 0 \tag{1}$$

where the subscript i of a function denotes the partial derivative with respect to its ith argument.

Of course if $V_3 = 0$ so that pollution does not affect welfare, equation 1 reduces to $\pi = -F_1$, or world price = domestic marginal rate of transformation so that free trade is optimal from a producer perspective as well. In the case where $V_3 < 0$

so that pollution affects welfare adversely, equation 1 can be rewritten as

$$\pi + V_3(P_1F_1 + P_2)/V_2 = -F_1 \tag{2}$$

Now $(P_1F_1 + P_2)$ is the *net* marginal change in pollution as the output of good 2 increases: it is the sum of the direct marginal change P_2 from the increase in output of good 2 and the indirect marginal change P_1F_1 from the fall F_1 in output of good 1 induced by the increase in the output of good 2. Thus if $P_1F_1 = P_2$ is negative (resp. positive) so that the net change in pollution from an increase in the output of good 2 is negative (resp. positive), the domestic rate of transformation of good 2 for good 1 is larger (resp. smaller) than the world price of good 2; that is, if an increase in the output of good 2 reduces (resp. increases) pollution, since pollution is an uninternalized *domestic* externality, the output of good 2 should be subsidized (resp. taxed) relative to its world price. This optimal rate of tax or subsidy will in general be different in a trading optimum as compared to autarky. Nonetheless, welfare in a free-trading optimum will be no less than under autarky.

This is a straightforward application of the standard theory of domestic distortions to what, in the present instance, is a production externality.[81]

A4.1.2 Small Country, Purely Domestic Pollution, Abatement Possible by Spending Resources

Let K_a, L_a denote the amount of capital and labor respectively devoted to abatement. Let $\bar{K}$, $\bar{L}$ denote the aggregate endowment of capital and labor. Now the transformation function is $X_1 = F(X_2, \bar{K} - K_a, \bar{L} - L_a)$ and pollution is $P=P(X_1, X_2, K_a, L_a)$.

As before, with given X_1, X_2, K_a, and L_a, clearly free trade is optimal from a consumer perspective. As such, opening the economy to trade in consumption, while keeping production at autarky optimum levels, cannot reduce welfare. The indirect utility is as before $V(\pi, Y, P)$ where $Y = X_1 + \pi X_2$.

The first-order conditions for the optimal (interior) choice of production of X_2 and of resources K_a, L_a devoted to abatement are

$$V_2(F_1 + \pi) + V_3(P_1F_1 + P_2) = 0 \tag{3}$$
$$V_2F_2 + V_3P_3 = 0 \tag{4}$$
$$V_2F_3 + V_3P_4 = 0 \tag{5}$$

First, equations 4 and 5 imply $F_2/F_3 = P_3/P_4$; that is, the marginal rate of substitution of capital and labor is the same in commodity production (i.e., F_2/F_3) as in pollution abatement (i.e., P_3/P_4).

Second, equation 3 is the same as equation 1 so that the conclusion that if an increase in output of 2 reduces (resp. increases) pollution it should be subsidized (resp. taxed) relative to its world price remains even with abatement possibilities. Only, now, the effect of or pollution of an increase in output of 2 is evaluated given the optimum levels of resources devoted to abatement.[82]

Finally, the result that welfare in a free-trading optimum is no less than under an autarky optimum continues to hold, though in general the optimal production tax or subsidy could be different in the two optima. Again this is a straightforward implication of the standard theory of domestic distortions.

A4.1.3 Large Country, Purely Domestic Pollution, Active Trade Policy with No Retaliation, Abatement Feasible

It should be evident from the analysis of the small-country model that, as long as pollution is a purely domestic distortion, standard theory should go through when a *purely* international distortion, namely, the ability to influence the terms of trade (which is not internalized by private domestic agents) is added. We confine ourselves to demonstrating this result for the case where abatement is possible. The same results can be easily seen to hold for the case when abatement is not possible.

Since terms of trade are now endogenous, it is more convenient to work with the direct utility function

$$U[F(X_2,\bar{K}-K_a,\bar{L}-L_a)+\pi(E_2)E_2,X_2-E_2,P(F,X_2,K_a,La)]$$

where E_2 represents the net exports of good 2 and $\pi(E_2)$ the average price (in terms of good 1) per unit of good 2 exported. The choice variables are X_2, E_2, K_a,L_a. The corresponding first-order conditions for an interior maximum of U are

$$U_1F_1 + U_2 + U_3(P_1F_1 + P_2) = 0 \quad (6)$$
$$U_1(\pi_1E_2 + \pi) - U_2 = 0 \quad (7)$$
$$-(U_1 + U_3P_1)F_2 + U_3P_3) = 0 \quad (8)$$
$$-(U_1 + U_3P_1)F_3 + U_3P_4) = 0 \quad (9)$$

From equation 7 it is seen that the domestic marginal rate of substitution between good 2 and good 1 – that is, U_2/U_1 – equals the *marginal revenue* (in terms of good 1) per unit of exports of good 2 at the optimal level of exports. The U_2/U_1 equals the marginal terms of trade and differs from the average terms of trade by the term π_1 E_2. The difference is the standard optimal tariff to exploit market power.

From equations 8 and 9 it is clear that the marginal rate of substitution between capital and labor in goods production – that is F_2/F_3 – equals that in pollution abatement – that is P_3/P_4. Rewriting equation 6 as

$$-F_1 = U_2/U_1 + U_3(P_1F_1 + P_2)/U_1$$

it is seen that the domestic marginal rate of transformation between goods 1 and 2 – that is, $-F_1$ – differs from the domestic marginal rate of substitution U_2/U_1 by the addition of $U_3(P_1F_1 + P_2)/U_1$. By assumption, pollution hurts welfare so that U_3, the marginal utility of pollution is negative, while U_1, the marginal utility of consumption of good 1, is positive. Thus the additional term is positive, zero, or negative according as the net addition to pollution of an increase in production of good 2 – that is, $(P_1F_1 + P_2)$ – is negative, zero, or positive. For example, if the net addition to pollution is positive so that the additional term is negative, it follows that, in addition to an optimal tariff (equation 7) to exploit market power in external markets, an optimum tax [of $U_3(P_1F_1 + P_2)/U_1$] on the production of good 2 is needed to allow for the *purely domestic distortion* of pollution.

It is evident that the feasibility of abatement does not affect the algebraic form of equations 6 and 7 on which the preceding result (about the need for an optimum tariff and a production tax) is based. As such the absence of the possibility of abatement does not affect the result.[83] Also, it should be obvious that welfare with trade restricted by an optimum tariff would be no less than under autarky.

The rest of the world's offer curve to the home economy – that is, $\pi(E_2)$ – in the preceding analysis in principle could be viewed as a function $\pi(E_2,T^*)$ of home exports E_2 and foreign tariffs on home imports. Thus, given Cournot behavior, the home economy's optimal tariff will be a function (the home reaction function linking the optimal tariff T^*. Similarly, there will be a foreign reaction function linking the optimal tariffs of the rest of the world to the home economy's tariff. As is well known since the work of Harry Johnson (1954), the intersection of the two reaction functions is the Cournot-Nash equilibrium of the tariff game. And such an equilibrium is not Pareto optimal from a global perspective.

A4.2 GLOBAL POLLUTION

4.2.1 Small Country, Global Pollution

We begin, in this section and the next, with *national welfare* maximization, and then consider, in sections A4.2.3 through A4.2.8, questions relating to global Pareto optimality (i.e., "world welfare").

Assume now that the pollution is global; that is, its effect cuts across (some or all) national borders. In this case, the pollution function may be rewritten as $P[F(X_2,\bar{K} - K_a,\bar{L} - L_a) + X_1^*,X_2 + X_2^*,K_a + K_a^*,L_a + L_a^*]$ where the starred variables X_2^*,K_a^*,L_a^*, respectively denote the output of good i (i = 1, 2) and the capital and labor devoted to abatement in the rest of the world.

Implicit in this formulation are two strong assumptions: first, only global levels of outputs, and not their distribution between countries, affect global pollution, second, only global expenditure of resources on abatement, and not their distribution between countries, matters. The latter in effect postulates the *same technology* of abatement among countries in the sense that at any level of *aggregate* resources devoted to abatement, the marginal reduction in pollution achieved by a marginal increase in *domestic* resources devoted to abatement is the same as that achieved by a marginal increase in *foreign* resources devoted to abatement. But of course this statement does not necessarily imply that the same amount of resources will be devoted to abatement at home and abroad in any equilibrium. In section A4.2.7 we relax these assumptions.

Since by assumption a small country cannot affect the prices at which it trades with the rest of the world through its trade policy, there is no channel by which it can affect the commodity or factor prices in the rest of the world.[84] If we assume Cournot behavior in that the small country takes the rest of the world's outputs and pollution abatement resources as given, it is easily shown that the results of section A4.1.2 continue to hold: free trade is optimal and the domestic marginal rate of substitution between capital and labor should be the same in goods production and pollution abatement.

However, the assumption of Cournot behavior is rather artificial in this case. It is more natural to assume that if the country is "small," it will behave as if its shares of global outputs and global resources devoted to abatement are negligible. Thus it will treat pollution P as if it is a constant $\bar{P}$ that cannot be influenced by its action. Clearly, it is optimal for such a country not to devote any resources to pollution abatement; that is, it will free ride on the rest o the world's expenditure of resources for abatement. It follows that if the trading system consisted a large number of small countries in this sense, no country will spend any resources on abatement: this is the analogue of the "tragedy of the commons" in the use of common property resources.

A4.2.2 Large Country, Pollution Global, Cournot Behavior with Respect to Both Tariffs and Resource Allocation for Abatement Abroad

For simplicity consider a trading world of two countries. For any given level of foreign tariff T^* and resource allocation for abatement K_a^*, L_a^*, the home economy's terms of trade π depends on its own exports E_2. Thus the direct utility of the home economy could be written as

$$U[F(X_2,\bar{K} - K_a,\bar{L} - L_a) + E_2\pi(E_2,T^*),X_2 - E_2, P]$$

where $P = P[F(X_2,\bar{K} - K_a,\bar{L} - L_a) + X_1^*,X_2 + X_2^*,K_a + K_a^*,L_a + L_a^*]$. Note that, since the pollution is now global, the utility function is different from that in section A4.1.2 insofar as it additionally includes *foreign outputs* that generate pollution and *foreign inputs* that abate it (since both determine the amount of foreign pollution).

The first-order conditions for an interior maximum of U with respect to X_2, E_2, K_a, L_a are

$$U_1F_1 + U_2 + U_3(P_1F_1 + P_2) = 0 \quad (10)$$
$$U_1(\pi_1E_2 + \pi) - U_2 = 0 \quad (11)$$
$$-(U_1 + U_3P_1)F_2 + U_3P_2 = 0 \quad (12)$$
$$-(U_1 + U_3P_1)F_3 + U_3P_4 = 0 \quad (13)$$

As is to be expected, given Cournot behavior (concerning both foreign tariffs and resource-abatement expenditures), these are exactly the same algebraically as equations 6 through 9. In other words, corresponding to each specified $(X_1^*,X_2^*,T^*,K_a^*,L_a^*)$, we have a home output $X_2(X_1^*,X_2^*,T^*,K_a^*,L_a^*)$, optimal tariff

$T(X_1^*,X_2^*,T^*,K_a^*,L_a^*)$, and home expenditure of resources $K_a(X_1^*,X_2^*,T^*,K_a^*,L_a^*)$, $L_a(X_1^*,X_2^*,T^*,K_a^*,L_a^*)$. These three represent the *home* reaction functions to foreign outputs X_1^* *and* $X_2^*(X_1^*$ *and* X_2^* are on the foreign transformation function, so that only one of them is independent), tariff T^*, and resources K_a^*,L_a^* allocated for abatement. It should be noted that, unless the utility function is additively separable in pollution, the domestic marginal rate of substitution (MRS) U_2/U_1 will be a function of foreign outputs and abatement resources. As such, from equation 11, it follows that the domestic optimal tariff will be a function not only of foreign tariff as usual, but also of foreign outputs and abatement resources.

Analogously one defines *foreign* reaction as a function of given values of the home outputs, tariff, and resource allocation for abatement. The "intersections" of the home and foreign reaction functions represent the Nash equilibrium values of outputs in the two countries and T^N, T^{*N}, K_a^N, K_a^{*N}, L_a^N, L_a^{*N}. As is well known, such Nash equilibria are not Pareto optimal.[85]

A4.2.3 Global Pareto Optimal Allocations

Pareto optimal allocations, on the other hand, are derived by maximizing a non-negatively weighted sum of the welfares of the two countries. It is more convenient to write the two utility functions as $U[C_1, C_2P]$ and $U^*(C_1^*, C_2^*P)$ where C_i, C_i^* represent the consumption of commodity $i(i = 1, 2)$ and P pollution

$$P = P[X_1 + X_1^*,X_2 + X_2^*,K_a + K_a^*,L_a + L_a^*) \quad (14)$$
$$X_1 = F[X_2, \bar{K} - K_a,\bar{L} - L_a) \quad (15)$$
$$X_1^* = F^*[X_2^*,\bar{K}^* - K_a^*,\bar{L} - L_a^*) \quad (16)$$

Market clearance implies

$$C_1 + C_1^* = X_1 + X_1^* \quad (17)$$

and

$$C_2 + C_2^* = X_2 + X_2^* \quad (18)$$

Maximization of $\alpha U + (1–\alpha)U^*$ (where $0 \leq \alpha \leq 1$) with respect to C_1, C_2, C_1^*, C_2^*, X_2, X_2^*, K_a, K_a^*, L_a, L_a^* subject to equations 17 and 18 after substituting equations 14, 15, and 16 into U and U^* yields the following first-order conditions for an interior maximum:[86]

$$\alpha U_1 - \lambda_1 = 0 \quad (19)$$
$$\alpha U_2 - \lambda_2 = 0 \quad (20)$$
$$(1–\alpha)U_1^* - \lambda_1 = 0 \quad (21)$$
$$(1–\alpha)U_2^* - \lambda_2 = 0 \quad (22)$$
$$[\alpha U_3 + (1–\alpha)U_3^*](P_1F_1 + P_2) + \lambda_1 F_1 + \lambda_2 = 0 \quad (23)$$
$$[\alpha U_3 + (1–\alpha)U_3^*](P_1F_1^* + P_2) + \lambda_1 F_1^* + \lambda_2 = 0 \quad (24)$$
$$[\alpha U_3 + (1–\alpha)U_3^*]P_3 - (\lambda_1 + \alpha U_3P_1)F_2 = 0 \quad (25)$$
$$[\alpha U_3 + (1–\alpha)U_3^*]P_4 - (\lambda_1 + \alpha U_3P_1)F_3 = 0 \quad (26)$$

$$[\alpha U_3 + (1-\alpha)U_3^*]P_3 - [\lambda_1 + (1-\alpha)U_3^*P_1]F_2^* = 0 \quad (27)$$
$$[\alpha U_3 + (1-\alpha)U_3^*]P_4 - [\lambda_1 + (1-\alpha)U_3^*P_1]F_3^* = 0 \quad (28)$$

From equations 19–22, it follows that the marginal rate of substitution (MRS) between goods 1 and 2 in consumption is the same in the two countries; that is, $U_2/U_1 = U_2^*/U_1^* = \lambda_2/\lambda_1$ regardless of the value α. Thus, from a consumer perspective, there is free trade in a Pareto optimum.

However, from equations 23 and 24, it is seen that the marginal rate of transformation (MRT) between goods 1 and 2 at home, $-F_1$, equals $\lambda_2/\lambda_1 + (1/\lambda_1)[\alpha U_3 + (1-\alpha)U_3^*](P_1F_1 + P_2)$; and abroad, $-F_1^*$ equals $\lambda_2/\lambda_1 + (1/\lambda_1)[\alpha U_3 + (1-\alpha)U_3^*](P_1F_1^* + P_2)$. Thus MRT at home (resp. abroad) differs from the common MRS by $[1/\lambda_1][\alpha U_3 + (1-\alpha)U_3^*][P_1F_1 + P_2]$ (resp. $[1/\lambda_1][\alpha U_3 + (1-\alpha)U_3^*][P_1F_1^* + P_2]$). This term is easily interpreted: $[\alpha U_3 + (1-\alpha)U_3^*]$ is the global welfare effect of a marginal increase in pollution, that is, the shadow price of a unit of pollution again in global welfare units; λ_1 is, as noted earlier, the shadow price of good 1. Thus the ratio of these two terms represents the global shadow "price" of a marginal unit of pollution in units of good 1, and at Pareto optimum it is the *same* in the two countries. The term $(P_1F_1 + P_2)$ is the net pollution effect of a marginal increase in the production of good 2 at home. The product of all three terms is thus in units of good 1 per unit of good 2 and represents the trade-off between the pollution of the two goods at home through the relative global welfare effects they have through pollution. Thus, at a Pareto optimum, the home MRT between the two goods must equal the sum of their relative welfare effects through their consumption – that is, λ_2/λ_1 – and their relative welfare effects through pollution, which is the second term. An analogous condition applies in the foreign country.

If we interpret the difference between MRS and MRT as a shadow production tax or subsidy on good 2 it is seen from equations 23 and 24 that this tax/subsidy would be the same in the two countries if $F_1 = F_1^*$ at an optimum, that is, if the MRT is the same in the two countries. At the same time, it is evident from equations 25–28 that the marginal rate of substitution between capital and labor is the *same* in the two countries in *all* activities, whether production or abatement. Thus, if we interpret the marginal rate of substitution as the shadow wage-rental ratio, it is the same in the two countries. With shadow commodity prices the same, factor price equalization follows. If the available technology of production of goods is the same in the two countries, then with factor price equalization the shadow production tax/subsidy rates will be the same in the two countries. The global Pareto optimal solution will require tax harmonization!

The first-order conditions relating to MRT in the two countries, taken together with the fact that MRS is the same in the two countries, imply that free trade combined with an appropriate production tax or subsidy is the appropriate policy associated with a Pareto optimum. However, in general, if the value of α is set *exogenously*, trade between the countries need not be balanced so that a lump sum income transfer from the country running the trade surplus to that running the deficit would be required to support the chosen Pareto optimum. But α can be chosen *endogenously* to ensure that no transfers are needed; that is, trade is balanced. A heuristic argument for the existence of such an α is as follows (the existence of such a unique α is shown for a special case in section A4.2.7). Set $\alpha = 1$ so that the foreign economy's welfare receives a zero weight. Clearly, at the associated Pareto optimum, the foreign economy in effect transfers its entire income to the home economy. The reverse happens when α is set at zero. Thus, by continuity, at some α between 0 and 1, the required transfer will be zero. However, the implementation of the associated Pareto optimum involves the use of information on the welfare effect of pollution in *both* countries for devising the appropriate taxes and subsidies in each.

A comparison of the first-order condition relating to home MRT with the analogous conditions in the Cournot-Nash case of section A4.2.2 makes it clear that, in the latter, each country ignores the effect of its production choice on foreign welfare through pollution so that the resulting Nash equilibrium cannot be Pareto optimal.

A4.2.4 Deviant Behavior by One Country, Global Pareto Optimality

The implementation of the global Pareto optimum with or without transfers involves the use of a set of optimal production taxes or subsidies in each country and the expenditure of appropriate levels of resources on pollution abatement. Suppose for instance, however, that one of the countries, say the home country, is required to devote a positive amount of capital and labor to abatement in supporting the Pareto optimum. If it deviates and, for example, does not spend any *resources* on abatement, we may ask whether a restricted Pareto optimum is still attainable. Will it involve the use of trade policy?

Referring back to the first-order condition (equations 19–28) characterizing a Pareto optimum, we see now that conditions 25 and 26 relating to the capital K_a and labor L_a devoted to abatement by the home country no longer apply. But the remaining conditions continue to hold. Therefore, free trade along with an appropriate set of production taxes and subsidies continues to support a restricted Pareto optimum.

Of course, the reason why a restricted Pareto optimum is achievable with free trade even though the home economy devotes no resources to abatement is obvious: since by assumption the externality of pollution arises from *production*, no deviation from free trade with respect to *consumption* is called for.

Indeed this argument goes even further. Suppose, for instance, that for whatever reason the home economy not only devotes no resources to abatement but also chooses production levels different from those associated with an unrestricted Pareto optimum. This assumption means that conditions 23, 25 and 26 no longer apply. However, equations 19–22 continue to apply so that free trade with respect to *consumption* continues to be optimal. And since equation 24 still applies, the foreign economy has to levy an optimal production tax or subsidy to sustain this further-restricted Pareto optimum. The home economy can, of course, sustain its deviant behavior through a variety of means.

It should be noted that, from the perspective of a global Pareto optimum, countries are symmetric. As such, which country, namely the home or the foreign country, deviates in its behavior is immaterial to the characterization of the restricted Pareto optimum. In the preceding analysis, if the foreign, rather than the home, country does not devote as many resources as it should in supporting an *unrestricted* Pareto optimum, conditions 27 and 28 rather than 25 and 26 no longer apply. But this difference does not affect the conclusion that free trade, along with an appropriate set of production taxes and subsidies, supports a *restricted* Pareto optimum.

A4.2.5 Shadow Factor Price Equalization

In the model of section A4.2.3, the shadow factor prices are equalized at the chosen Pareto optimum; whether or not there is international factor mobility is therefore irrelevant. However, such shadow factor price equalization need not always occur. The considerations that lead to the shadow factor price equalization in section A4.2.3 are as follows:

1. At a global welfare optimum in which a *positive* amount of each commodity is consumed in each country, the shadow commodity prices for consumers (in global welfare units) have to be the same in both countries.

2. The shadow price of pollution (in welfare units) is also the same in both countries.

3. If each country is devoting a positive amount of *each* factor to pollution abatement, then because one country's factor is a perfect substitute for the other country's in pollution abatement, and the price of pollution is the same in the two countries; the marginal value of each factor in pollution abatement must be the same in the two countries; and it follows that the shadow price of each factor in global welfare units is equalized between countries. Also, because the consumer shadow price of each commodity in *welfare* units is the same in the two countries, we see by taking the ratio of shadow factor price to the shadow consumer price of either commodity that the equalization of shadow factor prices in *commodity* units follows.

Thus, shadow factor prices (in any commodity unit) cannot be equalized if any of the preceding considerations do not apply. For example, if consumers in the home country do not consume the first commodity while foreign consumers do, the marginal rate of substitution of the two goods in consumption at home will differ between countries. As such, factor prices in commodity units could differ between countries even if they are equalized in welfare units.

A4.2.6 Efficiency and Equity: Possible Conflicts

The Analytical Argument

A globally Pareto optimal allocation of resources is *efficient* in two senses. It is *distributionally* efficient in the sense that there is no other feasible allocation that could make one country better off without making some other country worse off. It is also *productively* efficient in the sense that the allocation across countries of production, and hence of pollution generated by production, is such that there is no other feasible allocation that will increase the consumption of some commodity in a country without reducing the consumption of any other commodities anywhere or increasing pollution, or alternatively will reduce pollution without at the same time reducing the consumption of some commodity somewhere. The pure gain in moving to an efficient allocation from an inefficient one could be distributed among countries to make at least one country better off without hurting others.

While a Pareto optimal allocation is thus *efficient*, it need not be *equitable*. For example, an allocation that uses all of the world's resources to maximize just one country's welfare is Pareto optimal but hardly equitable. On the other hand, an equitable allocation in the sense of maximizing a *global* welfare function that incorporates equity considerations would also be Pareto optimal as long as the global welfare function is increasing in each country's welfare. Thus such an equitable allocation is necessarily Pareto optimal and hence efficient in both senses.

The preceding arguments suggest that there needs to be no conflict between equity and efficiency. Indeed this would be the case if instruments exist that would sustain an equitable Pareto optimal allocation. For example, a market mechanism for resource allocation, *supplemented* by lump sum *transfers* as needed between countries, could sustain such an allocation. However, if transfers are infeasible, then an equilibrium market allocation (without transfers) need not be equitable. Then achieving a more equitable allocation will involve in this case the sacrifice of efficiency in one or both senses.

Illustrations

A suggestive illustration of a possible conflict between efficiency and distributional equity is shown in Figure 1. The marginal cost of pollution abatement in the United States is seen to be above that in Brazil at all levels of pollution to be abated up to $\bar{P}$. As such, it will be cost efficient for only Brazil to engage in pollution abatement up to $\bar{P}$. For Brazil also to bear the full cost of such abatement would be deemed (at least by Brazilians) inequitable!

Consider also the following simple version of the model of section A4.2.3. Take two countries. The home (resp. foreign) country has $\bar{H}$ (resp. $\bar{H}^*$) hectares of virgin forest. A hectare of this forest, if cleared and planted with wheat (resp. rice), will produce 1 ton of what (resp. rice), and release μ (resp. μ^*) litres of pollutants into the environment. Left as forest land, on the other hand, that hectare would have removed γ (resp. γ^*) litres of pollutants from the environment.

Home utility U is given by

$$U = \theta_1 \log C_1 + \theta_2 \log C_2 + \theta_3 \log (\bar{P} - P) \qquad (29)$$

where $1 \geq \theta_i \geq 0$, $\theta_3 \equiv 1 - \theta_1 - \theta_2$, C_1 is the consumption of wheat, C_2 is the consumption of rice, P is the quantity of (net) pollutants in the economy and $\bar{P}$ is the maximum amount of pollutants consistent with survival. Analogously, foreign utility U^* is given by

$$U^* = \theta_1^* \log C_1^* + \theta_2^* \log C_2^* + \theta_3^* \log (\bar{P} - P) \qquad (30)$$

where $1 \geq \theta_i^* \geq 0$, $\theta_3^* \equiv 1 - \theta_1^* - \theta_2^*$.

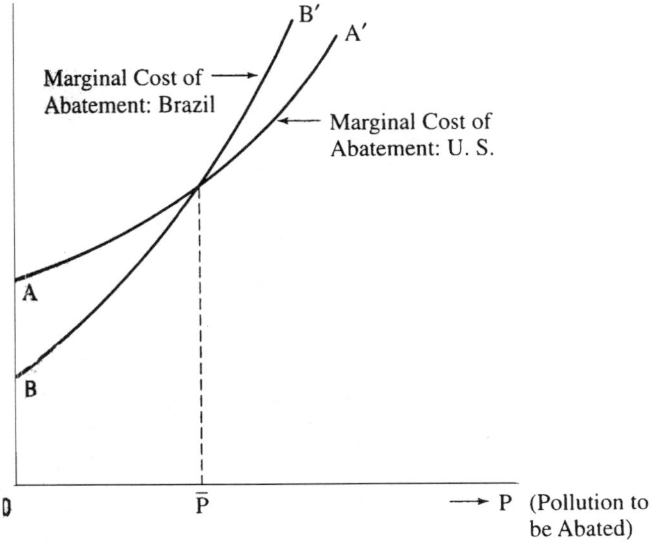

FIGURE 1 Efficiency and Equity with Global Pollution: Partial Equilibrium.

Clearly, in this model we have

$$C_1 + C_1^* = X_1 \equiv \text{Output of wheat} \tag{31}$$
$$C_2 + C_2^* = X_2^* \equiv \text{Output of rice} \tag{32}$$
$$\begin{aligned} P &= \mu X_1 + \mu^* X_2^* - y(\bar{H} - X_1) - y^*(\bar{H}^* - X_2^*) \\ &= (y + \mu)X_1 + (y^* + \mu^*)X_2^* - y\bar{H} - y^*\bar{H}^* \end{aligned} \tag{33}$$

As in section S4.2.3, Pareto optimal allocations are derived by maximizing $[\alpha U + (1-\alpha)U^*]$ for $0 \le \alpha \le 1$. The resulting production, pollution, consumption, and welfare levels can be characterized as follows.

In this simple model, the efficient combinations of X_1, X_2^*, and P (in the production sense) are given by equation 33 where obviously $0 \le X_1 \le \bar{H}$ and $0 \le X_2^* \le \bar{H}^*$. It can be shown that the efficient values of X_1, X_2^*, and P associated with the Pareto optimum corresponding to α are given by[87]

$$X_1 = \left[\frac{\alpha\theta_1 + (1-\alpha)\theta_1^*}{y + \mu}\right][\bar{P} + \mu\bar{H} + \mu^*\bar{H}^*] \tag{34}$$

$$X_2 = \left[\frac{\alpha\theta_2 + (1-\alpha)\theta_2^*}{y^* + \mu^*}\right][\bar{P} + \mu\bar{H} + \mu^*\bar{H}^*] \tag{35}$$

$$\bar{P} - P = [\alpha\theta_3 + (1-\alpha)\theta_3^*][\bar{P} + \mu\bar{H} + \mu^*\bar{H}^*] \tag{36}$$

The consumption of wheat and rice in the two countries in the Pareto optimum is given by

$$C_1 = \left[\frac{\alpha\theta_1}{\alpha\theta_1 + (1-\alpha)\theta_1^*}\right]X_1; \qquad C_1^* = \left[\frac{(1-\alpha)\theta_2^*}{\alpha\theta_1 + (1-\alpha)\theta_1^*}\right]X_1 \tag{37}$$

$$C_2 = \left[\frac{\alpha\theta_2}{\alpha\theta_2 + (1-\alpha)\theta_2^*}\right]X_2^*; \qquad C_2^* = \left[\frac{(1-\alpha)\theta_2^*}{\alpha\theta_1 + (1-\alpha)\theta_2^*}\right]X_2^* \tag{38}$$

The welfare levels U and U^* in the Pareto optimum are given by

$$U = (\theta_1 + \theta_2)\log\alpha + \theta_3\log[\alpha\theta_3 + (1-\alpha)\theta_3^*] + \theta_1[\log\theta_1 - \log(y + \mu)] \\ + \theta_2[\log\theta_2 - \log(y^* + \mu^*)] + \log(\bar{P} + \mu\bar{H} + \mu^*\bar{H}^*) \tag{39}$$

$$U^* = (\theta_1^* + \theta_2^*)\log(1-\alpha) + \theta_3^*\log[\alpha\theta_3 + (1-\alpha)\theta_3^*] + \theta_1^*[\log\theta_1^* - \log(y + \mu)] \\ + \theta_2^*[\log\theta_2 - \log(y^* + \mu^*)] + \log(\bar{P} + \mu\bar{H} + \mu^*\bar{H}^*) \tag{40}$$

The shadow prices (in global welfare units) of goods 1 and 2 and "clean" air (i.e., $\bar{P}$–P) for consumers are, respectively,

$$\lambda_1 = \left[\frac{(\alpha + \mu)}{\bar{P} + \mu\bar{H} + \mu^*\bar{H}^*}\right], \quad \lambda_2 = \left[\frac{\alpha^* + \mu^*}{\bar{P} + \mu\bar{H} + \mu^*\bar{H}^*}\right], \quad \lambda_3 = \frac{1}{\bar{P} + \mu\bar{H} + \mu^*\bar{H}^*} \tag{41}$$

Note that the shadow prices do not depend on α. Two further observations are in order.

First, it can be easily shown now that as α increases from zero to 1, U increases and U^* decreases. Eliminating α between equations 39 and 40 yields the utility possibility frontier of U^* as a function of U. The value of consumption at home (resp. abroad), namely $\lambda_1 C_1 + \lambda_2 C_2$ (resp. $\lambda_1 C_1^* + \lambda_2 C_2^*$) exceeds disposable income $\lambda_1 X_1$ (resp. $\lambda_2 X_2^* \lambda$) by $\alpha\theta_2 - (1-\alpha)\theta_1^*$ [resp. $(1-\alpha)\theta_1^* - \alpha\theta_2$]. Thus an income transfer of $\alpha\theta_2 - (1-\alpha)\theta_1^*$ from country 2 to country 1 is implicit in the preceding Pareto optimum. No transfer will be required only for $\alpha = \theta_1^* / (\theta_1^* + \theta_2)$. (The reason that consumer disposable income is the value of production at consumer prices is that a lump-sum tax or subsidy needed to finance the wedge between consumer and producer prices has to be subtracted [or added] to the value of production at producer prices [i.e., income at factor cost] to arrive at disposable income at market prices.)

Second, inspection of equations 35–36 also reveals that if $\theta_i = \theta_i^*$ (i = 1, 2, 3) so that both countries have identical tastes, efficient production and pollution levels (X_1, X_2^* and P) are independent of α. Thus the choice of α affects only the distribution of the fixed outputs of X_1 and X_2^* between the two countries for consumption purposes. In this case, the utility possibility frontier is given by

$$U^* = (\theta_1 + \theta_2)\log\left[1 - e^{-(\delta - U)/(\theta_1 + \theta_2)}\right] + \delta, \qquad -\infty \leq U \leq \delta \tag{42}$$

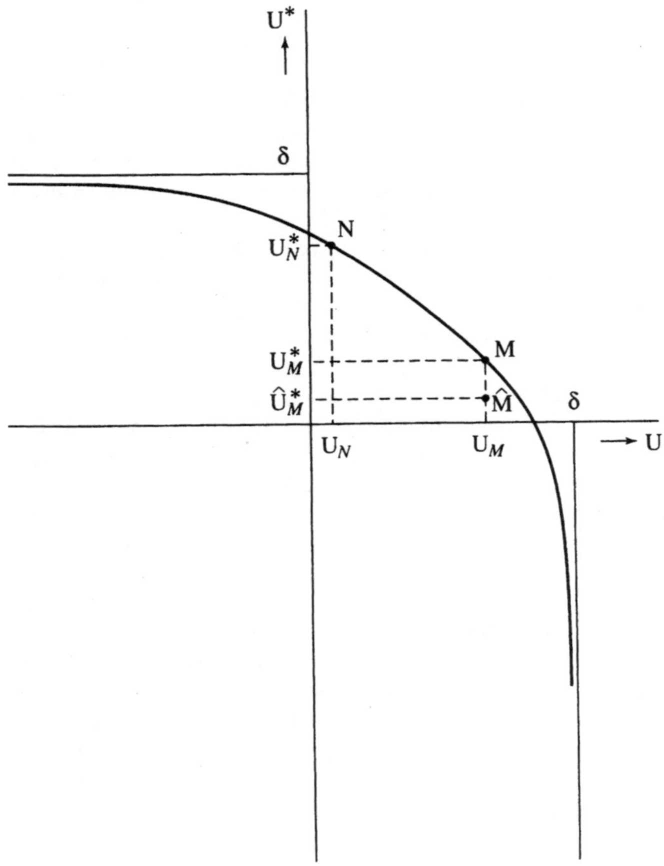

FIGURE 2 Efficiency and Equity in World Pollution: General Equilibrium

where $\delta = \theta_1[\log\theta_1 - \log(y+\mu)] + \theta_2[\log\theta_2 - \log(y+\mu) + \theta_3 + \log(\bar{P}+\mu\bar{H}+\mu^*\bar{H}^*)$. It can be seen from equations 39 and 40 that as $\alpha \to 0$, $U \to -\infty$, and $U^* \to \delta$, and as $\alpha \to 1$, $U \to \delta$ and $U^* \to -\infty$. In fact U^* is a concave function of U as depicted in Figure 2 for the case $\delta > 0$. It is seen that δ represents the maximal utility that *either* country would achieve if *global* resources are used to maximize only its utility – in other words, the weight placed on the other country's utility in the global welfare function is zero. With the countries being identical in tastes, this maximal utility is the same for both countries.

We may now use this simple method, with the added simplification of *identical tastes*,[88] to illustrate efficiency-equity conflicts in two different ways.

(1) Suppose first that income transfers between the countries are infeasible so that the only feasible Pareto optimal allocation is that corresponding to $\alpha = \theta_1/(\theta_1 + \theta_2)$ (point N in Figure 2 which assumes identical tastes). If, say, the welfare

U_N of the home economy at N is deemed too low and an increase of it to U_M is deemed desirable, had transfers been feasible, the point M on the utility possibility frontier would have been the optimal way (i.e., with the least loss of foreign welfare) of achieving such an increase. With transfers infeasible, the welfare of the foreign economy would have to be reduced below U_M^* (say to $\hat{U}_M^*$) for achieving such an increase. Thus the loss ($U_M^* - \hat{U}_M^*$) is the loss from distributional inefficiency (in departing from Pareto optimality) incurred in order to achieve equity, given that transfers are infeasible.

(2) However, the no-transfer Pareto optimal allocation N might be deemed unsatisfactory for a reason other than its being inequitable; the associated global pollution levels may be viewed as "too high." This might happen if it is believed that one or both countries attach "too low" a value to clean air in their preferences. In the context of our simple model, if preferences are the same in the two countries, a natural way to express this concern is to set an upper bound $\hat{P}$ on pollution levels. Now from equation 36 it is seen that $P = \bar{P} - [\alpha\theta_3 + (1-\alpha)\theta_3^*](\bar{P}+\mu\bar{H}+\mu^*\bar{H}^*)$. If tastes are identical so that $\theta_3 = \theta_3^*$, then recall that P is independent of α and equals $\bar{P} - \theta_3(\bar{P}+\mu\bar{H}+\mu^*\bar{H}^*)$. If this exceeds $\hat{P}$, then there is no feasible Pareto optimum with or without transfers that can achieve the upper bound $\hat{P}$. If it is less than or equal to $\hat{P}$, the upper bound is respected at all Pareto optima.

Let us consider the case where $\bar{P} - \theta_3(\bar{P}+\mu\bar{H}+\mu^*\bar{H}^*) > \hat{P}$ so that the upper bound represents a binding constraint. Of course, if we give up all production and consumption, net pollution P will be negative, since the pollutant-absorbing capacity of the virgin forests will come into full play then. As such, it is feasible to meet the bound $\hat{P}$ by reducing production relative to the levels at a Pareto optimum. It can then be shown that the *efficient* way of achieving $\hat{P}$ without transfers is to *reduce* the output of X_1 and X_2^* by the same proportion so that $X_1 = \beta X_1^0$, $X_2 = \beta X_2^{*0}$ where X_1^0 *and* X_2^{*0} are the values given by equations 34 and 35, and $\beta = \left(\dfrac{\hat{P}+\bar{\mu}\bar{H}+\mu^*\bar{H}^*}{\bar{P}+\bar{\mu}\bar{H}+\mu^*\bar{H}^*}\right)(1-\theta_3)$.[89] Clean air – that is, $\bar{P}-\hat{P}-$ goes up relative to $\bar{P}-P^0$ by the factor $\left(\dfrac{1-\beta(1-\theta_3)}{\theta_3}\right)$. This *reduces* the welfare of each country by the *same amount* – $(\theta_1+\theta_2)\log\beta - \theta_3[\log(1-\beta(1-\theta_3)) - \log\theta_3]$. While such a reduction is efficient in meeting the bound $\hat{P}$ on pollution, the incidence might be viewed as inequitable if the post-reduction welfare level of one of the countries is relatively low. Once again, meeting the bound and being equitable at the same time will then mean deviating from efficiency.

What happens in the *general case* in which the two countries do not have identical tastes so that $\theta_3 \neq \theta_3^*$? It is then seen from equation 36 that pollution P is an increasing (resp. decreasing) function of α if $\theta_3^* > \theta_3$ (resp. $\theta_3^* < \theta_3$). This observation is not surprising, since θ_3 (resp. θ_3^*) is analogous to the "share" of clean air in the home economy's spending and, as α increases, the home economy's share in world spending increases. Hence, if the "share" of clean air in the home economy's spending is less than that of the foreign economy, pollution increases as a greater share of world spending accrues to the home economy.

Now, for concreteness, assume that $\theta_3^* > \theta_3$ so that pollution increases with α. Then, as long as there exists an $\hat{\alpha}$ $(0 < \hat{\alpha} < 1)$ at which pollution equals $\hat{P}$, pollution will be less than $\hat{P}$ for *all* α in the interval $0 < \alpha < \hat{\alpha}$. Of course, unless the no-transfer value of α– that is, $\theta_1^* / (\theta_1^* + \theta_2)$ – is less than $\hat{\alpha}$, the bound $\hat{P}$ cannot be met at a Pareto optimal allocation if transfers are ruled out: efficiency will have to be sacrificed again in the interest of equity.

Our analysis of this model has then illustrated the following key propositions:

(a) As long as lump-sum income transfers between countries are feasible, it is possible to achieve a resource allocation that is at the same time *distributionally efficient* in the sense that relative to it, any other allocation will make at least one country worse off in terms of consumer welfare, *productivity efficient* in the sense that relative to it in any other allocation there will be less output of at least one commodity or greater pollution, and *equitable* in the sense of maximizing a global welfare function that incorporates distributional equity among countries while being an increasing function of each country's welfare.

(b) if such transfers are infeasible, at least one of the preceding three desiderata has to be given up. For example, a distributionally and productively efficient allocation without transfers was shown to exist that was not deemed equitable. Achieving equity then involves a sacrifice of efficiency in both sense.

(c) Equity was judged in propositions a and b by a global welfare function that was solely a function of the welfare of consumers in each country as perceived by them. In other words, the welfare evaluations of each country's consumers were respected. If, for example, these evaluations are deemed inappropriate because they attach too little weight to global pollution, then an efficient allocation without transfers that is equitable (in the sense of proposition) may not be satisfactory from the perspective of a global welfare function that overrides consumer weighting of global pollution. Once again, to achieve a satisfactory allocation, either efficiency or equity, in the sense of proposition, or a both have to be given up.

A4.2.7 Country-Specific Pollution Generation and Abatement

As noted earlier, the preceding analysis of global pollution assumed that the outputs of two countries (resp. the resources devoted to pollution abatement) were perfect substitutes for each other in the generation of pollution (resp. in abatement). This assumption is easily relaxed. Consider again the case of global Pareto optimality of section S4.2.3. Let the pollution function (equation 14) be replaced by

$$P=P[F(X_2, \bar{K}-K_a, \bar{L}-L_a), X_2, K_a, L_a, F^*(X_2^*, \bar{K}^*-K_a^*, \bar{L}^*-L_a^*), X_2^*, K_a^*, L_a^*] \quad (43)$$

First-order conditions (equations 19–22) still hold, and as such free trade with respect to consumption continues to be optimal. Conditions 23, 25 and 26 still hold (recall that subscript i of P continues to denote the partial derivative with respect to its ith argument, except P now has eight, instead of four, arguments). Equation 24 is replaced by $[\alpha U_3 + (1-\alpha)U_3^*][P_5 F_1^* + P_6] + \lambda_1 F_1^* + \lambda_2 = 0$. Equations 27 and 28 continue to hold with P_3 replaced by P_7 and P_4 by P_8.

The only significant result that is different from section A4.2.3 is that, while *within each country* the marginal rate of substitution between capital and labor is the same in goods production and pollution abatement, this common rate is not in general the same in the two countries. As such, the factor price equalization result need no longer hold. Also, with the outputs and resources devoted to pollution abatement in the two countries not being perfect substitutes for each other in pollution generation and abatement, respectively, the efficiency-equality conflict discussed in section A4.2.6 is more likely.

A4.3 PREVIOUS CONTRIBUTIONS OF RELEVANCE TO OUR ANALYSIS

There is a significant volume of scholarly literature on trade and the environment, most of it published in the last three years of so.[90] The literature is diverse in incorporating environmental considerations into economic models and in the policy questions addressed. It is beyond our scope to provide a critical survey and assessment of this literature.

Before discussing the two contributions most closely related to this Chapter, however, it is worth pointing out that we have mostly confined our analysis to "first-best" policies in a context where environmental externalities or other distortions are present. We did so primarily because it is well known that (1) when a number of distortions are present, removing or reducing a subset of them need not be welfare-improving and that whether it is or not would depend on the specific circumstances; and (2) when first-best policies are infeasible, other policies might exist that will improve welfare over laissez-faire, but in general the ranking of such policies according to the net welfare improvement they bring about is not possible (while of course in particular circumstances it might be).

In the literature, a frequently posed question is whether moving from autarky to free trade would be welfare improving in situations where trade-environment interactions are present, and, of course, answers vary depending on assumptions about other policies. This is just another illustration of the first of the two well-known results stated in the preceding paragraph. After all, the welfare superiority of free trade over autarky depends on the absence of other distortions.

The contributions that come closest to our Chapter are by Markusen (1975, 1976). Markusen (1975) models pollution much in the same way as we do except that, in his case, the production of only one of the two commodities (the same one in each country) generates global pollution and no abatement is possible. His analysis of "first-best" policies for maximizing national welfare is the same as for our case of a large country but without abatement possibilities (section A4.2.2): an optimum tariff combined with a production tax is first-best optimal.

He then considers the case when the first-best combination is infeasible and in turn examines the use of consumption taxes only, tariffs only, and production taxes only, as second-best policy instruments. He finds that the formulas for the calculation of some second-best instruments contain components of opposite algebraic signs so that taken together they lead to an ambiguous sign for the instrument. This result means, first, that whether the instrument will be a tax or subsidy or neither (i.e,. laissez-faire) will depend on the numerical balance between the positive and negative components, a balance that can only be decided empirically. Second, even if a second-best instrument has an unambiguous sign, it does not mean that its use will produce a superior welfare outcome compared to another instrument whose second-best value is of ambiguous sign. This is an illustration of the second of the well-known results: second-best policy rankings are circumstance-dependent.

Markusen (1976) models pollution the same way as Markusen (1975). But now the policy issues are considered not from the perspective of a single large country that faces no retaliation or ignores it even if it is possible, but in the context of two countries that are "small" relative to the rest of the world from the perspective of commodity trade but whose production-generated pollution affects the welfare of both. Each government has production and trade taxes as policy instruments at its disposal.

Markusen first solves for the optimum tax structure for each when it takes the other's tax structure as given (Cournot behavior) thus leading to Cournot-Nash equilibrium tax structure in the usual fashion. The Cournot-Nash equilibrium is then compared with two types of cooperative equilibria – one without transfer payments and the other with transfer payments. Three conclusions are derived. First, for any distribution of world resources, there exists some set of allocations that make both countries better off relative to some suboptimal equilibrium. Second, in the absence of transfer payments, there exists a set of cooperative solutions that achieve such an allocation. Third, if transfer payments are permitted, Pareto optimal allocations that make both countries better off relative to the Cournot equilibrium are attainable. These conclusions are clearly similar to some of ours relating to Nash equilibria and global Pareto optimality.

NOTES

We have profited from the comments on an earlier draft by several project participants, especially Ken Abbott, Christopher Bliss, Drusilla Brown, Alessandra Casella, Alan Deardorff, Robert Hudec, Al Klevorick, Brian Langille, Virginia Leary, Andre Sapir, and John Wilson, at a conference at the Minnesota Law School in July 1993 and at a Washington, DC, conference in October 1994. The comments of Claude Barfield, Steve Charnowitz, Dan Esty, William Nordhaus, Susan Rose-Ackerman, and Karl-Göran Mäler have been very helpful. While we take joint responsibility for the entire chapter, the blame for any errors in the text must be assigned to Bhagwati and in the Appendix to Srinivasan!

1 By CCII, we mean harmonization of standards within the *same* industry across different trading countries.

2 This, of course, is the central issue addressed later in this chapter.

3 The suspension of trade generally, i.e., the use of trade "sanctions" (to promote human rights, for instance) is a related but different issue that we do not discuss in this chapter in depth.

4 As in argument 2.

5 The difficulties posed by the GATT, and now the WTO, for the environmentalists extend to GATT law (i.e., Dispute Settlement Panel findings) in regard to the ethical-preference issue as well. The general issue of GATT law on the entire range of relevant

questions concerning the environment is addressed by Frieder Roessler in Chapter 2 in Volume 2 of this work.

6 *International Pollution Deterrence Act of 1991*, Statement of Senator David L. Boren, Senate Finance Committee, October 25, 1991.

7 We will be considering several objections to this view, of course, before reaching this conclusion.

8 The entire range of the factors (philosophical, economic, and political) that are currently prompting the drive toward CCII harmonization is reviewed and synthesized by Bhagwati in Chapter 1. See also the discussion in Daniel Esty, *Greening the GATT* (Washington, DC: Institute for International Economics, 1994), pp. 108–114, 156–167.

9 "Bushism, Found: A Second-Term Agenda Hidden in Trade Agreements," *Harper's Magazine*, September 1992, p. 44.

10 Cf. J. Bhagwati and M. Kosters, eds, *Trade and Wages* (Washington, DC: American Enterprise Institute, 1994). Several trade economists share this skeptical view; see the most recent review in Jagdish Bhagwati, "Trade and wages: Choosing among alternative explanations," *Federal Reserve Bank of New York Economic Policy Review*, January 1995.

11 Cf. J. Bhagwati, "Free traders and free immigrationists: Friends or foes?" (mimeo) (New York: Russell Sage Foundation, 1992).

12 The prominent U.S. role in the UN Conference on Population in Cairo in September 1994 may be explained, at least in part, in this fashion.

13 Cf. Appendix, section A4.1.1.

14 Cf. Appendix, section A4.1.2.

15 Thus, any unfixed domestic distortion, such as failure to have optimal pollution taxes or adequate institutional arrangements to prevent the overuse of commons, for instance, can lead to immiserization under free trade vis-à-vis autarky. Cf. the review in Bhagwati (1971). Also see the recent writings of Graciela Chichilinsky, Peter Lloyd, and others on this question.

16 Cf. Appendix, section A4.1.3.

17 Cf. the contribution of D. Brown, A. Deardorff, and R. Stern (Chapter 5). The answer eventually depends on how the offer curve of the lower-standard country shifts with the harmonization up.

18 The conditions under which tax harmonization will occur in a globally Pareto optimal solution are discussed in section A4.2.3 of the Appendix.

19 Cf. Appendix, section A4.2.4.

20 Cf. Appendix, section A4.2.1.

21 Cf. Appendix, section A4.2.2.

22 We should also state the related but distinct proposition that diversity of standards across countries will be observed as the norm in competitive equilibrium and, besides, will change with trade and hence, income (as implicit, of course, in our preceding analysis and in the Appendix). This proposition is also derived, in the context of a model where standards are characterized as having some of the characteristics of "public goods" in each of two trading countries and enter directly the utility functions in these countries, by Alessandra Casella in Chapter 3. The focus of our analysis instead is on the issue of CCII harmonization and on the question of standards diversity when welfare maximization is being pursued (and may require departure from a laissez-faire competitive equilibrium).

23 This phrase has passed even into the latest annual report of the Council of Economic Advisers as part of a definition of "competitiveness" that Paul Krugman has castigated in a recent article in *Foreign Affairs*.

24 If the country is large, then we must substitute an optimal tariff for free trade in this sentence.

25 Thus recent judicial determinations in the United States have undermined the public

law that had grown up earlier with strong support for environmentalism, not reflective of costs and benefits, for the possibility of "takings" in the public environmental interest and in regard to standing and judicial review. The earlier public law literature is well represented by Abram Chayes, "The role of the judge in public law litigation," *Harvard Law Review*, 89 (1976), and Ronald Dworkin, *Law's empire*, 1986; and it is also well developed in India, in regard to standing (for NGOs etc.) in particular, in the public interest litigation developed in the Supreme Court. The reverse movement in the United States can be seen from cases such as *Lucas v. South Carolina Coastal Council* and *Nollan v. California Coastal Commission* on takings, *Lujan v. National Wildlife Federation and Lujan v. Defenders of Wildlife* on standing, and *Competitive Enterprise Institute v. National Highway Traffic Safety Administration* and *Corrosion Proof Fittings v. EPA* on judicial review. The last area has, in particular, seen the increased judicial scrutiny of the cost-benefit aspects of executive actions implementing legislated regulation. The U.S. Congress is itself currently in the midst of an intense battle over precisely this question, with the New Democrat Clinton administration much more open to cost-benefit analysis than the older Democrats.

26 The question of democracy is addressed, from a different perspective, in section 4.4.3.

27 An in-depth review and synthesis of the theoretical literature on this question is provided by John Wilson in his chapter for the project, "Capital mobility and environmental standards: Is there a theoretical basis for a race to the bottom?" (Chapter 10 of this volume). We therefore only sketch the nature of the argument here.

28 Wilson, Chapter 10.

29 Cf. Arik Levinson's chapter for the project, "Environmental regulation and industry location: International and domestic evidence" (Chapter 11 of this volume). Levinson looks at both the international and the domestic evidence (e.g., interstate locational decisions in the United States, since states have different standards), having himself produced first-rate work in the latter genre.

30 Cf. Levinson, Chapter 11, citing for instance, work by Baumol and Oates, Low, etc.

31 Levinson, Chapter 11, cites work by Hamilton, Baldwin, and Welles, and Walter on voter participation, in particular.

32 Levinson, Chapter 11, cites this explanation from the work of Gladwin and Welles, and Knögden. The argument requires that the transaction costs of diverse choices are large enough to offset the forgone advantage of meeting each standard only as necessary and not beyond. Besides, it does not apply to single-plant firms or to subsidiaries that act as more or less independent decision makers.

33 Again, the argument requires that the advantages of being "ahead of the curve" offset the advantages of conforming to lower standards now and adapting or retooling later when the higher standards emerge.

34 Cf. Levinson, Chapter 11, citing Pearson.

35 Eg., the (static and dynamic) arguments underlying Explanation 2 imply that CCII differences will be disregarded by multinationals in any event, with their plant-design choice gravitating toward the higher-standard technology everywhere and therefore locational choices becoming independent of CCII differences in standards.

36 Cf. Levinson, Chapter 11.

37 To our knowledge, the countervailing of *implicit* subsidies would be a novel principle in GATT law on subsidies as well, and is not to be contemplated with equanimity in view of its explosive potential; it is probably for this reason that the concept of remedy used by the proponents of harmonization of standards is that of AD rather than of CVD (countervailing duties on foreign subsidies).

38 Cropper and Oates (1992, pp. 675–676).

39 Questions raised by "values"-related differences in CCII standards are considered separately later in this chapter.

40 This statement, of course, does not apply equally to trade in highly differentiated products like autos where one can get fixated on specific countries, e.g., Japan.

41 See Bhagwati, "American Rules, Mexican Jobs," *New York Times*, March 24, 1993.

42 Recall our analysis, based on Arik Levinson's review, Chapter 11.

43 One of the important reasons for such nonharmonization (documented by Joel Slemrod in Chapter 6) is that horizontal equity among firms from different countries abroad can conflict with the desire to have horizontal equity among one's firms at home and one's firms abroad. This problem comes up quite directly in regard to personal income taxation where the U.S. practice is to tax on basis of citizenship while the practice elsewhere is to tax on basis of residence. The former ensures horizontal equity between U.S. citizens at home and abroad but, given the residence-based taxation practice of other nations, leads to lack of horizontal equity between, say, U.S. and French citizens in Manila or New Delhi where U.S. citizens must continue to pay U.S. income taxes (subject to some exemptions) while the French citizens do not have to pay French income taxes. The questions raised by the U.S. practice of exercising income tax jurisdiction on its citizens abroad, through the citizenship rather than residence nexus, have been extensively studied by modern economists cognizant of the extensive international personal mobility today. Cf. Jagdish Bhagwati and John Wilson, eds, *Income taxation and international personal mobility* (Cambridge, MA: MIT Press, 1991).

44 Insofar as it involves suspension of trade access by a country for products that are produced by processes that are disapproved of, it is also GATT-*illegal* as per the first Tuna-Dolphin Panel finding, and as discussed in section 4.4.

45 This "break in the ranks" occurs when there are diverse priorities at stake. Among single-issue NGOs, as on child labor, we can expect more international solidarity, of course.

46 August 15, 1992, p. 4. The magazine is published in New Delhi and enjoys a large circulation.

47 GATT, *Annual Report* (Geneva, Switzerland, 1991), pp. 33–34.

48 Steve Charnovitz, "GATT and the environment: Examining the issues," *International Environment Affairs*, 4(3), Summer 1992, p. 211. This is an interesting, thought-provoking, and lucidly argued but ultimately unpersuasive critique of the GATT report (note 47) and of the Dolphin-Tuna Panel Report.

49 Cf. GATT, *Annual Report* (1991), pp. 33–34.

50 Cf. Charnovitz, "GATT and the environment," p. 213.

51 The recently activated GATT Group on Environment Measures and International Trade has among its tasks the examination of the trade effects of packaging and labeling requirements intended to protect the environment. It has been examining the packaging and labeling questions in depth.

52 It is not just that the budgets of the poor countries are financially strapped. It is also that few parliaments would sanction expenditure of the huge amounts of money that are needed to take out ads in the Western papers and to hire lobbyists in Washington. The only democratic exception seems to be Mexico, which had, at the end of 1991, as many as 71 lobbying firms in the United States registered as "foreign agents" acting on behalf of NAFTA.

53 We are talking here of unilateral actions. Where a substantial plurilateral or multilateral consensus is achieved on a suspension of trade access, the cost imposed will generally be higher.

54 Jessica Matthews has argued that sometimes unilateralism has enabled the United States to provide leadership on important issues. But, even if this were true, it would not justify unilateralism. After all, just because dictatorships may sometimes be beneficial, we would not permit them and renounce our loyalty to democracy.

55 Charnovitz, "GATT and the environment," pp. 206–207.

56 So, you are not a "consequentialist" but one who has an "absolute" moral value. You may not expect to change Mexican behavior; you may even be hurting only yourself. But you may be doing what you think duty or virtue compels. It is worth noting, however, that one does not have to deny Mexico access to the U.S. market to avoid eating a "defiled product." After all, by not eating any tuna whatsoever and by directing political action in boycotts or education instead of seeking official embargoes, one can hurt the market for Mexican tuna as well. As noted earlier, the market pressure induced by such an action could also lead Mexican fishermen to abandon dolphin-unsafe fishing methods in order to regain lost markets.

57 There is, of course, a "moral hazard" problem: countries may become deliberately sinful to be bribed into virtue. But we doubt this is likely to be a serious problem, since the compensation in practice is likely to continue to be in form of other trade concessions in lieu of the one withdrawn.

58 Ibid., pp. 204–205.

59 Cf. Jackson, (1992), pp. 1241–42.

60 This point is argued in section 4.4. It may, however, be useful to clarify the matter so as to eliminate any ambiguities and doubts in the matter.

61 Section 301 actions aimed at securing new trade concessions, rather than at securing compliance with treaty-defined trade objections, fall into this class of problems, of course. On their GATT-inconsistency, see Jagdish Bhagwati and Hugh Patrick, eds, *Aggressive unilateralism* (Ann Arbor: Michigan University Press, 1991), especially the contributions by Hudec and Bhagwati.

62 These questions are addressed with far greater authority by Frieder Roessler, legal counsel to the GATT, in Chapter 1 of Volume 2 of this work. Also see Chapters 2 and 3 by Robert Hudec and Daniel Farber.

63 Nearly all cases can be fitted into one or both of these categories. Thus producing chickens in batteries may be objected to as cruel, fitting it into category 1. Overfishing in the commons to which I have access fits into category 2. If you use your forests in an "unsustainable" way, I may object to it because I think that it is bad per se, i.e., category 1, or because it affects global warming and hence me, i.e., category 2, or because of both reasons.

64 GATT, *Annual Report* (1991), pp. 22–23.

65 The GATT law on this general question, and its relatively more environmentally friendly nature relative to the interstate "Dormant Clause" doctrine in the United States are the subject of the penetrating analysis by Daniel Farber and Robert Hudec in their chapter for this project (Chapter 2 in Volume 2). They distinguish between the "facially discriminatory" and the "facially neutral" (but nonetheless discriminatory, whether "indirectly" and "incidentally" or otherwise) regulations, analyzing how GATT and U.S. jurisprudence apply to each of these in regard to their implications for trade that lead to litigation.

That the GATT law is essentially more environmentally friendly was borne out also by the GATT panel finding in the EU versus the Unites States case on U.S. fuel conservation measures in September 1994, which upheld much of the U.S. law as consistent with the GATT, even when the conflict seemed compelling prima facie.

66 Gottfried Haberler, *Theory of International Trade* (London: William Hodge, 1936), p. 339. Haberler cited this amusing case as an instance of the manner in which countries evaded the obligation of the most favored nation clause.

67 As we will argue, a challenge to recycling and packaging requirements cannot be ruled out on the ground that alternative, less-trade-restricting measures are possible and should be undertaken.

68 From the economic perspective, a domestic firm acting strategically may also be able

to persuade its government to enact higher standards whose effect is to make the cost of entry by foreign rivals, which must tool up to meet these higher standards, disproportionately higher (since the domestic firm has a significantly higher proportion of its sales in its own market). Higher standards in this case would then be in reality a protectionist technique for making market access by foreign firms more expensive.

69 Cf. Charnovitz, "GATT and the environment," pp. 213–214. For the Thailand case, see GATT, *Basic Instruments and Selected Documents, 37S/200* (Geneva, Switzerland). Also see Sty, *Greening the GATT*, p. 48.

70 Cited in Charnovitz, "GATT and the environment," p. 214.

71 Cf. ibid., p. 251. Charnovitz calls this the "proportionality" issue, but it is really a "trade-off" issue.

72 This was the issue addressed to a panel of trade and legal scholars at the Conference on the Morality of Protectionism at the New York University Law School in November 1992. It is quoted in Robert Hudec's excellent contribution, "'Circumventing' Democracy: The Political Morality of Trade Negotiations," New York University *Journal of International Law and Politics*, vol. 25. 1993, pp. 311–322.

73 Some issues are, of course, similar to those raised in the case of domestic environmental problems. Thus, we must ask again, How convincing is the science being invoked to spur action? Ironically, some of those who attack the use of science to attack environmental regulations in challenging phytosanitary standards defend the use of science in urging action on global problems. The fickle nature of science in these matters is evident from the history of the ozone problem. Scientists in the United States were in the forefront in suggesting the link between CFCs and ozone-depletion, leading in 1978 to the prohibition of the use of CFCs in aerosol spray cans. The Europeans were skeptical: so was the Reagan administration. The discovery of the big hole in the ozone layer in Antarctica in 1984 turned almost everyone around, leading to the Montreal Protocol in 1987 and the further change therein in 1990 to eliminate CFCs by A.D. 2000.

74 The theoretical analysis of the instrument is in the Appendix, section A4.1.3, and, more fully, in Markusen (1975).

75 This would clearly be a case where the process that generates the *physical* transborder extentiality is being objected to and a trade measure against it is being legitimated, as distinct from the "*values*" objection to a process as discussed earlier.

76 This is the conclusion reached by Aparna Guha in a dissertation at Columbia University, examining the options before Canada in relation to the acid rain from the United States. She is currently studying the possibility of a market in permits to use fossil fuels in U.S. electricity generation where Canada could bid and pay herself to reduce the acid rain being generated in the United States. This approach would require, of course, that the permits be segmented by the states that generate the acid rain that comes across to Canada, else the cost to Canada could become prohibitive. There is much excellent work on the acid rain problem, including by Karl-Göran Mäler and his associates in Stockholm.

77 Of course, the question of single-country use of a second-best tariff policy can be raised here just as well as in the preceding case, but this question has raised no interest in the global-pollution context.

78 Cf. Appendix, section A4.2.6 on this question.

79 This efficiency is only in the sense of cost minimization when pollution anywhere equally affects a single target such as CO_2. The number of permits may, however, be too small or too large, and getting it right by letting nonusers also bid (and then destroy permits) is bedevilled by free rider problems.

80 In this appendix, unless otherwise stated, we will simply *assume* that the relevant set of first-order conditions indeed characterize a unique solution to the optimization

problem under consideration. We do not go into the assumptions on the production, utility, and pollution functions that will ensure that this will be the case.

81 Cf. Srinivasan (1987) and Bhagwati (1971).

82 Note also that we do not have a reason to subsidize the use of abatement technology.

83 Of course, the precise values of the optimum tariff and subsidy would in general differ depending on whether or not abatement is feasible.

84 Even though the trade flows of a small economy by definition have no influence on the terms at which the flows take place, such flows could influence the output in the rest of the world. This is best seen in a Ricardian model in which the small open economy specializes in producing its exportable good while the rest of the world (ROW) is incompletely specialized and the equilibrium world prices are the autarky prices of the ROW. With the opening of trade with the small economy, ROW still consumes its autarky consumption bundle while production adjusts to accommodate the trade flows from the small economy. Although policy-induced changes in the trade flows of the small economy do not affect equilibrium world prices, they do affect the production in ROW and, hence, pollution, if pollution is a by -product of production.

85 Since the home (resp. foreign) country takes the foreign (resp. home) country's outputs and resources allocated for abatement as given, each country's reaction function with respect to the variables it chooses (X_2, K_a, and L_a for the home country and X_2^*, K_a^*, and L_a^* for the foreign country) are functions of the values of the variables for the other country taken as given. Nash equilibrium is a mutually consistent set in the sense that each country's choices as obtained by substituting the other country's choices in its reaction function, when substituted into the latter's reaction functions, yield the latter's choices.Thus $X_2(X_1^{*N}, X_2^{*N}, T^{*N}, K_a^{*N}, L_a^{*N})$ etc. when substituted in the reaction function $X_2^*(\ )$ will yield back X_2^{*N} and vice versa. We are assuming that such Nash equilibria exist. The existence issue is a complex one.

86 The variables λ_1 and λ_2 are the Lagrangean multipliers associated with the constraints of equations 17 and 18, respectively; these are shadow prices in global welfare units of good 1 and 2, respectively.

87 It is assumed that the parameters and endowments are such that the feasibility constraints $X_1 \leq \bar{H}$ and $X_2^* \leq \bar{H}^*$ hold.

88 The more general case of different tastes is briefly discussed on page 212, however.

89 Its efficiency can be demonstrated by showing that this solution satisfies the conditions for Pareto optimality subject to the requirements that pollution does not exceed. $\hat{P}$ and there are no transfers. In particular, we can show that the shadow cost of pollution in global welfare units will be the same in the two countries, though higher than its value at the no-transfer Pareto optimum without a binding upper-bound constraint on pollution.

91 Among the important contributions, aside from those reviewed in the Appendix, are Lloyd (1992), Snape (1992), and Baumol and Oates (1988). There are many others on issues such as the "race to the bottom" that are not addressed intensively in this chapter but are the foci of other authors in this project.

REFERENCES

Baumol, William, and Wallace Oates, 1988. *The theory of environmental policy*, 2nd ed. Cambridge, England: Cambridge University Press.

Bhagwati, Jagdish, N. 1971. "The generalized theory of distortions and welfare." In J. Bhagwati, R. Jones, R. Mundell and J. Vanek, eds, *Trade, balance of payments, and growth: Papers in international economics in honour of Charles P. Kindelberger*. Amsterdam: North Holland.

Cropper, Maureen, and Wallace Oates. 1992. "Environmental economics: A survey." *Journal of Economic Literature*, 20 (June): 675–740.

Johnson, Harry. 1954. "Optimum tariffs and retaliation." *Review of Economic Studies*, 21 (55); 152–153. Reprinted in H. G. Johnson, *International trade and economic growth* (London: Allen and Unwin, 1958).

Lloyd, Peter. 1992. "The problem of optimal environmental policy choice." In Kym Anderson and Richard Blackhurst, eds, *The greening of world trade issues*. New York: Harvester/Wheatsheaf.

Markusen, James, 1975. "International externalities and optimal tax structures." *Journal of International Economics*, 5:15–29.

Markusen, James. 1976. "Cooperative control of international pollution and common property resources." *Quarterly Journal of Economics*, 90:618–631.

Snape, Richard. 1992. "The environment, international trade and competitiveness." In Kym Anderson and Richard Blackhurst, eds, *The greening of world trade issues*. New York: Harvester/Wheatsheaf.

Srinvasan, T. N. 1987. "Distortions." In J. Eatwell, M. Newgate, and P. Newman, eds, *The new Palgrafe*, 865–867. London: Macmillan.

4. INTERNATIONAL LABOR STANDARDS AND TRADE: A THEORETICAL ANALYSIS

D. K. Brown, A. V. Deardorff and R. M. Stern

5.1 INTRODUCTION

THE INTERACTION OF LABOR STANDARDS and international trade policy is not, as we will note, a new issue. Nonetheless, it has assumed new importance because of the concerns of labor interests in the United States and elsewhere that labor issues were ignored in the Uruguay Round of Multilateral Trade Negotiations and therefore should be placed high on the agenda of any future negotiating round. Issues of labor standards were also at the center of the public debate surrounding the North American Free Trade Agreement (NAFTA). Prominent among the objections to the NAFTA were concerns that labor standards are not enforced at a sufficiently high level in Mexico, and therefore that the competition that will ensue from the NAFTA will place U.S. domestic industries at a disadvantage vis-à-vis their Mexican competitors. The result, it is feared, is that either U.S. firms will shut down or move production to Mexico, or that pressure will be put on the United States to lower labor standards domestically.[1] Because of these concerns, President Bill Clinton placed labor standards on his list of three issues for which side agreements had to be negotiated before bringing the NAFTA to Congress for approval.

While issues of labor standards have obviously taken on a high profile in policy discussions and negotiations, there has been comparatively little theoretical analysis of the connections between labor standards and trade. It is our purpose in this paper to explore these connections more fully. In contrast to and complementing Bhagwati and Srinivasan (1995), who examine principally whether diversity of standards is compatible with the case for free trade, our focus will be on the welfare and other effects of standards themselves, and whether it is in a country's interest to adopt common standards internationally.

After first reviewing the institutional and historical background of labor standards and trade in section 5.2, we will devote the rest of the paper to examining several theoretical approaches to the issue. In section 5.3, we begin with a partial equilibrium analysis of standards as a general problem, not limited necessarily to labor standards. Our first conclusion is that if one abstracts from effects of labor standards on a country's terms of trade, then the general economic interest of a country will determine the level of its labor standards independently of standards that exist abroad. Similarly, to the extent that countries agree internationally on the implementation of a common standard, it is not necessarily the case that each country's self-interest is in establishing an international standard most like its own. Rather, their position in international trade, as either a net exporter or net importer of those goods most affected by labor standards, will determine whether they favor international standards that are high or low.

The reason for this result turns out after all to have to do with the terms of trade, and we therefore turn in section 5.4 to several models that focus explicitly on the effects of standards on the terms of trade. They differ in the extent to which countries are assumed to be specialized in production, and in whether the standards themselves merely divert resources from production in all sectors, or whether they instead raise production costs directly in particular sectors. In all cases, in this section of the paper, we confine attention to standards that are imposed exogenously, rather than explicitly modeling the market failure to which they may be a response.

In section 5.5 we make a first attempt at modeling the market failure, considering a case in which standards take the form of occupational health and safety regulations. Looking at a case in which workers choose among industries that differ in their inherent riskiness of illness or accident, we allow firms to select endogenously the levels of occupational safety that they provide, at some cost, and also the wage that they will pay their workers. With homogeneous preferences over safety and wages on the part of workers, or with enough competitive firms to tailor their offerings to heterogeneous worker preferences, there is no apparent market failure. If the government nonetheless intervenes, mandating a higher standard than is provided endogenously, then we work out the effects that this standard will have, in a context of international trade, both on the level of worker safety and on the trade, terms of trade, and welfare of the country as a whole. We then modify the model to allow for heterogeneous workers. With more kinds of worker preferences than there are firms to cater to those preferences, this heterogeneity causes a market failure that may plausibly be the basis for policy. We examine this case too, showing the possibly perverse effects that such standards may have in the context of international competition.

In section 5.6 we summarize the main results of our theoretical inquiries and conclude by examining the implications for the international harmonization of labor standards.

5.2 LABOR STANDARDS IN HISTORICAL PERSPECTIVE

5.2.1 Definition and General Principles of Labor Standards

Because labor standards are multifaceted, it is useful to begin by detailing the most important standards and by outlining the general principles involved in their interpretation and implementation.[2] For this purpose, we shall follow the definitions and principles set out by Lyle (1991, pp. 20–31). These are summarized in the Appendix. It should be noted that the definitions and principles listed in the Appendix do not cover all aspects of international worker rights. Rather, they are intended to highlight those worker rights standards that are set forth in U.S. trade law, but not to give the full legal text. The standards include (1) freedom of association, (2) the right to organize and bargain collectively, (3) freedom from forced labor, (4) a minimum age for employment, and (5) acceptable conditions of work, including a minimum wage, limitations on hours of work, and occupational safety and health rights in the workplace. We shall have more to say later in this chapter on these standards when we address issues of modeling and analysis of the presence or absence of particular standards in the context of international trade and the effects of harmonization of standards between trading countries.

5.2.2 Trade Effects of Intercountry Differences in Labor Standards

As will be noted in more detail later, there has been long-standing concern in the world economy about the absence or relatively weak official acknowledgment and enforcement of labor standards, especially in developing countries. The sources of concern have been both ethical and economic. It has been maintained on ethical grounds that there are certain basic human rights that are universal to mankind, and that governments everywhere should therefore be urged or maybe even coerced to institute measures that will insure that these rights are available to their citizens. The economic argument is that countries that do not guarantee and enforce these rights domestically may have an undue cost advantage in their export trade insofar as private costs do not fully reflect the social costs that would incorporate various standards. This argument presumes that the labor standards are defined to be absolute and universal rather than matters to be decided by sovereign nations. Of course, the issue becomes immediately ambiguous if it is recognized and granted that the choice of labor standards may depend on a country's stage of development and per capita income, and therefore that the weights attached to standards in an individual nation's social welfare function may differ. Clearly, many of the world's developing countries have found themselves in a situation historically of opting for standards lower than those that prevail in richer neighboring countries, and many continue to do so today.

In more advanced countries in which high labor standards are articulated and legally enforced, private and social costs will presumably be reconciled through policy. There may be a perceived disadvantage for the country's firms, however, as import-competing firms may argue that they cannot compete effectively against imports from countries with lower labor standards. Exporters may likewise argue that they also cannot compete effectively in third markets against foreign firms whose costs are artificially low because of the absence or weak enforcement of labor standards abroad. Import-competing and exporting firms in the high-standards country may respond to this situation by instituting measures to adjust to the domestic standards by undertaking capital-labor substitution, or, depending on their market power, by depressing wages. Exporting firms may also decide to relocate some of their production to foreign locations with lower standards. Another conceivable consequence is that efforts may be made to induce the government authorities to weaken or remove what are believed to be particularly onerous and costly standards.

To avoid all this, it seems appealing to urge or require that the foreign government raise its standards to the same levels as in the high-standard nation. If the foreign nation resists, the high-standard nation may wish to take punitive measures of some kind that are designed to bring about the desired change. Such actions could involve imposing import restrictions or some other type of sanction that will be costly to the foreign nation.

There is evidently, therefore, a range of responses that may occur in the high-standard country, and it is not always clear what the economic effects of the responses may be. As will be developed more fully in our theoretical discussion, the economic effects of certain responses may be counterintuitive and indeed counterproductive from a welfare point of view.

The preceding discussion abstracts from the political economy of protectionism and trade liberalization insofar as the focus is on the particular issue of the presence or absence of effective labor standards. What is missing is that both import-competing and export firms and workers may use issues of lower foreign labor standards to further their own narrow interests to the detriment of their nation's welfare. Thus, for example, there may be pressure for trade restrictions or some other restrictive measures ostensibly aimed at getting the foreign nation to raise its labor standards. In such an event, we encounter the same problem that is found generally when a government is requested to intervene in trade, namely, how to separate the ostensibly genuine motive from the more purely protectionist motive. It is also possible that forcing developing countries to adopt cost-raising labor standards may be harmful to their economic interests and could interfere with their efforts to pursue less interventionist and more export-oriented economic policies.[3,4]

5.2.3 International Monitoring and Enforcement of Labor Standards

As noted by Hanson (1983, pp. 11ff.), the call for international legislation dealing with labor standards dates from the first half of the 19th century in Europe.[5] These early movements were motivated in large measure by ethical considerations and were designed especially to improve working conditions in relation to hours of work, women's and children's labor, the use of hazardous materials, and so on. The links between labor standards and trade were recognized then and later. But, as Alam (1992, p. 13) points out, the early reformers generally took free trade as a given and desirable objective and sought to use moral suasion and international agreements to deal with differences in labor standards. Various international meetings were convened in the later part of the 19th century and in the first part of the 20th century to deal with international labor standards on ethical as well as competitiveness grounds. By and large, however, the results of these (and later) efforts could be characterized as "rather modest" on the whole (Charnovitz, 1987, p. 580).

Following World War I, as Part XIII of the Treaty of Versailles of 1919, the International Labor Organization (ILO) was founded. The methods and principles set out in the ILO construction deal with all conceivable aspects of labor standards, although no explicit trade sanctions are included. As stated in ILO (1988, p. 4), ILO action designed to promote and safeguard human rights takes three main forms: (1) definition of rights, especially through national adoption of ILO conventions and recommendations; (2) measures to secure the realization of rights, especially by means of international monitoring and supervision but not by imposition of trade sanctions; and (3) assistance to nations in implementing measures, particularly through technical cooperation and advisory services. Since World War II, the role and influence of the ILO regarding labor standards have been central to the declarations and efforts of the United Nations and associated regional organizations designed to protect and promote human rights.

As noted by Charnovitz (1987, pp. 566–567) and Alam (1992, p. 16), issues of alleged unfair competition involving labor standards were addressed in Article 7 of Chapter II of the 1948 (Havana) Charter of the (stillborn) International Trade Organization (ITO): "The members recognized that unfair labor conditions, particularly in the production for export, create difficulties in international trade, and accordingly, each member shall take whatever action may be appropriate and feasible to eliminate such conditions within its territory." Since the General Agreement of Tariffs and Trade (GATT) was conceived with a more narrow mandate in mind, it did not address issues or labor standards, except in Article XX(e), which provides for prohibition of goods made with prison labor.

Charnovitz (1987, p. 574) notes that as early as 1953 the United States proposed (unsuccessfully) adding a labor standards article to the GATT. The proposed standard, which was supported by organized labor, was very broad and would have empowered GATT members to take measures against other countries under GATT Article XXIII. The United Stats continued to push for negotiation of a GATT article on labor standards in both the Tokyo and Uruguay rounds of multilateral trade negotiations. While receiving some support from other GATT member countries, the U.S. efforts continued to be unsuccessful.[6] The issue of labor standards in the GATT is thus in a state of limbo. However, in its April 1994 statement at the Marrakesh signing of the Uruguay Round accords, the United States put the international community on notice that it intends to pursue issues of labor standards in future multilateral negotiations.

Issues of worker rights also have been given prominence in the European Community (EC) because of concern over low-wage competition from some EC member countries. It is interesting that many of the arguments that have been voiced in the United States about the potentially detrimental effects of imports from developing countries with lower labor standards have been made in the EC context as well. As De Boer and Winham (1993, p. 17) note, the issue of a Community-wide social charter was first broached in 1972. Subsequently, with the issuance in 1985 of the white paper intended to remove remaining barriers to trade and creation of a single market, the Community Charter of Fundamental Social Rights for Workers was drafted in 1988. This charter was adopted in 1989 on a voluntary basis by all EC members except the United Kingdom. It was hoped to incorporate the Social Charter into the Maastricht Treaty in December 1991, but this action was opposed once again by Britain. The Social Charter was subsequently approved by the other eleven EC members, but on a voluntary basis and not as part of the Maastricht Treaty.[7]

The issue of a social charter for North America was brought up in the context of NAFTA as a possible means of protecting the interests of workers.[8] It is interesting, accordingly, to consider what lessons, if any, the experience of the

EC has for NAFTA. The answer appears to be not much. First, the EC efforts to forge a social charter have to be regarded in the broad context of the integration process that is intended to harmonize social programs and policies in the EC member countries.[9] Second, while limited in amount, the EC provides financial transfers to the less advanced and lower-income regions and countries in the Community to assist with structural adjustment and development. Being a free trade agreement, the NAFTA does not contemplate an EC type of economic and eventual political union, and, at least for now, funds have not been set aside to deal with problems of low-wage workers. This is not to say of course that there is no scope for the harmonization of labor standards in the NAFTA. In this connection, Weintraub and Gilbreath (1993) favor a tiered agreement on issues of labor standards, with the timing of the implementation of particular standards geared to increases in Mexican real wages.[10] But there is a catch to all this, as Watson (1993) points out, since a North American social charter would affect Mexico asymmetrically and have detrimental effects by trying to force up Mexican real wages. It would also constitute perhaps an unwarranted intrusion into Mexican sovereignty. Watson's conclusion, therefore, is that it would be preferable to forgo completely a North American social charter, in the expectation that the NAFTA may increase Mexican real wages, and to provide technical and financial assistance to Mexico to help them raise and maintain their standards.[11]

We have provided a brief historical overview of efforts to deal with international labor standards on a global and regional basis, and we have made some reference to the unsuccessful U.S. efforts to include labor standards on the agenda of the GATT negotiations. This should not be taken to mean, however, that U.S. policy has remained otherwise silent on these issues. Rather, the opposite is the case as, in the last decade, the United States has introduced a number of unilateral policy measures dealing with labor standards, to which we now turn.

5.2.4 Labor Standards in U.S. Trade Policy and Law

The evolution of labor standards in U.S. trade policy and law is set forth in Table 1. The earliest prohibitions of imports were directed against imports made by prison and forced labor. A fair labor standards provision was included in the National Industrial Recovery Act (NIRA) of 1933, but the NIRA was subsequently judged by the Supreme Court to be unconstitutional. Beginning in the 1980s, it is evident that there have been a number of legislative actions establishing criteria for eligibility for trade preferences, as in the cases of the Caribbean Basin Economic Recovery Act (CBERA) of 1983 and the 1984 renewal of the Generalized System of Preferences (GSP). Adherence to worker rights was made a condition in a 1985 amendment covering the activities of the Overseas Private Investment Corporation. In 1986, U.S. firms in South Africa were required to adhere to fair labor standards, and similar conditions were attached to the 1987 U.S. participation in the Multilateral Investment Guarantee Agency of the World Bank.[12] Finally, the denial of worker rights was made actionable under Section 301 of the 1988 Omnibus Trade and Competitiveness Act. The 1988 Trade Act also expanded the requirements of the Departments of State and Labor to submit periodic reports to Congress on human rights abuses and foreign adherence to

TABLE 1 *Evolution of Labor Standards in U.S. Trade Policy Legislation*

Year	Act	Labor Standards Provisions
1890	McKinley Act	Prohibited imports made by convict labor.
1930	Tariff Act	Prohibited imports of goods made by convict labor, forced labor, or indentured labor under penal sanction.
1933	National Industrial Recovery Act (NIRA: judged unconstitutional by U.S. Supreme Court in 1935)	Imports permitted only if produced according to U.S. domestic fair labor standards, including the right to organize and bargain collectively, limits on maximum hours of work, and minimum wages.
1974	Trade Act	Directed the president to seek the adoption of fair labor standards in the Tokyo Round of GATT negotiations.
1983	Caribbean Basin Economic Recovery Act (CBERA)	Criteria for eligibility as a beneficiary country extended to include the degree to which workers are afforded reasonable workplace conditions and enjoy the right to organize and bargain collectively.
1984	Generalized System of Preferences (GSP) Renewal Act	Criteria for eligibility as a beneficiary country extended to include whether or not the country has taken, or is taking, steps to afford its workers internationally recognized worker rights defined as including freedom of association, the right to organize and bargain collectively, freedom from forced labor, minimum age for the employment of children, and acceptable conditions of work with respect to wages, hours of work, and occupational safety and health.
1985	Overseas Private Investment Corporation Amendments Act	The corporation is to insure, reinsure, guarantee, or finance a project in a country only if the country is taking steps to adopt and implement internationally recognized worker rights as defined for GSP purposes.
1986	Anti-Apartheid Act	Made it incumbent on U.S. firms employing more than 25 persons in South Africa to follow a code of conduct that includes fair labor standards.

Table 1 *continued*

Year	Act	Labor Standards Provisions
1987	U.S. participation in Multilateral Investment and Guarantee Agency of World Bank	Made U.S. participation conditional on countries affording internationally recognized worker rights to their workers.
1988	Trade Act (Omnibus Trade and Competitiveness Act)	Made the systematic denial of internationally recognized worker rights (as defined above) by foreign governments an unfair trade practice and liable for U.S. countermeasures where such denials cause a burden or restriction on U.S. commerce.

Source: Adapted from Alam (1992, p. 25).

internationally recognized worker rights. It is thus evident that labor standards have become explicitly linked with U.S. trade (and investment) policy in a number of different legislative measures in the past decade.

It is noteworthy that the CBERA and GSP stipulations on labor standards are linked with U.S. preferential trade concessions. In the case of the CBERA, the stipulations were made advisory, but they are mandatory for continued GSP eligibility. As Lyle (1991, p. 9) notes, official U.S. investigations of worker rights under the GSP are carried out by an interagency subcommittee of the Trade Policy Staff Committee, which includes members from the Office of the U.S. Trade Representative and several cabinet departments. Investigations of worker rights violations are initiated in response to petitions from interested parties, using information contained in the State Department's annual country reports on human rights, reports from U.S. embassies and consulates, ILO findings, and other pertinent information, including public hearings. Recommendations are made to the president, who has the final say in determining continued GSP eligibility. If GSP privileges are removed or suspended, a country must reapply to have the privileges reinstated.

In April 1991, GSP privileges were removed from Sudan, and in prior years similar actions were taken with respect to Burma, the Central African Republic, Chile, Liberia, Nicaragua, Paraguay, and Romania. The U.S. experience with GSP may thus provide some useful insights into the design and implementation of policies and procedures governing trade-linked labor standards in other contexts. Perhaps the most noteworthy features are that trade concessions can be withdrawn if investigation concludes that labor standards are not being upheld, and that evidence of a change in policies abroad is a condition for reinstatement of the concessions.[13]

Having set the context and discussed some of the possible consequences of intercountry differences in labor standards and experiences in the monitoring and enforcement of labor standards globally, regionally, and with reference especially to the United States, we turn now to our central task of the theoretical modeling and analysis of international labor standards.

5.3 INTERNATIONAL STANDARDS COORDINATION – A SIMPLE MODEL

In this section we use a partial equilibrium model to examine how standards in general may be set by countries acting individually and how these countries would be affected if instead they were to coordinate on a common standard. In a world with countries that are too small to affect their terms of trade, we will argue that if governments act in their independent national interests, then they will set possibly diverse standards that will be optimal from the point of view of the world.[14] However, it will be in the interests of particular groups of producers within these countries to press for higher standards abroad than would otherwise obtain. Also, it will be in the countries' national interests (including both producers and consumers) to press for either higher or lower standards for the world as a whole depending upon whether, as countries, they are net exporters or net importers of the good in question.

The theoretical modeling of labor standards in international trade is complicated by the fact that, in any country large enough for the world to care about it, standards that affect trade also affect the terms of trade. This statement is true not only of labor standards, but of other standards as well, and this problem is a common one for any analysis of policies and regulations that are intended to deal with externalities and other social concerns in a context of international trade. The effects of such policies on international prices are undoubtedly important, and we will explore them more fully and carefully in subsequent sections of this paper. However in almost all cases, these terms of trade effects are not the central concern of proponents of such policies, and to include them in the analysis inevitably intertwines the concerns of the policy advocates with the effects of trade in ways that cloud, rather than clarify, the issues.

Therefore, in this first theoretical section, we attempt to consider the general problem of international policy coordination in a way that will most clearly capture the concerns of the policy advocates, and thus in a way that abstracts from effects on the terms of trade. This task is not easy. For one country to have no effect on its terms of trade, it must be small. For a particular trading partner, whose policies the first country wishes to influence, also to have no effect on world prices requires that it too be small. But if that assumption is true, the first country will care about the second country's policy on only moral grounds.[15] We look here at a world of many countries, each one of which is assumed to be too small to affect world prices. Each country's interest is then in its own policy choice, plus the collective choices of the other countries. In this context, no country on economic grounds would care about the policy choices of other individual countries. They would, however, care about international agreements that might alter the policy choices of all other countries collectively.

In this context, as we will later explain more fully, we model a standard as a policy that raises the costs of firms while at the same time providing a benefit to

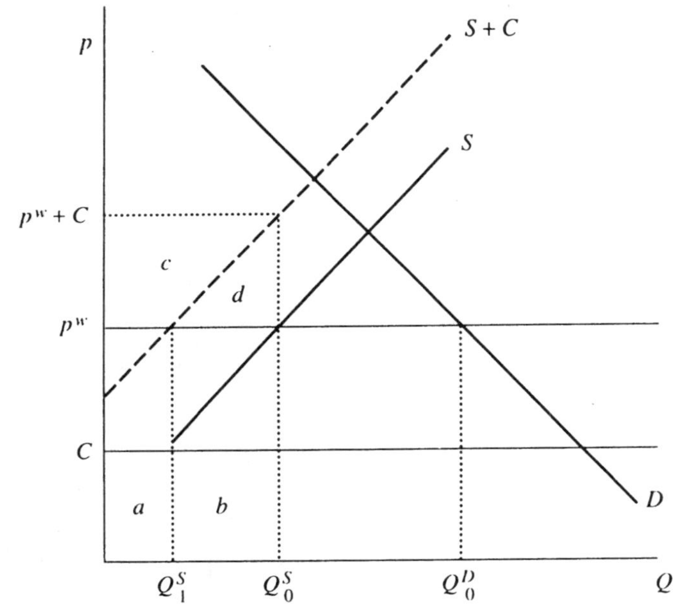

FIGURE 1 Partial Equilibrium Effects of a Standards Policy in a Small Country.

society as a whole. At the end of section 5.4 we will discuss the mechanisms by which the particular labor standards mentioned in section 5.2 do not fact raise costs.

Consider then a partial-equilibrium, perfectly competitive model of many small countries, each of which supplies and demands a good that is traded freely by all. World supply and demand are the sums of the individual-country supplies and demands, and these interact to determine a world price that is taken as given by all. The situation of a representative importing country is shown in Figure 1. The world price is p^w, the country's supply and demand curves in the absence of any policy are S and D, with D intersecting p^w to the right of S because we have selected a country that imports the good.

Suppose now that the behavior of suppliers in the absence of any policy is such as to impose an additional cost on society that is not captured in the supply curve. This could be an external diseconomy of the usual sort (such as pollution), or, to accord better with our topic of labor standards, it might be a measure of the societal opprobrium associated with, say, employing children. For this section of the paper at least, it does not matter what the source of the social cost is, merely that it exist and be somehow quantifiable.

To quantify the social cost in a relevant way, however, we must also consider what will be done about it. There is one cost that is appropriate if the suppliers are allowed to continue their behavior unchanged and nothing is done about it. There is a second that is appropriate if suppliers continue their behavior that the government devotes its own resources to undo the damage. And there is a third cost that is appropriate if the suppliers are required to discontinue the offending behavior, the cost of doing so then being borne by the suppliers themselves. Presumably an optimal policy will select whichever of these alternatives, or a combination of them, imposes the lowest cost on the country as a whole. It will also clearly require that the suppliers bear this cost at the margin, either by paying a production tax equal to it, or by directly changing their means of production, since otherwise their choice of output would be higher than optimal. To capture all this, then, we include in Figure 1 a curve representing this minimum social cost per unit of output C and assume that it represents both the cost of optimally solving this problem and an addition to the costs of suppliers when the solution is implemented.

We will speak, then, of a "standards policy" as one that adds this social cost C to the costs of private firms for all levels of output, and at the same time eliminates a cost to society at least equal to C. The supply curve in the presence of the standard is then $S + C$, the private supply curve S displaced between the social cost C.

The effects of the standard are easily seen from the figure. Because the country is small, the world price is unchanged, as is the domestic quantity demanded Q_0^D. Quantity supplied to the domestic market by domestic suppliers falls, however, from Q_0^S to Q_1^S, and the quantity of imports increases by this same amount.

As for welfare effects, demanders are of course unaffected, since they still buy the good at the unchanged world price. Suppliers bear the increased cost C of production due to the policy, and their welfare would have been unchanged if the price had risen to $p^w + C$. Since it did not, they lose producer surplus equal to area c in the figure. Society, on the other hand, gains at least the areas $a + b$, recalling that C represented the least-cost way of dealing with the social cost, and was therefore no larger than the cost itself in the absence of the standard. The country as a whole, therefore, gains at least the triangular area d, since by construction $c + d$ is equal to $a + b$.

All of this was done taking the world price as given, which the country, as a small open economy, was bound to do. No standard was imposed in the rest of the world, and as suppliers would surely remind us, the imposition of the standard has cost them dearly. However, there is no question that the standard was a desirable policy: the country gained more from its imposition than the suppliers lost, and assuming as usual that they could somehow be compensated if it were viewed as desirable to do so, the country's welfare has gone up. The absence of a standard abroad may have altered the size of the gain, as we will soon see, but it cannot have undermined it totally.

Nor is there a case here for interfering with trade. Suppliers, of course, would welcome a tariff equal to C along with the standard, so that the domestic price would rise exactly enough to offset all cost to them. But if this was done, we would have the usual deadweight losses associated with a tariff, and welfare would fall, not rise. Thus free trade remains here the optimal policy, even though the standard was not matched by standards abroad.

Suppose, however, that the standards *were* matched by standards abroad. That is, suppose that all other countries were in exactly the same situation as this one (except that some export rather than import the good), and that they too responded by setting the standard C. In that case, at the initial world price p^w, all suppliers would supply less and the world price would have to rise. To determine how much it would change, we would need to construct the relevant curves, but that is not necessary. Given the same standard in all countries, it is clear that the world price could not rise as high as $p^w + C$, since if it did, all supplies would remain at their initial level (see Figure 1), while all demands would fall. Therefore, we can be sure that a common standard of C set by all countries would lead to a rise in world price by something less than C. Exactly how much it would rise depends, as usual, on the various supply and demand elasticities, and need not concern us here.

Figure 2, then, shows the situation with such a common standard. The suppliers' cost still rises by C, but now the world price also rises by a fraction of that amount, and the suppliers' loss in producer surplus is confined to the smaller area c (which is smaller than c in Figure 1). Society still gains at least the area $a + b$ (which still sums to $a + b$ in Figure 1), but now demanders also lose from the rise in price. The loss in consumer surplus is area $e + f + g + h + i + j$, giving a net effect on the country as a whole of $+d - (h + i + j)$. As drawn, this change in country welfare is negative, and would be so for any country that imports a significant amount of the good in comparison to its domestic production. The reason is that consumers of the imported good do not share at all in the social benefit of the standards imposed abroad, but bear part of the cost due to the rise in world price.

This outcome would be reversed if the country were an exporter of the good. In that case (and also if the country were an importer but of only a small amount), as the reader can verify, the losses of both producer and consumer surplus are more than made up for by the gain from eliminating the social cost.

We set out in this section to abstract from effects on the terms of trade and to focus theoretical attention only on the sorts of effects that seem to be the concern of the advocates of labor standards. The small country assumption worked well for this purpose so long as we considered only standards in one country. But as we have just seen, once multilateral standards are considered, terms-of-trade effects inevitably play a role. It is quite possible for a country to lose from imposing a standard, even when that standard is optimally configured from the point of view of undoing or correcting a social cost, simply because of the country's position in the trade of the good involved. A country that imports a good on which a standard is imposed is likely to lose from the standard because of the rising cost to its consumers. A country that exports such a good, on the other hand, has a more than normal interest in obtaining multilateral standards.

This, especially for an importing country, is very much at variance with stated arguments of most advocates of standards, in the labor arena and elsewhere. The reason may be that these advocates often have a point of view that is narrower than that of the country as a whole, perhaps identifying only with producers. Or they may recognize the consumers' interests but reject them as being illegitimate, on the grounds that consumers were benefiting immorally from the low price permitted by the absence of a standard previously. Whatever may be the case, it is useful here to be able to separate the several welfare effects of a standard, and this our partial equilibrium model is nicely suited to do.

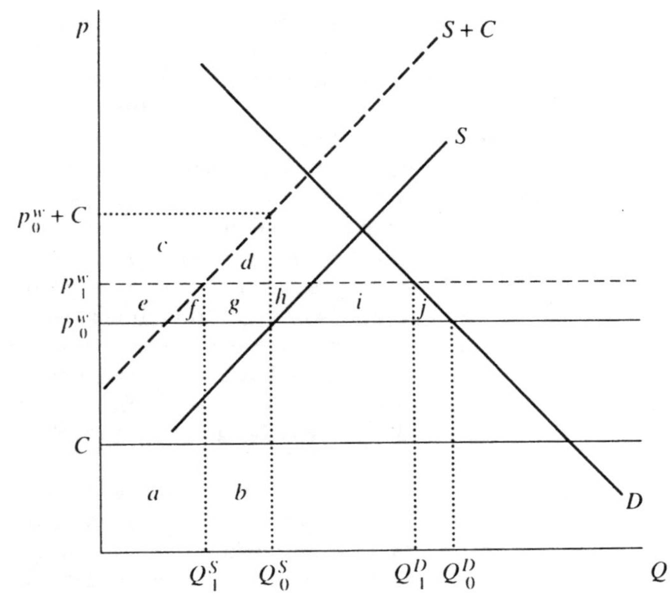

FIGURE 2 Partial Equilibrium Effects of a Common International Standard in a Small Country.

That is, in comparing Figures 1 and 2, one can easily see why countries are reluctant to impose standards unilaterally, even when those standards would raise welfare in the country overall. As long as the interest of the policy makers is to give greater weight to producer interests and to social costs than they do to consumer interests, then it is quite natural to press for multilateral standards. These will achieve greater reduction in social cost worldwide, and they will lessen (though not remove) the burden on producers.

So far we have assumed that multilateral standards are set all at the same level. If the problem at hand were a social cost that was the same, per unit of production, for all countries, then that would be a natural assumption. But in fact, we have already noted in passing, countries often disagree as to the level of cost associated with a particular market failure, sometimes for cultural reasons, sometimes because of differences in levels of development. Suppose then that the social costs C were to vary across countries.

Without a multilateral standard, countries would each have an incentive to impose standards at the level of their own social cost, as we saw in Figure 1, and this choice would indeed be optimal for the world as a whole. The collective effect of these diverse standards would be qualitatively the same as shown in Figure 2, except that there would be no assurance that the world price would rise by less than the size of a particular country's standard. High-standard countries would find the world price rising by substantially less than their own standard, and thus have their producers bear a larger proportion of the cost. Low-standard countries would, in contrast, experience price increases that would be larger in comparison to their own standards and that might even be larger absolutely than the standards themselves. In that case, their producers would gain, not lose, from the multilateral standards.

It is this possibility, presumably, that motivates demands that the standards of different countries be "harmonized," which in this case may be taken to mean set at the same level. As this model makes clear, however, there is nothing in the economics of the situation that calls for such harmonization. On the contrary, world efficiency is best served by letting each country set its standard in accordance with its own needs and perceptions of cost. To do otherwise – to require that all countries impose the same standards – will mean that some countries impose higher standards than the corresponding social costs or that others will impose lower standards than social cost. Either way, outputs will then be set inappropriately low or high, as the case may be, and welfare will not be maximized.

To conclude this section, let us return one final time to the terms-of-trade effects that we tried so hard to exclude. Suppose now that some countries are not in fact small, but instead that they can influence the terms of trade through their policies. How they will behave will of course depend on the direction of their trade in the product in question. Any standard they set, regardless of their pattern of trade, will cause the output of their own producers to fall and will then lead to a rise in the world price. If they import the good, as does the country in Figure 1, and if they attempt to maximize their entire country's welfare, then this worsening of the terms of trade will lead them to cut back on the policy, setting a standard that is lower than the social cost. Exporters, in contrast, recognizing that their standards not only correct the social cost but also improve their terms of trade, will set their standards higher than social cost.

This is exactly the kind of outcome that we sought to avoid in this section, for it means that standards are being used for purposes that have nothing to do with the problems they are ostensibly intended to solve. But the result does have an interesting and perhaps rather surprising implication. Exporting countries are presumably those with lower cost, as a result, one hopes, of comparative advantage. Since, as we have just seen, it is exporters who have the incentive to set standards too high, and importers who have the incentive to set standards too low, it follows that standards will be used to bring costs closer together across countries.

Throughout this discussion, we have confined our attention to a single industry in partial equilibrium. This approach is appropriate for problems that in fact arise in only one or a small number of industries, as long as those industries are small relative to other markets in the economy. For some kinds of standards, that may well be the case. But for labor standards, which are likely to apply across the board to all industries, it certainly is not. We used partial equilibrium here, as we said, in an effort to abstract from terms-of-trade effects, and to decompose the effects of standards into those on producers and consumers. But it is time to leave this framework and turn instead to models of general equilibrium. We begin this task in the next section.

5.3.1 Summary

Let us sum up what this partial equilibrium analysis has told us. We have modeled a standard as policy that imposes additional cost on domestic firms, the purpose being to correct an externality of some sort that imposes a cost on society that would not otherwise be borne by the firm. The first result is that, if countries are too small to affect their terms of trade and if the social cost of the externality is borne only by the country where the firm is located, then domestic policies that internalize the externality are welfare improving from the points of view of both the individual country and the world as a whole. This is the case whether or not the partner country also imposes a standard. Furthermore, trade sanctions that punish trade partners for failing to do so are not beneficial.

Pressure for international standards may nevertheless emerge, in part since separate interests within each country desire different outcomes. For obvious reasons, producers that are subject to these standards would prefer not to be. At the same time, producers would also prefer that higher standards be set abroad, since these will raise world prices to their own benefit. Therefore, for example, if optimal standards are diverse across countries, producers in the high-standard countries will press for adoption of a common standard worldwide, even though that would not be socially optimal.

National interests also diverge from the optimum when it comes to finding international agreement on the level of standards to set. Since national welfare (including both producers and consumers) rises with the world price of a net export and falls with the world price of a net import, and since standards tend to raise world prices, net exporters will press for higher-than-optimal international standards while net importers will press for lower-than-optimal ones. This observation is true even though individually, as small countries, the standards they would set for themselves would be optimal.

Finally, allowing countries to be large enough to influence world prices by their own actions, these incentives to distort standards for terms-of-trade purposes also extend to the setting of their own standards. Net exporters, for example, will set standards higher than optimal, since high standards will secure the additional benefit of a higher world price and improved terms of trade.

5.4 EFFECTS OF IMPOSED LABOR STANDARDS ON TRADE AND THE TERMS OF TRADE

In this section we examine how standards alter welfare in a large country, and how this effect depends on the resources that are used by the standard itself.[16] Depending on the particular model that applies, we find that countries now have an incentive to set standards either too high or too low, and that there is a clear case for some form of coordination, if not full harmonization, to achieve the world optimum. In one case, where countries specialize completely in different traded goods, each country's standard will act like any restriction and thus improve its terms of trade. Such countries will set standards too high, will prefer that other countries set no standards at all, and will need to coordinate to reduce the level of standards that would be arrived at independently. In a second case, where countries produce the same tradable goods but in different proportions, the effect of a labor standard depends on the resources that it withdraws from world production of tradable goods. If the standard, say, uses primarily labor, then it will make labor more scarce, raise the world prices of both labor and labor-intensive goods, and improve the terms of trade of labor-abundant countries. Because countries now experience the same price changes from labor standards but differ in the welfare implications of these price changes, standards will now be set too high in some countries and too low in others, making it desirable for both that the world harmonize on a level of standards somewhere in between.

In contrast to the previous section, where we tried to abstract from terms of trade effects, we begin our general equilibrium analysis by examining effects that a country's labor standards may have precisely on its trade and terms of trade. For this purpose we initially ignore whatever distortions may exist in the economy that provide the reason for the labor standards, and assume instead that they are simply imposed exogenously. This assumption does not mean that the standards are without purpose, but it does mean that their purpose is not to offset or correct a distortion in the economy that would in turn have its own effects on production and trade, and that might change with the imposition of the standard. We will consider such distortion-correcting labor standards in section 5.5.

For now, consider a generic labor standard Z that may be imposed at some level in a country and that uses resources that would otherwise be used for production. We will consider several different models of trade and of the interaction between the labor standards, production, and trade, in order to determine how the standard will alter the country's output and trade, its potential to gain from trade, and the terms of trade between it and the rest of the world. We will also consider the issue of harmonization of labor standards in these models, asking how a country's welfare will be affected by standards abroad, and how these standards, if set optimally, will interact with one another.

Once again the standard is modeled simply as a policy that raises cost of production, now being explicit about which resources are used up in this process. At the end of the section we will discuss how the particular labor standards described in section 5.2 relate to this theoretical formulation.

5.4.1 Model 1: Labor Standards in a Specialized Economy

We consider first a country that is specialized in the production of a single tradable good X, which it exports in exchange for a second tradable good that it does not produce, Y. The potential imposition of a labor standard takes the form of producing a nontraded good Z at some level, and this production withdraws resources from the production of tradable X. It is not necessary, in this model, to be specific about what these resources are. Instead we merely assume a production possibility frontier (PPF) between X and Z that summarizes the trade-off.

Consider Figure 3. In the top quadrant appear a family of indifference curves, indicating the welfare that the country derives from consumption of the two

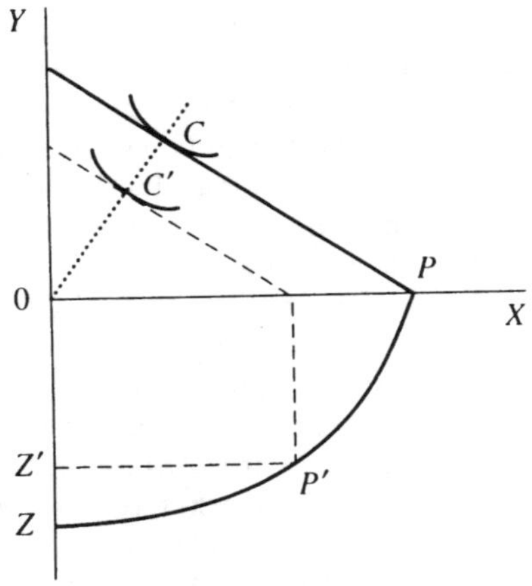

FIGURE 3 General Equilibrium Effects of a Standards Policy in a Specialized Economy.

traded goods *X* and *Y*. The downward-sloping straight lines also indicate, for some particular world prices, the rate of exchange between the two goods.

The bottom quadrant shows the PPF between *X* and Z. Initially, without any labor standard, Z is set at zero and production is at point *P*. A portion of the output of *X* is exported in exchange for *Y*, and the country consumes at point C.

When a labor standard is imposed at some level Z', production moves to point P', less *X* is produced, and less is also exported in exchange for *Y*. As long as both tradable goods are normal goods, consumption of both will fall, to point C', as will the quantities of trade. Assuming for simplicity that preferences are homothetic, consumption and trade all decline by the same percentage, equal to the fall in the output of *X*.

Clearly the country loses welfare in terms of what it derives from consuming the traded goods. That result does not mean that the standard was ill-advised, however, since we have not specified its purpose. If we assume that there is a benefit to be obtained from the standard – one that is separable from the benefits of consuming *X* and *Y* and that does not alter the economics of the *X* and *Y* industries – then presumably the standard could be set optimally, balancing the marginal benefit from the standard against the marginal cost in consumption.

If the country were small, this would be the end of the story, since the reduced trade would have no effect on equilibrium world prices, or on anything else of concern to the foreign economy. If the country were small, however, its labor standards would not be an international issue. We therefore assume for the rest of this section that the countries we consider are large enough to influence their terms of trade.

The direction of the effect is obvious. Since at initial prices the country both exports less of *X* and imports less of *Y*, the world price of good *X* will rise relative to *Y*. That is, the country's terms of trade will improve. This is a benefit to the country imposing the standard, and a cost to its trading partner.

Now, consider the issue of harmonization. At one level the question is simply whether a country will benefit more by imposing a labor standard unilaterally, or would instead do better getting its trading partner to impose the same standard. To answer that question, we need first to know how a standard imposed by the other country will affect welfare at home. In this model the answer is clear: since the other country is specialized in good Y and will withdraw resources from its production if it imposes a standard, the foreign labor standard has an effect on world prices that is opposite to that of a domestic standard. If we use a standard, it improves our terms of trade; if they use one, it improves theirs but worsens ours. Thus each country would prefer to go it alone.

At a slightly deeper level we can assume that each country's labor standard will be set optimally, given the standard of the other, and we can ask how the standards will differ depending on whether they are set noncooperatively or cooperatively (harmonization). In this mode, because each country's standard imposes a negative external effect on the other by altering the terms of trade, each will have an incentive to set too high a level of the standard. If countries can cooperate, they will need to harmonize their labor standards to *lower* levels than they would set unilaterally.[17]

This result, which is quite different from the kind of harmonization that one sees called for by labor activists, arises because the effect of the labor standard that is driving the result is quite different from what labor activists are likely to have in mind. In section 5.5 we will try to consider alternative models that are closer in spirit to the views of labor. Nonetheless, the possible terms-of-trade effect of a labor standard is certainly a valid one, and also a potentially important one that can arise in general equilibrium. It should be taken into account in any complete analysis of international labor standards.

The terms-of-trade effect will not, however, always work in this direction. This first model with complete specialization is quite special in that regard, as we will now see.

5.4.2 Model 2: A Heckscher-Ohlin Model with Economy-Wide Labor Standards

Suppose now that the countries produce both of the traded goods, using two factors of production and identical, constant-returns-to-scale production functions in the manner of the Heckscher-Ohlin trade model. For this model, assume that labor standards are again imposed separately from production of the tradable goods, so that they simply withdraw a portion of the factors that would have been available for production of tradable goods. How a standard affects output and trade now depends on the factor intensity of the standard itself – that is, the ratio of the factors withdrawn from tradable production as a result of the standard – in comparison to the factor intensities of the tradable goods.[18]

Consider Figure 4a. The outer PPF between tradable goods X and Y shows the maximum outputs of the two goods if all of the home country's (A's) resources are devoted to their production. We assume that good X is labor intensive and that the home country is labor abundant, so that in free trade equilibrium it produces at P, consumes at C, and exports good X to the world market.

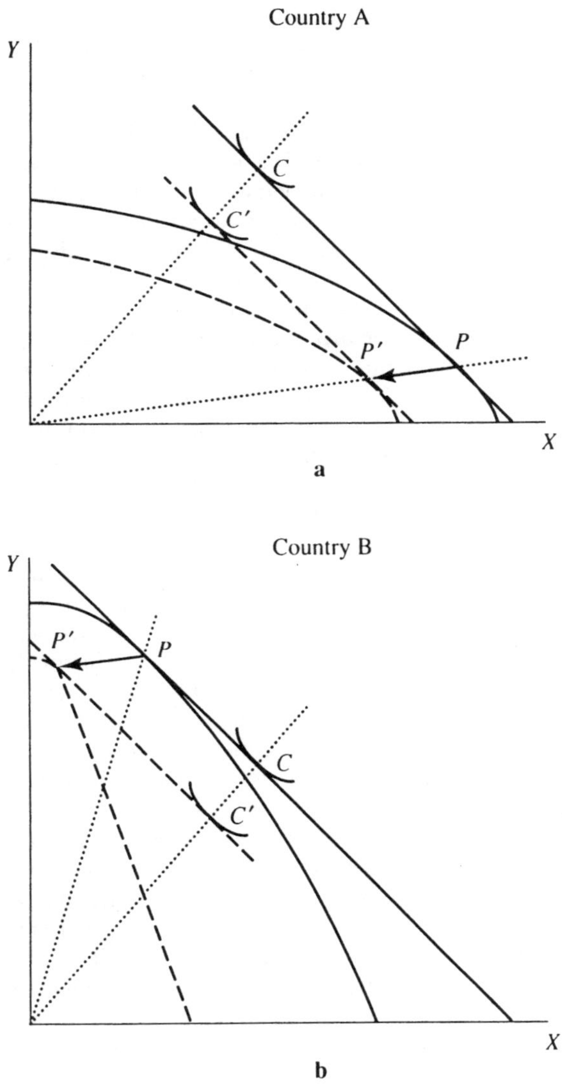

FIGURE 4 General Equilibrium Effects of Economy-Wide Labor Standards in a Heckscher-Ohlin Model.

If a labor standard is now imposed, this will use up some of the labor and capital that underlie the outer PPF, and will therefore shift it inward. The direction of the shift depends on the factors used by the standard. A especially simple but special case is shown in the figure, where the PPF is shifted proportionally inward by the standard. This would happen if the standard withdrew the two factors in the same proportions as they exist in the endowment of country A.

In this special case, we find once again that the standard will unambiguously, at initial prices, cause a fall in the country's trade. This in turn will cause its terms of trade to improve when we allow for equilibrium on the world market.

However, the similarity with Model 1 ends here. It is not the case that the same labor standard imposed in the other country will improve *its* terms of trade. As shown in Figure 4b, the foreign PPF shifts inward, not proportionally, but rather in the same direction as that of country A, assuming that the labor standard there requires the factors in the same proportion as in the home country. But since the foreign country produces the goods in quite different proportions, because of its greater abundance of capital, this is a shift that is very much biased toward continuing to produce its export good.

In fact, since the ratio of the drops in output of the two goods is the same as the ratio of production in the home country, and since this is less than the common ratio of consumption in both, it must be the case that the foreign country's production of good X falls by more than its consumption, and it actually increases its demand for good X from the world market. Hence, a labor standard that matches in its factor requirements the factor endowments of the home country will necessarily improve the home country's terms of trade regardless of which country implements it.

More generally, what matters in this model for the effect of a labor standard on the world market and the terms of trade is how the factor requirements of the standard compare to the factor requirements of *world* production. If a standard uses, say a higher ratio of labor to capital than is available in the world market, then it will withdraw from tradable-goods production – in either country where it is implemented – amounts of factors that will reduce the country's output of the labor-intensive good relative to its consumption of that good. As a result, such a labor standard will raise the world relative price of the labor-intensive good, regardless of who exports it.

Thus the only completely neutral standard will be one that uses factors in the same proportion as world endowments. Any other labor standard will tilt the world prices in favor of one country or the other. Considering the harmonization issue, this finding means that a labor-abundant country will get an extra terms-of-trade benefit from a labor-intensive standard, and will tend to overprovide it, while a capital-abundant country will experience a loss and will tend to underprovide it. Harmonization in favor of a more uniform standard will therefore be desirable from the world-efficiency perspective.

5.4.3 Model 3: A Heckscher-Ohlin Model with a Standard that Raises Production Cost

In our analysis up to now, labor standards were assumed simply to divert resources from the country as a whole. Here we allow for the standard to be implemented within an industry in a manner that raises the industry's cost. For simplicity we allow for the standard in only one of the two industries of a Heckscher-Ohlin model.

Figure 5a shows the PPF for a home country exporting the labor-intensive good X prior to imposition of a labor standard. The effect of a labor standard will be to increase the factor requirements of production in X, and therefore to shift the PPF inward. The exact nature of that shift, however, depends on how factor requirements in the industry are changed by the labor standard.

A simple possibility is shown in Figure 5: the standard is Hicks neutral in the sense that it raises the required amounts of both factors in the same proportion and therefore leaves the shapes of all X isoquants unchanged. Were one to draw the Edgeworth production box for this situation, the standard would leave the efficiency locus unchanged in appearance, with only the levels of X output along it reduced by the percentage of the increased cost. Thus the PPF is shifted proportionally to the left in Figure 5a, with the level of output of X that corresponds to each level of Y being cut by a fraction.

It follows immediately that, once again, at given prices of the goods the country will trade less. This result in turn will cause an improvement in its terms of trade to clear the world market.

At the same time, in Figure 5b, the same shift in the PPF of the partner country causes it to trade more, and this outcome also will lead to a further improvement of the home country's terms of trade. As in the case of economy-wide labor standards in Model 2, it is the standard itself that favors one country or the other, and not the identity of the country that implements it.

Figure 5 shows only one very special case. A labor standard in an industry could just as easily increase the industry's factor requirements in ways that are biased toward one factor or the other, and this bias would change the way that the PPF shifts because of the standard.[19] We will not go through any more of these cases here, but will merely note that the result just found, of a standard that raises the world price of the industry where it is imposed, is in some sense the normal outcome but is not inevitable. On can construct a case in which a standard imposed on an industry actually leads the relative output of that industry to expand and drives down its price. That, however, is a rather skewed and unusual outcome.

5.4.4 Factor Requirements of Labor Standards

Having identified the importance of the "factor requirements" of labor standards for their effects on trade, let us pause a moment and relate our discussion to our earlier list of labor standards noted in the Appendix. In what sense can actual labor standards be accurately modeled as diverting factors from other uses, and which factors do they divert?

Freedom of Association and Right to Organize: These two standards do not, in any obviously important way, divert resources. Presumably a small amount of labor is needed to administer a labor union, for example, but this must be a negligible aspect of a union's economic effects.

Freedom from Forced Labor: If an economy is making use of forced labor, the question here must be whether that labor would continue to be available if it were not forced to work, presumably at a higher wage. If at least some of the forced workers would choose not to work, or not to work as much, then this

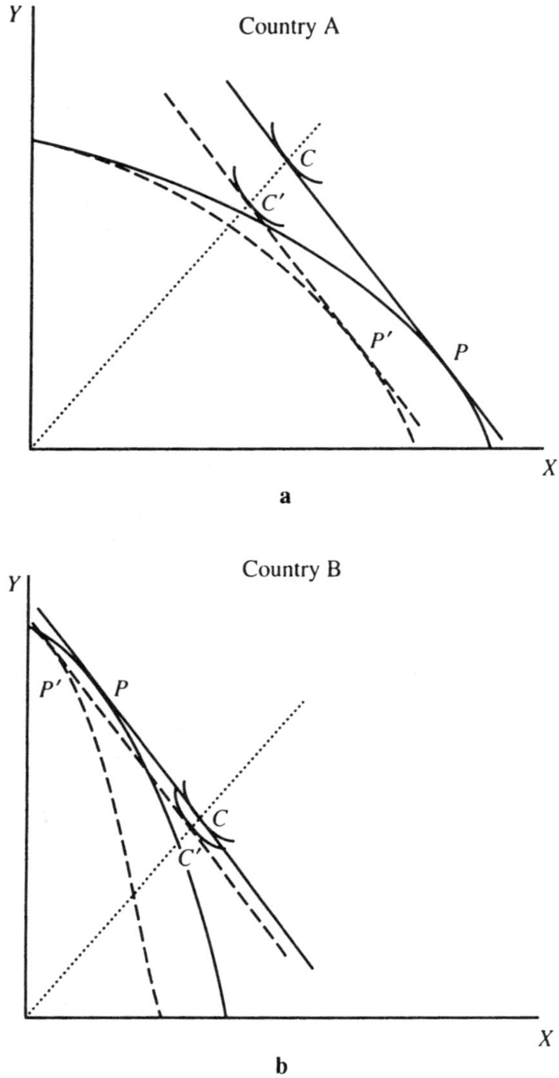

FIGURE 5 General Equilibrium Effects of an Industry Labor Standard in a Heckscher-Ohlin Model.

standard will reduce the supply of labor to the economy. It is a purely labor-using standard.

Minimum Age for Employment: A standard that prohibits children from working simply removes them from the labor force. It too is a purely labor-using standard.

Minimum Wage: A minimum wage does not obviously alter the quantity of factors available, but only, supposedly, their price. However, if one believes that labor markets function well, then an effective minimum wage will price out of the market some marginal workers, and the labor force will be reduced. In this sense, a minimum wage is, again, a labor-using standard.

Hours of Work: An upper limit on hours of work, if it is effective (and not merely circumvented by workers taking second jobs), is a straightforward reduction in the labor force. It too, then, is labor using.

Occupational Safety and Health: OSH regulations are therefore the only standard we consider that may not be purely labor using. These regulations may well require investments in capital (safer machines) or land (to reduce overcrowding) in order to be implemented. Depending on the nature of the particular regulation, therefore, and the technologies available for satisfying it, OSH regulations could easily be less labor intensive than world production as a whole.

In summary, with the exception of OSH regulations, most labor standards appear to be primarily labor using. That is, they remove a portion of a country's labor force that would otherwise be available. Such standards will tend to make labor more scarce in the countries where they are implemented. This scarcity will in turn increase the world prices of labor-intensive goods, improving the terms of trade of those countries that export labor-intensive goods and worsening the terms of trade of others. Thus it would appear that the general economic interests of advanced countries, whose comparative advantage presumably is based on factors other than labor, would favor limiting the spread of these standards rather than imposing them on the less-developed world. Similar conclusions or the opposite, however, could apply to OSH regulations, depending on the factors required for their implementation.

All this, however, neglects the role of any distortions that may exist and provide the basis for having labor standards in the first place. We now turn to the modeling of such distortions and their interaction with standards and trade.

5.5 ENDOGENOUS WORKING CONDITIONS AND LABOR STANDARDS

In the preceding sections we have analyzed two aspects of labor standards in international trade (1) correcting market failure due to the presence of an externality in an international trade environment, and (2) the resource costs of labor standards and their implications for the terms of trade. In the first of these cases, where we dealt with market failures, we did not identify the source of the market failure, but we did make the assumption that the government had the ability to correct the externality.

However, much of the labor literature on occupational safety and health is devoted to analyzing specific sources of market failure and the tools used by governments to address these problems.[20] Generally, it is found that establishing minimum labor standards rarely corrects, or even partly corrects, labor-market failure associated with worker safety.

In this section, we analyze legally mandated minimum safety standards using a model in which occupational safety and health are endogenously determined. First, we consider a setting in which the market is able to provide the socially optimal level of worker safety. In this case, government intervention in the form of a minimum safety requirement naturally reduces social welfare, both nationally and from a world point of view.

We then turn to evaluate a market that is not able to provide the socially optimal level of worker safety because of heterogeneity of worker preferences over working conditions and wages. The existence of a market failure raises the possibility that the government might usefully intervene. However, in the case analyzed here, we find that government-mandated working conditions will not restore Pareto optimality.

Our conclusions concerning international bargaining over labor standards depend, as in section 5.3, on whether the minimum safety requirement is imposed on the export industry or on the import-competing industry. The implications for working conditions are more surprising. A minimum safety standard always improves working conditions in the industry in which it is imposed. In addition, as long as the labor standard is applied in the capital-intensive sector, then wages and working conditions improve in all sectors of the economy. This is the case in both regulated and unregulated industries. However, if the standard is imposed in the labor-intensive sector, then workers in all sectors of the economy are made worse off. Money wages decline in all industries. Safety rises in the regulated sector, but not by enough to compensate for the fall in wages. Finally, both wages and safety actually decline in the unregulated sector.

5.5.1 Endogenous Safety without Market Failure

Generally, if labor markets are perfectly competitive and sufficiently deep, then firms and workers will choose the Pareto optimal level of safety in each plant. In this case, government intervention that establishes a minimum safety level is, of course, not defensible on efficiency grounds. Nevertheless, governments occasionally attempt to raise standards despite the absence of an identifiable market failure. Therefore, it is useful to analyze the implications of minimum standards for wages, working conditions, and international trade when labor markets are functioning efficiently.

The sufficient conditions for Pareto optimality when the safety level is endogenous are well established (see Dickens, 1984):

1. All markets are perfectly competitive.
2. Firms set safety and wage levels to maximize profits.
3. There is a large enough number of workers and firms such that for the safety level chosen by the firm there exists some wage at which the firm can hire any amount of labor it wants but can hire no labor at a lower wage.
4. Workers and firms have perfect knowledge of wage and safety levels at all other firms.
5. There are no external economies.

Obviously, Pareto optimality can fail for several reasons. One case will be discussed in this section. However, consider, first, safety setting in an economy that satisfies the efficiency conditions listed.

Suppose, as in section 5.4, that there are two goods: X the labor-intensive export good and Y the capital-intensive import-competing good. Labor and capital are taken to be freely mobile between sectors and traded in perfectly competitive markets.

For present purposes we will take technology to be Cobb-Douglas, so that

$$X = K_x^{\alpha} L_x^{(1-\alpha)} \quad (1)$$
$$Y = K_y^{\beta} L_y^{(1-\beta)}$$

where $\beta > \alpha$

There is some danger to workers producing both X and Y, but each firm can improve working conditions if it chooses to do so. We assume that safety is produced using the same technology required to produce a unit of X. Further, the X sector is taken to be inherently more dangerous than the Y sector, so that it takes $g_x > 1$ times as much expenditure per worker in the X sector to achieve a particular level of safety compared to what would be required for the same level of safety per worker in the Y sector. Finally, all workers are assumed to have identical preferences over safety and money wages.

There are three basic conditions that characterize firm behavior in the labor market. First, for each firm in sectors X and Y, the cost of providing the worker with a wage-safety combination must equal the worker's marginal value product. That is

$$p_x MP_L^x = p_s g_x + w_x \quad (2)$$
$$p_y MP_L^y = p_s + w_y \quad (3)$$

where p_i and w_i, i = x, y, are goods prices and wages in sector i, and p_s is the price of a unit of safety in sector y. Second, workers must be indifferent between the X-sector and Y-sector wage-safety combinations. This indifference implies that

$$U(s_x, w_x) = U(s_y, w_y) \quad (4)$$

Third, cost-minimization requires that each firm choose a wage-safety combination so that the worker's marginal rate of substitution between safety and wages equals the ratio of the wage to the price of safety. That is,

$$MRS_{s,w}(s_x, w_x) = \frac{w_x}{g_x p_s} \quad (5)$$

$$MRS_{s,w}(s_y, w_y) = \frac{w_y}{p_s} \quad (6)$$

These labor-market conditions are depicted in Figure 6. For each industry, the worker's indifference curve is tangent to the line that depicts all combinations of safety and money wages that cost the firm the worker's marginal value product. In addition, the level of utility achieved by a worker in sector X is the same as that in sector Y.

Two points are worth noting about this equilibrium. First, the marginal-value product of labor in the X sector is higher than in the Y sector. This relationship can be seen by comparing the wage-intercept of the X-iso-labor-cost line to that of the Y-iso-labor-cost line in Figure 6. The economic intuition is straightforward. Since safety in the X sector is more expensive than in the Y sector, it costs an X firm more money to provide a particular real income to one of its workers than for a firm in the Y sector. Hence, an X-sector worker must have a higher marginal value product than a Y-sector worker.

Second, suppose that we hold the world prices constant while increasing the capital intensity of production in both sectors. Then the marginal value product of labor must rise at a slower rate in the X sector than in the Y sector.

To see this point, recall that equilibrium in the capital market requires that

$$p_x, MP_K^x = p_y MP_K^y \tag{7}$$

or at constant world prices

$$\hat{MP}_K^x = \hat{MP}_K^y \tag{8}$$

where the circumflex indicates percent change. For the purposes of the assumed technology, this condition can be written as

$$\hat{MP}_K^x = -(1-\alpha)\hat{k}_x = -(1-\beta)\hat{k}_y = \hat{MP}_K^y \tag{9}$$

where k_x and k_y are the capital-labor ratios in the X and Y sectors, respectively.

The implication for the labor market, however, is that, since $\alpha < \beta$

$$\hat{MP}_L^x = \alpha\hat{k}_x = \frac{\alpha(1-\beta)}{1-\alpha}\hat{k}_y < \beta\hat{k}_y = \hat{MP}_L^y \tag{10}$$

for $\hat{k}_x, \hat{k}_y > 0$. That is, there is a magnification effect on the marginal value product of labor in the Y sector.

Now, let the government impose a minimum safety standard in sector X that exceeds the equilibrium level in Figure 6, holding world prices fixed. In the new equilibrium, Y-sector firms are not constrained by the minimum standard, so that the worker's safety-wage indifference curve must still be tangent to the Y firm's labor isocost curve. However, X-sector firms are not so characterized. For these firms it is merely necessary that the worker's indifference curve pass through (or touch) the X firm's labor isocost curve at the minimum safety level. Tangency is not required, since competing firms are legally prohibited from reducing cost by trading off worker safety for higher wages.

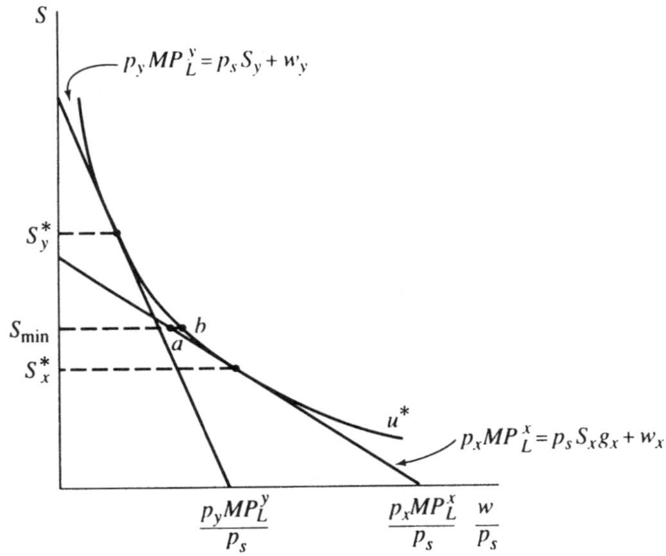

FIGURE 6 The Trade-off between Wages and Safety for Firms and Workers in Two Sectors.

These conditions are clearly not satisfied at the minimum safety level in Figure 6. If the firm pays the safety-wage combination at *b*, it can hold on to its workers, but it is then paying those workers more than their marginal value product. On the other hand, if the firm pays the safety-wage combination at a, then it will lose all of its workers to the *Y* sector.

The government might expect that the new standard will cause the real wage to rise. However, this is not the case. In order to satisfy the labor-market-clearing conditions, raising the real wage requires that we expand the labor-intensive sector *X*. All firms would become more capital intensive so that the marginal value product of labor would rise and the two labor isocost lines in Figure 6 would begin to shift out. However, as noted previously, the *X*-sector isocost will shift out proportionately less than the *Y*-sector isocost. Therefore, it will be impossible to find a pair of isocost curves that satisfies the equilibrium conditions as characterized earlier.

Contracting the labor-intensive *X* sector has the opposite effect. As capital intensity falls, the marginal product of labor in the *X* sector falls more slowly than in the *Y* sector. The isocost curves shift left, rendering a new equilibrium as depicted in Figure 7.

Clearly, the safety in the *X* sector has risen. We can see, though, that as long as safety is a normal good, safety in the *Y* sector has fallen, since real income of workers declined.

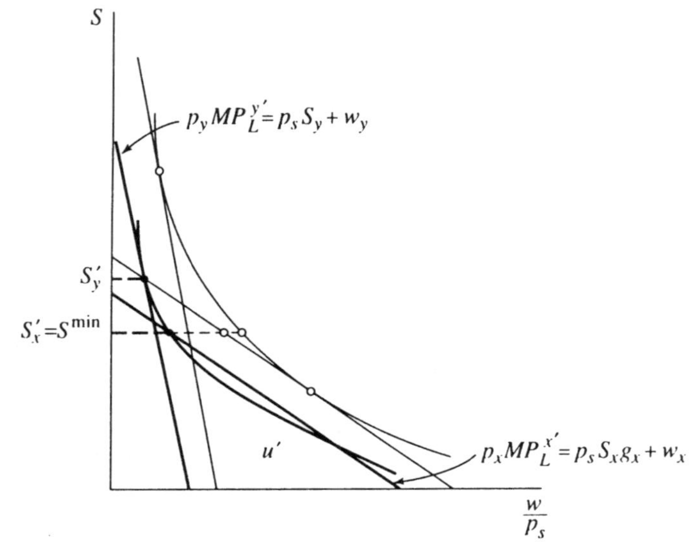

FIGURE 7 Effects of a Minimum Safety Requirement.

Now consider the consequences for international trade. We can see that X production has fallen. Since X is the export good, it is likely that the terms of trade will improve with the standard. A similar standard in the partner country will also contract X supply onto the world market, further improving the home country's terms of trade. Therefore, the home country might seek an international standard if its objective is to improve its terms of trade or, more likely, if the home country is concerned with the level of employment in the X sector.

It is interesting to consider reversing the factor intensity ranking, letting X be the capital-intensive sector. In this case, increasing capital intensity in both sectors will cause the iso-labor-cost curve in the X sector to shift out faster than the Y sector. A minimum labor standard that affects only industry X, then, would require a contraction of the X sector, thereby raising the real wage, increasing the capital intensity of production, and shifting the iso-labor-cost curve in the X sector out faster than in the Y sector.

Unlike the previous case in which the X sector is labor intensive, the standard *raises* the real wage. In addition, the safety level rises in *both* sectors even though the standard binds only on the X sector. Nevertheless, if world prices are variable, the terms of trade would still improve with the standard as long as it is imposed in the export sector. Thus an international standard would be desirable from the point of view of the home country. Conversely, a country's interest in harmonization on terms-of-trade grounds would be reversed if the standard were applied to the import-competing sector.

Our analysis of models with endogenous safety comports well with the model discussed in section 5.4. As before, the trade status (export or import) of the industry in which government intervention occurs determines the terms-of-trade effects associated with the standard. In addition, the terms of trade improve for the exporter of the relevant good no matter which country imposes the standard.

The two classes of models differ, though, in their predictions concerning worker safety. In the previous section we assumed that the standard would improve working conditions. By contrast, in models with endogenous safety, if a standard is imposed in the labor-intensive sector, then real wages fall economy-wide and the level of safety actually falls in the capital-intensive sector. We can be guaranteed that working conditions improve for all workers only if the minimum standard is imposed in the capital-intensive sector.

5.5.2 Endogenous Working Conditions and Market Failure

We turn now to consider a case in which the market does not give rise to efficient working conditions. One labor-market failure can come about even in a perfectly competitive environment if worker attitudes toward risk are highly heterogenous and nonuniformly distributed across the labor force. In this case, we find that if attitudes toward risk are normally distributed across workers, then safe plants that hire safety-conscious workers may not be safe enough. That is, workers preferring a safer plant but lower wages could compensate their co-workers preferring higher wages in a less safe plant. By contrast, the more dangerous plants may be too safe given the distribution of non-safety-conscious workers employed.

For the purposes of this model we will retain the assumption that the X sector is the labor-intensive export sector and Y is the capital-intensive import-competing sector. Worker attitude toward safety, however, will be handled somewhat differently.

We will make two assumptions concerning worker preferences: (1) no two workers have the same set of preferences over safety and money wages; and (2) near the mean of the distribution of preferences over safety and money wages, workers are more similar to each other than in the tails. We impose one final condition: there is a floor below which labor employment in a particular firm cannot fall. As we will see, without this condition, each plant would employ only one worker.

To get a sense of this model, consider the wage-safety trade-off for two industries, X and Y, with X as before requiring greater expenditure to achieve a given level of safety. Each firm must choose a safety-wage combination along its industry isocost line. Now, however, the available workers have varying preferences for safety and wage income. Rather than having to offer a safety-wage package that all workers will regard as equivalent to what is available elsewhere, each firm can target a group of workers and tailor its safety-wage package to the members of that group. Equilibrium requires that each employee like the compensation package at least as much as others available, and thus that the marginal employee be indifferent between his or her employer's package and those packages that are most similar offered by other firms. The heterogenous preferences are shown in Figure 8 by several indifference curves, each for a different worker.

Recall that there is a minimum number of workers required for each firm. In the case shown, that number of workers supports three firms, numbered 1, 2,

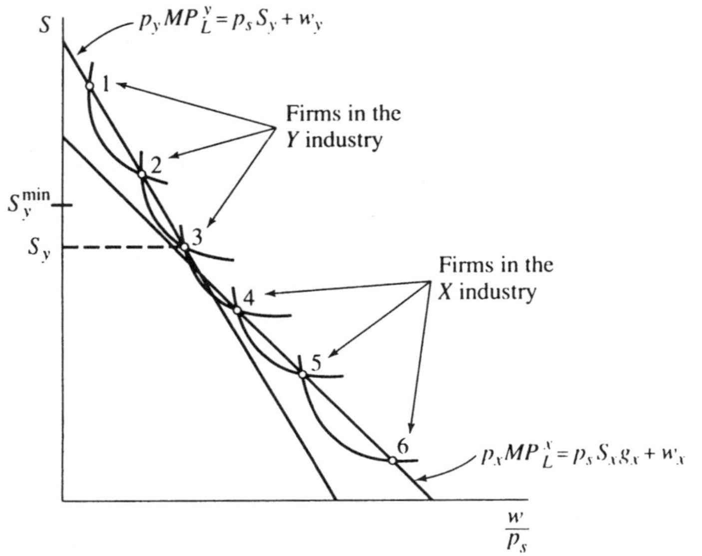

FIGURE 8 Two Industries with Heterogeneous Worker Preferences.

and 3, that number of workers supports three firms, numbered 1, 2, and 3, in the safer industry Y, plus three other firms, numbered 4, 5, and 6, in the more dangerous industry X.

Firm 1 has selected the highest level of safety and the lowest wage, and employs only workers from the safe tail of the preference distribution. Firm 2 selects somewhat less safety and a higher wage, employing the next group of workers. The indifference curve connecting the safety-wage packages of firms 1 and 2 is that of the marginal worker, who would be indifferent between the two firms. Continuing down and to the right in the figure, the safety-wage choices of firms 3 through 6 are shown, together with the corresponding indifference curves of the marginal workers in each case. There are also, of course, some lucky inframarginal workers (indifference curves, not drawn) for whom their current job is unequivocally more attractive than the next best alternative.

Note a couple of points about Figure 8. First, for each marginal worker, because the indifference curve passes below the isocost line, there are many safety-wage combinations that are more attractive to the worker and cheaper for the firm. However, a new entrant who tries to locate between two plants, to capture the marginal workers, will not be able to attract a sufficiently large number of workers to meet the minimum start-up size.

A corollary, no firm would ever locate so as to hire more than the minimum number of workers. Otherwise, an entrant could come in, offer a cheaper wage-safety combination, and still hire enough workers to undertake production.

Second, plants toward the center of the distribution have more similar safety levels than plants out in the tails. This conclusion follows from our assumption that in the center, the safety-wage trade-off is densely populated with workers. It also implies that the marginal-worker indifference curves pass further below the isocost lines at the tails of the distribution than they do toward the center. That is, workers in the tails are less satisfied with wages and working conditions than those with preferences closer to the mean.

The safety level within a plant has properties very much like a public good. Pareto optimality is achieved if the average marginal rate of substitution between wages and safety at each plant is equal to the price of safety.[21] As long as each plant is drawing equally from workers who prefer more safety and workers who want less safety, then the condition for Pareto optimality will be satisfied. However, if the entire distribution of worker tastes has a central tendency, as we assume, then our condition for efficiency will fail to obtain.

There is much debate among labor economists as to the direction of the resulting bias in plant safety. The model described here is strongly disposed to the conclusion that plants safer than average are, in fact, not safe enough, whereas plants more dangerous than average are too safe, given the allocation of workers across plants. This result follows from the fact that each plant draws more workers from an extreme of the wage-safety distribution than from the center. As a consequence, the distribution of preferences at each plant is skewed despite the fact that the overall distribution of worker preferences is symmetric.

Take, first, the plant located at the mean of the worker distribution. If the distribution of worker preferences is symmetric, then the central plant hires half of its employees from the population of workers that prefer more wages and less safety than average, and the other half from those who prefer more safety and less wages. This one plant, therefore, is likely to meet the requirement of Pareto optimality that the average MRS is equal to the firm's relative price of safety.

Now consider the adjacent next-safer plant. The central plant and the next-safer plant are going to divide the workers lying between them on the distribution. We can see, though, that since the distribution of workers is more dense close to the central plant than the next-safer plant, the central plant will be able to attract more of these intermediate workers than the next-safer plant. In order for the next-safer plant to acquire a full complement of workers, therefore, it must hire more than half of its workers from the group that would prefer an even safer plant.

The opposite is the case for plants below the mean. We conclude then that the presence of a central tendency in worker preferences will cause plants more safe than the mean to be too dangerous for the workers that they employ, whereas the plants that are more dangerous than the mean are too safe for the workers employed.

The consequent market failure, then, requires that safe plants become even safer. The government may therefore attempt to introduce a minimum safety standard that applies only to the safer of the two industries. Such a policy is depicted in Figure 8.

Suppose that we consider a minimum safety standard in the *Y* sector that is between the safety levels of the two most dangerous plants in this sector. Clearly, if the most dangerous *Y* plant tries to move from its current position and locate at the minimum standard, it will not be able to attract enough employees to meet the start-up requirement.

Further, the most dangerous plant employed in the *Y* sector must shut down. The owners of the next most dangerous plant now realize that they can lower costs by offering less safety and higher wages. This is the case because they no longer have to compete with the *Y* sector's most dangerous plant for workers. They are bounded, of course, by the minimum safety standard.

Some of the resources released by the most dangerous *Y*-sector plant will find their way to the *X* sector. The resulting increase in production of the labor-intensive good will raise the real wage and shift both labor isocost curves outward. However, as before, the *Y*-sector isocost line will shift out faster than the *X*-sector iscost line.

A new *X*-sector plant will open up at a position like *a* in Figure 9. Such a plant could not have existed in the absence of a minimum standard in sector *Y*. For without the minimum standard, a *Y*-sector firm could have located at point b, stolen of firm a's labor, and still broken even.

It is unclear what happens to the level of safety in the economy. The average level of safety rises in both sectors, but the more dangerous industry has expanded and the safer industry has contracted.

However, in any event, the market failure has not been corrected. The safe plants are still too dangerous and the dangerous plants are still too safe given the employees working at these plants.

The terms-of-trade effects are similar to those in the previous model. If the industry targeted for the minimum standard is in the import sector, then terms of trade deteriorate, and an international standard will make the home country worse off. Otherwise, the standard improves the terms of trade, and harmonization is attractive.

5.5.3 Summary

In the previous sections of this chapter we analyzed international bargaining over labor standards under the presumption that the government could usefully intervene to correct labor market failure. In this section we considered whether commonly used government policies, such as occupational safety and health regulations, do in fact have the desired effect.

We found that, under fairly reasonable assumptions, the labor market is capable of generating an efficient level of worker safety, so that no government intervention is necessary. Working conditions may vary across plants and industries, but this variability is largely a reflection of varying worker attitudes towards risk.

Nevertheless, the assumptions necessary to guarantee efficient working conditions may not apply in all industries. However, in most cases of market failure, government-mandated minimum working conditions will not restore Pareto optimality. We examined the case of heterogeneity of worker preferences over risk and money wages, and found that safety standards did little to correct the market failure.

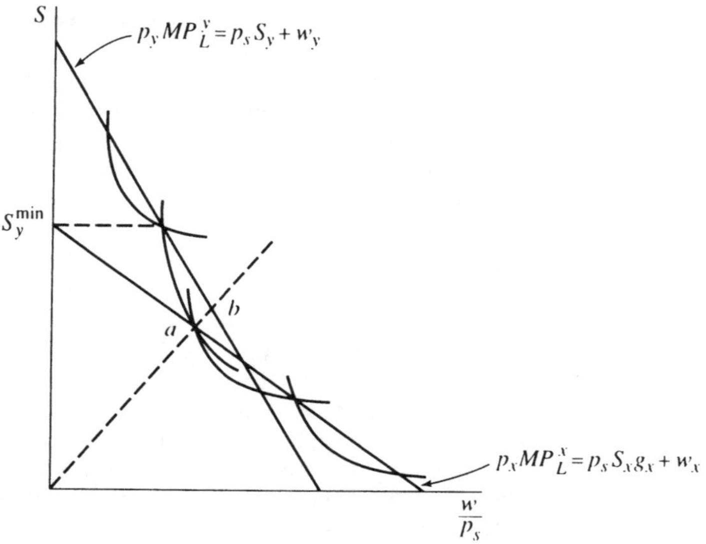

FIGURE 9 Minimum Safety Standard with Heterogeneous Worker Preferences.

Moreover, minimum safety standards can hurt the very workers they are intended to protect. A minimum standard applied to the labor-intensive sector will reduce money wages for workers in all sectors of the economy, and safety will decline in the unregulated sector. Safety rises in the regulated sector but not by enough to compensate for the lower money wages.

We can be certain that workers gain from the standards only if the standard is applied to the capital-intensive sector. In this case wages and safety levels rise in all sectors of the economy, whether regulated or not.

5.6 CONCLUSIONS AND IMPLICATIONS FOR INTERNATIONAL HARMONIZATION OF LABOR STANDARDS

Historically, labor standards began to emerge in the middle of the 19th century for reasons that had little to do with international goods trade. Reforms were generally concerned with the welfare of disadvantaged labor groups such as women, children, and prisoners. In some cases, the objective of the reforms was to eliminate techniques of production that had such horrible health consequences for workers that the reformers could not believe that the workers would take these jobs if they were aware of the dangers. The interest in international standards turned more on the desire to eliminate certain practices worldwide than on the desire to alter the trade in goods or gain an advantage in trade.

Over time, the pursuit of international labor standards has taken on a more protectionist tone. In some cases the protectionist intent is barely disguised. In fact, it is quite commonly feared that countries with below-average labor standards are gaining unfair advantage in trade.

In analyzing the economics of international labor standards we have sometimes found support for this view. However, the consequences of harmonization depend very much on the market setting. Frequently, harmonization is not found to be in the interest of the high-standard country. Some of the results of our analysis are summarized in the following list:

Summary of Main Results

1. In a price-taking environment, standards that are least-cost methods of fixing a market failure, like internalizing an externality, are welfare improving whether or not trade partners behave similarly. Welfare gains associated with setting price equal to social marginal cost are not contingent upon correct pricing in the rest of the world. Intervention in trade to punish foreigners who do not comply would not be welfare improving, since a price-taking economy cannot affect world prices.

2. Point 1 does not imply that a small country has no interest in international labor standards. On the one hand, action by all foreign governments could raise the world price of the affected goods, a result that would be beneficial to domestic producers of the good.

Domestic consumers would, of course, be made worse off because they would suffer an increase in price but might not benefit from the improved allocation of foreign resources. However, domestic consumers could benefit despite the increase in price if the labor standard has a moral basis, such as eliminating child or forced labor.

On the other hand, if home-country consumers do not benefit from foreign standards, and if the domestic sector is small enough, a small country could actually be made worse off by an internationally coordinated attempt at correcting a market failure. But even so, such a country may still pursue harmonization if producers have a disproportionate role in policy making.

3. World welfare is best served when all countries internalize external effects. However, for cultural or economic-development reasons, the external cost of a labor-market abuse often varies by country. In such a case, harmonizing on an international standard will not produce an efficient outcome.

Pressure to harmonize may still be applied, nevertheless, particularly by countries where the externality is large. For these countries, the cost of the standard borne by their producers will exceed the increase in the world price. Governments may therefore seek relief for their producers by demanding harmonization.

4. The standards themselves may have resource costs. In most cases, such as freedom from forced labor, child labor laws, maximum hours limitation, and a minimum wage, the standard is labor using. Or, as in the case of child labor laws that increase education, they may be unskilled labor using but skilled labor augmenting. These standards can be analyzed in the same manner as a change in the endowment of labor.

However, other standards, such as occupational safety, require resources other than labor. The factor proportions of the safety industry then play a role in determining the effects of safety standards.

5. In a setting in which each economy is completely specialized in production, any standard that diverts resources away from the production of goods will contract the supply of exports to the world market. A terms-of-trade gain then results.

A partner country imposing a standard will also improve its own terms of trade, thereby hurting the home country. Thus each country should prefer to go it alone.

Because standards not only have a direct beneficial effect on labor but also improve a country's terms of trade, each country may be tempted to set a standard above the level necessary to correct any market failure that may exist. In such a setting, therefore, noncooperative behavior will leave the world with standards that are above the Pareto optimal level. International cooperation will be called for, but, as with tariffs, the treaty will call for a mutual lowering of labor standards.

6. The result under point 5 is quite fragile, however. Once we move away from a model with complete specialization to a Heckscher-Ohlin model, the outcome is quite different. Surprisingly, the terms-of-trade effect of a labor standard is entirely independent of the country that imposes the standard. The only parameter that matters is the factor proportions employed in implementing the standard relative to the world's factor endowments.

If the standard has a higher capital-labor ratio than the world's endowment of capital relative to labor, then the price of the capital-intensive good will rise on the world market. The capital-abundant country will gain, whether or not it was the source of the standard.

In such a setting, the capital-abundant country will tend to want a high labor standard, whereas a labor-abundant country will want a low standard. Harmonization would, therefore, improve world efficiency.

7. Labor standards that apply to only one industry have a similar property. Gains from the standard are determined by the country that exports the affected good, not the country that imposes the standard.

8. Finally, we explicitly modeled the market for safety. First we considered the case in which the market chooses the efficient level of safety. The results under point 7 carry over to the endogenous safety model. A standard will improve the terms of trade if applied to the export sector but worsen the terms of trade if applied to the import sector.

There are no curious features of this model. The imposition of the safety standard will raise real wages only if the regulated sector is capital intensive. Otherwise, real wages fall. This is a consequence of the Stolper-Samuelson theorem. Also, if the regulated sector is capital intensive, then the safety level will rise in both the regulated and unregulated sectors.

The gains from trade are difficult to establish in this model because government intervention introduces a distortion into the economy. However, gains are more likely if the export rather than the import sector is regulated, because increasing the price of the export good reduces the distortion caused by the regulation.

We then turned to a model in which excessive worker heterogeneity gives rise to a market failure. As in the efficient endogenous safety model, terms of trade improve if the regulated sector is also the export sector.

This model can also be used to illustrate that minimum safety standards frequently do not address the underlying market failure. Informational externalities are sometimes offered as an explanation for government regulation of working conditions. However, as in the heterogeneous worker model, a minimum safety level does not correct the market failure.

It should be evident from the foregoing summary that we have relied on a variety of models that have been designed to reflect settings in which different national characteristics may determine the outcome of the introduction of labor standards. Our intention accordingly has been to investigate the relationships between labor standards and trade primarily on a theoretical level. While our effort is by no means the final word on the subject, it appears to us that a fruitful next step would be to identify the interest groups and industries that are seeking to influence policy making in the design and implementation of international labor standards in different nations and to assess the economic effects of alternative policies.

5.6.1 Implications for International Harmonization of Labor Standards

Harmonization as a principle of negotiation in the GATT has served us well when applied to tariffs. It is established from a world-welfare point of view that harmonization on a zero tariff is best. This follows from the remarkably robust result that intervention at the border is virtually never a first-best policy.

It is natural to try to carry over the principle of harmonization to other aspects of negotiations, such as environmental and labor standards. Unfortunately, the principle that serves us so well with tariffs cannot be appropriately applied to the regulation of internal policies.

It is true that world welfare is best served by eliminating market failures where they exist, and the labor market is no exception. To the extent that labor standards are the appropriate remedy, then national governments should certainly enact them. However, there is little to suggest that such market failures are uniform across countries and, therefore, should be countered with similar measures. Hence, international harmonization of labor standards cannot be supported from a world-welfare point of view.

Furthermore, each country has a strong incentive to correct the market failures that exist within its borders. Therefore, there is not a strong case for international pressure to do so.

Our first conclusion, then, is that we should expect diversity in working conditions as the norm. As a terminological matter, it seems inappropriate to label as "unfair" the trade that follows from differences in labor standards as long as the labor standards are consistent with efficient resource use.

There is one important exception, however, to this conclusion. There are some cases in which labor standards are designed for income redistribution rather than to correct a market failure. Slave labor and child labor are two obvious examples. In the latter case, there are certainly efficient allocations that are highly inequitable, especially where children are concerned.

The international imposition of labor standards is even more difficult to defend because standards as commonly enacted rarely if ever address existent market failures. In our theoretical analysis, we offered as an example a minimum safety standard that was intended to address the market failure associated with diversity in tastes between wages and working conditions for workers within a plant. We found that the minimum standard raised real wages only if they were imposed in the capital-intensive sector. Otherwise, real wages fell economy-wide, and safety declines in the sector were not bounded by the minimum safety standard. Furthermore, the standard did not correct the market failure.

We turn now to consider the likely effect of harmonization on high- and low-income countries. First, do high-income countries gain from imposing standards on low-income countries?

On the one hand, low-income countries tend to be abundant in unskilled labor. Minimum standards that impose restrictions on hours worked, child labor, prison labor, and the like remove some labor from the workforce. According to Heckscher-Ohlin type reasoning, the effect will be a contraction in the supply of labor-intensive production on the world market. As a consequence, the terms of trade of low-income countries will rise at the expense of high-income countries, thus making high-income countries worse off.

On the other hand, if the labor standard happens to be imposed in the capital-intensive sector, then the low-income countries will expand their export of labor-intensive goods. In this case, the terms of trade of the high-income countries will turn to their advantage.

Of course, the objective of labor standards in high-income countries may not be to raise national welfare, but rather to protect their scarce factor (unskilled labor). Labor standards in low-income countries will support this objective, but they will do so only by lowering welfare of both the high-income countries and the world as a whole.

In any event, the important point to realize here is that the gains from trade for the high-income countries do not depend on efficient resource use in low-income countries. The gains from trade stem simply from the opportunity to trade at prices other than autarky prices. Therefore, high-income countries should be willing to trade with low-income countries whether or not they have optimally configured labor markets.

This conclusion naturally raises the opposite question. Do low-income countries gain from having standards imposed upon them? There are several reasons why this might be the case.

First, for various reasons a breakdown in the political process may prevent governments from enacting legislation that corrects a market failure. An international requirement to do so, therefore, may be politically useful. However, it must be kept in mind that, for this argument to be compelling, we would have to be confident that the required policy does indeed correct the labor-market failure. This point has yet to be demonstrated, as we discussed previously.

Second, as a historical matter, the right to organize has been a precursor to the development of democratic institutions. Supporting nascent labor organizations may be a legitimate activity for existing democracies.

Third, as noted earlier, standards that withdraw labor from the market will contract the supply of labor-intensive goods. The terms of trade of the low-income countries will therefore improve as a consequence. However, again, it should be kept in mind that the reason the low-income countries are gaining stems from the fact that the standard is helping labor to collude and exercise market power by withdrawing their services from the market. This outcome may be in the interest of the workers, but it lowers world welfare.

We finally come to the question of whether it would be appropriate to countervail against low-standard countries. There are some conditions under which countervailing would be counterproductive or unjustified. For example, if all countries in the world are essentially price takers, then a countervailing action by one country against another will serve only to reduce the welfare of the countervailing country and have no effect on the exporter.

More realistically, it seems entirely likely, indeed certain, that efficient use of the world's resources will require varying labor standards across countries. These varying labor standards will probably give rise to some trade flows. However, it seems inappropriate to punish countries whose exports are stimulated by low standards as long as the trade of these countries is consistent with the efficient use of productive resources.

Countervailing may be justified if labor standards that are necessary for efficient resource allocation have not been enacted. In this case, the absence of labor standards could depress the wages of unskilled workers worldwide. However, it should be noted that a countervailing duty in this case could lower wages in the offending country, thereby further worsening working conditions in the low-income country.

Consider a duty imposed by a high-income country on the labor-intensive exports from a low-income country. Within the high-income country, the duty will have the desired effect. The price of labor-intensive goods will rise, pulling up the return to labor. In contrast, the opposite will occur in the low-income country. The duty will lower the price of exports of the labor-intensive good. As a consequence, the return to labor in the low-income country will tend to fall.

To sum up, we would have to say that the case for international harmonization of labor standards is rather weak. As genuinely motivated as such calls for international harmonization may be, the theoretical case has not been made. Furthermore, it is likely that international harmonization of labor standards will have unintended adverse consequences for the very people they are intended to protect.

APPENDIX

Worker Rights Standards

1. Freedom of Association
   - A. Definition: The right of association concerns relations between unions and governments and involves the right of workers and employers
     1. to establish and join organizations of their choosing without previous authorization;
     2. to draw up their own constitutions and rules, elect their representatives, and formulate their programs;
     3. to join in confederations and affiliate with international organizations; and
     4. to be protected against dissolution or suspension by administrative authority.

B. General principles
   1. Freedom of association applies to everyone *except* military and police.
   2. Unions should be independent of the government or ruling party.
   3. Restrictions on the right to strike are legitimate only for government service (civil servants engaged in the administration of the state) and "essential services" (only those services whose interruption would endanger worker or public safety and health). When denied, there should be an effective alternate process for mediation, arbitration, and settlement of grievances.
   4. Unions' civil liberties must be respected.
   5. Unions may form and join federations, confederations, and international confederations.

II. The Right to Organize and Bargain Collectively

A. Definition: The right to organize and bargain collectively concerns relations between unions and employers and involves the right of workers
   1. to be represented in negotiating the prevention and settlement of disputes with employers;
   2. to protection against interference with union activities;
   3. to protection against acts of antiunion discrimination; and
   4. to protection against refusal of employment, dismissal, or prejudice resulting from union membership or participation.
   5. Government should promote processes for voluntary negotiations between employers and workers and their organizations.

B. General principles
   1. Voluntary collective bargaining should be protected by law and should be practiced.
   2. Antiunion discrimination by employers should be illegal.
   3. Speedy and effective processes should exist to review union/worker complaints of antiunion discrimination.

III. Forced Labor

A. Definition: Forced labor should be prohibited and suppressed in all its forms. Although there are certain exceptions, forced labor refers to work or service exacted from any person under the menace of penalty and for which the person has not volunteered. "Menace of penalty" includes loss of rights or privileges as well as penal sanctions.

B. General principles
   1. Forced labor should *never* be used for the following purposes:
      a. economic development.
      b. to enforce racial, social, national, or religious discrimination.
      c. as political coercion or education, or punishment for holding or expressing political views opposed to the established political, social, or economic system.
      d. for labor discipline.
      e. as a punishment for having participated in legal strikes.
   2. The following do not constitute "forced labor" as defined under the international standards:
      a. certain forms of prison labor, *only* when imposed following conviction for a crime in a court of law.

b. national service obligations (compulsory military service and normal civic obligations).
c. genuine emergency, limited to a "sudden, unforeseen happening, calling for instant countermeasures, such as war, calamity or threatened calamity such as earthquakes, floods, pestilence, etc."
d. minor communal services, defined as services performed by community members in the direct interest of the community.

IV. Minimum Age Employment
A. Definition: The minimum age standard aims at the effective abolition of child labor by raising the minimum age for employment to a level consistent with the fullest physical, mental, and social development of young people.
B. General principles
1. The minimum age for employment should be set no lower than 15, with an option for a lower minimum of 14 for developing countries with a level of economic development that makes the realization of the higher standard impossible. Countries that set the minimum age at the lower level, however, should be trying to progressively change conditions so that they can meet the higher standard.
a. Exceptions: light work is permissible for 13–15 year-olds; minimum age of 18 for dangerous work; work in connection with education or training; participation in artistic performances.
2. Minimum age legislation should cover all economic activity, not just employment under contract.
3. Education should be provided for all children and should be compulsory. The minimum age for employment shall not be less than the age for completion for compulsory schooling.
4. Minimum age legislation should have an effective enforcement system that includes an adequate number of inspectors and penalties that serve as effective deterrents. Penalties should include fines and/or imprisonment.

V. Acceptable Conditions of Work
A. Definition: The standards for acceptable working conditions provide for the establishment and maintenance of systems, adapted to national conditions, that provide for minimum working standards: wages that provide a decent living for workers and their families; working hours that do not exceed 48 hours per week, with a full 24-hour rest day; a specified annual paid holiday; and minimum conditions for protection of the safety and health of workers.
B. Basic principles
1. Minimum wage principles
a. There should be a national, statutory minimum wage.
b. It should be set realistically, preferably as a result of an open, public or tripartite process, with certain specified criteria..
c. Wages should be protected, that is, paid in money, and workers should be able to choose where and how they spend their wages.
2. Hours of work

   a. Working hours should not exceed 48 hours per week, with a full 24-hour rest day. Workers should have a specified annual paid holiday.
   b. Overtime should be regulated, remunerated at a higher rate than for "normal" working hours, and prohibited from exceeding a certain number of hours in a given period.
3. Safety and health principles
   a. Workers should have health and safety rights in the workplace, including a complaint process for hazardous conditions and the right to remove themselves from hazardous situations.
   b. The right should set health and safety standards as part of an open, public, or tripartite process.
4. Enforcement principles
   a. There should be a legislatively mandated enforcement system for minimum wage, hours of work, and safety and health.
   b. Inspectors should have the right to enter the workplace, should have access to workers and their representatives, and have the right to issue citations for violations.
   c. Workers and unions should be protected against adverse action in filing complaints.
   d. Penalties for violations should not be limited to warnings, but should include fines and prison sentences.

Note: As stated in Lyle (1991, p. 20): "These are not intended to be legal definitions, nor to encompass the entire spectrum of internationally recognized worker rights. Rather, they represent general guidance intended merely to highlight the basic principles behind each of the five internationally recognized worker rights found in U.S. trade law."

Source: Adapted from Lyle (1991, pp. 20–31).

NOTES

We wish to thank Asad Alam, Jagdish Bhagwati, Steve Charnovitz, Robert Hudec, Greg Schoepfle, participants in the July 1993 Fairness-Harmonization Project Meeting and the September 1994 project conference, and members of the International Economics and the Labor Economics seminars at the University of Michigan for helpful comments on earlier versions of this paper.

1 For a theoretical evaluation of this "race to the bottom" problem, see Wilson (1995). An assessment of this issue, taking the empirical aspects into account, can be found in Bhagwati and Srinivasan (1995), Klevorick (1995), and Levinson (1995).

2 For additional details and perspective on the history of labor standards, see Leary (1995).

3 The view being expressed here is at variance with the view of the so-called neo-institutionalists, who argue that the imposition of labor standards may have positive welfare and growth effects. These positive effects may result from the labor-income-raising effects of capital-labor substitution, greater harmony in the workplace, more

emphasis on worker training, and increased incentives for productivity-enhancing investments. For a more complete statement of this neoinstitutionalist position and a critique of the "neoclassical" view with its emphasis on comparative advantage and the gains from (free) trade, see Hanson (1983, esp. pp. 53–63), Herzenberg (1988), Kochan and Nordlund (1989), Office of Technology Assessment (1992, esp. pp. 77–78), Portes (1990), and Singh (1990).

4 Bhagwati (1995) provides further insight into the issues involved in the arguments made in support of reducing the diversity of institutions and policies among trading nations. See also Howse and Trebilcock (in process) and Schoepfle and Swinnerton (1994).

5 This section is based in large measure on Alam (1992, esp. pp. 10–44). Charnovitz (1986, 1987, 1992), Hanson (1983, esp. pp. 11–32), and ILO (1988).

6 See Marshall (1990) for a forceful argument in favor of trade-linked labor standards as part of the GATT system and Charnovitz (1992) for some recommendations on GATT actions regarding labor standards.

7 The highlights of the EC Charter of Fundamental Social Rights are summarized in De Boer and Winham (1993, pp. 36–37), and the full text is to be found in Commission of the European Communities (1990). See also Campbell (1990). For an analysis of the economic effects of social protection in the EC, see Abraham (1994).

8 A useful reference is Lemco and Robson (1993).

9 Bhagwati (1995) notes that the EC can be viewed as representing a process of building a *federal* political structure, close, say, to those of the United States. Canada, and India, and therefore having a set of *minimum* labor standards makes *political* sense. See Sapir (1995) for a review of the process of social harmonization in the EC from the 1950s to the present. Sapir concludes that, while there have been noteworthy efforts to formalize the objectives of EC social policies, the implementation of explicit measures has remained limited and is not likely to change at least in the near future.

10 In connection with the NAFTA debate, Bhagwati (1995) notes that he favored asking for some minimum labor standards because the NAFTA could be construed as a *preferential* gift to Mexico for which something could be asked in exchange. Notwithstanding this suggestion, it seems apparent that the EC model became the prototype for a number of nongovernmental organizations that were seeking to introduce explicit labor standards requirements into the NAFTA, which were reflected in the side agreements on the environment and labor that were negotiated.

11 Further support for this view is to be found in Morici (1993) and Garcia Rocha (1990). It will be interesting, accordingly, to analyze the content and potential economic effects of the side agreement on labor issues in the NAFTA that has been negotiated among the three NAFTA nations.

12 See Perez-Lopez (1993) for a discussion of voluntary codes of conduct that have been proposed for U.S. corporations operating in countries with allegedly questionable labor practices.

13 See Dorman (1989) for an evaluation of the procedures and decision-making criteria regarding worker rights in the implementation of the U.S. GSP; case studies of El Salvador, Malaysia, and Chile; and recommendations for improving the procedures and decision-making criteria in investigating alleged violations of worker rights standards. The reports prepared by the Bureau of International Labor Affairs (ILAB) are also worth noting. They include evaluations of worker rights in export-processing zones (see U.S. Department of Labor, 1989–90, and Schoepfle, 1990), child labor, worker rights restrictions in East Asia, and characteristics of the informal sector in a number of developing countries (see U.S. Department of Labor, 1992, and Schoepfle and Perez-Lopez, 1993). For some background discussion of the issues involved in the renewal of the GSP in late 1994, see Lande and Dybner (1994).

14 Note that we are referring here to purely domestic externalities as compared to transborder externalities. Bhagwati and Srinivasan (1995) distinguish the two types of externalities, noting that the Pareto optimality proposition applies only to domestic externalities. Labor standards involve domestic externalities, except in cases in which one country may affect standards in another country due to a "good" or "bad" example or because there may be a "race to the bottom." We shall abstract from such possibilities.
15 For a discussion of moral considerations, see Bhagwati (1995).
16 The models of this section, as well as many of the results, draw heavily on Alam (1992).
17 Asad Alam has pointed out to us that if countries are symmetric, in the sense that the terms-of-trade gain to one is of the same magnitude as the terms-of-trade loss imposed by the other when each raises its labor standards, any cooperative solution would neutralize the terms-of-trade effects. Both countries would still gain, however, so long as the level of the standard is such that the marginal benefit exceeds the marginal cost from reduced consumption.
18 It should be clear that this problem is identical to that of the effects of accumulation of factors of production. In that sense, our results are merely applications of known results and techniques from the literature begun by Rybczynski (1955).
19 The results may also change if preferences are nonhomothetic.
20 See U.S. GAO (1993) for comparative information on the design and operation of occupational safety and health programs in the United States and Canada and references to earlier reports comparing the United States and Mexico.
21 See Dickens (1984) for demonstration.

REFERENCES

Abraham, Filip, 1994. "Social protection and regional convergence in a EMU." *Open Economies Review* 5:89–114.

Alam, Asad. 1992. "Labour standards and comparative advantage." Unpublished doctoral dissertation, Columbia University.

Bhagwati, Jagdish. 1995. "The demands to reduce domestic diversity among trading nations." Chapter 1 in this volume. [Refers to J. N. Bhagwati and R. E. Hudec (eds), *Fair Trade and Harmonization. Prerequisites for Free Trade? Vol. 1: Economic Analysis.* MIT, 1996.]

Bhagwati, Jagdish, and T. N. Srinivasan. 1995. "Trade and the environment: Does environmental diversity detract from the case for free trade?" Chapter 4 in this volume.

Campbell, Duncan C. 1990. "EC 1992: The social dimension at issue," in Jorge F. Perez-Lopez. Gregory E. Schoepfle, and John Yochelson, eds. *EC 1992: Implications for U.S. workers*. Proceedings of a Working Roundtable, jointly sponsored by the U.S. Department of Labor and Center for Strategic and International Studies. *Significant Issues Series*, 12:97–124.

Charnovitz, Steve. 1986. "Fair labor standards and international trade," *Journal of World Trade Law* 20:61–78.

Charnovitz, Steve. 1987. "The influence of international labour standards on the world trading regime: A historical review." *International Labour Review*. 126:565–584.

Charnovitz, Steve. 1992. "Environmental and labour standards in trade." *The World Economy*, 15:335–356.

Commission of the European Communities. 1990. *The Community Charter of Fundamental Social Rights for Workers*, European File 6/90. Brussels: Commission of the European Communities.

De Boer, Elizabeth, and Gilbert R. Winham. 1993. "Trade negotiations, social charters, and the NAFTA." In Jonathan Lemco and William B. P. Robson, eds, *Ties beyond trade: Labor and environmental issues under the NAFTA*. Canadian American Committee: C. D. Howe Institute (Canada) and National Planning Association (U.S.A.).

Dickens, William T. 1984. "Occupational safety and health regulation and economic theory." In William Darity, Jr., ed., *Labor economics: Modern views*. Boston: Kluwer-Nijhoff.

Dorman, Peter. 1989. *Worker rights and U.S. trade policy: An evaluation of worker rights conditionality under the general system of preferences*. U.S. Department of Labor, Office of International Economic Affairs. Bureau of International Labor Affairs. Washington, DC: U.S. Government Printing Office.

Garcia Rocha, Adalberto. 1990. "Mexico." In Stephen A. Herzenberg, Jorge Perez-Lopez, and Stuart K. Tucker, eds, *Labor standards and development in the global economy*. Washington, DC: U.S. Department of Labor, Bureau of International Labor Affairs.

Hanson, Gote. 1983. *Social clauses and international trade: An economic analysis of labour standards in trade policy*. New York: St Martin's Press.

Herzenberg, Stephen A. 1988. "Institutionalizing constructive competition: International labor standards and trade." Economic Discussion Paper 32, U.S. Department of Labor, Bureau of International Labor Affairs, Office of International Economic Affairs, Division of Foreign Economic Research.

Howse, Robert, and Michael J. Trebilcock. In process. "The fair trade free-trade debate: Trade, labour and the environment," University of Toronto.

International Labor Organization (ILO). 1988. *Human rights: A common responsibility*. International Labor Conference, 75th Session, 1988. Geneva: ILO.

Klevorick, Alvin K. 1995. "Reflections on the race to the bottom." Chapter 12 in this volume.

Kochan, Thomas A., and Willis Nordlund. 1989. *Reconciling labor standards and economic goals: An historical perspective*. U.S. Department of Labor. Office of International Economic Affairs, Bureau of International Labor Affairs. Washington, DC: U.S. Government Printing Office.

Lande, Stephen, and Ariel Dybner. 1994. "The future of the U.S. Generalized System of Preferences," Overseas Development Council, *Policy Focus*, No. 5.

Leary, Virgina A. 1995. "Workers' rights and international trade: The social clause (GATT, ILO, NAFTA, U.S. Laws)." Chapter 5 in Volume 2 of this work.

Lemco, Jonathan, and William B. P. Robson, eds. 1993. *Ties beyond trade: Labor and environmental issues under the NAFTA*. Canadian American Committee: C. D. Howe Institute (Canada) and National Planning Association (U.S.A.).

Levinson, Arik. 1995. "Environmental regulation and industry location: International and domestic evidence." Chapter 11 in this volume.

Lyle, Faye. 1991. "Worker rights in U.S. policy." *Foreign Labor Trends*, 91–154. U.S. Department of Labor, Bureau of International Labor Affairs. Washington, DC: U.S. Government Printing Office.

Marshall, Ray. 1990. "Trade-linked labor standards." In Frank J. Macchiarola, ed., "International trade: The changing role of the United States." *Proceedings of the Academy of Political Science*, 37:67–78.

Morici, Peter. 1993. "Implications of a social charter for the North American Free Trade Agreement." In Jonathan Lemco and William B. P. Robson, eds, *Ties beyond trade: Labor and environmental issues under the NAFTA*. Canadian American Committee: C. D. Howe Institute (Canada) and National Planning Association (U.S.A.)

Office of Technology Assessment (OTA). Congress of the United States. 1992. *U.S.–Mexico trade: Pulling together or pulling apart?* Washington, D.C.: U.S. Government Printing Office.

Perez-Lopez, Jorge F. 1993. "Promoting international respect for worker rights through business codes of conduct." *Fordham International Law Journal*, 17:1–47.

Portes, Alejandro. 1990. "When more can be less: Labor standards, development, and the informal economy." In Stephen A. Herzenberg, Jorge Perez-Lopez, and Stuart K. Tucker, eds, *Labor standards and development in the global economy*. Washington, DC: Bureau of International Labor Affairs.

Rybczynski, T. M. 1955. "Factor endowment and relative commodity prices," *Economica*, 22:36–41.

Sapir, André, 1995. "Trade liberalization and the harmonization of social policies: Lessons from European integration." Chapter 15 in this volume.

Schoepfle, Gregory K. 1990. *Labor standards in export assembly operations in Mexico and the Caribbean*. U.S. Department of Labor, Bureau of International Labor Affairs. Washington, DC: U.S. Government Printing Office.

Schoepfle, Gregory K., and Jorge Perez-Lopez, eds. 1993. *Work without protections: Case study of the informal sector in developing countries*. Washington, DC: U.S. Department of Labor, Bureau of International Labor Affairs.

Schoepfle, Gregory K., and Kenneth A. Swinnerton, eds. 1994. *International labor standards and global economic integration: Proceedings of a symposium*. Washington, DC: U.S. Department of Labor, Bureau of International Labor Affairs.

Singh, Ajit. 1990. "Southern competition, labor standards and industrial development in the North and South." In Stephen A. Herzenberg, Jorge Perez-Lopez, and Stuart K. Tucker, eds, *Labor standards and development in the global economy*. Washington, DC: U.S. Department of Labor, Bureau of International Labor Affairs.

U.S. Department of Labor, Bureau of International Labor Affairs (ILAB). 1989–90. "Worker rights in export processing zones." *Foreign Labor Trends*, FLT 90–132, including Volume 2, "Worker rights in export processing zones: Mexico." Washington, DC: U.S. Government Printing Office.

U.S. Department of Labor, Bureau of International Labor Affairs (ILAB). 1992. *International worker rights: Child labor, special categories in East Asia, informal sector*. Biennial Report to Congress. Washington, DC: U.S. Department of Labor.

U.S. General Accounting Office (GAO). 1993. *Occupational safety and health: Differences between programs in the United States and Canada*. GAO/HRD-94-15FS (December).

Watson, William. 1993. "A skeptical view of the social charter." In Jonathan Lemco and William B. P. Robson, eds, *Ties beyond trade: Labor and environmental issues under the NAFTA*. Canadian American Committee: C. D. Howe Institute (Canada) and National Planning Association (U.S.A.).

Weintraub, Sidney, and Jan Gilbreath. 1993. "The social side to free trade." In Jonathan Lemco and William B. P. Robson, eds, *Ties Beyond Trade: Labor and environmental issues under the NAFTA*. Canadian American Committee: C. D. Howe Institute (Canada) and National Planning Association (U.S.A.).

Wilson, John Douglas. 1995. "Capital mobility and environmental standards: Is there a theoretical basis for a race to the bottom?" Chapter 10 in this volume.

5. The Seeking of a World Competition Code: Quixotic Quest?

J. Davidow

There is an American tradition, personified by idealists such as Jefferson and Wilson, of believing that the United States has developed new and better freedoms that can be extended to the whole world. Seekers after this goal have tended to die with their dreams unfulfilled, if not totally frustrated.

Such a death occurred in 1979, when Corwin Edwards succumbed to a stroke at age 73. Edwards devoted his career to supporting and spreading antitrust doctrine. He was policy planning director for Thurman Arnold in the Justice Department's Antitrust Division, and then chief economist of the Federal Trade Commission. In numerous books and articles, he explained and advocated competition policy of the American style, i.e., grounded in the economic case for free markets but also motivated by a political suspicion of unchecked private economic power.[1]

Shortly before the defeat of Germany, President Roosevelt personally embraced the anticartel philosophy of Edwards and the Antitrust Division, and expressly linked this policy to the embryonic United Nations. Roosevelt wrote:

> During the past half century the United States has developed a tradition in opposition to private monopolies. The Sherman and Clayton Acts have become as much a part of the American way of life as the Due Process clause of the Constitution. By protecting the consumer against monopoly these statutes guarantee him the benefits of competition.
>
> Unfortunately, a number of foreign countries, particularly in continental Europe, do not possess such a tradition against cartels. On the contrary, cartels have received encouragement from these governments. Especially is this true with respect to Germany. Moreover, cartels were utilized by the Nazis as governmental instrumentalities to achieve political ends. . . . Defeat of the Nazi armies will have to be followed by the eradication of these weapons of economic warfare. But more than elimination of the political activities of German cartels will be required. Cartel practices which restrict the few flow of goods in foreign commerce will have to be curbed. With international trade involved, this end can be achieved only through collaborative action by the United Nations.[2]

After World War II, Edwards went to Japan to work on the de-cartelization of that country and the development of an antitrust law there.[3]

Also just after the war, the United States and Great Britain jointly proposed creation of an international trade organization. In 1948, Edwards was a key part of the U.S. delegation when fifty-three nations met in Havana and drafted the charter of such an organization. Article V of the ITO Charter condemned a list of restrictive business practices, defined as:

(1) Fixing of prices, or of terms or conditions to be observed in the purchase, sale, or lease of any product.
(2) Exclusion of enterprises from, or allocation or division of, any territorial market or field of business activity, or allocation of customers, or fixing of sale or purchasing quotas,
(3) Discrimination against particular enterprises;
(4) Production limitations or quotas;
(5) Prevention of development or application of technology or invention, whether patented or not, or withholding of same with the result of monopolizing an industrial or commercial field.
(6) Illegal extension of rights under patents, trademarks, or copyrights, and
(7) Any similar practices which the Organization may declare, by a majority of two-thirds of the Members present and voting, to be restrictive business practices.[4]

The ITO Charter was submitted at one session of the U.S. Congress, which adjourned without voting on the measure. It was never resubmitted, the State Department apparently having concluded that it would not be ratified. Some opponents of the Havana Charter were not averse to its provisions on restrictive business practices (RBPs) but were critical of its support for international commodity agreements and hostile to its declarations on foreign investment and full employment. The representative of the National Association of Manufacturers (NAM) said of the charter's provisions "they contain a mild – a very mild – indictment of private cartels, while opening the gates widely to intergovernmental ones."[5]

There were those, like Edwards and Sigmund Timberg of the Antitrust Division, who therefore rationalized that the ITO Charter was rejected in the United States because of the controversial provisions favoring commodity stabilization agreements and worldwide full employment, rather than because of its RBP provisions, and that therefore a separate international antitrust agreement would still have a chance for U.S. support.[6]

In 1952, Edwards headed the American delegation to a UN ad hoc committee under the Economic and Social Council (ECOSOC) which, on the motion of the United States, was delegated to draft restrictive business practice rules and an implementing procedure. Timberg acted as secretary to the group. The committee's report surveyed the existing state of anti-trust or anticartel law in the ten or so nations which provided information on that subject. It concluded that there were great disparities in the treatment of cartels and restrictive business practices, but that there had been substantial progress toward the development of new and stronger legislation in this area as compared to the period prior to World War II. The committee's final recommendation was extremely similar to that contained in the Havana Charter. In essence, the proposal was that the same list of restrictive practices be promulgated, and that a UN body with an executive board be available to arrange consultation between states affected by such practices or for investigation of complaints presented by member states, to be followed by findings and possible requests that members take remedial measures in accordance with their own laws and procedures. Practices required by national law would not be subject to investigation.[7]

In the following year, substantial opposition developed to the recommendations of the UN committee. The report was condemned by the International Chamber of Commerce and the National Association of Manufacturers.[8]

In March 1955, the U.S. representative to the United Nations withdrew American support for the concept of an international body for the control of restrictive business practices. He stressed that the substantial differences that then existed between national laws and policies in regard to competition would make it very difficult for a multinational body to determine which business practices are harmful and which are not, and would also make it unlikely that recommendations of the UN commission could be or would be effectively carried out in all countries. In closing, the U.S. delegate stated:

> The elimination of harmful restraints on international trade and the furthering of the development of free competitive enterprise continue to be basic objectives of this country's economic policy. In the present circumstances, however, the endeavor to effectuate a plan of international co-operation along the lines envisaged by the current proposals might well prejudice rather than promote the attainment of these objectives.
>
> It is therefore the opinion of the United States Government that present emphasis should be given not to international organizational machinery but rather to the more fundamental need of further developing effective national programmes to deal with restrictive business practices, and of achieving a greater degree of comparability in the policies and practices of all nations in their approach to the subject.[9]

In the years following the abandonment of the ECOSOC antitrust proposal, the United States did help achieve substantial progress in strengthening national antitrust laws and beginning antitrust cooperation within groups smaller than the United Nations. With American assistance and encouragement, the European Coal and Steel Community in 1951 and then the European Common Market in 1957 adopted treaties and regulations aimed at preventing restrictive business practices.[10]

Recalling these events in a book written in 1967, Edwards concluded that while there was an excellent case for regional control of restrictive business practices, a global agreement was impractical because many states used restraints of trade as a weapon against other countries and rejected private enterprise as the optimum form for economic activity. He stressed that "[d]evelopment of a common policy towards cartels and monopolies is possible, if at all, only within a free trade area or in a setting in which public and private restrictions are reduced to a roughly comparable extent."[11] Noting also the wide differences among nations concerning regulatory methods and concepts of due process, he concluded:

> In the light of the difficulties which have been summarized above, international collaboration to control restrictive business practices cannot be global. It cannot

> succeed if it includes countries that are widely divergent in their legal and political systems or in the place that they give to private enterprise. It cannot succeed if it undertakes a program that is markedly inconsistent with the commercial policies of the participating states. It cannot succeed if the participating states do not have a substantial degree of common experience as to the nature of the business enterprises and of business practices. If it includes any substantial number of states that are without experience in domestic control of restrictive business practices, it must be seriously handicapped. Comprehensive collaboration, such as was contemplated by those who drafted the ITO charter and the ad hoc committee's report, is not now practicable.[12]

Thus, Edwards's reflection in retirement was that he had been wrong in 1948 and 1953 in believing that a global code for the control of RBPs was feasible or politically acceptable. Nor did he believe that the conditions of 1967 were significantly more favorable.

Despite Edwards's pessimism, the issue of international antitrust principles refused to die. It was revived in the 1970s in connection with increasing political controversy about investment and marketing practices of multinational corporations. Also, the issue was pushed by a group that had played no significant role in the debates of the 1940s, the developing countries.

ANTITRUST DEVELOPMENTS AT UNCTAD

Although no "International Trade Organization" was created in Geneva following the failure of the Havana Charter, in 1964 a United Nations Conference on Trade and Development (UNCTAD) was established in that city. This organization achieved a membership as large or larger than that of the UN General Assembly. Its mission, however, was solely to focus on furthering the trade and development of the "southern" nations of the world, who negotiated as a bloc called the "Group of 77," while the West was styled as "Group B" and the East as "Group D."

At its third planning conference in 1972, UNCTAD took up the topic of controlling "restrictive business practices adversely affecting the trade and development of developing countries."[13] Further work followed in 1974 and 1975 on codes of conduct.

Developing countries' pressure for international RBP rules was undoubtedly the primary factor in rejuvenating UN activity in this field, but the peculiarity of the South's approach often threatened to stalemate the negotiations it demanded. The southern states made their understandable interest in securing development, control of foreign investment, and legitimization of national measures the preoccupation of the United Nations and of their versions of these codes of conduct, initially to the almost complete exclusion of the concepts of free competition, free trade, and international law. Restoring these fundamentals became the key task of the North.

The Group of 77 countries stressed in the earliest drafts of their codes that international RBP rules should not impede but endorse southern cartels "in defense of" their primary commodities. Their national enterprises were to be accorded special and preferential treatment so they could achieve countervailing power against firms from developed countries. Codes should be legally binding, but developing countries' national officials should be free to exempt RBPs for national policy reasons. Besides their specific points, there was a basic difference in approach: Western nations were prepared to condemn, and to seek limited forms of international cooperative action against, those traditional restrictive business practices which would likely injure international trade and development, particularly that of developing countries. The Group of 77 countries sought international endorsement of the concept that all corporate conduct that was injurious to, or not positively helpful for, their development should be branded as restrictive and altered to their specification.

A central feature of the new approach of the 1970s was the effort to link the issue of restrictive business practices to disputes concerning activities of multinational corporations. Obviously, those restrictive business practices that occur in international trade and investment are committed by businesses engaged in such commerce. Such firms, unless they deal solely in exports, are by definition "multinational" or "transnational" companies. But the most relevant questions are whether major transnational enterprises have accounted for a substantial or increasing number of offenses in recent years, or more than firms that only export, or than the local firms with which they compete abroad. The considered judgment of Western enforcement officials is that the answer to all these questions is in the negative. In the late 1930s, it was estimated that 30 or 40 percent of world trade in manufactures was controlled by cartels.[14] Many of these cartels were highly organized, operated with impunity, and could have their agreements enforced in the courts of hospitable countries like the United Kingdom and Germany.[15] In the quarter century after the end of World War II, civil and criminal prosecutions by U.S. antitrust agencies, the spread of antitrust laws to almost all OECD countries, and million-dollar-plus fines by an aggressive EEC competition directorate caused traditional cartel practices to become rare, episodic and usually ineffective unless backed by home governments.

In a perceptive article on multinational enterprises, Detlev Vagts of Harvard Law School argued in 1970 that while MNEs may occasion antitrust problems because of their mergers, joint mergers, and dominance of small markets, their primary clashes with host states will more likely stem from five major types of issues that are not really antitrust problems.

1. Management strategies that are inconsistent with national development goals,
2. Transfer pricing causing customs and tax disputes,
3. Exclusive use, or non-use or non-transferral, of patents and know-how,
4. Repatriation of earnings,
5. Termination of investments.[16]

It has been the intermixture of these issues with conventional antitrust questions that delayed and complicated UNCTAD RBP and transfer of technology negotiations.

In 1974, the United Nations recruited a group of "Eminent Persons" to report on problems caused by MNEs. In the section of their report dealing with competition questions, the Eminent Persons recommended that transnational enterprises should be required to report restrictions on their export and purchasing policies to host governments, that governments should agree to prohibit the market allocation of exports by multinational corporations (except when such allocations secure other benefits for the countries concerned), that preparatory work in appropriate UN bodies should be undertaken for the adoption of an international antitrust agreement, and that pending such an agreement, home countries should show restraint in applying their antitrust policies if other governments were affected.[17] The most controversial of the recommendations was the one that appears to condemn market allocation. This recommendation was obviously not unanimous even within the group, particularly in regard to market allocations within a single MNE, or ones based on patent rights and technology licensing. Notwithstanding this recommendation, and despite their strong pro-developing country emphasis, the Eminent Persons warned: "Most countries should be careful not to discourage the transfer of technology by rejecting a measure of control over its use which may be inseparably linked to its wider advantages. Such advantages usually accompany wholly-owned or majority-controlled affiliates rather than minority-owned ventures."[18]

Some of the free economy Eminent Persons explained their views at length. Ryutaro Komiya, Professor of Economics at Tokyo University, observed that

> one cannot ask a majority-owned subsidiary of a multinational corporation to compete with its parent or with other majority-owned subsidiaries of the group. The branch offices of a bank cannot be required to compete with each other or with the head office, whether in one country or internationally. There is no country whose antitrust laws require that the parent and its majority-owned subsidiaries compete with each other.
>
> . . . [A] third type of market allocation arrangement, namely territory arrangements accompanying patent and know-how licensing, is very different from other restrictive practices, since it is based upon the proprietary right to patents and know-how. The main difficulty here is that a perspective licensor is often unwilling to let a prospective license use the technology and wants simply to export products from the home country, unless he is somehow protected at least to some extent from competition with the licensee. Thus, total prohibition of territorial restriction accompanying patent and know-how licensing will certainly retard, rather than promote, the transfer of technology, and will not be beneficial to the developing countries. Moreover, exclusive licensing arrangements are generally not illegal in most countries.[19]

Another group member, Hans Schaffner, former President of Switzerland, pointed out that "it would be completely unrealistic in many other cases to expect or demand that intense competition should be fostered between a parent and its offshoots abroad. This is particularly clear where the latter depend to a large extent on a continuous flow of sophisticated technology service from their parent."[20]

In 1977, the OECD published the results of a three-year study of multinational enterprises by its experts on restrictive business practices.[21] The report concluded that MNEs can produce substantial beneficial effects on national and international competition, as by entering concentrated markets dominated by local firms. It was acknowledged that MNEs are often large, and often compete in major oligopolistic markets, so that their restrictive business practices, when they do occur, will often be of great significance. The report goes on to emphasize that

> large national enterprises may present many problems similar to those just discussed. Restrictive practices of multinational enterprises do not differ in terms of competition theory or in terms of the substantive antitrust rules of Member countries. It does not therefore seem necessary or appropriate to seek to create different substantive antitrust laws for national and multinational enterprises. Such different substantive antitrust rules could have the effect of handicapping some competitors as against others.

In considering whether there were any antitrust problems peculiar to MNEs, the OECD experts concluded that the most significant of these were procedural problems in obtaining information or relief abroad, and problems of conflict of national policies and jurisdiction.[22]

In regard to the issue of market allocation within a multinational enterprise, the experts concluded as follows:

> Competition laws and practices in the OECD Member nations generally provide that intra-enterprise practices such as allocation of functions among branches or subsidiaries of a single enterprise are not considered in themselves as an unreasonable restraint of trade. Holding such parties unlawful would be likely to discourage internal growth and decrease efficiency. It might also force upon competition authorities the impracticable task of seeking to create and maintain competition within a single enterprise on an ongoing basis. In no case have arrangements within the same legal entity, such as between branches or operating divisions of the same company, been held to be unlawful. Even in cases involving separate legal entities under common control, findings of illegality have been rare and have been based upon exhaustive factual analysis of the particular cases.

In light of this analysis, they recommended no change at this time in relation to the treatment of intracorporate arrangements.[23]

In 1974, a group of RBP experts invited by UNCTAD, mainly from academia, met and formulated an initial report on restrictive practices, including tentative RBP rules for enterprises.[24] This report was not endorsed by the Trade and Development Board of UNCTAD, except for the experts' call for further meetings, this time among experts representing governments. Accordingly, UNCTAD authorized a second, and then a third, ad hoc group of experts, designated by governments. Their mandate included (1) the identification of restrictive business practices likely to injure international trade, particularly the trade and development of developing countries; (2) the formulation of principles and rules to deal with such practices; (3) the development of systems for information exchange and collection; and (4) the formulation of a model antitrust law for developing countries. The ad hoc groups of experts each met about six times over a two-year period, until all parts of the mandate except negotiation of principles and rules were largely accomplished.[25]

Also in the early 1970s, developing countries began to press UNCTAD to work on a "Code of Conduct for the Transfer of Technology" which would, *inter alia*, condemn RBPs imposed by licensors. Serious negotiation began during 1975.

During 1976, the Western countries, plus Japan, partly because of a desire to stay ahead of the UN and UNCTAD work on MNE issues, promulgated their own thirty-nine-point code of conduct for multinational enterprise under the auspices of the OECD. The OECD code includes four competition principles. These reflect a more conservative approach than that of the ITO and ECOSOC codes. Monopolization is condemned only when a dominant position in a relevant market is abused by means of specific conduct such as certain acquisitions, refusals to deal, predatory practices, price discrimination, and patent abuse. Participating in a cartel is to be avoided, but only when the cartel is not permitted by "applicable" law. Multinational corporations, it is stated, should permit their purchasers, distributors, and licensees to buy, sell, and export freely, but may restrict such freedom when doing so is justified by trade conditions, the need for specialization, or sound commercial practice. The guidelines, reflecting enforcement officials' recognition of the importance of procedural and information problems in regulating the competitive conduct of multinational enterprises, contain a final principle stressing the duty of MNEs to consult and cooperate with authorities of directly affected countries in regard to competition investigations, and to furnish requested information if the adequate safeguards for its confidentiality are provided by the requesting government.[26]

At UNCTAD in Geneva between 1976 and 1980, during many weeks of difficult negotiating sessions each year, and after two diplomatic-level conferences, agreement was reached on principles and rules for the control of restrictive business practices. About 70 percent agreement was reached on the restrictive licensing chapter of a code of conduct for the international transfer of technology.[27] Transfer of technology, which was more closely associated with developing country demands for a "New International Economic Order" than were RBPs, was initially pursued with great political vigor at the United Nations and reached the diplomatic conference stage earlier, in 1977, as opposed to 1979 for RBPs. On the other hand, for a number of important reasons transfer of technology RBP rules are more difficult to negotiate than traditional anticartel RBP rules, which caused the diplomatic-level conferences on this subject in 1977 and 1978 to be partially stalemated, and the 1980 fourth transfer of technology conference to fail while the RBP conference was succeeding.

The highly politicized nature of the transfer of technology issue led the Group of 77 to put forward an ambitious and confrontational text, combined with a demand that the code be legally binding, and to be largely unwilling to compromise issues unacceptable to the West.[28] Second, developed countries, which had traditionally encouraged innovation and its disclosure and transfer by granting important exclusive rights to inventors through national patent systems, legal protection of trade secrets and know-how, and international protection under the Paris Convention, have accepted, within a narrow range of debate, the legal principle that industrial property rights are a proper exception to antitrust laws, entitling a licensor to set price, quantity, field of use, and territorial and other conditions consistent with the scope and duration of the relevant rights but not to go beyond or abuse those rights.[29] Developing countries, whose inventors secured only a tiny percentage of all protected inventions, even within their own countries, were largely unwilling to accept the concept that owners of technology should be granted any rights to restrict transfer but instead insisted that they should be required to license or sell the technology to developing country recipients on a "no strings attached" basis.[30]

The success of the conference on an RBP Code partially results from the fact that transnational enterprises, under the threat of harsh sanctions from at least U.S., German, and Common Market antitrust laws, appear to have substantially abandoned many traditional cartel practices, except for those allowed or encouraged by governments, such as export associations.[31] On the other hand, UN studies indicate that restrictions in technology transfer agreements, such as export prohibitions designed to protect home or third markets, remain in relatively common use.[32] In fact, developing country regulations limiting repatriation of profits have actually encouraged trying clauses or other restrictions designed to extract money from the country. Thus, while for developed countries to agree to rules against traditional cartel practices would usually involve only symbolic concessions or hypothetical difficulties (except for the issues of export cartels and intraenterprise restrictions), weakening the restrictive rights of licensors might well involve the surrender of real advantages currently being exercised. Accordingly, Western delegates, representing the patent bar as well as the antitrust bar of their countries, insisted on the negotiation that each rule explicate in detail when a restriction would be justified, as well as when it would not.

A final irony of the transfer of technology negotiation has been that some Group of 77 nations, particularly of Latin America, who desired the code in order to universalize their stringent national laws, came to realize that lengthy bargaining with developed country experts was resulting in an exception-ridden document that would tend more to undermine their harsh rules than to endorse them. Thus, a resolution of the UNCTAD conference in May 1979 stated that the third transfer of technology conference, in November, would be the "concluding" conference, to signal that the Group of 77 preferred breaking off the negotiations to having the West gradually eat away at the international level the gains developing countries had achieved nationally and regionally through weakening the regime of supplier hegemony in technology transfer.[33] This threat was not carried out after the third conference, and a fourth conference was adjourned after it reached an impasse.

The two UNCTAD codes were and are being negotiated on a global basis, among nations with vastly different economic systems and degrees of experience with and attitudes toward the control of RBPs, and without any guarantee that a code's adoption will coincide with a global free trade system or a rule against state-organized cartels. Edwards's prediction of 1967 was that global rules lacking the prerequisites just discussed would not succeed. Success, however, has many meanings, particularly in the ephemeral realms of international politics and "soft" international law. By the end of 1987 UNCTAD's global antitrust principles were endorsed by the UN General Assembly, based on the success of the 1980 RBP conference. These principles are more comprehensive, more detailed, and more balanced between obligations of governments and enterprises than were the drafts of 1948 and 1953. But it is doubtful that they would have been ratified by all major states if put in treaty form. Nor does it seem probable that the codes by themselves, or by means of the forms of implementation that will be acceptable to most nations, will substantially reduce the prevalence of RBPs. The most important questions are whether principles negotiated to be acceptable in the political context of the late 1970s, particularly its emphasis on rapid development and achievement of a New International Economic Order, can retain enough clarity of meaning and philosophy to provide a basis on which the United Nations of the 1990s can build a system to protect competition at least comparable to the GATT in acceptance, neutrality, and effectiveness, and can be developed into a system that has some working effectiveness.

TEXTS AND ISSUES

Much of the remainder of this paper will attempt to deal with these questions by examining the texts negotiated or still at issue in terms of substance as well as problems of implementation and effectiveness.

Scope of Application

Defining the scope of application for an international code of conduct on RBPs was a task greatly complicated by political considerations. The West has generally pressed for broad coverage imposing like rules on both state-controlled and private enterprises, and on both transnational enterprises (TNEs) and the local enterprises with which they compete. Socialist states initially insisted that abuses stem only from private TNEs and sought to narrow the scope of application accordingly. Developing countries tended to favor "universal" application to foreign enterprises of East and West, and favored exceptions based on their national laws, or on special preference principles, which would favor or exempt their enterprises or allow their officials to permit RBPs when doing so would secure some development goal.

In the RBP code, it is stated expressly that the rules are universally applicable to all types of enterprises engaged in commerce, including those owned or controlled by states.[34] The principles and rules apply to all acts and practices having the requisite effects, regardless of whether such practices involve enterprises in one or more countries.

For purposes of the UNCTAD RBP rules, "restrictive business practices" are defined as acts or agreements that through an abuse of a dominant position of market power, "limit access to markets or otherwise unduly restrain competition, having or being likely to have adverse effects on international trade, particularly that of developing countries, and on the economic development of those countries."

The definition reflects compromise achieved by ambiguity which is potentially controversial. The stress on effect on trade and development, especially of developing countries, suggests that adverse effect on developing countries is a test in determining whether conduct is a restrictive business practice. However, the better reading appears to be that the definition does not define any offense, since those are defined in a later section. In the definition, there is no word "*or*" preceding the reference to having an adverse effect on trade and development. Thus, the definition must be read to state that an offense exists when a practice abuses a dominant position by limiting access to markets or unduly restraining competition, *and* such practice has an adverse effect on trade or development. The text exempts from the principles and rules all enterprise conduct which is directly caused by intergovernmental agreements.

The scope of application of the Transfer of Technology Code is not yet fully agreed. All groups concur that the code is "universally" applicable to all states and to all transactions in which a supplying party, private or state owned, transfers technology internationally to an acquiring party. Developing and socialist states would also apply the code to similar transactions within a state between the subsidiary of a foreign firm and a local reciprocent. Developed countries, objecting that such a rule would subject subsidiaries to more stringent rules than their local rivals, would leave the regulation of all intrastate transactions to local law. A suggested compromise would apply the code to those intrastate transactions in which the subsidiary acts as an intermediary in transferring technology developed abroad.[35]

In regard to exceptions, a text proposed by the Group of 77 and partially supported by Group D would exempt those practices that competent national authorities of the technology-acquiring country decide to be in its public interest. Group B so far argued that such an exception is unnecessary.

General Principles and Objectives

There are five agreed objectives of the restrictive business practice rules. These include ensuring that RBPs do not interfere with trade liberalization, encouraging efficiency through the creation and protection of competition, promoting consumer interests, eliminating disadvantages that may result from the RBPs of transnational corporations and other enterprises, and providing rules that can be emulated at national and regional levels.

A subsequent section sets forth general principles that are agreed upon. These call for action at national, regional, and international levels to eliminate restrictive business practices, collaboration between governments at bilateral and multilateral levels for this purpose, creation of international mechanisms to facilitate exchange and dissemination of information among governments in regard to RBPs, and the creation of means to facilitate the holding of multinational consultations relating to RBPs and their control. The principle is also agreed that the provisions of the rules should not be construed to justify conduct by enterprises that is unlawful under applicable national legislation.

Two of the most controversial issues in the negotiations on the RBP Code concerned exceptions for conduct approved by developed country governments and special treatment for conduct important to the trade and development of developing countries. The South opposed the former principle and the North the latter one. Compromise was achieved by accepting both concepts, but in less absolute terms than desired by their proponents. Principle C–6 urges that "due account" be taken of the extent to which conduct has been accepted or required under applicable legislation or regulation, bearing in mind the desirability that such laws and regulations should be clearly defined and public and the need to achieve the most comprehensive possible application of the principles and rules. Similarly, states, particularly of developed countries, are instructed by principle C-7 to "take account" in their control of restrictive practices of the needs of developing countries to promote the establishment of domestic industries and encourage economic development through regional arrangements among themselves.

Both principles embody the concept of "comity" in international antitrust enforcement, an idea that has been approved by U.S. courts in a number of recent rulings on antitrust jurisdiction over foreign events.[36]

In the Transfer of Technology Code, there is an agreed section on special treatment for developing countries, but it deals with governmental assistance to developing countries and in no way suggests that their enterprises may commit offenses condemned by the RBP chapter of the code. The only reference there to private transfers is the principle that developed countries should "facilitate access, to the extent practicable, to technologies whose transfer is subject to private decisions."

Principles for Governments

A major innovation in the modern UN codes is that they contain principles for governments as well as for enterprises. Both the ITO and ECOSOC rules consisted simply of lists of restrictive practices from which enterprises should refrain. The only principle for governments was that they should enact legislation that would cause the elimination of such practices. Yet the experience in the ensuing decades was that far more international problems arose from attempts at state enforcement of antitrust laws against foreigners or foreign transactions than from the issue of prevention of international antitrust violations. The extraterritorial application of U.S. antitrust law occasioned a whole series of significant diplomatic problems and even engendered blocking legislation by a number of other nations.[37] Similarly, when the Common Market Commission attempted to apply its antitrust law to activities outside the territory of the member states, or to gather information from neighboring countries, diplomatic problems and efforts at thwarting jurisdiction were quickly encountered.[38] It is instructive that when the OECD considered the international application of antitrust law, its first major agreement, reached in 1967, concerned itself primarily with the duty of one state to notify another of antitrust actions that might affect the important interests of the other.

In both the UNCTAD RBP principles and rules and the Transfer of Technology Code, the idea of setting forth principles for governments as well as for enterprises was quickly introduced and accepted by all groups, and has remained an integral part of the texts.

Section E of the UNCTAD RBP principles sets out in substantial detail principles and rules that states should follow at the national, regional, and subregional level. A clause urges states to adopt and improve legislation for the control of restrictive business practices. The next one suggests they should base their legislation on the principle of eliminating behavior or acts that abuse dominant positions, limit access to markets, or otherwise unduly restrain competition, and that have adverse effects on trade or development.

The key provision is the third, which instructs that when states do control restrictive business practices, they should ensure treatment of enterprises that is fair, equitable, and in accordance with established procedures of law, and that laws and regulations should be readily and publicly available. Group B insisted on additional language in the provision that national RBP laws should be not only fair and equitable, but also "non-discriminatory." The Group of 77 eventually accepted this concept by adding language that enterprises should all be treated "on the same basis."

Paragraph E(4) commits states to seek appropriate measures to prevent the use of restrictive practices within their competence when it comes to their attention that such practices adversely affect international trade and development. Under paragraph 5, when states obtain information from enterprises that contains legitimate business secrets, they are obliged to accord such information reasonable safeguards normally applicable in this field.

There was a proposed paragraph 6, supported only by Group B, which, like the OECD recommendation of 1967, would have committed states contemplating enforcement action that would affect important interests of other states to notify those states of such action, preferably sufficiently in advance to facilitate consultation. The Group of 77 countries opposed on the grounds that they did not want to encourage diplomatic protests against their RBP cases. The clause was dropped as part of an overall compromise.

Paragraph 7 was a particularly important and controversial text. It dictated that states should take measures to prevent their legislation or administrative procedures from "fostering" the participation of enterprises in cartels when such participation would cause a dominant position of market power likely to have adverse affects on international trade or development. There were two disagreements over the wording of this provision. The Group of 77 would have preferred that the provision be directed particularly at developed countries, but this was not accepted by Group B. Group B, on the other hand, would have limited the provision to condemning participation of enterprises in "international" cartels, which arguably would have made the provision inapplicable to export arrangements involving companies selling out of a single nation.[39] Both the Group of 77 and Group D insisted that the provision should condemn national export cartels. The clause was ultimately dropped because no consensus was reached on it. The primary argument for reaching agreement to prevent export cartels was that the alternative is export warfare. This argument has some basis in recent events, though some export cartels are used to reduce trade surpluses and thus prevent trade wars. Also, it was difficult to devise a neutral principle concerning what should be condemned and what allowed. An unqualified condemnation of export cartels would have ignored the reality that many of them lack market power and are designed merely to achieve minor economies of scale in selling abroad. Moreover, such a condemnation would not have prevented other practices, such as merger of exporting firms or government-controlled export, that eliminate export competition even more effectively than does an export association.

The principles for enterprises also provide that states should institute notification procedures for obtaining such information from enterprises as is necessary for the control of restrictive business practices.

Provision 8 commits states with greater expertise in the control of restrictive business practices, on request, to share their experience with, or otherwise provide technical assistance to, other states wishing to develop such systems. Lastly in this section, a ninth provision urges states, on request or at their own initiative, to supply publicly available information, and possibly other information, necessary for its control of restrictive business practices to a requesting, interested state.

In the Transfer of Technology Code, the issue of rules for states had an opposite genesis. The Group of 77 wished to have a document proclaiming the unfettered right of recipient states to screen technology transfers. Developed states agreed to recognize the right of states to adopt measures concerning the "evaluation, negotiation and registration" of agreements, but in addition demanded text declaring that national regulation must be consistent with "international law." Thus, they indirectly raised the controversial issues of whether national regulation of technology transfer contracts could be deemed an expropriation of rights, and whether such a taking would necessitate prompt, adequate, and effective compensation.[40]

Though not conceding the appropriateness of an international law standard, the developing nations eventually agreed that national regulations "should be applied equitably, in accordance with established procedures of law." Group B has pressed for guarantees also of "fundamental fairness" and enforcement that is "without discrimination." The socialist countries, Group D, joined in the demand for a nondiscrimination standard.

The chapter affirms the right of a nation to govern the "terms and conditions and the duration of transfer of technology transactions," but counterbalances this right with the admonition that regulation should "promote a favorable and beneficial atmosphere for the international transfer of technology . . . under mutually agreed, fair and reasonable terms and conditions" which "take into account differing factors . . . such as local conditions."[41]

Lastly, strenuous negotiation produced a closing paragraph that, though somewhat tautological and obscure, attempts to balance respect for industrial property protection with development objectives: "Each country adopting legislation on the protection of industrial property should have regard to its national needs of economic and social development, and should ensure an effective protection of industrial property rights granted under its national law and other related rights recognized by its national law."

Principles and Rules for Enterprises

Section D of the UNCTAD RBP principles and rules sets forth principles and rules for enterprises, including transnational corporations. It is provided, first, that enterprises should conform to the RBP laws of the countries in which they operate and be subject to the RBP laws and agencies there. Concern was expressed by business groups that this provision might imply a very broad theory of enterprise unity under which a host country would be presumed always to have antitrust jurisdiction over a foreign parent owing to the operations there of its subsidiary. Both the intent and the better reading of the langauge are that it is neutral on this complex issue. The definition of enterprise includes parents, subsidiaries, and the entity as a whole, but since they all cannot possibly be relevant in each instance, the only reasonable construction is that "enterprise" refers to the relevant parts of the whole, depending on standards such as which parts are operating in a country or are actually involved in the RBP in question.[42]

A second provision states that enterprises should cooperate with competent authorities in the countries in which they operate, and in particular should provide information such as details of restrictive arrangements required for RBP control. Information is to be provided even if it is located in foreign countries, unless such production is prevented by the applicable law or established public policy of the country where it is located.

Provision 3 deals with restrictive business practices of a cartel nature, and, after much hard negotiation on the parent-subsidiary issue, finally reads as follows:

> 3. Enterprises, except when dealing with each other in the context of an economic entity wherein they are under common control, including through ownership, or otherwise not able to act independently of each other, engaged on the market in rival or potentially rival activities, should refrain from practices such as the following when, through formal, informal, written or unwritten agreements or arrangements, they limit access to markets or otherwise unduly retrain competition, having or being likely to have adverse effects on international trade, particularly that of developing countries, and on the economic development of these countries.
> (a) agreements fixing prices including as to exports and imports;
> (b) collusive tendering;
> (c) market or customer allocation arrangements;
> (d) allocation by quota as to sales and production;
> (e) collective action to enforce arrangements – e.g., by concerted refusals to deal;
> (f) concerted refusal of supplies to potential importers;
> (g) collective denial of access to an arrangement, or association, which is crucial to competition.

This text is somewhat less clear than it appears to be. A "price-fixing" arrangement might set a maximum rather than a minimum price,[43] might merely fix profits overnight,[44] or might fix a price as a standard, e.g., medical fees for insurance compensation, with all sellers knowing they are free to charge a higher or lower price.[45] The legality of such practices would involve fine points of law and policy, with results varying from country to country. Moreover, in most countries workers, through unions, are free to fix the price they will demand for their labor; farmers are free, through cooperatives, to fix the prices for their crops going to market; and certain regulated industries, such as shipping conferences, are free to fix prices, possibly subject to public filing and review. In most countries, because of an inward theory of jurisdiction and a mercantilist trade policy, exporters are free to fix prices for products that will be sold only in other countries. It is often not forbidden for firms to form a joint venture to mine or manufacture a product, with the designated manager of the joint venture being allowed to fix the price of the product to be sold on behalf of the partners in the venture. Lastly, almost any form of price fixing might be ordered by, or authorized by, national law or a national official.

Thus, a UN code banning even well-known, relatively clear offenses like price fixing is nowhere near as certain a guide as it might seem. To a considerable extent, the sections of the document dealing with objectives, definitions, scope of application, exceptions, and general principles could clarify some of the ambiguities. Nevertheless, in most legal systems, rulings or guidelines issued by enforcing authorities, combined with decisions by a tribunal, would be needed to resolve subtle or unanticipated cases. Relying on voluntary compliance, or on separate interpretations by each UN member nation, will probably not produce uniform conduct or interpretations in regard to many of the most important behavioral questions, though particularly heinous forms of price fixing, such as secret bid rigging, will almost certainly be nearly universally condemned in theory and practice.

The other major horizontal cartel practices – market allocation, customer allocation, boycotts, etc. – raise essentially the same issues as those just discussed in relation to price fixing. The prohibitory rule is easy to draft, and securing agreement on it is not politically difficult, but major issues of interpretation and application remain.

The issue of how to deal with single-firm conduct, or with restrictive vertical agreements imposed by a stronger firm on a weaker one, is complicated by differing views – sometimes even within a single legal system – about what are the proper purposes of antitrust measures. The primary objective of all, or at least most, antitrust laws is to preserve the competitive process by deterring private restraints on it. A secondary, more political objective is to prevent the concentration of economic power. Third, there is a desire to control unfair methods of competition, though these may purposely be left to private tort law rather than be made part of public law. It is usually not an objective of RBP law to ensure that strong firms treat weak firms fairly in a commercial sense. But that issue has clouded the treatment of abuse of a dominant position, particularly in the context of technology transfer.

In the UNCTAD RBP negotiations, it was decided, as in the OECD guidelines, to deal with issues of single-firm conduct under the concept of "abuse of a dominant position of market power in a relevant market." The *Alcoa* case's concept of "monopolization" as primarily a structural offense requiring structural relief has not always found favor even in the United States, where recent decisions have moved quite close to an abuse standard.[46]

Eight types of conduct were listed as being potentially abusive when employed to limit access to markets or unduly restrain competition:

> 4. Enterprises should refrain from the following acts or behaviour in a relevant market when, through an abuse or acquisition and abuse of a dominant position of market power, they limit access to markets or otherwise unduly restrain competition,

having or being likely to have adverse effects on international trade, particularly that of developing countries, and on the economic development of these countries:

(a) predatory behaviour towards competitors, such as using below cost pricing to eliminate competitors;

(b) discriminatory (i.e. unjustifiably differentiated) pricing or terms or conditions in the supply or purchase of goods or services, including by means of the use of pricing policies in transactions between affiliated enterprises which overcharge or undercharge for goods or services purchased or supplied as compared with prices for similar or comparable transactions outside the affiliated enterprises;

(c) mergers, takeovers, joint ventures or other acquisitions of control, whether of a horizontal, vertical or conglomerate nature;

(d) fixing the parties at which goods exported can be resold in importing countries;

(e) restrictions on the importation of goods which have been legitimately marked abroad with a trademark identical or similar to the trademark protected as to identical or similar goods in the importing country where the trademarks in question are of the same origin, i.e., belong to the same owner or are used by enterprises between which there is economic, organizational, managerial or legal interdependence and where the purpose of such restrictions is to maintain artificially high prices;

(f) when not for ensuring the achievement of legitimate business purposes, such as quality, safety, adequate distribution or service:

  (i) partial or complete refusals to deal on the enterprise's customary commercial terms;

  (ii) making the supply of particular goods or services dependent upon the acceptance of restrictions on the distribution or manufacture of competing or other goods;

  (iii) imposing restrictions concerning where, or to whom, or in what form or quantities goods supplied or other goods may be re-sold or exported;

  (iv) making the supply of particular goods or services dependent upon the purchase of other goods or services from the supplier or his designee.

It was also agreed to include a note stating that whether a particular practice was abusive should be examined in terms of its purpose and effects in the actual situation, with reference also to the economic relationship of the firms involved, to any special conditions or economic circumstances in the relevant market, to whether the practice is of a type usually treated as acceptable under national and regional RBP laws, and to whether its effects are consistent with the purposes and objectives of the principles and rules.

Developing and socialist countries would have included excessive pricing as an abuse. Certain Group B nations, however, particularly the United States, Canada, and Australia, have always reasoned that a firm illegally monopolizes a market only when it engages in exclusionary conduct. High prices invite entry and thus are the opposite of exclusionary.[47] On the other hand, the RBP laws of at least West Germany, the United Kingdom, and the EEC are applicable to instances of excessive pricing.[48] The compromise was to tie the issue of excessive pricing to the discriminatory pricing offense, since even in the United States a seller can violate the Robinson-Patman anti-price discrimination act by charging a higher price to a disfavored consumer as well as by charging a lower price to a favored one.

The definition of "dominant position of market power" referred to enterprises that not only alone, but also when "acting with a few others," are in a position to control a relevant market. This reference would normally apply to concerted domination of a market. Even if it were interpreted to apply to parallel conduct amounting to "shared" or "joint" monopolization of a market, it would still be entirely consistent with existing Common Market and West German Law regarding dominant positions,[49] but might involve a more controversial point under laws such as the American or Canadian antitrust statutes.[50] Nevertheless, the effect of the provision is essentially conservative, since nothing in the principles and rules defines being a member of a "shared monopoly" as an offense in itself. The effect of the substantive provisions, when combined with the definition, is to create a rule that offenses like price discrimination and tying arrangements are objectionable only when engaged in by one or a few of the leading firms dominating an industry. In a number of Group B jurisdictions, such as the United States and the EEC, these practices could be illegal even when engaged in by a nondominant firm.[51]

That provision D(4) (iv) focuses on trademark-related antitrust abuses in the UNCTAD RBP exercise, rather than in the Transfer of Technology Code, results partially from a formal Group B position, namely, that "naked" trademark licenses should not be deemed transfers of technology but should be covered instead by general RBP rules. In fact, there are precedents in the OECD countries condemning efforts by dominant firms to use licensed or assigned trademarks to prevent the importation of genuine parallel imports legitimately bearing the same mark where the purpose is to avoid competition, rather than to protect buyers from confusion or disappointment.[52] Curiously, the trademark area is one of the few in which under Western law the imposition of the restriction on an affiliated firm tends to make the practice more objectionable rather than less.[53]

The Group of 77 would have attacked the use of marketing strategies to hinder imports or exports by related enterprises as the high point of their effort to introduce investment and development issues regarding multinational enterprises into the RBP rules. Group B has rejected such a rule not only on this basis, but also because it could be so vague as to cast doubt on the legitimacy of countless management decisions by multinationals. Moreover, Group B contended that provisions (v) (a) and (v) (c) in paragraph 4, dealing with unreasonable refusals to deal and restrictions on sale or resale, dealing with unreasonable refusals to deal and restrictions on sale or resale, provide adequate rules against any such practice by a multinational enterprise that would have the effect of entrenching a dominant firm, or injuring a competitor, in an unjustifiable manner. Western experts were prepared to tie the issue of parent-subsidiary export restraints to the doctrine of abuse of a dominant position of market power, but not to treat such restrictions as cartels. A practical example is the U.S. Justice Department's suit against the Everest and Jennings wheelchair company, a firm with about 70 percent of the U.S. market, which prevented its English affiliate from selling its lower priced chairs to American buyers. The complaint charged Everest and Jennings not with a conspiracy in violation of section 1 of the Sherman Act, but with monopolization and attempted monopolization in violation of section 2. The case was settled on the basis of "affirmative" relief, not only removing all restrictions on exports of foreign wheelchairs from E&J affiliates to the United States, but obligating the parent company to reward managers of its affiliates for making such exports.[54] Nevertheless, even this case falls far short of the rule suggested by the developing countries. The ruling applied to a multinational enterprise with a dominant market position that was preventing export to the market in which it was dominant, not to every multinational enterprise preventing exports to any market. Also, the E&J case challenged a refusal to sell for export to America a product that already was for sale and for which the buyer was prepared to pay the customary price, when the refusal was solely for the purpose of protecting the higher price structure of the parent in the United States. The Group of 77's attack on marketing strategies preventing or hindering exports is potentially applicable to much more defensible business conduct by MNEs. It now appears that UN delegates can reconcile the two positions into a sensible RBP rule, perhaps by reserving the broader investment issues for inclusion in the general code of conduct for TNEs being negotiated by the United Nations in New York.[55]

One of the more disputed antitrust offenses was the abuse of transfer pricing by overcharging or underpaying subsidiaries. Western opposition was based partially on a matter of principle. Group B delegates contended that transfer pricing is more properly treated as a tax or investment question than an antitrust issue. Transfer pricing is assigned a separate chapter in a general code of conduct for TNEs.

It is likely that, in the context of taxation, the United States and other developed countries would support the principle that parent-subsidiary transactions should be made on an arm's-length basis, compared to equivalent transactions.[56] But this does not conclusively settle whether or under what circumstances transfer pricing should be treated as an antitrust offense. Group B was prepared to support a text based on the OECD competition guideline, which condemns discriminatory pricing, including transfer pricing among affiliated firms, that is used as a means of adversely affecting competition outside those firms. Clearly, if a transfer price is to a wholly owned subsidiary and does not alter resale prices, there appears to be no competition issue at all. The colorful phrasing of this point is that the antitrust laws are indifferent to corporate self-abuse.[57]

As has been noted earlier, negotiation of the substantive rules concerning restrictive technology transfer practices has been a slower, more difficult, and more painstaking process than was negotiation of substantive rules in the RBP code. The developing countries sought in their original draft to outlaw or make unenforceable a list of forty practices encompassing virtually every form of control a licensor could seek in regard to a licensee.

The developed countries were initially prepared to condemn only eight licensing restrictions, and even most of those only when "reasonable" in the circumstances. Gradually, the chapter narrowed to twenty practices, fourteen accepted in principle by all groups and six more pressed for by the developing countries or socialist states. Only four practices were in fully agreed text, with five more all agreed except for the modifier "unreasonably" insisted upon by Group B.

The conflict over the extent to which RBP prohibitions should be applied to parent-subsidiary restrictions, eventually settled conservatively in the UNCTAD RBP rules, remains in the introduction (*chapeau*) to the RBP chapter in the Transfer of Technology Code. The Group B text states that restrictions "for the purpose of rationalization or reasonable allocation of functions between parent and subsidiary" should "normally" not be considered contrary to the chapter unless amounting to an abuse of a dominant position of market power within the relevant market. The Group of 77 text states that the rules are applicable to parent-subsidiary relations, but that "such practices may be considered as not contrary . . . when they are otherwise acceptable and which [*sic*] do not adversely affect the transfer of technology."

It is essentially agreed that a licensor should not impose obligations extending beyond the life of the industrial property rights, should not seek to prevent the licensee from challenging the validity of a patent, should not prevent research or development into new products or processes, should not require the licensee to grant back exclusive sales or representation rights except where the licensee is acting as a manufacturing subcontractor, and should refrain from entering into patent pools that unduly restrain competition. Most of these rules have analogues in U.S. and Common Market law.[58]

Other rules demanded by the developing countries, such as prohibitions against restrictions on the use of local personnel or restrictions on adaptation of the technology to local conditions, do not commonly arise as RBP issues in developed countries, but text was found that compromises what seem to be more investment or commercial than competition issues. The transformation of these provisions by negotiation from the simple prohibitions demanded by the Group of 77 to complex, carefully balanced rules is exemplary of the hard bargaining involved in drafting this code. The negotiated texts read as follows:

> *Restrictions on Use of Personnel*
> [Unreasonably]**#requiring the acquiring party to use personnel designated by the supplying party, except to the extent necessary to ensure the efficient transmission phase for the transfer of technology and putting it to use or thereafter continuing such requirement beyond the time when adequately trained local personnel are available or have been trained, or prejudicing the use of personnel of the technology acquiring country.
>
> *Restrictions on Adaptations*
> Restrictions which [unreasonably]** prevent the acquiring party from adapting the imported technology to local conditions or introducing innovations in it, or which oblige the acquiring party to introduce unwanted or unnecessary design or specification changes, if the acquiring party makes adaptations on his own responsibility and without using the technology supplying party's name, trade or service marks or trade names, and except to the extent that this adaptation unsuitably affects those products, or the process for their manufacture, to be supplied to the supplying party, his designates, or his other licenses, or to be used as a component or spare part in a product to be supplied to his customers.

Undoubtedly, the most important and hotly contested issue in the RBP chapter of the Transfer of Technology Code has been how permissive to be in regard to export restrictions imposed by a technology supplier. Such restrictions restrain international trade and may hinder the development of the recipient state. On the other hand, they often reflect the basically national and territorial nature of industrial property rights. Moreover, they frequently are the *sine qua non* for licensing and transferring valuable know-how to a developing country where lower labor or raw material costs might otherwise permit successful invasion of the technology supplier's home market or other markets where it has granted or retained exclusive rights.

The United States has usually applied its antitrust laws to export restrictions only in the context of *cross-licences* between powerful companies who are using the restrictions to divide up world markets.[59] Even when the restrictions are based on pure know-how licenses, the relevant test is whether the licenses were necessary for the development of competitive products, and whether the restrictions are of reasonable scope and duration.[60] Common Market rulings are hard on export restrictions within that market, but not outside of it.[61]

In the context of the technology code negotiations, the debate over export restrictions has tended to center on when they are acceptable, rather than when they are not. Group B would have been content with a rule stating that export restrictions are bad when they are of unreasonable scope in terms of the products and countries they seek to cover, or when their duration exceeds that of the technology rights being transferred. Pressed to state when export bans are permissible, Group B took the position that they are justified when they prevent export to countries where the technology is legally protected, where the know-how is still secret, or where others have been licensed. Group D, which is relatively conservative on certain industrial property questions, supported the first and third justifications, but would not agree that know-how licensing justified export restraint. The Group of 77 has reluctantly indicated that it might acknowledge a supplier's right contractually to ban export to a country where the goods could in any event be excluded as infringing rights there, or to countries where others have been licensed for production. The insistence on licensing for production is consistent with a long-standing developing country position that technology rights should not be internationally protected when they are used to protect a market whose technology is not being exploited.[62] Group B has recognized this position in negotiations over revision of the Paris Convention for the protection of industrial property rights by agreeing to the validity of "march-in" compulsory licensing rights after three years or so of nonuse, but the issue is more complex in regard to know-how that is being constantly licensed or transferred for various purposes.[63] Moreover, Group B has been unwilling to accept the principle that it is impermissible to license "exclusives" for a group of countries except when production is contemplated in every one of them.

An important and largely agreed provision prohibits conditioning the transfer of a particular technology on the acceptance by the recipient of additional technology, goods, or services that he does not want, unless such tying is required to maintain quality where the supplier's name is used or to fulfil the specific obligations of a guarantee (it is noted here that the supplier should specify ingredients rather than tying, if feasible). Developing countries were so anxious to cause the "unbundling" of technology they purchase that they secured agreement that "avoiding undue or unnecessary packaging" of technology is a stated objective of the Code of Conduct.[64] There is a long history of Western antitrust cases condemning tying clauses in technology licenses, so agreement that there would be a provision on this topic was easy to obtain, though difficult negotiations accompanied the formulation of the exceptions to the rule.

Other carefully worded agreed texts define when a supplier may or may not restrict the right of the recipient to deal in competing products or technologies or to publicize the products resulting from the transferred technology in his own way.

A provision condemning supplier regulation of prices to be charged by a technology recipient remains bracketed because of insistence by the United States and a few other group B countries that this practice is sometimes justifiable, particularly when there is only one licensee who is not in competition with the supplier.[65]

Agreement on a fourteenth provision is blocked by a small but significant difference in conception between the Group of 77 and Group B about the nature of know-how licensing. The developing countries have pressed for a rule condemning all restrictions or obligations that continue after the conclusion of a technology transfer arrangement, while the West would allow restrictions based on know-how that is still secret. The Group of 77 position would mean that if a firm licenses know-how for five years, it may not thereafter seek to prevent the licensee from continuing to make products based on that technology, or otherwise using or disclosing it. The conceptual argument is that you can sell knowledge but not lease it, since it cannot be erased from people's minds. Group B espouses the more conventional view that what happens to the know-how or use of it after the arrangement is a matter of commercial bargain. If the know-how has remained secret at the end of the contract, it should not be illegal for the licensor to have contracted for its return and its nonuse and nondisclosure. Interestingly, a U.S. Court of Appeals upheld approximately the Group of 77 theory in a two to one decision, but was promptly reversed by a unanimous Supreme Court, which held that the unfortunate licensee could be held to its bargain even when the know-how had become public and was being used by others who paid no royalty.[66] However, it should be noted that the American case involved only an obligation to pay royalties, not a ban on use which might have been found more anticompetitive. Also, the developing countries stress that Western cases are based on the assumption of fair bargains among equals, while the purpose of the Code of Conduct is to redress a perceived inequality of bargaining power resulting in one-sided agreements.

Provisions 15 through 20 would prohibit limitations on volume or field of use, abusive of quality controls, required use of trademarks, required payment in equity shares, insistence on arrangements of unlimited duration, and limitations on use of technology "already imported." Not one of the provisions would clearly be illegal under most Western RBP laws, though certain of the practices could be considered objectionable if employed to achieve market division or significant restraint of competition.[67] The twentieth practice, moreover, is so purely development oriented that no acceptance of it seems possible. Western suppliers of technology do not seem likely to accept the principle that if they have licensed technology to a recipient in a particular country, they thereafter may not prevent the recipient from disseminating it to others and may not charge new royalties to later licensees.

Legal Nature and Implementation

Difficult issues in the UNCTAD negotiations on both the RBP and the Transfer of Technology Codes have concerned the legal nature and implementation of the rules being formulated. The position of Group B on their legal nature has been long-standing, clear, and adamant: The agreed rules or principles should be viewed as guidelines to be accepted on a voluntary basis by agreeing states and recommended by them to their enterprises. In the spring 1976 meeting of the UNCTAD RBP experts, the developed country experts offered the following text:

> [P]rinciples for governments should be voluntary because of the greatly varying states of development among members of the United Nations and the divergencies in approaches to restrictive business practice, a field in which many member countries had no legislation or little experience. . . . [P]rinciples for enterprises should also be voluntary, since, in the foreseeable future, national or regional law, as perhaps guided by model laws, would be the most appropriate instrument for the enforcement of binding rules on enterprises. . . . There exists no worldwide international machinery for the enforcement and interpretation of any conceivable worldwide restrictive business practice rules, and little likelihood, given the wide divergence in national objectives, attitudes and experience in this field, that countries would be prepared to create and accept binding international enforcement and adjudication. . . . [A]ny attempt to enforce general principles for enterprises separately in each nation would lead to wide variations in interpretation, procedures and sanctions . . . this would be unfair and inequitable, would create an unstable and unpredictable atmosphere in which enterprises would be forced to operate, and could exacerbate conflicts among nations. On the other hand, voluntary principles could help to harmonize international opinion about restrictive business practices, shape the general behaviour of most enterprises, and facilitate international co-operation.

In drafting the codes, Group B was prepared only to agree to "encourage" its enterprises to "follow" the rules, rather than to "ensure" that they "conform" to the rules, as the Group of 77 would have preferred.[68]

The Group of 77, stressing that multinational enterprises in particular should not feel free to disregard these new international norms, for some time insisted that the words "shall refrain" rather than "should refrain" precede the listing of offenses to be avoided. Also, they initially insisted that the Transfer of Technology Code expressly obligate states to agree to an "internationally legally binding Code of Conduct on the transfer of technology."[69]

Nevertheless, the developing country position has been far less clear or consistent on this issue than appears on the surface of the texts. In the transfer of technology negotiations, when it became certain that the West would not agree to a binding code, the Group of 77 agreed to create a review committee that would reexamine the code and its legal nature after five years. But the Group of

77 would not publicly acknowledge that acceptance of this alternative signaled abandonment of its original position. In the UNCTAD RBP negotiations, the Group of 77 never expressly came out in support of a legally binding set of rules, probably because of the extreme sensitivity of OPEC nations and some other developing countries that the rules might boomerang against the practices of their national enterprises.

Moreover, the developing countries made it obvious that they do not favor international adjudication of rights and wrongs in RBP matters, particularly if the issue is the fairness of national treatment of a foreign enterprise.[70] Thus, the binding nature of the rules for enterprises was to be achieved essentially by national action in furtherance of the international agreement. For developed countries this would necessitate an extreme form of extraterritorial application of their antitrust or RBP laws. For instance, if an American firm licenses technology to Brazil with a clause restricting exports to China that is arguably violative of the RBP chapter of the Code of Conduct, Brazil can invalidate the restriction under its national law even without a binding international code. If Brazil for some reasons wants the United States to invalidate the restriction, U.S. courts would face innumerable problems of jurisdiction and evidence. Nor would it be clear that Brazil would accept the result if U.S. courts found the restrictions reasonable and not violative of the code. If China wishes to have either Brazil or the United States invalidate the restriction, and both refuse to do so, it is totally unclear how such a dispute could be resolved absent an international tribunal.

Wester countries are fully aware of, and reconciled to, the fact that even voluntary international guidelines can be promptly enacted as binding national law by any country wishing to do so, or adopted as a sort of investment pledge an enterprise must adhere to as a condition of doing business in a country. Developing countries have so far shown little inclination to make an antitrust code binding, as in the European Common Market, by means of an international commission armed with subpoenas and sanctions and an international court endowed with exclusive jurisdiction. Rather, they seem to favor the approach espoused by the United States in UN bribery code negotiations, namely, urging that signatories should bind themselves to amend national law to achieve conformity with the standards of the code. Such an approach in the antitrust or transfer of technology context could have the ironic and unworkable effect of obligating TNE home bases like the United States and the EEC to seek to engage in enforcement of antitrust laws on an even more extraterritorial basis than that which has previously caused substantial diplomatic controversy.

But the reality was that the West, the Communist nations, and the more conservative or nationalistic of the developing countries were unwilling to accede to a binding antitrust or technology code in the foreseeable future. Thus, after agreement by all groups that neither code would be binding at present, the remaining issues centered on the delineation of implementation, review, and consultation procedures that were consistent with the nonbinding nature of the rules.

In both UNCTAD negotiations, the developed country position in regard to implementation was to favor approximately the same approach as in the OECD, though with somewhat greater hesitation about agreeing to even as extensive a review process as was acceptable in the friendlier and more reliable confines of the OECD. The 1976 OECD declaration provides for a limited form of follow-up and implementation. It was agreed there that the Investment Committee of the OECD should examine and review "issues" arising under the guidelines. Such review was not to involve judging the practices of a single enterprise in a particular situation, though enterprises would be permitted to participate in a review when their information would be pertinent. Lastly, it was provided that the operation of the guidelines would be reviewed in general terms after three years (in 1979) in order to determine whether they should be altered or supplemented. Since 1976, the guidelines have been promulgated and endorsed, have been cited in a number of diplomatic negotiations and a few legal briefs, and have been used by the Investment Committee in the review of at least one controversy concerning the behavior of a multinational enterprise in which they appear to have caused an alteration in corporate behavior (in a labor relations matter).[71] They were thoroughly reviewed in 1979, but only one small change was made.

The most substantial implementation provision of the UNCTAD RBP rules is a procedure for consultation at the request of a state, particularly a developing country, when it believes that bilateral diplomacy is appropriate in regard to an issue concerning control of restrictive business practices. States agree to give full consideration to such requests and, upon agreement as to subject matter and procedure, to consult in good faith. It is then stated that if the states involved so agree, a report on the matter should be made available to interested states or international organizations. The Group of 77 also would have provided that, with the permission of the involved states, any unresolved matter arising out of a consultation on restrictive business practices should be brought to the Trade and Development Board of UNCTAD in order that it might consider what further action might be taken to resolve the issue. Group B successfully opposed any such "conciliation" procedure.

An additional section provides that states should implement the agreed provisions by means of appropriate national legislation and regulation. A second provision in the section commits states to the creation of a permanent group of experts within a committee of UNCTAD to monitor implementation and to make proposals for possible improvements in the principles and rules.

In the negotiations on the Transfer of Technology Code, it is agreed in regard to implementation that states that have accepted the code should "take appropriate steps at the national level to meet their commitment to the Code." In addition, it is agreed that a committee of UNCTAD should provide a forum for exchange of views among states on matters related to the code, particularly on its application and experience gained in its operation. The committee is authorized to undertake studies and research for the purpose of furthering the aim of the code, to invite and consider studies from other parts of the UN system, to collect and disseminate information relating to the code, to make appropriate recommendations, and to organize symposiums and workshops about the application of the provisions of the code. Group B has so far rejected an additional provision that would empower the committee to provide a forum and procedure for negotiations and consultations between states concerning the interpretation or application of the code.

It is agreed that the committee shall review the implementation and application of the code five years after its adoption and make a decision whether to recommend an additional UN conference to revise all or part of the code for its improvement or further development.

Past experience suggests that consultation procedures will more likely be used to complain about antitrust investigations or prosecutions than to seek relief against an RBP. A study by the OECD in 1977 shows that the first paragraph of its 1967 resolution, calling for notification of enforcement proceedings, and usually in fact resulting in consultations about those proceedings, has been employed more than 150 times, by a large number of nations.[72] The second paragraph of the 1967 resolution, dealing with enforcement cooperation, has been used far less frequently. The 1973 resolution, dealing directly with the elimination of international restrictive business practices, has never been used, nor has the 1960 GATT consultation procedure on RBPs.[73] Thus, it appears that national law, not international cooperation or conciliation, remains the major method for eliminating those restrictive business practices that nations are willing to prevent or punish, while the only popular topic for consultation is conflict of jurisdiction and of national interests involved when one state attempts to investigate, prevent, or punish an alleged restrictive business practice involving nationals of another state.

Why is it that consultation is seldom used to attack RBPs? First of all, the adversely affected state is seldom totally dependent on aid from the home state of the TNE. It may have laws to control RBPs, or it can enact them. It may also control mergers, licensing, or pricing by means of investment or technology transfer screening laws. It may well be able to rely on an "effects" doctrine or on the presence of a branch to establish jurisdiction.[74] Second, most restrictive arrangements are discovered after they end, or cease upon being discovered. Consultation is not particularly helpful in obtaining punishment for past violations, or damages to compensate customers or other victims. Lastly, many modern states do not accept the premise that they are responsible for the behavior of "their" enterprises abroad. Moreover, they would likely be reluctant to seek to restrain conduct occurring outside their territory and probably not violative of their law, or as to which facts are unknown or in dispute.

On the other hand, in light of agreement on the creation of committees empowered to gather information concerning experience under the codes as well as to discuss "issues" arising under them, it seems likely that indirect pressures for avoidance of certain RBPs or of certain governmental encouragement of them will result from such multilateral consultations. The latter would probably be workable if carried out with UNCTAD's emphasis on consensus rather than on voting by nation. This approach, although slow and tending toward generalities, avoids embarrassing the leading home countries of TNEs by means of lopsided majority votes, and forcing them into defensive postures.

CONCLUSION

The subject of international antitrust codes is full of paradoxes. As has been discussed earlier here, in 1967 Corwin Edwards wrote that global approaches to control of RBPs could not succeed for many reasons, mostly related to differences in national laws, in degree of development, and in attitudes towards the free market system. Yet, in 1968 Edwards agreed to become a consultant to UNCTAD to outline new projects for UN involvement in the control of RBPs.[75] The subject of restrictive business practices is obviously too important to be ignored internationally in the age of the multinational corporation. And the United States was and is too dedicated to antitrust law and too expert in it to play any international role short of leadership. Such leadership will be crucial to ensure that the UN RBP Code and the permanent committee of experts function in neutral, procompetitive ways.

It seems likely that some suspicion about UN rules will persist in American business circles. The NAM and the Chamber of Commerce led the opposition to the codes, but eventually came to support the RBP Code as finally adopted. Originally, U.S. business organizations expressed concern that any UN antitrust agreement would involve undue exceptions or preferences for developing country and state enterprises, would not sufficiently recognize the reasons for parent company control of subsidiaries, would so embrace development goals as to lose its identity as a competition code, and would be so vague as to be open to changing and abusive interpretations.[76] It was also argued that the exclusion of intergovernmental agreements – such as OPEC – from the code would vitiate its usefulness.

Many of these criticisms were important in shaping a final text that the United States and multinational companies could support. Some of the objections, however, appear in retrospect to have been excessive or unfounded. There was undoubtedly reason for concern that wholesale acceptance of the Group of 77's initial positions in the transfer of technology and RBP negotiations would have threatened the procompetitive rationale of antitrust regulation and might have involved endorsement of discriminatory treatment of Western enterprises, with the long-run effect of discouraging foreign licensing, trade, and investment rather than facilitating them on more acceptable terms. But the outcome of the negotiations has been strongly conservative of basic antitrust positions. The logic of the discipline almost always triumphed over hastily improvised efforts to graft investment and development politics upon established antitrust doctrines. More importantly, early recognition in these negotiations that control of RBPs is much more a problem of disputes between governments about when and how to prevent, allow, or even encourage RBPs than a problem simply relating to enterprise behavior led to a careful balance in the texts between rules for states and rules for companies.

In late 1974, the developing countries pushed a "Charter of Economic Rights and Duties" through the UN General Assembly, over the reservation of the United States, the United Kingdom, the Federal Republic of Germany, and a few other Western states, in an attempt to create a new principle of international law legitimizing unfettered national sovereignty over natural resources and foreign investment.[77] As Oscar Schachter has perceptively pointed out, the effect, paradoxically, was just the opposite: The very recourse to international declarations strengthened the principle that economic regulation by nations is indeed subject to international rules, however permissive those may be in a given document.[78] The transfer of technology and RBP exercises have carried forward this trend in a much more obvious way. Developing countries have won the principles that enterprises have no more right to engage in RBPs against weak states than against strong ones, and that all states have the right to enact and enforce legislation in this field. The price for these principles has been agreement to rules that tend to establish what is acceptable commercial conduct as much as what is unacceptable, and to rules that specify such duties as fair treatment and respect for confidentiality that states owe to foreign enterprises involved in RBP disputes. These tough, specialized negotiations in the UNCTAD forum have eroded much of the *carte blanche* for arbitrary regulation contained in the Charter of Economic Rights and Duties.

The relation of the UNCTAD RBP principles to the legitimization of commodity cartels like OPEC is somewhat more complex. The Charter of Economic Rights and Duties stated unequivocally that producer cartels are good and that no state should interfere with them. Significantly, the Western alternative to this text was not a condemnation of such cartels but rather a demand that consumer countries should be included in the negotiation of any such "stabilization agreements." The UNCTAD RBP principles largely bypass the OPEC issue by providing that restrictive business practices are practices by enterprises, not by states themselves, and by exempting intergovernmental agreements. The possibility that OPEC needs the cooperation of enterprises to function and that the RBP text on exemptions based on state approval may be read to require the approval of consumer states might justify discussions or consultations about OPEC or similar cartels in an UNCTAD RBP forum, but there seems no likelihood that such requested consultation would even be accepted, much less cause modification of a major commodity cartel among producer governments.

International antitrust rules are justified not only by free market or free trade principles, but also by the concept that restraint or cartelization of international markets is a sovereign prerogative and therefore that private enterprises may not engage in such activities except under rules set down by states. This concept reflects fundamental American conceptions of the separation of private and state economic activity. Condemning restrictive business practices by enterprises in an antitrust code while leaving the issue of OPECs to state-to-state diplomatic relations is entirely consistent with this approach.

In the long run, UN antitrust principles, combined with continuing international work and study in the antitrust field, may help to create a climate unfavorable to OPECs, much as U.S. antitrust principles justified the fight to de-regulate American industries cartelized in the 1930s.[79]

During this active period of formulation RBP principles at the international level, it is too early to make a final assessment or prediction about the value of what has been or will be achieved. Some successes are evident. Controlling restrictive business practice has been accepted as an international goal, justified largely on the basis of a free market rationale. Discrimination against foreign enterprises has been avoided, while the principle of fair treatment has been firmly established. The seeds for useful institutional work internationally at the expert level have been planted.

In regard to the larger issues, measurement of success will turn on the modesty of one's conception of what is presently possible. Final codification of a body of law like antitrust that varies widely and does not exist in many countries is almost certainly not feasible. Direct international investigation and punishment of individual restrictive practices seems equally unlikely in the near future, given nations' insistence on sovereignty and the diversity, even conflict, of their interests. But increased international publicity about, and a subsequent reduction in, certain types of RBPs seems more attainable as a positive result of these exercises. Transforming grievances about multinational enterprises from political rhetoric into specific issues about which experts can analyze facts and negotiate rules can be a significant step in reducing North–South tensions and improving the climate for investment. All in all, there seem to be good grounds for judging the work of the last five years as being a success.

NOTES

#Two asterisks following bracketed words denote text proposed by Group B.

1 Edwards's writings include *Economic and Political Aspects of International Cartels*, U.S. Congress, Senate, A Study for the Subcommittee on War Mobilization of the Committee on Military Affairs, 78th Cong., 2d Sess. (Washington, D.C.: Government Printing Office, 1944); *Maintaining Competition: Requisites of a Governmental Policy* (New York: McGraw-Hill, 1949); *Big Business and the Policy of Competition* (Cleveland: Western Reserve University Press, 1956).

2 Public letter, Franklin D. Roosevelt to Cordell Hull, Sept. 1944, quoted by Edwards in his article, "The Possibilities of an International Policy Toward Cartels," in *A Cartel Policy for the United Nations* (New York: Columbia University Press, 1945), p. 97.

3 Edwards's work in Japan is described in Eleanor M. Hadley, *Antitrust in Japan* (Princeton: Princeton University Press, 1970), pp. 125–26.

4 Title V of *Havana Charter for an International Trade Organization*, Department of State Publication no. 3206, Commercial Policy Series no. 114 (Washington, D.C.: Government Printing Office, 1948). The negotiation is described in Dale Furnish, "A Transitional Approach to Restrictive Business Practices," *International Lawyer* (1970), 4:322–27.

5 See U.S. Congress, House, Hearings before the Committee on Foreign Affairs, 81st Cong., 2d Sess., on H.R. Res. 236 (Washington, D.C.: Government Printing Office, 1950), p. 564. See also *ibid.*, p. 419.

6 See Sigmund Timberg, "Restrictive Business Practices as an Appropriate Subject for United Nations Action," *Antitrust Bulletin* (1955), 1:410.

7 Report of the Ad Hoc Committee on Restrictive Business Practices, ECOSOC, Official Records, 16th Sess., Supp. no. 11, UN Doc. E/2380 (1953), pp. 12–18.

8 See Corwin D. Edwards, *Control of Cartels and Monopolies* (Dobbs Ferry, New York: Oceana, 1967), pp. 234–35.

9 UN Doc. E/2612/Add.2 (1955), p. 5. See Furnish, "Restrictive Business Practices," p. 327.

10 The ECSC rules are discussed in Edwards, *Cartels and Monopolies*, pp. 243–79. The Common Market rules are examined, e.g., in James A. Rahl, "European Common Market Antitrust Laws," *Antitrust Law Journal* (1971), 40:810.

11 Edwards, *Cartels and Monopolies*, pp. 325–26.

12 *Ibid.*, p. 327.

13 UNCTAD Res. 73 (III), May 19, 1972, discussed in L. Robert Primoff, "International Regulation of Multinational Corporations and Business – the United Nations Takes Aim," *Journal of International Law and Economics* (1976), 11:288–89.
14 See Fritz Machlup, "The Nature of the International Cartel Problem," in *A Cartel Policy*, pp. 11–12.
15 See Ben W. Lewis, "The Status of Cartels in Post-War Europe," in *ibid.*, pp. 25–46.
16 Detlev Vagts, "The Multinational Enterprise: A New Challenge for Transnational Law," *Harvard Law Review* (1970), 83:739.
17 *The Impact of Multinational Corporations on the Development Process and on International Relations* (New York: United Nations, 1974, Sales no. E. 74.II.A.5).
18 *Ibid.*, p. 69.
19 *Ibid.*, p. 111.
20 *Ibid.*, p. 143.
21 OECD, *Restrictive Business Practices of Multinational Enterprises* (Paris: OECD, 1977).
22 *Ibid.*, p. 58, paras. 193 and 194.
23 *Ibid.*, pp. 59 and 63, paras. 200 and 212.
24 UN Doc. TD/B/C.2/119/REv. 1 (1974).
25 See UNCTAD, Report of the Second Ad Hoc Group of Experts on Restrictive Business Practices (Geneva United Nations, 1976, TD/B/C.2/AC.5/6); UNCTAD, Report of the Third Ad Hoc Group of Experts on Restrictive Business Practices on its Sixth Session (Geneva: United Nations, 1979, TD/B/C.2/AC.6/20).
26 OECD, *International Investment and Multinational Enterprise* (Paris: OECD, 1976), discussed in Joel Davidlow, "Some Reflections on the OECD Competition Guidelines," *Antitrust Bulletin* (1977), 12:441.
27 The background of these conferences is discussed in Mark R. Joelson, "The Proposed Codes of Conduct as Related to Restrictive Business Practices," *Law and Policy in International Business* (1977), 8:857–61. See also UNCTAD Res. 89(iv) (1976), and UNCTAD Res. 103(v) (1979).
28 See generally Marcus B. Finnegan, "Code: A Panacea or Pitfall? *Les Nouvelles* (June 1978), pp. 74–75.
29 See generally Joel Davidow, "U.S. Antitrust Laws and International Transfers of Technology: The Government View," *Fordham Law Review* (1975), 43:733; Marcus B. Finnegan, "The Burgeoning Development of the Common Market Competition Rules and its Impact on International Licensing," *Mercer Law Review* (1976), 27:519.
30 See Pubwash Code, UN Doc. TD/B/AC.11/L.12 (1974); Surendra Patel, "Transfer of Technology and Developing Countries," *Foreign Trade Review* (January–March 1972), 6.387.
31 See J. D. Gribbin, rev. of OECD, *Export Cartels*, Report of the Committee of Experts on Restrictive Business Practices, 1974, *Antitrust Bulletin* (Summer 1976), 21(2): 343–44.
32 One such study is UNCTAD, Major Issues Arising from the Transfer of Technology to Developing Countries, UN Doc. TD/B/AC.11/10/Rev. 1 (1974).
33 UNCTAD Res. 113(v), June 3, 1979.
34 UNCTAD. The Set of Multilaterally Agreed Equitable Principles and Rules for the Control of Restrictive Business Practices, UN Doc. TD/RBP/CONF/10 (April 1980) (hereinafter referred to as RBP Code), Scope of Application, provision 4.
35 See UNCTAD, Draft International Code of Conduct on the Transfer of Technology, UN Doc. TD/CODE TOT/20 (1979) (hereinafter cited as TOT Code), provision 1.4 and n. 6.
36 Mannington Mills v. Congoleum Corp., 595 F. 2d 1278, 1296 (3d Cir. 1979); Timberlane Lumber Co. v. Bank of America, 549 F. 2d 597, 612 (9th Cir. 1976).

37 See Note, "Discovery of Documents Located Abroad in U.S. Antitrust Litigation: Recent Developments in the Law Concerning the Foreign Illegality Excuse for Non-production," *Virginia Journal of International Law* (1974), 14:747; International Law Association, *Report of the Fifty-first Conference Held at Tokyo* (London: ILA, 1965) (collection of diplomatic protests), pp. 565–92.

38 One such matter was the *Hoffman-La Roche Vitamins* case. Hoffman objected that the Commission was using this information obtained through a breach of the Swiss Criminal Code, but this contention was rejected in a decision of the Commission (76/642/EEC of June 9, 1976). The informant was prosecuted *in absentia* by the Swiss Government, discussed in Jeremy Lever, "Aspects of Jurisdictional Conflict in the Field of Discovery," in *Proceedings of Fifth Annual Fordham Corporate Law Institute on International Antitrust* (New York: Harcourt, Brace, Jovanovich, 1979), p. 358.

39 This distinction would approximate the present state of U.S. law, under which national export cartels are exempted by the Webb-Pomerene Act of 1918, 15 U.S.C. §§ §§ 61–66 (1976); but cartel agreement between a U.S. export cartel and a foreign one is not permitted. United States v. United States Alkalai Export Ass'n, 86 F. Supp. 59 (S.D.N.Y. 1949).

40 See Don C. Piper, "On Changing or Rejecting the International Legal Order," *International Lawyer* (1978), 12:293.

41 TOT Code, provision 3.1.

42 Illustrative of the highly factual nature of this determination are Zenith Radio Corp. v. Matsushita Elec. Inc., 402 F. Supp. 262 (E.D. Pa. 1975) (parent-sub treated as an entity); and Williams v. Canon, Inc., 432 F.Supp. 376 (C.D. Cal. 1977) (insufficient contacts found between parent and sub). See generally, OECD, *Restrictive Business Practices*, pp. 40–54; Joseph Griffen, "The Power of Host Countries Over the Multinational: Lifting the Veil in the European Economic Community and the United States," *Law and Policy in International Business* (1974), 6:375.

43 This practice would violate U.S. antitrust law. *See, e.g.*, Albrecht v. Herald Co. 390 U.S. 145 (1968). However, it is almost never attacked by the Justice Department or the Federal Trade Commission. The rule is criticized in Philip Elman, "Petrified Opinions' and Competitive Realities," *Columbia Law Review* (1966), 66:625.

44 Chicago Board of Trade v. United States, 246 U.S. 231 (1918).

45 *See, e.g.*, United States v. American Society of Anesthesiologists, Inc., 473 F.Supp. 147 (E.D. Pa. 1979).

46 United States v. Aluminium Co. of America, 148 F. 2d 416, 426 (2d Cir. 1945). See Laurens H. Rhinelander, "The Roche Case: One Giant Step for British Antitrust," *Virginia Journal of International Law* (Fall 1974), 15:34–35.

47 See Rhinelander, "The Roche Case" pp. 34–35. United Brands Co., [1975–2] Comm. Mkt. Rep. (CCH) ¶ 9800; Corwin D. Edwards, "American and German Policy Toward Conduct by Powerful Enterprises: A Comparison," *Anti-trust Bulletin* (1978), 23:100.

48 See Edwards, "American and German Policy," pp. 93–94; Kurt Markert, "The New German Antitrust Reform Law," *Antitrust Bulletin* (1974), 19:135; Valentine Korah, "Interpretation and Application of Article 86 of the Treaty of Rome: Abuse of a Dominant Position within the Common Market," *Notre Dame Lawyer* (1978), 53:768.

49 See Treaty Establishing European Economic Community, *United Nations Treaty Series*, 298:11, Art. 86, March 25, 1957; European Economic Commission, *Report by the Commission on the behavior of the oil companies in the Community during the period from October 1973 to March 1974* (Brussels: European Communities, 1977), pp. 154–55. Under German law, see section 22 of the German Law Against Restraints of Competition, July 27, 1957; see also Kurt Markert, "The Control of Abuses by Market-Dominating Enterprises Under German Antitrust Law," *Cornell International Law Journal* (Summer 1978), 11:275.

50 See Edward H. Levi, "The Antitrust Laws and Monopoly," *University of Chicago Law Review* (1947), 14:153; Richard A. Posner, "Oligopoly and the Antitrust Laws: A Suggested Approach, *Stanford Law Review* (1969), 21:1562; W. T. Stanbury and G. B. Reschenthaler, "Oligopoly & Conscious Parallelism: Theory, Policy & Canadian Cases," *Osgoode Hall Law Journal* (1977), 15:617–700.

51 In the United States, the Robinson-Patman Act prohibits price discrimination by any seller. See Corwin D. Edwards, *The Price Discrimination Law* (Washington, D.C.: Brookings Institution, 1959). Tying arrangements are also condemned by U.S. law whenever the party using them has sufficient economic power in the tying product to appreciably restrain competition. Northern Pac. Ry. v. United States, 356 U.S. 1 (1958). The Treaty of Rome, Article 85(d) and (e), condemns price discrimination and tying arrangements by parties whenever those practices have as their object or effect the restraint of competition, and regardless of whether the parties have a dominant position cognizable under Article 86.

52 See generally, OECD, *Restrictive Business Practices relating to Trademarks* (Paris: OECD), 1978). *See also* the EEC cases Grundig-Consten, [1966] E.C.R. 299, and Sirena, [1971] E.C.R. 69.

53 *See* Unites States v. Guerlain Inc. 155 F.Supp. 77(S.D.N.Y.), *dismissed,* 172 F.Supp. 107 (S.D.N.Y. 1959); 19 C.F.R. §133.21(b) and (c).

54. United States v. Everest & Jennings Intl., Civ. No. 77–1648 R (C.D. Cal. 1977), [1979–1] Trade Cases (CCH) ¶ 62508, at 76,961 (Feb. 5, 1979).

55 For instance, the OECD Guidelines on International Investment and Multinational Enterprises ("Competition Guidelines") provide in guideline 5 on general policies that MNEs should "allow their component entities freedom to develop their activities and to exploit their competitive advantage in domestic and foreign markets, consistent with the need for specialization and sound commercial practice." This provision is not treated as an antitrust principle; but as an investment policy. The Competition Guidelines are an annex to the OECD Declaration on International Investment and Multinational Enterprises of June 21, 1976.

56 In the OECD Guidelines for Multinational Enterprises, the second taxation guideline warns against use of "transfer pricing which does not conform to an arms length standard" to violate national laws.

57 The relevant OECD text is Competition Guideline 1(e). Two U.S. antitrust cases, Gottesman v. General Motors Corp., 310 F.Supp. 1257 (S.D.N.Y. 1970), *aff'd*, 436 F. 2d 1205 (2d Cir. 1971), and Trans World Airlines v. Hughes, 449 F. 2d 51 (2d Cir. 1971), *rev'd on other grounds*, 409 U.S. 363 (1973), suggest that tying arrangements by a parent company to "bleed" an affiliate may be actionable under the antitrust laws at the behest of minority stockholders.

58 *See* Brulotte v. Thys Co., 379 U.S. 29 (1964), and A.O.I.P. v. Beyrard, 17 Comm. Mkt. L.R. D14 (1976) (condemning restrictions after expiration); Lear, Inc. v. Adkins, 395 U.S. 653 (1969), and Davidson Rubber, 11 Comm. Mkt. L.R. D52 (1972) (condemning "no-challenge" clauses); Transparent Wrap Mach. Corp v. Stokes & Smith Co., 329 U.S. 637 (1947), and Raymond-Nagoya, [1973] Comm. Mkt. Rep. (CCH) § 9513 (applying a rule of reason to grant-back clauses). See generally Mark R. Joelson, "United States Law and the Proposed Code of Conduct on the Transfer of Technology," *Antitrust Bulletin* (1978), 23–835.

59 *Compare* United States v. National Lead Co., 332 U.S. 319 (1947), and United States v. Imperial Chem. Indus., 100 F. Supp. 504 (S.D.N.Y. 1951) (condemning cross-licensing international cartels) *with* Brownell v. Ketchum Wire & Mfg. Co., 211 F. 2d 121 (9th Cir. 1954), and Dunlop Co. Ltd. v. Kelsey-Hayes Co. 484 F. 2d 407 (6th Cir. 1973) (upholding export restrictions on one-way licenses).

60 *See* Foundry Services Inc. v. Beneflux Corp. 110 F. Supp. 857 (S.D.N.Y. 1953). Shin

Nippon Koki Co. v. Irvin Industries, Inc., [1975–1] Trade Cases (CCH) ¶60.347, 66.438 (N.Y. Sup. Ct. 1975); U.S. Department of Justice, *Antitrust Guide for International Operations* (Washington, D.C.: Government Printing Office, 1977), pp. 28–32.

61 *Compare* Consten and Grundig-Verkaus GmbH v EEC Comm'n, [1966] Comm. Mkt. Rep. (CCH) ¶7618, and Centrafarm B.V. v. Sterling Drug, Inc., 14 Comm. Mkt. L.R. 480 (1974) *with* Raymond-Nagoya, [1973] Comm. Mkt. Rep. (CCH) ¶9513 (1973).

62 See UNCTAD, The Role of the Patent System in the Transfer of Technology to Developing Countries, UN Doc. TD/B/AC.11/19/REv.1 (1975), pp. 47–52.

63 *See* United States v. Westinghouse Elec. Corp. 471 F. Supp. 532 (N. D. Cal. 1978), *appeal filed*, No. 794109 (9th Cir. 1979). See generally, Miles W. Kirkpatrick and Steven P. Mahinka, "Antitrust and the International Licensing of Trade Secrets and the Know-How: A Need for Guidelines," *Law and Policy in International Business* (1977), 9:725.

64 TOT code, Provision (viii).

65 *See* United States v. General Elec. Co., 272 U.S. 476 (1926), discussed in Lawrence A. Sullivan, *Handbook of the Law of Antitrust* (St. Paul: West, 1977), ¶ 185, pp. 541–54.

66 Aronson v. Quick Point Pencil Co., 99 S.Ct. 1096 (1979), *rev'g* 567 F. 2d 757 (8th Cir. 1977).

67 See Sullivan, *Antitrust*, ¶ 186, pp. 554–62.

68 TOT Code, preamble, provision 11, p. 2.

69 *Ibid.*, provision 13.

70 This can be seen in the Group of 77's insistence that codes be enforced by national, not international, means, and that granting exemptions should be the right of national officials.

71 Roger Blanpain, *The Badger Case and the OECD Guidelines for Multinational Enterprises* (Amsterdam: Kluwer-Deventer, 1977).

72 OECD, Report on the Operation of the 1967 Council Recommendation Concerning Cooperation Between Member Countries on Restrictive Business Practices Affecting International Trade During the Period 1967–1975, reprinted in *Antitrust Bulletin* Summer 1977), 22:459:85.

73 See UNCTAD, International Consultation and Conciliation Procedures Aimed at Facilitating Control of Restrictive Business Practices, UN Doc. TD/B/C.2/AC.5/3 (1975); Joel Davidow and Lisa Chiles, "The United States and the Issue of the Binding or Voluntary Nature of Codes of Conduct Regarding Restrictive Business Practices," *American Journal of International Law* (April 1978), 72:265–68.

74 See OECD, *Restrictive Business Practices*, pp. 35–45.

75 Edwards was a principal author of a paper entitled "Study of Certain Restrictive Business Practices Adopted by Private Enterprises of Developed Countries," UN Doc. TD/B/C.2/54 (1968). This study was made pursuant to Resolution 25(II) of the second UNCTAD Conference.

76 U.S. industry's position is reviewed in David G. Gill, "The UNCTAD Restrictive Business Practices Code: A Code for Competition?" *International Lawyer* (1979), 13:607.

77 See Charles N. Brower and John B. Tepe, "The Charter of Economic Rights and Duties of States: A Reflection or Rejection?" *International Lawyer* (1979), 13:607.

77 See Charles N. Brower and John B. Tepe, "The Charter of Economic Rights and Duties of States: A Reflection or Rejection of International Law," *International Lawyer* (1975), 9:295.

78 Oscar Schachter, "The Evolving International Law of Development," *Columbia Journal of Transnational Law* (1976), 15:16.

79 See chapter 4. "Participation of Competition Officials in the Formulation and Implementation of Regulatory Regimes and Programs" in OECD, *Competition Policy in Regulated Sectors* (Paris: OECD, 1979).

6. Welfare Effects of Global Patent Protection

A. V. Deardorff

INTRODUCTION

THE URUGUAY ROUND of Multilateral Trade Negotiations has included a major effort by the industrialized countries especially to bring the protection of intellectual property rights under the auspices of the General Agreement on Tariffs and Trade (GATT). The purpose is primarily to extend such protection to countries that currently provide it only weakly or not at all, particularly certain developing countries. This paper will explore one aspect of the economics of this issue, emphasizing in particular the possible adverse welfare effects that would be caused by extending intellectual property protection to all countries of the world. The argument will be formalized in terms of a particularly simple model of patent protection, though the principles apply as well to other forms of intellectual property protection such as copyrights.[1]

As is well known, a primary reason for providing patent protection is to permit inventors to earn a return on their inventions, and therefore to provide an incentive for technology to advance. The cost of providing patent protection, however, is that it permits the patent-holder to exercise monopoly power over the market for the new product, and this prevents the benefits of the new product from being enjoyed optimally by consumers. It is for this reason, some have argued, that patent protection is granted for only a limited time, so as to achieve a desirable balance between incentives to invent and gains to consumers from products after they have been invented.[2] I will argue that the same sort of trade-off may also justify limiting patent protection geographically, as well as over time.

Such a geographical limitation on the coverage of patents is most likely to be desirable when inventive activity is concentrated in one part of the globe, while the benefits from inventions can be enjoyed equally by consumers worldwide. To make the point, I will therefore focus on a particular very simple theoretical model of inventions and patents that has these properties in extreme form.

In the context of this model, I will show first that the trade-off between incentives to invent and the subsequent enjoyment of inventions does justify the use of patent protection, at least as a second-best policy in the country where invention occurs.[3] Thus, the principal motive most often discussed for extending patent protection around the world is indeed present in my model. However, I will then show that extending this protection to other countries is very likely to be harmful to them, in spite of the fact that they will benefit from increased inventive activity. In those circumstances, if the world as a whole does gain from extending patent protection, it is only in the inventing countries that these gains are experienced, and in fact, they gain even more than the world as a whole because they gain at the rest of the world's expense.[4]

Finally, I show that it is even possible for the world as a whole to lose from extending patent protection, and that such a loss *must* occur, in the context of my model, as the coverage of patent protection is extended to the entire world. Thus, a case can be made, in terms of world welfare, for limiting the coverage of patent protection to less than the entire world.

I recognize that the model in which I demonstrate this result is far from general, and that there are many considerations that are absent from the model that could undermine it. I will discuss several of these in the concluding section. Nor would I argue by any means that the efforts in the Uruguay Round have been misguided. I do not doubt that a good case can be made for extending patent and other intellectual property rights into a number of countries where they currently do not exist, or are only laxly enforced. However, the case for universal patent protection is not a clear one, as my analysis demonstrates, and the concerns of some developing countries that they will be exploited by patent protection are not without foundation.

I. AN ECONOMIC ANALYSIS OF PATENT RIGHTS

A Single Invention in a Single Country

Consider first the case of a single invention. At a research cost of R, an inventor has designed a new product that can be produced by anyone at a constant marginal production cost of c. Individual consumers have a demand for the new product that is described by their inverse demand function,

(1) $p = a - bq.$

With n identical consumers, the inverse market demand function is

(2) $p = a - (b/n)q$

which is graphed in Figure 1 as the curve DD.

Competitive production. Suppose that the inventor is *not* granted a patent. Then anyone at all will be able to produce the new good, and a perfectly competitive market price equal to the marginal cost, c, will be established. The competitive out will be

(3) $q^c = n\dfrac{a-c}{b},$

and consumers will earn a surplus of

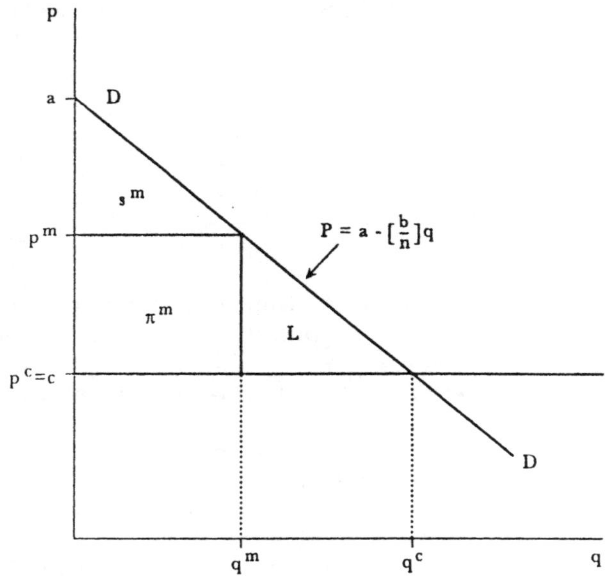

FIGURE 1 Welfare effects of monopoly pricing of a single invention.

$$(4)\qquad s^0 = \int_0^{q'} [a-(b/n)q-c]\,\mathrm{d}q = \frac{n}{2}\,\frac{(a-c)^2}{b}.$$

There will be no monopoly profits earned on the invention, and the inventor will have lost entirely the cost of research, *R*. None the less, given that the product has already been invented, this competitive outcome is also optimal in the sense of maximizing joint consumer and producer welfare, and the consumer surplus in equation (4) is therefore superscripted with an *o* for optimal.

Monopolized production. Now suppose instead that a patent is granted to the inventor. The inventor will now be able to charge a monopoly price that maximizes the monopoly profit on production,

$$(5)\qquad \pi = (p-c)\,q,$$

where p is given by the market demand function, (2). It is seen that, because demand is linear and marginal cost is constant, the monopoly output will be exactly half of the competitive output,

$$(6)\qquad q^m = {}^1\!/_2 n\frac{a-c}{b}$$

with a monopoly price halfway between cost c and the demand parameter a,

(7) $p^m = {}^1/_2(a+c)$,

and monopoly profit

(8) $\pi^m = {}^1/_4 n \dfrac{(a-c)^2}{b} = {}^1/_2 s^0.$

As noted here and as illustrated in Figure 1, monopoly pricing in this linear case extracts exactly half of the optimal consumer surplus in the form of monopoly profit.

Consumers in this monopoly situation derive an even smaller surplus:

(9) $s^m = \displaystyle\int_0^{qm} [a-(b/n)q-p^m]\,\mathrm{d}q = {}^1/_8 n \dfrac{(a-c)^2}{b} = {}^1/_4 s^0,$

that is, only one-quarter of what they would have obtained with perfect competition. The benefit to society as a whole of having the invention produced by a monopoly includes both the monopoly profit and the consumer surplus, and is therefore three-quarters of the benefit that would have accrued under competition:

(10) $b^m = \pi^m + s^m = {}^3/_4 s^0.$

Therefore, there is a deadweight loss of one-quarter of the optimal consumer surplus that is attributable to monopoly pricing.

This is illustrated in Figure 1, where the demand curve DD and the constant marginal cost c give rise to competitive (and optimal) output of q^c at a price $p^c = c$. A patent that grants monopoly power to the patent-holder cuts output in half, raises price, and creates a deadweight loss that is labelled L. However, the advantage of the patent is also indicated in that the patent holder now earns the monopoly profit π which then provides some return on the cost of the invention.

Unfortunately, even this return may not be enough to compensate the inventor for a worthwhile invention. If we now consider the *ex ante* problem of whether the invention was worthwhile, it is clear that the invention would have been worth the cost to society as long as the optimal consumer surplus, s^o, were to exceed the cost of research, R. Since only half of s^o, i.e. π, accrues to the patent-holder, one would expect that some worthwhile inventions will not be created, even when there is patent protection. Patents are therefore an imperfect method of fostering invention, both because they lead to monopoly distortions of consumer choice, and because they fail to foster all worthwhile inventions. This latter point will be made more clearly if we now consider multiple inventions and bring the choice of the level of invention explicitly into the analysis.

Multiple Inventions in a Single Country

The case of multiple inventions will be most tractable if we consider a continuum of them and hence abstract from the indivisibility of individual inventions and the discontinuities that this would imply. As long as the actual number of inventions is large, this simplification will not matter appreciably for the results.

Suppose then that inventions are indexed by non-negative real numbers, . Let $a(z)$, $b(z)$, $c(z)$ and $R(z)$ be the demand and cost parameters for invention z, as in the analysis above. Then let $s^o(z)$ be the optimal consumer surplus corresponding to invention z, as in (4), but normalized to be expressed per unit of research cost. That is,

$$(11) \quad s^0(z) = \frac{n}{2} \frac{[a(z) - c(z)]^2}{b(z)} \Big/ R(z).$$

Without loss of generality, let inventions be ordered so that

$$(12) \quad z_1 > z_2 \Rightarrow s^0(z_1) \leq s^0(z_2).$$

Because of the assumed linearity of demand and cost, this ordering of inventions by optimal consumer surplus will also be the ordering by monopoly profit, and therefore the inventions that will be undertaken will always be those with the lowest indices, z, up to some cutoff point.

I will measure the level of invention by its research cost. Hence if all inventions from $z = 0$ to some $z = \hat{z}$ are invented, then the total cost of invention, I, will be

$$(13) \quad I(\hat{z}) = \int_0^{\hat{z}} R(z)\, \mathrm{d}z.$$

Since $\mathrm{d}I(\hat{z})/\mathrm{d}\hat{z} = R(\hat{z}) > 0$, the function $I(\cdot)$ is monotonic and can be inverted. I therefore re-express the optimal consumer surplus of the marginal invention in terms of I, the total cost of invention:

$$(14) \quad s^0(I) = s^0[I^{-1}(I)].$$

From (12) to (13), $s^o(I)$ is also weakly monotonically decreasing in I. What it represents is the optimal consumer surplus per dollar of research obtainable from the marginal dollar of research, given that I dollars have already been spent on all inventions yielding a greater surplus per dollar.

From the earlier analysis of a single invention, it follows that various properties of a monopoly equilibrium can also be calculated from $s^o(I)$. In particular,

$$(15) \quad \pi^m(I) = {}^1\!/_2 s^0(I)$$

is the monopoly profit, per dollar of research, from the marginal invention, and

(16) $s^m(I) = {}^1/_4 s^0(I)$

is the consumer surplus, per dollar of research, from the marginal invention, given that production is monopolized.

From their derivation, it is clear that these functions ought actually to be step functions, declining discontinuously at each level of investment that completes the full research cost, $R(z)$, of the marginal invention. For simplicity, however, I will assume that the number of inventions is large, so that these functions can be approximated as continuous. Further, and much more restrictively, I will assume that these functions are linear, represented by

(17) $s^0(I) = n(f - gI)$,

where f, $g > 0$ are parameters of this linear function and n, as before, is the number of consumers in the country.

Population is included here explicitly in order to facilitate analysis of the two-country case below. It appears multiplicatively because of its role in (4). Note, therefore, that $f - gI$ is the optimal consumer surplus per dollar of research for a representative consumer and that, from (4), $f = [a(z) - c(z)]^2/2b(z)$ for $z =$ 0, highest-priority invention. The slope parameter g indicates the rapidity with which diminishing returns to invention set in. A particular level of invention, $\bar{I} = f/g$, represents the total research cost of all available inventions whose products would be demanded if competitively priced and thus provides an upper bound on the level of invention that will actually take place.

Competitive invention. I can now examine the equilibrium levels of invention and welfare under various scenarios. The competitive case is simplest, because nothing happens. Without patent protection, the level of invention will be zero in this model, since there will be no way for any inventor to recover the cost of research. Levels of total consumer surplus, S^c, and monopoly profit, Π^c, will also be zero:

(18) $I^c = S^c = \Pi^c = 0.$

Optimal invention. The optimal level of invention, I^0, will include all inventions that yield an optimal consumer surplus greater than their cost of research, and hence whose optimal consumer surplus per dollar is greater than 1. Thus, from (17),

$$(19) \quad I^0 = S^{0-1}(1) = \frac{nf-1}{ng}.$$

Since the optimal consumer surplus is obtainable only if products are competitively priced, the monopoly profits corresponding to this optimal level of invention be zero:

(20) $\Pi^0 = 0.$

The total consumer surplus obtained in this optimal situation will then be found by adding across all inventions the optimal consumer surplus per dollar, multiplied by the research cost of each invention. With the assumed continuity of the surplus function, s^0, this addition is accomplished by integration:

$$(21)\quad s^0 = \int_0^{I^0} s^0(I)\,\mathrm{d}I = \int_0^{(nf-1)/ng} n(f-gI)\,\mathrm{d}I = \frac{(nf)^2-1}{2ng}.$$

Finally, the net gain to society from this optimal level of invention is the sum of the consumer and producer gains (the latter being zero in this case) minus the research cost, I^0, of the inventions:

$$(22)\quad N^0 = S^0 + \Pi^0 - I^0 = \frac{(nf)^2-1}{2ng} - \frac{nf-1}{ng} = \frac{(nf-1)^2}{2ng}.$$

Monopolized invention. If inventors are protected with patents, then production will take place under conditions of monopoly, as discussed above. The level of invention will be that which equates the monopoly profit from the marginal invention to its research cost, or in other words which equates the monopoly profit per dollar to unity. Thus,

$$(23)\quad I^m = S^{m^{-1}}(1) = S^{0^{\,1}}(2) = \frac{nf-2}{ng}.$$

The level of monopoly profit is obtained by integrating the profit function from (15) and (17), i.e.

$$(24)\quad \Pi^m = \int_0^{I^m} {}^1\!/_2 s^0(I)\,\mathrm{d}I = \int_0^{(nf-2)/ng} {}^1\!/_2 n(f-gI)\,\mathrm{d}I = \frac{(nf)^2-4}{4ng},$$

while the level of consumer surplus is obtained by integrating (16):

$$(25)\quad S^m = \int_0^{I^m} {}^1\!/_4 s^0(I)\,\mathrm{d}I = \int_0^{(nf-2)/ng} {}^1\!/_4 n(f-gI)\,\mathrm{d}I = \frac{(nf)^2-4}{8ng},$$

Summing (24) and (25) and subtracting (23), the net gain to society from invention in the patent-protected monopoly situation is

$$(26)\quad N^m = S^m + \Pi^m - I^m$$
$$= \frac{(nf)^2-4}{8ng} + \frac{(nf)^2-4}{4ng} - \frac{nf-2}{ng} = \frac{(nf-2)(3nf-2)}{8ng}.$$

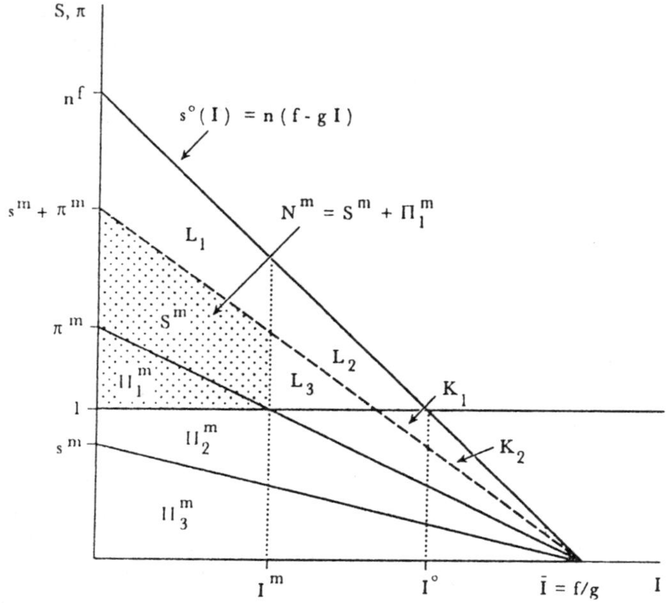

FIGURE 2 Welfare effects of many inventions per dollar of research.

These results are illustrated in Figure 2. The uppermost curve represents the optimal consumer surplus per dollar cost of research, and is drawn as the straight line $n(f - gI)$. Its intersection with the horizontal line at 1 indicates the socially optimal level of invention, so long as goods once invented are also produced optimally. The total consumer surplus generated by this level of invention is the area under the $s^0(I)$ curve between $I = 0$ and $I = I^0$. The net gain to society, however, is smaller by the cost of research, and is therefore given by the area of the triangle under s^0 (I) and above 1.

As was found from the analysis of a single invention, the monopoly profits, π^m, and the consumer surplus in the presence of monopoly, s^m, are one-half and one-quarter, respectively, of s^0. These are therefore also drawn in Figure 2 as straight lines, starting from correspondingly lower intercepts and ending at the same level of invention $\bar{I}$. Since monopolists earn only π^m per dollar of research, patent rights will foster invention only up to the point where these monopoly profits equal one dollar. Thus, the level of invention with patent protection is shown as I^m.

With this construction, the total profits from all inventions up to I^m are given by the area under π^m, shown in Figure 2 as the sum of areas Π_1^m, Π_2^m and Π_3^m. Consumer surplus is the area under s^m between 0 and I^m, which is equal to Π_3^m, but is shown separately by first adding together π^m and s^m in the line $s^m + \pi^m = (3/4)s^0$. Consumer surplus is then the area S^m, below this line and above π^m. The total net benefit to society due to inventions up to I^m is the sum of consumer surplus and profit, minus the cost of research. Since the latter is the area of the rectangle under the horizontal line at 1, this net benefit is simply the shaded area, $S^m + \Pi_1^m$.

Comparing this with the larger triangle of optimal social benefit from invention, there is a deadweight loss of areas $L_1+L_2+L_3$. Area L_1 represents the loss of consumer surplus arising from the monopoly pricing of products that are invented. Area L_2+L_3, on the other hand, represents the consumer surplus that is forgone because less than the optimal amount of invention takes place, even when inventors are granted monopoly patent rights. The total deadweight loss is calculated from (22) and (26) as[5]

$$(27) \quad N^0 - N^m = \frac{(nf-1)^2}{2ng} - \frac{(nf-2)(3nf-2)}{8ng} = \frac{nf^2}{8g}.$$

Multiple Inventions in Two Countries

Suppose now that there are two countries, A and B. All invention takes place in country A, but once a good has been invented the technology is known and it can be produced in either country, subject of course to any limitations imposed legally by patent rights. Consumers in the two countries have identical individual demand functions for all goods. Populations (numbers of consumers) in the two countries are n^A and n^B respectively. It will be convenient to define

$$(28) \quad n = n^A + n^B$$

and to express results in terms of n and the fraction of the world's population that is country A:

$$(29) \quad y = \frac{n^a}{n}.$$

As before, let (1) represent the common individual inverse demand functions for a particular good, so that the market inverse demand functions in the two countries are

$$(30) \quad p^J = a - (b/n^J)q^J, \quad J = A, B.$$

With marginal cost, c, of producing the good common to both countries, the optimal consumer surplus for the good in country J is

$$(31) \quad s^{0J} = \frac{n^J}{2}\frac{(a-c)^2}{b} = n^J\tilde{s},$$

where $\tilde{s}$ is the optimal *per capita* consumer surplus for the good.

As before, let inventions be ordered by decreasing values of $\tilde{s}/R$, and assume that these values can be expressed as a linear function of I. That is,

$$(32) \quad \tilde{s}(I) = f - gI$$

is the optimal *per capita* consumer surplus per dollar of research for the marginal invention, given that I dollars have been spent inventing all goods of equal or greater $\tilde{s}/R$. The relevant values of consumer surplus and monopoly profits for the two countries can then also be expressed in terms of this linear function. First, multiplying the *per capita* consumer surplus in (32) by population,

$$(33) \quad s^{oJ}(I) = n^J (f-gI), J=A,B,$$

is the total optimal consumer surplus per research dollar in country $J=A,B$ owing to the marginal invention at level of invention I (and would be received by consumers in country J if the good were competitively priced there). From this, again exploiting the linearity of demand, properties of the monopoly equilibria can be found as well:

$$(34) \quad \pi^J(I) = {}^1/_2 s^{0J}(I) = {}^1/_2 n^J (f-gI), \qquad J=A,B,$$

is the monopoly profit per dollar of research to be obtained by selling the product of the marginal invention in country J at the monopoly price. Similarly,

$$(35) \quad s^{mJ}(I) = {}^1/_4 s^{0J}(I) = {}^1/_4 n^J (f-gI), \qquad J=A,B,$$

is the consumer surplus per dollar received by consumers in country J from the marginal invention if they pay the monopoly price.

It is now possible to calculate the totals of consumer surplus and monopoly profit for different patent protection regimes by first using (34) to identify the level of invention that will take place, and then integrating these various functions. The two regimes that I will consider are 'restricted patent protection', in which patent protection is provided only in country A, and 'extended patent protection', in which protection is extended to country B as well.

Restricted patent protection. With patent protection only in country A, monopoly profits will be earned only there, and invention will take place up to the point where

$$(36) \quad \pi^A(I^r) = 1.$$

Using (34) and (29), it follows that

$$(37) \quad I^r = \frac{ynf - 2}{yng}.$$

Integrating (35) up to this level of invention and using (29), the level of total consumer surplus in country A may be found as

$$(38)\quad S^{rA} = \int_0^{I^r} \frac{1}{4} n^A(f-gI)\,\mathrm{d}I = \frac{y^2n^2f^2-4}{8yng},$$

Monopoly profits are made only in country A, and thus may be found by integrating (34) for country A alone. Since (34) is just twice (35), profits are found immediately as twice (38):

$$(39)\quad \Pi^r = \Pi^{rA} = \frac{y^2n^2f^2-4}{4yng}.$$

Finally, because patent protection is limited to country A, consumers in country B have access to a competitive supply of all invented goods. Their total consumer surplus is therefore obtained by integration (33) for country B:

$$(40)\quad S^{rB} = \int_0^{I^r} n^B(f-gI)\,\mathrm{d}I = \frac{(1-y)(y^2n^2f^2-4)}{2y^2ng}.$$

The net gain to all residents of country A, including their monopoly inventors, is their consumer surplus plus their monopoly profit, minus the cost of invention. Using (37), (38) and (39),

$$(41)\quad N^{rA} = S^{rA} + \Pi^r - I^r = \frac{(ynf-2)(3ynf-2)}{8yng}.$$

The net gain to all residents of country B includes only their consumer surplus, $N^{rB}=S^{rB}$, in (40). Together, these give the net gain for the world as a whole as

$$(42)\quad N^{rW} = N^{rA} + N^{rB} = \frac{(ynf-2)[y(3ynf-2) + 4(1-y)(ynf+2)]}{8y^2ng}.$$

All of this is illustrated in Figure 3, which replicates Figure 2 for country A in the top panel and for country B, upside down, in the bottom panel. With monopoly profits earned only in country A, invention takes place up to I^r, where the marginal per-dollar profit in country A, π^A, intersects the horizontal line at 1. Gross profits are then the area under π^A, or $u_1+u_2+u_3$. Consumer surplus in country A is area u_1. Since the cost of invention, I^r, is the area u_1+u_2, the net gain for country A is u_1+u_3.

Meanwhile, consumers in country B get a free ride, receiving the optimal, or competitive, consumer surplus equal to area $v_1+v_2+v_3$.

Extended patent protection. If patent protection is now extended to country B as well as country A, then an invention once patented in country A will also entitle the inventor to monopoly profits in country B.[6] With potential investors knowing this, invention in country A will take place up to the point where the total profits from the two sources from the marginal invention just covers the cost of research. Thus,

$$(43) \quad \pi^A(I^e)+\pi^B(I^e) = 1.$$

Using (34), this can be solved to yield

$$(44) \quad I^e = \frac{nf-2}{ng}.$$

As before, the totals of consumer surplus and monopoly profits in the two countries can be found by integrating (34) and (3) up to I^e. In country A this gives

$$(45) \quad S^{eA} = \int_0^{I^e} \frac{1}{4} n^A(f-gI)\, dI = \frac{y(n^2f^2-4)}{8ng},$$

and

$$(46) \quad \Pi^{eA} = \int_0^{I^e} \frac{1}{2} n^A(f-gI)\, dI = \frac{y(n^2f^2-4)}{4ng},$$

where Π^{eA} is now only a portion of the total profits.

In country B the inventors from country A also earn monopoly profits equal to

$$(47) \quad \Pi^{eB} = \int_0^{I^e} \frac{1}{2} n^B(f-gI)\, dI = \frac{(1-y)(n^2f^2-4)}{4ng}.$$

Consumers in country B now get only the reduced consumer surplus of the monopoly case:

$$(48) \quad S^{eB} = \int_0^{I^e} \frac{1}{4} n^B(f-gI)\, dI = \frac{(1-y)(n^2f^2-4)}{8ng}.$$

Total profit is

$$(49) \quad \Pi^e = \Pi^{eA} + \Pi^{eB} = \frac{n^2f^2-4}{4ng},$$

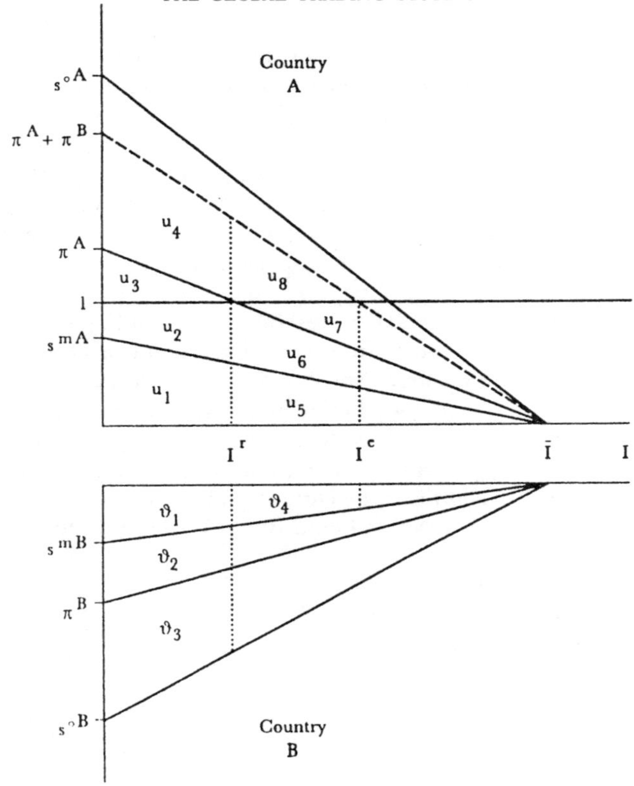

FIGURE 3 Welfare effects in two countries of inventions in one, with restricted and extended patent protection.

which is the same expression found in the single-country case in (24), since the monopolist inventors are now treating the world as essentially a single market. The net gain to country A is found from (44), (45) and (49):

$$(50) \quad N^{eA} = S^{eA} + \Pi^{e} - I^{e} = \frac{nf - 2}{8ng}\,[(2 + y)(nf + 2) - 8].$$

Finally, the net gain to country B is again just its gain in consumer surplus,

$$(51) \quad N^{eB} = S^{eB}.$$

The net benefit to the world is therefore

$$(52) \quad N^{eW} = N^{eA} + N^{eB} = \frac{(3nf - 2)(nf - 2)}{8ng}.$$

To illustrate these results in Figure 3, the marginal profit earned in country B, π^B, is first added to π^A in the top panel. The level of invention with extended patent protection, I^e, is then found where this new line crosses the horizontal line at 1. In country A, consumer surplus expands to include u_5, while profits now include u_5+u_6 earned on sales in country A as well as $u_4+u_7+u_8$ on sales to country B. Deducting the research cost, I^e, the net benefit to country A is $u_1+u_3+u_4+u_5+u_8$.

Consumers in country B now earn only the monopoly consumer surplus under s^{mB} for all goods up to I^e. Thus their total benefit is now v_1+v_4.

Comparison of restricted and extended regimes. It is clear from Figure 3 that residents of country A gain unambiguously from extending patent protection to country B. Consumers in A get consumer surplus from the additional goods that are invented, as shown by the area u_5. The monopolist inventors in country A also gain the even larger area u_4, which is the monopoly profit on sales to country B of goods they would have invented anyway, plus u_8, the excess monopoly profits in both markets on the additional inventions. Formally, the gain to country A from extending patent protection is found from (41) and (50) to be

$$(53)\quad N^{eA} - N^{rA} = \frac{2(1-y)}{8yng}[yn^2f^2 - 2(1-y)].$$

As long as

$$(54)\quad ynf - n^Af > 2,$$

so that I^r in (37) is positive, (53) is also positive, verifying the gain to country A.

Residents of country B, on the other hand, are likely to lose. The monopoly pricing of the goods they were previously getting competitively causes them to lose three-quarters of the optimal consumer surplus on those goods. In Figure 3 this loss is area v_2+v_3. In return for this they do get consumer surplus on the new goods whose invention is stimulated by the extended protection, but even on these they only get the monopoly consumer surplus, shown as v_4 in Figure 3. If v_2+v_3 is greater than v_4, as drawn in the figure, they lose.

Formally, the change in welfare for country B is found from (40) and (48) to be

$$(55)\quad N^{eB} - N^{rB} = -\frac{1-y}{8y^2ng}[3y^2n^2f^2 + 4(y^2 - 4)].$$

If ynf is only slightly greater than required in (54), this will be negative regardless of the value of y alone. That is,

$$(56)\quad ynf = n^Af > \sqrt{\frac{16}{3}} = 2.31$$

is sufficient for (55) to be negative. Alternatively, as long as the fraction of the world's population that is located in the innovating country, y, is sufficiently large, then country B will lose. If

$$(57) \quad y^2 > \sqrt{\frac{16}{4 + 3\, n^2 f^2}},$$

then (55) will also be negative.

Clearly, much depends on the size of the two populations, together with the parameter f. The latter represents the intercept of the optimal consumer surplus function, and hence the per capital consumer surplus optimally obtainable from the highest priority invention, per dollar cost of research needed for that invention. Condition (54) merely requires that this highest-priority invention yield a total benefit to the population of country A that is twice its cost. Likewise, condition (55) implies that, if the per dollar benefit from the highest-priority invention for the world, nf, is, say, ten times its cost (nf=10), then country B will be hurt by extending patent protection if the share of world population in country A is greater than only 16/304=5.3 per cent. Thus, it seems quite likely that (55) will indeed be negative under plausible circumstances.

Turning finally to effects on the world as a whole, these can be observed in Figure 3 by first noting that area u_4 and v_3 are equal, so that part of the gain to country A cancels directly with part of the loss to country B. This leaves the net effect on the two countries together as $u_5+u_8+v_4-v_2$. As drawn in Figure 3, it appears that the three areas of gain are together larger than the single area of loss, v_2, and that the world gains here from extending patent protection.

This is not inevitable, however, as Figure 4 shows. There, the relevant portions of Figure 3 are reproduced, but the proportions are changed. As a result, the three areas of gain from extended patent protection, shown as the shaded areas u_5, u_8 and v_4, are much smaller than in Figure 3, while the area of loss, the cross-hatched area v_3, is larger. As drawn, the latter area is larger than the former, and the case drawn is therefore one in which extended patent protection lowers welfare of the world as a whole.

How do Figures 3 and 4 differ? In drawing Figure 4, I attempted to capture what would happen if population were shifted from country B to country A, thus expanding all of the amounts of surplus and profit in country A and contracting them in country B. By doing this, the level of invention in the restricted protection equilibrium is made larger, since inventors in A have a larger protected market, and at the same time the scope for expanding invention still further by extending protection is reduced.

To check that this is a correct interpretation, consider the more formal expression for the gain to the world from extending protection. From (42) and (52),

$$(58) \quad N^{ew} - N^{rw} = \frac{1-y}{8y^2 ng}(16 - 4y - n^2 f^2 y^2).$$

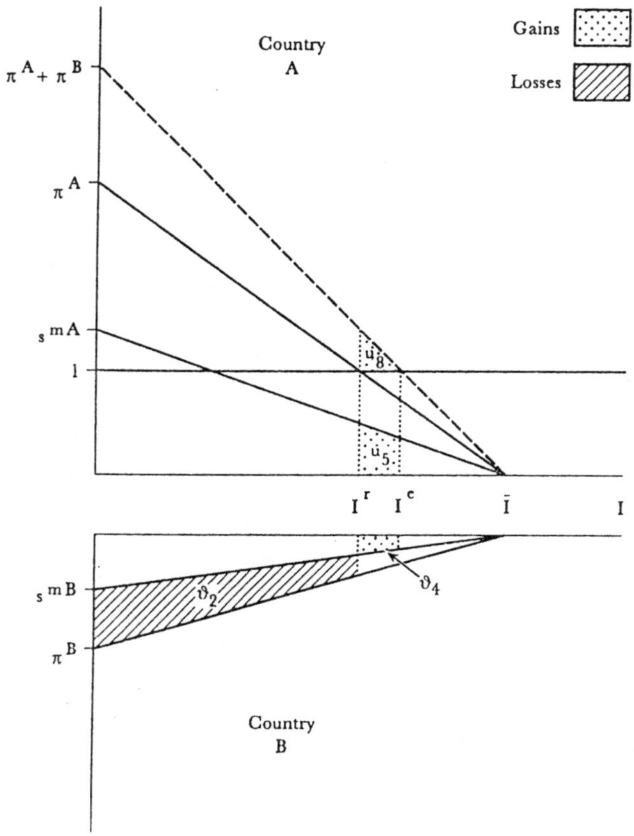

FIGURE 4 World welfare effects of extending patent protection to a relatively small country.

The sign of this depends on the expression in parentheses. Setting that expression equal to zero for $y = 1$, it follows that if

(59) $nf > \sqrt{12} = 3.46$,

then (58) will be negative for y sufficiently close to 1. I will assume from here on that (59) is indeed satisfied, that is, that the most desirable invention would yield a surplus for world consumers at least three-and-a-half times its cost.

Under the assumption, then, the world as a whole loses from extended patent protection once the portion of the world already covered by patent protection is sufficiently large. In particular, it cannot be optimal from a world welfare standpoint for patent protection to be extended to the entire world.

II. CONCLUSIONS AND QUALIFICATIONS

I have now shown what I set out to show: that under specified circumstances it is not optimal to extend patent protection to all countries of the world. The reason for this result is implicit in the analysis. Patent protection has the offsetting effects of, on the one hand, permitting inventors to earn monopoly profits on their inventions and thus stimulating inventive activity and, on the other hand, distorting consumer choice by monopoly pricing. If all innovation originates in one part of the world, then extending patent protection to a broader and broader area does have these two effects, but there are diminishing returns to the first of them. That is, as more and more of the world is already covered by patent protection, the extra market that can be covered, and hence the extra invention that can be stimulated by extending patent protection still further, becomes smaller. Thus, at some point the costs due to extending monopoly pricing to existing inventions come to outweigh the benefits of generating new ones.

Many assumptions are explicit, and others implicit, in this analysis, and the results depend to varying degrees upon all of them. Let me conclude by suggesting my own judgements as to the importance of some of these assumptions for the main result.

Location of Invention

First, it is not crucial to world welfare, though it may be to the individual countries, that no invention take place in country B. If inventors in both countries had a chance of creating the inventions of the model and of patenting them wherever patent protection is available, then some of the monopoly profits that I have modelled as accruing to country A would accrue instead to inventors in country B. With free trade, however, the same levels of invention would take place in equilibrium, and levels of world welfare would be the same.

Identical Demands

On the other hand, it is crucial that *per capita* demands for invented goods be the same, or at least similar, in both countries. If they are not – if some inventions would be demanded more in country B than in country A – then an important benefit to extending patent protection to B is missing from the model. Patent protection in country B will stimulate precisely those inventions that are of particular importance to B's population, and thus will yield a greater benefit to B than to A. This possibility would therefore increase the net gain, both to country B and to the world as a whole, of extended patent protection.

Linearity

The analysis here has been greatly facilitated by assuming that demands for goods were linear and that the function relating optimal surplus to the level of invention was linear as well. Linearity of demand seems of comparatively minor importance:

what really matters is that there be some welfare loss arising from monopoly pricing, and this would be the case for a wide variety of demand functions.

Linearity of the surplus function is a bit more critical, as is seen in Figure 3, for example. If the curves were not linear, there would be the possibility that they would, say, turn sharply downward just to the right of I^r. In that case, there would be very little additional invention stimulated by extending patent protection, and the case against it would be strengthened. In contrast, if the curves were to flatten out just to the right of I^4, the I^e might be pushed to a much higher level, and the benefits to extending patent protection would be increased. Thus, the cases for and against extending protection can be materially altered by the curvature and position of these curves. On the other hand, in the absence of any information about what these curves do in fact look like, the linear case seems to be about as neutral as one could hope for.

Transmission of Information

I have assumed here that, once an invention is discovered, the information about how to produce it is freely available worldwide. This is important, since otherwise production could not take place at all in country B in the absence of patent protection, and the main source of loss arising from extending protection, both for country B and for the world as a whole, would be removed. It is of course true that information about many new inventions is not costlessly transmitted abroad, and that extending patent protection may therefore be beneficial to the extent that it stimulates the transfer of technology. On the other hand, the demands for protection on the part of the innovating firms in the United States and other advanced countries make it clear that, in at least some industries, information about new products is diffusing without patent protection much more readily than the innovating firms would like.

I am sure that many other objections to this model can and will be raised as discussion proceeds. It may well be that extending patent protection to a larger part of the world is in fact in the interest of the world as a whole, and perhaps even in the interests of some of the developing countries who may resist such change. All I have tried to establish is the intellectual legitimacy of the position that worldwide patent protection may not be desirable. I am inclined to believe, on the basis of this model and other considerations discussed in Deardorff (1990), that at least the very poorest of countries should be exempted from any new agreement that is made to extend patent protection under the GATT.

ACKNOWLEDGMENTS

I have received helpful suggestions from many people, including John H. Jackson, Jim Levinsohn, Jeff Mackie-Mason and Robert M. Stern, as well as from participants in The University of Michigan Law School seminar that Professor Jackson and I taught together in winter 1989 on the subject of intellectual property protection. Helpful comments were also made by participants at the Western Ontario-Michigan conference on TRIPs and TRIMs in Washington,

D.C. in April 1989 and by participants in the Research Seminar in International Economics at The University of Michigan. I received partial support in writing this paper from a Ford Foundation to the Institute of Public Policy Studies of The University of Michigan for a program of research on trade policy.

NOTES

1 Trademarks, on the other hand, seem to play a distinctly different role from patents and copyrights, and I would not extend the argument to them.
2 See Nordhaus (1969) and Scherer (1980).
3 A first-best policy would eliminate the monopoly distortion and somehow subsidize invention more directly. However, given the difficulty of measuring the value of inventive activity for this purpose, this may not be feasible.
4 Chin and Grossman (1990) have also made this point elegantly in the context of a somewhat different model of process innovation. They too found the possibility of a welfare loss for the world as a whole as a result of extending patent protection, though they did not relate it to the portion of the world that is covered.
5 It is intriguing – though not at all important, as far as I can see – that this expression turns out to be so simple. Nothing that nf and f/g are the vertical and horizontal intercepts of the s^0 line in Figure 2, this expression for net loss is exactly one-quarter of the area of the triangle formed by s^o and the two axes. Since $s^m + \pi^m = (3/4)s^0$, this means that the awkwardly shaped area $L_1+L_2+L_3$ is actually equal to the triangle between $s^m+\pi^m$ and s^0. This implies that the area L_3 is equal to the area K_1+K_2, a result that can also be shown using the traditional tools of plane geometry. The proof, which I leave to interested readers or their highschool-age children, uses the fact that the vertical line above I^m is broken into four equal segments by the lines that cross it.
6 It is not necessary, of course, that the inventor also be the producer in country B. The inventor can license someone else to produce there and can extract the monopoly profit by setting the licence fee at an appropriate level.

REFERENCES

Chin, Judith C. and Grossman, Gene M. (1990). Intellectual property rights and North–South trade. In Ronald W. Jones and Anne O. Krueger (eds), *The Political Economy of International Trade: Essays in Honor of Robert E. Baldwin*. Cambridge, Mass.: Basil Blackwell, pp. 90–107.

Deardorff, Alan V. (1990). Should patent protection be extended to all developing countries? *The World Economy*, 13, 497–507.

Nordhaus, W. D. (1969). *Invention, Growth, and Welfare: A Theoretical Treatment of Technological Change*, Cambridge, Mass.: MIT Press.

Scherer, F. M. (1980). The economics of the patent system. Chapter 16 in *Industrial Market Structure and Economic Performance*. Boston: Houghton Mifflin, pp. 439–58.

7. Efficiency and Distributional Implications of Global Restrictions on Labour Mobility

B. Hamilton and J. Whalley

1. INTRODUCTION

Much of the recent North–South debate has been concerned with such issues as commodity price stabilization programs, debt write-offs, the long-term deterioration in Southern terms of trade (which some economists consider contentious) and protectionist trade policies in the North. Relatively little has been heard about controls on inward labour migration to the North from the South,[1] despite the widespread recognition of the potential quantitative dominance of immigration controls in the North as a source of LDC loss.[2]

This paper takes as its point of departure the (apparent) total absence of any calculations of possible worldwide impacts from the removal of immigration controls. A simple procedure for calculating efficiency gains from liberalized global labour migration is outlined and some speculative 'order of magnitude' calculations reported as to the potential worldwide efficiency gain from either removal or partial modification of immigration controls in developed countries.

Although wide bounds are obtained on the estimates presented due to various adjustments to the data used, large annual worldwide efficiency gains always result from removing immigration controls. While LDCs do not realize all of the gains from liberalized migration policies, their share is large enough to suggest that the immigration control issue may well be many orders of magnitude more important for the South than other issues discussed thus far in the North–South debate. The implication is that if Southern negotiators are interested in promoting the aggregate welfare of their (current) citizens, they should argue much more passionately than hitherto for liberalization of immigration controls in the North. A further implication is that if modest gains are made by the South in terms of a current agenda which excludes immigration policies but are accompanied by even harsher immigration controls in the North, the South may well be a significant net loser. Results of partial relaxation of controls emphasize that much larger gains per migrant occur with the first rather than last transferee. Even a small relaxation in existing controls is thus important since the marginal gains are so large.

Since the calculations reported yield such strong policy implications, a number of qualifications are clearly stated since the assumptions used are highly simplified and the data are imprecise. The importance of the issue and the desirability of ballpark estimates motivate the exercise, rather than exactness of forecast. Perhaps the most extreme criticism of the calculations would be that the assumptions made prior to the calculations dictate the conclusion, and that alternative assumptions could be made which would make the entire efficiency gain estimate disappear. Such an assumption would be that all differences in wage rates across countries merely reflect productivity differentials from differing qualities of labour. In this case, removing immigration controls in the North would have no impact on labour mobility since immigration restrictions are not binding. The recent waves of illegal immigration into the U.S. from Mexico, Haiti, and elsewhere clearly suggest that this position is too extreme, but some account must clearly be taken of productivity differentials.

A further assumption is that the worldwide labour supply is fixed. Under this assumption, removal of Northern immigration controls results in a worldwide efficiency improving labour reallocation. If, however, a perfectly elastic (Malthusian) labour supply function were to be assumed in LDCs the effect of removing Northern immigration restrictions would be that wage rates in all regions would fall and the worldwide labour supply expand.

The reader's attention should also be drawn to a number of features neglected in the analysis. If outward migration is selective rather than general, departing residents having LDCs may well be the best trained and most highly educated (as currently). The human capital transfer accompanying such selective outward migration may drive down wage rates of lower skilled labour remaining and worsen worldwide income distribution. Selective migration could be generated by taking relocation costs explicitly into account, which is not done here. Indeed, the distributional issue of who gains and who loses within the group who reside in LDCs prior to removal of controls in the North may indeed be a major reason why little is made of this issue by the South. Another neglected feature of the present analysis is that user fees for education services in LDCs typically do not cover the human capital loss from outmigration, inflicting further losses on those who remain.

In addition there are obvious political pressures for resistance to inward migration into the North by labour groups who will likely see wage rates driven down. This, presumably, provides the main reason why extensive liberalization will not occur. The impacts on those who reside in the North before the changes are captured in the calculations reported through induced changes in wage rates between regions; labour in the North is a major loser and capital typically gains.

2. METHODOLOGY FOR THE CALCULATIONS

In order to calculate the worldwide efficiency gains from a removal of immigration controls, a number of assumptions are made which enable the change in the allocation of labour by region in the world economy to be calculated for alternative groupings of countries into regions. In this section, the basic methodology for the calculations is outlined.

To illustrate our methodology we first consider the case where production in each of a number of countries or regions is characterized by a linear marginal revenue product of labour schedule. Each region produces a single homogeneous product; capital is fixed by region; labour is paid its marginal product in each

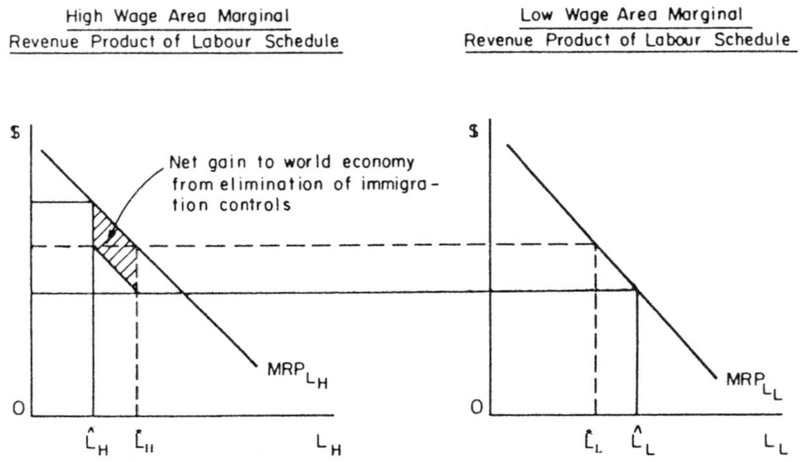

FIGURE 1 Exposition of gain from removal of immigration controls in the linear marginal revenue product of labour case.

region; and the worldwide labour supply is fixed. Differences in wage rates occur only because of restrictions on inward migration of labour into high wage areas. The return to immobile capital in each region is the area under the marginal revenue product of labour schedule less labour costs.

Figure 1 illustrates this situation for the case where a low and a high wage region are involved. For each region the linear marginal revenue product of labour schedule reflects diminishing marginal productivity of labour in that region. In the presence of controls, the allocation of labour between the region is (L_H) and $\hat{L}_L$. Employment in the high wage area $\hat{L}_H$ reflects the restrictions on the inflow of labour since controls produce the higher wage rate. The effect of removing immigration controls is to allow labour to flow from the low wage to the high wage region, and to equalize the wage rate. Labour employment in the low wage region contracts from $\hat{L}_L$ to $\hat{L}_L$ and expands in the high wage region from L_H to $\hat{L}_H$.

The expansion of labour employment in the high wage region yields an increase in the value of product in that region. Labour use contracts in the low wage region and a production loss occurs. Since we assume a single output which is homogeneous across regions, the areas of gain and loss may be superimposed one on the other since the full employment assumption implies that the change in labour allocation in the two regions has to be the same. The area of net gain from elimination of immigration controls is represented in fig. 1. This diagram is similar to that used by Harberger (1966) in his discussion of the productive efficiency effects of distortions in the corporate tax in the U.S.

If we were to use the linear marginal product assumption, it would be possible to use national accounts and employment data to specify the marginal revenue product schedules in each region. A method which could be used to do this is

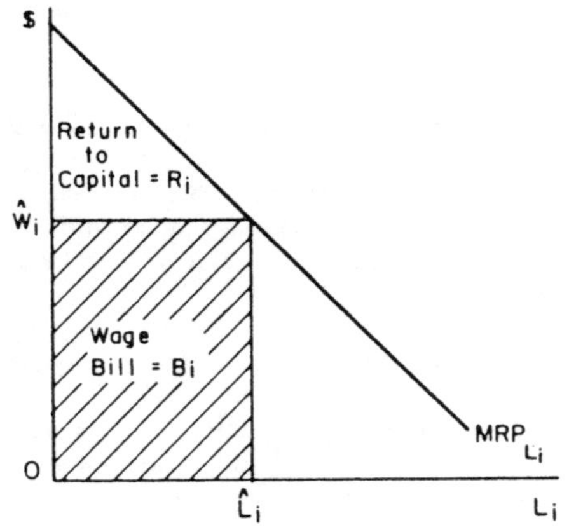

FIGURE 2 Use of national accounts and employment data to infer marginal revenue product of labour schedule

illustrated in fig. 2. If national accounts and other data can be used to give an observation on the wage bill in region i, B_i, then from GNP accounts the return to capital in region i, R_i, is determined. The point estimate of the elasticity of the marginal revenue product schedule with respect to L_i, evaluated at the observed labour employment $\hat{L}_i$, is $-2R_l/B_i$.[3] R_i, $\hat{L}_i$, and B_i are observable, and from this data it is possible to calculate both the rate, $\hat{W}_i$, corresponding to employment of $\hat{L}_i$, and the elasticity of the schedule. $\hat{W}_i$ and $\hat{L}_i$, along with the elasticity provide all the characteristics of the linearized marginal revenue production function for each region.

To find the allocation of labour between regions in the no immigration control regime an iterative search can be used. This is a relatively simple calculation to program on a computer which, even with dimensions of around 180 (approximately the number of countries in the world excluding those with very small populations), requires minimal amounts of execution time. In high dimensional cases, the calculation of the gain to the world economy from removal of immigration controls proceeds as in the two country case by adding the changes in value of product in expanding and contracting regions.

The method we use to calculate the efficiency gains from liberalized migration controls dispenses with the linear marginal revenue product schedules outlined in fig. 1 and, instead, generates these schedules directly from an aggregate production function for each of the regions. The steps involved are outlined in table 1. For each region a CES production function is used and the substitution parameter p_i is specified. This implies a value for the elasticity of factor substitution in production for each region. The employment and factor share data for each region discussed above are used along with the assumption that factors are paid their marginal products before the immigration controls are removed to determine the parameters δ_i. This uses the first-order conditions for cost minimization and the observations on factor use and factor returns. A choice

TABLE 1 *Method of calculating global efficiency effects of modifying immigration controls*

Step 1	–	For each region an aggregate CES production function is used, $Y_i = A_i[\delta_i K_i^{-pi} + (1 - \delta_i)L_i^{-pi}]^{1/-pi}$.
Step 2	–	Extraneous values of p_i for each region are assumed.
Step 3	–	From the assumption that factors receive their marginal product in each region in the presence of existing controls, value of δ_i are determined from the ratio of first-order conditions.
Step 4	–	Units are assumed for the output produced in each region such that one unit sells for \$1. The GNP values for the region, K_i, L_i, p_i, and δ_i are used to solve for A_i.
Step 5	–	Using production function parameters, an iterative procedure is used to calculate the change in labour allocation after modification of immigration controls consistent with (a) (in the removal case) equalized *MRP* of labour in all regions; (b) full employment of the fixed labour supply.
Step 6	–	The gain from removal of immigration controls is calculated as the change in the value of total world product.
Step 7	–	The procedure can be repeated for alternative extraneous values of the parameters p_i in each region.

of units for the homogeneous output allows the scale parameter A_i to be determined in the production function in each region.

These estimated production function parameters can then be used to calculate the change in labour allocation across regions after modification or removal of immigration controls. In the removal case, an equalized marginal revenue product of labour across regions is found, consistent with full employment of the fixed worldwide labour supply.

This procedure is similar to that represented in table 1, except that the marginal revenue product schedules are no longer linear. Instead, non-linear schedules derived from production functions for each region are used in numerically determining (on the computer) the labour allocation by country after immigration controls have been modified or removed. In cases where only partial removal of controls occurs, we allow only part of the difference between each region or country's wage rate and the global mean wage rate to be eliminated. All regions have the same percentage difference between their own wage rate and the global mean removed, and a new labour allocation is sought, consistent with both the specified partial liberalization and full employment of the fixed labour supply.

The gain (or loss) to the world economy in either case can be calculated as the change in the value of the total world product between the existing and new policy regimes. This procedure can be repeated for alternative extraneous values of the parameters p_i in each region.

3. DATA AND ASSUMPTIONS

To implement the method described above, data drawn from a number of different sources are used, and in the process some key assumptions are made. In the main calculations reported, data on a 7-region country classification used in a different context by Whalley (forthcoming) are adopted due to the convenience of using data already assembled. Two alternative groups of countries are also considered to assess the effect of disaggregation by country on results.

The data used by Whalley rely on 1977 GNP per capita in U.S. dollars taken from the World Bank Atlas (1979). Countries of the world are grouped into seven regions outlined in table 2; the EEC, US, Japan, other developed countries, OPEC (oil producers), new industrialized countries and less developed countries. GNP per capita in U.S. dollars is calculated for each region. The World Bank Atlas also provides data on population for 1977 for each country, which are similarly aggregated to produce population by region. Table 2 indicates the large differences in U.S. dollar GNP per capita by region and also the concentrating of population in LDCs. Data on factor shares between capital and labour in each of the seven regions are taken from Whalley (n.d.); these data rely on U.N. sources. These two pieces of data provide an observation on the wage bill which, in turn, directly produces an estimate of the wage rate once labour employed is known.

Two different types of calculations are made, referred to as 'unadjusted' and 'adjusted'. In the unadjusted calculations data are used in crude form with population data used as a proxy for the workforce. This is clearly a poor assumption since population will exceed workforce in each region. In adjusted calculations approximate fractions representing the ratio of population to the workforce for each region are used.

There are also problems of interpretation with international GNP data which affect the calculations, especially the divergence between official and purchasing power parity exchange rates highlighted by Kravis et al. (1975). This issue motivates further adjustments to explore robustness of results to the data used. Finally, differential labour efficiency factors by region are used to allow for variations in labour productivity by region.

These adjustments have a dramatic effect on estimated global efficiency gains because their effects compound. Because of their importance they are listed in table 3. Adjustments for the ratio of the size of the work-force to population assume that in rich regions (1–5) the workforce is 60% of the population but only 40% in poor regions (6 and 7). These adjustments crudely reflect demographic patterns. To adjust for differences in efficiencies of labour across regions, labour in newly industrialized and less industrialized countries is assumed to be less efficient than labour in developed countries. Two alternative differential efficiency factors of one-half and one-third are used in adjusted calculations. Finally, in making adjustments for differences between purchasing power parity and official exchange rates in converting GNP data into U.S. dollars, figures from Kravis et al. (1975) are used in a manner similar to the correction factors used in Whalley (1980). Here correction factors by region are applied rather than by income level as in the earlier. In cases where all 179 countries in table 2 are considered, the same correction factors are assumed to apply to all countries within each region.

In addition to differences between adjusted and unadjusted calculations, further variations occur with respect to the groups of countries used. Calculations are made not only for the equalization or partial removal of differences in wage rates

TABLE 2 *Classification of countries into regions and summary features of each.*[a]

	Countries included in regions			
Region 1 (EEC)	Belgium Denmark France	Ireland Italy	Luxemburg Netherlands	U.K. W. Germany
Region 2 (U.S.)	United States			
Region 3 (Japan)	Japan			
Region 4 (Other Developed)	Albania Australia Austria Bahamas Barbados Bermuda Bulgaria Canada	Czechoslovakia E. Germany Finland Fr. Polynesia Gibraltar Greece Greenland Guam	Hungary Israel Malta New Zealand Norway Poland Portugal Puerto Rico	Romania Samoa Spain Sweden Switzerland U.S.S.R. Virgin Isl. Yugoslavia
Region 5 (OPEC) (oil producers)	Bahrain Brunei Indonesia Iran	Iraq Kuwait Libya	Nigeria Oman Qatar	Saudi Arabia Un. Arab. Em. Venezuela
Region 6 (N.I.C.)	Argentina Brazil Chile Costa Rica Cyprus Ecuador Fiji	Fr. Guyana Hong Kong Jamaica Korea Lebanon Macao Malaysia	Martinique Mexico Neth. Antil. N. Caledonia Pacific Islands Panama Singapore	Surinam Taiwan Trinidad Turkey Uruguay
Region 7 (L.D.C.)	Afghanistan Algeria Angola Antigua Bangladesh Belize Benin Bhutan Bolivia Botswana Burma Burundi Cameroon Cape Verde Ce. Africa	Dm Kampuch Egypt El Salvador Ethiopia Gabon Gambia Ghana Grenada Guadeloupe Guatemala Guinea Guinea-Bis Guyana Haiti Honduras	Madagascar Malawi Maldives Mali Mauritania Mauritius Mongolia Morocco Mozambique Namibia Nepal New Hebrides N. Guinea Nicaragua Niger	Sao Tome Senegal Seychelles Sierra Leone Solomon Is. Somalia S. Africa Sri Lanka Sudan Swaziland Syrian A R Tanzania Thailand Togo Tonga

Chad	India	Pakistan	Tunisia
China	Ivory Coast	Paraguay	Uganda
Colombia	Jordan	Peru	Upp Volta
Comoros	Kenya	Philippines	Vietnam
Congo	Kiribati	Reunion	Yemen A R
Cuba	Korea	Rwanda	Yemen PDR
Djibouti	Laos Fdr	St Kitts	Zaire
Dominica	Lesotho	St Lucia	Zambia
Dominion Rp.	Liberia	St Vincent	Zimbabwe

Summary features of regions

	1977 GNP/Capita in $U.S.	1977 Population in billions	1977 GNP in $ bill. (U.S.)
Region 1 (EEC countries)	6283	0.3	1629
Region 2 (U.S.)	8751	0.2	1897
Region 3 (Japan)	6511	0.1	737
Region 4 (other developed countries)	3848	0.5	2024
Region 5 (OPEC)	10000.3[b]	0.3	303
Region 6 (newly industrialized countries)	1306	0.4	461
Region 7 (less developed countries)	325.1	2.4	773
Total	1863	4.2	7824

[a]All figures used are taken from the World Bank Atlas for 1977 and grouped according to the blocs listed above. An important point is that all conversions into U.S.$ made in constructing the World Bank Atlas are at market or official exchange rates, and there is a widespread view that relative to a 'purchasing power parity' calculation this substantially underestimates $GNP/capita in most LDCs. The most widely quoted estimates of 'purchasing power parity' premia are in Kravis et al. (1975).

[b]This seemingly low figure for OPEC arises from the inclusion of Nigeria as a large population member of OPEC.

between the seven regions indicated in table 2, but also across all 179 countries in table 2, and between aggregated 'rich' and 'poor' regions (regions 1 to 5 are assumed 'rich' and regions 6 and 7 'poor'). In the individual country case to simplify the calculation factor shares are assumed to be the same for any country within each of the seven groups.

4. RESULTS OF CALCULATIONS

In table 4 estimates of the annual worldwide efficiency gains from free mobility

TABLE 3 *Adjustments made to data used in unadjusted case.*

(A) Population/workforce
Crude correction for size of labour force to population. Workforce assumed to be 60% of population in developed country regions (1–5), but only 40% in developing country regions (6 and 7).

(B) Efficiency units
Differential efficiencies of labour assumed by region. Labour in Regions 6 and 7 (NICs and LDCs) assumed to be (a) one-half, and (b) one-third as efficient as labour elsewhere in alternative calculations.

(C) Exchange rates
Crude correction for purchasing power parity premium over official exchange rates, using estimates from Kravis, et al. (1975). Premia relative to the U.S. dollar used are 1.24 for the EEC, 1.47 for Japan, 1.87 for other developed, 2.32 for OPEC, 2.32 for NICs, and 3.49 for LDCs. [See Whalley (1980, p. 274).]

TABLE 4 *Estimates of annual worldwide efficiency gains from free labour mobility – unadjusted cases, $ trillion 1977.*

Removal of controls on labour mobility between	Elasticities of substitution in production in all regions 1.5	1.25	1.0	0.75	0.25
(1) All countries listed to table 2	16.02	14.46	12.28	9.26	5.80
(2) The 7 regions listed in table 2	15.41	13.82	11.52	8.58	5.52
(3) The 'rich' and 'poor' regions listed in table 2	7.02	6.81	6.49	5.92	4.74
Worldwide GNP in 1977			7.82		

of labour are reported for the unadjusted case for different values of the elasticity of substitution in production in all regions. In spite of the sensitivity of the values of substitution elasticities, these results suggest large gains from the removal of global immigration controls. In most cases the gain exceeds worldwide GNP generated in the presence of the controls suggesting that immigration control is one of the (and perhaps the) most important policy issues facing the global economy. A large portion of the gain is accounted for by labour migration occurring between the aggregated rich and poor regions. Relatively little additional gain results from labour migration occurring between individual

TABLE 5 *Estimates of annual worldwide efficiency gains from partial liberalization of migration restrictions – unadjusted 7-region calculations ($ trillion 1977).*

% Reduction in difference between region and global wage rates	Elasticities of substitution in production in all regions				
	1.5	1.25	1.0	0.75	0.5
1	0.74	0.61	0.48	0.35	0.23
2	1.52	1.23	0.96	0.70	0.45
4	3.12	2.50	1.91	1.36	0.85
6	4.59	3.71	2.82	1.98	1.22
8	5.81	4.79	3.68	2.57	1.55
10	6.76	5.70	4.45	3.11	1.86
20	9.36	8.28	6.99	5.25	3.09
40	11.92	10.41	8.83	7.11	4.65
60	13.78	12.00	9.91	7.71	5.22
80	14.99	13.28	10.92	8.23	5.41
100	15.41	13.82	11.52	8.58	5.52

countries beyond the gain from migration between the seven major regions. The impact of restrictions on labour mobility is thus clearly an issue between rich countries as a bloc and poor countries as a bloc rather than between individual countries.

Table 5 reports results from allowing partial removal of immigration controls in the unadjusted case for the 7-region calculation. These calculations involve allowing for only partial removal of the difference between each region's wage rate and the global mean wage rate. The most important feature of this table is the large gains arising from only small amounts of migration. This reflects the fact that marginal efficiency gains are larger for initial units of migrating labour since the marginal product differences are largest in the initial phases of migration. With elasticities equal to 1.5 in each region, over 40% of the total potential gain is realized when only 10% of the wage differential is eliminated, and 5% of the gain for a 1% reduction. This suggests that small changes in global migration restrictions are especially important since their marginal effects are large.

Table 6 reports results from elimination of immigration controls in the seven region case with the various adjustment factors outlined above. Since these adjustment factors compound one with another in reducing the measured wage rate differential on an effective labour units basis, in combination they sharply reduce the estimate of global efficiency gains. While this is disturbing from the viewpoint of producing firm estimates of the effects, the key role of these adjustments is hardly surprising. Combining work force/population, exchange rate, and labour efficiency adjustments reduces measured wage rate differentials between rich and poor regions by an order of approximately 20 (i.e. 2 x 3.5 x 3). This highlights the need for a more accurate assessment of these parameters in

TABLE 6 *Estimates of annual worldwide efficiency gains from global removal of immigration controls – adjusted 7-region calculations ($ trillion 1977)*

	Elasticities of substitution in production of all regions				
	1.5	1.25	1.0	0.75	0.5
No adjustment (table 4)	15.41	13.82	11.52	8.58	5.52
Adjustments					
PW	11.04	9.93	8.36	6.36	4.30
EX	12.11	11.08	9.80	8.09	5.46
EU	6.59	5.91	4.99	3.84	2.68
EU2	8.83	7.94	6.70	5.14	3.55
EU+PW	5.09	4.56	3.82	2.93	2.04
EX+PW	7.69	7.03	6.24	5.24	3.72
EX+EU[a]	3.29	2.96	2.58	2.14	1.55
EX+PW+EU	2.07	1.84	1.6	1.34	1.05
EX+PW+EU2[a]	3.29	2.96	2.58	2.14	1.55

Notation for adjustments
PW – Population workforce adjustment
EX – Exchange rate adjustment
EU – Labour efficiency units correction using factors of 1:3
EU2 – Labour efficiency units correction using factors of 1:2

[a]These two produce the same result since the *PW* + *EU2* adjustment compound to the same adjustment as *EU*.

any future work if more than a broad impression of possible orders of magnitude is sought.

Table 7 reports the distributional impacts of liberalized migration restrictions in the unadjusted 7-region cases. Panel (A) shows both the sharp changes which occur in wage rates and the adjustments between regions. With an elasticity of substitution of 0.5, four regions gain labour and three lose; but with the higher elasticity value of 1.5 only one region gains labour while six have labour outflows. Because only one region expands labour use in the 1.5 elasticity case, this case may be regarded as especially implausible. Wage rates rise in labour losing regions and fall in labour receiving regions. The changes in the return to capital by region in panel (B) emphasize the feature that capital owners in labour gaining regions are made better off, and in labour losing regions are made worse off. The incentive for labour unions in high wage countries to oppose liberalization of immigration restrictions is thus clearly shown.

Fig. 3 displays the global Lorenz curves for the worldwide income distribution before and after removal of immigration controls in the 179 country unadjusted

TABLE 7 *Distributional impacts of removal of immigration controls – 7-region unadjusted case*

Region	Elasticities of substitution in production in all regions 1.5	1.25	1.0	0.75	0.5
(A) % change in wage rates to non-migrating labour					
1	23.7	9.6	–12.1	–39.7	–67.7
2	–27.9	–36.2	–48.8	–64.8	–81.2
3	27.2	12.7	–9.6	–38.0	–66.8
4	72.0	52.3	22.2	–16.1	–55.1
5	1750.2	1538.7	1214.8	802.3	382.6
6	624.3	541.5	414.7	253.2	88.9
7	1718.4	1510.6	1192.2	786.8	374.3
(B) % Change in return to capital by region					
1	–25.7	–13.3	22.6	99.4	184.1
2	396.3	526.6	695.3	760.9	659.3
3	–24.9	–14.5	14.7	76.5	148.2
4	–61.5	–60.0	–40.4	52.3	242.7
5	–37.7	–47.5	–59.1	–69.1	–65.8
6	–62.7	–72.2	–81.1	–84.9	–61.6
7	–94.3	–98.9	–100.0	–100.0	–100.0

case using elasticities of substitution of 0.5. The Lorenz curves are drawn using GNP/capita by country and assuming that in each case the distribution of income within each country is uniform. While this is only one of the cases considered here, the sharp move towards equality clearly shows the dramatic effects on worldwide equality which are possible from modifying immigration restrictions. These effects are much larger, for instance, than those likely from increases in aid flows to Lima target levels.

5. CONCLUSION AND POLICY IMPLICATIONS

Although highly speculative, the calculations reported here clearly suggest large potential worldwide efficiency gains from moving toward a worldwide labour market free of immigration controls. Gains to the world economy in many of the unadjusted cases exceed existing worldwide GNP; in the adjusted cases gains are smaller but still large. Thus, while the main conclusion of this paper may not be surprising, it is the potential quantitative size of the effects involved that is striking.

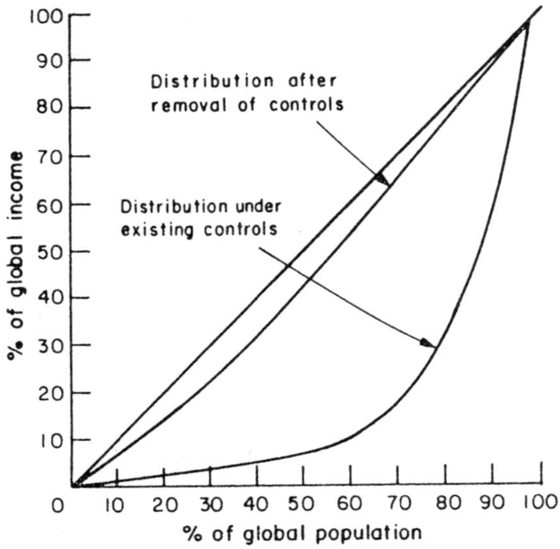

FIGURE 3 Global distributional effects of removing immigration controls: Lorenz curves for 179 country unadjusted cases with substitution elasticities of 0.5.

To place the results here in the context of current policy debates, it is useful to compare the results to some of the estimates of effects from policy initiatives on some of the more actively discussed issues in the North–South debate. Cline (1979) presents a 'best guess' numerical evaluation of possible impacts of policy initiatives under the North–South dialogue including commodity price stabilization, cancellation or rescheduling of LDC debt, relaxation of trade protection in the North on LDC exports, and increased aid flows. A best guess offered by Cline is that annual gains to LDC's from a series of 'optimistic' policy changes on these fronts could be in the range of $40 billion/year. Cline also describes the impact of liberalized migration on developing countries as potentially 'very large'. The calculations reported here suggest that the gains from liberalized labour mobility are likely to dominate developing country gains from non-migration initiatives. The implication thus appears to be that liberalization of worldwide migration could possibly be the single most important issue in current North–South exchanges for the South. Citizens of LDCs could thus be well served if demands for removal of immigration controls in the North were more forcefully presented, instead of allowing the other proposals which have so far preoccupied negotiations on a new international economic order to take centre stage. Even small steps towards liberalization are important because effects are large at the margin. Finally, concessions to the South in North–South forums may be of little value if at the same time immigration restrictions in the developed would are further tightened.

NOTES

The calculations reported in this paper are an outgrowth of work on a project on trade liberalization supported by the Ford Foundation under their competition in International Economic Order. We are grateful to Emmanuel Jimmenez, a seminar group at Western Ontario, and an unnamed referee for helpful comments on an earlier draft.

1 Trade theorists might argue that the factor price equalization theorem makes such a discussion unnecessary. The approach here assumes wage rate equalization is to be achieved through unimpeded international labour flows rather than free mobility of goods with internationally immobile factors. Whether factor price equalization would hold were all impediments to goods trade in the world economy removed remains a contentious issue, though most trade economists appear to regard factor price equalization as a theoretical possibility rather than an empirical proposition.

2 As long ago as 1967 Harry Johnson remarked that '. . . immigration policies of developed countries, which generally discriminate severely against immigrants from less developed countries, especially the poorly trained and educated, may be said to lie at the core of the development problem' [Johnson (1967, p. 107], and more recently Gerry Heleiner (1979) has argued that '. . . most important "imperfection" in world markets is that which exists in the market for labour, particularly unskilled labour. The world labour market is severely segmented by the fact of immigration restrictions'. [Helleiner, in: Cline, ed. (1979, p. 365).]

3 This follows from fig. 2, since the return capital, R_i, is the arena below the marginal value product of labour schedule and above the labour rectangle. Thus $Ri = -{}^1/_2\hat{L}_i \cdot (\partial MRP_{Li}/\partial L_i) \cdot \hat{L}_i$, and $(\partial MRP_{Li}/\partial L_i) = -2(R_i/\hat{L}_i^2)$. Thus $(\partial MRP_{Li}/\partial L_i).(\hat{L}_i/\hat{W}_i) = (-2R_i/B_i)$.

REFERENCES

Cline, W. R., ed., 1979, Policy alternatives for a new international economic order. An economic analysis (Praeger, New York).

Harberger, A. C., 1966, Efficiency effects of taxes on income from capital, in: M. Krzyaniak, ed., Effects of the corporation income tax (Detroit, MI).

Helleiner, G. K., 1979, World market imperfections and the developing countries, in: W. R. Cline, ed., Policy alternatives for a new international economic order: An economic analysis (Praeger, New York).

Johnson, H. G., 1967, Economic policies toward less developed countries (Praegar, New York).

Kravis, I. B., Z. Kenessey, A. Heston and R. Summers, 1975, A system of international comparisons of gross national product and purchasing power (Johns Hopkins Press, Baltimore, MD).

Whalley, J., 1980, The worldwide income distribution: Some speculative calculations, Review of Income and Wealth, Sept., 261–275.

Whalley, J., n.d., Trade liberalization among major trading areas (MIT Press, Cambridge, MA) forthcoming.

World Bank Atlas, 1979 (World Bank, Washington, DC).

8. Competition Policy and the Global Trading System

B. Hoekman

1. INTRODUCTION

The issue of whether multilateral disciplines on private anti-competitive practices are desirable has been the subject of discussion for many years. Competition law and policy disciplines were on the agenda of the negotiations to establish an International Trade Organisation (ITO) after the Second World War. As is well known, the ITO never came into being, and the General Agreement on Tariffs and Trade (GATT) only took over the ITO provisions on restrictive business practices in a 'best endeavours' clause (Art. XXIX GATT). Since then developing countries have pursued the topic in the UN context, while the OECD has been dealing with the issue for many years in the context of its Competition Law and Policy Committee. These efforts resulted in various 'codes of conduct,' none of which is legally enforceable.[1] Prospects for substantive negotiations on multilateral disciplines relating to competition law increased with the decision of the first Ministerial meeting of the World Trade Organisation (WTO) in December 1996 to establish a working group on the topic. The working group was given two years to study issues relevant to the interaction between trade and competition policy. Despite the longstanding interest in, and deliberations on, the topic, much work will be required to determine a possible negotiating agenda.

Different rationales have been suggested for launching negotiations. They include a view that anti-trust disciplines are required to enhance WTO market commitments; a perception that anti-trust rules are necessary to constrain the use of anti-dumping; a belief that the (potential for) exercise of market power by global multinationals requires a global competition code; and the possibility that governments may be able to use anti-trust laws as an instrument to circumvent WTO obligations. This paper discusses the desirability and feasibility of alternative negotiating agendas aiming at an international agreement on trade-related anti-trust principles (TRAPs). Section 2 reviews the major options. The desirability of these alternatives is evaluated in Section 3, using three criteria: (i) enhanced access to foreign markets (a trade negotiator's criterion); (ii) economic efficiency and welfare (an economist's criterion); and (iii) whether it strengthens the WTO-based trading system. Although the second and third of these criteria will be considered most relevant by economists, the first criterion is included because it reflects the objectives of many proponents of putting anti-trust on the WTO agenda. Section 4 discusses the feasibility of alternative options. Section 5 concludes.

Three basic arguments are made. First, introducing competition law (antitrust) on the WTO negotiating agenda could foster efficiency and strengthen the trading system. Not surprisingly, however, many options will not lead to this result, and much depends on the specifics of the proposal that is on the table. From an efficiency perspective the rationale for a TRAPs agreement is not very compelling. Second, if negotiations are launched, the potential costs and benefits for developing countries of feasible TRAPs agreements appear limited. Options that would be very beneficial – in particular initiation of a process of replacing anti-dumping actions with domestic competition law enforcement – will confront significant opposition, especially by interest groups in industrialised countries. Third, the best feasible option from an efficiency, market access and trading system perspective may be the introduction of antitrust-related regulatory disciplines in the context of 'standard' issue-specific negotiations of the type that have traditionally been pursued in the GATT/WTO setting.

2. THE MAJOR OPTIONS

Many suggestions have been made regarding competition law and the WTO, ranging from a global competition code (harmonisation of substantive rules) to doing nothing (competition between competition regimes). What follows, briefly discusses the major options. Clearly many variants can be (and have been) proposed, and some proposals can be combined with others. The options identified below can be regarded as among the most important 'types' of agreement that might be pursued.

a. Option 1 — Minimum Anti-trust Standards

In 1993, the so-called Munich group of competition law experts created a Draft International Anti-trust Code (Fikentscher and Immenga, 1995). The establishment of an International Anti-trust Authority is envisaged, which would have the task of enforcing a set of common, harmonised anti-trust rules in all contracting parties (through the offices of national competition authorities). It would have the power to request domestic competition authorities to initiate an investigation and to challenge implementation of the Code before an International Anti-trust Panel. The rules proposed are detailed, and include *per se* prohibitions for specified horizontal and vertical restraints. They would have direct effect: private parties could invoke them before national courts. The Code would be an Annex IV agreement under the WTO, i.e., a plurilateral treaty applying only to those WTO members that sign it.[2] Scherer (1995) has made a proposal along similar lines, suggesting that agreement be sought on a number of minimum standards: 'the most likely candidates are export and import cartels, serious abuses of dominant positions in the world market, and merger approval procedures' (Scherer, 1996, p. 18). An International Competition Office would start enforcing the agreed standards seven years after its creation, and employ national competition authorities to support its investigations. Participants initially would be allowed to exempt three industries from the ban on export cartels. A difference with the Munich proposal is that the focus is much more on anti-competitive practices that directly affect trade.

An EU Group of Experts has suggested that agreement be sought in the WTO context on specific business practices that impede trade, *without* creating a new international institution (EU Commission, 1995). Enforcement of the common minimum standards would be the responsibility of national anti-trust authorities. The agreement again would be plurilateral in nature. In addition to the substantive rules – *per se* prohibitions on horizontal restraints and export cartels; complemented by a rule of reason approach to other practices – the proposal includes notification requirements, positive and negative comity obligations,[3] and subjecting firms that have been granted special or exclusive privileges to the agreed competition standards. The WTO would enforce the agreement; dispute settlement provisions would be extended to private anti-competitive practices.

b. Option 2 – Introduce Anti-trust Law Criteria in Anti-dumping

A frequent proposal is to establish linkages between competition law disciplines and anti-dumping. The most far-reaching suggestion is to abolish anti-dumping altogether and replace it with (domestic) anti-trust.[4] Less radical options include allowing anti-dumping actions to be contested (*ex ante* or *ex post*) on the basis of anti-trust considerations and introducing competition law-type thresholds and criteria into the anti-dumping process. Examples of the latter include using a 'relevant market' instead of 'like product' approach to defining the product market in an investigation; including an injury to competition standard; allowing for competition-based defences by exporters (e.g., 'meeting the competition' or lack of market power); and abolishing provisions allowing for suspension of anti-dumping investigations following negotiation of 'voluntary' price undertakings.[5]

c. Option 3 – Extend the Reach of WTO 'Nonviolation' Dispute Settlement Mechanisms

Instead of negotiating substantive anti-trust disciplines (as under option 1), the reach of WTO dispute settlement procedures could be extended to cover entry-restricting business practices that are tolerated by a government. In principle, governments may use anti-trust as a substitute for trade policies that are prohibited by the WTO. Art. XXIII: 1 of the GATT already allows WTO members to challenge actions by governments that, although not illegal under WTO rules, nullify or impair concessions obtained in trade negotiations (so-called non-violation disputes).[6] Until a dispute between Kodak and Fuji was brought to the WTO in 1995, the provision had not been used to challenge non-enforcement of anti-trust law.[7] In part this reflects a need to show that the nullification is caused by a government measure that was not 'reasonably' foreseeable at the time the trade concessions were negotiated. In the anti-trust context the problem is whether non-enforcement or the discriminatory application of competition law constitutes a 'measure.' Use of non-violation dispute settlement might be facilitated by seeking agreement that non-enforcement of national anti-trust law is a government 'measure' and weakening the 'reasonable expectations' language (Hindley, 1996).[8]

d. Option 4 – Give the WTO a Competition Advocacy Role

Another alternative is to give the WTO secretariat a competition advocacy mandate. In national jurisdictions there is a good case for allowing competition agencies to monitor the competitive impact of government polices as well as enforce competition laws (Khemani and Dutz, 1995). A number of developing countries and economies in transition have granted their competition agencies the right to comment on or oppose government policies that restrict competition (Boner, 1995).[9] A similar task could be given to the WTO. One forum for this could be the WTO's Trade Policy Review Mechanism under which the trade policy stance of all WTO members is periodically subjected to a detailed report by the WTO Secretariat which is the basis for a review by the WTO Council. Such reports could be expanded to include not just policies that are subject to WTO disciplines but also the application of antitrust law, including the impact of exemptions.[10]

e. Option 5 – Prohibit Anti-trust Exemptions Allowing Private Restrictions on Trade

Rather than pursuing a set of minimum common standards for anti-trust law, it has been proposed that the focus be limited to policies that allow private practices that directly restrict trade. For example, Messerlin (1996) among others has argued there is a case for prohibiting pro-cartel provisions of national competition laws (e.g., exemptions for export cartels that have no effect on the domestic market). Under this approach attention would be focused narrowly on government measures and policies that allow such practices. GATT in principle already prohibits import *and* export quotas; this would then be extended to anti-trust exemptions that have an equivalent result. As discussed below, it may be difficult to pursue this path without also addressing the behaviour of state monopolies or firms granted exclusive rights.[11]

f. Option 6 – Pursue Sector-Specific Agreements or Commitments

Yet another alternative is to avoid the general topic of anti-trust but seek to introduce competition criteria into specific WTO Agreements.[12] Some efforts in this direction have already been made. For example, the Agreement on Safeguards prohibits the use of voluntary export restrictions, orderly marketing arrangements and similar measures on either exports or imports, including compulsory import cartels, and states further that WTO members are to refrain from encouraging or supporting the use of measures with equivalent effect by public *or* private enterprises (Art 11:3). Negotiating attention might therefore be focused on specific sectors or policies. A noteworthy example of such an approach is the recently concluded agreement to liberalise access to basic telecommunications services under the auspices of the General Agreement on Trade in Services (GATS). Telecommunications markets are frequently characterised by dominant suppliers that control bottleneck or essential facilities. Negotiations therefore centred in part on matters such as interconnection obligations and competition safeguards.[13] These principles were negotiated in recognition of the fact that private dominant players in the telecoms market, left free to make decisions about how to treat other suppliers, could frustrate negotiated market access and national treatment commitments. While the principles that were negotiated are regulatory in nature, in principle commitments could pertain to the enforcement of anti-trust disciplines.[14]

g. Option 7 – Keep TRAPs Completely Off the WTO Agenda

A final option is not to introduce anti-trust on the negotiating agenda of the WTO in any shape or form. Proponents of this view argue that efforts should be devoted to expanding the reach and depth of bilateral and plurilateral cooperation between the competition agencies of the major industrialised countries, including application of the principle of positive comity.[15] The presumption is that in the WTO setting, priority should be given to more 'traditional' government policies that discriminate against foreign producers, including not only trade barriers but also investment restrictions, government procurement practices and policies that reduce competition in serve markets. The basic argument is that trade and investment liberalisation is the most powerful co-competitive instrument available.

3. EVALUATING THE OPTIONS

Three criteria are useful in evaluating the desirability of alternative TRAPs options: (i) the extent to which they enhance market access opportunities for foreign firms; (ii) their likely impact on national welfare (economic efficiency); and (iii) whether they strengthen the multilateral system (WTO).[16] The market access yardstick is one that is used by many proponents of putting anti-trust on the WTO agenda. They argue that inadequate anti-trust enforcement allows incumbent firms to block or attenuate foreign competition.[17] Clearly a focus on market access is not necessarily welfare improving. Market access negotiations may give rise to market-sharing deals and 'voluntary' import expansion agreements that are anti-competitive. Or, to give a more specific example, suppose negotiators agree that foreign takeovers of domestic firms should not be constrained. Suppose further that a large foreign firm that previously contested the market through exports takes over a large domestic competitor. An anti-trust authority may have good reasons to block such foreign direct investment because of the associated reduction in competition. If it is constrained in this, domestic consumers may suffer the consequences. The basic tension that arises is that while competition policy is nationally blind, market access-based negotiations and agreements are not. An attempt to summarise the possible impacts is made

TABLE 1 *Assessing the Options*

Option	*Market Access*	*Welfare*	*Systemic Impact*
1. Minimum standards for anti-trust law	0	+/-	+/-
2. Introduce anti-trust criteria in anti-dumping	+	+	+
3. Expand non-violation dispute settlement	0	+/0	+/-
4. Competition advocacy	0	+/0	+/-
5. Rules on anti-trust exemptions for 'cartels'	+/0	+/-	+/0
6. Sector-specific disciplines	+	+/-	+/0
7. Keep trade and anti-trust separated	0	0	0/-

Notes:
+ indicates positive impact, – a negative impact, and 0 no impact. More than one symbol indicates that a range of outcomes is possible.

in Table 1, with a + sign indicating a positive impact, a – sign a negative impact, and a 0 no impact. Not surprisingly, in many cases a range of outcomes is possible.

a. Market Access

An agreement to abide by minimum anti-trust standards is not likely to do much to enhance the contestability of markets for foreign firms. In markets where minimum standards imply a strengthening of anti-trust law enforcement (mostly developing economies), this may not have much of an impact on the conditions of competition for foreign firms if more traditional trade and investment barriers are not reduced first.[18] Conversely, in industrialised country markets minimum standards will be of little relevance as they will already be satisfied. In contrast, attaining greater consistency between existing WTO rules on anti-dumping and anti-trust criteria would be of great benefit in terms of guaranteeing market access conditions for exporters and reducing uncertainty. As of mid-1996, WTO members maintained 776 anti-dumping measures – either anti-dumping duties or price undertakings by affected exporters (Table 2). Of these, 72 per cent were imposed by high income countries, the rest by developing countries. Of the new investigations launched between July 1994 and June 1996 (a total of 317), over two-thirds were directed against firms from developing countries. As the Uruguay Round agreements to eliminate the Multifibre Arrangement are implemented, the use of anti-dumping may rise.

Even though high income countries account for the lion's share of anti-dumping cases, some 15 low and middle income countries also initiated anti-dumping investigations in 1994–95 (Table 2). An increasing number of developing countries and economies in transition either have or are in the process of adopting anti-dumping laws. At the last count, over 50 developing and transition economies had such legislation (WTO, 1996).[19] Given that developing country trade accounted

TABLE 2 *Anti-dumping Investigations and Measures in Force, 1994–95*

Country	*Number of Initiations During 7/94–6/95 Against:*		*Measures in Force as of 6/95*	*Number of Initiations During 7/95–6/96 Against:*		*Measures in Force as of 6/96*
	LMICs	*HICs*		*LMICs*	*HICs*	
Argentina	5	1	3	26	16	28
Australia	3	3	86	6	2	86
Brazil	9	3	18	1	0	20
Canada	1	8	91	3	3	96
Chile	2	0	2	2	2	0
Colombia	1	0	6	5	0	7
EU	31	6	178	16	3	76
Guatemala	n.a.	n.a.	n.a.	1	0	n.a.
India	8	1	5	3	2	8
Israel	n.a.	n.a.	n.a.	0	4	n.a.
Japan	0	0	2	0	0	3
Korea	3	0	6	1	6	9
Mexico	18	0	42	2	1	61
New Zealand	8	1	22	7	2	26
Peru	4	0	n.a.	4	0	2
Philippines	2	1	n.a.	0	0	n.a.
Singapore	2	0	0	0	0	2
South Africa	7	2	15	8	7	15
Thailand	0	0	1	0	0	1
Turkey	2	0	38	0	0	38
US	21	9	305	10	6	294
Venezuela	1	0	n.a.	5	0	4
TOTAL	128	35	820	100	53	776

Notes:
HIC = high income countries; LMICs = low and middle income countries, including transition economies.

Source: 1995; Finger and Winters (1996); 1996: WTO (1996). Data are from reports to the WTO by member countries.

for some 32 per cent of global trade in 1993,[20] anti-dumping is well on the way towards becoming a global problem. The first best option from a market access perspective is clear: abolish anti-dumping. But even a less ambitious approach of introducing anti-trust-consistent criteria into anti-dumping enforcement would improve access conditions in both industrial and developing country markets.[21]

Expanding the reach of WTO non-violation dispute settlement would facilitate raising anti-trust-related issues in the WTO and generate information on what types of practices are considered most problematical by government. However, the focus of such disputes will be on the circumvention of liberalisation commitments, not on improving market access *per se*. Moreover, absent agreement on minimum anti-trust standards, the remedies that may be suggested by a WTO panel cannot affect the national application of anti-trust law – at best a complainant country will be offered compensation. This is unlikely to enhance market access conditions for the firm that brought the complaint. At most, the information generated may help to mobilise domestic groups that are negatively affected. The same conclusion applies to the greater advocacy option and extending WTO rules to ban anti-trust exemptions for private practices that restrict international trade. Export cartels presumably are intended to restrict supply (raise prices) – so that market access is not an issue. Import cartels (or monopolies) certainly can restrict market access. If permitted, they are likely to have government involvement as this would otherwise run foul of existing anti-trust regimes in major trading nations. Indeed, to the extent that there is a (political) rationale for restricting imports, it is more probable that such import restrictions will be achieved through state-trading, which is permitted under the GATT. The implication of this is that any attempt to impose disciplines in this area will have to extend to state trading as well.[22]

Turning to issue-specific negotiations, existing WTO agreements where anti-trust-type obligations might be negotiated include those on trade-related intellectual property rights (TRIPs), trade-related investment measures (TRIMs), services (GATS) and government procurement. Allowance is already made in the TRIPs agreement to apply anti-trust-like criteria (e.g., in deciding to require compulsory licensing), while the TRIMs agreement makes reference to possible future discussions on the need for anti-trust disciplines.[23] In the procurement context, it is well known that firms may have an incentive to collude in bidding for public contracts. If domestic firms do so with an incentive to collude in bidding for public contracts. If domestic firms do so with a view to excluding foreign bidders, this may not result in a violation of the Government Procurement Agreement (GPA). Such practices must be combated through domestic anti-trust enforcement and through the appropriate design of bidding mechanisms (see e.g., Mattoo, 1997; and Wood, 1997). From a market access perspective, however, it is not at all clear that anti-trust enforcement will help given that it is nationality blind, focuses on efficiency and is horizontal, not sector-specific.[24]

b. Efficiency

From an efficiency perspective, in principle there is a clear rationale for adopting and enforcing anti-trust rules. Although an open trade and investment regime is a powerful device to promote competition, it may not be adequate in the face of concerted efforts by domestic firms to collude and restrict entry. If non-tradable sectors (e.g., distribution services) are controlled by domestic manufactures and there are restrictions on foreign investment, imports may be restricted and prices be higher than otherwise. Whether anti-trust enforcement will improve national welfare depends on the substantive rules that are adopted and on their enforcement. As in any area of regulation, care must be taken that the specific disciplines that are adopted are appropriate to the economic situation of the country and that competition agencies are professionally staffed and shielded from rent seeking, capture and political influence.[25]

That 'one size fits all' does not apply to anti-trust is amply illustrated by the widely diverging laws and policies of OECD countries. Differences exist on virtually all aspects of competition law, be it the treatment of mergers, resale price maintenance, parallel imports, the weights that should be given to actual versus potential competition, what constitutes an abuse of a dominant position, and so forth. This reflects differences in objectives, priorities, and economic philosophy.[26] There is substantial agreement in the literature that horizontal restraints – collusion between firms in the same industry to restrict output or fix prices – are anti-competitive and should be banned (assuming that the objective of competition law is to foster efficiency). Two types of such restraints are relevant: those that impact on the domestic market; and those imposed by domestic firms that affect other countries. The latter, which are exemplified by export cartels, are often explicitly allowed by national competition laws as long as the agreements do not have a detrimental effect on the home country market. The Webb-Pomerene Act in the US is a prominent example.

Domestic horizontal restraints should be a matter of concern for domestic anti-trust authorities, and presumably most jurisdictions would ban such practices. While a TRAPs agreement banning horizontal restraints in domestic markets would benefit countries that allow such practices, it is unclear why a linkage to a trade forum (the WTO) is required to induce governments to ban them. Possibilities include political economy constraints and/or a lack of administrative capacity. The former presumably will extend beyond the question of horizontal practices to anti-trust more generally, i.e., passing legislation. If there are constraints on the development of anti-trust legislation, any TRAPs agreement requiring minimum standards in the area of horizontal restraints will be insufficient to ensure efficient outcomes. National anti-trust laws must address the whole range of possible anti-competitive practices if they are to be effective. In practice, implementation may be the bigger problem. That is, national legislation may prohibit horizontal restraints, but the anti-trust authorities do not have the resources to enforce them. This cannot be solved by a WTO agreement, but requires cooperation among anti-trust authorities (technical assistance) as well as political support from the government. Assistance is already available from a variety of sources, and this will continue to be the case independent of a WTO agreement. It can be noted that in such situations it is particularly important that the trade and investment regime is liberal, as foreign competition should be a powerful source of market discipline that attenuates the feasibility of maintaining horizontal restrictions.

Export cartels may permit firms to exploit greater market power in foreign markets. The resulting transfer of income (profits) to domestic firms may increase the welfare of the home country, explaining the permissive attitude that is often taken by national competition laws.[27] Little up to date information is available concerning the prevalence and impact of export cartels. Studies undertaken in the 1970s suggest that perhaps some two per cent of US, UK, and German exports were 'assisted' by export cartel exemptions (Rahl, 1981). In general, the economic significance of export cartels is considered to be minor, due largely to the threat of anti-trust enforcement by large entities such as the US and the EU. As noted by one scholar, 'a global cartel engaging in the traditional restraints of market allocation or price fixing could probably not operate today because its scope would cause it to violate in some respect both US and EC anti-trust laws, and probably those of a good many other nations as well' (Rahl, 1981, p. 250). Rahl goes on to note that rather than seeking to negotiate away anti-trust exemptions for export cartels, a policy of attacking them through the application of national anti-trust would be simpler and more effective.

Developing countries may benefit from export cartels involving their firms, and these benefits may outweigh the costs associated with imports controlled by foreign export cartels. Although developing countries have traditionally been concerned about the scope for multinational enterprises to exploit their market power in developing country markets, there is very little information regarding the prevalence and net impact of export cartels on developing countries. Whether a negotiated ban on export cartels would be beneficial to developing countries is therefore unclear. However, experience with commodity agreements illustrates the difficulty of exercising market power. The pursuit of 'strategic' trade policies – of which toleration of export cartels is an example – requires a great deal of information if it is to be welfare enhancing, and account must be taken of possible retaliation by trading partners.

The toleration of export cartels in national anti-trust law is inconsistent with the GATT ban on quantitative export restrictions (Art. XI),[28] but consistent with the permissive approach towards the use of export taxes, which are not subject to GATT rules. Economic incentives suggest that elimination of anti-trust exemptions require cross-issue linkages/tradeoffs (i.e., side payments). Any agreement to ban export cartels will have to be complemented by multilateral disciplines on government policies that have an equivalent effect, i.e., the current freedom to impose tariffs on exports, maintain/create export monopolies, or grant firms exclusive rights and privileges (Hoekman and Mavroidis, 1994).

With respect to non-horizontal practices (e.g., vertical restraints, abuse of a dominant position, mergers), it is well known that apparent restrictions on competition may be justified on efficiency grounds.[29] Most laws therefore allow competition agencies to make judgements in such cases following a so-called 'rule of reason' approach. The differences across countries in rules and practices, as well as the latitude for the exercise of judgement that is embodied in the rule of reason approach, suggests that seeking the adoption of common norms for non-horizontal restraints is not desirable. Diverging anti-trust law and practice reflect differences in preferences, priorities, economic systems, administrative capacity, etc.[30]

More can be said in favour of multilateral agreement on the procedural and administrative aspects of competition laws in order to ensure transparency and due process. Existing WTO agreements on issues such as product standards, government procurement or intellectual property have a few key substantive provisions (e.g., non-discrimination; 20 year patent protection) which are complemented by very detailed procedural and 'due process' requirements that are intended to ensure that policies are transparent and the key rules are not easily circumvented. Any competition agency should ideally have a number of features, including transparency of the administrative mechanisms, regulations and procedures; separation of investigation and prosecution from adjudication functions; expeditious and transparent proceedings that safeguard sensitive business information; provisions for imposing significant penalties; and checks and balances to guarantee due process, including the right of appeal, reviews of decisions, and access to information on legal and economic interpretations (Khemani, 1994). A TRAPs agreement embodying such principles could help to ensure that these desirable features are realised in all WTO members.

The option of introducing competition policy criteria into anti-dumping rules is likely to be welfare enhancing as it reduces the threat of contingent protection, both in export markets and at home. It is well established that the economic rationale for anti-dumping is quite limited and that anti-dumping regimes can be very costly for the countries that implement them (Finger, 1993). As mentioned previously, an increasing number of developing countries have adopted anti-dumping laws – or are in the process of doing so. Thus, for these countries disciplining anti-dumping is not just an issue of expanding exports, but also one of reducing costs for domestic users of imports in developing countries.

The welfare implications of expansion of non-violation dispute settlement are also likely to be positive as this is an additional instrument to ensure that liberalisation commitments will be implemented. An important advantage of this option over others is that it goes beyond competition law-related issues. In principle, any measure that nullifies a trade liberalisation commitment can be contested. In this respect non-violation is a 'strong' form of competition advocacy. Giving the WTO such an advocacy mandate would also be beneficial as it would generate information on the economic effects of government policies. More important, it could provide incentives for the establishment of domestic counterpart institutions. The latter is particularly important for developing countries. Domestic 'transparency institutions' and competition agencies have long been promoted by trade policy and competition analysts who argue that public information on the costs and benefits of government policies is required in order to countervail rent-seeking activities (see e.g., Finger, 1982). A multilateral competition advocacy role may help to support the creation and operations of such institutions.[31]

Sector- or issue-specific agreements may or may not increase efficiency. As discussed earlier, such agreements are likely to focus on market access, which does not necessarily imply greater competition and welfare. Although in principle governments should be expected to adopt regulatory regimes and competition policies that maximise welfare, in practice lobbying by interest groups will lead to economic inefficiencies. External pressure can then be a catalyst for changes that are welfare improving. This is of course the main raison d'être for multilateral trade negotiations. Whatever the outcome of sectoral or issue-specific negotiations, anti-trust *per se* is unlikely to enter into the picture given its horizontal focus. Indeed, keeping anti-trust out of the picture may help to ensure that issue-specific agreements are efficiency enhancing, as anti-trust remains an independent policy domain that is unconcerned with 'market access.' However, regulatory commitments that are informed (inspired) by anti-trust considerations or criteria may be very helpful in ensuring that negotiated market access commitments are not only realised but are efficiency enhancing.

c. Systemic Implications

Whether an option will strengthen the trading system depends importantly on whether it will: (i) reduce the scope for using anti-trust to circumvent WTO obligations; and (ii) close other holes and loopholes in existing WTO agreements. Of the various options, only disciplining anti-dumping and the scope of anti-trust exemptions for trade-restricting cartels (including state-trading) appear beneficial in terms of strengthening the trading system, as these will remove existing holes in the WTO. As regards the latter, it has already been mentioned that Art. XI GATT already prohibits quantitative import and export restrictions, and GATT panels have interpreted this Article relatively broadly in terms of what measures are covered.[32] The adoption of a prohibition on private cartels with an equivalent effect would be consistent with the objectives and wording of Art. XI. The other options all have potential downside risks as well as benefits. Many, if not most, 'anti-trust'-related disputes in the trade context have concerned practices which are not horizontal (e.g., access to distribution systems). As minimum standards are unlikely to extend to such practices, adoption of anti-trust legislation that is limited to minimum standards may do little to strengthen the trading system. If the minimum standards revolve around procedural transparency and due process-enhancing disciplines, there may be enforcement and implementation-related benefits associated with a WTO agreement. Although these may not be very large because panels may not be able to propose effective remedies, there is potentially value in being able to use multilateral dispute settlement procedures for the adjudication of disputes concerning procedure. It could help to foster greater consistency and coherence of decisions and practices of WTO members in the anti-trust area.

Expanding the reach of non-violation-based dispute settlement has the potential to both strengthen and stress the system. From a systemic perspective it is beneficial that actions be brought to the WTO; from a national perspective it is valuable to be able to 'deflect' pressures for action to the multilateral level – allowing firms access to an objective fact-finding mechanism may be enough in many instances to 'clear the air.' Moreover, if it helps to prevent the use of unilateral remedies, this also will be a valuable systemic benefit. Conversely, the fact that WTO panels will be requested to look at the *effects* of enforcement or non-enforcement of national anti-trust laws could increase the pressure on the system. One reason is because of the implied reliance on 'judicial activism' as opposed to negotiated disciplines (Jackson, 1996). In effect the WTO would be made into a court of appeal for (a subset of) anti-trust decisions by members, but panels will not have the ability to impose remedies that will change the status quo, as the substantive provisions of national anti-trust law will not be regulated by the WTO. This may induce greater use of unilateral measures that are 'motivated' by the finding of the panel. Clearly there is a significant danger in pursuing this course.

Similarly, the competition advocacy option may be detrimental to the trading system if it results in criticism of practices where there is legitimate scope for different conclusion under a 'rule of reason' approach. It will also imply an additional burden on the WTO Secretariat, which would need to be given a much greater analytical capacity than it has today. Finally, the systemic implications of sector or issue-specific agreements are not likely to be detrimental. After all, this has been the standard operating mode of the GATT/WTO.

4. FEASIBILITY OF ALTERNATIVE AGREEMENTS

Summing up, disciplining anti-dumping, prohibiting anti-trust exemptions for cartels (extended to state-trading), and issue/sector-specific agreements are likely to enhance both market access and strengthen the WTO. However, in terms of efficiency only the anti-dumping option (a subset of the issue-specific approach) appears unambiguously beneficial. How feasible might it be to attain the various options?

a. Minimum Standards

At least 37 developing countries and economies in transition already have competition legislation, and another 21 are in the process of revising or adopting such laws (Table 3). Although the substantive obligations of these laws will differ, as will enforcement standards, in most cases existing statutes will tend to be most stringent with respect to horizontal restraints. This suggests that achieving agreement on minimum standards will respect to such practices may well be feasible. Greater difficulty may be experienced concerning the procedural and administrative disciplines, as this may well constitute more of a threat for vested interests that oppose greater competition. As noted before, agreement on common norms with respect to vertical restraints is highly improbable given the significant differences in approaches across countries and the need for a 'rule of reason' approach.

b. Anti-trust and Anti-dumping

Recent regional integration agreements suggest that agreements to link anti-trust to anti-dumping will not be easy to achieve. A commitment by Central and Eastern European countries to apply EU competition rules did not eliminate the threat of contingent protection by the EU. Anti-dumping remains applicable to trade flows. The same is true, in the EU's recent agreements with the Mediterranean countries (Galal and Hoekman, 1997). Similarly, the North American Free Trade Agreement also maintains anti-dumping for internal trade flows. Despite the Canadian government's great interest in disciplining the use of anti-dumping (with a stated preference for abolition) negotiators were unable to agree to replace anti-dumping with anti-trust enforcement. However, there are regional agreements where the anti-dumping option has been repealed in favour of competition law enforcement. Examples are the European Economic Area, the Australia–New Zealand Closer Economic Relations Trade Agreement and most recently the free trade agreement negotiated between Chile and Canada. In the first two cases achieving such agreement took a long time, and was conditional upon substantial harmonisation of competition and related policies, including subsidies.[33]

Whatever the feasibility of linking anti-trust and anti-dumping in the regional context, informal proposals to pursue such a linkage in the WTO have been confronted with strong opposition. This reflects the preferences of both the anti-

TABLE 3 *Adoption of Competition Law in Developing and Transition Economies*

Countries with Legislation				*Memo: Countries in the Process of Adopting Legislation*
Country	*Status*	*Country*	*Status*	
Africa				Cameroon
Algeria	1995	Mali	1992	Egypt
Côte d'Ivoire	1991	South Africa	1979	Jordan
Kenya	1988	Tunisia	1991	Gabon
Asia				Ghana
China	1993	Sri Lanka	1987	Morocco
India	1969; 1991	Taiwan	1991	Senegal
Pakistan	1970	Thailand	1979	Zambia
South Korea	1980			Zimbabwe
Latin America				Indonesia
Argentina	1919; 1946; 1980; under rev.	Jamaica	1993	Malaysia
Brazil	1962; 1994	Mexico	1992	Philippines
Chile	1959; 1973	Peru	1991; 1994	Ecuador
Colombia	1959; 1992	Venezuela	1992	El Salvador
Transition Economies				Paraguay
Belarus	1992	Latvia	1991	Albania
Bulgaria	1991	Moldova	1992	Armenia
Czech Republic	1991	Poland	1990	Azerbaijan
Estonia	1993	Romania	1991	Croatia
Georgia	1992; under rev.	Russia	1991	Macedonia
Hungary	1990	Slovakia	1994	Tajikistan
Kazakstan	1991; 1994	Ukraine	1992	Vietnam
Kyrgyzstan	1994	Uzbekistan	1992; 1994	

Note:
This list of countries is not necessarily comprehensive.
Source: World Bank, Competition and Strategy Group.

trust community and the proponents of anti-dumping laws in a number of high-income countries. Discussion of minimum anti-trust standards is not rejected by either group; what is opposed is making any agreement on TRAPs 'too' trade-related. Many anti-trust authorities are hesitant about becoming drawn into trade policy, given the different objectives in practice of the two policy communities. While in principle favouring the introduction of competition principles into anti-dumping laws there is concern about involving anti-trust offices in the trade policy process. The fear is that this might end up 'corrupting' anti-trust enforcement by shifting the focus from protection of competition to protecting domestic firms from foreign competitors.

Supporters of anti-dumping are strongly opposed to any anti-trust-related involvement in the enforcement of such law (Rosenthal and Silliman, 1996; and Stewart, 1996). For example, they argue that anti-dumping focuses on what is recognised by the WTO to be an 'unfair' practice, that the appropriate disciplines and remedies were recently re-negotiated with great difficulty in the Uruguay Round, and that:

> anti-dumping policies as articulated in the [GATT] Agreement on Article VI better promote rational resource allocation between countries than national competition policies . . . [and] since there are no internationally agreed rules on competition policy, it is at a minimum premature to discuss a merger of one area into another (Stewart, 1996, p. 3).

If anything, it is argued by Stewart, competition policy has significant lessons to learn from anti-dumping law. These propositions suggest that anti-trust authorities do have potential cause for concern. The apparent confluence of interest between defenders of strong anti-trust laws and the anti-dumping lobby may create a powerful coalition against any attempt to ensure that a TRAPs agreement introduces anti-trust principles into the contingent protection process, especially anti-dumping.

Making WTO anti-dumping rules more competition friendly may therefore be difficult to attain. This would be particularly detrimental to developing countries, who have much to gain from the introduction of competition principles in this area. Clearly a necessary condition for introducing anti-trust criteria into anti-dumping rules will be significant 'concessions' in other areas by developing countries. Whether enough concessions can be made to overcome the anti-dumping lobby, and whether any resulting benefits will be worth these concessions are open questions.

c. Non-violation Dispute Settlement

Clearly a necessary condition for this option is that countries have national anti-trust legislation. Many developing nations do not and will therefore have to adopt such provisions. However, as mentioned earlier, a large number of countries already have competition legislation or are in the process of drafting such laws (Table 3). This is therefore not a binding constraint. The fact that GATT contracting parties did not avail themselves of this provision in the past, even though in principle it offers the opportunity to allege that non-enforcement of anti-trust or measures supporting anti-competitive practices nullified benefits, suggests that extension may not be that easy to achieve. This is an approach that grants substantial discretion to panelists, and governments may fear that they tread on a slippery slope (Blackhurst, 1994; and Jackson, 1996). The outcome and repercussions of the recent decision by the US (supported by the EU) to bring a non-violation complaint to the WTO alleging that Fuji has restricted Kodak's ability to contest the Japanese market by engaging in anti-competitive practices should help governments to decide how far down this track they are willing to go.

d. Competition Advocacy

Granting the WTO a competition advocacy mandate requires acceptance by members to be subjected to multilateral surveillance. Until the Trade Policy Review Mechanism (TPRM) was adopted in the late 1980s there was little reason to be optimistic regarding the willingness of members to do so.[34] In principle the rationale for accepting greater competition advocacy is the same as that underlying the TPRM: although a government may not like to be subjected to review as it can lead to pressure to change policies (both by domestic lobbies and foreign trading partners), the quid pro quo is that all other WTO members are in the same situation. As long as competition advocacy is restricted to a trade-related focus, i.e., there is a 'trade effects' justification for analyzing the impact of particular practices or situations, agreement may be feasible.

e. Anti-trust Exemptions

A necessary condition for obtaining agreement to discipline export cartels through removal of national anti-trust exemptions will be that all WTO members perceive this to be in the national interest. This in turn will require a determination of the costs and benefits of removing such exemptions, this being a necessary condition for ascertaining the need for side payments (i.e., compensating 'losers' in other areas). It is therefore difficult to determine *ex ante* whether agreement is likely to be feasible. More research is required in this area. Moreover, as noted previously, concurrent discussions will be required to discipline the ability of governments to achieve outcomes analogous to those that might be attained through anti-trust exemptions: state-trading and taxation of exports. Clearly this will not be easy to achieve. But it can be recalled that Art. XI GATT already prohibits quantitative import and export restrictions and can be used to contest the use of policies with an equivalent effect (Hoekman and Mavroidis, 1994; and WTO, 1995, p. 314).

f. Issue-specific Agreements

Sectoral or issue-specific agreements should be feasible in principle; as in any negotiation the acceptability of a proposal will depend on its impact on individual WTO members. Past experience demonstrates that agreement on a wide variety of issues is possible, although many that would be welfare enhancing may not be feasible because of opposition by powerful interest groups (viz. the anti-trust-anti-dumping option). Such specific agreements – the recent basic telecom agreement is an example – may embody regulatory commitments that have competition policy elements. Achieving agreement on such principles should be easier than seeking a consensus that general anti-trust laws be applied in particular ways.

5. CONCLUSIONS

The demandeurs for WTO negotiations on anti-trust are largely industries in high income countries that wish to have additional levers and policy handles to increase their access to foreign markets. The current dispute between Kodak and Fuji is a good example, and also serves to illustrate that the issue is not a North–South one. There is no clear North–South divide on any of the possible TRAPs options discussed in this paper. Even with respect to an issue such as anti-dumping many developing countries that have passed the relevant legislation may prefer not to restrict the reach of this instrument, while countries such as Japan have traditionally pushed for greater disciplines.

Given the nascent nature of competition law in many developing countries, the implications of a TRAPs negotiation are potentially greater than for industrialised ones with well-developed anti-trust regimes. However, taking into account the feasibility of alternative options, from a developing country perspective the possible downside risk attached to the TRAPs agenda seems limited. The option that in principle has the greatest potential for reducing welfare – harmonisation of substantive competition rules – will in all probability be limited at most to a prohibition on certain horizontal restrictions. Although even this is uncertain given that it will do little in market access terms, there are few if any efficiency rationales for tolerating horizontal restrictions on the domestic market. Thus, there should not be a major concern regarding an agreement that includes this. However, the detailed content and substance of the specific rules and criteria of anti-trust law are best left for sovereign states to pursue independent of the multilateral trading system. In this connection the most that can be said for minimum standards is if agreement pertains to 'procedural' norms for the implementation and enforcement of competition laws (transparency, 'due process'). Although many developing countries have anti-trust legislation, enforcement may be uncertain or inconsistent. Allowing for 'procedural' dispute settlement cases under which panels would restrict themselves to determining whether national law was applied correctly may help ensure consistency and diffuse tensions.

The only option that in principle should enhance market access conditions, improve efficiency (welfare), and strengthen the trading system is the introduction of anti-trust criteria into anti-dumping. The most beneficial outcome would be the abolition of anti-dumping, but the likelihood of this occurring is not high, to say the least. The probability of a significant expansion of the reach of non-violation dispute settlement procedures is also not very high, given that many governments will regard this a 'slippery slope'. Whether agreement to ban private practices that restrain international trade will prove possible is quite uncertain. Much will depend on the evaluation of governments regarding the net benefits associated with the status quo, which also permits state-trading and export taxes. Without new empirical research to determine the prevalence and economic impact of cartels and state trading, it will be difficult for policymakers to formulate a negotiating position. Perhaps the most likely outcome on a TRAPs negotiating agenda is an enhanced 'competition sensitivity' in sector and issue-specific market access negotiations. This has the potential to be beneficial in terms of market access, efficiency and strengthening the trading system, and also appears to have little downside risk. If governments are serious about enhancing the 'competition-friendliness' of the WTO and wish to signal that they take anti-trust-related issues seriously, such negotiations should include efforts to discipline anti-dumping.

The conclusion drawn by James Rahl almost 20 years ago regarding the significance of private cartels in international trade applies as well to the more general topic of introducing anti-trust into the WTO:

> no one should believe that private cartels, though they can be extremely damaging, represent the most serious kind of inference with free trade today. The various governmentally created restraints, including tariffs, quotas, miscellaneous other trade barriers, commodity agreements, orderly marketing arrangements, anti-dumping orders, subsidies, national preference requirements in buying, pervasive regulation of some industries, and state trading monopolies, surely add up to far more restraint of international competition than do cartels (Rahl, 1981, p. 242).

This has certainly been the perception of governments engaged in multilateral trade negotiations, and it is reflected in the Uruguay Round agreements that deal with many of these topics. But very much still remains to be done in these 'traditional' areas of governmental restraints on trade.

Providing governments with the option of multilateral dispute settlement to contest actions of other governments that effectively nullify trade liberalisation commitments has always been a key role of the GATT. Although its effectiveness has been limited at times, this has partly been a reflection of the preferences of governments not to use (test) the system. With the strengthening of multilateral dispute settlement procedures under the WTO, the scope for using existing mechanisms has increased. The Kodak-Fuji case may be an indication that governments are becoming more willing to pursue this path. If further development of issue- and sector-specific liberalisation agreements includes efforts to incorporate pro-competitive regulatory disciplines where appropriate, the WTO trading system will be in a good position to ensure that trade liberalisation and market access commitments will not be circumvented by other policies, including anti-trust.

A good case can be made that anti-trust and trade policy should remain independent. Anti-trust is a policy that is (should be) aimed at achieving efficient outcomes by protecting the competitive process, unconstrained by market access (nationality) considerations. Efforts to liberalise access to markets – the raison d'être of the WTO system – will complement and affect anti-trust enforcement, but only in rare circumstances will anti-trust enforcement be the optimal instrument to deal with market access 'problems.' Trade and investment liberalisation should therefore continue to be pursued on a priority basis. Of particular importance in this connection is liberalisation of services, including sectors such as distribution and transport. Commitments made by WTO members on services are quite limited, with developing countries in particular fully opening up only a small set of service activities to foreign competition. Liberalisation of trade in services in particular could help to diffuse pressures for 'action' in the anti-trust area (e.g., with respect to distribution-related disputes).

NOTES

This is a substantial revision of World Bank Policy Research Paper 1735. The author is indebted to Joel Davidow, David Richardson, Petros Mavroidis, Matsuo Matsushita, David Tarr, as well as three anonymous referees for the discussions. Shayan Khemani kindly provided the data reported in Table 3. The views expressed are personal and should not be attributed to the World Bank.

1 See Davidow (1981) for a discussion of developments in the 1960s and 1970s; Lloyd and Sampson (1995) provide an overview of the various multilateral instruments and fora that have addressed competition issues.

2 See Hoekman and Kostecki (1995) for a discussion of such agreements.

3 The notion of positive comity appeared alongside traditional negative comity in the September 1991 cooperation agreement in anti-trust between the EU and the United States. According to the traditional (negative) comity principle, sovereign states will consider important interests of other states when exercising their own jurisdiction. Positive comity shifts the initiative to the state whose interests are affected, which is given the legal option of requesting another state to initiate appropriate enforcement proceedings to address the petitioning country's concerns (Art. V of the agreement). See Ham (1993) for a discussion of the EU–US agreement.

4 Arguments favouring the abolition of anti-dumping have been made for many years. See, e.g., Caine (1981).

5 See e.g., Wood (1989 and 1996), Messerlin (1994 and 1996), Schöne (1996) and Hoekman and Mavroidis (1996).

6 See Hoekman and Mavroidis (1994) for a discussion.

7 In 1982 the EC requested the establishment of a working party under Art. XXIII:2 on the basis that the benefits of successive negotiations with Japan were not realised because of 'a series of factors peculiar to Japan' that inhibited imports. This was a so-called situation complaint under Art. XXIII:I(c), but was ultimately never pursued (see Bronckers, 1985 and WTO, 1995, p. 670).

8 Graham and Richardson (1994) have suggested that in the case of anti-trust-related trade disputes the application of domestic competition legislation first be reviewed by a multilateral panel of experts, and that invocation of non-violation proceedings be made conditional upon the panel finding that national competition laws were not appropriately applied. This may not have much of an impact on the status quo, however, as the focus of attention is not on the effective circumvention of WTO commitments. In principle what is required for this option to be useful is the introduction of an 'equivalent effect' test, i.e., anti-trust policies effectively result in a situation that is prohibited under the WTO, or that effectively nullifies a previously negotiated market access concession.

9 The motivation for this is that in economies that have a history of government intervention and where industry is often highly concentrated, enforcement of competition law will need to be supplemented by competition policies that support the objectives of the law. In addition, there will often be a need for 'educating' enterprises, legislators and officials regarding the objectives and application of competition legislation.

10 More generally, the WTO secretariat could be given a mandate to undertake research on the competitive effects of other government policies as well. Examples would be to look at the impact of differences in product standards and certification requirements, or the behaviour of state-trading entities and firms with exclusive rights on the contestability of markets.

11 The proposal by the EU group of experts for a minimum standards agreement (see option 1) notes the need for addressing issues related to grants of exclusive rights and state trading.
12 The anti-dumping-anti-trust option noted earlier is a special case of this general approach in that the introduction of anti-trust criteria is a second-best solution to the first-best option of replacing anti-dumping with national anti-trust enforcement.
13 Typical firm-based access barriers in telecoms include a denial of network interconnection, a refusal to provide interconnection on commercial terms, and misuse of commercial information. See Hoekman, Low and Mavroidis (1996).
14 Another option would be to attempt to strengthen Article IX GATS, which recognises that business practices of service suppliers may restrain competition and thus trade in services but imposes no obligations regarding the scope and enforcement of competition policy. Members are only obliged to supply publicly available non-confidential information of relevance to a competition-related matter if so requested by another Member. Expansion of Art. IX to include substantive obligations would imply agreeing to common anti-trust disciplines for all services. This would be akin to proposals under option 1, as the rationale for limiting WTO-based anti-trust disciplines to services (and not goods) is unclear.
15 See footnote 3.
16 It is assumed in the subsequent discussion that any agreement will be enforced by national authorities, with the WTO being the forum for communications and dispute settlement.
17 The recent nonviolation case brought by the US government on behalf of Kodak is illustrative, as the claim is that Kodak's market share has been constrained by actions by Fuji that induce distributors not to carry Kodak.
18 Unfortunately, despite the interest in the topic, very little empirical work has been undertaken to determine to what extent anti-trust enforcement (or the lack thereof) has reduced the ability of foreign firms to contest a market.
19 The following developing country and transition economies have notified anti-dumping legislation to the WTO: Argentina, Barbados, Bolivia, Botswana, Brazil, Brunei Darussalam, Chile, Colombia, Costa Rica, Côte d'lvoire, Cuba, Czech Republic, Dominican Republic, Ecuador, Egypt, El Salvador, Guatemala, Republic of Guinea, Honduras, Hungary, India, Indonesia, Israel, Jamaica, Kenya, Korea, Macau, Malawi, Malaysia, Maldives, Mauritius, Mexico, Morocco, Nicaragua, Pakistan, Paraguay, Peru, Philippines, Poland, Romania, St Lucia, Senegal, Slovakia, Slovenia, South Africa, Sri Lanka, Surinam, Swaziland, Thailand, Trinidad & Tobago, Tunisia, Turkey, Uganda, Uruguay, Venezuela, and Zambia.
20 Two thirds of which involved sales of goods by industrial to developing economies, while the remainder consisted of South-South trade (World Bank, 1996).
21 As noted by Schöne (1996) and Messerlin (1996), the majority of anti-dumping duties would not have been imposed if anti-trust methodologies had been applied.
22 Here again it is perhaps worth noting that little empirical work has been done to determine the prevalence and impact of trade-restricting cartels. The same applies to state-trading.
23 See Hoekman and Kostecki (1995) for an introduction to these agreements and references to the literature.
24 Indeed, as noted earlier, an emphasis on market access may result in less efficient competition outcome as 'nationality-blindness' may be a necessary condition for efficiency.
25 See, e.g., the contributions in McChesney and Shughart (1995) on problems of capture. This may be especially problematical in developing countries with a tradition of government intervention in the economy. In such contexts, instead of focusing on

anti-competitive behavior, the anti-trust authority may end up as a price control body or enforcer of private contracts. If the probability of this occurring is significant a government may be better off not adopting an anti-trust law and the related enforcement institutions.

26 For much more comprehensive discussions on this topic, see Boner and Krueger (1992), Boner (1995), and Khemani and Dutz (1995).

27 See e.g., Scherer (1995). Auquier and Caves (1979) analyse the effects of – and optimal policy towards – exemptions from competition law for 'rent extracting' behaviour by home country firms on export markets.

28 'No prohibitions or restrictions other than duties, taxes or other charges, whether made effective through quotas, import or export licences *or other measures*, shall be instituted or maintained by any contracting party on the importation of any product of the territory of any contracting party or on the exportation or sale for export of any product destined for the territory of any other contracting party' (Art. XI:1 GATT, emphasis added).

29 See, e.g., Tirole (1988), Carlton and Perloff (1994), Viscusi et al. (1995), Khemani and Dutz (1995), and Philips (1995).

30 A major problem in this regard is that the WTO method of reciprocal bargaining is simply not suited to anti-trust. It works well when the policies on the table have little economic justification, especially when used by all countries (i.e., import restrictions), but breaks down when there are good reasons why countries may want to have different types of regulation (as with anti-trust). In such cases Pareto improvements are very difficult to attain, even if side payments are possible.

31 Some countries have given anti-trust offices a mandate to scrutinise government policy, including privatisation and trade policies, for their impact on competition. A problem that arises for any agency that pursues such a mandate is that it may confront opposition by interests that benefit from a particular situation. This may result in attempts to constrain the agencies mandate directly, or in efforts to reduce its budget. A TRAPs agreement could help to sustain the work of such entities.

32 See WTO (1995, pp. 314–54) for a summary of the case history.

33 For a discussion of New Zealand, see Ahdar (1991). More generally, see Hoekman and Mavroidis (1996) and Schöne (1996).

34 See Hoekman and Kostecki (1995) for background on the TPRM.

REFERENCES

Ahdar, R. (1991), 'The Role of Antitrust Policy in the Development of Australian–New Zealand Free Trade,' *Northwestern Journal of International Law & Business*, **12**, 317–34.

Auquier, A. and R. Caves (1979), 'Monopolistic Export Industries, Trade Taxes, and Optimal Competition Policy,' *Economic Journal*, **89**, 559–81.

Blackhurst, R. (1994). 'Competition Policies: National Versus Multilateral Jurisdiction,' *Aussenwirtschaft*, **49**, 223–9.

Boner, R. A. (1995), 'Competition Policy and Institutions in Reforming Economies,' in C. Frischtak (ed.), *Regulatory Policies and Reform: A Comparative Analysis* (Washington DC, The World Bank).

Boner, R. A. and R. Krueger (1992), *The Basics of Antitrust Policy* (Washington DC, The World Bank).

Bronckers, M. (1985), *Selective Safeguards in Multilateral Trade Relations* (Deventer).

Caine, W. K. (1981), 'A Case for Repealing the Antidumping Provisions of the Tariff Act of 1930,' *Law and Policy in International Business*, **13**, 681.

Carlton, D. and J. Perloff (1994), *Modern Industrial Organization* (New York: Harper-Collins).

Davidow, J. (1981), 'The Seeking of a World Competition Code: Quixotic Quest?', in O. Schachter and R. Hellawell (eds), *Competition in International Business: Law and Policy in Restrictive Practices* (New York: Columbia University Press).

European Commission (1995), 'Competition Policy in The New Trade Order: Strengthening International Cooperation and Rules' (Report of the Group of Experts, mimeo).

Fikentscher, W. and U. Immenga (eds) (1995), *Draft International Antitrust Code* (Baden-Baden: Nomos Verlag).

Finger, J. M. (1982), 'Incorporating the Gains from Trade into Policy,' *The World Economy*, **5**, 367–77.

Finger, J. M. (ed.), (1993), *Antidumping: How it Works and Who Gets Hurt* (Ann Arbor: University of Michigan Press).

Finger, J. M. and L. A. Winters (1966), 'What Can the WTO Do for Developing Countries' (World Bank, mimeo).

Galal, A. and B. Hoekman (eds) (1977), *Regional Partners in Global Markets: Limits and Possibilities of the Euro-Med Initiative* (London: Centre for Economic Policy Research).

Graham, E. and J. D. Richardson (1994), 'Summary of the Institute of International Economics Project on International Competition Policy,' COM/DAFFE/CLP/Td(94)42 (Paris: OECD, April).

Ham, A. (1993), 'International Cooperation in the Antitrust Field and in Particular the Agreement Between the USA and the Commission of the EC,' *Common Market Law Review*, **30**, 571–95.

Hindley, B. (1996), 'Competition Law and the WTO: Alternative Structures for Agreement,' in J. Bhagwati and R. Hudec (eds), *Fair Trade and Harmonization* (Cambridge: MIT Press).

Hoekman, B. and M. Kostecki (1995), *The Political Economy of the World Trading System* (Oxford: Oxford University Press).

Hoekman, B. M. and P. C. Mavroidis (1994), 'Competition, Competition Policy and the GATT,' *The World Economy*, **17**, 121–50.

Hoekman, B. and P. C. Mavroidis (1996), 'Dumping, Antidumping and Antitrust,' *Journal of World Trade*, **30**, 27–52.

Hoekman, B., P. Low and P. C. Mavroidis (1996), 'Regulation, Competition Policy and Market Access Negotiations: Lessons from the Telecommunications Sector,' in E. Hope (ed.), *Competition Policy in an Integrated Global Economy* (London: Routledge, forthcoming).

Jackson, J. H. (1996), 'Issues of Dispute Settlement in the WTO System: Comment', in *The Emerging WTO System and Perspectives from East Asia*. Joint US–Korea Academic Studies, **7** (Washington DC: Korea Economic Institute of America).

Khemani, S. (1994), 'Competition Law: Some Guidelines for Implementation,' FDP Note No. 14 (The World Bank).

Khemani, R. S. and M. Dutz (1995), 'The Instruments of Competition Policy and Their Relevance for Economic Development,' in C. Frischtak (ed.), *Regulatory Policies and Reform: A Comparative Analysis* (Washington DC: The World Bank).

Lloyd, P. and G. Sampson (1995), 'Competition and Trade Policy: Identifying the Issues After the Uruguay Round,' *The World Economy*, **18**, 681–705.

Mattoo, A. (1997), 'Economic Theory and the Procurement Agreement,' in B. Hoekman and P. Mavroidis (eds), *Law and Policy in Public Purchasing: The WTO Agreement on Government Procurement* (Ann Arbor: University of Michigan Press).

McChesney, F. and W. Shughart (eds) (1995), *The Causes and Consequences of Antitrust: The Public Choice Perspective* (Chicago: University of Chicago Press).

Messerlin, P. (1994), 'Should Antidumping Rules be Replaced by National or International Competition Rules?,' *Aussenwirtschraft*, **49**, 351–74.
Messerlin, P. (1996), 'Competition Policy and Antidumping Reform,' presented at the conference, The World Trading System: Challenges Ahead (Institute for International Economics, Washington DC), 24–25 June.
Philips, L. (1995), *Competition Policy: A Game-Theoretic Perspective* (Cambridge: Cambridge University Press).
Rahl, J. (1981), 'International Cartels and Their Regulations,' in O. Schachter and R. Hellawell (eds), *Competition in International Business* (New York: Columbia University Press).
Rosenthal, P. and C. Sillman (1996), 'The Limits of Competition Law in the Current WTO Context,' presented at a conference, Antidumping and Competition Policy: Complements or Substitutes? (Center for Applied Studies in International Negotiations, Geneva, 11–12 July).
Scherer, F. M. (1995), *Competition Policies for an Integrated World Economy* (Washington DC: Brookings Institution).
Scherer, F. M. (1966), 'International Trade and Competition Policy,' in E. Hope (ed.), *Competition Policy in an Integrated Economy* (London: Routledge, forthcoming).
Schöne, R. (1996), *Alternatives to Antidumping from an Antitrust Perspective*, Dissertation No. 1830 (University of St Gallen).
Stewart, T. (1996), 'Why Antidumping Laws Need Not Be Cloned After Competition Laws Nor Replaced By Such Laws,' presented at a conference, Antidumping and Competition Policy: Complements or Substitutes? (Center for Applied Studies in International Negotiations, Geneva, 11–12 July).
Tirole, J. (1988), *The Theory of Industrial Organization* (Cambridge: MIT Press).
Viscusi, W. K., J. Vernon and J. Harrington (1995), *Economics of Regulation and Antitrust* (Cambridge: MIT Press).
Wood, D. (1989), 'Unfair' Trade Injury: A Competition-based Approach,' *Stanford Law Review*, **41**, 1153–80.
Wood, D. (1996), 'How to Make Antidumping Laws more Competition-Friendly,' presented at a conference, Antidumping and Competition Policy: Complements or Substitutes?, Center for Applied Studies in International Negotiations (Geneva, 11–12 July).
Wood, D. (1997), 'The WTO Agreement on Government Procurement: An Antitrust Perspective,' in B. Hoekman and P. Mavroidis (eds), *Law and Policy in Public Purchasing: The WTO Agreement on Government Procurement* (Ann Arbor: University of Michigan Press).
World Bank (1996), *Global Economic Prospects* (Washington DC: World Bank).
World Trade Organisation (1995), *Analytical Index: Guide to GATT Law and Practice*, 6th Edition (Geneva: WTO).
World Trade Organisation (1966), 'Report of the General Council to the 1996 Ministerial Conference,' Vol. 2 (Geneva: WTO).

9. Linking Negotiations on Trade and Foreign Direct Investment

R. McCulloch and R. F. Owen

I. INTRODUCTION

National Policies toward foreign direct investment constitute an important class of nontariff trade distortions. Surprisingly, although the Tokyo Round of multilateral trade negotiations focused its efforts on nontariff barriers, the trade-distorting effects of policies toward foreign direct investment were largely ignored. Now, however, the relationship between trade and investment issues has been formally brought into the GATT framework, as US and Canadian negotiators attempt to resolve conflicts over restrictions imposed on US-based firms by the Canadian Foreign Investment Review Agency.

This paper explores the relationship between trade and investment policy, and discusses theoretical and policy questions raised by a linkage of international negotiations on trade and investment. Section II of the paper deals with host-country policies toward foreign direct investment and their impact on trade. The section presents data on the incidence of host-country policies affecting US subsidiaries world-wide as well as detailed information on foreign subsidiary performance and regulatory policies in Canada, the most important host country for US direct investments abroad. Section III draws on various strands of the theoretical and empirical literature on trade and foreign direct investment to analyze avenues of interaction between trade and investment policies as co-determinants of the location of production. Section IV evaluates the potential benefits and pitfalls from a linkage of trade and investment issues in the GATT or in bilateral negotiations between the United States and its major trading partners. Some conclusions and suggestions for further research are presented in section V.

II. NATIONAL INVESTMENT POLICIES AND THEIR IMPACT ON TRADE

The phenomenal growth of foreign direct investment by multinational corporations has stimulated an equally phenomenal growth of research intended to sort out the complicated benefits and costs for home and host countries and the implications for global efficiency. Although no consensus has emerged from that research, most national governments have drawn their own conclusions and have proceeded to encourage, limit, or otherwise regulate the activities of multinational corporations (MNCs). In this section we analyze the motives, forms, and consequences of host-country regulation of foreign investment, focusing on the relationship to trade flows. A central conclusion is that policies toward foreign investment do exercise a potentially important influence on trade flows through both direct and indirect channels. Moreover, a comparison of the economic performance of foreign subsidiaries with that of their domestic counterparts strongly suggests that the trading behavior of MNCs is itself an important reason underlying the perceived need for host-country regulation of MNC activities.

Why and How Host Countries Regulate Foreign Direct Investment

Host countries appear to view direct foreign investment as a necessary evil of national economic life. The literature abounds with anecdotal evidence of MNC excesses (especially but by no means exclusively in developing host countries), and virtually no host country is willing to allow MNCs completely free reign within its borders. Yet even fewer nations have gone to the opposite extreme of excluding foreign investment. Rather, various national policies are applied in an effort to extract maximum benefits from foreign direct investments.

Although schemes for maximizing national benefits are as varied as the economic systems and philosophies that give rise to them, an increasing number of host countries now follow a "carrot-and-stick" approach toward foreign direct investment. The carrot consists of foreign investment incentives such as favorable tax treatment, below-market loans, and protection via tariffs or nontariff barriers from potential competitors for the domestic market. The stick consists of a variety of "performance requirements"—restrictions on the established subsidiary with regard to export or import levels, techniques of production, levels of employment, or such diverse matters as local research and development, repatriation of profits, and financial arrangements. The carrot-and-stick combination allows host governments to promote national objectives without eliminating incentives for investment. With performance requirements alone, a significant cost is imposed on investors, so that some portion of the potential flow of new investment would be deflected to other locations. However, when incentives arc provided as well, the overall profitability of investing in a given country may be unaffected or even increased.[1]

Nationalism and xenophobia no doubt provide much of the necessary political support for host-country regulation of foreign direct investment. However, serious economic arguments in favor of regulatory policies almost always center on market imperfections. Experts agree that the existence of foreign direct investment virtually requires a significant departure from conditions approximating perfect competition. Accordingly, standard neoclassical analyses favoring nonintervention on economic efficiency grounds do not apply. Host-country measures to regulate foreign direct investment fall into two somewhat overlapping categories intended to correct two distinct types of market imperfections: market power and externalities in production.

The first category consists of measures to offset "restrictive business practices" that are part of the monopolistic or oligopolistic parent firm's global profit-maximization strategy. While long lists of such practices have been compiled, the most important relate to restrictions on exporting (particularly when a subsidiary has been created to serve a protected local market), required imports of components or complementary products, and limitations on the subsidiary's further use of the parent firm's unique technology. Typical performance requirements can thus be viewed as placing limits on the parent firm's ability to maximize global profits by controlling the operation of its subsidiaries.

Performance requirements are also designed to take account of positive externalities from MNC operations within a given country. Many host countries, especially LDCs, seek foreign investment precisely for its anticipated positive externalities, particularly technology transfer through on-the-job training of the local workforce. Measures that mandate vertically integrated production operations, set levels for various categories of local employment, or require local research and development activities all seek to increase the nation's social payoff from direct investment through enhanced production externalities.

National regulation of foreign direct investment has been widely analyzed from the perspective of global economic efficiency as well as that of costs and benefits to home and host country, yet surprisingly little has been done except at the most abstract level to integrate the analysis of foreign investment with that of tariffs and other barriers to trade. This is a significant gap, since some of the most frequently employed performance requirements are obviously intended to affect trade of multinationals directly through explicitly specified minimum export and maximum import levels (local content requirements).[2] In addition, both investment incentives and performance requirements are likely to have a pervasive indirect effect on trade through their influence on decisions regarding the location and operation of MNC subsidiaries. These interrelationships of direct investment, trade, and policies to regulate them are highlighted in this paper.

Economic Performance of Foreign Subsidiaries: The Canadian Case

Host-country concerns that motivate regulation of foreign direct investment are based on observed or anticipated differences in the unconstrained behavior of foreign subsidiaries and domestically controlled firms. Although there is considerable evidence in the literature of large differences in the performance of subsidiaries and domestic firms,[3] we focus here on evidence from recent data for Canada. These findings are particularly interesting in light of Canada's importance as a host country, its high level of industrialization, and its recent policies toward foreign (overwhelmingly US) direct investment.

Canada is unique among industrialized nations in the extent of MNC involvement in its economy, with foreign subsidiaries accounting for about 60% of total sales and total assets in manufacturing. In several extractive industries, foreign control is equally high. Indeed, until recently Canada was the world's most important host country (it has now been surpassed in absolute although not relative terms by the United States). Accordingly, the benefits and costs of foreign direct investment have been a traditional focus of controversy in Canadian politics, and activities of MNCs are frequent targets of nationalistic critics.

Recent Canadian policy toward foreign investors raises concerns in the United States for several reasons.[4] First, the United States–Canadian trade and investment relationship is large enough to be important for its own sake. Canada is the largest US trading partner and the most important host country for US foreign investment. (From the Canadian viewpoint, the importance is even greater. Approximately 70% of Canadian trade is with the United States, and US-based firms account for 90% of all foreign investment in Canada.) Second, the recent emphasis on nontariff trade distortions in the Tokyo Round of multilateral trade negotiations makes the Canadian policies conspicuous as yet another variety of policy with important direct and indirect effects for trade. Third, because Canada is the largest host country for US investment, and also a country in a highly favorable situation to use national regulation to increase its share of the gains from MNC activities, Canadian policies and their results may provide advance notice of what is to be expected in other host countries.

Yet Canada is far from being a typical host country. Canada's potential ability to dictate terms to multinational firms operating within its borders far exceeds that of any developing host country. The more attractive the host country, the more conditions it is able to impose in dealings with multinationals without much loss in the volume of inward investment. The greatest leverage can be exercised by a host country "with a large, dynamic, resource-rich economy, a stable and capable government with high-quality infrastructure and low transactions costs."[5] This profile puts Canada at the top of the list of host countries capable of wielding considerable influence on the activities of foreign investors through national regulation. And, unlike the United States, Canada is small enough as a *home* country relative to any other host country that retaliation (at least in kind) by other nations is a minor consideration.

A statistical analysis reveals striking disparities with regard to import propensities and R&D performance between foreign subsidiaries and domestic firms in Canada. Recently released data on Canadian imports by domestic- and foreign-controlled enterprises indicate that, overall, foreign-controlled firms are responsible for over 80% of Canadian imports and that these firms have an average import propensity (as measured by the ratio of imports to sales) nearly four times greater than that of domestic firms.[6] Moreover, foreign subsidiaries' imports are overwhelming sourced from the home country (87% in the case of the United States, 74% for other countries). In several industries the relative import propensities of foreign subsidiaries are dramatically higher. In the service sector, for example, the import propensity of foreign subsidiaries is nearly twenty times that of domestic firms. Moreover, the US–Canadian Auto Pact has been associated with a significant increase in the import propensities of US firms in Canada. At the manufacturing and wholesale stages, the import propensities of US auto firms are now respectively 7.0 and 8.6 times as great as those of domestic firms.

Paralleling these disparities are differences in the ratios of R&D expenditures to sales for Canadian domestic firms and foreign subsidiaries. On average, Canadian firms undertake more than twice as much R&D activity relative to sales as their foreign counterparts; in 87 out of 115 manufacturing industries, the ratio of R&D expenditures to sales is higher for Canadian domestic firms.[7]

This is consistent with the standard prediction that most R&D activities of multinational corporations will be concentrated in the home country.

These statistics provide a clear empirical basis for Canada's concerns regarding the economic performance of susidiaries. Nonetheless, these disparities in mean import and R&D propensities, while impressive, are not conclusive proof of differences in performance between subsidiaries and domestic firms. Rigorous econometric analysis would control for firm size, diversification, and other pertinent characteristics of these firms.

Canadian Policy toward Foreign Investment

After decades of successful wooing of foreign investors and perennial consternation over the extent of foreign ownership, Canada developed during the 1970s an explicit mechanism for screening new inward direct investments. Established by the Foreign Investment Review Act of 1972, Canada's Foreign Investment Review Agency (FIRA) began in 1974 to oversee new MNC activities in Canada[8] and to ensure that these investments provide benefits to Canada as well as to their foreign owners. Although virtually all nations impose some restrictions to entry by MNCs, the Canadian policy represents the most explicit example of entry control.[9] All proposed investments must gain FIRA approval. Evaluation by FIRA is supposed to be on the basis of ten criteria, including impact on Canadian employment and productivity, contribution to technology, use of Canadian resources, and expanded exports.

Since the vast majority of projects submitted to FIRA are eventually approved, it appears that whatever benefits (apart from noneconomic ones, e.g., psychological or political) derived are not from screening out undesirable investments but rather through the effect on the actual terms of specific investments. Evaluation of the results is inevitably subjective, since it is impossible to know how foreign investors would have acted in the absence of the new policies. On the basis of its early activities, some observers dismissed the FIRA as a relatively innocuous and ineffective measure intended primarily to defuse criticism from Canadian nationalists.[10] But recent events suggest that at least to some American firms, the effects are both real and potentially very important.

The activities of the Foreign Investment Review Agency have been a source of US–Canadian frictions since the agency began screening foreign takeovers of Canadian companies in 1974.[11] Since 1981, US officials have been concerned by FIRA-imposed terms for takeovers and new investments as distortions of US trade in goods and services. Contribution to Canadian trade performance is a part of the "significant benefit" potential investors must demonstrate in order to win FIRA approval. Specific examples of recent FIRA deliberations involving US-based firms seem to support the contention that FIRA is using its authority to influence trade.

In the case of Gannett, a New York publisher, acquisition of a Canadian billboard company was approved only after Gannett agreed to purchase Canadian newsprint for its US operations.[12] Gannett also agreed to "sell" laser printing technology to a Canadian firm for a token $1.[13] In another publicized case, Apple Computer was allowed to enter the Canadian market after agreeing to buy

Canadian-made parts, where competitive, and to recommend Canadian-made computer peripheral equipment to its dealers world-wide.[14]

From the perspective of Canadian officials, its screening procedures merely assure that new investments will be advantageous to the nation. The Foreign Investment Review Act does not set specific minimum levels for exports or for utilization of Canadian inputs. Rather, potential investors themselves set such targets for their proposed activities, presumably in order to gain prompt FIRA approval. Nonetheless, the United States claims that recent Canadian practice conflicts with that nation's obligations under the GATT; a formal complaint was made by the United States within the GATT framework on February 17, 1982.[15] What ultimately happens in the US–Canadian dispute will presumably set a legal precedent for other cases, at least where GATT members are involved. However, many developing nations, whose use of investment incentives and performance requirements is more extensive than that of industrialized nations, are not GATT members. For the United States, the most important of these in terms of trade and investment ties is Mexico.

Department of Commerce data on US subsidiaries in Canada indicate that the systematic influence on FIRA activities has been relatively minor, at least through 1977.[16] Commerce compared the percentage of investment incentives and performance requirements reported for Canadian subsidiaries organized or acquired before 1970 with those organized or acquired between 1970 and 1977 (the latter period includes the first three years of FIRA operation). The data showed a decrease in the number of reported incentives (16% in the later period compared with 19% for the earlier period) and an increase in the percentage of reported performance requirements (6% in the later period in comparison to 4% for the earlier period). However, the Commerce Department report suggests that these figures understate the present extent of FIRA influence and that a larger percentage of subsidiaries affected by performance requirements would be found for later years, as "the 1977 benchmark data does not cover the period in which we believe the incidence of performance requirements in Canada to have increased significantly."

A report on other nations' investment incentives and performance requirements prepared for a private committee of US companies and labor unions goes further, contending that "Canadians have . . . succeeded in forcing foreign investors to conform with their national trade policy without regard for the interests of other states or the efficient international allocation of production."[17] The report emphasizes that FIRA's criterion of "significant benefits" to Canada explicitly includes the effects on utilization of "Canadian parts, components and services and on Canadian exports." It notes that about a third of all proposals approved by FIRA specified some export-related benefits, while nearly two-thirds included some commitment to resource processing or procurement in Canada. However, it is not possible to infer from these statistics the extent to which FIRA distorts trade. Even without the screening process, in the course of pursuing their own interests many foreign-controlled enterprises would export, while most would make use of Canadian parts or processing. However, the report stresses that approved investments *are* monitored for compliance with the terms and conditions of the proposal and that the Act provides for enforcement of these terms.

Other Foreign Government Policies Affecting US Direct Investment

While no other host country is as important to US-based multinationals as Canada, recent data on the experience of US affiliates world-wide indicate that Canada's active regulation of foreign direct investment is paralleled by policies in other nations. Data collected by the US Department of Commerce from US parent companies (with mandatory reporting)[18] show that as of 1977 about 14% of US affiliates world-wide were subject to performance requirements of some kind, while about twice as many—26%—were subject to investment incentives.

Among the most significant investment incentives are tax concessions, tariff concessions and subsidies—respectively 2, 8, and 9% of US affiliates were subject to these. Not surprisingly, tariff incentives are used more frequently by developing countries, whereas tax incentives are used extensively by both groups. Minimum local labor requirements accounted for over half of all performance requirements; there were also significant numbers of minimum export requirements, maximum import levels, and minimum local input requirements (of US affiliates, respectively 2, 3, and 3% were subject to these latter).

Across industries, there are important differences in the extent to which investment policies affect subsidiaries. In manufacturing transportation equipment the level of both investment incentives and performance requirements (respectively 41 and 27%) is substantially higher than for most other industries. Other industries with particularly high levels of investment incentives include food products and electrical machinery, while more than one-quarter of US affiliates in mining are subject to some form of performance requirements.

These data also show significant differences across countries in the extent of host-government measures. Although the overall level of reported investment incentives was approximately equal between developed and developing countries, the latter use performance requirements far more frequently (25 vs. 6%). Differences are even greater from country to country. For example, in South Korea and Taiwan over one-half of all foreign subsidiaries benefit from some form of investment incentive, whereas more than half of all subsidiaries in Libya, Peru, Venezuela, and Chile are subject to performance requirements. The high reported incidence of these measures for some individual countries, the substantial cross-country variation in their specific forms, and the much higher average use of performance requirements by developing countries all suggest that regulation of this kind may be central to some nations' strategy for industrial development. Accordingly, international negotiations to limit these trade-distorting measures are likely to encounter major obstacles.

III. THE INTERACTION BETWEEN TRADE AND INVESTMENT POLICIES

Any case for linking trade and investment negotiations must rest on the strength of the relationship between commercial policy and investment policy as co-determinants of the location of economic activity. Mutual gains from trade reflect an appropriate international division of labor, with production processes located according to comparative advantage. In recent decades, however, multinational corporations have become a primary vehicle for the "internationalization of production." Responding to differentials in cost and profitability world-wide, MNCs break down into many separate steps production processes that begin with extraction of raw materials and end with distribution and service of final products; each step in the complex operation is moved to the location most advantageous to the firm. The significance of multinational activities for international trade flows is obvious from available data. In the case of the United States, for example, approximately half of total exports involve multinational corporations, while a quarter consist of intra-corporate transactions and are thus potentially affected by MNC transfer-pricing policies.[19]

Trade Barriers and Foreign Direct Investment

In a world without trade barriers or other distortions, the process of internationalization would imply not only that each good is produced at the location offering lowest cost, but that each step in its production is located so as to minimize overall cost of serving a particular market. Of course, under real-world conditions, production cost differentials reflecting comparative advantage are just one of several important factors determining the location of economic activity. Location decisions arc also influenced by tariffs, quantitative trade restrictions, taxes, and subsidies, as well as by national policies toward foreign investment. Thus, changes in trade barriers may have important implications for direct investment decisions. Conversely, the efficiency and distributive effects of trade barriers depend crucially upon the extent of induced capital flows, so that policies toward foreign investment may have an important although indirect influence on the consequences of protection and the gains from trade liberalization.

Ultimately, the impact of tariffs and nontariff barriers, including restrictions on foreign direct investment, depends crucially on the degree to which foreign investment and trade are substitutes or complements. Initial evidence from research on the role of tariff levels in explaining the distribution of foreign investment across manufacturing industries in Australia, Canada, and Europe established the role of high tariffs or other barriers to trade as investment incentives for MNCs seeking to sell in the protected market.[20] Likewise, the role of protection in attracting foreign investments to developing nations has been well documented in the literature evaluating import-substituting industrialization policies. However, several recent studies for Canada have found little support for the substitutability hypothesis, so that the overall evidence on this issue appears to be inconclusive.[21]

Although the relationship between trade barriers and foreign investment has been used mainly as a way to explain differences in the extent of MNC activity across industries within a country, the same logic suggests that *discriminatory* trade barriers may promote investment flows between particular countries. Selective trade restrictions used by the United States to slow down the growth of its imports from Japan and certain other nations have undoubtedly contributed to the rapid growth of Japanese foreign investment in the United States, especially by firms that have already incurred substantial costs in developing a US market for their products. For similar reasons, Japanese firms may have accelerated their foreign investments in Asian developing countries not affected by voluntary export restraints and orderly marketing agreements on trade with the United States, resulting in faster relocation of production than would have occurred on the basis of changing relative costs alone.

Direct Investment in the Product Cycle

A large part of MNC production and trade is linked to innovation and the international dissemination of new technology, as described in the now-familiar international product cycle. The product cycle implies links between trade and investment policy through its associated "foreign investment cycle" for the innovating firm, and also has implications for the complementarity/substitutability issue.

According to the product-cycle scenario, a new product is developed first for an important home market. Products that succeed at home then become candidates for exporting. At this stage, foreign direct investments by the firm are typically complementary to its export performance, e.g., distribution and service facilities abroad. Indeed, some foreign investment in these forms is virtually essential to export success.[22] Later on, as the world market for the new product grows, the successful product becomes standardized and imitations begin to appear. At this point, the innovating firm is likely to shift production to foreign subsidiaries on the basis of relative cost advantage. Although production by foreign subsidiaries is often seen as a substitute for exports, establishment of foreign subsidiaries may be "defensive," simply allowing the innovating firm to retain its share in a market that would otherwise be lost to competitors with production facilities more advantageously located. Finally, if the relative cost advantage of foreign production is important, the home market may eventually be served through foreign production. But even at this stage, the internationalization of production still implies the possibility of continuing exports of components and services or of complementary products by the parent firm.[23]

Each step in the product cycle and associated foreign investment cycle represents a managerial decision based on comparative costs along with trade and investment policies. In particular, trade barriers *or* investment incentives abroad should accelerate the transition from exporting to establishment of foreign production subsidiaries. Likewise investment incentives abroad, especially paired with implicit or explicit export performance requirements, encourage the innovating firm to serve its own home market through imports, while import-limiting performance requirements tend to cut down on complementary flows of components or related products in the latter stages of the cycle.

Trade Barriers and the Competitiveness of MNCs

Because a key difference between MNCs and domestic firms is the degree of internationalization of production, changes in trade barriers will have important effects on their relative competitiveness.[24] General reductions in trade barriers, such as those negotiated in the Kennedy and Tokyo Rounds, may increase incentives for foreign investment *globally* by allowing MNCs greater latitude for internationalization of production according to comparative advantage. Trade liberalization tends to increase the advantage of international firms over domestic ones, as MNCs are better able to capture the potential efficiency gains from reduced barriers, especially in the short term. If effective protection rates fall, domestic firms encounter increased foreign competition, whereas MNCs have the ability to serve an established domestic market by imports. Moreover, in light of their substantially higher import propensities (see section II), foreign subsidiaries are likely to enjoy greater cost reductions than domestic firms as a result of across-the-board tariff reductions. Thus, for a country like Canada, with a large existing *stock* of foreign investment, participation in the multilateral trade negotiations may have actually improved the competitive position of foreign subsidiaries and exacerbated the foreign domination of industry, notwithstanding the role played by protection in attracting the foreign capital in the first place.

A further consequence of the MNCs' "international technology" is that scale economies in any particular stage of production can have important implications for the effects of trade policy on investment patterns and of investment policy on trade patterns. Multilateral trade liberalization should promote investments to centralize production activities subject to important scale economies.[25] Moreover, in the presence of scale economies, trade barriers, investment inventives, and/or export performance requirements can lead to a reversal of the pattern of trade that would be implied by comparative advantage alone.[26] In the case of export performance requirements, the subsidiary once established may exceed the minimum level set by the host country—so that the requirement appears, misleadingly, to be redundant. In fact. the requirement in this instance may have played an important role in determining the size of the production subsidiary established in the host country; once the fixed costs have been committed, the higher export level is determined by the firm's own profit calculations.

Implications of Imperfect Competition

As our discussion of innovation and scale economies has already acknowledged, multinationals thrive where markets deviate in important ways from the standard competitive assumptions. This suggests an additional and important source of complications in analyzing the interaction between policies toward trade and investment. For example, to the extent that MNC strategy is based on price discrimination across separated national markets, tariffs and import or export restrictions may have effects quite different from those predicted under perfect competition.[27] More generally, policy prescriptions based on the purely competitive case have doubtful relevance where trade flows are dominated by multinational firm transactions. More theoretical analysis explicitly incorporating an economic motive for direct investment is required.[28]

IV. IMPLICATIONS FOR NEGOTIATING STRATEGIES

Section II of this paper argues that host-country regulation of foreign direct investment, while an established prerogative of sovereign nations, also constitutes a potentially important class of nontariff trade distortion. Section III indicates a number of ways in which trade and investment policies interact, with implications for the volume, direction, and terms of trade. Taken together, this material suggests that there is a logical link between negotiations on trade and negotiations on investment. The 1982 US decision to bring its investment dispute with Canada to the GATT makes this link a matter of current practical interest as well. In this section we explore some questions raised by bringing trade and investment issues together in the GATT or in other bilateral or regional negotiations. While the previous sections draw on available data and widely accepted theory, here our approach is speculative, intended primarily to provoke debate and stimulate further research, rather than to provide a final answer to a difficult question.

Nontariff Barriers and the Tokyo Round

The Tokyo Round signaled a belated recognition that trade policy trends in the 1960s and 1970s have been increasingly in conflict with a fundamental principle of the GATT—that trade intervention for legitimate national objectives should take exclusively the form of tariffs, "which constitute a known and constant barrier that it is possible for a foreign producer to overcome if he is competitive enough . . ."[29] Despite the success of the Kennedy Round in negotiating important across-the-board reductions in tariff rates, the lasting gains achieved in terms of freer international trade have been called into question by the subsequent proliferation of nontariff distortions.[30] In part, this trend undoubtedly reflects substitution of other policy tools to achieve largely unchanged domestic objectives once met by tariff protection. The Kennedy Round succeeded in reducing tariff protection but had no significant effect on the motives for protection or the power of domestic interest groups, whose appeals now elicit trade-distorting policies of unprecedented variety and sophistication. However, the increased prominence of nontariff distortions is also a natural consequence of a major change in the role of governments. Trade flows have inevitably been affected along with domestic economic activity as governments exercise a greatly expanded mandate for intervention and regulation in areas once left primarily to private action. As a result, rather than the known, constant, and ever-decreasing barriers envisioned by framers of the GATT, contemporary trade policy is characterized by "its very complexity, subtlety and potential to inflict damage . . ." In comparison with the straightforward protectionism of the 1930s, "we have moved in the trade sphere, as in the military, from a conventional to a thermo-nuclear world."[31]

The Tokyo Round negotiations, which produced "codes of conduct" governing certain nontariff trade barriers, implied a major redefinition of GATT's role and domain. The codes of conduct represent the first formal multilateral effort to regulate the broad range of government policies that directly or indirectly (even at times inadvertently) favor domestic producers over their competitors abroad. By focusing attention on the panoply of government actions that can influence the volume, direction, and terms of trade, the Tokyo Round in effect made a matter for multilateral negotiation and GATT surveillance of policies previously regarded as sovereign nations' unilateral prerogatives.

Investment Issues and the GATT

The logic of the Tokyo Round seems to apply in the case of policies toward foreign direct investment. However, host countries have increasingly assumed the right to regulate new foreign investment. Although somewhat more controversial, many nations have also sought to alter the terms of established foreign investment, i.e., to change the rules of the game once appreciable sunk costs are involved. Thus, unlike international negotiations on trade liberalization, where there is considerable agreement regarding relatively neutral rules and disagreement is focused more on the specific applications of these rules, the underlying principles of international negotiations on investment are themselves likely to be controversial, with host and home countries pursuing antithetical objectives. Furthermore, the potential division between host and home countries corresponds roughly to the division between developing and developed countries.[32] This suggests both that the United States, by far the world's most important home country in absolute terms, plays an asymmetrical role in international negotiations relating to investment and that the most important potential gains may involve countries which are simultaneously important home and host countries of multinationals, in particular, the United States and certain other industrial nations.[33] Accordingly, whether investment issues should be brought into the GATT process or linked to trade issues in bilateral or regional negotiations is perhaps better viewed in practical terms: specifically, is a linking of investment and trade negotiations likely to produce more desirable outcomes than the status quo (in which there is virtually no international framework governing policies toward foreign investment), or alternatively, a hypothetical situation in which a separate international agency or GATT-like agreement deals with all issues related to investment?[34]

Obviously, this question has no ready answer. To begin with, current knowledge of the importance of investment policies as trade distortions is at best sketchy. Although the data summarized in section II suggest that the influence of such policies is pervasive, there is at present no evidence that the economic costs are large, either in absolute terms or relative to that of other nontariff barriers—including many important ones yet to be addressed successfully by the GATT, e.g., safeguards.[35] Any practical argument for bringing investment issues under the GATT umbrella would have to be bolstered by quantitative documentation of their trade-distorting impact.

A more basic issue is that as with other governmental policies affecting trade, GATT success in limiting trade-distorting practices in the investment area ultimately depends upon the willingness of its members to surrender national sovereignty in a politically sensitive area. Despite the successful efforts of the Tokyo Round in negotiating the new codes on nontariff barriers, the degree to which members are willing *in practice* to accept limits on their domestic options in order to promote collective goals remains in doubt. To extend the GATT's fragile achievements in this difficult area to a set of issues as sensitive and politically explosive as host-country regulation of foreign direct investment could be premature and counterproductive.

A related consideration is that any GATT-sponsored effort to limit host country prerogatives on efficiency grounds might well be interpreted as further evidence that the GATT remains primarily a rich man's club dedicated to preservation of the status quo in the world economy. Given present North–South differences on foreign investment issues and the role of the United States in the dispute currently before the GATT, initiatives to extend the GATT mandate to include host-country investment regulation (or even just trade-related investment performance requirements) have the potential of reversing the modest progress made in the Tokyo Round toward bringing less-developed countries into fuller participation in the GATT.[36] For this reason, a GATT code on investment may well have to incorporate an explicit double standard for developed and developing nations, as has already been instituted in the Tokyo Round for a number of other areas. Yet, even this will not necessarily diffuse opposition from developing nations in the GATT, since the major developing host countries are "middle income" nations near the point of "graduation" from special and preferential status.[37]

Finally, bringing together trade and investment issues, whether within the GATT or outside, carries all the well-known advantages and disadvantages of issue linkage. Issue linkage has the important virtue of enlarging the potential for mutual gains. In practice, however, this means that technical economic issues tend to be submerged by other, "larger" considerations such as military and strategic objectives. In fact, to a certain degree the successes of the GATT may be attributed to the Agreement's rather narrow scope. The more ambitious International Trade Organization (ITO), whose intended role in the trade area was eventually assumed by the GATT, would have had jurisdiction as well over investment issues (and, among others, international commodity agreements). The US Senate's dissatisfaction with the investment provision played an important role in the Senate's failure to ratify the ITO Charter.

Negotiating Outside the GATT

Does a linkage of trade and investment policy issues in the case of bilateral negotiations between the United States and other individual nations or regional groups provide greater potential benefits and fewer pitfalls? In the instance of the United States and Canada, the extent of the trade and investment relationships between the two nations implies a rich agenda of bilateral economic issues for negotiation,[38] while the relatively similar economic and political attitudes of the two reduce the likelihood that negotiations will move quickly from the economic sphere into unrelated foreign policy concerns.

Even here, however, serious obstacles remain. Since the offending trade targets in the US–Canadian case are set by the investing firms themselves rather than by the FIRA or by Canadian statute, it is not obvious what concessions short of abolition of FIRA and elimination of its screening function would be acceptable to the United States. Given the present domestic political climate in Canada and the fact that foreign investment there is overwhelmingly by US-based firms, such an offer is unlikely to be forthcoming from Canadian negotiators. The US decision in early 1982 to take the issue to the GATT suggests that at least from the official US point of view, a trade-investment linkage within the GATT framework offers greater promise than the bilateral approach.

In comparison, US–Japanese bilateral negotiations on economic issues may offer considerable potential for a mutually beneficial linkage of trade and investment issues without the same difficulties. In its current quest for bilateral trade balance (so-called trade reciprocity) with Japan, the United States has stressed a variety of nontariff barriers to trade. In view of the recognized complementarity between foreign direct investment and exporting and Japan's highly restrictive policies toward inward foreign investment, a logical step for US negotiators would be to emphasize liberalization of Japan's barriers to foreign investment.

In North-South and especially US–South relations, the domestic political acceptability of direct negotiations to reduce LDC screening and regulation of foreign direct investment is even more problematic than in the Canadian case. However, there continue to be important potential gains from North–South negotiations on trade issues, and success in this area would also tend to reduce the perceived need on the part of Southern nations for trade-distorting investment regulation. Because past rounds of multilateral trade negotiations focused primarily on trade among the industrial nations, they have left unexplored a major source of mutual gains from trade liberalization along lines of comparative advantage.

On average, developing nations have much higher import barriers than the United States or other industrial nations. These are in part a legacy of import-substitution policies and in part a reflection of the sideline role that developing nations have played in the reciprocal bargaining process of the GATT. On the other hand, the United States, along with most industrialized nations, affords much higher than average protection to manufacturing industries that compete directly with rapidly growing LDC exports—notably textiles and apparel, but also a growing number of other products. This pattern of protection has had two important effects on North–South economic relations. On the trade side, it has slowed down the adjustment of North–South trade flows in *both directions* to changing patterns of international competitiveness. On the investment side, it may have dampened the rate of direct investment in areas of current and future LDC comparative advantage, while maintaining incentives for inefficient import-substituting investments. The latter are often assembly or packaging operations that merely substitute imports of parts or bulk products for imports of final products, at high cost to consumers in the protected local market. Such a misdirection of investment contributes to the observed high import propensities and poor export performance that are a key source of Southern dissatisfaction with MNC practices.

Given the current pattern of protection, reciprocal North–South trade liberalization offers the potential for important mutual gains. Unlike most other proposals to increase the access of Southern exporters to Northern markets, e.g., the Generalized System of Preferences, reciprocal liberalization offers tangible gains to *Northern* nations in the form of increased export opportunities for their own products, so that the domestic political appeal is far greater.[39] An additional consideration is that reciprocal trade liberalization by itself would tend to improve the export performance of subsidiaries in developing countries and to increase the amount of foreign investment in areas of comparative advantage. This in turn could reduce the perceived need on the part of developing nations for investment incentives and trade-distorting performance requirements.

V. CONCLUSIONS

The trade-distorting effects of national policies toward foreign investment are a new and potentially important concern for policymakers. Our work here has been primarily exploratory, intended to present information, provoke debate, and suggest avenues for future research on this subject. The major focus of the paper is the relationship between trade policy and foreign investment policy. We have examined this relationship from several perspectives: the extent to which investment policies influence trade, the role of MNC trade performance as a motivation for national regulation of investment, the ways in which trade and investment policies interact as co-determinants of the location of production and pattern of trade, the implications of trade liberalization for the relative competitiveness of MNCs and domestic firms, and considerations affecting the prospects for a future link between trade and investment negotiations in the GATT or outside.

Some specific conclusions of the analysis are summarized by the following points:

(1) Host-country regulation, while an established prerogative of sovereign nations, also constitutes a potentially important class of nontariff distortion, at least when measured in terms of frequency. However, little information is yet available about the quantitative impact of investment regulation on trade flows. Detailed studies, both across industries and across countries, are needed.

(2) US subsidiaries in virtually every host country are affected to some degree by investment incentives and performance requirements, although their incidence and form varies significantly across countries and by industry. The importance of performance requirements is much greater on average for developing countries than for industrialized countries. This suggests that performance requirements of various kinds may be central to some nations' preferred strategy for industrial development. Accordingly, these nations may be reluctant to negotiate reductions in their sovereignty in this area.

(3) In the specific case of Canada, the most important host country for US investment and probably the nation best able to alter the terms of foreign investment within its borders, striking differences with respect to importing and R&D performance of subsidiaries and domestic firms provide a clear empirical basis for Canada's perceived need for active regulation of foreign direct investment. However, the trade-distorting impact of Canadian regulation is difficult to document. The screening procedure gives potential investors an incentive to stress the export and domestic-content requirements of their proposals. Trade targets are set by the firms themselves, although in light of the impact of promised trade performance on the prospects for speedy approval.

(4) Because a key difference between MNCs and domestic firms is the degree of internationalization of production (as documented in this paper for the Canadian case), general reductions in trade barriers tend to increase the advantage of multinational firms over domestic ones, especially in the short term. For a country like Canada with a large existing stock of foreign investment, multilateral trade liberalization probably exacerbated the foreign domination of industry by improving the competitive position of foreign subsidiaries relative to their domestic counterparts.

(5) The timing of the international product cycle and its associated direct investment cycle has important implications for the United States, whose comparative advantage is in production of new goods. Managerial decisions that determine timing are crucially affected by trade barriers and by host countries' policies toward foreign direct investment, both incentives and performance requirements.

(6) Because the typical environment for MNC activity deviates in important ways from the standard competitive assumptions, the interaction between trade and investment policies may include effects quite different from those predicted under perfect competition. Policy prescriptions based on the purely competitive ease thus have doubtful relevance where trade flows are dominated by multinational firm transactions. Theoretical analysis explicitly taking account of the economic motive for direct investment is required.

(7) Negotiations on trade issues are facilitated by the dual role of every nation as importer and exporter. As a consequence, there is considerable agreement regarding rules, and disagreement is focused on the specific applications of these rules. In contrast, the underlying principles of international negotiations on investment are themselves likely to be controversial, with home and host country pursuing antithetical objectives. This suggests that the greatest potential gains from negotiations are for the group of countries with important interests as both home and host countries, in particular, the United States and some other industrial nations.

NOTES

Comments on this paper by the Middlebury Conference participants are gratefully acknowledged. Dr. Asim Erdilek also provided helpful comments. The work was supported in part by National Science Foundation Grant No. PRA-8116448.

1 We do not attempt to evaluate the effectiveness of host-country regulation in achieving national objectives. It is worth emphasizing, however, that regulatory intent and actual outcome do not necessarily coincide.
2 Allocative consequences of such performance requirements have been analyzed by Munk (1969) and Grossman (1981).
3 For example, Brash (1966) and Safarian (1966).
4 The recent controversy centers on Canadian policies restricting the activities of US-controlled subsidiaries. A decade earlier, US-Canadian conflict resulted from the effects on US trade of incentives offered to other foreign investors. In response to grants, subsidized loans, and preferential tax treatment, the French-owned Michelin tire company established two production plants in Nova Scotia to produce steel-belted radial tires for the North American (primarily US) market. The United States treated the estimated value of the Canadian incentive package as an export subsidy and applied a countervailing duty on imports of Michelin tires from the two plants. See Volpe (1976).
5 Hawkins and Walter (1980).
6 Statistics Canada (1981).
7 Based on data used in Owen (1982).

8 Including foreign takeovers of Canadian firms and expansion into new activities by foreign firms already established in the Canadian market.
9 Hawkins and Walter (1980).
10 For example, see Spero (1981).
11 *Wall Street Journal,* May 7, 1975.
12 *Wall Street Journal,* February 16, 1982.
13 *Business Week,* November 23, 1981, p. 43.
14 *Wall Street Journal,* February 16, 1982.
15 *New York Times,* February 18, 1982.
16 Department of Commerce (1981b).
17 Labor-Industry Coalition for International Trade (1981).
18 US Department of Commerce (1981a). The responses relating to investment incentives and performance requirements are summarized in US Department of Commerce (1981b).
19 Data cited by Corden (1974).
20 For example, Brash (1966), Safarian (1966), Horst (1972a, 1972b), Scaperlanda and Mauer (1969), and Schmitz and Bieri (1972).
21 Including Hewitt (1975), Orr (1973, 1975), and Owen (1982). One possible explanation of the apparently conflicting evidence is that, given substantial fixed costs of entry, subsidiaries established in a protected market may remain profitable to operate even after protection is reduced.
22 Bergsten, Horst, and Moran (1978).
23 Ibid.
24 Obviously, the strength of this argument depends on the "true" source of MNC advantage and thus ventures into an area of unresolved conflict among the experts. See, e.g., Kindleberger (1969), Magee (1977), and Aliber (1970).
25 Where scale economies are relatively unimportant, reduced trade barriers may have an opposite effect. To reduce risk from a variety of country-specific sources, MNCs may follow a diversification approach, establishing production facilities in a number of countries.
26 Horst (1971).
27 Ibid.
28 One such analysis is Markusen (1980).
29 Johnson (1965).
30 The classic reference is Baldwin (1970), who notes the potential trade-distorting effects of investment policies only in passing.
31 Curzon (1981).
32 Notable exceptions to this division are Canada, Australia, and South Africa.
33 Not entirely coincidentally, the OECD has succeeded in formulating a voluntary code governing many aspects of foreign investment.
34 Goldberg and Kindleberger (1970) are credited with this proposal. Dunning (1974) has argued for what he terms an issue- or problem-oriented approach that would treat trade and investment policies together as part of a "General Agreement on International Production." Also see Vernon (1974).
35 On what the Tokyo Round left undone, see Corbet (1979).
36 Indeed, developing countries have been working through the United Nations Center on Transnational Corporations on their own investment code, which reaffirms the right of host countries to regulate foreign direct investment.
37 On preferential treatment and graduation of LDCs, see Frank (1977).
38 See Grey (1981) for a comprehensive discussion.
39 See the discussion of targeted most-favored-nation liberalization of trade in McCulloch (1981).

REFERENCES

Aliber, Robert Z., 1970. "The Theory of the International Corporation: A Theory of Direct Foreign Investment," in C. P. Kindleberger (ed.), *The International Corporation.* Cambridge, Mass.: MIT Press.

Baldwin, Robert E., 1970. *Non-tariff Distortions of International Trade.* Washington, D.C.: Brookings.

Bergsten, C. Fred, Thomas Horst, and Theodore Moran, 1978. *American Multinationals and American Interests.* Washington, D.C.: Brookings.

Brash, D. T., 1966. *American Investment in Australian Industry.* Canberra: Australian National University Press.

Corden, W. M., 1974. *Trade Policy and Economic Welfare.* London: Oxford University Press.

Corbet, Hugh, 1979. "The Importance of Being Earnest about Further GATT Negotiations," *The World Economy,* September, pp. 319–341.

Curzon, Gerard, 1981. "Neo-protectionism, the MFA and the European Community," *The World Economy,* September, pp. 251-262.

Dunning, John H., 1978. "The Future of the Multinational Enterprise," *Lloyds Bank Review* July 1974. Reprinted in Bela Balassa (ed.), *Changing Patterns in Foreign Trade and Payments.* New York: Norton.

Frank, Isaiah, 1979. "The Graduation Issue for LDCs," *Journal of World Trade Law,* May/June, pp. 289–302.

Goldberg, Paul M., and Charles P. Kindleberger, 1979. "Toward a GATT for Investment: A Proposal for Supervision of the International Corporation," *Law and Policy in International Business,* Summer, 295–325.

Grey, Rodney de C., 1981. *Trade Policy in the 1980s: An agenda for Canadian–U.S. Relations.* Montreal: C. D. Howe Institute, September.

Grossman, Gene, 1981. "The Theory of Domestic Content Protection and Content Preference," *Quarterly Journal of Economics,* November, pp. 583-603.

Hawkins, Robert G., and Ingo Walter, 1980. "Multinational Corporations: Current Trends and Future Prospects," in *The International Economy: US Role in a World Market.* Washington, D.C.: Joint Economic Committee of the Congress Of the United States December 17.

Hewitt, Gary K, 1975. "U.S. Penetration of Canadian Manufacturing Industries." Ph.D. thesis, Yale University.

Horst, T., 1972. "Firm and Industry Determinants of the Decision to Invest Abroad: An Empirical Study," *REStat,* August, pp. 258–266.

——, 1972. "The Industrial Composition of US Exports and Subsidiary Sales to the Canadian Market," *American Economic Review,* March, pp. 37–45.

——, 1971. "The Theory of the Multinational Firm: Optimal Behavior Under Different Tariff and Tax Rates," *Journal of Political Economy,* September/October.

Johnson, Harry G., 1965. *The World Economy at the Crossroads.* Montreal: Canadian Trade Committee, Private Planning Association of Canada, April.

Kindleberger, Charles, *American Business Abroad: Six Lectures on Direct Investment.* New Haven, Conn.: Yale University Press.

Labor-Industry Coalition for International Trade, 1981. *Performance Requirements.* Washington, D.C.: Labor-Industry Coalition for International Trade, March.

Magee, Stephen P., 1977. "Information and the Multinational Corporation:: An Appropriability Theory of Direct Foreign Investment," in J. N. Bhagwati (ed.), *The New International Economic Order: The North–South Debate.* Cambridge, Mass.: MIT Press.

Markusen, James R., 1980. "Multinationals and the Gains from Trade: A Theoretical Analysis Based on Economics of Multi-plant Operation." Institute for International Economic Studies, University of Stockholm, Seminar Paper No. 160, October.

McCulloch, Rachel, 1981. "Gains to Latin America from Trade Liberalization in Developed and Developing Countries," *Quarterly Review of Economics and Business*, Summer, pp. 231–258.

Munk, B., 1969. "The Welfare Costs of Content Protection: The Automotive Industry in Latin America," *Journal of Political Economy*, January/February.

Orr, Dale, 1973. "Foreign Control and Foreign Penetration in the Canadian Manufacturing Industries." Unpublished paper, July.

——, 1975. "The Industrial Composition of US Exports and Subsidiary Sales to the Canadian Market: Comment," *American Economic Review*, March, pp. 230–234.

Owen, R. F., 1982. "Inter-industry Determinants of Foreign Direct Investments: A Canadian Perspective," forthcoming in A. Rugman (ed.), *New Theories of the Multinational Enterprise*. New York: St. Martin's.

Scaperlanda, A. E., and L. J. Mauer, 1969. "Determinants Of US Direct Investment in the *EEC*," *American Economic Review*, September, pp. 558–568.

Spero, Joan Edelman, 1981. *The Politics of International Economic Relations*. New York: St. Martin's, pp. 102–134.

Statistics Canada, 1981. *Canadian Imports by Domestic and Foreign Controlled Enterprises*. Ottawa: Ministry of Supply and Services.

US Department of Commerce, 1981. *U.S. Direct Investment Abroad*. Washington, D.C.: US Department of Commerce, April.

US Department of Commerce, Office of International Investment, 1981. *The Use of Investment Incentives and Performance Requirements by Foreign Governments*. Washington, D.C.: US Department of Commerce, October.

Vernon, Raymond, 1974. "Competition Policy Toward Multinational Corporations," *American Economic Review*, May, pp. 276–282.

Volpe, John, 1976. *Industrial Incentive Policies and Programs in the Canadian–American Context*. Montreal: Canadian–American Committee, January.

10. Patents and Pharmaceutical Drugs: Understanding the Pressures on Developing Countries

J. Nogues

I. INTRODUCTION

In September 1989 – the deadline for a U.S. investigation – Argentina announced that within two years it would submit a draft law extending patent protection to pharmaceutical products. One year earlier – on 20 October, 1988 – the U.S. Federal Register published the list of goods on which the United States would retaliate by increasing *ad valorem* tariff rates to 100 per cent on imports from Brazil; this country had refused to negotiate patent protection to pharmaceutical drugs. On 18 December 1987, the European Community (EC) removed Korea from the list of countries eligible for GSP (Generalized System of Preferences) treatment. The reason: Korea had refused to grant EC manufacturers the same intellectual property protection it affords to U.S. exporters. The European Community, Japan and the United States have all tabled proposals at the Uruguay Round for significantly greater homogeneity and higher protection of Intellectual Property Rights (IPRs) – patent protection to pharmaceuticals probably being the most significant item on this agenda – around the world. The proposals are directed at developing countries, which, so far, have resisted.

This list – which goes on – of bilateral and multilateral actions raises a question: why all these pressures on developing countries? The hypothesis of this article is that part of these pressures evolve as a reaction to institutional and competitive changes that have taken place in the pharmaceutical drug markets of industrial countries. Most importantly, these changes refer to tighter drug safety and efficacy regulations and to increased competition from generic drugs. At the same time, besides patents, other policies of developing countries – such as trade barriers, price controls and, also most importantly, the adminstration of regulations – also have an impact on the competitive positions of different firms. Nonetheless, this article focuses on developments taking place in industrial countries.

The plan of the article is as follows: Section II will review the world-wide pattern of patent policies and the pressures from industrial countries on developing countries for modification of patent laws in general, and pharmaceutical drugs in particular. Section III presents the evidence on the relative importance of patents for the pharmaceutical industry. Section IV discussed changes in effective patent duration as modified by regulatory policies. Section V presents evidence on the growing importance of competition between brand names and the generic drug industry and the impact of this competition on drug prices. Section VI presents some final remarks.

II. PRESSURES ON DEVELOPING COUNTRIES

The purpose of this section is to highlight the pressures put by industrial countries for reforming patent policies in the Less Developed Countries (LDCs). It first presents the world-wide pattern of patent protection for pharmaceutical drugs and the proposals for reform of patent policies tabled at the multilateral trade negotiations of the Uruguay Round. Subsection 1 will also argue that, for the first time in modern economic history, industrial countries have come to an agreement on "appropriate" patent protection. Subsection 2 will provide a brief discussion of some of the bilateral actions taken by industrial countries against developing countries; the existing patent policies of many of these countries are quite different from the proposals of industrial countries. Finally, subsection 3 will provide a brief discussion of the economic interests at stake.

1. Patent Protection for Pharmaceuticals

While today a great majority of industrial countries provide patent protection for pharmaceutical drugs, there are many developing countries that do not. Nevertheless, it should not be concluded that patent protection for pharmaceuticals has a long tradition in industrial countries. For example, it was only in 1949 that the United Kingdom introduced patent protection for pharmaceutical drugs. Also, many other industrial countries have only recently introduced patents for pharmaceuticals, including France, 1960; Germany, 1968; Japan, 1976; Switzerland, 1977; Italy, 1978; and Sweden, 1978. Thus, among industrial countries, for many years the pharmaceutical industry was one of the few that remained unprotected by patents. Even today some industrial countries such as Australia, Finland, New Zealand and Norway, still refuse to grant patent protection to pharmaceuticals; Spain will introduce it only in 1992 (Lobo, 1988).

Furthermore, at different times, industrial countries enforce a system of patent licences that restricts the monopoly of patent-owner quite significantly. This is the case, for example, in Canada and the United Kingdom. Other countries – including the United States – have used antitrust legislation to control license agreements. For example, when discussing the patent system in general, Scherer asserts that ". . . compulsory licensing has been specified as a remedy in more than 100 antitrust cases, making available some 40,000 to 50,000 patents at 'reasonable' royalties or (in a few instances) royalty free . . ." (Scherer, 1980, p. 397).

On the other hand, many developing countries have not yet introduced patent protection for pharmaceuticals. As a matter of fact, the pharmaceutical industry is the one most often excluded from patent protection in developing countries.[1] The World Intellectual Property Organization (WPO) has listed 48 countries (WIPO, 1988) as not providing patent protection for pharmaceutical products:[2] Argentina, Australia*, Bolivia, Brazil*, Bulgaria, Chad, China, Colombia*, Cuba,

Czechoslovakia, Ecuador, Egypt, Finland, German Democratic Republic, Ghana, Greece, Hungary, Iceland, India, Iran, Iraq, Korea, Lebanon, Libya, Malawi*, Mexico*, Monaco, Mongolia, Morocco, New Zealand*, Norway, Pakistan, Peru, Poland, Portugal, Romania, the Soviet Union, Spain (until 1992), Syria, Thailand, Tunisia, Turkey, Uruguay, Venezuela, Vietnam, Yugoslavia, Zambia* and Zimbabwe*.

As can be seen from the above list, there are many countries that provide patent protection for pharmaceutical processes, but not pharmaceutical products. A process-patent protects the product only if it is produced with it. Since small modifications of a formula create many ways of producing a chemical compound, process-patents are generally viewed as providing weak protection for pharmaceutical drug companies. Furthermore, in developing countries the courts have often interpreted the exclusion of pharmaceutical product patents as a policy for enhancing competition in the drug market. Thus, when cases of process-patents have been brought to trial, the courts have usually turned down demands to use these patents to protect the monopoly power of the product.

Thus, a significant part of the developing world provides weak patent protection for pharmaceutical drugs; very often patent protection is not provided or, if provided, it is not legally strong. This situation has become an issue for multilateral negotiations between developed and developing countries. Also, the lack of patent protection for pharmaceutical drugs has triggered numerous bilateral actions of industrial against developing countries. According to Benko (1988), these complaints refer to the characteristics of both the international and domestic patent regimes. Industrial countries argue that the international patent regime is inadequate because a number of countries have not signed some of the international agreements and also because they provide no enforcement or dispute settlement mechanisms. Furthermore, industrial countries complain that the domestic patent regimes of many developing countries are inadequate because: patent protection is too short; some industries such as pharmaceuticals are excluded; the legal enforcement of patent rights is weak; and too much emphasis is given to compulsory licensing.

At the Uruguay Round, industrial country negotiators – including those of the European Community, Japan and the United States – have proposed, among other things, that patents should be offered in all fields; that they should last for 20 years from date of application; that compulsory licenses should be applied only in extraordinary circumstances; and that there should be a strong dispute settlement mechanism. The few developing countries that have tabled proposals on intellectual property rights – for example Brazil and India – oppose these reforms. The only exception is Korea, which has tabled a proposal very similar to that of the industrial countries.

Thus, it might be concluded that from an historical perspective the current situation finds industrial countries in quite general agreement on a policy issue – patent protection in general and pharmaceutical drugs in particular – where until not long ago important differences were observed among them. Explaining this is not easy, but at the very least it can be said that neither theory nor empirical research provide support for the current state of affairs. There is no theory of patents powerful enough to provide those in favor of the above-mentioned patent policies with strong support (Braga, *et al.* 1990). The most general economic model of patents is that of Nordhaus (1969); in this model it is only under a very particular set of parameter values that the industrial countries' proposals can be defended.[3]

On the other hand, empirical research has shown that social returns to research and development (R&D) are quite high and generally higher than private returns (Mansfield, 1986); this evidence is used to support patents. Furthermore, the evidence is only for industrial countries; research on the social rate of return of drug innovation in developing countries has not been undertaken and the reason appears to be simply that these countries do not undertake drug research.

2. Bilateral Policies and Actions

In March 1987, only a few months after the Uruguay Round had been launched, Mr Gerald J. Mossinghoff, President of the U.S. Pharmaceutical Manufacturers Association (PMA), declared that they were working with the U.S. Congress to get it to enact ". . . the intellectual property revisions of the Omnibus Trade bill that would *strengthen the hand of the U.S. Government* in urging all of our trading partners to respect our rights in inventions and trademarks . . ." (PMA, 1987, emphasis added). Shortly after, the U.S. Omnibus Trade Act of 1988 was passed, modifying the administrative provision of bilateral trade instruments. The most significant changes for the pharmaceutical industry were introduced to Section 301 of the Trade Act of 1974 (henceforth Section 301). This Section provides for the enforcement of U.S. rights under international trade agreements and for the relief from ". . . unfair practices of foreign governments which can be unjustifiable, unreasonable, discriminating or which burden or restrict U.S. commerce."

If in Section 301 investigation the foreign country is found to be "violating" U.S. rights and it does not correct its policies, the United States Trade Representative (USTR) – in charge of the Section 301 investigations – can recommend the use of retaliatory measures. The Omnibus Trade Act introduced important changes to Section 301; changes which, according to Grinols (1988), would make it easier for the United States to expand the number of Section 301 cases, increase the likelihood of finding the investigated country was acting unfairly, and most likely increase the magnitude and duration of the retaliatory measures.

Also, among the changes introduced, is a mandate for the USTR to identify priority countries that deny adequate and effective protection of intellectual property rights; currently India is on this USTR list. The United States has threatened to use Section 301 in more cases than those actually investigated. For example, under strong pressure, Korea passed legislation in 1986 that would allow patent protection for pharmaceutical products (Gadbaw, 1988). However, the attack on Korea's patent policies did not come only from the United States. In December 1987, the European Community removed Korea from the GSP because it did not provide adequate patent protection for the R&D-intensive pharmaceutical industry (WIPR, 1988).

Under similar pressures, other countries have announced that they will introduce patent protection for pharmaceutical products, e.g., Mexico (Gwym, 1988) and Argentina (Nogués, 1990). But retaliatory threats have not always ended with positive changes by developing countries. Probably the most notorious case has been the retaliatory action against Brazil, undertaken after completion of a Section 301 investigation. Among other things, this investigation – initiated by the PMA – estimated the injury to U.S. firms, because of absence of patent protection for pharmaceutical processes and products. Because Brazil did not satisfy the demands made by the PMA, the United States increased *ad valorem* tariff rates to 100 per cent on an important number of goods imported from Brazil (U.S. Federal Register, 24 October 1988).[4]

It is quite clear from all this that developing countries have confronted, and continue to confront, significant pressures from industrial countries in order for them to introduce patent protection for pharmaceutical products. The choices for developing countries have narrowed; either they increase protection to intellectual property and in particular extend patent protection to pharmaceutical drugs, or otherwise suffer actual or threatened retaliatory actions by industrial countries.

3. The Economic Interests at Stake: A Preliminary Discussion

What would the pharmaceutical companies of industrial countries gain from the introduction of patent protection in developing countries? How important are these gains? The first question is easy to answer, but the second has only recently begun to be analyzed. Essentially, introduction of patent protection would put an end to the era of copying brand-name pharmaceutical drugs by domestic companies of developing countries. After patent protection is introduced, only brand-name companies will be the "legal" suppliers of patented drugs.

Regarding the importance of the pharmaceutical drug market and the loss to copiers, the PMA has made estimates of some countries: these are presented in Table 1. Part of the pharmaceutical drug market in these countries is supplied by patent-owners, but part is also supplied by copiers; the proportion supplied by the latter type of firm varies between countries, being highest in India (36.1 per cent) and lowest in Brazil (5.5 per cent).[5] Overall, in the four countries mentioned in Table 1, the PMA estimates that the sale of copied drugs amounts to US$1.4 billion per year. The speed at which domestic copiers would lose their market to patent-owners depends, in part, on whether patent protection would be enforced retroactively. In the absence of retroactive enforcement, the rate of market loss of copiers will partly depend on the rate of introduction of new patented drugs.

The US$1.4 billion is a fraction of the world-wide sales of R&D-intensive pharmaceutical companies; it is likely that this fraction has increased. It is certainly one of the reasons why the pharmaceutical drug companies are pressuring developing countries. But the central hypothesis of this article is that these pressures are also triggered by changes which have occurred in industrial countries. The R&D-intensive industry seeks to maintain and regain the market share that has been increasingly lost to the generic drug industry. A major component for achieving this goal is to increase patent protection.

TABLE 1 *Estimates of increased income of pharmaceutical companies holding patents (US$m)*

	Countries				
Variables	Argentina	Brazil	India	Mexico	Total
1. Pharmaceutical market size	1,200.0	2,000.0	4,200.0	1,000.0	8,400.0
2. Patented pharmaceutical market	771.0	1,750.4	2,546.0	852.5	5,919.9
2.1 Sales by domestic firms of copied drugs	231.0	93.8	920.0	136.5	1,381.3
2.2 Sales of drugs by firms who are patent-owners	540.0	1,656.6	1,626.0	716.0	4,538.6
3. Percentage share of U.S. companies*	45.0	50.0	45.0	50.0	not applicable

*Refers to share of sales of U.S. companies in total sales by multinationals.
Source: MacLaughlin, *et al.* (1988).

III. THE IMPORTANCE OF PATENTS TO THE PHARMACEUTICAL DRUG INDUSTRY

This section makes three points. First, patents are important, but only to a few industries, one of which is pharmaceutical drugs (Subsection 1 below). Second, the importance of patent protection for this industry comes from the strength that it provides in litigations (Subsection 2 below). Finally, although patent protection is important to only a few industries, the pharmaceutical drug industry happens to be among the most R&D-intensive and invests an important proportion of aggregate R&D.

1. The Inter-Industry Importance of Patents

There is a general presumption that patents are an important instrument for allowing inventors to appropriate the returns from inventions. Evidence accumulating in recent years shows that patents are far more important for some inventions and industries than for others. Probably the pioneering study to throw light on this issue was undertaken by Mansfield (1986). His figures are reproduced in Table 2; they show by industry and for the early 80s, the percentage of inventions that would not be developed or introduced into the market in the

TABLE 2 *Percentage of inventions that would not have been developed or introduced in the absence of patent protection**

	Percentage that would not have been introduced	Percentage that would not have been developed
Pharmaceuticals	65	60
Chemicals	30	38
Petroleum	18	25
Machinery	15	17
Fabricated metal products	12	12
Primary metals	8	1
Electrical equipment	4	11
Instruments	1	1
Office equipment	0	0
Motor vehicles	0	0
Rubber	0	0
Textiles	0	0

*Some inventions that were developed in this time period (1981–83) were not introduced then, and some inventions that were introduced then were not developed then. Thus, the left-hand column of the table refers to somewhat different inventions than does the right-hand column.
Source: Mansfield (1986).

absence of patent protection. According to these figures, the pharmaceutical drug industry comes at the top of each list.

Mansfield's conclusions received important support from a comprehensive study undertaken by Levin, *et al.* (1987). This study examined the relative importance of different ways of protecting the inventor's returns on his inventions. The authors prepared a comprehensive questionnaire and interviewed research managers from 130 U.S. industries. One set of questions included the views of these managers regarding the importance of alternative means of appropriating the return from the innovations made by their enterprises; patents to prevent duplication; patents to secure royalties; industrial secrets; lead-time; learning advantages; and sales and/or service efforts. The authors distinguished between process and product innovations and the answers were rated on a one-to-seven scale. The study showed that on average the most important means of appropriating the returns in process and product innovations are lead-time and sales/service efforts; in contrast, patents to secure royalty income on process and product innovations were only 65 and 67 per cent as important as lead-time and sales/service efforts respectively.

Table 3 from Levin, *et al.*, answers a similar question to that raised in Mansfield (1986), namely what is the inter-industry importance of patents for appropriating the returns from innovation. Again the answers are rated on a one-to-seven scale.

TABLE 3 *Effectiveness of process and product patents as a means of protecting the returns from industrial innovation*

Industry	Process Patents	Product Patents
Pulp, paper and paperboard	2.6	3.3
Cosmetics	2.9	4.1
Inorganic chemicals	4.6	5.2
Organic chemicals	4.1	6.1
Drugs	4.9	6.5
Plastic materials	4.6	5.4
Plastic products	3.2	4.9
Petroleum refining	4.9	4.3
Steel mill products	3.5	5.1
Pumps and pumping equipment	3.2	4.4
Motors, generators and controls	2.7	3.5
Computers	3.3	3.4
Communications equipment	3.1	3.6
Semiconductors	3.2	4.5
Motor vehicle parts	3.7	4.5
Aircraft and parts	3.1	3.8
Measuring devices	3.6	3.9
Medical instruments	3.2	4.7
Full sample	3.5	4.3

Source: Levin, *et al.* (1987).

The figures in this table show that patents are most important in protecting the process and product innovations of the drug industry; these patents were rated 40 and 51 per cent higher than the industrial averages for processes and products respectively. Furthermore, "... only five of 130 industries rated product patents to prevent duplication higher than six (out of seven) points ..." (Levin, *et al.*, p. 795). Drugs were one of the five.

The importance of patents for the pharmaceutical drug industry is not restricted to the United States. For example, in a classic study of the British patent system, Taylor and Silberston assert that the "... pharmaceutical industry stands alone in the extent of its involvement with the patent system ..." (Taylor and Silberston, 1973, p. 231). Clearly then, in industrial countries, patents are a crucial policy instrument in determining the returns to innovative efforts in a core-group of industries and particularly for pharmaceutical drugs.

2. The Inter-Industry Strength of Legal Protection

There are several hypotheses as to why the importance of patents differs so markedly between industries. For example, in some industries, such as consumer electronics, the rate of innovation and product differentiation is so fast that lead-times are the most natural way of appropriating the returns from innovation. On the other hand, many innovations may not be patentable in the sense of satisfying the requirements for a patent; namely, that the invention is novel, that it has utility and that it is non-obvious. But even if an invention were patentable, it could be that because a patent discloses valuable information, the owner would prefer to keep it secret. This could be particularly important when the inventor fears that the courts will not protect his patent rights.

Precisely this legal aspect is an important factor that explains the significance of patents to the pharmaceutical industry; to quote, the "... most probable explanation for the robust finding that patents are particularly effective in chemical industries is that comparatively clear standards can be applied to assess a chemical patent's validity and to defend against infringement. The uniqueness of a specific molecule is more easily demonstrated than the novelty of, for example, a new component of a complex electrical or mechanical system. Similarly, it is easy to determine whether an allegedly infringing molecule is physically identical to a patented molecule; it is more difficult to determine whether comparable components of two complex systems do the same work in substantially the same way." (Levin, *et al.*, p. 798). This quote could also be extended to pharmaceutical drugs for which, as said, patents are the most important means of appropriating the returns from R&D.

3. The Relative Importance of R&D Invested by the Private Pharmaceutical Industry

The amount of R&D undertaken by the private pharmaceutical drug industry is very high. First, firms in this industry typically invest a minimum of around 10 per cent of their sales in R&D. But in some countries like the United States, this proportion increased during the 1980s and – according to the PMA – reached 16 per cent in 1988. This contrasts with the economy-wide average R&D investment as a proportion of the gross domestic product (GDP) of industrial countries which stands at around 2.5 per cent (Evenson, 1990). This puts the pharmaceutical firms among the most intensive R&D industries of industrial countries. Second, these firms are generally huge; in 1982 each of the 30 largest pharmaceutical drug companies of the world had sales above US$1 billion. Third, in absolute terms, the total amount of R&D invested by pharmaceutical firms in industrial countries is enormous. For example, according to PMA reports, investment in R&D of private U.S. pharmaceutical firms exceeds US$7 billion; the industry is proud to remind the general public that this is higher than the total investment undertaken by the U.S. National Institute of Health for biomedical research (emphasized by the PMA in the Washington Post, 17 November 1989, p. A60). Such a figure also represents close to 10 per cent of all U.S. R&D investment.[6]

Summing up, only in a few industries do patents appear to be a major instrument for fostering technological innovation and diffusion; in the great majority, innovation appears to be triggered by market conditions. One of the few industries where patents are a major instrument for protecting intellectual property is pharmaceutical drugs. Although these drugs are easily copied – with or without the information disclosed in the patent (Mansfield, 1985) – they are unique innovations and, therefore, the legal protection provided by patent litigation is clearly in favor of innovating firms. Finally, although for many industries patents are generally unimportant as a means of appropriating the returns from R&D, given the size of R&D invested by the private U.S. pharmaceutical drug companies, one may conclude that patents are an important instrument in protecting a non-negligible portion of the output of the total R&D of industrial countries.

IV. SAFETY REGULATIONS, PRODUCTIVITY OF R&D AND EFFECTIVE PATENT DURATION: THE CASE OF THE UNITED STATES.[7]

This section makes essentially two points. First, there are two approaches to deal with the fact that pharmaceutical drugs can be a source of serious health risks; these approaches can be biased towards the market mechanisms, or towards a governmental enforced regulatory system. The history of the United States – and other industrial countries – shows a clear drift towards the second approach (Subsection 1 below). Second, the stringent regulations introduced in the United States during the early 1960s, has had clear effects on the costs and productivity of R&D undertaken by private pharmaceutical companies. Furthermore, increased safety and efficacy regulations have reduced the effective patent protection, thus reducing the profits per dollar invested in R&D (Subsection 2 below). This has been an important argument in defending this industry's request for longer patent duration; it is also a factor in explaining the industry's demand for higher protection in developing countries.

1. Market-Induced Information Flows versus Government Safety Regulations

The purpose of this section is to discuss the effects of the changing regulatory environment of pharmaceutical drugs in the United States. Safety regulations in the area of these drugs are justified with the argument of market failure. The problem is that pharmaceutical drugs can be a source of serious risk; in fact, some fatal cases associated with their consumption have shaped the nature of regulations in the United States as well as in other countries. The problem is essentially one of incomplete and/or inaccurate information which is more serious in the case of new and relatively undertested drugs. The solution, or at least the reduction in health risks, lies in improved information on positive and negative effects of drugs.

Two ways to reduce health risks can be envisaged: market-oriented and government-oriented. In a market-oriented approach, the quality and quantity of information on drug therapy would rely mainly on the quality of the doctors and the professional management of manufacturing enterprises. Presumably, the degree of market success of these agents would be linked to their professionalism.

Furthermore, potentially abusive behavior by these agents would be checked by other institutions; the law would define the boundaries under which behavior by doctors and firms could remain unpunished. The government could also reinforce the market by directly providing or enticing private parties to improve and disclose the best information possible.

An alternative approach would suggest that because the market is unreliable for these purposes, it is preferable to introduce a centralized regulatory agency. This alternative course of action is likely to be taken when the perceived risks of relying on the market remains very high. The U.S. pharmaceutical drug history demonstrates this latter approach; today the U.S. government shares major responsibility for negative health consequences that could arise from the marketing of risky drugs. The first law regulating pharmaceuticals was the Pure Food and Drug Act of 1906. This law prohibited adulteration and mislabelling of food and drugs. The aim of the law was to improve the quality of information, and the role of government was essentially to prosecute violators and, when necessary, withdraw their products from the market.

In 1938, the Food, Drug and Cosmetic Act tightened regulations on pharmaceutical drugs. The law was passed after several hundred children died as a consequence of the combination of sulfanilamide and the poisonous diethylene glycol, which had been marketed without toxicity tests. The new law required firms to submit a new drug application (NDA) to the Food and Drug Administration (FDA), demonstrating that the drug was safe. The application was automatically approved in 60 days unless the FDA recommended otherwise. These regulations remained unchanged until 1962.

In spite of the tighter regulations between 1938 and 1962, R&D continued to increase and during those years major medical discoveries – particularly in the area of antibiotics – were introduced. In fact, in terms of profits, the pharmaceutical industry was one of the best performers. The performance was so visible that in the early 1960s, Senator Estes Kefauver began a series of Congressional hearings with the aim of reducing the market abuses of pharmaceutical drug companies which were claimed to be associated with patent rights. Senator Kefauver advocated the introduction of compulsory licensing. At the same time, the thalidomide case occurred, and the nature of the discussions on the pharmaceutical industry shifted from one of market abuses to one of product safety. In 1962 the Kefauver-Harris Amendment to the Food, Drug and Cosmetic Act of 1938 was passed. The major provisions of the Amendment include a requirement of efficacy and the establishments of FDA regulatory controls. Furthermore, the provision to approve a new drug application within 60 days was repealed; the FDA is now quite free to take whatever is necessary for approving a drug.[8]

2. Consequences of the 1962 Drug Safety Regulations

The new regulations have made the U.S. government switch from a role of legislating for improving market performance to one of regulating directly via the FDA. As a consequence, the duration and stringency of the tests that the FDA requires for approving new drugs increased considerably. The average industrial phase of testing for toxicology and effectiveness is estimated to be 6.4 years. It is only after 2 to 15 volumes of material and 10 to 100 volumes of raw data that the firm is ready to submit to the FDA an application for approval.

In 1963, the average time it took the FDA to decide on a new drug was 14 months. By 1979, the average time had increased to 35 months and in 1986 wit was 37 months. As a consequence of the increased and lengthier tests, the average time to develop a new drug from start to market is around 10 years – a major factor in reducing effective patent protection – and the average cost per approved pharmaceutical drug has increased to US$125 million.[9] This cost includes those associated with all (successful and unsuccessful) new chemical entities that begin clinical testing.

The regulations also had severe consequences on the productivity of R&D. For example, after 1962, the number of new drugs marketed in the United States declined from around 50 per year to 20 in 1986. Some observers have attributed this decline to the depletion of research opportunities, but the bulk of the evidence suggests that this was primarily associated with the 1962 regulations. This is borne out not only by time-series analysis made by the United States but also by cross-section analysis.

The consumer loss from lower drug innovations as well as the fact that even approved drugs are introduced with an important lag in relation to other countries can be substantial. The counterpart benefits of the new drug regulations have apparently been small. For example, Peltzman (1974) has estimated that the cost of avoiding the introduction of ineffective drugs could be four times higher than the benefits that would accrue if more and faster introduction of drugs were allowed.

The question has also been looked at in an international perspective by comparing the United States with Europe, which has less stringent regulations. Perhaps because of this, between 1964 and 1975, Europe discontinued the marketing of five drugs. The benefits for the United States of not having introduced these drugs – because Europe learned before of the risks – has not been estimated, but there is agreement that these benefits probably have been small.[10] An indicative and serious case, in terms of health consequences in the United States, was Zomax, a prescription painkiller. After more than two years this product was withdrawn from the U.S. market in early 1983 when reports showed that severe allergy reactions could occur. Later, in 1985, a study by the FDA concluded that Zomax had probably been a factor in 14 deaths and in 403 life-threatening reactions. This case led to numerous litigations against McNeil Pharmaceutical, a subsidiary of Johnson and Johnson, and the producer of Zomax (Washington Post, 25 October 1988). The conclusion from this is that, in spite of heavy regulations, health risks continue to exist. There also is little evidence that the consumer benefits in the United States, where regulations apparently are much stricter, are higher than in other countries.

Finally, it could be argued that more stringent regulations have reduced the number of ineffective drugs being introduced into the market. While this might be true, it appears that the proportion of ineffective to total new drugs did not decline after 1962.[11]

In summary, the evidence for the United States shows that increased regulations have had a clear impact on the average time it takes from the moment when research on a new chemical compound starts until the moment when the FDA approves the new drug for marketing.[12] This has reduced the effective patent protection and today the protection is much shorter for the pharmaceutical industry than it is for other industries. In addition, several institutional changes introduced during the 1980s have facilitated competition from generic drugs. This, plus the fact that patents are a powerful instrument for sustaining drug prices, implies that the rate of profit per dollar of R&D must have declined with the extension of generic drug competition.

V. INCREASING COMPETITION FROM GENERIC DRUGS

During the 1980s, there have been a number of policy changes which have facilitated competition from generic drug companies in the United States. Subsection 1 below reviews some of these policies, and Subsection 2 reviews the impact of generic drug competition on prices.

1. Institutional Changes and Generic Drug Competition

Traditionally, the R&D-intensive pharmaceutical firms could count on a number of institutions for lengthening the impact of patent protection after their expiration. First, anti-substitution laws meant the pharmacist could sell to customers only the brand prescribed by the physician. These laws in effect extended the effective patent life beyond the legal life. In fact, the first entrant into a new drug market had a privilege that in some cases extended the monopoly position well beyond the statutory patent duration (Gorecki, 1986; Comanor, 1986; McRae, *et al.*, 1985). This situation was facilitated by misinformation or underinformation to the consumer, who takes decisions based fundamentally on what his/her physician and pharmacist recommend (Hall, 1986). Such recommendations can overcome important price differentials which usually develop between brand-names and generic drugs.

The 1984 Patent Restoration Act – to be discussed below – which facilitated the introduction of generic drugs, came at around the same time that other institutional changes were being introduced. First, the elimination of anti-substitution laws in practically all U.S. states permitted the pharmacist to suggest to the client the existence of a generic equivalent to the prescribed drug. The consumer choice can only be avoided when the physician explicitly prescribes that the patent should consume a drug from a specific company.

Other U.S. policies which foster the consumption of generics are cost-containment policies, such as limited reimbursement lists. Also, Medicaid programs and even private insurance companies, are recommending the use of generics. All this implies that, in general, once patent protection expires, competition from the generic-producing companies becomes important as soon as the FDA approves these drugs for marketing; in fact, as will be seen, the 1984 Patent Act reduced FDA regulations for generic drug approval. To quote "... The experience of two leading pharmaceuticals, Valium and Inderal, that have experienced generic competition for the first time this year illustrates these trends.

These two drugs have lost approximately one quarter of their respective market shares on new prescriptions to generic products selling at price discounts of 20 per cent or more. This has occurred within the first three months of generic availability. Another leading pharmaceutical, Indocin, has lost approximately half its market share in only its second year of generic competition. These rates of sales' losses are far in excess of historical patterns in pharmaceuticals, or what was experienced only a few years ago . . ." (Grabowski and Vernon, 1989).

The extent of competition from generic drugs is apparently much more important than that which these two cases show. For example, the combined U.S. market share of the 13 widely prescribed generic drugs has increased during the 1980s from around 30 to 60 per cent of total drug sales.[13] This trend is expected to increase as patents on major selling drugs expire in the early 1990s.

The R&D-intensive pharmaceutical firms can overcome this competition by increasing patent duration and/or by becoming more productive, i.e., by introducing drugs in the market at a faster rate. The figures show that the productivity of R&D continues to remain stagnant. For example, according to reports by the PMA, between 1984 – when effective patent duration was extended – and 1989, R&D by the U.S. pharmaceutical industry increased from a little less than US$4 billion to 7.3 billion. In spite of this, for years the trend in the annual number of new drugs approved by the FDA has not changed significantly.[14] In part, this should be attributed to the lag between initial research and final FDA approval. If the productivity of R&D in the drug industry continues to remain stable, competition from the generic drug industry will be likely to continue to increase. For example, it is estimated that the market of major drugs whose patents will expire during the 1990s is around US$10 billion and an important part of this market will be lost to generic drugs.[15]

2. The Impact of Generic Competition on Drug Prices

Disentangling the role of patents on drug prices is a difficult task, particularly which other regulations – including price controls – are imposed. Furthermore, although patents provide a monopoly, prices will also reflect the extent of competition among different patented drugs in given therapeutic classes. In spite of the difficulties of analyzing the impact of patents on drug prices, two patterns tend to appear quite neatly. First, generic drug prices are well below brand-name prices; also, an important share of the market is taken by generic drugs. Second, the price of drugs appears to be systematically lower in countries that do not provide patent protection for pharmaceuticals.

(a) The impact of generics on drug prices. It has often been noticed that generic drugs enter the market at high discounts *vis-à-vis* the brand-names. The extent of such price differentials is best studied in markets with free prices. In this regard, the United States is generally believed to have one of the freest pharmaceutical drug markets in the world.[16] For example, Scherer (p. 390) reports that for many years Pfizer sold the antibiotic Tetracycline at US$30.60 per 100 capsules. When Pfizer's patent was challenged, competing firms sold the generic product at US$2.50 per bottle. Furthermore, Schere asserts that many ". . .

similar cases of price-cost-margins in order of 90 percent for patented drug products have been identified. . . ."

Other examples illustrate the impact of generic drug introduction. One hundred tablets of 2mg pills of Valium are wholesale priced at around US$30, while the generic Diazepan sells for around US$15. One hundred tablets of 600mg pills of Motrin are wholesale priced at around US$25, while the generic Ibuprofen is priced at around US$14. Another example, made by the President of the American Association of Retired Persons, asserts that its members pay US$15.95 for a three-month supply of Bolar's version of Dyazide and US$31.95 for the Smith Kline brand-name product. The same source asserted that there might be a ten-to-one difference in the price of different arthritis drugs (*The Wall Street Journal*, 6 September 1989). Similar price differences are found in many other examples of drugs that have gone off patents such as Aldomet, Amixil, Inderal, etc.[17]

Finally, major reductions in drug prices after patent expiration have also been reported in other countries. For example, Taylro and Silberston report that ". . . U.K. price reductions of the order of a quarter to a half or more have been noted at this stage of the life-cycle of important patented drugs." (Taylor and Siblertson.)

In conclusion, over time patents appear to be a major factor in sustaining drug prices. Also, the appearance of generic competition is a significant factor in bringing these prices closer to marginal production costs (see also U.S. Congress, 1986); the market becomes more competitive, not perfectly competitive.

(b) The cross-country evidence. Prices of pharmaceuticals also differ significantly among countries. Table 4 shows a cross-country comparison of an index of 1975 prices of identical packages of pharmaceutical products. After fitting a simple econometric model Schut and Van Bergejk concluded that a ". . . . strong positive relationship between price level and per capital GDP is found, a 10 per cent increase in per capita income being associated with on average 8 per cent higher drug prices. The implementation of direct price control measures by the government results on average in a 20 per cent price reduction, while government policies such as bulk purchasing through a centralized government agency, promotion of the use of generics and, to a lesser extent, excluding patent protection seem to be successful in lowering the general price level of pharmaceuticals." (Schut and Van Bergeijk, 1986 p. 1141.)

The ordinary least-square estimation yielded the following results:

$$P = \underset{(6.04)}{38.53} + \underset{(6.69)}{1.43}\ \frac{GDP}{N} + \underset{(1.16)}{7.08}\ PP - \underset{(-2.30)}{15.72}\ DPC - \underset{(-1.50)}{11.12}\ IPC + e$$

$$R^2 = 0.78$$

where P = price index of pharmaceuticals; GDP = gross domestic product; N = population; PP = dummy for patent protection; DPC = dummy for price controls; and IPC = dummy for indirect price-control measures.

Looking at the econometric results – according to which the patent dummy variable was not statistically significant – one might be tempted to conclude that

TABLE 4 *Cross-country prices index of pharmaceuticals (1975)*

Country	Price Index Pharmaceuticals	Country	Price Index Pharmaceuticals
Malawi*	60.83	Ireland*	73.58
Kenya*	50.63	Hungary	57.25
India	31.71	Poland	53.98
Pakistan	38.76	Italy	69.01
Sri Lanka*	15.22	Spain	69.68
Zambia*	96.58	United Kingdom*	71.19
Thailand	48.01	Japan	81.88
Philippines*	51.14	Austria	139.53
South Korea*	35.10	Netherlands*	137.29
Malaysia	70.74	Belgium*	101.73
Colombia	48.07	France*	91.56
Jamaica*	46.13	Luxemburg*	100.27
Brazil	63.83	Denmark*	157.56
Mexico	69.68	Germany (F.R.)*	152.52
Yugoslavia	48.24	United States*	100.00
Iran	70.42	Uruguay	69.95

*Listed in Schut and Van Bergejk as providing patent protection.
Source: Schut and Van Bergeijk (1986, Table 2). Patent information for 1988 and WIPO (1988).

in terms of pharmaceutical prices, developing countries would neither suffer nor benefit from patent policies. But the low statistical significance of the patent dummy variable can be explained by at least three factors. First, the authors do not distinguish between patent protection for pharmaceutical products and processes. For example, the authors listed South Korea and Zambia as providing patent protection for pharmaceuticals when, in fact, they only provide such protection to processes. More importantly, the authors do not provide an idea of the extent of regulations; one could presume that the price-control dummy variable picks up part of the impact of patents, i.e., dismantling price controls would result in a relatively higher price increase of patented drugs. Finally, one would expect patent protection to have particularly strong price effects in countries where the law clearly stands in favor of the patent holder. It is far from clear whether in developing countries patent rights are strongly protected by the law (see, for example, Gadbaw and Richards, 1988).

Probably, the most that can be concluded from the figures in Table 4 is that the industrial countries which enforced patent protection (the United Kingdom, the Netherlands, Belgium, France, Luxemburg, Denmark, Germany and the United States) also showed high prices of pharmaceutical products. In contrast, developing countries paid prices for pharmaceuticals which on average were only 42 per cent of those paid in industrial countries providing patent protection.

Furthermore, industrial countries like Italy and Japan, that in 1975 did not provide patent protection for pharmaceuticals, also showed quite a high price of pharmaceuticals. This observation lends support to the assertion that pharmaceutical companies charge what the market will bear.

Summing up, the previous section showed how increasing regulation had reduced effective patent life. In spite of this, investment in R&D by the industry has continued to increase, but productivity – measured in new drug approvals – continues to stagnate. In this section it has been argued that a number of institutional changes have facilitated competition from the generic drug industry and that generally such competition has a major downward effect on drug prices. Thus, the trend that emerges is one where the profits of the R&D-intensive pharmaceutical industry are squeezed by the double effect of government regulations and generic drug competition.[18] What strategies have the industry followed in order to confront this situation?

VI. STRATEGIES OF THE R&D-INTENSIVE PHARMACEUTICAL INDUSTRY

The R&D-intensive pharmaceutical industry has followed a number of strategies in order to overcome the negative impact of the factors discussed in the previous section. These strategies can be classified as market-based or policy-determined.

1. Market-Based Competition Strategies

A market-based competition strategy should be understood as a strategy that is developed and implemented within a stable framework of regulations and incentives. Based on this interpretation, the R&D-intensive pharmaceutical industry has developed a number of strategies. First, several brand-name companies have decided to produce generic drugs themselves. This has been done, among others, by Squibb, Warner-Lambert, American Cynamid and Ciba-Gigy. It has been estimated that these companies now supply 25 per cent of the prescription for generic versions of drugs that have had patents expire since 1980 (*The Wall Street Journal*, 6 September 1989, p. B1).

Another strategy has been to request the FDA to reclassify some of their patented drugs from prescription drugs to over-the-counter drugs. This would familiarize the customer with the medicine before patent expiration, thus reducing the extent of generic competition once the patent expires.

Other strategies have included mergers. Probably 1989 witnessed one of the most active merger years in the history of the pharmaceutical industry. The most visible mergers were those between Bristol Meyers and Squibb from the United States, with combined annual sales of US$3.8 billion, and Smith Kline Beckman from the United States and Beecham from the United Kingdom (now Smith Kline Beecham) with sales of US$3.6 billion. A common factor underlying this industrial restructuring appears to be the increasing costs of R&D.[19] It would seem that many firms now consider that size is a most important factor in overcoming the barriers imposed by high R&D costs and also to benefit from economies of scale that apparently exist in the R&D process. These mergers would therefore increase the probability of coming up with new drugs with important market potential. While this is true, a declining number of pharmaceutical companies and increasing concentration might eventually affect competition – among other things – by reducing the number of competing drugs within therapeutic classes (Jadlow, *et al.*, 1987).[20]

2. Policy-Determined Strategies

In addition to the market-based competition strategies that the pharmaceutical industry has developed, it has also organized itself to lobby and seek for higher rents through policy changes. The industry has a powerful argument, namely, that the social rate of return of its investments in R&D is high. It is useful to quote Mansfield on his views of rates of return to innovation in the U.S. industry generally: ". . . practically all of the studies carried out to date indicate that the average social rate of return also seems high, generally in the neighbourhood of 30 to 50 per cent. As in the case of studies cited in the previous section, there is a variety of very important problems and limitations inherent in each of these studies. But recognizing this fact, it nonetheless is remarkable that so many independent studies based on so many types of data in so consistent a set of conclusions . . ." (Mansfield, 1986).

This conclusion implies that a marginal increase in R&D would be beneficial to society. In order to have the incentive to do this, the industry needs to appropriate a greater share of the rents produced by its innovations. This can be done in a number of ways but most importantly by seeking longer patent protection at home and stronger patent protection abroad. Section II reviewed the discussion of patent policies of developing countries; this section will review the subject in industrial countries. In addition, the industry seeks to obtain other preferential policies such as subsidies for R&D, additional funds for the FDA to accelerate the drug approval process, increasing the regulatory barriers to market generics by making the bioequivalency test between different brands come closer to one another, less stringent cost contaminant policies, less supervision on private sector pricing policies, lobbying against proposals for compulsory licensing, making it easier to transform prescription drugs to over the counter drugs, reduction in the burden of regulations for drug approval, etc.[21]

As the time required for approval of new drugs increased, and the patent office continued to arrive at a decision much faster than the FDA, the average effective patent life declined. For example, Eisman and Wardell (1981) estimated an average effective patent life for new pharmaceutical drugs of 13.6 years and 9.5 years in 1966 and 1979 respectively. This appears to be lower than in other countries. For example, for a common sample of drugs, in the United States it took from the initial stage to FDA approval an average of 10.5 years, while it averaged only 5.4 years in other countries (Mossinghoff, 1987).

As the effective patent duration declines so does the private rate of return to R&D and the incentive to undertake this type of activity. In September 1984, after many years of lobbying by the industry, the Drug Price Competition and Patent Restoration Act was passed as U.S. law. It has two major components.

First, it restores part of the patent life which drugs had lost as the pre-market testing process by firms and the FDA – as a consequence of the 1962 reforms – lengthened. It should be mentioned that this is the first time since 1861 that the patent terms in the United States have been changed, and it changed in favor of one industry. The second major change of the Act is that it facilitates the entry of generic drugs.

The extension of patent life provided by the new law is equal to the sum of the drug application review time by the FDA plus one half of the clinical testing time. The maximum extension is five years and no extension beyond 14 years of effective patent life will be allowed. For the drugs introduced in the U.S. market between 1976 and 1981 the average effective patent life – had the law been applied during those years – would have increased from 8.9 to 11.8 years, i.e. by 33 per cent.

This is a significant increase and had other things remained unchanged, the measure would have boosted the returns to R&D. But the other legislative change, facilitating the introduction of generic drugs into the market, has apparently compensated the R&D incentive effects of longer effective patent duration. Under the new law, a generic drug company can market a product by demonstrating to the FDA that the drug is bioequivalent to the original one. This is a low-cost experiment which contrasts with the lengthy and costly tests these generic companies were required to undertake. Because the tests undertaken by the original innovator were confidential, the FDA required similar tests by the generic drug company. But by demonstrating bioequivalency, these tests are not necessary, the new law has thus not only facilitated the introduction of generics but also eliminated duplicative testing.

What has been the impact of the 1984 Patent Restoration Act? In terms of the long-run incentives for R&D, the Act does not appear to have had a significant effect. Under different assumptions regarding the extent of the loss of sales to generic drugs, Grabowski and Vernon (1989) estimated that the returns to R&D of the innovative pharmaceutical firms, contingent upon the changes introduced by the new law, remained, on average, quite unchanged; the faster generic drug approval process approximately counteracted the R&D incentives of longer effective patent duration. Nevertheless, in the short run, the new regulations facilitating the approval of generics has implied that these drugs have taken a significant share of the market. In the aggregate, it was mentioned above that the combined U.S. market share of the 13 widely prescribed generic drugs has increased during the 1980s from around 30 to 60 per cent. More specifically, the generic drugs share in total prescriptions is now higher than 50 per cent in the following therapeutic classes: cardiovascular, anti-diabetes, tranquilizers, anti-arthritis, antibiotics and analgesics (HKS, 1990). Summing up, a global analysis of the industry concludes that the short-run impact of the 1984 Patent Restoration Act has favored the generic drug companies (Kaitin, *et al.*, 197).

Pharmaceutical firms of other countries have not remained passive to changes in U.S. regulations and patent protection. For example, for some time the major EC pharmaceutical firms have been pressing the European Commission for longer patent protection. These firms claimed that longer effective patent protection in the United States and Japan, as well as longer gestation periods attributable to increasing regulations, makes the extension of effective patent protection necessary. The European Commission is now studying legislation that would extend such protection by two years and legislation providing this or higher protection is likely to be approved in 1990.

Finally, it can be noted that the further apart in time – from the moment research on a new drug starts – a dollar of income is earned, the lower the present value. Thus, for the same amount of time gained, a dollar of income from shortening the length of FDA regulations is worth more than a dollar of income gained from longer patent protection; it should also be remembered that such a dollar is earned at the end of the patent life. Likewise, for any given drug, one dollar of earnings from the introduction of patent protection in developing countries is worth more than one dollar of earnings from the extension of patent protection in industrial countries.

Summing up, this section has shown that the R&D-intensive industry has developed a set of complex strategies in order to meet competition from the generic drug industry. Part of this strategy is market-oriented, but an important part is also policy-determined. The industry is a highly regulated one, and each regulation is a source of negotiations between the industry and the government; over time, this dynamic interaction between industry and government knits the web and nature of regulations. But among all of the regulations, patent protection stands high on the agenda of the industry; patents sustain very high drugs prices. In turn, these profits finance R&D whose output provides tomorrow's competitive edge. Section II showed the pressures the industrial countries put on developing countries for increasing patent protection to pharmaceutical drugs; this section has shown that within industrial countries such protection has already been granted. Nevertheless, the time dimension of patents suggests that for similar levels of income, the introduction of patent protection in developing countries is worth more to brand-name companies than the extension of patent protection in industrial countries.

VII. FINAL REMARKS

This article has offered a discussion on the question of why there are pressures on developing countries for introducing and/or reinforcing patent protection to pharmaceutical drugs. The story is that patent protection is an important component of a complex strategy developed by the R&D-intensive pharmaceutical drug companies of industrial countries to meet market competition. For legal and economic reasons, patents – as the article shows – are fundamental instruments for allowing the drug-inventing companies to appropriate the returns from their innovations. Patents sustain high prices, which in turn provide rents to undertake further R&D, which in turn allows the invention of new drugs, etc., etc. In recent years, increasing drug regulations have implied that effective patent protection to the R&D-intensive pharmaceutical drug companies has eroded. Furthermore, competition from the generic drug companies has increased quite significantly. Finally, the potential size of developing countries' markets for patented drugs is no longer trivial. Thus, restoring patent protection in industrial countries and making developing countries introduce patent protection, has become part – albeit an important part – of R&D-intensive pharmaceutical companies' strategies to regain market share.

NOTES

The author would like to express his appreciation for comments received from Bela Balassa and Paul Meo.

1 Other products and/or processes that are quite often excluded from patent protection are animal varieties, methods for treatment of human or animal body, plant varieties, biological processes for producing animal or plant varieties, food products and computer programs (WIPO, 1988).

2 An asterisk indicates that patents for pharmaceutical processes are also excluded.

3 This particular set of parameter values includes the productivity of research and development (R&D) which is expected to differ quite significantly among industries and countries.

4 Brazil used to be on the USTR watch list, but was deleted in 1990 for having made progress in a number of issues; trade liberalization policies were an important factor. On 2 July 1990 this progress also led the United States to lift the retaliatory tariff of the Section 301 pharmaceutical case. Finally it should be said that Brazil challenged the U.S. Section 301 action in a GATT dispute settlement panel.

5 These proportions have varied quite drastically over time as economic conditions and regulatory behavior have come to benefit multinational companies or domestic companies. See for example Katz and Groisman (1988) for the case of Argentina.

6 Among the 30 largest pharmaceutical companies, 14 are from the United States, 12 are European and four from Japan (*The Financial Times*, 4 November 1989, p. 23).

7 This section draws from Grabowski and Vernon (1983).

8 The thalidomide case had world-wide implications on the nature of regulations for drugs. For a discussion of the changes introduced in the United Kingdom see Hartley, *et al.* (1966). But in spite of the changes, the U.S. regulations are believed to be among the most stringent in the world.

9 Estimated by the Pharmaceutical Manufacturers Association (*The Washington Post*, 17 November 1989, p. A–60).

10 There has also been a case of a new drug – Oraflex – that was introduced into the U.S. market and later discontinued, when in Europe – where the drug had been introduced before – it was noticed that in some cases it had severe side-effects.

11 An alternative hypothesis – suggested by Jorge Katz – is that the increased regulations and testing could have provided a further source of learning from which the industry and the population at large has benefited. As far as can be ascertained, the importance of this hypothesis remains unknown.

12 There are also reports arguing that a similar trend has occurred in the European Communities. See for example Hartley, *et al.*

13 *The Wall Street Journal*, *Genetic Drug Scandal Creates Opening*, 6 September 1989.

14 For example, during the consecutive years between 1980 and 1989, the number of new drugs approved by the FDA was 12, 27, 28, 14, 22, 30, 20, 21, 20 and 23.

15 The patents of the following major drugs will expire in the indicated year. Seldane (Dow Chemical, 1992), Tagament (Smith Kline, 1994). Zantac (Glaxo/Sandoz, 1994); Pepcid (Merck, Johnson and Johnson, 2000). Naprosyn (Syntex/Procter and Gamble, 1993); Fedene (Prizer, 1992); and Nicorette (Dow Chemical, 1992). (*The Wall Street Journal*, 5 June 1989, p. B1.)

16 This does not mean that free pricing is always allowed. See, for example, a discussion of the debate on this issue published in *The Washington Post* of 11 June 1989 (p. H1) and the recent control on the AIDS drug, AZE by which the government brought down the annual cost of treatment from US$8,000 to US$6,000.
17 One might ask what explains the post-patent pricing strategy of brand-name companies when they allow such significant price-differentials with their competing generic drugs. One plausible explanation is that over their life, brand-name drugs create a clientele of relatively wealthy doctors and patients who, in spite of low-priced generic drugs, prefer to remain loyal to the medicine they have been prescribing and taking.
18 See Joglekar and Patterson (1986) for evidence of declining profits to R&D.
19 This is often mentioned in the newspaper articles announcing the mergers. See for example: *The Financial Times*, 4 August 1989, article, *In the Grip of Takeover Fever*. Increasing drug competition within therapeutic categories has also been a factor. For example, it has been mentioned that sales of Smith Kline's anti-ulcer drug, Tagamet, was losing market to Glaxo's drug Zantac. In contrast, Beecham has two promising drugs: Eminase, for heart problems, and the anti-arthritis Reliflax (*The Wall Street Journal*, 31 July 1989), which as part of the merger agreement, Smith Kline is expecting to profit from.
20 As a consequence of these mergers, the proportion of total sales made by the four largest firms increased from 21.3 to 24.1 per cent.
21 A presentation of these demands by the U.S. industry is made in Pharmaceutical Manufacturers Association (1987).

REFERENCES

Benko, Robert, *Intellectual Property Rights and the Uruguay Round*, The World Economy, June 1988.

Braga, Carlos, Robert Evenson and William Lasser, *Intellectual Property Rights: A Survey*, The World Bank, mimeo, 1990.

Comanor, William, *The Political Economy of the Pharmaceutical Industry*, Journal of Economic Literature, September 1986.

Eismna, Martin and William Wardell, *The Decline in Effective Patent Life of New Drugs*, Research Management, January 1981.

Evenson, Robert; *Intellectual Property Rights, Inventions, Technology Purchase and Piracy in Economic Development: An International Comparative Study*, (mimeo), 1990.

Gadbaw, R. Michael, *Republic of Korea*, in Gadbaw, R. Michael and Timothy Richards (eds.), 1988.

Gadbaw, R. Michael and Timothy Richards, *Intellectual Property Rights: Global Consensus, Global Conflict?*, Westview Press, 1988.

Gorecki, Paul, *The Importance of Being First: The Case of Prescription Drugs in Canada*, International Journal of Industrial Organizations, 1986, pp. 371–395.

Grabowski, Henry and John Vernon, *The Regulation of Pharmaceuticals: Balancing the Benefits and Risks*, American Enterprises Institute, 1983.

Grabowski, Henry and John Vernon, *Longer Patents for Lower Initiation Barriers: The 1984 Drug Act*, The American Economic Review, Papers and Proceedings, May 1989.

Grinols, Earl, *Procedural Protectionism: The American Trade Bill and the New Protectionist Mode*, (mimeo), 1988.

Gwynn, Rosemary, *Mexico*, in Gadbaw and Richards (eds), 1988.

Hall, K. L., *Pharmaceuticals in the Third World: An Overview*, The World Bank, PHN Technical Note, 1986.

Hartley, K., R. Lavers and K. Maynard, *Regulation and Development Times in the U.K. Pharmaceutical Industry*, Scottish Journal of Political Economy, November 1966.

HKS (Hemant K. Shah), *HKS Genetic Drug Industry Monitor*, 1 April 1990.

Jadlow, Joseph, Janice Jadlow and Shirley Yu, *Risk, Rivalry and Innovation: The Case of Ethical Drugs, Revista Internazionale di Scienze Economiche e Commerciali*, 1987, pp. 593–608.

Joglekar Prafulla and Morton Paterson, *A Close Look at the Returns and Risks of Pharmaceutical Re-D*, Journal of Health Economics, 1986, pp. 153–177.

Katin, Keneth and A. Gene Trimble, *Implementation of the Drug Price Competition and Patent Term Restoration Act of 1984: A Progress Report*, Journal of Clinical Research and Drug Development, 1987, pp. 263–275.

Katz, Jorge and Silvio Groisman, *La Industria Formacutica en Argentina: Periodo 1983–1988*, paper presented to the *Seminario Sobre el Uso Racional de los Medicamentos*, México.

Levin, Richard C., Alvin Kelvorick, Richard Nelson and Sidney Winter, *Appropriating the Returns from Industrial Research and Development*, Brookings Paper on Economic Activity, No. 3, 1987.

Lobo, F., *La Evolucion de las Patents sober Medicamentos en los Paises Desarrollados, Sistema Economico Latinoamericano (SELA)*, mimeo, Carcas, 1988.

MacLaughlin, Janet, Timothy Richards and Leigh Kenny, *The Economic Significance of Piracy*, in Gadbaw and Richards (eds) 1988.

McRae, James and Francis Tapon, *Some Empirical Evidence on Post-Patent Barriers to Entry in the Canadian Pharmaceutical Industry*, Journal of Health Economics, 1985, pp. 43–61.

Mansfield, Edwin, *How Rapidly Does New Industrial Technology Leak Out?* Journal of Industrial Economics, December 1985.

Mansfield, Edwin, *Patents and Innovation: An Empirical Study*, Management Science, February 1986.

Mossinghoff, Gerald, *Public Policy Challenges to the Pharmaceutical Industry*, in PMA, 1987.

Nordhaus, William D., *Invention, Growth and Welfare*, MIT Press, 1969.

Nogués, Julio, *Patents, Distortions and Development*, The World Bank, PPR Working Paper Series No. 315, 1990.

Pharmaceutical Manufacturers Association, *Preserving the Environment for Innovation: The Challenge to Society and Industry*, Pharmaceutical Manufacturers Association, May 1987.

Peltzman, Sam, *Regulation of Pharmaceutical Innovation: The 1962 Amendments*, American Enterprise Institute, 1974.

Scherer, Frederick M., *Industrial Market Structure and Economic Performance*, Rand McNally, Chicago, 1980.

Sherwood, Robert, *Intellectual Property and Economic Development*, Boulder, Westview Press, 1990 (forthcoming).

Schut, Frederick and Peter Van Bergeijk, *International Price Discrimination: The Pharmaceutical Industry*, World Development, 1986, pp. 1141–1150.

Taylor, C. T. and Z. H. Silbertson, *The Economic Impact of the Patent System: A Study of the British Experience*, Cambridge University Press, 1973.

Temin, Peter, *Technology, Regulations and Market Structure in the Modern Pharmaceutical Industry*, Bell Journal of Economics, Autumn 1979.

Thalidomide: A Brighter Side, *The Economist*, 15 July 1989.

U.S. Congress, House of Representatives on Energy and Commerce, Subcommittee on Health and Environment, Prescription Drug Price Increases Serial No. 99–58, 99th Congress, 1st Session, Washington, D.C., U.S. Government Printing Office, 1986.

World Intellectual Property Organization, *Existence, Scope and Form of Generally Internationally Accepted and Applied Standard/Norms for the Protection of Intellectual Property*, WIPO, WO/Inf/29, September 1988.
WIPR (World Intellectual Property Report), South Korea, February.

11. National Sovereignty and the World Trade Organization

D. Palmeter

I. INTRODUCTION

The World Trade Organization (WTO) came into existence on 1 January 1995 as the culmination of the Uruguay Round of trade negotiations that had concluded the year before. It did not come into existence quietly. Critics as diverse as Ralph Nader on the left to Patrick Buchanan on the right, with Ross Perot somewhere in between, denounced the WTO.

Though the criticism has abated somewhat, it has hardly gone away. This criticism is based on many factors: simple protectionism; fear of the rapid change and disruption that is characteristic of the modern economy – "globalization"; concern that the WTO and the increased trade it is intended to foster will both damage the environment and limit our ability to protect it; resentment that WTO obligations may restrict us in expressing moral disapproval of some of the world's governing regimes through trade sanctions.

Many of these criticisms directly or indirectly invoke loss of national sovereignty as a concern. In particular, there is fear that the WTO, through its dispute settlement system, threatens the integrity of our laws dealing with the environment, and our sovereign right to protect our environment, as well as our health and safety. There is also outrage that WTO Agreements may limit the ability of states, such as Massachusetts, to express their sentiments with regard to human rights by refusing to purchase goods from firms that do business in countries with repressive regimes, such as Burma (Myanmar). I believe that criticisms of this kind are uninformed and that they mischaracterize the WTO and its dispute settlement process. Today I hope to induce you to agree.

The way I hope to do that is first to give you some background on the WTO and its dispute settlement process. Then, I propose to examine the actual application of WTO dispute settlement in two environmental cases, and discuss the issues presented in a pending case involving human rights issues. The first environmental case was first to go through the entire WTO process. It involved a challenge by Brazil and Venezuela to a regulation issued by the U.S. Environmental Protection Agency dealing with pollutants in gasoline. I should disclose that I advised Brazil in this matter, but I will try to keep my remarks objective. The second environmental case is a very recent one involving restrictions on the import of shrimp from countries that do not require their fishermen to use devices designed to prevent the killing of sea turtles. The human rights case concerns the Massachusetts law sanctioning companies doing business in Burma. Further disclosure: there is a constitutional challenge to the Massachusetts law presently before the federal court in Boston. My firm is involved in that challenge. The constitutional questions have no bearing on the WTO matters we will be discussing.

II. BACKGROUND

The Uruguay Round of trade negotiations that gave birth to the WTO was the eighth and final round of negotiations conducted under the auspices of the General Agreement on Tariffs and Trade, known as GATT. GATT was a multilateral trade agreement that grew out of the aftermath of World War II. In its 47 years of existence, GATT served as the forum for eight rounds of tariff-cutting negotiations, as well as a focal point for continuing contact by its Parties.

GATT was a complex agreement, but it was based on three core "constitutional" Articles, which remain fundamental in the WTO. In fact, the 1947 GATT has been brought into the WTO word for word, where it is now part of "GATT 1994". Thus, panels still wrestle with whether the matters before them are or are not consistent with GATT.

The first core constitutional provision of GATT, set out in Article I, is "most-favoured-nation" treatment, which is an unusual way of saying "normal" treatment. It means that each GATT Party, and now each WTO Member, receives the same tariff treatment as the "most favoured" Party or Member – in other words, they are treated the same. Any favour granted to one is granted to all. The second principle, set out in Article II, is tariff-binding. This is simply a promise not to raise tariffs above agreed levels. The third principle, set out in Article III, is "national treatment". It means that once foreign goods have entered the national market of another Member, once the bound tariff is paid and import formalities are completed, foreign goods will be treated the same as domestic goods for a tax and all other regulatory purposes.

These broad principles, like any broad principles, are sometimes easier to state than to apply. GATT was less than a year old when its first dispute arose, a dispute involving the most-favoured-nation obligations. One GATT party complained that another was applying a 5 percent consular tax to imports from some countries and a 2 percent tax on imports from others. Article 1 of GATT requires that "charges of any kind" be non-discriminatory, and the issue was whether consular taxes were "charges of any kind". The Chairman of the meeting at which the complaint was made ruled that they were. It was as simple as that. The official report, in its entirety, states:

> "In response to a request for an interpretation of the phrase 'charges of any kind' in paragraph 1 of Article 1 with respect to consular taxes, the Chairman ruled that such taxes would be covered by the phrase 'charges of any kind'."[1]

This is how dispute settlement began, with a simple ruling from the chair in 1948. A question arose concerning the interpretation of the Agreement, and it was resolved in a way that was acceptable to the parties by a ruling of the presiding officer. Over time, the complexity of the question increased, and the chair began to refer them to working parties composed of the disputants and any others interested in the issue. Eventually this evolved into a system of panels composed of delegates from parties not involved in the dispute who heard argument from the disputants. Still later, non-delegates, usually academics and retired government officials, began serving as panelists from time to time.

While we commonly refer to this system as "dispute settlement", that term was used only part of the time in GATT. More often, the term "conciliation" was used, reflecting GATT's diplomatic origins and the diplomatic procedures that governed it.

One characteristic of this system reflected its origin as a multi-party agreement: the requirement that concurrence of the entire membership was necessary for any action, including the adoption of dispute settlement reports. Nothing in GATT gave the chair the authority to decide that dispute in 1948. Canada's Dana Wilgress simply was in the chair when the question was raised and he ruled. Any party, most particularly the party he ruled against, could have objected. But no one did, and that was the key to the GATT dispute settlement.

Reports of working parties and, later, of panels were brought before the entire membership. Objection – usually by the losing party – was enough to prevent their adoption. Dissatisfaction with this system, primarily by the United States, led to the adoption of the WTO's Understanding on Rules and Procedures Governing the Settlement of Disputes – the "DSU."

III. WTO DISPUTE SETTLEMENT

The move from GATT to the WTO very much reflects a move away from a diplomatic approach to solving problems toward a juridical approach. Brazil's ambassador to the WTO, Celso Lafer, has used the term "thickening of legality" to describe the change.[2] Vestiges of the diplomatic remain in dispute settlement, as we shall see, and at times these have provided ammunition for critics of the WTO.

Formal dispute settlement begins with a request for consultations from the complaining party to the potential defendant. This is a relatively non-controversial remnant of the system's diplomatic heritage. The hope is that through consultations, a solution can be reached that will avoid litigation. In reality, however, in many instances extensive discussions between the governments concerned will already have occurred well before a request for formal consultations is made. Frequently, a decision to request consultations in reality is a decision to start the formal process.

If consultations do not produce a solution, the complaining party may request the Dispute Settlement Body – the DSB – to establish a panel. The WTO Secretariat presents the names of possible panelists to the parties. These names are drawn from a list of qualified individuals maintained by the Secretariat, and includes names provided by Members. If the parties cannot agree on three names, either party eventually may ask the Director-General to name the panel. This has happened on occasion, although Members generally refer to avoid it as too unpredictable.

After panelists are agreed upon or are named by the Director-General, the process begins. The parties submit written briefs and meet with the panel, and then repeat the process with rebuttal briefs and a second meeting. The panel subsequently presents an interim report to the parties, on which they may comment and point out errors. Needless to say, the losing party tends to find more errors than the prevailing party.

The panel gives whatever consideration it deems appropriate to the comments of the parties on the interim report, and then issues its final report first to the parties and, about two weeks later, to the entire membership. In theory, the interim report is confidential; it is intended to give the parties a chance to settle the case before the report is made public. But leaks to the press of the results of interim reports are notorious, and some have argued that the interim report should be eliminated. The opportunity for final negotiations provided by the interim report procedure is another vestige of the WTO's diplomatic ancestry. On at least one occasion, however, it has worked. In a dispute between Canada and the European Communities, the parties settled after they received the final report but before it was made public.

This raises what is perhaps the most common criticism of the process: confidentiality. Americans, used to government in the sunshine, to open hearings and open judicial processes, mistrust the confidentiality that prevails in WTO dispute settlement, particularly the absence of public hearings. The two meetings the panel normally holds with the parties are closed to the public. Outsiders not only may not participate as *amicus curiae*; they may not even attend and observe. All of this secrecy smacks of the Star Chamber to us.

But closed panel meetings are another vestige of the WTO's diplomatic ancestry that many Members continue to value. Those Members had little enthusiasm for following the lead of the United States and others in establishing a legalistic system in the first place. In the view of many in the WTO, a system structured more for diplomatic conciliation than for legalistic conclusions is preferable. The result was a compromise that put in place a legalistic system but retained some of the diplomatic. Clearly, a process that is viewed as an effort to conciliate works better in private than in public, even in the U.S. domestic legal system. Mediators and conciliators – who try to reconcile such disparate antagonists as warring spouses and labour and management – work in private.

If you view dispute settlement in this light, closed meetings make sense. If you view it as I do, as legal process, closed panel meetings do not make sense. But they are hardly sinister. The present system is a compromise, and like many compromises, it may not always make logical sense. Eventually, everything relevant is made public. The arguments of the parties are set out in exhaustive detail in the reports – the main reason why they are so lengthy. This language is approved by the parties themselves. And, of course, as with court opinions, the determinations of the panels are set out in detail, giving us all ample opportunity to criticize.

Once a panel report has been issued – by being circulated to all the Members of the WTO, at which time it is also released to the public – it will be adopted unless it is appealed or unless there is a consensus not to adopt. Since it is highly unlikely that the winning party would join a consensus not to adopt a decision in a case it just won, adoption is all but automatic.

This is just the opposite of the GATT system where decisions were not adopted unless there was a consensus to do so, consensus required agreement of the losing party. While the losing party agreed to adopt GATT reports in about 90 percent of the cases, a number of reports in important cases were blocked and others were adopted only after several years. Change in this system of blockage and delay was an important negotiating goal of the United States in the Uruguay Round, spelled out explicitly in the Omnibus Trade and Competitiveness Act of 1988. There is some irony in the fact that the WTO dispute settlement system is largely a result of U.S. efforts, insisted upon by a Congress many of whose members now denounce it. Perhaps that has something to do with the observation of Former Secretary Lloyd Bentsen, who, as chair of the Senate Finance Committee, had to remind his critical colleagues:

> "If we want tough rules and a just and effective dispute settlement system when we are plaintiffs in a case, we also have to live with the same rules when we are defendants."[4]

The right to appeal from a panel decision is another extremely important innovation of the Uruguay Round. There was no appeal in the GATT. The Uruguay Round negotiators believed, however, that with the new system of near automatic adoption of reports, appellate review was necessary. The Appellant Body, a semi-permanent group of seven members, three of whom serve on a particular case, was the result. There is nothing like it in the entire field of public international law. Even the International Court of Justice in The Hague is a court of first instance from which there is no appeal.

The Appellate Body reviews issues of law covered in a panel report, and legal interpretations developed by the panel. It may uphold, modify or reverse the legal findings and conclusions of the panel, and once it has done so, its report, together with the panel report as possibly modified by the appellate decision, is subject to automatic adoption unless there is consensus to the contrary.

That, in rather a large nutshell, is the WTO dispute settlement procedure in the abstract. It is now time to examine how it works in practice.

IV. UNITED STATES – STANDARDS FOR REFORMULATED AND CONVENTIONAL GASOLINE

On 1 January 1995, the day the WTO came into existence, a regulation issued by the Environmental Protection Agency (EPA) known as the Gasoline Rule, also became effective. The Gasoline Rule implemented a portion of the Clean Air Act by setting quality standards for gasoline. These quality standards encompassed many properties of gasoline, such as maximum content for sulfur and benzene, minimum content for oxygen, maximum rate of evaporation, and several performance requirements designed to reduce or limit emissions of volatile organic compounds, toxic air pollutants, and nitrogen oxides. The regulation required the use of "reformulated" gasoline in major metropolitan areas, such as Los Angeles, where air pollution from auto emissions was severe. In the rest of the country, "conventional" gasoline could continue to be used. Congress was concerned, however, that producers of cleaner reformulated gasoline would just dump the pollutants removed in its production into the remaining conventional gasoline, thereby merely moving the pollution around rather than reducing it. So Congress specified that all conventional gasoline had to meet a statutory baseline based on average 1990 gasoline quality. This would prevent the impurities removed from reformulated gasoline being dumped into conventional gasoline. EPA was directed to implement this requirement by regulation.

The logical way for EPA to proceed would have been simply to require that all gasoline met the average 1990 standard. But EPA was faced with a political problem. Meeting a single, uniform standard would be far easier for some refiners in the United States than for others. All domestic refineries are located in someone's congressional district and in someone's state, which means that at least one Member of the House of Representatives and two Senators would not be pleased if an EPA regulation resulted in the shutting down of a local refinery, with the loss of its jobs, and a possible increase in the price of gasoline in the area.

This phenomenon did not escape the notice of the EPA. The Agency was charged with issuing a regulation that would ensure that gasoline quality by 1 January 1995 was at least as good as the average quality of 1990. But not all gasoline produced in 1995 could meet the average of all gasoline in 1990. So the EPA hit upon an ingenious idea: each refiner would be required, on average, to produce gasoline that met its own, individual 1990 average. If every refinery produced to its own 1990 average, then the quality of 1995 production normally could be expected to meet the overall 1990 average.

Two factors could interfere with this result. One would be if the market shares of the domestic refiners in 1995 and subsequent years differed from their 1990 shares. The other was imports. The EPA addressed both problems with the same measure. It provided that for the domestic refiners, their individual baselines would apply only up to the amount produced by that refinery in 1990. Production above that amount would be subject to the simple statutory baseline that the averages were calculated to reach. This was not foolproof, of course, because if one refiner reduced its production below its 1990 levels, that alone would change the overall mix. But the EPA considered this to be a remote possibility at best.

With imports, the EPA did not believe it could effectively apply its 1990 individual baseline methodology to foreign refiners. It expressed doubt that foreign refiners had the records necessary to establish the qualities of their 1990 gasoline, and it expressed doubt that it had the ability to audit the foreign refiners even if they had the data.

Another, more likely, reason slipped out during congressional hearings on the Gasoline Rule. Mary Nichols of the EPA told a Senate Committee that one of the reasons she had not followed a staff recommendation that foreign refiners be given individual baselines was that the regulation was hard enough on the domestic petroleum companies and "that it was appropriate, if we had a choice, to lean in the direction of doing something that would favour their competitive position *vis-à-vis* the [foreigners]."[5] In any event, while the United States imported large volumes of crude petroleum, imports of finished gasoline were comparatively small, less than 5 percent of the market. So the EPA applied the statutory baseline to all imported gasoline.

Brazil and Venezuela, the major foreign suppliers of gasoline to the United States, objected. The Gasoline Rule, they argued, was inconsistent with the national treatment requirements of GATT because it treated imports less favourably than domestic gasoline. The United States denied the claim, arguing that the Rule did not treat imports less favorably and, even if it did, it was excused by Article XX of the GATT, which permits the use of measures otherwise inconsistent with GATT's requirements if, among other things, they are necessary to protect human, animal or plant life or health; or if they relate to the conservation of exhaustible natural resources.

The first argument was based on the fact that since the statutory baseline applied to imports represented the average that the individual baselines were intended to meet, imports, on average, were treated no less favourably than domestic production, on average. The panel rejected the argument. While the averages might be the same, the panel reasoned, the components were not treated in the same manner. Imported gasoline that was chemically identical with domestic gasoline would not be permitted under the Rule. This was a denial of national treatment, and was not overcome by the fact that some domestic gasoline, which exceeded the baseline requirements applied to imports, also would not meet the EPA's standard because it did not measure up to the individual baseline requirements applicable to its producer.

The panel also rejected the argument that the Rule was "necessary" to protect human, plant or animal life or health. While no doubt it contributed to the wellbeing of humans, plants and animals, it was not "necessary" in the sense that there were no viable alternatives, such as applying the same standard to both imports and domestic production.

The more difficult issue was so-called "XX(g)" issue, which also figured importantly in the other environmental case we will be discussing, the one that concerns U.S. restrictions on the import of shrimp. Article XX permits measures that otherwise would be inconsistent with WTO/GATT obligations if the measures qualify for any one of ten listed exemptions, and if they are consistent with the Preamble to Article XX. Paragraph (g) of Article XX exempts measures "relating to the conservation of exhaustible natural resources if such measures are made effective in conjunction with restrictions on domestic production or consumption."

A 1988 GATT panel report, on a U.S. claim against Canada, held that the phrase "relating to" in Article XX(g) should be interpreted to mean "primarily aimed at". None of the parties in the *Gasoline* case disputed this interpretation. Brazil and Venezuela adopted it for the obvious reason that it is a far tougher standard for the United States to meet than "relating to". The United States was in the awkward position of not being able to oppose a legal interpretation it previously had advanced with success. The panel concluded that the Gasoline Rule was not "primarily aimed" at the conservation of an exhaustible natural resource because the "baseline establishment methods at issue in this case were not primarily aimed at the conservation of natural resources."[6]

The panel said that it saw no connection between the less favourable treatment of imported gasoline that was chemically identical to domestic gasoline, and the objective of improving air quality in the United States. Further, the panel reasoned, treating imports the same as domestic production would not hinder the United States in its pursuit of conservation policies.

The Appellate Body disagreed. The question was not, it held, whether the less favourable treatment was primarily aimed at the conservation of a resource, but whether the measure itself was. The measure, the Appellate Body held, was the Gasoline Rule itself and it most certainly was primarily aimed at the conservation of an exhaustible natural resource, namely clean air.

In most legal systems, that would have ended the work of the appellate tribunal. The case would have been remanded to the lower tribunal for any further proceedings necessary. In this case, the remand order would have instructed the panel to consider the other claims of Brazil and Venezuela which had not been addressed by the panel because, having reached a decision on one ground, the panel did not consider the additional claims, But the WTO Appellate Body does not possess remand authority. Consequently, it went ahead itself with the analysis that normally would be conducted by the panel on remand, and quickly reached the Preamble to Article XX, called, in the francophone civil-law world of Geneva, the *chapeau*. This introduction to the ten specified exceptions, such as measures that relate to exhaustible natural resources, requires that the measures not be applied in a manner that would constitute a means of arbitrary or unjustifiable discrimination or a disguised restriction on international trade. The Gasoline Rule, the Appellate Body held, failed this test. The discrimination was arbitrary and unjustifiable and, in the view of the Appellate Body, amounted to a disguised restriction on international trade.

Both sides declared victory, the United States because its Article XX(g) appeal was upheld, Brazil and Venezuela because the Appellate Body upheld the findings of the panel in their favour. The question was, what would the United States do about it. The United States had three options:

(i) it could ignore the report;
(ii) it could leave the regulation as it was and offer to compensate the complainants for their lost trade with lower tariffs on other products; or
(iii) it could bring the measure into conformity.

There were two ways it could bring the measure into conformity:

(i) apply the statutory baseline applicable to imports to domestic production; or
(ii) make individual baselines available to foreign refiners on terms no less favourable then those available to domestic refiners.

If the United States chose to do nothing, Brazil and Venezuela eventually would have been permitted to retaliate against U.S. exports – "suspend concessions" in WTO parlance. The right to do this has provoked the ire of critics who set it as the club with which the WTO beats the United States into surrendering its sovereignty. It is no such thing, as I will point out shortly.

Negotiating compensation presents two difficulties: first, the other party has to agree to it, and second, compensation which lowers tariffs on other products is likely to be greeted with less than total enthusiasm by the domestic industry making those products. Imagine the U.S. Trade Representative explaining to an industry why the United States had agreed to lower tariffs on its products in order to keep in place a discriminatory rule that favoured the oil industry.

Applying the statutory baseline to domestic production as well as to imports would have been contrary to the reason for the entire Rube Goldberg rule in the first place: the domestic refiners did not want to have to meet that standard. That left application of the domestic rule to imports, and that is what the EPA did. After fifteen months, it published a revised rule in the Federal Register.

But the story is not over. An association of domestic gasoline refiners and an independent importer have challenged the new rule as contrary to the requirements of domestic administrative law. The case is presently before the U.S. Court of Appeals for the District of Columbia. We shall soon see whether there is to be another chapter in this story.

V. UNITED STATES – IMPORT PROHIBITION OF CERTAIN SHRIMP AND SHRIMP PRODUCTS

The second environmental case we will look at dealt with regulations issued by the Department of State implementing the Endangered Species Act. These regulations required the use of turtle-excluding devices (TEDS) in nets used by ships trawling for shrimp. They applied first to U.S. shrimp and later to shrimp caught in the Caribbean and western Atlantic. However, the U.S. Court of International Trade ruled that limitation of the TED requirement to the Caribbean and western Atlantic was contrary to the statute. Accordingly, in 1996 the TED requirement was imposed on a world-wide basis. This chronology had a decisive impact on the ultimate resolution of the case by the WTO Appellate Body.

India, Pakistan, Thailand, and Malaysia, four suppliers subject to the 1996 world-wide extension of the TED requirement, argued that the ban on their exports was inconsistent with Article XI of the GATT, which broadly prohibits import bans, and that the action could not be justified under Article XX. The United States appealed the panel's conclusions with regard to Article XX. The Appellate Body affirmed the result reached by the panel, although, as with *Gasoline*, with a different legal approach. The panel had said that its duty was to determine whether that type of measure, if adopted by other Members, would threaten the world trading system. The panel found that it would, because this could mean that Members would be required to comply with conflicting measures at the same time. In other words, if instead of reaching an international agreement on whether and how sea turtles and other endangered species should be protected, each Member made its own rules and then required every other nation to follow them, there would no longer be an international system. There would be chaos.

The Appellate Body concluded that the panel ruled too broadly. The import ban, which the United States acknowledged was inconsistent with Article XI, was not excused by Article XX, in the view of the Appellate Body, simply because it discriminated. The *chapeau* of Article XX, the Appellate Body noted, does not permit discrimination between countries where the same conditions prevail, yet the import ban did not take into account any of the conditions which might have prevailed in the territories of other Members. Further, it said, shrimp caught by methods identical to those employed in the United States were excluded simply because they were caught in waters of countries that had not been certified by the United States as having a TEDS programme. In addition, the United States negotiated agreements with one group of countries, those in the greater Caribbean area, but not with others. This was discrimination against the others.

This last point may be the key to calm resolution of this matter. The reason for the discriminatory pattern of negotiations was that, initially, the State Department interpreted the statute as requiring action only as to the countries in the greater Caribbean area. However, State was sued by some environmental organizations and was ordered by the Court to apply the embargo on a global basis. Thus, there was virtually not time for State to negotiate with the complaining countries.

But, from State's point of view, there was a *Deus ex Machina*. The Appellate Court reversed the judgment of the lower Court, thus giving the State Department a freer hand for the time being. Possibly, just possibly, the time can be used to reach a broader agreement on how best to save sea turtles, which might include ways other than ways particular to the United States. It is worth noting in this regard that the complaining countries claimed that they too had taken measures to protect turtles and that these measures, applied in the conditions that prevailed in these territories, were more protective of turtles than TEDS.

The United States will be given time to implement the ruling. In most cases that time has been fifteen months. During that period, the government will consult with Congress and interested groups, and then reach a decision.

VI. MYANMAR (BURMA) SANCTIONS

Moral revulsion with the Burmese military dictatorship and admiration for the pro-democracy activities of Nobel Laureate Aung San Suu Kyi understandably have prompted many to want to express their revulsion and their admiration. In 1996, the Commonwealth of Massachusetts expressed itself with a law that restricts state authorities and state agencies in procuring goods and services from any person doing business in Myanmar. It does so by imposing an automatic price penalty of 10 percent on bids for state purchases from companies doing business in or with Myanmar.

If the citizens of Massachusetts choose to adopt such a policy – and put their money where their collective mouth is by paying more for state-purchased goods than they otherwise might – who is to question them? Well, the European Communities and Japan question them, and, after months of negotiations, early last month they asked for the establishment of a dispute settlement panel to consider the Massachusetts sanctions.

Both the EC and Japan contend that the Masschusetts sanctions are inconsistent with the provisions of the WTO Agreement on Government

Procurement. A look at the basis of those allegations will bring the issue of sovereignty into perspective, both as it might apply to that dispute and as it applies generally, including the environmental disputes we have discussed.

In the GATT, government procurement was an exception to the national treatment requirement discussed above – the requirement that once foreign goods have entered the national market of another Member they will be treated the same as domestic goods. Governments could continue to "buy American" or whatever, without acting in a manner inconsistent with their GATT obligations. This was modified somewhat in 1979 with the adoption of a Government Procurement Agreement, known as the GPA. About twenty GATT Parties agreed at the time to open their government procurement to imports. The GPA continued through the Uruguay Round, but little was changed. It remains one of two "plurilateral" agreements in the WTO, that is, agreements that are optimal. Members may adhere or not, as they wish. The GPA is not "multilateral". (The other plurilateral agreement is the Agreement on Civil Aircraft.)

From the perspective of the United States, there is a further noteworthy fact. The GPA does not just open all government procurement to imports. It is a far more complicated bargain. Some Members have larger government sectors than others, and they believed that just opening up all government procurement would disadvantage them. The other Members, with smaller government sectors, believed the disadvantage was the reverse: that their exporters were barred from sales to important parts of the public sector in other countries that were in the private sector in their own. Utilities are an example. In the United States they are largely investor-owned and can buy from wherever they wish; in many other countries, at least until the recent wave of privatizations, they were government-owned and tended to buy only from national suppliers. There was a further problem. National governments may commit themselves, but in the territories of some Members, subnational procurement, at the state and local level, is far more important than in others.

The problem presented by these asymmetries was resolved by a system of affirmative inclusions in the Agreement. Members specified the entities whose procurement would be covered. They added or subtracted from their offer list, depending upon what was forthcoming from others: the Ministry of Agriculture from Country A, the Ministry of Commerce from Country B and so on.

The constitutional authority of the federal government to include purchases by state agencies in the U.S. list ran from the highly questionable to the non-existent. The political authority to bind the states against their wishes was, in any event, non-existent. Still, inclusion of procurement by state governments would significantly increase the bargaining power of the United States. Therefore, the federal government requested that states make portions of their procurement open to imports under the terms of the GPA, and more than thirty of them have done so. Among them is Massachusetts, which agreed to apply the GPA to the procurements of eleven of its agencies.

The EC and Japan claim that these eleven Massachusetts agencies are included in the GPA commitment of the United States, and that the sanctions are inconsistent with the national treatment requirements of the GPA. From their perspective, the United States and Massachusetts made an agreement in 1994 and broke it in 1996. Whether the action of Massachusetts in fact is inconsistent with the obligations it voluntarily assumed, remains to be seen. Assuming that the panel finds against Massachusetts, however, it is instructive to look at the issue of sovereignty in light of what could occur if the panel finds in favour of the EC and Japan.

VII. WTO REMEDIES – COMPENSATION AND RETALIATION

The first thing to note about all of these cases is that they deal with an agreement, with what amounts to an international contract. The cases are tantamount to cases for breach of contract. To be sure, the contract involved is complex, and just what is required is not always clear. Like many agreements reached by negotiation, particularly negotiation by politicians, some problems may be papered over deliberately in the hope that the problem may never arise or, if it does arise, it will be dealt with later.

The way these problems are dealt with is a rational way that grew out of the initial experience, back in 1948, when the Chairman ruled that consular taxes are "charges of any kind" within the meaning of Article 1 of the GATT. One party states that another has acted in a manner inconsistent with its agreement; the other denies it. Neutral third parties are asked to look into the dispute and to make a recommendation. The WTO dispute settlement system, with all of its new formalities, is in the end, no more than an elaboration on this structure.

So what happens when the neutral third parties conclude that one of the parties indeed has acted in a manner inconsistent with its obligations? Remember that in discussing the *Gasoline* case, we noted that the options available to the United States were:

(i) to bring the measure into conformity;
(ii) to keep the measure and offer compensation to our trading partners; or
(iii) to do nothing and accept eventual retaliation from our trading partners in the form of increased barriers to our exports.

These choices are what upset many of the critics of the WTO. They see the threat of retaliation as effectively compelling exercise of the first option. Bringing the measure into conformity they see as surrendering sovereignty to international bureaucrats. Alfred Eckes, former chairman of the U.S. International Trade Commission, asserts that we are forced to bow to the dictates of those international bureaucrats or face "heavy fines".[7]

Eckes' statement is typical of the exaggeration and misrepresentation that characterizes so much of the criticism of the WTO. You can read the text of the Dispute Settlement Understanding from start to finish and you never will find a reference to fines, heavy or otherwise. The sole remedy available to a WTO Member that wins its case against the measure of another, if that measure is not changed and an adequate compensation is not forthcoming, is, effectively, cancellation of the bargain. There are no fines, no penalties. There simply is a determination that, if one side backs out of its bargain, the other side may do the same.

It is hard to see how this interferes with the defending party's sovereignty. To the contrary, to the extent that there is a sovereignty-restraining commitment, it is on the complaining party, not the defending party. If one nation has the sovereign right to act as it pleases, so does every other nation, including the sovereign right to decide how it will react to the actions of others. It really is this second exercise of sovereignty that WTO Members agree to restrain.

Look, for example, at the Massachusetts sanctions case. Two years ago, Massachusetts exercised its claimed right to impose the measure. The EC and Japan disagreed, but what did they do? For two years they complained and negotiated, but they did not act. Now they have acted, but only by starting dispute settlement proceedings in the WTO. As sovereigns, of course, they are free to do as they please without going to the WTO. But they have agreed to do otherwise; they have agreed not to exercise their sovereign right to take any action they please in a manner that is inconsistent with the WTO commitments they, and the United States, have made.

The parties to the WTO Agreements have taken a step back from the Hobbesian abyss of the unbridled exercise of their sovereign rights. To be sure, they retain those rights, but they have agreed to limit their exercise in exchange for a like agreement from other Members. They have agreed to curb their exercise of private vengeance.

Interestingly, this is where legal systems begin – where societies take steps to control private retaliatory activities. Law in ancient Athens was based on the efforts of the community to restrict the self-help activities of its citizens. Roman Law, Germanic Law, and English Common Law began the same way – with efforts to limit the blood feud. We can see the same thing today in sports: no matter what the other player did, the player who retaliates will get called for a foul.

In trying to control the blood feuds and the fouls of international trade, in a complex, changing and interdependent world, the Members of the WTO are not usurping any nation's sovereignty – they are agreeing only to limit the exercise of their own sovereignty when they believe such a limitation is to their advantage.

There is nothing sovereignty-threatening about this. Governments have agreed to limit the exercise of their sovereignty on numerous occasions in numerous ways. That's what treaties are all about, and the treaty power of the United States is as old as the Constitution itself.

The question is always whether a particular agreement – a particular limitation of sovereignty – is an advantageous agreement. In answering this question with regard to the WTO, it is worth noting that the trading system governments have established has contributed significantly to the prosperity of the post-World War II world. Export trade has grown at a much faster pace than purely domestic trade. Jobs in the export trade by pay considerably more, on average, than jobs in purely domestic trades. The economic benefits of the system are hard to dispute.

Perhaps more important than the economic benefits, however, the trading system governments established by agreeing to limit the exercise of their sovereignty has contributed significantly to diminishing the kinds of trade frictions that, in the Hobbesian world of the past, the world of war-by-all-against-all, led too often to bloodshed. This is no small achievement, and should not be lost sight of in the current trade debates and the debates to come.

NOTES

This is the text of the Rockefeller Lecture delivered on 27 October 1998 at The Nelson A. Rockefeller Center at Dartmouth College.

1 BISD II/12.

2 The World Trade Organization Dispute Settlement System 11, 1996, Gilberto Amado Memorial Lecture, United Nations, 1996.

3 *Several Disputes Settled "Out of Court"*, WTO Focus, August–September 1996, No. 12, p. 4.

4 138 Cong. Rec. S1111, 6 February 1992.

5 Oversight of the Reformulated Gasoline Rule, Hearings before the Committee on Environment and Public Works, United States Senate, 103d Cong. 2d Sess. 30, 22 April 1994 (testimony of Mary Nichols, Assistant Administrator, Office of Air and Radiation, Environmental Protection Agency).

6 Gasoline Report, paragraph 6.40.

7 Alfred E. Eckes, Jr., *Opening America's Markets: U.S. Foreign Trade Policy Since 1776*, Univ. N. Carolina, Press, 1995, p. 284.

12. Regulatory Protectionism and the Law of International Trade

A. O. Sykes

Among the most vexing and persistent disputes in modern international commercial relations involves a European prohibition on the sale of beef from animals treated with certain growth hormones. The use of hormones to fatten beef cattle is widespread in the United States, and hence the European regulation affects United States beef exporters significantly.[1] The United States has maintained that the prohibition is disguised protectionism designed to benefit European beef producers, while the European Union has insisted that it is a sensible public health measure designed to protect its citizens against the possible risks of ingesting hormone residues. After many years of bilateral wrangling,[2] the World Trade Organization ("WTO") has now ruled that the European regulation is not reasonably necessary to the attainment of a legitimate health objective and, consequently, that it violates WTO law.[3] The dispute continues, however, as the United States and the European Union debate what must be done to bring Europe's behavior into compliance with WTO law.

The "beef hormones" decision raises many interesting legal and factual issues. This Article, however, focuses on a broader puzzle, a puzzle that is nicely illustrated by the legal rules governing transatlantic trade in beef. Although Europe has now been told that its beef hormone regulations are an unjustified protectionist measure that violates international law, it continues to maintain a hefty tariff on imported beef products.[4] Further, should beef imports in the future exceed a specified increase over historical levels, an additional and substantial "special safeguard" tariff may be imposed.[5] Likewise, should increased imports of beef "cause or threaten serious injury" to the European beef industry, Europe would be entitled to use temporary additional protective tariffs or quantitative ceilings on imports (quotas) to remedy the problem[6] And finally, Europe (like the United States) maintains hefty farm subsidies. To cattle growers in particular, Europe is permitted to bestow an annual subsidy of nearly 2 billion ECU without violating its commitments to limit agricultural subsidies.[7] Needless to say, subsidies too are a form of protectionism that lower costs for domestic producers and allow them to compete more effectively against imports.

What is going on here? Why are protective tariffs, subsidies, and quotas (under specified circumstances) perfectly legal under WTO law, while protectionism in the form of a regulatory measure such as the hormones regulation is illegal? This Article undertakes to answer this question using some rudimentary economics of international trade melded with simple public choice theory.

Some terminology is useful at the outset. Government regulation[8] of product markets[9] can increase the costs of production for firms outside the regulating jurisdiction ("foreign firms") more than it increases costs for firms inside the regulating jurisdiction ("domestic firms") and thereby confer a competitive advantage on domestic firms. I define "regulatory protectionism" as any cost disadvantage imposed on foreign firms by a regulatory policy that discriminates against them or that otherwise disadvantages them in a manner that is unnecessary to the attainment of some genuine, nonprotectionist regulatory objective. Regulatory protectionism can result either from substantive regulatory requirements from the mechanisms used by regulators to ensure compliance with substantive requirements (the "conformity assessment" process). It need not be deliberate and may result simply from regulators' failure to appreciate the trade impact of their policies.

To give a few examples, a nation may regulate the pharmaceutical market by requiring government approval of new drugs before they may be sold. If, however, the regulatory authorities require foreign pharmaceutical manufacturers to engage in more testing and clinical trials than domestic manufacturers with no apparent health justification for this difference in treatment, regulatory protectionism arises. Similarly, a policy prohibiting the use of some food preservative in imported foodstuffs, but allowing its use domestically, would constitute regulatory protectionism.

Such cases of overt discrimination provide the clearest examples, but, as the beef hormones case illustrates, facially non-discriminatory policies may also constitute regulatory protectionism. The European regulation at issue in the beef hormones case imposes a cost disadvantage on foreign suppliers from nations that permit the use of growth hormones, because it requires them to undertake costly measures to certify their exports as hormone-free.[10] European beef producers, however, need not concern themselves with the measures, because hormones are purportedly not used at all in Europe. And because this cost disadvantage results from a regulation that is not necessary to attain any legitimate public health objective (according to WTO findings), it constitutes "regulatory protectionism" as defined in this Article.

It is easy to imagine other examples of facially neutral regulatory protectionism. Transportation regulators might require that all new automobiles sold in the domestic market be equipped with a particular type of airbag that is only manufactured domestically, even though other types of airbags manufactured abroad (and available more cheaply to foreign automobile manufacturers) are just as safe and effective. Or regulators might require all products of a certain type to be tested at a particular laboratory that surreptitiously expedites the processing of domestic goods, even though other laboratories could perform the job adequately.

By contrast, some regulations have a protective effect (raising the costs of foreign firms more than the costs of domestic firms), but are nondiscriminatory and necessary to attain a genuine, nonprotectionist regulatory objective. In legal parlance, they might be called the "least restrictive means" to obtain that objective. For example, a nation may wish to attain a higher level of air quality than others and may require all automobiles sold in the domestic market to meet comparatively stringent hydrocarbon emissions standards. Foreign manufacturers may have higher unit costs of compliance – perhaps they sell few vehicles into the country in question and thus are unable to reap the same scale economies or learning-by-doing economies in regulatory compliance that accrue to domestic firms with larger sales volumes. But if the regulation is nondiscriminatory and no less restrictive alternative is available to meet air quality goals, then the measure does not constitute regulatory protectionism as defined in this Article.

So defined, regulatory protectionism is economically inefficient, in part for the same reasons that protectionism of any sort is inefficient. Protectionism draws high cost domestic firms into the market while excluding low cost foreign firms, and it prices out of the market some consumers who would be willing to purchase goods at a price exceeding the marginal cost of production of efficient suppliers.[11] What previous work has not appreciated, however, is that in most cases regulatory protectionism causes additional deadweight losses that make it considerably more inefficient than other instruments of protection such as tariffs, quotas, and subsidies. Accordingly, the societal returns to legal constraints on regulatory, protectionism are greater, other things being equal, than the social returns to constraints on other protectionist instruments. This proposition, developed in Section I, is the principal normative point of this Article.

Section II develops some connected positive claims about the law of international trade. The analysis draws on a blend of public choice theory and the theory of optimal contracts. It posits that trade agreements may be understood as sophisticated contracts among the self-interested political officials representing each member nation. These actors are not concerned with "welfare maximization," as that phrase is conventionally used by economists, but with the maximization of their own political fortunes as measured by votes, campaigns contributions, and the like.[12] This perspective, when melded with the welfare analysis in Section I, yields two sets of insights.

First, from a political standpoint, regulatory protectionism is an inferior form of protectionism for nations that are unconstrained in their trade policies. But after a nation enters into a trade agreement, circumstances may arise that tempt political officials to employ regulatory protectionism due to constraints on their ability to use other preferred protectionist instruments. It is in the mutual interest of political actors who bind themselves to trade agreements to disable themselves from behaving in this fashion if possible and to encourage renegotiation of the agreed-upon constraints on the politically "efficient" instruments of protection instead. Further, the degree of trade protection afforded by regulatory measures may be difficult to quantify, and the transaction costs of reciprocal trade negotiations can be lowered if protectionism is restricted to more transparent instruments such as tariffs. This line of reasoning affords a "political economy" explanation for the fact that regulatory protectionism is prohibited under the treaty creating the WTO even though various other forms of protectionism are permissible (albeit subject to constraint). The lesson here is but a special case of a more general insight developed in the literature on public choice and regulation – where the self-interest of political actors requires an inefficient transfer of rents to well-organized interest groups (here, domestic industries that seek insulation from foreign competition), it is often best to make that inefficient transfer as efficiently as possible.[13]

Second, regulations that are nondiscriminatory and necessary to the attainment of legitimate, nonprotectionist regulatory objectives will not be prohibited in politically savvy trade agreements. Such measures will be permitted (although they will be a possible subject of future trade negotiations) even though the burden on international commerce may be great and the domestic regulatory benefits may be small. The political economy explanation for this claim rests on the disjunction between economic efficiency and political efficacy, and the extreme difficulty of fashioning legal rules to identify measures that are politically undesirable from the perspective of trade negotiators even though essential to domestic regulatory goals. Accordingly, politically savvy parties to trade agreements will prefer to negotiate directly over such measures rather than entrust their policing to courts or similar tribunals. The law of the WTO is again consistent with this claim, as the legality of regulatory measures in no way turns on a "balancing" of regulatory benefits and commercial burdens.

Section III concludes with some comparative observations on the treatment of protective regulations in other legal systems, including the North American Free Trade Agreement ("NAFTA"), the European Union, and the United States federal system. The treatment of regulatory protectionism in each legal environment is quite similar to that of the WTO – all systems tend to prohibit it. The treatment of nondiscriminatory regulatory measures that have protective effects but are essential to the promotion of legitimate regulatory objectives varies slightly more across systems; for the most part, however, the treatment is similar to that of the WTO. Hence, all four systems that I examine appear broadly consistent with the political economy analysis.

I. THE WELFARE ECONOMICS OF REGULATORY PROTECTIONISM

Governments have an array of devices at their disposal for protecting domestic industries against outside competition. Taxes on imports (tariffs), restrictions on the quantity of imports (quotas), and subsidies to domestic producers are common instruments of protection. Regulations that disadvantage foreign suppliers relative to domestic firms are a fourth option. Still others can be imagined.

These alternative instruments of protection are by no means equivalent. In particular, although tariffs, quotas, and subsidies can be quite similar in their impact on welfare (though not identical), regulatory protectionism is systematically more pernicious, often by a wide margin. A simple, partial equilibrium comparison of policy instruments makes the point.

Figure I depicts a competitive market for a single good in an importing nation. To keep the diagram as simple as possible, I make the "small country" assumption and imagine that the importing nation can purchase all of the good that it wishes from abroad at the "world price" *P*. Nothing essential would change, however, if I assumed instead that supply curve for the imported good were upward sloping.[14] The domestic supply curve (initially) is *S*, and the domestic demand curve is *D*. With no intervention into the market by the government, total consumption

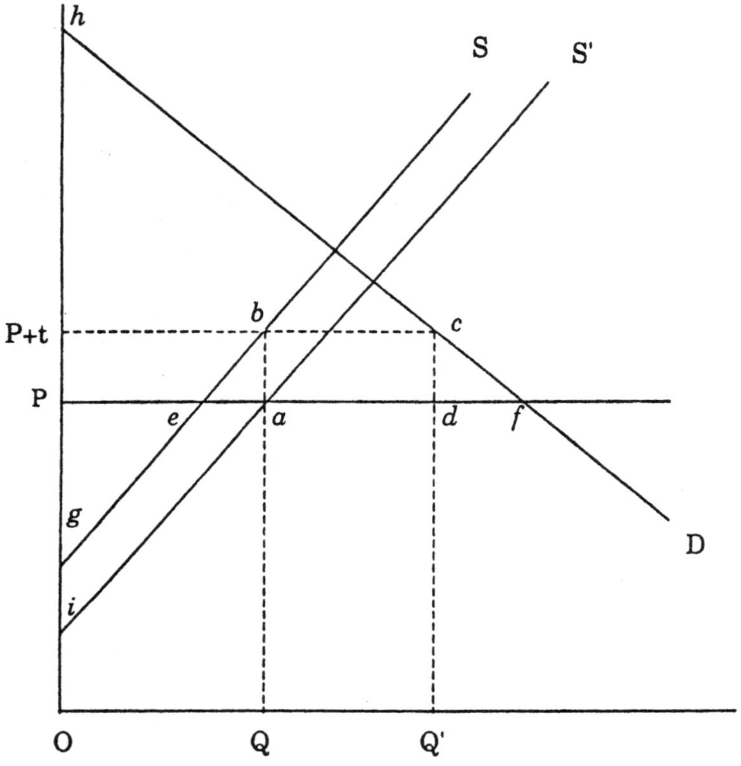

FIGURE 1

would be determined by the intersection of the demand curve *D* with a horizontal line at the world price *P* (the horizontal distance *Pf*). Domestic firms would supply a quantity equal to *Pe*, and imports would supply the remaining consumer demand *ef*. Domestic consumer surplus would equal *hfP*, while domestic producer surplus would equal *Pge*.

Let us suppose, however, that the government decides to protect the domestic industry so that it can achieve a higher level of profit or employment. For concreteness, suppose that the government wishes to confer surplus on domestic producers in an amount *Pai*, or that it wishes to induce domestic output of *Q* (both options result in the same surplus for domestic firms). Consider the government's options. A tariff equal to *t* on all units of the imported good will increase the price of the good to consumers to the level *P+t*. Consumption will then equal *Q'*, with domestic production of *Q* and imports of *A'-Q*. Domestic producer surplus rises to *(P+t)bg*, which is equal to *Pai*. Consumer surplus has fallen to *(P+t)ch*, but government revenue on the *Q'-Q* units of imports is now *(Q'-Q)t*, equal to the area *abcd*. Making the welfare comparison to the level of surplus that exists without government intervention, the sum of consumer surplus, producer surplus, and government revenue is now less by the two "deadweight loss" triangles *eba* and *cdf*.

As an alternative to a tariff, the government might impose a quota restricting imports to *Q'-Q*. Price would rise and the market would clear when domestic production reached *Q* at the price *P+t*. Such a quota would have the same impact on consumer and producer surplus as the tariff of *t*, but it would not generate any revenue for the government (unless the rights to import under the quota were auctioned). Instead, the "quota rents" *abcd*, equal to the tariff revenue under the tariff system, would be captured by the entities with the right to import under the quota. For example, if admission to the domestic market were offered to the foreign sellers that were first in line, those sellers would be able to command the elevated price *P+t* for their merchandise and would receive an additional *t* per unit by comparison to the scenario without government intervention. The difference between the tariff and the quota, therefore, is not in the amount of surplus, but in who captures it.[15]

A third option is a subsidy. If the government offers domestic producers a payment equal to *t* per unit of output, the effect is to shift the supply curve downward to *S'*. The domestic industry will produce *Q* and earn a surplus equal to *Pai*, while imports will equal *af*. Here, consumer surplus no longer declines relative to the scenario without intervention, but deadweight loss remains nonetheless. The reason is that government now makes an expenditure on the subsidy equal to *Qt*, which is equal to the area *bgia*. Part of this amount – *geai* – is a transfer to domestic producers that increases their surplus. The remainder, equal to the area of the triangle *eba*, is deadweight loss. Though not reflected in the diagram, a further deadweight loss exists as a result of the taxes necessary to raise the government revenue for subsidy. When this factor is added to the analysis, it is apparent that one cannot rank the welfare effects of subsidies, tariffs, or quotas. Plausibly, their effects are similar in many settings, and any differences will depend on the circumstances.

Now consider a fourth option – a regulatory measure calculated to disadvantage foreign suppliers. Such a measure might take many forms, as indicated in the introduction, but for concreteness let us suppose that the government announces the following policy: Any foreign supplier who desires to sell a unit of the good in the market of the importing nation must provide an agent to sit on a flagpole for one hour and cluck like a chicken. Let us further assume that the market wage for an hour of sitting and clucking is *t*.[16] Foreign suppliers who can sell elsewhere at the price *P* will now demand *P+t* to sell in this market. The market will once again clear at that price, just as in the case of the tariff and the quota. Imports will equal *Q'-Q* and domestic production will equal *Q*. Consumer surplus will be the same as in the case of the tariff or quota, and domestic producer surplus will be the same. But now the deadweight loss may be far greater than it is with the other protectionist instruments. Instead of the triangle *eba* and *cdf*, it will equal the entire area *ebcf* if we assume that the agent who sits and clucks earns no surplus because he can command a wage of *t* per hour elsewhere (if the regulation merely diverts that agent from some productive activity with wage *t* so that the agent receives no real benefit from the government's regulatory protectionism).

The difference between the regulatory measure and the alternative instruments of protection (tariffs, subsidies, and quotas) is that an amount equal to the area of the rectangle *abcd* is preserved as surplus for *somebody* under each of the alternative instruments. The government captures it as tariff revenue under the tariff option, consumers retain it under the subsidy option, and whoever holds the rights to import captures it under the quota option. Under the regulatory option, by contrast, the surplus can be completely destroyed because of the socially wasted expenditure of t per unit of imports.

This analysis requires two caveats. First, if the mandated increase in costs under regulation confers surplus on someone (such as the clucker, in my example), the additional deadweight loss from regulatory protectionism will be smaller than the full regulatory compliance cost per unit. But it will be the rare case in which additional waste is absent. Thus, suppose that the wage of t is better than the wage that the clucker can earn elsewhere (call it w). Then, a rectangle of surplus equal to $(t\text{-}w)$ $(Q'\text{-}Q)$ will be transferred to cluckers, and the additional deadweight loss from regulatory protectionism will be less than *abcd* – to be precise, it will equal $w(Q'\text{-}Q)$. Only if w is zero, however, will the welfare loss from regulatory protectionism be no worse than the welfare loss from other forms of protectionism. That is, unless the resources consumed by regulatory protectionism have zero value in alternative uses – a situation that should be very much the exception than the rule – regulatory protectionism will destroy more surplus than other protectionist instruments.[17]

Second, the "rectangle" of surplus that is preserved under the tariff, quota, or subsidy option may be the target of rent seeking by interest groups, and their expenditures in pursuit of that surplus may represent a social cost. With the tariff, for example, interest groups may expend resources lobbying the government to transfer the tariff revenue to them through some new government expenditure program. Or with the quota, interest groups hoping to obtain the right to import under the quota, and the associated quota rent, may spend resources, lobbying for that right. Consequently, some of the rectangle will likely be dissipated through efforts by interest groups to secure it. But it seems exceedingly unlikely that this possibility could reverse the conclusion that regulatory protectionism is worse from a welfare standpoint than other forms of protectionism. Rational interest groups will not spend more on efforts to secure the surplus than the expected returns from those expenditures, and hence we would expect their total expenditures to be less than the surplus at stake (in other words, less than the area of the rectangle *abcd*) – rent seekers on average should earn at least a competitive rate of return on their efforts. Further, interested group expenditures in pursuit of the available surplus will often involve transfers (for example, campaign contributions) rather than expenditures that amount to deadweight loss. For these reasons, rent seeking almost certainly will not dissipate the entire "rectangle" that the tariff, quota, or subsidy otherwise preserves. By contrast, regulatory protectionism can destroy all of it. And where it does not – because it confers surplus on the factors of production used in regulatory compliance (the first caveat above) – rent seeking by the beneficiaries of regulatory protectionism will dissipate a portion of their surplus as well. Hence, the net social surplus (left over after all deadweight costs from rent seeking have been netted out) should still be systematically greater with a tariff, quota, or subsidy than with regulatory protectionism.[18]

The lessons here are general. Although my hypothetical clucking requirement is rather silly and implausible, regulatory protectionism, as I have defined it, is the economic equivalent. By definition, it raises the costs of foreign suppliers (or the domestic imports with whom they deal) by inducing an expenditure of resources for no purpose (or with no effect) other than to raise the price of imported goods. Whether those resources are consumed in superfluous inspection services, pointless labeling or "safety" requirements, or unnecessary requirements that foreign sellers establish a domestic "presence," the economic analysis remains the same. A comparable degree of protection against foreign competition could be achieved, at lower economic cost, by employing one of the more efficient protectionist instruments. Accordingly, if protectionism is to be tolerated at all, societal economic welfare will be greater if it is channelled into the less destructive devices for achieving it.

II. POSITIVE THEORY AND THE STRUCTURE OF WTO OBLIGATIONS

The WTO, which supplants the General Agreement on Tariffs and Trade ("GATT"), embodies detailed commitments on scores of issues spanning hundreds of pages of legal text and additional thousands of pages of product by product, service sector by service sector, and country by country obligations.[19] My focus here is on a subset of the provisions contained in these agreements – those pertaining to traditional instruments of protection such as tariffs, quotas, and subsidies on the one hand, and those pertaining to regulatory protectionism in product markets on the other. The goal is to explain the structure of these provisions using a blend of public choice theory (or political economy theory) and the theory of optimal contracts.

Before developing the theoretical analysis, however, I will lay out the legal landscape. Section A considers the WTO rules regarding tariffs, quotas, and subsidies. It discusses how the WTO agreements permit signatories to employ these traditional instruments of protection, albeit subject to substantial limitations, including some that preclude the introduction of *new* tariffs, quotas, or subsidies that would frustrate the expectations created by reciprocal trade concessions. Section B then argues that the WTO agreements *prohibit* regulatory protectionism, as I have defined it, in goods sectors. By contrast, regulatory measures that have protective effects but that are also necessary to the achievement of an apparently genuine regulatory objective other than protectionism are allowed.

The theoretical analysis is developed in Section C. My essential claim is that this structure of permissible and impermissible protectionism can be understood as a part of an optimal "contract" among self-interested political actors.

A. The WTO Rules on Tariffs, Quotas, and Subsidies

The heart of the GATT – predecessor to the WTO – was a set of reciprocal commitments among signatories to lower their tariffs below the high levels that had emerged in the 1930s. Pursuant to these "tariff bindings," nations covenanted product by product not to charge a tariff above the negotiated "bound rate."[20] Periodic negotiations throughout the history of the GATT and the WTO have produced a steady reduction of the bound rates on most goods imported into most countries (less so in developing countries). But tariffs are not illegal. Rather, signatories have a right to charge any tariff they want unless they have negotiated a binding with respect to the particular good in question. Further, bindings can be renegotiated upward, at a price of course, if nations find them too low.[21]

The drafters of the original GATT recognized that tariff commitments would be of little value if signatories could substitute quotas instead.[22] Accordingly, to protect expectations under the tariff bindings, the GATT contained a general prohibition of quotas that carried over into the WTO.[23] But this prohibition was subject to a number of exceptions relating to, inter alia, the use of quotas to ensure the efficacy of agricultural price support schemes, to overcome balance of payments difficulties, to protect declining industries, and to protect human, animal, and plant life or health.[24] The drafters even included an elaborate provision on how to administer quotas to avoid undue trade discrimination, anticipating that quotas would be used regularly despite the general prohibition.[25] Thus, like tariffs, quotas are in no meaningful sense illegal, and they remain in use by many countries in many goods sectors. Quotas are, however, quite constrained and are not to be used unless they can be justified under one of the exceptions to the general prohibition. Further, in some instances, the introduction of a new quota will trigger a requirement that trading partners be "compensated" (through alternative trade concessions) for the adverse impact on their exports.[26]

Much the same thing may be said about subsidies. The original GATT agreement provided that subsidies to domestic producers, with the exception of subsidies applicable only to exports, were generally exempt from legal restrictions.[27] The signatories quickly realized that a *new* subsidy to domestic firms could frustrate the market across expectations under a tariff binding and thus developed a rule that new subsidies to domestic producers of goods covered by tariff bindings are impermissible unless adequate trade compensation is paid.[28] The GATT also authorized unilateral countermeasures against subsidized imports known as "countervailing duties," which a signatory could use at its discretion if subsidized imports were "such as to cause or threaten material injury" to domestic competitors.[29] But there was no attempt in the original GATT or during its subsequent evolution to prohibit subsidies in general. And, although the WTO introduced some new and quite interesting constraints on subsidies, they are still tolerated in many settings even if their only apparent justification is to insulate domestic firms from foreign competition (especially in the agricultural sector). Thus, like tariffs and quotas, subsidies are not in general illegal, but they are constrained in important ways, particularly insofar as nations may wish to introduce new subsidies for products with bound tariffs.

B. The WTO Rules on Regulatory Protectionism

Regulatory impediments to trade have been a subject of considerable and growing negotiation throughout the history of the GATT and the WTO. During the recent Uruguay Round of multilateral trade negotiations, two extensive agreements concerning regulatory barriers to trade were concluded – the WTO Agreement on Technical Barriers to Trade ("TBT Agreement")[30] and the WTO Agreement on the Application of Sanitary and Phytosanitary Measures ("SPM Agreement").[31] The SPM Agreement, part of the Agreement on Agriculture, primarily concerns measures to protect human, plant, or animal health from hazards relating to agricultural products – food safety regulations being the paradigmatic example. The TBT Agreement applies to all other product market regulations.

Although the term "regulatory protectionism' is mine and is found nowhere in the text of the WTO accords, the TBT and SPM Agreements nevertheless prohibit regulatory protectionism as here defined in product markets. The legal principles that accomplish this task may be broken down into six categories.

1. Facial discrimination: the national treatment principle

It is exceedingly difficult to imagine a principled justification for substantive regulatory requirements that apply to foreign firms only. The conformity assessment system for foreign merchandise may differ from that in place domestically to be sure, but a requirement that foreign sellers achieve a level of safety, quality, or any other regulatory objective that domestic firms need not achieve seems transparently protectionist, with rare exception.[32] Accordingly, a covenant against regulatory protectionism must generally prohibit such regulatory policies.

The legal principle that condemns additional requirements for foreign firms is known generally in the WTO system as the "national treatment principle," which forbids governments from treating imported goods differently than domestic goods. With particular reference to product market regulations, the TBT and SPM Agreements both contain tight national treatment requirements.[33]

2. Policing protectionist motives: the sham principle and scientific evidence requirements

An additional weapon against regulatory protectionism is the "sham principle," under which the actions of regulators may be directly reviewed for importer motive. A "sham" arises where the purported high-minded objectives of regulation are disingenuous and the real motive is found to be protectionist – where the regulatory measures are "a disguised restriction on international trade."[34] The sham principle is related to nondiscrimination principles in that evidence of discrimination is powerful evidence of protectionist motives, but it has the potential to reach nondiscriminatory regulations as well when their true objective is to disadvantage foreign firms. Also related to the sham principle are rules that require nations to provide credible scientific evidence to support claims made by domestic regulators, such as claims relating to health and safety risks. Such rules may be strengthened by a requirement that sensible procedures be followed in assessing the need for regulation in the first instance.

The WTO Agreements embrace these antiprotectionist devices. The TBT Agreement provides: "Members shall ensure that technical regulations are not prepared, adopted or applied with a view to or with the effect of creating unnecessary obstacles to international trade."[35] The corresponding language in the SPM Agreement states that "[s]anitary and phytosanitary measures shall not be applied in a manner which would constitute a disguised restriction on international trade."[36] Both agreements further require regulators to engage in a proper assessment of the risks and other matters relating to the regulations in question before promulgating them.[37] The SPM Agreement is particularly strong in this regard, with a lengthy article devoted to the principles of risk assessment.[38] These provisions in particular were central to the ruling in favor of the United States in the beef hormones dispute.[39]

3. The information deficiencies of regulators: comment requirements and reference to international standards

As noted earlier, regulatory protectionism need not result from a calculated effort to raise rivals' costs. Inadvertence, indifference and information deficiencies on the part of domestic regulators can also produce important regulatory trade barriers.[40] One device for addressing this problem is a procedural requirement that regulators consider comments on proposed regulations before promulgating them. Advance comment requirements allow foreign firms to provide regulators with information bearing on the wisdom of their proposed regulations, including information about the costs of compliance to foreigners and alternative methods to achieve the regulatory objective at lower compliance cost. Both the TBT and SPM Agreements thus require regulators to publicize new regulatory proposals and to allow reasonable time for comments by foreign parties before adopting them (with appropriate exceptions for urgent matters of health, safety, or security).[41]

Another important device for remedying the information deficiencies of regulators involves using international standards. A number of international institutions develop and publish voluntary product standards (including standards relating to quality, health, and safety,[42] and it is often desirable that regulators use these standards in their own national regulations.[43] International standards are typically produced only after an extensive exchange of information among countries and thus tend to avoid some of the problems that may result when national regulators act on the basis of limited information. In addition, because international standard-majority voting requirement,[44] the existence of an international standard can reflect a high level of agreement about its acceptability and the absence of a major constituency that would be disadvantaged by its implementation. Accordingly, unless a pertinent international standard is demonstrably inadequate to achieve a particular regulatory objective, its use often will constitute the least trade disruptive method of achieving that goal. The WTO Agreements thus impose an obligation to employ international standards whenever they suffice to achieve the domestic regulatory objective.[45]

Finally, just as it is valuable for regulators to use international standards when possible, it is valuable to have international standards established on the basis of the best information available. Accordingly, to improve the quality of information at the international level, the WTO Agreements require national regulators to participate in the activities of the international standardizing bodies "within the limits of their resources."[46]

4. Information costs and the costs of regulatory surprise for foreign firms: the role of notice and publication requirements

Firms invariably incur costs to learn about the regulatory systems in the various markets that they serve. They may need to translate regulations into another langauge, hire lawyers to explain the regulations to them, and even incur substantial costs trying to identify who is in charge of regulating particular matters and where their regulations may be found in an accessible form. These costs tend to be greater for foreign firms than for domestic firms and bureaucratic systems abroad. Similarly, foreign firms may be disadvantaged unnecessarily by regulatory change or "surprise." Greater advice notice of impending regulatory changes can confer at least a transitory competitive advantage. And because domestic firms tend to be better informed about and more involved in their own political systems than foreign firms, the costs of regulatory surprise seem likely to fall more heavily on foreign firms.

Publication requirements under the WTO address the unnecessary costs that foreign sellers may incur in attempting to learn about existing regulations and how to comply with them. The key provision in each Agreement concerns the establishment of designated "enquiry points" – in effect, national clearinghouses for information about all regulations with which foreign products must comply.[47] These requirements not only avoid unnecessary costs to foreign firms by reducing search costs, but also reduce costs associated with the uncertainty that some regulation may have been overlooked.

Notice requirements, which require the publication of new regulations substantially in advance of their effective date (barring emergencies), address the unnecessary costs of regulatory surprise. Accordingly, both the TBT and SPM Agreements contain substantial notice requirements.[48]

5. Avoiding other unnecessary costs of regulatory compliance: the least restrictive means requirement

Regulatory objectives often can be achieved in a variety of ways. Food safety can be promoted by inspecting processing facilities, for example, or by testing the finished product. Fire safety can be promoted by chemically treating otherwise flammable materials or using nonflammable materials. When an objective can be achieved in a variety of ways, firms may differ as to which method is the cheapest for them. This difference is especially likely in international commerce, where technologies and input prices will vary from country to country. Regulations that require their objectives to be achieved in limited ways that are advantageous to domestic firms can thus confer an inefficient economic advantage on them.[49] Likewise, exporting firms can become subject to redundant regulatory requirements that increase their costs of doing business without being necessary to the attainment of regulatory objectives in the firms' export markets.[50]

One solution is to require that regulations be drafted at the highest possible level of generality that suffices to meet regulatory goals; put differently, the law can require that regulators employ the least restrictive means necessary to achieve their objectives. This, for example, a regulation governing fire doors in commercial buildings might be drafted to require a certain burn-through time for every door, but should not be drafted to require the use of particular materials or particular thicknesses where satisfactory performance can be achieved without them. Similarly, a regulation concerning automobile emissions might be drafted to require that emissions of particular pollutants fall below certain levels, but should not be drafted to require the use of a particular emissions control technology when others are available or may become available. The general principle that these examples illustrate is that product performance regulations are almost always preferable to product design regulations.

Even if nations attempt to draft regulations in such a manner as to employ the least restrictive means, however, limited information may handicap their efforts. Other nations may employ regulatory means that achieve the same objectives in a way not initially recognized by the importing nation. Where this problem arises, importing nations can avoid regulatory protectionism by accepting the regulations of other nations as equivalent in response to an appropriate petition – in legal parlance, they can afford each other "mutual recognition."

Each of these ideas finds its way into the WTO Agreements. The least restrictive means principle is embodied in the requirement that regulations not be more trade restrictive than "necessary" to the attainment of their legitimate objectives.[51] The corollary preference for performance rather than design regulations appears expressly in the TBT Agreement.[52] Finally, both the TBT and SPM Agreements encourage mutual recognition in appropriate cases.[53]

6. Additional obligations with respect to conformity assessment

The principles set forth to this point can be applied not only to the substantive regulations of national governments, but also to the methods used to ensure compliance with them. For example, regulations that require goods to be tested at a particular laboratory or by a particular method when equally good alternatives are available can surely inflate the costs of conformity assessment necessarily. Requirements for testing or inspection by nations of the importing nation, or testing or inspection on the soil of the importing nation, may also be unnecessary and invite abuse and capture.

Accordingly, the WTO Agreements specifically extend most of the principles set forth above to conformity assessment. A national treatment obligation exists,[54] sham principles apply,[55] a general least restrictive means requirement is in place,[56] nations shall not require information that is not reasonably necessary to conformity assessment,[57] nations must process imported goods as expeditiously as they process domestic goods,[58] nations may not site testing facilities so as to disadvantage foreign goods,[59] notice and publication requirements apply,[60] and nations are required to use international conformity assessment standards where they will achieve their purposes.[61] Among other things, these requirements prohibit nations from engaging in selective enforcement of facially non-discriminatory regulations.

* * *

In summary, the TBT and SPM Agreements contain a wide variety of principles that collectively have the effect of preventing member nations from deliberately or inadvertently engaging in regulatory protectionism. Any such measure – whether in the form of a substantive regulation or a procedure for assessing conformity with a substantive regulation – can be reached under one or more of the legal obligations set out above.

Notice, however, what the WTO Agreements do *not* prevent. Nations that genuinely wish to pursue nonprotectionist regulatory objectives may do so as long as scientific evidence supports the regulatory policy (or during an interim period of scientific uncertainty) and as long as the least trade restrictive measures are employed to achieve the regulatory goal. The *stringency* of a given regulation on a given subject, therefore, is of no concern to the WTO. Nor are the trade effects of stringent regulations, even if large, as long as the regulation complies with the obligations set forth above. The system neither requires nor permits any "balancing" of the adverse trade effects of regulation against the importance and the regulatory goals to be achieved.

C. The Political Economy of the WTO Rules

1. The prohibition on regulatory protectionism

When nations enter into cooperative agreements on matters of mutual interest, we might expect that such agreements, much like private contracts, would result in a state of affairs in which the welfare of one party cannot be enhanced without detriment to the welfare of another (Pareto optimality). This notion is no doubt correct most of the time, but the "welfare" measure for the parties needs to be specified with some care.

It is a commonplace in the economic literature on trade policy to observe that consumer interests, which are strongly implicated by national trade policy, are poorly organized and vastly underrepresented in the political calculus. Likewise, not all producer interests are equally well-organized or influential. These facts explain the emergence of tariffs, quotas, and other trade restrictive measures in the first instance, despite their adverse effect on national economic welfare in most cases.[62]

Just as conventional welfare economics cannot afford an adequate explanation of national trade policies formulated in isolation, so too does it fail to provide an adequate explanation for the particulars of cooperative trade agreements. For if trade agreements such as those that comprise the WTO had as their objective the maximization of economic welfare in the conventional sense, the level of protection permissible in accordance with such agreements would be negligible.[63] Yet, as indicated above, tariffs, quotas, and protective subsidies are widespread in the WTO system (although they are subject to important constraints on their magnitude, a key point as shall be seen). A convincing positive theory of cooperative trading arrangements, therefore, cannot rest on conventional welfare economics, but must instead explain why the political optima embodied in trade agreements deviate importantly from economic welfare optima.

The public choice perspective on international trade agreements begins with the observation that trade agreements are compacts not among nations, but among their self-interested political officials. These officials are typically interested in maximizing their political fortunes measures by such things as votes, campaign contributions, and government revenues that can be spent in various ways to secure political support. Thus, a Pareto optimum achieved the Pareto frontier for the political officials who enter the agreement on behalf of their countries, subject to the internal political constraints that confront each official.[64] If this perspective is correct, trade agreements will result in changes in national trade policy only if such changes enhance the political fortunes of signatory politicians by generating net votes or campaign contributions, by raising government revenues that can be used for other politically valuable purposes, or by benefiting them (net) in some other way.

This analysis provides a ready explanation for the observation that trade agreements tend to be trade liberalizing rather than trade restricting. When nations formulate trade policy in isolation (as they did in the 1930s before GATT), they may take the trade policies of other nations as largely fixed.[65] The trade policy battle then tends to be fought mainly by import-competing interests who favor protection and certain well-organized import-consuming interests who favor liberalization. When nations have the opportunity to cooperate, however, export interest groups become more important players, for they can then reward their political officials for securing better access to foreign markets during the course of trade negotiations. Because the pro-trade export interests have more influence on policy when nations are cooperating rather than acting in isolation, the result is a greater degree of trade liberalization when nations act cooperatively than when they act unilaterally.[66]

The public choice perspective also can explain why trade agreements do not achieve complete liberalization. Trade concessions on tariffs reduce government revenues directly, a fact that may be troublesome to incumbent politicians for a variety of reasons. Likewise, not all export interest groups are equally well-organized, and some import-competing interest groups are exceptionally well-organized and influential at any given point in time. It would be quite surprising if the coalition of export interests and import-consuming interests favoring liberalization triumphantly all the time in every industry in every country, and indeed it does not. Rather, trade liberalization only occurs to the extent that the consumer and export interest groups who benefit from it are well-organized and prevail in the political process over the import-competing interest groups (and perhaps the politicians concerned about tariff revenue) who resist trade liberalization.

The same perspective further suggests why political officials acting either unilaterally or cooperatively would not be indifferent among the various instruments of protection available to them, and why regulatory protectionism has come to be so disfavored in the trading community. Return for a moment to the analysis accompanying Figure 1 above, which presents a welfare comparison of tariffs, quotas, subsidies, and regulatory protectionism.[67] In that comparison, each instrument is used to achieve the same level of protection for import-competing domestic firms. The reader will recall that tariffs and quotas are then similar in their welfare consequences, except that tariffs create government revenue whereas quotas tend to confer an equivalent amount of surplus on private sector firms that hold the property rights to import under the quota. Subsidies are also potentially similar to tariffs and quotas in their welfare effects, except that the potential tariff revenue becomes consumer surplus, and subsidies introduce distortions elsewhere associated with taxation in other markets. Regulatory protectionism, by contrast, destroys considerable additional surplus that can be as large as the foregone rectangle *abcd* of tariff revenue, quota rents, or consumer surplus that exists under the other three options.

This welfare comparison suggests a very simple political economy analysis that can explain why regulatory protectionism would be prohibited in the trading community while the other protectionist instruments are not. It rests on the eminently plausible assumption that the political fortunes of officials in trading nations tend to rise as producer surplus in their economies increases, other things being equal, and as their government revenue increases, other things being equal.

Using this assumption, consider first the political interests of officials setting trade policy in isolation from other nations. An official desiring to protect a domestic industry under these circumstances may prefer a tariff to any other instrument of protection. The reason is that the tariff yields government revenue and the other instruments do not. In cases where foreign retaliation is of great concern, however, or where officials prefer to bestow surplus directly on well-organized domestic producer groups (perhaps because of constraints on how officials may spend the tariff revenue), a quota may be preferred to a tariff. The quota can be structured to "bribe" foreign producers with quota rents to discourage foreign retaliation, or can be structured to bestow quota rents directly on domestic importers. Occasionally, a subsidy may dominate a tariff or quota from a political standpoint if domestic consumers of the good in question are quite well-organized (most likely a consuming industry) and would punish their politicians for a loss of consumer surplus attributable to protection. Thus, it is not difficult to imagine scenarios in which any one of these three instruments might be the first choice for protection a domestic industry.

But what about regulatory protectionism? Unlike the tariff, it produces no government revenue. Unlike the quota, it creates no quota rents to be bestowed on domestic importers, or on foreign producers who might otherwise move their governments to retaliate. And unlike the subsidy, it does nothing to preserve consumer surplus in the market in question. In short, regulatory protectionism seems demonstrably inferior to each of the alternatives from the perspective of political officials setting trade policy in isolation. They can achieve the same level of protection for any domestic industry using a tariff, quota, or subsidy, while conferring additional surplus on the treasury, on foreign suppliers or domestic importers, or on domestic consumers, and reaping the attendant political rewards.

Consequently, if nations were unconstrained in their ability to use the protectionist instrument that they most prefer, we would expect to see very little regulatory protectionism. Each nation acting unilaterally would almost always choose one of the alternative policies.

Now consider the situation that confronts parties to a cooperative trade agreement. In particular, let us suppose that nations have constrained themselves in their ability to employ tariffs, quotas, and subsidies by virtue of trade agreement. This is a realistic description of the WTO, as shown above, because of the widespread existence of tariff bindings and the associated constraints on any quotas and subsidies that would frustrate expectations associated with the bindings. Let us further assume that nations take all of these commitments and constraints seriously and would incur a substantial reputational penalty or retaliatory sanction should they deviate from them. Finally, imagine for a moment that the hypothetical trade agreement embodies no constraints on regulatory protectionism.

On these assumptions, the temptation to use regulatory protectionism seemingly arises where it did not exist before. The reason is quite simple: import-competing interests would always like more protection. And if the trade agreement permits nations to afford such protection through regulatory measures and not through other measures, regulatory protectionism would become a tempting way to provide it. Among other things, it might be used in a way that constitutes implicit cheating on the bargain, frustrating the expectations created by tariff bindings through a regulatory protection loophole.

If cheating is the concern, of course, a complete prohibition on regulatory protectionism might seem unnecessary. Rather, parties to a trade agreement could simply adopt the same rule that the WTO applies to subsidies – just as a new subsidy program that frustrates the expectations associated with a tariff binding is impermissible but subsidies in general are not, so might new regulatory protectionism be prohibited. Yet, if the analysis above is right, *all* regulatory protectionism will be new following the entry into force of the trade agreement, since there is no reason to utilize it prior to the establishment of constraints on the preferred instruments of protection. Hence, a complete prohibition on regulatory protectionism and a prohibition on new regulatory protectionism will amount to the same thing. Accordingly, we might expect trade agreements generally, and the WTO in particular, to prohibit regulatory protectionism altogether. At least for the WTO, that expectation has already been shown to be correct in practice.

Much the same conclusion can be reached another way, albeit using a somewhat stronger assumption about the welfare functions of political officials. In particular, suppose that the expected joint political surplus of officials who are parties to the bargain increases with the *sum* of global producer surplus and government revenue. Put differently, suppose that ex ante, producer groups in general are expected to be equally well-organized and influential, and that officials are indifferent between a dollar of producer surplus (which they will be rewarded for generating) and a dollar of government revenue (which they can use to bestow largesse and thus induce political rewards). Though no doubt oversimple,[68] this assumption does generate the result that tariffs or quotas will always dominate regulatory protectionism – an inspection of Figure 1 reveals that tariffs and quotas both generate a larger sum of producer surplus and government revenue than regulatory protectionism at any given level of protection. If regulatory protectionism always moves political officials off their Pareto frontier, it will be in their interest to prohibit it.

To this conclusion I add one clarification and two observations about the further benefits of a prohibition on regulatory protectionism. Trade agreements, like private contracts, are subject to ex ante uncertainty and thus to changing circumstances that may (from a political standpoint) warrant departures from prior commitments. This set of issues lies at the heart of some previous work on the GATT escape clause, which suggests that the reimposition of protection for an industry in economic difficulty may at times be justifiable as a politically valuable adjustment of trade commitments.[69] When such circumstances arise, a mechanism for the adjustment of commitments is required. And, if the adjustment of commitments with respect to tariffs, quotas, and subsidies were unduly costly, regulatory protectionism might be useful as the lesser among evils. In fact, however, the WTO system contains elaborate provisions facilitating the renegotiation of tariff commitments that make this concern quite implausible. Article XXVIII of GATT 1994 provides for the renegotiation of any tariff commitment, for example, and protects the expectations of other parties with a compensation requirement.[70] Article XIX provides for the reimposition of protection for troubled (and thus politically vocal) industries using tariffs and quotas.[71] Thus, it should always be better to renegotiate over the more efficient instruments of protection than to introduce the costs of regulatory protectionism.

One additional benefit of a prohibition on regulatory protectionism relates to an observation made in the introduction to this Article – regulatory protectionism need not be deliberate. Regulators may act often with limited information, or without meaningful input from those affected by their decisions. This problem is likely to be particularly acute when those disadvantaged by regulation are foreign firms. International legal agreements that prohibit regulatory protectionism, such as the TBT and SPM Agreements of the WTO, require central governments to pay much greater heed to the implications for their regulations for trade. In significant part, these agreements may be aimed not just at deliberate cheating but also at the costs of inattention and inadvertence in a diffuse bureaucracy. Otherwise, the unwitting destruction of joint surplus through regulations that unnecessarily burden foreign suppliers may become a serious problem. Efforts to avoid such problems by international agreement ensure that protection is afforded only where it is, on balance, politically valuable, and only in a manner that destroys as little surplus for well-organized interest groups as possible.

A second additional benefit of a prohibition on regulatory protectionism relates to the problem of quantifying the amount of protectionism in the system in order to facilitate reciprocal market access negotiations. The central objective of the original GATT, now furthered by the WTO, was to make politically valuable, reciprocal market access commitments to enable exporters to expand their sales.[72] In the course of negotiation over these commitments, officials needed to know what they were giving and what they were getting. Tariffs provide a clear metric in this regard. A 20 percent tariff will inflate the price of imports to consumers by 20 percent, other things being equal. Exporters and their representatives can thus evaluate the impact of tariffs on export prices rather easily and thereby assess the market access opportunities at differing tariff rates. Regulatory protectionism, by contrast, is much less transparent in its effects. Consider the beef hormones example in the introduction. A prohibition on the importation of hormone-raised beef will raise costs of exporters by some amount that relates to the costs of segregating animals treated with hormones from those not so treated, the costs of certifying that the animals were properly segregated, and so on. These costs may be quite uncertain and variable – are they comparable in their effects on trade to a 10 percent tariff? a 20 percent tariff? The answer may be quite unclear, and thus it is helpful for negotiators to have protectionism channeled into an instrument such as a tariff that has a more readily identifiable impact on prices and market access opportunities.[73]

2. The absence of balancing

What remains for discussion from the political economy perspective is the absence of any "cost-benefit" or "balancing" rule within the WTO to weed out regulatory measures that serve genuine nonprotectionist objectives where the regulatory benefits are small and the adverse trade impact great. Much of the explanation for this absence lies in the fact that such welfare-reducing measures (using "welfare" in the conventional sense of modern welfare economies) need not be welfare-reducing from a political standpoint. Indeed, if rigorous cost-benefit analysis were the touchstone of policy, virtually all tariffs, quotas, and subsidies would fall to pass muster because of the deadweight losses evident in Figure 1. Those measures, and others like them, survive because political officials care not only about the magnitude of costs and benefits, but also about their incidence. Modest benefits to a well-organized interest group can readily outweigh larger costs to a diffuse and poorly organized interest group in the political calculus.

For the same reason, objective cost-benefit analysis is not the proper metric from a political perspective for the evaluation of nonprotectionist regulations that have an adverse trade impact.[74] The constituency favoring a regulation may be well-organized and influential, and the constituency that suffers from it (and particularly from the adverse trade effects) may be poorly organized. A simple balancing of the economic costs and benefits of the regulation can mask these important distributional concerns.

To be sure, the political officials who enter a trade agreement such as the WTO ideally might like to subject regulations with important adverse effects on foreign trade to a political cost-benefit analysis, asking whether the net impact of the regulation on the political interests of WTO members is positive or negative.[75] I have already argued that regulatory protectionism fails such a cost-benefit test and is accordingly prohibited. But where the regulation in question advances some genuine regulatory objective other than protectionism, only a case-by-case analysis of its political costs and benefits can determine whether it is a net benefit or a net detriment from a political standpoint. Categorical prohibitions, such as those described above, are no longer useful.

But legal tribunals will have great difficulty conducting any sort of political cost-benefit analysis on a case-by-case basis. Scientific and economic exports can provide much of the information necessary for a tribunal to engage in conventional cost-benefit analysis, but the information for an assessment of the political interests of national officials, and the intensity of the concerns on each side, will be largely inaccessible. Moreover, political officials likely would be appalled at the thought of an international tribunal balancing the political considerations on each side and transparently upholding or striking down regulations on political grounds. I suspect that virtually all political officials would prefer to maintain the illusion that regulation is undertaken solely for high-minded reasons.

Accordingly, the WTO does not entrust its dispute resolution process with the task of balancing the political costs and benefits of national regulations that are necessary to the attainment of genuine regulatory goals other than protectionism. Once a regulation is determined to have this property, it is simply upheld under both the TBT and SPM Agreements. Of course, where a legally permissible regulation has considerable adverse effects on export interests abroad and is of little political value to the officials in the importing country, another avenue exists for getting rid of it – negotiation. A side payment by officials in the exporting nation(s), in the form of a concession on other trade matters or perhaps some unrelated matter of mutual interest, can induce officials in the importing nation to change its policy. As Ronald Coase noted long ago, such negotiation alone can suffice for parties to achieve a Pareto optimum as long as the transaction costs of bargaining are small enough.[76]

Indeed, a Coasean perspective can organize the entire political economy analysis. Officials who enter trade agreements seek to attain their political Pareto frontier. To a considerable degree, they do so through sector-by-sector, product-by-product bargaining over tariffs and other instruments of policy, resulting in highly detailed commitments on each imported and exported good. Likewise, when circumstances change and one party introduces a new policy that affects the welfare of others, the same process of detailed bargaining can restore the Pareto optimum. But bargaining is costly; to economize on bargaining costs it is at times useful to have categorical rules that apply to all products and markets, enforced by a dispute resolution system. This option is appealing when optimal behavior is more or less the same in all product markets, and when that optimal behavior can be achieved by a legal rule that is reasonably precise and straightforward to apply. Regulatory protectionism, as I have defined it, is always suboptimal from a political perspective and can be defined in its particulars by a set of fairly clear legal rules – the rules described in Section B above. The task of policing regulatory protectionism is thus an appropriate one for the quasi-judicial dispute resolution of the WTO. By contrast, it is exceedingly difficult to devise a workable and palatable legal rule to condemn regulatory measures that are necessary to nonprotectionist regulatory goals but that are nevertheless undesirable because of their trade impact. As a result this task is left to case-by-case bargaining.

III. SOME COMPARATIVE NOTES ON OTHER TRADING ARRANGEMENTS

The WTO is by no means the only trading arrangement that confronts the problems of regulatory protectionism. Others include the NAFTA, the European Union, and the United States federal system. If the analysis to this point is right, we might expect strong pressures to prohibit regulatory protectionism in all of these systems. Each of them imposes substantial constraints on the tariffs, quotas, and subsidies that subsidiary jurisdictions might otherwise use to protect their firms from foreign competition. These constraints should in turn lead to pressure to use highly wasteful regulatory protectionism if it is not effectively prohibited. We might also expect that nonprotectionist regulatory measures would be treated with less hostility, even where their effects on trade are great. A quick review of the law of these other systems suggests that these expectations are borne out in the main.

A. The NAFTA

The NAFTA is an agreement under which Canada, Mexico, and the United States afford significant tariff preferences to each other that are not afforded to other trading nations.[77] Like the WTO, it includes constraints on quotas and subsidies to avoid frustrating expectations under the negotiated preferences.

The NAFTA was negotiated more or less concurrently with the negotiations that led to the WTO, and the proposals in each tended to filter through the other. Perhaps not surprisingly, therefore, the provisions of the NAFTA relating to regulatory protectionism bear striking resemblance to those of the Uruguay Round TBT and SPM Agreements. Both the NAFTA chapters on technical barriers[78] and on sanitary and phytosanitary measures[79] incorporate by now familiar WTO principles including the national treatment requirement; the sham principle; obligations to give reasons; notice, publication, and comment requirements; obligations to use international standards; and least restrictive means principles. The chapters extend these obligations both to substantive regulations and to conformity assessment.

Although there are a number of modest differences in wording between the pertinent NAFTA and WTO provisions,[80] the NAFTA, like the WTO, can fairly be said to prohibit regulatory protectionism.[81] Similarly, the NAFTA is tolerant of nondiscriminatory regulatory measures that have protective effects but that can be justified as essential to nonprotectionist objectives – NAFTA too requires no "cost-benefit" balancing between regulatory benefits and adverse trade impact.

B. The European Union

The European Union, like the NAFTA, affords trade preferences to its members. It has the familiar property of constraining the use of protectionist instruments that nations would ordinarily want to use, thereby raising the danger of regulatory protectionism as a substitute.

1. Legislative response

Unlike the WTO and the NAFTA, the European Union has legislative authority that can be used to address regulatory protectionism. That authority has been used extensively. The Treaty Establishing The European Community ("Treaty of Rome") authorized the European Council of Ministers,[82] upon a proposal from the European Commission,[83] to issue directives to "approximate" (in other words, harmonize) the measures of Member States that "directly affect the establishment or functioning of the common market."[84] The old approach to harmonization through Council initiatives involved the product-by-product promulgation of detailed technical regulations. Products that met the specifications could circulate freely within the Community, although Member States were sometimes free to require their own producers to meet a different set of technical specifications. In the mid-1980s, the Commission and the Council embraced a new approach that delegates the detail work to others. For the most part, the Council limited itself to setting out the "essential requirements" that products must meet relating to matters such as health, safety, environmental protection, and consumer protection.[85] The Council can then refer the task of formulating detailed standards that meet the essential requirements to Europe-wide standardization organizations. Once the detailed requirements are established, Member States must conform their national laws and regulations to them, subject to an "escape clause" that permits nations to deviate on grounds such as public morality; protection of human, animal, and plant life and health; protection of intellectual property; and protection of the environment. A product that conforms to the resulting standards, or that conforms to national measures deemed "equivalent" by the Commission, is presumed to meet the essential requirements and is entitled to be marketed freely within the Community, again subject to an escape clause.[86]

For product regulations covered by either old or new harmonization directives, a clear consequence of a directive is the elimination of any regulatory protectionism that might result from differences in the substantive regulations promulgated by national regulators. Although the escape clauses permit Member States to adopt more stringent regulations where they can justify them on the basis of goals other than protectionism, any cost disadvantage imposed on foreign firms due to differences in regulatory requirements will require justification before the Commission and perhaps the European Court of Justice as well.

Like the WTO, the European Union has also taken additional steps to eliminate regulatory protectionism that may result from regulatory "surprise" or from information deficiencies on the part of regulators. A 1983 Mutual Information Directive[87] requires national standard-setting organizations and regulators to notify the Commission and certain European standard-setting organizations of proposed standards or regulations before their adoption. With respect to regulations in particular, Member States must notify the Commission of proposed regulations. The Commission then disseminates that information to other Member States. Either the Commission or another Member State may object to a proposed regulation and request that it be modified to avoid adverse trade effects. The Commission may also opt to prepare a harmonization directive on the subject. In either case, final adoption of the proposed regulation must be delayed until the matter is resolved.[88]

The global approach to conformity assessment[89] is another important innovation. It encourages all parties involved in certification and testing – both product manufacturers and third-party testing laboratories – to embrace European quality control standards to govern their activities. And once the European quality assurance standards are in place, additional guidelines specify when and where the necessary testing and certification for each product will occur. These guidelines minimize the cost and intrusiveness of testing and certification while still meeting essential regulatory objectives.[90]

2. Judicial response

Article 30 of the Treaty of Rome provides that: "Quantitative restrictions on imports and all measures having equivalent effect shall, without prejudice to the following provisions, be prohibited between member-States."[91] Among the subsequent provisions in the Treaty, one pertinent to regulatory measures is Article 36: "The provisions of Articles 30 to 34 shall not preclude prohibitions or restrictions on imports . . . justified on grounds of public morality, public policy or public security; the protection of health and life of humans, animals or plants; the protection of national treasures . . .; or the protection of industrial and commercial property. Such prohibitions or restrictions shall not, however, constitute a means of arbitrary discrimination or a disguised restriction on international trade."[92] This structure should by now seem quite familiar – protectionism is prohibited, bona fide regulation to achieve other objectives is not.

These Articles of the Treaty raise a number of interpretive issues, implicitly left to the Commission and to the Court of Justice. It was settled quickly that Article 30 would have broad applicability and, in particular, that it would encompass all manner of regulatory barriers.[93] A 1969 directive from the Commission stated that product regulations can have an "equivalent effect" to quantitative restrictions.[94] In the view of the Commission, product regulations application to imports exclusively ("distinctly applicable measures") were automatically covered by Article 30, and regulations application to domestic and imported goods alike ("indistinctly applicable measures") would be covered or not in accordance with a balancing test. It was necessary to inquire whether "the restrictive effects on the free movement of goods are out of proportion to their purpose," and whether "the same objective can be attained by other means which are less of a hindrance to trade."[95] This early interpretation by the Commission goes beyond mere prohibition of regulatory protectionism, of course, and hints at a more general balancing of regulatory benefits against the costs of trade reduction. In 1974, the Court of Justice took an even more expansive view of the measures that might run afoul of Article 30 in the case of *Procureur du Roi v Dassonville*:[96] All trading rules enacted by Member States which are capable of hindering, directly or indirectly, actually or potentially, intra-Community trade are to be considered as measures having an effect equivalent to quantitative restrictions."[97] The *Dassonville* formulation makes no distinction between distinctly and indistinctly applicable measures and requires no balancing test as under the 1969 directive. It does require actual or potential "hindrance" of trade, a concept that has proven illusive to define. Because any regulation or conformity assessment measure that prohibits the importation of a good or substantially increases the cost of importation would surely qualify, however, the details of the "hindrance" concept need not detain us.

The Court later backed away from the broad sweep of its *Dassonville* test in a case known popularly as *Cassis de Dijon*.[98] The Court held that "disparities between the national laws . . . must be accepted insofar as those provisions may be recognized as being necessary in order to satisfy mandatory requirements relating in particular to the effectiveness of fiscal supervision, the protection of public health, the fairness of commercial transactions and the defence of the consumer."[99] The list of mandatory requirements to which the court refers was subsequently held not to be exhaustive.[100] After *Cassis*, therefore, the Court applies a two-tier test: For measures applicable to imports exclusively, the Member State must justify them on the basis of the Article 36 criteria noted above.[101] Measures that are applicable to both domestic and imported goods, however, may be justified on the basis of mandatory requirements not enumerated in Article 36. Those that fail this test cannot be applied against imports, and the *Cassis* decision itself indicates that the Court will scrutinize the purported nonprotectionist justifications for a regulation closely.[102] Further, a presumption exists that products lawful in one State ought to be allowed into another, and the Court can force a kind of "mutual regulation" where the regulations in force in the exporting nation achieve all the legitimate objectives of the importing nation, even if they do so in a manner that differs from the importing nation's own approach.[103]

In sum, the jurisprudence of the European Court of Justice has evolved in a manner quite similar to the WTO rules. Discriminatory regulations are extremely difficult to sustain, and nondiscriminatory regulations with adverse trade impact must employ the least trade restrictive means for the attainment of nonprotectionist regulatory goals. Mutual recognition will be required where no violence to legitimate regulatory objectives will occur. Finally, despite some hints to the contrary in earlier statements by the Commission, there is little "balancing" of non-protectionist regulatory benefits against the burden on commerce.

C. The United States Federal System

The inefficiencies of noncooperative trade policies under the Articles of Confederation are said to have provided much of the impetus for the Constitution of the United States.[104] Like the other trading arrangements above, the Constitution imposes a number of restrictions upon the use of traditional protectionist instruments by the states, such as a prohibition upon export of import duties without the consent of Congress.[105] It also grants to Congress the "power . . . to regulate Commerce with foreign Nations, and among the several States"[106] (the Commerce Clause), thereby affording Congress the power to constrain state action expressly through statutory enactments. But not all restrictions on state activities in the commercial sphere are express. State policies that are in tension with federal regulatory policy may be deemed implicitly preempted by the federal regime.[107] And, even when the Congress has taken no action on a subject pursuant to the Commerce Clause, state action may be found to violate the Constitution because of the negative implications of that clause – the so-called dormant or negative Commerce Clause.[108]

This allocation of powers has much to say about the treatment of regulatory protectionism within the United States. Congress has eliminated regulatory trade impediments in many areas (though sometimes as an incidental consequence of federal regulation). The Food, Drug, and Cosmetic Act, for example, establishes a federal mechanism for the approval of prescription drugs that preempts state drug regulation.[109] The Federal Communications Act affords the FCC authority to establish television broadcast formats.[110] The Ports and Waterways Safety Act,[111] by promulgating safety rules for the design of tanker vessels, preempts more stringent state standards.[112] Innumerable other examples might be offered.

Yet, many regulatory barriers remain outside the scope of federal legislation, even under the implied preemption doctrine. States and localities maintain their own building codes, health regulations, pollution control regulations, and a wealth of other product-related measures. These regulations are a source of impediments to commerce domestically and have been a matter of considerable interest internationally.

The WTO accords afford *foreign nations* some legal basis for challenging these state regulations on the basis of the principles laid out earlier. State regulations that are inconsistent with the requirements of the TBT and SPM Agreements can place the United States in violation of international law and thus lead to initiatives by the federal government to correct the problem.[113]

Another source of constraints on protectionist state and local regulations, which can be invoked directly by domestic and foreign firms affected by those regulations, is the dormant Commerce Clause. Modern analysis in dormant Commerce Clause cases begins with the question of whether the challenged practice effectuates a "legitimate local public interest, and its effects on interstate commerce are only incidental."[114] If any discrimination against interstate commerce is to be tolerated in pursuit of a legitimate interest, it must be because of the absence of adequate "nondiscriminatory alternatives."[115] Finally, whenever a demonstrable burden on interstate commerce exists, with or without discrimination against out-of-state producers, the Court will weigh the interests of state against the burden. Discriminatory policies are likely to be struck down under this balancing analysis, while nondiscriminatory policies are "upheld unless the burden imposed on [interstate] commerce is clearly excessive in relation to the putative local benefits."[116]

On its face, this doctrine automatically invalidates any substantive state regulation that creates regulatory protectionism as defined in this Article. It requires national treatment in virtually all cases absent a compelling regulatory justification for its absence, and the balancing test implies a least restrictive means requirement.[117] More generally, any time a regulatory measure is not necessary to achieve some state regulatory objective other than protectionism, the burden on commerce is self-evidently "excessive in relation to the putative local benefits."

Accordingly, the dormant Commerce Clause has been used regularly to invalidate state measures that amount to regulatory protectionism.[118] Examples of measures struck down by the courts include: a prohibition by one state on imports from another that display a quality standard developed by the other state;[119] a requirement that milk be pasteurized and bottled locally;[120] prohibitions on the importation of food products from outside a defined radius in which state inspectors would operate;[121] a requirement that eggs imported from out of state be stamped with the two letter postal code for the state of origin;[122] and requirements that domestic electric utilities either continue to use domestic high sulfur coal or incur substantial regulatory burdens for failing to use it.[123]

To be sure, the operation of the dormant Commerce Clause has proven controversial in some respects, particularly as to the application of the balancing test. Determining whether the local public interest is "legitimate," whether nondiscriminatory alternatives are "adequate," and whether the local benefit outweighs the burden on commerce can require difficult value judgments that judges have no special capacity to make and that are ordinarily entrusted to the political branches of government. Further, if balancing of interstate burden against local benefit is taken seriously, it requires a wealth of empirical information that often will be unavailable in United States courts. For these and other reasons, commentators are often critical of dormant Commerce Clause doctrine, as are a number of prominent jurists. Laurence Tribe suggests that: "The Supreme Court's approach to Commerce Clause issues . . . often appears to turn more on *ad hoc* reactions to particular cases than on any consistent application of coherent principles."[124] Now Chief Justice Rehnquist wrote in a 1981 dissent: "The true problem with today's decision is that it gives no guidance whatsoever to these States as to whether their laws are valid or how to defend them . . . . We know only that [the challenged state] law is invalid and that the jurisprudence of the 'negative side' of the Commerce Clause remains hopelessly confused."[125] Among the law and economics scholars, Frank Easterbrook and Edmund Kitch have argued that the dormant Commerce Clause strays beyond the limits of judicial competence[126] and may even be unnecessary given the realities of competition and the incentives for cooperation among the states.[127]

It is instructive that these criticisms are directed mainly toward the balancing analysis in cases that purport to weigh the importance of the state's regulatory goals against the attendant burden on commerce. Where the state's proffered nonprotectionist objective seems genuine and the state has employed the least restrictive means to achieve it, it is indeed difficult to imagine how a court is to determine whether the attendant burden on commerce nevertheless outweighs that objective. But such cases, by definition, are not cases of regulatory protectionism. Whatever the particular criticisms of dormant Commerce Clause doctrine, therefore, even the critics seemingly exhibit near consensus on the idea that regulatory protectionism as it is defined here ought to be, and is, prohibited under the dormant Commerce Clause. The battle joins when courts go beyond that prohibition to strike down nonprotectionist regulations that unavoidably place significant burdens on commerce.

On this set of issues, perhaps the United States can learn from the international agreements that confront the same problems. The pattern in the WTO, the NAFTA, and the European Union is much the same: balancing regulatory benefits and burdens is neither authorized nor undertaken in the judicial or quasi-judicial process. When a regulatory objective appears to be genuine and nonprotectionist, all that is required is the least trade restrictive means to achieve it. The remaining burdens on commerce resulting from heterogeneous domestic regulations and conformity assessment systems are left to case-by-case negotiation in the WTO or the NAFTA, or to the European government in Brussels in the case of Europe. The regularity of that pattern *perhaps* suggests its wisdom and thus may support the suggestion by a number of jurists and commentators that United States courts ought to steer clear of balancing bona fide regulatory benefits against commercial burdens in dormant Commerce Clause cases. I do not want to overstate the point, however, as I have merely made the case that a balancing analysis is unlikely to be a part of a politically savvy trade agreement — it is unlikely to move signatory officials toward their Pareto frontier. Whether it may nevertheless be defended on independent normative grounds is a distinct issue, although I suspect that the argument against it from a political efficiency standpoint — the inability of the judicial process to measure the relevant costs and benefits accurately — may counsel against it more generally.

CONCLUSION

Protection against foreign competition can be conferred through a range of policy instruments with variable welfare consequences. Regulatory protectionism is generally the most pernicious of the familiar techniques. It holds little temptation for savvy political officials who are free to select among the alternative instruments of protection, and emerges only after those officials become constrained in their choice of policy instruments. This Article has suggested a political economy basis for expecting a prohibition on regulatory protectionism to emerge in multilateral trading arrangements, and has shown that a prohibition is in fact present in the WTO, the NAFTA, the European Union, and the United States federal system. This regularity is striking. It is also fortunate as a normative matter, as it channels protectionism into the instruments that do the least damage.

Regulatory measures can have protective effects, however, without constituting "regulatory protectionism" as defined herein – measures that are nondiscriminatory and are essential to the attainment of some regulatory objective other than protectionism may burden foreign firms. The WTO and NAFTA are tolerant of such measures, and, after a brief flirtation with judicial balancing of the benefits and burdens, the European Union is largely tolerant of them as well. United States doctrine is more murky, and judicial balancing of regulatory benefits and commercial burdens is still undertaken to some extent. This aspect of United States law has been the subject of intense criticism, however, and if the political economy analysis herein cannot settle the debate as a normative matter, it can at least help us to understand its genesis.

NOTES

Frank & Bernice J. Greenberg Professor of Law, University of Chicago. I have received useful comments on earlier versions of this paper from Lucian Bebchuk, Louis Kaplow, and from seminar participants at Columbia, Harvard, NYU, and the annual meeting of the American Law and Economics Association. I am grateful to the Bradley and Scaife Foundations for financial support.

1 For a description of the early history of the dispute, see Office of the United States

Trade Representative, *Unfair Trade Practices: European Community Hormones Directive*, 52 Fed Reg 45304 (1987).

2 The dispute began in 1985 when, in conjunction with its ban on the domestic use of growth hormones, the European Community banned the importation of beef from nations that permit growth hormones to be given to cattle for human consumption. This import ban was to become effective in 1988. Id. The United States complained, and subsequent European intransigence led President Reagan to impose retaliatory tariffs against European exports under Section 301 of the Trade Act of 1974. Presidential Proclamation 5759, *Increasing the Rate of Duty on Certain Products of the European Community*, CPR 1987 Comp 189. The European Union later modified its regulation to permit beef imports from countries that allow the use of growth hormones if the imported beef could nevertheless be certified as hormone-free. But because compliance with the certification process was expensive, and much United States beef still was excluded by it, the United States continued its retaliatory tariffs for certain imports although suspending the increased duty for others. See Office of the United States Trade Representative, *Modification to the Determination To Impose Increased Duties on Certain Products of the European Community*, 54 Fed Reg 31398 (1989).

3 See WTO, *EC Measures Concerning Meat and Meat Products* (Hormones), Complaint by the United States, Report of the Panel, WT/DS26/R/USA, Aug 18, 1997; *EC Measures Concerning Meat and Meat Products* (Hormones), Report of the Appellate Body, WT/DS26/AB/R, Jan 16, 1998. Both are available online at <http://www.wto.org/wto/ddf/ep/public.html> (visited Nov 10, 1998).

4 For example, the tariff on carcasses or half carcasses is presently 20 percent plus 2763 ECU per ton, which will gradually decline to 12.8 percent plus 1768 ECU per ton in accordance with European tariff concessions negotiated during the Uruguay Round of multilateral trade negotiations. See WTO, 19 *Legal Instruments Embodying the Results of the Uruguay Round of Multilateral Trade Negotiations Done at Marrakesh on 15 April 1994* 16212 (1994).

5 See id; WTO, *Agreement on Agriculture*, Art 5, reprinted in John H. Jackson, William J. Davey, and Alan O. Sykes, *1995 Documents Supplement to Legal Problems of International Economic Relations* 100–02 (West 3d ed 1995) ("*Documents Supplement*").

6 See GATT 1947, as amended, Art XIX, reprinted in *Documents Supplement* at 44–45 (cited in note 5).

7 See WTO, 19 *Legal Instruments Embodying the Results of the Uruguay Round* at 16955 (cited in note 4).

8 Throughout this Article, I use the term "regulation" as it is used in the WTO agreements, to refer to policies promulgated by governments with which compliance is *mandatory*. Regulations should be distinguished from "standards," with which compliance is *voluntary* and which may result from either government or private sector activity. See Alan O. Sykes, *Product Standards for Internationally Integrated Goods Markets* 13–14 (Brookings 1995).

9 Much of what I have to say bears on government regulation of service industries, labor markets, the environment, and similar areas, but these topics raise distinct issues that I will not address directly in this Article.

10 The certification process is expensive because cattle growers must keep track of which animals have been treated, make sure that the animals' carcasses are segregated at the packing house, and provide supporting documentation as required.

11 See, for example, Peter B. Kenen, *The International Economy* 17–19, 175–77 (Prentice-Hall 1985) (showing how opening trade by removing tariffs or quotas will increase consumer surplus in excess of any decrease in producer surplus). Section I

of this Article also elaborates on the economic inefficiencies associated with protectionism.

12 Other papers that draw on this perspective to explain important aspects of the law of international trade include Alan O. Sykes, *Protectionism as a "Safeguard": A Positive Analysis of the GATT "Escape Clause" with Normative Speculations*, 58 U Chi L Rev 255, 274–78 (1991) (using public choice theory to help explain the existence of the GATT escape clause); Alan O. Sykes, *The Economics of Injury in Antidumping and Countervailing Duty Cases*, 16 Intl Rev L & Econ 5 (1996) (evaluating injury analysis in antidumping and countervailing duty cases from the perspectives of welfare economics and public choice theory); Warren F. Schwartz and Alan O. Sykes, *Toward a Positive Theory of the Most Favored Nation Obligation and Its Exceptions in the WTO/GATT System*, 16 Intl Rev L & Econ 27 (1996) (using public choice theory to explain the most-favored-nation provision of the GATT and its exceptions).

13 See generally Sam Peltzman, *Toward a More General Theory of Regulation*, 19 J L & Econ 211 (1976); Gary Becker, *Comment*, 19 J L & Econ 245 (1976) (evaluating Peltzman).

14 The assumption of a perfectly elastic (flat) import supply curve here is unrealistic in an important sense – all costs of protectionism will be passed through to domestic consumers, and hence foreign suppliers will have no reason to complain about it. International rules restricting protectionism exist, of course, precisely because foreign suppliers do care about it. But as indicated in the text, the essential insight that I wish to develop with Figure 1 – that regulatory protectionism is typically far more damaging to social welfare than other forms of protectionism – holds regardless of whether the import supply curve is flat or upward sloping, and the "small country" assumption allows the reasoning to be presented in a diagram that is far less cumbersome.

15 This proposition oversimplifies but does no harm for present purposes. Important differences do exist between tariffs and quotas, for example, in imperfectly competitive markets. The notion that quotas are no worse than tariffs from a welfare standpoint in competitive markets is also questionable under many circumstances. For example, when quotas are allocated among supplier countries, they may not replicate the market shares that each nation would obtain under a most-favored-nation tariff system. Additional deadweight losses can then result because imported goods are no longer obtained from the most efficient suppliers. Such considerations may help to explain the general preference within the WTO system for tariffs over quotas, but nothing in the analysis to follow turns on such matters.

16 There is no loss of generality in this formulation. Whatever the precise form of regulatory protectionism, t simply represents the unit cost of resources consumed for the purpose of compliance with the protectionist regulation. It can be a direct expenditure as in my hypothetical, an opportunity cost (such as the foregone interest on the value of imported goods that sit around awaiting inspection or certification), or depreciation in the value of the goods themselves (as when delay in customs processing causes loss of perishable merchandise).

17 Of course, if regulatory protectionism creates insurmountable hurdles to imports that no resource expenditure could overcome, it is no different in its welfare consequences than a prohibitive tariff on an import quota of zero.

18 Put more formally, suppose that rent-seeking expenditures by interest groups destroy some fixed proportion of x of the surplus potentially available to those interest groups, where $x<1$. The assumption that $x<1$ is compelling, for otherwise rent-seeking expenditures would be irrational. Assume further that this proportion x is constant across all of the protectionist options – tariffs, quotas, subsidies, and regulation. It

follows that regulatory protectionism is inferior from a welfare standpoint to the alternatives as long as some of the rectangle *abcd* is consumed in regulatory compliance costs – had that part of the rectangle been preserved under a tariff, quota, or subsidy, only the fraction *x* of it would have been destroyed through rent seeking.

19 See *Agreement Establishing the World Trade Organization*, reprinted in *Documents Supplement* at 3–14 (cited in note 5).

20 The modern counterpart of the GATT legal obligation not to charge a tariff above the bound rate is created by GATT 1994, Art II, itself a part of the WTO agreements. GATT 1994 is reprinted in *Documents Supplement* at 79–96 (cited in note 5). Articles incorporated into GATT 1994 from GATT 1947 are reprinted in *Documents Supplement* at 15–78. The term "tariff binding" refers to a negotiated tariff ceiling; the term "bound rate" is the amount of the tariff permitted under that ceiling.

21 See GATT 1994, Art XXVIII (cited in note 20).

22 Indeed, some skeptical readers may wonder whether any of the rules of the system are really "binding" and meaningful, since members of the WTO can always quit and pursue whatever policies they wish or violate their obligations to see what happens. I (and others) have argued elsewhere, however, that the level of compliance with WTO rules is quite high because of the damage to reputation and the prospect of trade sanctions that attend deviation from the rules, and the importance to each member of retaining the benefits of the bargain. See Alan O. Sykes, *Constructive Unilateral Threats in International Commercial Relations: The Limited Case for Section 301*, 23 L & Pol Intl Bus 263, 266 (1992); Frieder Roessler, Warren F. Schwartz, and Alan O. Sykes, *The Economic Structure of Renegotiation and Dispute Resolution in the WTO/GATT System* 15–24, unpublished manuscript (on file with U Chi L Rev); Judith Hippler Bello, *The WTO Dispute Settlement Understanding: Less Is More*, 90 Am J Intl L 416 (1996). For details on the structure of dispute resolution under the WTO and the sanctions that may attend violation, see generally WTO, Annex 2, *Understanding on Rules and Procedures Governing the Settlement of Disputes*, reprinted in *Documents Supplement* at 366–90 (cited in note 5).

23 See GATT 1994, Art XI (cited in note 20); *Agreement Establishing the World Trade Organization*, Art II (cited in note 19).

24 See, for example, GATT 1994, Arts XI (agricultural price support schemes), XII (balance of payments), XIX (declining industries), XX (protection of human, animal, and plant life or health) (cited in note 20).

25 See id Art XIII.

26 See, for example, id Art XIX.

27 See GATT 1947, Arts III(8)(b) (exempting subsidies to domestic producers), XVI (exempting subsidies applicable only to exports from the Art III(8)(b) exemption) (cited in note 6).

28 See, for example, *EEC–Payments and Subsidies Paid to Processors and Producers of Oilseeds and Related Animal-Feed Proteins*, 37th Supp GATT BISD (1991), excerpted in John H. Jackson, William J. Davey, and Alan O. Sykes, *Legal Problems of International Economic Relations* 357-62 (West 3d ed 1995).

29 See GATT 1994, Art VI, para. 6 (cited in note 20). Countervailing duty was defined as "a special duty levied for the purpose of offsetting any bounty or subsidy bestowed, directly or indirectly, upon the manufacture, production or export of any merchandise." Id Art VI, para. 3.

30 The TBT Agreement is reprinted in *Documents Supplement* at 149–69 (cited in note 5). The TBT Agreement is a successor to the GATT Standards Code, negotiated during the 1970s. The TBT Agreement is considerably more comprehensive in its substantive provisions than the GATT Standards Code, and, unlike the Standards

Code, to which only a subset of the GATT membership acceded, the TBT Agreement applies to all WTO members.

31 The SPM Agreement is reprinted in *Documents Supplement* at 121–33 (cited in note 5). The covered measures include regulations to protect plants and animals from entry of diseases or pests; regulations to protect human and animal life from dangers associated with food additives or contaminants; measures to protect human health from diseases carried by plants or animals; and all measures intended to protect against the spread of pests. SPM Agreement, Annex A, Definition 1.

32 Occasionally, measures that might seem to discriminate against imports from a particular source could be justified because of dangers unique to that locale – "mad cow" disease, for example, may be limited for a time to Great Britain, and might justify a ban on British cattle imports only.

33 The TBT Agreement provides that "in respect of technical regulations, products imported from the territory of any Member shall be accorded treatment no less favourable than that accorded to like products of national origin and to like products originating in any other country." TBT Agreement, Art 2.1 (cited in note 30). The corresponding provisions of the SPM Agreement require member governments to "ensure that their sanitary and phytosanitary measures do not arbitrarily or unjustifiably discriminate between Members where identical or similar conditions prevail, including between their own territory and that of other Members." SPM Agreement, Art 2(3) cited in note 31). This softer language in the SPM Agreement is intended to permit "discrimination" of sorts when the relevant threat to human, animal, or plant life or health is associated with goods only from certain countries.

34 GATT 1994, Art XX (cited in note 20).

35 TBT Agreement, Art 2.2 (cited in note 30).

36 SPM Agreement, Art 2(3) (cited in note 31).

37 TBT Agreement, Art 2.2 (cited in note 30); SPM Agreement, Art 2(2) (cited in note 31).

38 The SPM Agreement requires members to ensure that "any sanitary or phytosanitary measure . . . is based on scientific principles and is not maintained without sufficient scientific evidence (except as an interim measure in the face of scientific uncertainty)." SPM Agreement, Art 2(2) (cited in note 31). Detailed risk assessment procedures are set forth in SPM Agreement, Art 5.

39 See text accompanying note 3.

40 Food additive regulations that prohibit additives not on an approved list, for example, may result in the prohibition of imports containing additives known elsewhere to be perfectly safe.

41 TBT Agreement, Art 2.9.4, 2.10 (cited in note 30); SPM Agreement, Annex B, paras 5(d), 6 (cited in note 31).

42 The International Organization for Standardization has jurisdiction to address design, safety, and quality concerns in product markets across the board, and publishes thousands of standards as a result of its work. The Codex Alimentarius, affiliated with the United Nations, focuses mainly on food safety issues. A miscellany of other entities with standard-setting functions includes the International Labor Organization, the International Telecommunications Union, the International Institute on Refrigeration, the International Commission on Illumination, and others. See Sykes, *Product Standards* at 58–60 (cited in note 8) (listing international standardization organizations).

43 See id at 61–62 (describing the problem of incompatible broadcast formats for high-definition television and suggesting that incompatibility could be avoided if nations followed standards set by the International Radio Consultative Committee).

44 See id at 59–60.

45 TBT Agreement, Art 2.4 (cited in note 30); SPM Agreement, Art 3(1), 3(3) (cited in note 31).

46 TBT Agreement, Art 2.6 (cited in note 30); SPM Agreement, Art 3(4) (cited in note 31).

47 TBT Agreement, Art 10.1 (cited in note 30); SPM Agreement, Annex B, para. 3 (cited in note 31). Developed country members also have an obligation to make all pertinent information available in English, French, and Spanish if requested to do so by another member. TBT Agreement, Art 10.5; SPM Agreement, Annex B, para. 8. For good measure, a specific nondiscrimination rule prohibits charging more for such information when it is sold to foreign firms than when it is sold to domestic firms. TBT Agreement, Art 10.4; SPM Agreement, Annex B, para. 4.

48 Any time a new regulation would depart from an established international standard, or would address an issue on which no international standard exists, advance notice must be given in the form of "notice in a publication at an early appropriate stage, in such a manner as to enable interested parties in other Members to become acquainted with it." TBT Agreement, Art 2.9.1 (cited in note 30). Substantially equivalent language in the SPM Agreement may be found in Annex B, para. 5(a) (cited in note 31). Direct notice must also be provided to the WTO Secretariat indicating what products would be covered by the proposed regulation and how it would depart from any relevant standards promulgated by international agencies. TBT Agreement, Art 2.9; SPM Agreement, Annex B, para. 5(b)–(c). Exceptions exist, as one might expect, where urgent matters of health, safety, or national security preclude this advance notice. TBT Agreement, Art 2.10; SPM Agreement, Annex B, para. 6. All regulations must also be "published promptly" when they are adopted. TBT Agreement, Art 2.11; SPM Agreement, Annex B, para. 1.

49 The caveat is that if conformity assessment costs are sufficiently lower under a system that limits the options allowed to achieve a given end, the savings may be worth the costs of foreclosing certain otherwise acceptable methods of achieving regulatory goals.

50 Meat packing plants in country A may become subject to the slaughtering process regulations of country B, for example, even though post-slaughter testing for various residues and contaminants by inspectors in country A is enough to ensure that the meat satisfies the health standards of country B.

51 The TBT Agreement provides that "technical regulations shall not be more trade-restrictive than necessary to fulfil [sic] a legitimate objective. . . . Such legitimate objectives are, inter alia: national security requirements; the prevention of deceptive practices; protection of human health or safety, animal or plant life or health, or the environment." TBT Agreement, Art 2.2 (cited in note 30). The SPM Agreement's version of this principle requires members to "ensure that any sanitary or phytosanitary measure is applied only to the extent necessary to protect human, animal or plant life or health." SPM Agreement, Art 2(2) (cited in note 31).

52 TBT Agreement, Art 2.8 (cited in note 30) ("Wherever appropriate, Members shall specify technical regulations based on product requirements in terms of performance rather than design or descriptive characteristics.").

53 The strongest requirement is contained in the SPM Agreement: "Members shall accept the sanitary or phytosanitary measures of other Members as equivalent . . . if the exporting Member objectively demonstrates to the importing Member that its measures achieve the importing Member's appropriate level of sanitary or phytosanitary protection." SPM Agreement, Art 4(1) (cited in note 31). The TBT Agreement is softer, requiring that "Members shall give positive consideration to accepting as equivalent technical regulations of other Members . . . provided they are satisfied that these regulations adequately fulfil [sic] the objectives of their own regulations." TBT Agreement, Art 2.7 (cited in note 30). This weaker language

amounts at least to an obligation to give reasons for refusing to accept regulations as equivalent, which should raise the costs of disingenuous refusals to do so.

54 TBT Agreement, Art 5.1.1 (cited in note 30); SPM Agreement, Annex C, para. 1(a) (cited in note 31).

55 TBT Agreement, Art 2.2; SPM Agreement, Art 2(3).

56 TBT Agreement, Art 5.1.2; SPM Agreement, Annex C, para. 1(e).

57 TBT Agreement, Art 5.2.3; SPM Agreement, Annex C, para. 1(c).

58 TBT Agreement, Art 5.2.1; SPM Agreement, Annex C, para. 1(a).

59 TBT Agreement, Art 5.2.6; SPM Agreement, Annex C, para. 1(g).

60 TBT Agreement, Art 5.6; SPM Agreement, Annex C, para. 1(b).

61 TBT Agreement, Art 5.4; SPM Agreement, Annex C, para. 1.

62 For an introduction to the welfare economics of protectionism, see Jagdish N. Ghagwati and T. N. Srinivasan, *Lectures on International Trade* 105-25 (MIT 1983); Kenen, *The International Economy* at 167–92 (cited in note 11).

63 Even when protectionist measures are plausibly beneficial from the selfish perspective of an importing nation – such as when the nation possesses monopsony power in world markets or can divert rents or positive externalities to its domestic industry from foreign industries – they are nevertheless usually detrimental from a global perspective. See generally Bhagwati and Srinivasan, *Lectures on International Trade* at 174–84 (cited in note 62); Paul R. Krugman, *Rethinking International Trade* 233–42 (MIT 1990).

64 See generally Robert E. Baldwin, *The Economics of the GATT*, in Peter Oppenheimer, ed. *Issues in International Economics* 82 (Oriel 1980) (analyzing the relationship between the political and economic objectives served by the GATT); Sykes, 58 U Chi L Rev at 274–78 (cited in note 12) (analyzing the political aspects of the GATT through the lens of public choice theory).

65 In economic parlance, they become Cournot-Nash actors. See Augustin Cournot, *Researches Into the Mathematical Principles of the Theory of Wealth* (MacMillan 1897) (originally published in 1838); John Nash, *Equilibrium Points in N-Person Games*, 36 Proc Natl Acad Sci 48 (1950).

66 The fact that nations acting unilaterally may sometimes anticipate retaliatory or conciliatory moves by other nations in response to their own does not change the analysis importantly – what matters is that negotiations over cooperative agreements make the returns to exporters much more precise and certain and thus increase their returns from participating in the trade policy process. See Sykes, 58 U Chi L Rev at 281 (cited in note 12).

67 See Section I.

68 It has been argued elsewhere that this assumption may not be a bad approximation of the ex ante reality that confronts trade negotiators, and that it may have considerable purchase in explaining the terms of trade agreements. For example, it can explain the existence of the most-favored-nation clause of the WTO/GATT system. GATT 1994, Art I (cited in note 20), which generally forbids tariff discrimination among trading partners (with some interesting and perhaps also explicable exceptions). See generally Schwartz and Sykes, 16 Intl Rev L & Econ 27 (cited in note 12).

69 See Sykes, 58 U Chi L Rev at 289–99 (cited in note 12).

70 GATT 1994, Art XXVIII (cited in note 20).

71 Id Art XIX. See also Roessler, Schwartz, and Sykes, *Economic Structure of Renegotiation and Dispute Resolution* at 11 (cited in note 22) ("[I]t may be politically efficient . . . to afford transitory protection to import-competing industries suffering severe dislocation, at the expense of growing and prosperous foreign competitors.").

72 See Baldwin, *Economics of the GATT* at 83–87 (cited in note 64).

73 One additional bit of history fits nicely with this political economy analysis. The GATT began in 1947 with a series of tariff bindings negotiated among the major trading nations of the time. Initially, the only constraints on regulatory protectionism were those of GATT Article III, the national treatment Article. But with time, due to the constraints on tariffs, quotas, and subsidies that the GATT introduced, regulatory barriers to trade became more important. During the Tokyo Round of trade negotiations during the 1970s, some GATT signatories responded by negotiating a "Standards Code" that went considerably beyond the national treatment requirement, though it fell well short of the obligations now embodied in the TBT and SPM Agreements. The perceived deficiencies in the Standards Code led to additional pressures to constrain regulatory protectionism, culminating in new WTO Agreements. The history of legal obligations under the GATT and WTO is detailed in Sykes, *Product Standards* at 63–86 (cited in note 8). In short, the international constraints on the traditional instruments of protectionism came first, and the more elaborate and detailed constraints on regulatory protectionism followed later as nations became increasingly creative in devising new forms of protective regulations. This pattern of legal developments lends support to the notion that regulatory protectionism is of little political utility in an environment where nations are unconstrained in their trade policies, but becomes important once their preferred instruments of protection are disabled.

74 This observation is hardly novel, at least not in the domestic context, as it underlies much of the modern economic theory of regulation. See, for example, George J. Stigler, *The Theory of Economic Regulation*, 2 Bell J Econ & Mgmt Sci 3 (1971); Peltzman, 19 J L & Econ 211 (cited in note 13); Richard A. Posner, *Theories of Economic Regulation*, 5 Bell J Econ & Mgmt Sci 335, 344-50 (1974).

75 As a formal matter, the inquiry would be whether the political benefit to officials who favored the regulation (presumably those in the importing country) outweighed the political detriment to officials who disfavored the regulation (presumably those in the adversely affected exporting countries, whose exporters are upset about a loss of market access). In theory, this interpersonal welfare comparison can be made using the "weights" that are implicit in the political Pareto optimum for the trade agreement in question. For a formal treatment, see Sykes, 58 U Chi L Rev at 300–03 (cited in note 12). If such a system could be implemented, all political officials could benefit on average so that ex ante – at the time the trade agreement is concluded – each official would find the system beneficial.

76 Ronald Coase, *The Problem of Social Cost*, 3 J L & Econ 1 (1960).

77 See generally North American Free Trade Agreement ("NAFTA"), reprinted in *Documents Supplement* at 489–710 (cited in note 5). Free trade agreements are authorized by Article XXIV of the original GATT, which remains part of the WTO system in GATT 1994. Article XXIV constitutes the principal exception to the most-favored-nation requirement of the WTO system that ordinarily prohibits discrimination among trading partners. To invoke the Article XXIV exception, parties to free trade areas must eliminate barriers to trade on "substantially all" trade between them. See GATT 1994, Art XXIV(5), (8) (cited in note 20).

78 NAFTA, Part Three, Technical Barriers to Trade, Chapter Nine: Standards-Related Measures (cited in note 77).

79 NAFTA, Part Two, Trade in Goods, Chapter Seven: Agriculture and Sanitary and Phytosanitary Measures, Section B ("NAFTA SPM Chapter") (cited in note 77).

80 For example, the NFTA SPM Chapter requires that no measure be maintained "where there is no longer a scientific basis for it." Id Art 712(3)(b). In the WTO SPM Agreement, by contrast, the obligation is not to be maintained "without *sufficient* scientific evidence." SPM Agreement, Art 2(2) cited in note 31) (emphasis

added). The NAFTA requirement can be read as less stringent (the difference between "some scientific basis" and "sufficient scientific evidence"), and if so, the NAFTA provision prevails in a dispute between the parties to the NAFTA. See NAFTA, Article 103 (cited in note 77).

81 For further discussion, see Sykes, *Product Standards* at 108–09 (cited in note 8) (discussing the NAFTA accords on technical barriers and SPMs).

82 The Council is the primary legislative body in Europe, from which most Community legislation emanates. It consists of country representatives (Ministers) that act in accordance with various voting rules, dependent upon the subject matter of the action. See *Treaty Establishing The European Community*, [1992] 1 CMLR 573, reprinted in Neville March Hunnings and Joe MacDonald Hill, eds, The Treaty of Rome Consolidated and the Treaty of Maastrict, Common Market Law Reports Reprints (Sweet & Maxwell 1992) ("Treaty of Rome").

83 The Commission is a group of distinguished citizens, acting in their individual capacity rather than under the direction of their home countries, charged with undertaking many of the initiatives required by the Treaty of Rome. Typically, as here, the Commission makes proposals to the Council, which then acts upon them, subject at times to the requirement that it seek advice from other entities such as the European Parliament. The Parliament has relatively little power. For a general description of the governmental structure of the Community, see Josephine Steiner, *Textbook on EEC Law* 10–19 (Blackstone 3d ed 1992).

84 Treaty of Rome, Art 100 (cited in note 82).

85 The 1989 "Machinery Directive" affords a nice illustration. *Council Directive of 14 June 1989 on the approximation of the laws of the Member States relating to machinery*, 1989 OJ (L 183) 9. It includes some general principles of safe construction for machinery, such as to "eliminate or reduce risks as far as possible," and to "take the necessary protection measures in relation to risks that cannot be eliminated." Id at (L 183) 15. It then proceeds to a higher level of detail, discussing the need for integral lighting for certain types of machinery, the importance of readily accessible devices to stop all moving parts, the need for controls to avoid accidents due to power supply interruptions, the need for measures to ensure stability against vibration and other disturbances, the importance of eliminating sharp edges, and on and on. Id at (L 183) 16–27. The directive thus addresses virtually every conceivable type of product hazard, and lays down general principles for avoiding each of them. Yet, the directive applies to a vast array of machinery products. Indeed, its application extends to virtually every product that in common parlance might be called a "machine," with a few enumerated exceptions such as "mobile equipment," "medical equipment," "steam vessels," "firearms," and several others. Id at (L 183) 11.

86 See Bernard van de Walle de Ghelcke, Gerwin van Gerven, and Koen Platteau, *The New Approach to the Elimination of Technical Barriers in the European Community*, 1990 BYU L Rev 1543, 1551–60 (dealing the European Community's product standards requirements).

87 *Council Directive of 28 March 1983 laying down a procedure for the provision of information in the field of technical standards and regulations*, 1983 OJ (L 109) 8, 9.

88 Id at (L 109) 8–11.

89 European Commission, *A Global Approach to Certification and Testing*, Common 89/209 of June 15, 1989, 1989 OJ (C 267) 3.

90 See generally id at (C 267) 15–24.

91 Treaty of Rome, Art 30 (cited in note 82).

92 Id Art 36 (emphasis removed).

93 See *Commission Directive of 22 December 1969 based on the provisions of Article 33(7), on the abolition of measures which have an effect equivalent to quantitative restrictions*

on imports and are not covered by other provisions adopted in pursuance of the EEC Treaty, 1970 OJ (L 13) 29.

94 Id.

95 Id at (L 13) 31.

96 [1974] ECR 837, 851 (holding that a provision of Belgian law "prohibiting the import of goods bearing a designation of origin where such goods are not accompanied by an official document . . . certifying their right to such designation constitutes a measure having an equivalent to a quantitative restriction").

97 Id at 852.

98 *Rewe-Zentral AG v Bundesmonopolverwaltung für Branntwein*, [1979] ECR 649 (*"Cassis de Dijon"*).

99 Id at 662.

100 The encouragement of cultural activities, for example, or the interest in maintaining "national or regional socio-cultural characteristics," can qualify as mandatory requirements. See Steiner, *Textbook on EEC Law* at 86–87 (cited in note 83) (listing cases after *Cassis de Dijon* that apply the mandatory requirements exception).

101 Article 36 requires some interpretation. With reference to regulatory barriers to trade, the two provisions of greatest relevance are the exception for measures to protect human, animal, and plant health, and the "public policy" exception. The latter has been construed very narrowly, however, and has proven to afford essentially no protection to Member States outside of a few areas of little pertinence here. See id at 95. Thus, as a practical matter, the only Article 36 exception likely to be of any use to the importing nation in a dispute is the health exception. Given the breadth of the *Dassonville* test for measures within the scope of Article 30, therefore, trade barriers that result from distinctly applicable regulatory measures will almost certainly be struck down unless a health justification can be shown.

102 (1974) ECR at 853.

103 A survey of cases may be found in Steiner, *Textbook on EEC Law* at 87–91, 96–97 (cited in note 83). For some illustrative decisions, see *EC Commission v Greece (Re Beer Purity Standards)*, [1988] 1 Common Mkt L Rep 813, 816–20 (holding that prohibitions on beer imports with certain additives violate Article 30 in substantial part because no scientific evidence could be adduced of any health hazard); *EC Commission v Germany (Re Purity Requirements for Beer)*, [1988] 1 Common Mkt L Rep 780, 799 (same); *EC Commission v United Kingdom (Re UHT Milk)*, [1983] 2 Common Mkt L Rep 1, 16 (holding that requiring an extra UHT treatment on imported milk and cream is unreasonable and thus violates Article 30 as equivalent to a quantitative restriction on imports); *EC Commission v United Kingdom (Re Imports of Poultry Meat)*, [1982] 3 Common Mkt L Rep 497, 519–20 (holding that import restrictions on food products violated Article 30 because the Court was unpersuaded that the health justifications were bona fide or that the least restrictive means had been employed); *EC Commission v Italy (Re Low-Fat Cheese)*; [1992] 2 Common Mkt L Rep 1, 16 (holding that the least restrictive means to protect consumers was labeling rather than prohibition on nonconforming products); *EC Commission v Germany (Re German Sausages)*, [1989] 2 Common Mkt L Rep 733, 741–42 (same); *Ec Commission v Germany (Re the Use of Champagne-Type Bottles)*, [1988] 1 Common Mkt L Rep 135, 143–44 (same); *Miro BV*, [1986] 3 Common Mkt L Rep 545, 559–60 (same).

104 See Laurence H. Tribe, *American Constitutional Law* 404–06 (Foundation 2d ed 1988).

105 US Const, Art I, § 10, cl 2.

106 Id § 8, cl 3.

107 See Tribe, *American Constitutional Law* at 479–501 (cited in note 104).

108 This listing of constitutional restrictions upon state actions that affect commerce is not intended to be exhaustive. Other and sometimes similar constraints emanate from the Privileges and Immunities Clause, the Equal Protection Clause, and a range of other provisions.

109 In general, the Act delegates the authority to promulgate regulations to an agency – the Food and Drug Administration – and allows the agency to decide whether to give its regulations preemptive effect. 21 USC §§ 301 et seq (1994).

110 47 USC § 151 (1994).

111 33 USC § 1221 (1994).

112 See *Ray v Atlantic Richfield Co*, 435 US 151, 168 (1978).

113 Note that the states are not per se bound by the WTO Agreements. But the United States is under an international obligation to police compliance by the states and, to avoid international sanctions for a violation, can bring an action to strike down inconsistent state laws. See Uruguay Round Agreements Act, 19 USC § 3512(B)(2)(A) (1994).

114 *Pike v Bruce Church, Inc*, 397 US 137, 142 (1970).

115 *Hunt v Washington State Apple Advertising Commission*, 432 US 333, 353 (1977).

116 *Pike*, 397 US at 142.

117 See Tribe, *American Constitutional Law* at 436–38 (cited in note 104).

118 The dormant Commerce Clause assuredly does less than, say, the WTO or the NAFTA to police the process by which regulations are promulgated and the attendant information and costs of regulatory surprise that may afflict foreign firms. This is perhaps an unavoidable consequence of a system that rests on ex post challenges to regulations through the judicial system as opposed to the renegotiation required under the WTO or the NAFTA. Further, these kinds of costs may well be less important in the United States federal system where language barriers are absent and transparency of government regulatory operations is more commonplace.

119 *Hunt*, 432 US at 350–54.

120 *Dean Milk Co v City of Madison*, 340 US 349, 356 (1951); *Dean Foods Co v Wisconsin Department of Agriculture*, 478 F Supp 224, 231–32 (W D Wis 1979).

121 *Miller v Williams*, 12 F Supp 236, 242 (D Md 1935).

122 *United Egg Producers v Department of Agriculture of Puerto Rico*, 77 F3d 567, 572 (1st Cir 1996).

123 *Alliance for Clean Coal v Bayh*, 72 F3d 556, 559–60 (7th Cir 1995); *Alliance for Clean Coal v Miller*, 44 F3d 591, 595–96 (7th Cir 1995).

124 Tribe, *American Constitutional Law* at 439 (cited in note 104).

125 *Kassel v Consolidated Freightways Corp,* 450 US 662, 706 (1981) (Rehnquist dissenting).

126 See Frank H. Easterbrook, *The Constitution of Business,* 11 Geo Mason U L Rev 53, 58 (1988); Edmund W. Kitch, *Regulation and the American Common Market,* in A. Dan Tarlock, ed, *Regulation Federalism and Interstate Commerce* 9, 46–47 (Oelgeschlager, Gunn & Hain 1981). Justice Scalia has at times expressed similar views. See *CTS Corp v Dynamics Corp of America,* 481 US 69, 95 (1987) (Scalia concurring) (arguing that the *Pike* inquiry is "ill-suited to the judicial function and should be undertaken rarely if at all"). Richard Posner, however, takes a more charitable view of the doctrine. See Richard A. Posner, *The Constitution as an Economic Document,* 56 Geo Wash U L Rev 4, 17 (1987) ("The 'negative' commerce clause is one device ... for preventing states from abusing their 'market power'."). For the argument that a proper constitutional interpretation does not support the creation of a dormant Commerce Clause by the judiciary, see Martin H. Redish and Shane V. Nugent, *The Dormant Commerce Clause and the Constitutional Balance of Federalism,* 1987 Duke L J 569.

127 Proposals for reform of dormant Commerce Clause doctrine abound. Easterbrook and Kitch impliedly argue that much of the dormant Commerce Clause doctrine ought be abandoned, leaving the Congress to police state malfeasance under the "positive' Commerce Clause. See Easterbrook, 11 Geo Mason U L Rev at 61 (cited in note 126); Kitch, *Regulation and the American Common Market* at 42–45 (cited in note 126). Donald Regan urged the Court to reject its "balancing" exercise in favor of an inquiry into whether the challenged practice has a "protectionist motive," an approach that he contends is followed already to a considerable degree in the guise of balancing language. Donald Regan, *The Supreme Court and State Protectionism: Making Sense of the Dormant Commerce Clause,* 84 Mich L Rev 1091 (1986). Saul Levmore favors greater attention to the question of whether a challenged practice imposes substantial costs on citizens of other states by exploiting state market power, or whether instead the economic costs of the practice are borne mainly within the jurisdiction. Saul Levmore, *Interstate Exploitation and Judicial Intervention,* 69 Va L Rev 563, 626–29 (1983). A similar proposal, though directed to the proper application of the "state action" doctrine under the antitrust laws, is that of Frank Easterbrook. See Frank H. Easterbrook, *Antitrust and the Economics of Federalism,* 26 J L & Econ 23, 45–49 (1983). For the argument that the aggregate efficiency consequences of state legislation will not depend systematically on whether the state is able to exploit non-residents, see Daniel R. Fischel, *From MITE to CTS: State Anti-takeover Statutes, the Williams Act, the Commerce Clause, and Insider Trading,* 1987 S Ct Rev 47, 74–78.

13. The Policy Harmonization Debate: What Can Developing Countries Gain from Multilateral Negotiations?

D. Tussie

INTRODUCTION

The attainment of domestically integrated economies in developing countries with reasonable levels of growth per capital GNP, free from massive dependence on foreign loans or grants, requires increased exports of processed and manufactured goods. Today a growing number of developing countries are adopting policies to allow faster growth of both exports and imports and for larger inflows of foreign direct investment. As they convert to market-based solutions, developing countries have also changed their defensive stance in the GATT. They have become committed upholders of genuine free trade principles and a rules-based system.

Sustainable outward-oriented growth by increasing numbers of developing countries requires internal commitment and an enabling external environment. Ironically, as more and more developing countries join the GATT, it has come under increasing pressure. Its principles have been put into question and it has ceased to be the principal vehicle with which the United States now conducts its trade policy. At the same time the issues on the agenda have been modified. Together, these changes have important implications for the developing countries. The restructuring of global bargaining arrangements has posed new challenges for the management of open economies.

The negotiation of the North American Free Trade Area (NAFTA) concurrently with the Uruguay Round has raised concern over the possibility of trade and investment diversion and, in general, over its exclusionary potential. In some regions, particularly Latin America, it has raised expectations of access to a "safe haven". The immediate impact of NAFTA on the final shape of the Uruguay Round seems to have been limited. Its longer-term system implications are still uncertain. But it is in this context that the failings or achievements of the Uruguay Round must be judged.

The Uruguay Round has been a milestone in international trade policy. It has converted the GATT and its successor, the World Trade Organization (WTO), into a legitimate forum for regulating the interplay between domestic policies and international interests. Its over-arching agenda and subsequent deadlock are testimony to the many dilemmas posed by the new trade agenda. Global harmonization of domestic practices has become an internationally negotiable proposition. Such a route could eventually lead to an international system whereby a set of norms, rules and economic policies must be accepted by every part as an entry fee for access to markets.

The purpose of this paper is twofold. It first examines the direction taken by the Uruguay Round negotiations as an indicator of what is in store on the agenda. It then queries what this direction might mean for developing countries. The final section makes some suggestions for future work.

A. THE NEW INTERNATIONAL TRADE AGENDA[1]

Negotiations in the GATT have always been the bedrock of world trade policy. GATT agreements set precedents and are points of departure for national trade policies as well as for regional integration schemes. In the early post-war years, trade policy was confined to deal only with policies that directly affected trade in goods. Tariffs and quotas were then the main impediments to trade. So from its inception the GATT was conceived as an instrument for the removal of tariffs on a most favoured nation (MFN) basis. This was seen to be the principal way of achieving free trade.

As GATT rounds proceeded, they removed a significant layer of tariffs applied by developed countries. By 1987, when the full extent of the Tokyo Round tariff reductions became effective during the course of the Uruguay Round, import-weighted average tariff rates reached about 4.3 per cent for the United States and 6 per cent for the EEC of Nine. For Japan which had brought forward the full implementation of its cuts by March 1983, the equivalent figure was 2.9 per cent. The tariff thus lost much of its traditional significance as an effective means of protection. For almost two-thirds of world trade the incidence of tariff costs is less than or equivalent to transport costs. The Uruguay Round will bring additional reductions of around 30 per cent. The international trading order of the 1990s within these parameters could be described as the most liberal since the First World War.

True, this aggregate picture hides the very significant corridors of international trade that have been subject to exceptions. At the sectoral and product level, in particular, tariff peaks and tariff escalation, according to the degree of processing for goods of export interest to developing countries, are notorious. At the same time that tariffs in developed countries have come to very low levels, non-tariff barriers have been increasing, particularly in the European Union and the United States. Non-tariff measures – and, more importantly, their incidence – are difficult to quantify. Therefore, it is not clear that such measures are now a more important impediment to trade than they were in the past. For some time UNCTAD has been calculating the share of imports into developed countries that is affected by non-tariff measures. As regards imports from all origins, the share of imports covered by non-tariff measures rose somewhat between 1981 and 1990, but the increase was modest (from around 16 to 17.5 per cent). The trade coverage ratio for imports from developing countries was considerably higher in both years, although the increase from 22.5 to 23 per cent was less significant (UNCTAD, 1991, p. 59).

Nonetheless, there can be little doubt that the impact of non-tariff measures is significant. Moreover, they are heavily biased against the exports of manufactures of developing countries, which concentrate on labour-intensive goods in which developed countries are losing competitiveness. In short, large segments of international trade have been partially excluded from the trend towards trade liberalization, which has been centred on trade among developed countries and in manufactured goods for which trade tends to be of an intra-industry kind.

In other words, the trade which has been liberalized is largely of a two-way nature in goods where both partners have production capacity and are at roughly equivalent levels of development. By contrast, one-way exports of developing to developed countries are subject to restrictions of both a tariff and a non-tariff nature.[2] The incorporation of developing countries into the international trading system remains fragmentary. The reason no longer lies in the derogations from GATT rules that they sought for development reasons. These could have played a part when import substitution was in full swing. But regardless of developing countries' trade policies, the goods they export – or could potentially export – have been increasingly excluded from GATT disciplines by the importers themselves.

Despite the exclusion of such trade corridors from meaningful liberalization, developed countries increased their expectations of what the system could deliver for them. Pressure was mounted for the GATT to assume new responsibilities. At the same time, the avalanche of unilateral liberalizations in a growing number of developing countries increased their own expectations as to what a properly functioning system must deliver in terms of market access.

In the course of the Uruguay Round, the GATT was pressed to its limit. It was confronted with the obstacle created by its own previous success in completing first the general removal of the tariff barriers of developed countries, and then the incorporation *en masse* of developing countries into its orbit.

Ceteris paribus, the first "peel of protection" of most economies was shed. With border measures receding, non-border measures applied by governments to shape competition perforce became more visible. They became negotiating matter. The accountability of governments for their trade and trade-related actions increased with their shedding of the outer layer of protection. A panoply of measures that were traditionally seen to have only indirect links into trade policy are now found to have "trade-interfering effects". To quote from the World Bank's Handbook, non-tariff barriers are considered to be "all public regulations and government practices that introduce unequal treatment for domestic and foreign goods of the same or similar production". Under such an extended net, they naturally "constitute the single most important obstacle to the growth of international trade" (Olechowski, 1987, p. 121).

A wider net over economic policy has been cast, the implication being that the dividing line between trade and other policies has become increasingly blurred; the distinction between border and non-border measures seems largely artificial. Lawrence (1993) has distinguished the integration achieved so far via the traditional tariff mechanism as "shallow integration". Freeing of trade was pursued by dealing with measures as they were reflected at the border. The Uruguay Round closed the era of shallow integration and gave way to a new policy arena "beyond the border" (Ostry, 1990). The concepts of "shallow" versus "deep" integration are largely equivalent to the concepts of negative and positive integration elaborated in traditional customs union theory. Reciprocal MFN tariff liberalization has given way to rule-making to reduce differences in the setting of competitive milieus. There is a fundamental difference between these two types of activities. The transition from one to the other points to deepening degrees of international integration, the progressive shift from separate national economies to global markets.

Put simply, liberalization had been routinely enacted on the basis of a calculation of concrete and immediate economic benefit. Since bargaining was essentially restricted to lowering border tariffs, there was no reason for agreeing on domestic policies. Bargaining came down to exchanging concessions over products on an item-by-item basis. The decision to liberalize became one of each government choosing the tariffs it wanted to set at the negotiating table.

Rule-making, in contrast, entails reaching an agreement over a framework of principles, norms, rules and decision-making procedures for transactions that will be spread over time. Once a government opens up to negotiate its national regulatory regimes, its autonomous economic management is gradually undermined; the country's economic policies are exposed, and they become intertwined with those of its negotiating partner until pressure to reduce difference grows. In place of domestic policies with international implications, there will be the integration of various domestic policies into an international one (Meyer, 1978).

The Uruguay Round was confronted with uncharted territory. At the same time, an ever growing number of countries from the developing and the disintegrating communist worlds joined the GATT and placed further strains on the system. The agenda for the Round contained a negotiating mandate spanning virtually every old and new trade and non-trade issue. The difficult task has been one of demarcation, that is, to determine those issues for which differences in domestic institutions could be tolerated and those which had to be addressed.

The Uruguay Round became stuck precisely over these questions, if albeit the apparent problem was disagreement over agriculture. Agriculture in many ways was the syndrome in which a myriad of complex factors converged. But even taken in isolation, inherent to the problem of agricultural negotiations was the question of what changes or alignments must be made in other policies in order to facilitate the freeing of trade. The question raised in the context of agriculture, just as in the Round more generally, was how much freedom of choice must governments sacrifice, and how legitimate are international agreements to shape the conditions of competition in domestic markets. Whenever the price of goods and services in a country varies excessively from a given internationally determined benchmark – whether this be brought about by subsidies, lax intellectual property protection or lower labour or environmental standards – the conditions of competition are affected. What is at stake is a delimitation of government intervention in the competition for global resources.

B. APPROACHES TO POLICY CONVERGENCE

As the content of the trade agenda shifts from negotiations over products for which national treatment was appropriate to negotiations over the policies that shape the conditions of competition, new principles are required.[3] Two solutions have in fact emerged to address the disruptive effects of domestic regulatory differences: harmonization and mutual recognition.[4]

Harmonization requires alignment of policy preferences to a specified benchmark. Intergovernmental negotiations are required to agree on the benchmark, transition period, conditions for enforcement, etc. The really serious hurdle of harmonization is that it involves hard choices between liberalization and other non-trade policy goals. The problems are such that previous well-established procedures for international negotiations are inadequate and even obsolete. Harmonization between countries with unequal bargaining strength, exemplified by the negotiations of the NAFTA or even the Strategic Impediments Initiative between the United States and Japan, will tend to be skewed in favour of the policy preferences of the more powerful. In this context, the smaller country will typically try to do its utmost to avoid linkages to policy areas outside a narrow – traditional – definition of trade policy with varying degrees of success (Kahler, 1993).

A second solution is mutual recognition of national rules and standards. The principle of mutual recognition accepts national diversities and allows a high degree of institutional competition. In other words, conformity to mutual recognition implies that lower (or less costly) standards on processes or products will have to be accepted. Competition is expected to lead eventually to convergence on the most efficient institutional arrangements. Because of the disruptive factor movements that competition can cause, it is an easier option to pursue among countries with small divergences in standards and policy preferences. It has been adopted by the European Union after a failed attempt to impose harmonization and centralized regulation. However, there is an exception to this generalization in the case of financial services for which regulatory harmonization will lead to an upward levelling of standards in many member States. Alternatively, it can be adopted among countries which vary in size and institutional settings, restricting it to policy domains in which variations in regulations do not produce excessive strains, or in cases where variations can be handled without resort to trade impediments. For imports not to be discouraged, specific technical aspects of the way goods are produced can be encapsulated. This might imply, for instance, that recourse to an import prohibition can be replaced by a labelling requirement (Pelkmans, 1987).

Both mutual recognition and harmonization are an endorsement that convergence will eventually take place. A new phase of international negotiations has been opened. A central point to be elucidated in the course of negotiations is how much convergence to pursue.

One way of addressing the problem is to look for mere correctives. This is the negative integration proposed in traditional customs union literature.[5] In this case agreement is sought on preventive action in so far as the freeing of trade from customs duties risks being nullified by such non-tariff barriers as technical or health standards, customs laws or procedures. The point of such negotiations is to determine to what extent such resorts involve evasion of free trade commitments via tariff substitutes. They result in commitments not to use policy tools that offset the effect of liberalization.

More far-reaching pressures for convergence hold that integration must be structural or positive. It ought to go beyond the tidying up of administrative procedures and must be undertaken in order to intensify free trade. Under this approach what ought to be harmonized are rules relating to the conditions of production. The question then is which policies are negotiable, how much equivalence is necessary and whether it is a requirement for freeing trade or the result of that process.

Negative harmonization aims to ensure that governments honour agreed-upon market access. It serves to lay the ground for tariff reductions to operate more effectively. Yet border measures are seen here to be the ultimate trade policy tool. Positive harmonization would aim at enforcing specific common rules that will define how exactly economic affairs are to be conducted.

In considering the problem of such positive or structural harmonization it is important to note some of the logical and procedure limits it confronts. Although most of these are problems of degree rather than of kind, the contention that structural harmonization must be exacted as a pre-condition for freer trade has a rather obvious logical flaw. Indeed, if the creation of a "level playing field" is carried to the extreme of establishing uniformity above all, international harmonization will be trade-impeding. The implication is that if economies are dissimilar they ought not to engage in trade with each other. Disintegration instead of deep integration will result. In the absence of a world doctrine in the various fields of safety, environmental standards, fair wage-setting procedures, etc., trade barriers are imposed.

In sum, a great deal of research, assessment and negotiation is required before an international consensus can be built on issues such as these. There are at the very least three layers to this discussion: what are the desirable lines of harmonization, what targets may be reasonably set and what methods may be legitimately used to implement them? These questions raise thorny political issues because they touch upon "distortions" that may be the deliberate choice of governmental policies designed to tackle priorities other than trade. Generally, they are inspired by considerations of social welfare; at other times they are engrained in local values and culture and are, as such, rather elusive non-tariff barriers (Bhagwati, 1991). Regional development, income distribution, national security and defense, and balance-of-payments equilibria are examples of objectives whose pursuit impinges on trade.

Not surprisingly, there is much unresolved controversy about how legitimate harmonization is, how far it should be taken and what policies must be incorporated. The road ahead is fraught with a morass of political, legal and economic difficulties.

C. THE POST-URUGUAY TRADING SYSTEM

The GATT system had not been predicated on making all countries identical. Like the principle of equal treatment before the law, it was justified on the opposite proposition that differences were many and various (Wolf, 1984). In fact, the system was designed to allow countries to trade despite and because of such differences. The proviso was that national treatment had to be ensured. The underlying philosophy was one of negative integration. The GATT aimed to remove tariffs and quantitative restrictions so that trade could be expanded and market signals could prevail. Thus, the innate ability of the GATT to constrain national governments, while at the same time leaving room for policy diversity, is limited.

But gradually the GATT has been pushed to extend its domain and seek positive integration goals. A good deal of the Final Act of the Uruguay Round is devoted to clarifying and extending GATT's aegis over non-tariff barriers that stem from domestic institutional divergences. The current road to dealing with variations in policy preferences and domestic differences has not included a wide acceptance of mutual recognition which could entail substantially greater competition.

The solution sought appears to be twofold. On the one hand, there is an attempt at harmonization within very broad bands of national discretion, as exemplified in the general agreement on trade in services. In other areas, much tighter harmonization is pursued, although with different implications for competition. On the issue of technical standards, tighter harmonization can be trade-encouraging rather than trade-impeding. The potential abuse of standards as trade barriers can be reduced by gradual harmonization, since this would cut down the scope for discretionary behaviour. Wide variations in standards mean that producers have to adapt to different requirements in different markets. The Uruguay Round seeks to guard against this eventuality, most notably through the agreement on technical barriers to trade. Moreover, increased transparency of standards may even have beneficial effects on the transfer of technology.

The agreement on intellectual property is a milestone in upward harmonization. The result of such harmonization is the extra-territorial protection of intellectual property rights and the gradual integration of this agreement into the broader framework of international economic law (Reichman, 1993). Prior to the Uruguay Round, in intellectual property protection – as in trade – the principle of national treatment obliged countries to follow disciplines on the form of protection, but freedom was allowed on the subject matter and the level of protection (Maskus, 1990). Now the Final Act of the Uruguay Round has introduced the obligation to set harmonized standards for six types of intellectual property: copyright, trademarks, geographical indications, industrial designs, patents and lay-out designs of integrated circuits. The rights of intellectual property holders and their time frames are also due to be harmonized. Patent-holders are granted rights for a 20-year-term without an explicit obligation to work the patent locally. Moreover, patentees are also granted exclusive rights of importation. Patentability is applied to all types of technology and extended to micro-organisms, food, chemicals and pharmaceuticals and the processes to produce them. In addition, the agreement lays out the obligations of governments for enforcing those rights under domestic law.

Global harmonization of intellectual property rights is based on debatable economic logic (Deardorff, 1990; Maskus, 1990; Subramanian, 1990). The adverse consequences for developing countries include higher royalty payments to foreign innovators; the corresponding loss of investment opportunities in domestic research and development; higher prices for products under monopoly rights; and greater dependence on imports in general. "On the bleakest view, a developing country stands to gain only when a foreign invention affords solutions of particular local utility that would not otherwise obtain sufficient investment in research and development" (Reichman, 1993, p. 5).

It is thus a testimony to the pressures towards positive harmonization when the conditions of competition depart in excess from an established benchmark. The procedure to lay down "minimum conditions" of intellectual property protection to which all countries are bound puts a brake on competition between national regulatory environments. Harmonization under this option is likely to result in fewer, rather than more, open markets for developing countries. The reason is twofold. When harmonization provides for upward alignment to industrial country standards, it inhibits market entry by developing countries. Contestability of markets is reduced and transaction costs in developing countries are increased.

The predicament for developing countries in the post-Uruguay Round trading system is now in direct relation to the problems inherent in developing rules of international cooperation on non-trade issues and practices. The search for new rules must allow developing countries to reap the benefits of specialization. The heightened commitment of developing countries to market-based policies has increased their interest in properly functioning markets abroad. In a globalizing world with intensified economic links, the proper functioning of international markets is decisive. This is most true of small open economies that are particularly exposed to trends in international markets and the uncompetitive behaviour of private agents.

Confidence-creating measures will be required to reduce mistrust and reservations if negotiations on non-trade issues in trade fora are to be taken on board. The WTO will have to do its utmost in the realm of dispute resolution to allow negotiated compromises to regulate the interplay between domestic policies and international interests, and thus curb resort to unilateral measures. Such actions should be forcefully resisted, not only to defend the existence of the multilateral process that the developed countries demanded in the first place, but also the integrity of the expanded WTO.

D. CONCLUSION

The reduced effectiveness of domestic protection to achieve competitiveness in a globalizing world economy led developing countries to participate actively in the Uruguay Round. Their stance changed significantly from the Round's beginning to its end. They came to understand that in exchange for market access, greater international obligations must be accepted with regard to their trade policies, and even other policies which are perceived as having an impact on international competitiveness. The prospect of expanded trade may legitimize some sacrifices. But expanded trade and more certainty of access must be consolidated.

The process of policy harmonization will have to be tailored to accommodate the capacity, the needs and the different paces of developing countries. To enable such accommodation, more time and effort will have to be dedicated to studying the appropriateness of rules and procedures in the unfolding agenda – an agenda which will mould the WTO. Rules and institutional procedures may not by themselves solve asymmetries. But the absence or inappropriateness of legal forms and procedures becomes a part of the problem and can make asymmetries insoluble.

A gradual and flexible approach seems more advisable for developing countries than upward harmonization regardless of economic rationale. Different levels of overall development, as well as development of the domestic judicial and administrative systems need to be accommodated. The approach with "bands of harmonization" should be given more thought. They are more advisable for the debate on labour and environmental standards, the "brand new" areas increasingly under discussion. These are also matters which hinge on the conditions of competition. The NAFTA solution, where enforcement of domestic laws is sought, needs to be considered.

Totally free access to the markets of industrial countries for manufactured exports is an unviable short-term proposition. But it is important to ensure that the debate over harmonization is not used – as was its not too distant relative, the concept of "market disruption" under the Multi-fibre Agreement (MFA) – to justify discrimination against developing countries. "Market disruption" was considered to stem from the dislocation produced by trade between low-wage and high-wage countries. The recent discussions on intellectual property, labour and environmental standards are in a way more awkward because they have taken a highly moralistic tone. To its credit, market disruption never carried any stigma attached to it. There was no accusation that the exporting low-wage country was doing anything improper (Dam, 1970).

Even though "market disruption" provided a cover for the MFA, it was accepted as being in the nature of the development process that wages reached different levels in different countries. The moralistic tone of present day discussions is regrettable because, in contrast to the MFA, which was initially conceived as a temporary expedient, accusations of social or environmental dumping posit trade measures as "the" solution. This does not mean that Western campaigners are wrong in trying to upgrade environmental protection or to abolish slavery, child exploitation or bans on trade unions. To the extent that the focus of the solution shifts away from these objectives *per se*, and concentrates on international harmonization to make countries comply via trade measures, the underlying problems facing poverty or the environment will remain unresolved.

The binary division in GATT, with all developing countries *de jure* and *de facto* free from any obligations, is indeed obsolete and should not be resuscitated. But a powerful case should still be made for "differentiation", and criteria for graduation should be adhered to. Per capital GNP, the contribution of manufacturing to GNP and to exports are good starting points. Careful thought must be given to establishing "bands of harmonization" around these criteria, so that the poorest countries can be allowed longer transition periods and even temporary derogations on specific issues bearing directly on competition. The experience of the European Union, with a mix of self-appointment and region-wide negotiations for "bands" in other issue areas, could provide some guidance. Institutional mechanisms should be established to:

(i) discriminate in which instances harmonization can be justified;
(ii) ensure that harmonization does not reduce transparency and contestability of markets;
(iii) guarantee that newly born standards do not inhibit the entry of developing countries.

All told, the spectre of a failed Uruguay Round held the risk of a potential scramble for safe regional havens, each country competing to arrive first with the most generous bid. The Uruguay Round clearly shows that the negotiation process functions. Despite greater demands than those historically placed on developing countries, the final agreement and the new WTO are an anchor to hold on to. This is important. A more balanced view of the costs and benefits of regional "safe heavens" can be reached with less anguish. Choice, not despair, leads to good bargaining and ultimately to sound marriages.

NOTES

1 Some of the ideas in this section were first developed in Agosin and Tussie (1993).
2 This hypothesis is spelt out in Tussie (1989); empirical verification can be found in de Castro (1989).
3 Jackson (1990, p. 99) proposes to pursue the original goals of the GATT via a new "organizational constitution", which would contain mostly procedural obligations, such as obligations to consult, to avoid actions harming other nations, to abide by dispute settlement results, and to provide fairness and transparency in domestic actions affecting international economic relations.
4 Kahler (1993) distinguishes a third alternative: disintegration or managed trade.
5 Harry Johnson *et al.* (1968) raised the question of how far harmonization ought to be sought as a prerequisite for freer trade. The present essay draws inspiration from that work, but raises the issue of harmonization from a different perspective, i.e. as the process unfolding as a result of trade liberalization.

REFERENCES

Agosin, Manuel R. and Diana Tussie (eds) (1993), *Trade and Growth: New Dilemmas in Trade Policy* (Basingstoke, United Kingdom: Macmillan).
Bhagwati, J. (1991), *The World Trading System at Risk* (Hemel Hempstead, United Kingdom: Harvester Wheatsheaf).
Dam, K. (1970), *The GATT: Law and International Organization* (Chicago and London: University of Chicago Press).
De Castro, Juan A. (1989), "Determinants of protection and evolving forms of North–South trade", *UNCTAD Review*, Vol. 1, No. 2.
Deardorff, A. V. (1990), "Should patent protection be extended to all developing countries?", *The World Economy*, Vol. 13, No. 4 (December).
Jackson, J. (1990), *Restructuring the GATT System* (London: Pinter Publishers and the Royal Institute of International Affairs).

Johnson, Harry, Paul Wonnacott and Hirofumi Shibata (1968), *Harmonisation of National Economic Policies under Free Trade* (Toronto: University of Toronto Press).

Kahler, M. (1993), "Trade and domestic differences", *America Latina Internacional*, Vol. 1, No. 1 (Spring).

Lawrence, Robert Z. (1993), "Futures for the world trading system and implications for developing countries", in M. Agosin and D. Tussie (eds), *Trade and Growth: New Dilemmas in Trade Policy* (Basingstoke, United Kingdom: Macmillan).

Maskus, K. (1990), "Innovation, intellectual property rights and the Uruguay Round", *The World Economy*, Vol. 13, No. 3 (September).

Meyer, F. V. (1978), *International Trade Policy* (London: Croom Helm).

Olechowski, A. (1987), "Non-tariff barriers", *The Uruguay Round: A Handbook on the Multilateral Trade Negotiations* (Washington, D.C.: World Bank).

Ostry, S. (1990), *Governments and Corporations in a Shrinking World* (New York: Council on Foreign Relations Press).

Pelkmans, J. (1987), "The new approaches to technical harmonization and standardization", *Journal of Common Market Studies*, Vol. 35, No. 3 (March).

Reichman, J. H. (1993), "Implications of the draft TRIPs Agreement for developing countries as competitors in an integrated world market", *UNCTAD Discussion Paper*, No. 73, November.

Subramanian, A. (1990), "TRIPS and the GATT paradigm: A tropical temperate view", *The World Economy*, Vol. 13, No. 4 (December).

Tussie, Diana (1989), *The Less Developed Countries and the World Trading System* (London and New York: Frances Pinter).

UNCTAD (1991), *Trade and Development Report* (Geneva and New York: United Nations).

Wolf, M. (1984), "Two-edged sword: Demands of developing countries and the trading system", in J. Bhagwati and J. Ruggie, *Power, Passions and Purpose* (Cambridge, Mass: MIT Press).

14. Trouble for Us and Trouble for Them: Social Regulations as Trade Barriers

D. Vogel

As the United States becomes more integrated into the global economy, U.S. health, safety, antidiscrimination, and environmental policies increasingly have international as well as domestic consequences. Some U.S. social regulations not only impose substantial costs on American industry while yielding little or no net gain to society, but they also disproportionately burden foreign producers seeking to do business here. The two regulatory programs that constitute the primary focus of this chapter, namely, fuel economy standards and rules for reformulated gasoline, fall into this characterization. These regulations have been either inefficient or ineffectual in advancing legitimate domestic health, safety, and environmental policy goals. At the same time, they have discriminated against imports.

Originally enacted in 1975 and most recently revised for model year 1989, corporate average fuel economy standards represent the cornerstone of American energy conservation policy. But the CAFE standards are a dubious means of conserving energy, especially when compared with fuel taxes, the policy adopted by virtually all other advanced nations.[1] In 1993 the European Community, at the behest of European luxury car manufacturers, requested the convening of a dispute settlement panel to hear their complaint that U.S. rules for determining compliance with CAFE standards were discriminatory and therefore violated the General Agreement on Tariffs and Trade.

Another group of regulations, the 1963 Clean Air Act and its amendments in 1967, 1970, 1977, and 1990, constitutes the most costly and important component of U.S. environmental policy.[2] Some of the provisions of these complex statutes have been criticized for foisting substantial costs on producers and consumers while producing relatively meager environmental benefits.[3] For example, in 1990 amendments began to regulate the content of automotive fuel to improve air quality in urban areas. In 1995 Venezuela filed a complaint against the United States with the newly established World Trade Organization, claiming that the method chosen by the Environmental Protection Agency to measure fuel cleanliness under the 1990 amendments discriminated against its petroleum exports to the United States.

This chapter explores the legislative and administrative histories of these two regulatory policies in detail and evaluates their effectiveness in relation to the goals they were intended to accomplish. The cases illustrate the close connection between the regulatory burdens imposed on domestic interests and the emergence of new nontariff trade barriers. The chapter concludes by suggesting that the "least trade restrictive alternative" is often in the best interest not only of foreign producers but of the United States as well.

U.S. FUEL ECONOMY STANDARDS

In 1975 Congress faced the challenge of formulating a long-term plan to reduce the nation's use of oil. At the time, federal price controls on fuel encouraged excessive consumption. Nowhere was this more apparent than in automotive fuel usage, which accounted for 25 percent of American energy demand and the dominant share of domestic petroleum consumption.[4] However, fearful of a political backlash from allowing gasoline prices to rise to world market levels (let alone adding to the prices with an additional fuel tax), Congress chose to shift the burden of conservation onto motor vehicle manufacturers. Indeed, the legislation that authorized the Energy Policy and Conservation Act of 1975, also *extended* the government's price controls on oil.[5]

The legislation approved by Congress established fuel economy standards for all passenger vehicles sold in the United States. These standards were based on the average fuel efficiency of all vehicles sold by each manufacturer. Beginning with the 1978 model year, the average fuel economy standard for all cars produced by each company was set at 18 miles a gallon. A few years later, corporate fuel efficiency standards were set for light trucks as well. Manufacturers whose average fuel economy fell below these standards were subject to fines. All standards were subsequently strengthened; since 1990 the CAFE requirement for passenger cars has been 27.5 miles a gallon.[6]

The Political Economy of CAFE

From the outset CAFE standards sought not only to conserve fuel but to do so in a way that protected the market share of domestic automakers. Congress could have furthered fuel efficiency by combining a tax on gas guzzlers with tax incentives for the purchase of fuel-efficient cars. But like imposing a gasoline excise tax, this action might have reduced the sales of the three major American manufacturers and boosted the market share of their Japanese competitors. As a House Ways and Means Committee report on the CAFE legislation explained, "Currently, many fuel-efficient cars are imported, and [our] Committee did not want the auto efficiency tax to provide a stimulus to increased imports of autos in view of the depressed state of the U.S. auto industry."[7] Corporate averaging represented a way of preventing Japanese companies from taking advantage of their strong lines of fuel-efficient vehicles. The concession by no means satisfied the domestic industry, which continued to oppose any mandatory fuel economy requirement as well as a gasoline tax. But by basing standards on corporate averages rather than the performance of individual vehicles, and by regulating automobiles rather than taxing fuel, Congress did attempt to protect the U.S. firms.

Congress also wanted to design the CAFE system in a way that would protect American jobs. The simplest way for domestic manufacturers to improve the average fuel efficiency of their fleets would have been to import smaller, more fuel-efficient cars from their subsidiaries in Europe and Asia. But this would have reduced domestic employment in an already depressed industry. The United Automobile Workers was prepared to support CAFE standards, but only if it could be assured that they would not cost jobs. Legislators responded to UAW pressure by establishing separate but identical standards for domestic (defined as having at least 75 percent domestic content) and imported passenger cars.

Thus Chrysler, Ford, and General Motors, which manufactured vehicles in the United States and also imported cars, would be required to meet CAFE targets for *both* categories of vehicles. American firms would therefore be unable to meet CAFE standards by averaging the fuel economy of their imports with their less fuel-efficient, domestically produced vehicles. By calculating domestic and imported fleets separately, Congress sought to force domestic manufacturers not only to make more efficient cars but to make them in the United States.

Bad Policy

These competitive distortions aside, the CAFE standards have other unfortunate features. Not the least of these is that the standards focus the entire effort to reduce fuel consumption at the point of purchase. This means that once a consumer has bought a (relatively) fuel-efficient vehicle, he or she has no further incentive to conserve energy by, for example, driving less, driving more slowly, or carpooling. On the contrary, because a new vehicle achieves higher mileage per gallon, motorists have every reason to drive more. In other words, as long as gasoline prices remain low, strict CAFE standards reduce the marginal cost of each vehicle mile. In fact, the average cost of driving an extra mile in the United States in 1994 was one-third less than in 1973.[8] The average annual number of miles traveled per vehicle increased from 9,500 in 1980 to slightly more than 12,000 in 1995, a period during which oil prices steadily decreased in real terms.[9] Between 10 and 30 percent of the potential fuel savings from CAFE has been lost as a result of this increased vehicle use.[10]

In addition, reliance on CAFE mandates has not always spurred the transition of the American automotive fleet to more fuel-efficient vehicles. Compliance with the gradual increase in fuel-economy standards has been expensive for American automobile companies, an expense that has been passed on to consumers in higher prices for all new vehicles. Moreover, about 60 percent of the increase in fuel efficiency is due to either a reduction in car weight or to smaller engine displacement, attributes American motorists have tended to dislike.[11] Arguably, CAFE has played a role in slowing the vehicular turnover rate, leaving older, fuel-guzzling vehicles on the road longer.

The average age of cars "on the road" has increased by two full years since the mid-1960s. "Peak demand for new cars in the 1980s was no higher than in the early 1970s, despite higher real GNP and the larger population."[12] Ironically, any part played by CAFE standards in reducing new car sales would depress employment in the automobile industry, thus undermining one of the aims of the CAFE strategy.

The impact of CAFE on fuel consumption has also been tempered by the decision to establish different regulatory standards for different kinds of vehicles.

Light trucks, which include pickups, vans, and sport utility vehicles, are required to meet standards of only 20.4 mpg, 7.1 mpg less than passenger vehicles.[13] In part because of this, they often offer a more favorable price-quality trade-off than do passenger cars, and their sales have therefore increased substantially. In 1995 more than 40 percent of the vehicles sold in the United States were in this category, thus helping to lower substantially the average fuel economy of all motor vehicles.[14] In 1994 the average fuel efficiency for the on-road fleet stood at 19.3 mpg, essentially unchanged from the mid-1980s.[15] Congress has made no effort to strengthen CAFE standards for the recreational vehicle category, which may in turn be related to the fact that American firms enjoy a comparative advantage in producing them.

Nearly twenty years of CAFE standards have certainly contributed to an improvement in overall fuel efficiency of new automobiles in the United States. Automobiles sold in the United States in 1990 averaged 28 mpg, twice the efficiency of vehicles produced during the 1974 model year.[16] CAFE deserves credit for this change, although higher gasoline prices in the late 1970s played a bigger role. But the energy conservation that CAFE has achieved could have been accomplished much more efficiently by a gasoline tax. Robert A. Leone and Thomas W. Parkinson concluded that a "gasoline tax required to match CAFE's conservation effect would have reduced producer and consumer welfare by 8 cents a gallon saved while the regulatory alternative actually reduced welfare by around 60 cents a gallon saved."[17] A study by Charles River Associates argues that a gasoline tax would have been far more effective than a fuel economy standard in both conserving petroleum and reducing carbon dioxide emissions.[18] Pietro Nivola and Robert Crandall estimate that a tax of (at most) 25 cents a gallon beginning in 1986 would have yielded as much, if not more, oil conservation as was achieved by CAFE through 1992.[19] Some critics argue that even a much smaller tax would have achieved the same results as CAFE has to date.[20]

Although CAFE has raised the fuel efficiency of new passenger vehicles, it has failed to lower fuel consumption below the levels of the early 1970s. Thanks to the steady increase in passenger miles driven since the early 1980s as well as the significant growth in sales of light trucks during the 1990s, both of which CAFE has perversely encouraged, or at least not discouraged, total fuel usage by all motor vehicles increased by 50 percent between 1970 and 1988.[21] Average motor fuel consumption per vehicle in the United States has remained twice as high as in Europe and Japan.[22] On a per capital basis, American motor fuel consumption is two to three times greater than in Europe and Japan, which imposed no fuel economy requirements on their automobile industries but have much higher gasoline prices. American gasoline consumption reached a record 7.79 million barrels a day in 1995.[23] As the centrepiece of the nation's energy conservation effort, CAFE has clearly fallen short.[24]

Consumer Safety

CAFE standards have also affected the safety of passenger cars. Automobile manufacturers have upgraded the fuel efficiency of new cars chiefly by reducing their weight. According to the National Highway Traffic Safety Administration (NHTSA), each 10 percent reduction in weight increases the fuel economy of new vehicle design by 8 percent.[25] Between 1974 and 1991 the weight of the average new car sold in the United States declined by 20 percent.[26] The doubling of fuel efficiency standards between 1975 and 1985 was due to a 1,000-pound reduction in average new car weight.[27]

But according to the NHTSA, large cars usually offer more protection in a crash than small cars. The greater vulnerability of the occupants of newer, lighter vehicles has been further heightened by the changing mix of vehicles on the road. In 1980 the NHTSA predicted that "with these smaller and lighter vehicles joining an increasing number of heavy trucks and older, heavier cars already on the road, the risk of death and serious injury will increase markedly."[28]

According to studies by Leonard Evans and by Crandall and John Graham, CAFE may have been indirectly responsible for perhaps 2,200 to 3,900 additional deaths for each model year's passenger cars in the ten years following their introduction.[29] Crandall and Graham predicted that cars produced under a standard of 27.5 mpg, which went into effect in 1990, would lead to a 14 to 27 percent increase in occupant deaths. Based on this estimate, the CAFE program is currently costing one additional fatality for every 2 million gallons of fuel saved. Doubtless, a tax on motor fuel would also have increased automobile deaths by inducing demand for lighter cars. But taxing fuel at least would not encourage owners of lightweight vehicles to increase their vehicle miles traveled. Unlike the less flexible CAFE solution, a tax would promote saving oil and lives by encouraging less driving, regardless of the weight of vehicles.

In 1985 the Council of Economic Advisers acknowledged CAFE's impact on automotive safety when it urged that the CAFE standard not be increased. Safety was subsequently raised in CAFE rulemaking hearings by the Insurance Institute for Highway Safety, the Competitive Enterprise Institute, and the National Safety Council. In a lawsuit by two public interest groups that challenged the EPA's decision to raise the fuel-efficiency level for the 1990 model year from 26.5 to 27.5, the plaintiffs argued that the Department of Transportation had not adequately addresed the linkage between CAFE and safety. Although the NHTSA has continued to doubt that CAFE might reduce motor vehicle safety, in 1990 it did cite the safety impact of fuel efficiency standards as grounds for opposing congressional proposals to increase the CAFE standard to 40 mpg. One administrator characterized the congressional initiative as sacrificing blood for oil.[30]

Distortions of Competition

Even the attempt by Congress to devise a way of protecting the American automobile industry while saddling it with additional regulatory costs has proved flawed. Initially, American firms considered CAFE preferable to a gasoline tax, since a tax might have abetted the market position of Japanese manufacturers. However, CAFE soon became a source of competitive advantage for the Japanese. Under its rules, companies are permitted to carry forward any excess credits over the 27.5 standard as potential offsets against future shortfalls and to carry back any excesses to compensate for past shortfalls. By the early 1990s, Japanese firms, which primarily produced small, relatively fuel-thrifty passenger vehicles, had accumulated large carry-forward credits, while General Motors and Ford incurred deficits. These accumulated credits enabled the Japanese producers to increase their sales of upscale cars without compromising fleet CAFE ratings. Japan, in other words, could export in much larger volumes precisely the kind of larger, more powerful models that claim the most profitable niche in the U.S. market. By contrast, the American companies have had to compromise on the designs of comparable vehicles in order to work off accumulated CAFE deficits. The upshot has been less overall fuel economy in the U.S. passenger car fleet but also further Japanese encroachment on the one market segment in which American manufacturers have been particularly competitive. So serious did this situation become that when Congress considered a proposal to raise CAFE standards in 1989, both the American automobile industry and the United Automobile Workers urged that the formula for calculating compliance with CAFE standards be altered.[31] The companies and the union demanded that all producers be required to improve the average fuel economy of their vehicles *proportionately*. This fix would have required Japanese producers to meet much higher standards than American firms because the average fuel economy of the cars Japan sold in the United States was higher to begin with. A spokesman for Chrysler explained, "The whole idea of the percentage increase is that everyone would be required to move upward."[32] Not surprisingly, the new formula was vigorously opposed by the Japanese automobile lobby. A representative of Toyota characterized it as "punishing people for good works."[33]

Not only did the proposed adjustment threaten to provoke another major Japanese–American trade squabble, but the requirement would likely have been flagrantly inconsistent with American obligations under GATT, because it would have required Japanese producers to meet a substantially higher standard than their American competitors. In any event, thanks to heavy pressure from domestic retailers and Japanese firms, Congress made no change in either the formula for calculating CAFE requirements or the requirements themselves. The Japanese continue to produce small to midrange vehicles in the United States, while using their credits to export high-performance luxury cars. (Japanese cars produced in the United States are counted as imports under CAFE because their domestic content is less than 75 percent, thus creating a further inducement for Japanese companies to keep the value added of their production facilities in the United States below the 75 percent threshold.) As Crandall commented, "the Japanese are being invited to compete in the highly profitable large and luxury car segments of the market by our own 'conservation' policies."[34]

CAFE and European Exports

The formula for establishing compliance with CAFE standards has improved the competitive position of the American automobile industry in one way: it has raised the price of European luxury cars sold in the United States. Because CAFE is calculated on the basis of the average fuel efficiency of the vehicles produced by each manufacturer, it has handicapped European makers who produce only the heavier, more powerful cars. Nearly all the vehicles manufactured by Jaguar, BMW, Volvo, Saab, Mercedes-Benz, Rolls-Royce, and Porsche are high-end products with relatively low mileage per gallon. As a result, these firms have been unable to comply with the increasingly strict CAFE criteria. In 1991, while cars exported by European manufacturers accounted for 4 percent of American sales, their manufacturers paid 100 percent of the CAFE penalties. Indeed, in the twenty-year history of the regulations, only European limited-line premium automakers have *ever* been subject to CAFE penalties.[35]

In 1985 the Environmental Protection Agency relaxed the fuel-economy standards for both passenger cars and light trucks after General Motors and Ford claimed they could not meet the original goals. The two companies were relieved of millions in penalties.[36] But European automobile firms have received no such solicitude. They have been required to pay the statutory fine of $5 for every tenth of a mile per gallon that their fleet average falls below 27.5, multiplied by the number of automobiles sold in the United States.[37] These fines have been substantial. In 1983 Jaguar missed the CAFE standard by over 7 mpg and was accordingly required to pay a CAFE penalty of $350 for each car it sold. Between 1985 and 1989 BMW paid CAFE penalties totalling $32 million, Mercedes-Benz $85 million, and Jaguar $27 million.[38] Only one major high-end European car exporter, Saab-Scania, met the 1989 CAFE standards, and that was because it offered cars with four-cylinder engines. Owing to these penalties, American customers were required to pay an additional $1,800 for a Jaguar XJ-S V-12 and $1,500 for the Mercedes 560 SEC sport coupe.

The GATT Trade Dispute

Matters came to a head in 1993. The European Union called for convening a GATT dispute settlement panel. In its complaint the EU charged that "the CAFE regulations are biased toward the full-line manufacturers [in other words, domestic manufacturers] that make both small, fuel-efficient and larger vehicles and limited-line manufacturers that produce mostly small vehicles."[39] The complaint also challenged two other American policies that it claimed discriminated against European automobile exports. One, the so-called gas-guzzler tax, is levied on passenger vehicles whose fuel economy is less than 22.5 miles a gallon. In contrast to the CAFE penalty, this tax is based on the fuel economy of particular models rather than on a corporate average. Established in 1978, the tax was doubled in 1991 and is now levied at a rate of $1,000 a vehicle.[40] To raise additional revenue the United States imposed in 1985 an excise tax on cars bought for business use and costing more than $16,000,. In 1991 this impost was amended to apply to all cars costing more than $32,000.

That year the three taxes plus CAFE penalties raised a total of $558 million, of which $494 million was paid by European car manufacturers.[41] The cumulative financial impact was far from trivial. For example, in 1992 Mercedes-Benz paid $216 million in fines and taxes, approximately $3,500 for each car sold in the United States. The EU charged that all three taxes were protectionist because they "individually and collectively have a discriminatory incidence on car imports."[42]

Although the EU's complaint addressed all three American rules, its challenge to CAFE attracted the most attention. American environmental and consumer groups have always strongly supported CAFE, not only defending it against its critics but frequently advocating efforts to tighten its standards.[43] Friends of the Earth sharply attacked the EU's case: "the EC cannot claim to be concerned about the development of the trade and environment debate if it persists in attempting to define . . . whether or not the environmental laws of another country are simply disguised trade barriers."[44] Trade analysts in the United States expressed concern that a GATT ruling against the United States would add to the international body's reputation as antienvironment, given that two of the three laws under challenge were designed to encourage conservation. This in turn would make it more difficult to secure legislative ratification of the Uruguay Round of multilateral trade negotiations. One environmental trade expert predicted, "The CAFE standards are so central to [U.S. clean air safeguards] that it will do the GATT a lot of harm if it does rule against the United States."[45]

The GATT Panel Decision

In its decision in the fall of 1994, the dispute panel found the taxes on gas guzzlers and luxury cars to be consistent with U.S. obligations under the GATT, but held that the CAFE provision requiring separate calculations for domestic and imported vehicles was not. The panel's examination of CAFE focused on the GATT consistency of two of its components: the fleet averaging procedure and the separate fleet accounting requirements for imported and domestic cars.

The panel found that both rules violated the GATT's article III, section 4, its national treatment provision, because they effectively treated domestic and foreign producers differently. GATT rules do generally permit signatories to impose whatever regulatory standards they wish on products sold within a nation's borders provided they treat like foreign and domestic products alike, even though they may disproportionately burden imported products. But CAFE requirements were not based on the characteristics of a particular product, that is, the fuel efficiency of the cars themselves. Rather, the requirements were imposed on companies and varied in part according to their ownership and nationality.

However, the panel then went on to note that GATT contains an exception to the national treatment clause. Article XX(g) permits contracting parties to adopt or enforce measures that are necessary "to conserve exhaustible natural resources," provided the measures are not used to discriminate arbitrarily against imports or employed as a disguised restriction of international trade.[46] The panel determined that the primary goal of the fuel averaging requirement was indeed to protect and conserve natural resources, thus arguably bringing it within the scope of article XX.

The panel noted that the EU was correct in suggesting that the American policy objective of promoting fuel efficiency could be achieved in ways that were less restrictive of trade, especially by increasing the minimal U.S. tax on gasoline. But it declined to hold the United States to a "least trade restrictive" standard. Rather, it concluded, all the United States was required to do was to demonstrate that the regulations it imposed were necessary to improve fuel economy.

But the panel could find no such justification for CAFE's separate fleet accounting standards; distinguishing between cars produced in the United States and those produced overseas was clearly not necessary to promote conservation in the United States. Indeed, the panel observed that the use of separate foreign and domestic fleet accounting standards actually undermined domestic fuel conservation because it "prevented manufacturers of large domestic cars from meeting the CAFE requirement for their domestic fleet by adding to it small foreign cars, or small cars made from foreign parts." This "placed small foreign cars and foreign parts in a less favourable competitive position with respect to small domestic cars and domestic parts."[47]

The panel also noted that the two sets of accounting requirements "placed large foreign cars in a less favourable competitive position with respect to large domestic cars" because they prevented "manufacturers of large foreign, but not domestic, cars from meeting their CAFE requirements for their imported fleet by adding to it small domestic cars." In short, the separate accounting requirements not only violated article III's national treatment rule but did so in such a way as to undermine rather than achieve the ostensible purpose of the CAFE standards. Accordingly, the panel concluded that "the CAFE regulation is inconsistent with Article III:4 and, to the extent that it is based on separate foreign fleet accounting, cannot be justified under Article XX (g) or Article XX (d)."[48]

This finding was hardly surprising: the separate accounting provision had been deliberately included in the original legislation at the insistence of the United Automobile Workers Union. Indeed, without the provision it was unlikely that the CAFE legislation would have been approved in the first place. What *was* surprising was the panel's failure to discern protectionist motives behind Congress's decision to base fuel economy on corporate fleet averages.

The United States was extremely pleased with the GATT panel ruling and urged that it be formally adopted by GATT itself. U.S. officials claimed that the panel had upheld the "core provisions" of the CAFE law. "The panel has emphatically rejected the European's claim that trade-neutral legislation intended to further energy conservation goals and protect the environment could be attacked because Chrysler, Ford, and GM invested and complied with the laws while Mercedes and BMW chose not to and had to pay penalties."[49]

U.S. officials also dismissed the significance of the one provision of CAFE that the GATT panel judged illegal. The trade representative's office indicated that it had no intention of changing the separate fleet accounting rule, claiming that the EU was not in a position to pressure the United States to make such a change because the rule in question did no economic harm to European manufacturers: "No European companies sell cars in the U.S. which qualify as domestic under CAFE, which sets a standard of 75 percent U.S. content."[50] Nor did the Japanese automobile producers appear to suffer as a result of this provision because even their American-made cars contained less than 75 percent domestic content.

The U.S. assessment of the GATT ruling, along with a refusal to modify the separate fleet accounting rule, was strongly criticized by the Europeans. An EU official stated: "We object to the fact that the U.S. appears unwilling to change the CAFE law, in the wake of a decision by a GATT panel that the law is discriminatory." He added that the U.S. posture did not bode well for the multilateral trade system or the World Trade Organization.[51]

Ironically, although both the American environmental groups and the Clinton administration expressed their delight, as well as their relief, at the outcome of the dispute, the episode ended up permitting the United States to continue an ill-conceived regulatory policy that not only distorts international trade but pursues conservation inefficiently. For in fact, the least trade-restrictive policy option is also the most sensible for American energy policy. A serious gasoline tax would not only lower fuel consumption at a fraction of CAFE's social cost, but would also avoid any discrimination among producers of European, American, and Japanese luxury vehicles. At the same time, the simple fuel levy would also benefit American manufacturers. Although substituting a tax for CAFE standards might reduce sales of oversized American cars, it would at least deprive Japanese competitors of the artificial competitive advantage CAFE inadvertently confers on them. Finally, by truly reducing the consumption of oil it would curb American dependence on foreign energy sources – a more useful policy objective than reducing American dependence on foreign cars.

The international dispute over the U.S. automotive fuel economy law did little to clarify or emphasize the shortcomings and contradictions of the U.S. approach to energy conservation in automotive transportation. An opportunity to better harmonize U.S. policy with the policies of major trading partners was lost. Neither the United States nor its trading partners are better off for this.

U.S. CLEAN FUEL STANDARDS

Because automobiles are a major source of air pollution, especially in urban areas, reducing automotive emissions has been a major focus of the federal government's effort to improve air quality. During the 1970s the regulatory efforts of the federal government focused on mandating changes in engine technology. In the late 1980s, as Congress began another major revision of the Clean Air Act, the focus shifted: the government began contemplating further reductions in automobile emissions by mandating changes in the composition and content of motor fuels, which had not yet been subject to regulation.

The drive for a federal clean fuel policy was initiated by the Bush administration, for whom it represented a way of reducing the nation's dependence on foreign oil and demonstrating the administration's commitment to a dramatic new approach to pollution control. The technological feasibility of the new regulatory strategy received a significant boost in 1989 when the Atlantic Richfield Company (ARCO) announced that it had developed a reformulated gasoline for use in older cars (ones not equipped with catalytic converters) that would significantly reduce their emissions. ARCO's market share immediately increased by 10 percent, and the issue of clean fuels moved to center stage in the environmental policy drama.[52]

Unfortunately, there is no such thing as a perfectly clean fuel. Not only do all fuels emit some pollution when burned by an internal combustion engine, but there are harmful environmental consequences associated with the production of all energy sources. The challenge the administration and Congress faced was to decide which regulatory standards the government wanted automotive fuels to meet. The challenge was especially critical because designing a wholly fuel-neutral regulatory standard is virtually impossible. Whatever emission requirements the government selected would invariably favor some fuels and discriminate against others. Not surprisingly, the most heated conflict over the 1990 Clean Air amendments centered on fuels.

The Bush administration originally favored the use of methanol, an alcohol fuel typically made from coal or natural gas. Methanol appeared able to reduce significantly hydrocarbon emissions, which would in turn reduce smog. However, adding methanol to gasoline might also increase emissions of formaldehyde, which is a carcinogen. Thus it was not clear that methanol would provide net environmental benefits in comparison with conventional gasoline. Moreover, the new fuel would be expensive. Although it costs as much as conventional gasoline to produce, it is 30 percent less efficient. It is also more corrosive and would require substantial changes in engine technology.

The Politics of Ethanol

At the same time, policymakers found themselves under heavy political pressure to mandate the use of another alternative fuel, ethanol. Ethanol is produced by distilling corn into alcohol. It can be mixed in a ratio of one part ethanol to nine parts gasoline to produce gasohol. Support for federal tax breaks and rules facilitating the use of ethanol in the nation's gasoline supply was led by a number of lobbies, including the Renewable Fuels Association, the Clean Fuels Development Coalition, and the National Corn Growers' Association. However, the most influential role was played by the Archer Daniels Midland Company, the major domestic producer of ethanol, nearly half of whose profits come from products either protected or heavily subsidized by the federal government. Dwayne Andreas, ADM's chief executive officer, is one of the most politically active businessmen in the United States.[53] During the 1992 presidential campaign, Andreas contributed more than $1.4 million in soft money (which goes to party organizations rather than individual candidates) and gave an additional $345,650 to various congressional and senatorial candidates. He was a major contributor to the campaigns of both George Bush and Bill Clinton, giving Bush more than $400,000 and Clinton $270,000. Within Congress the use of ethanol was championed by senators and representatives from corn-producing states, including the Senate majority leader and 1996 Republican presidential candidate, Robert J. Dole, another major beneficiary of Andreas's largess.

A central strategy of ethanol's promoters was to back regulations requiring that automotive fuel contain a relatively high minimum oxygen content, one that could only be met by blending conventional gasoline with 10 percent ethanol. Opponents, led by the petroleum industry, argued that fuel content regulations are, in effect, ethanol mandates. The oil companies preferred to use an alternative fuel called MTBE (methyl tertiary butyl ether), which is a methanol-derived fuel oxygenate. Not only can they produce this oxygenate themselves, but it is substantially easier to transport because it does not mix with water. However, gasoline mixed with MTBE cannot attain the oxygen level of ethanol.

Ethanol and Conservation

Efforts to promote the use of ethanol in automotive fuels date from the late 1970s when the Carter administration believed it would help secure energy independence. Gasoline with 10 percent ethanol was exempted from federal fuel excise taxes, and in 1980 the Department of Agriculture provided $341 million in loans to finance the construction of gasohol plants. Notwithstanding the tax preference for gasohol and the production subsidies, the market for gasohol remained relatively modest: motor fuels blended with ethanol constituted less than 1 percent of the total fuels market in 1980, though the level increased to 7 percent by 1990.[54]

Although the use of ethanol was originally justified as a way of reducing oil imports, it is not an energy-inefficient fuel. Not only does it cost twice as much to produce a normal gasoline, but making it may actually consume more energy than it generates. According to an application for federal subsidy submitted by ADM in 1979, its ethanol plant required 1,284 barrels of natural gas to produce 1,485 barrels of ethanol, thus producing a net energy gain of less than 15 percent of the total fuel produced. Moreover, this figure excludes the substantial energy consumed by growing the corn in the first place. Although one gallon of ethanol contains the energy equivalent of 76,000 Btus, the Department of Energy estimated in 1991 that making a gallon of ethanol required 85,000 to 91,000.[55]

Ethanol also contributes to increased energy use by reducing fuel economy, since each gallon of ethanol contains only two-thirds as much energy as gasoline. According to the Department of Energy, gasohol-fueled vehicles average 4.7 percent fewer miles a gallon than vehicles fueled by standard gasoline.[56]

Ethanol and Clean Air

More recently, the case for adding ethanol to gasoline has come to be defended on environmental grounds. But this justification is equally dubious. In fact, the Clean Air Act amendments of 1977 banned products such as ethanol precisely to *protect* the environment. In 1978 the EPA announced that "recent EPA and Department of Energy tests . . . show slight increases in nitrogen oxide emissions and substantial increases in evaporative hydrocarbon emissions" from cars using gasohol. However, since ethanol then amounted to only a minuscule share of the nation's gasoline sales, the EPA concluded that "there is no significant environmental risk associated with its continued use."[57]

Alcohol blends improve gasoline combustion but are also significantly more volatile than alcohol-free gasolines. A 1986 USDA report concluded that "evaporative emissions reported for ethanol blends are 5 percent to 220 percent above emissions for straight gasoline." A subsequent study reported that while gasohol would reduce carbon monoxide emissions by 25 percent, hydrocarbons would increase by as much as 50 percent and nitrogen oxide by 15 percent. Ethanol may also contribute to ozone pollution (smog) because it evaporates relatively quickly, especially in hot weather. Thus the National Academy of Sciences concluded that "using ethanol as a blending agent in gasoline . . . would not achieve significant air-quality benefits and, in fact, would likely be detrimental."[58]

The 1990 Clean Air Act amendments require that gasoline sold in areas where ozone levels exceed federal standards must have a Reid vapor pressure (the standard measure of fuel volatility) of nine pounds per square inch because, as the Senate Committee on Environment and Public Works duly observed, "evaporative hydrocarbon emissions . . . are now the most significant source of vehicle hydrocarbon emissions during the summer, when ozone formation is at its peak."[59] However, the amendments actually *relax* the volatility requirements for fuels containing 10 percent ethanol. When even this concession was not sufficient to permit the use of ethanol in the summer in some of the nation's largest and most polluted cities, ethanol's supporters persuaded the EPA to issue a waiver that would permit the use of this "clean" fuel in all areas of the United States throughout the year.

Defining Reformulated Gasoline

Under the terms of the 1990 Clean Air Act, to reduce smog, "only reformulated fuel could be sold in the nine smoggiest cities."[60] This, however, begged a critical question: how would reformulated gasoline be defined? The answer provoked a bitter battle for market share between ethanol producers and the oil industry. The oil industry wanted to be allowed to determine the composition of cleaner fuels. In his testimony before the House Commerce Committee, Charles J. DiBona, president of the American Petroleum Institute, pleaded, "Tell us how much polluting emissions should be reduced. Don't dictate the recipe for making the fuel. We want to make the best fuel we know how, not 'government gas.'"[61] But the ethanol lobby feared that if given the flexibility in fashioning fuel composition, oil refiners would primarily rely on MTBE because this oxygenate could be produced by the refiners themselves.

For its part, the Clinton administration strongly favored the use of ethanol both to increase farm income and to reduce dependence on imported oil. To ensure a market for ethanol, the EPA issued a proposed rule in June 1994 requiring that at least 30 percent of gasoline contains a "renewable oxygenate" by 1996.[62] This regulation, in effect, mandated the use of ethanol or its derivatives, since MTBE is derived from fossil fuels and therefore is not considered renewable.

Following the announcement of the renewable oxygenate requirement, forty-eight senators sent a letter of protest to EPA administrator Carol Browner. "This RFG [reformulated gasoline] rule," they said, "will create chaos in the market-place, cause serious deliverability problems, and unnecessarily increase the cost of RFG to consumers. Lastly, and most importantly, the rule will result in no clear environmental benefits."[63] The EPA's decision was also criticized by some environmentalists. A. Blakeman Early, the Washington representative for the Sierra Club, characterized the proposed rule as both illegal and bad policy, adding "It's not the role of the Clean Air Act to make mandatory markets for ethanol."[64] Senator Bill Bradley of New Jersey stressed that "no significant national environmental organization supports EPA's findings of environmental benefits" from the use of ethanol.[65] The administration's ethanol requirement was challenged on the floor of the Senate, where the vote primarily divided along geographic lines. Following a heated floor debate, the rule survived when Vice President Al Gore broke a tie vote in its favor.

The rule was subsequently struck down in federal court. In its decision the court reminded the EPA that "the sole purpose of the Reformulated Gasoline Program is to reduce air pollution," and that the agency itself had conceded that the use of ethanol might possibly make air quality worse.[66] What is more, the use of ethanol collided with the Clinton administration's commitment to reduce emissions of greenhouse gases because, in the words of EPA assistant administrator Mary Nichols, "the production of corn requires substantial amounts of energy, some of which results in greenhouse gas emissions."[67]

Although using ethanol would not benefit air quality and could harm it, its most important defect would be cost. According to the American Petroleum Institute, the EPA's ethanol mandate was projected to cost refiners $460 million a year, or 6 cents a gallon, to modify refinery facilities to blend ethanol for reformulated gasoline, to convert MTBE plants to produce ethanol-based oxygenates, and to modify product terminals and transport facilities. And this would be in excess of the extra cost of 5 to 10 cents a gallon to produce reformulated gasoline with MTBE. However, relatively few of these costs would have been visible to motorists comparing fuel prices because each gallon of ethanol sold in gasoline is exempt from part of the federal gasoline excise tax as well as part of state taxes. Indeed, the EPA's ethanol mandate was estimated to reduce federal and state taxes by $750 million a year.[68] As in the case of CAFE, the costs of the ethanol regime to the American public were hidden.

Subsidizing Farmers

The key to understanding the political economy of ethanol lies in the fact that requiring its use was, quite simply, a farm welfare program. Annual ethanol subsidies came to exceed $770 million. Such subsidies did increase farm income; demand for ethanol raised corn prices by an estimated 22 to 40 cents a bushel. But since most cost produced in the United States is used for feed grain, the ethanol program in fact increased costs to livestock producers by more than $1 billion a year, which in turn was passed on to consumers in the form of higher meat prices. Moreover, ethanol subsidies also harmed soybean farmers since corn by-products from ethanol production compete with soybeans. For a time, ethanol subsidies were depressing soybean sales by approximately $300 million. On balance, government-mandated ethanol production was costing farmers and taxpayers $4 for each $1 of extra farm income, making it a remarkably wasteful way of subsidizing farmers. According to a Department of Agriculture study, "Consumers would be much better off if they burned straight gasoline in their automobiles and paid a direct cash subsidy to farmers in the amount that net farm income would be increased by ethanol production."[69]

In sum, without extensive federal subsidies, which have amounted to approximately $550 million a year since 1978, little ethanol would be produced in the United States.[70] Pushing the use of ethanol in motor fuels not only distorts the marketplace for agricultural products, but by reducing tax revenues and requiring extensive government subsidies, contributes to the national budget deficit.

Further, although they have been touted in part as a way to reduce oil imports, federal ethanol subsidies hurt U.S. exports of corn by raising its price. Thus even as a form of economic mercantilism, the promotion of ethanol in motor fuels is perverse: it reduces imports of one commodity by decreasing exports of another.

Protecting Ethanol

The commitment to subsidizing domestic ethanol production has also affected American trade policies. For even if there were substantial environmental dividends from using ethanol, it would be in the national interests to have it supplied as inexpensively as possible. Yet thanks to political pressure from ADM, the United States has restricted imports of ethanol, thus assuring that virtually all ethanol used will be heavily subsidized by American taxpayers.

In 1980 the Carter administration was persuaded to impose a prohibitive tariff on ethanol imports despite the absence of any evidence that these imports, which came primarily from Brazil, were damaging domestic producers. Three years later, Congress enacted the Caribbean Basin Initiative to improve the access of Caribbean products to the U.S. market and thus strengthen the economies of the countries in that region; as long as at least 35 percent of a product's value originated in the Caribbean, it would be allowed to enter the United States duty free. Consequently, companies invested a total of several million dollars to construct plants in Jamaica and Costa Rica that could convert surplus European wine into ethanol. In 1984 the Customs Service ruled that because the conversion of wine into ethanol added more than 35 percent of the value to the finished product, this ethanol could enter the United States duty free.[71]

Although imports of ethanol from the Caribbean never exceeded 3 percent of the U.S. ethanol supply, American producers, led by ADM, wanted to further limit foreign competition. Congress responded in 1986 by raising the local value-added requirement for Caribbean ethanol to 70 percent, which effectively restricted all imports because Caribbean countries lacked any surplus agricultural stocks. This clause was slightly modified by the lawmakers in 1989, when they established a staggered set of local feedstock requirements for ethanol produced in the Caribbean. These still discriminated against ethanol imports, however.[72]

Questioning the Clean Fuels Policy

Partiality to ethanol has not been the only dubious feature of the Clean Air Act regulations. A primary purpose of this legislation is to improve air quality for the nearly 89 million Americans as of 1990 who live in nonattainment areas (cities where air quality does not meet federal standards for ozone concentration). The law defines *nonattainment* strictly and precisely: if the fourth-highest daily one-hour reading recorded on any monitor during the preceding three years shows an ozone concentration greater than 0.12 part per million, the area is not in compliance with federal ozone standards. If compliance were instead measured by the average reading, the number of nonattainment areas would decrease significantly. The average readings in the majority of cities classified as nonattainment areas exceed the federal standard in less than 1 percent of the hours monitored.[73] In fact, with the exception of Los Angeles, almost all nonattainment areas meet federal standards more than 99.4 percent of the time. Moreover most ozone comes from emissions from pre-1983 cars, which are gradually being phased out.[74]

Even more important, the precise nature and extent of the health effects of prolonged exposure to ozone have yet to be demonstrated, while the costs of reducing VOC (volatile organic compounds) emissions that produce ozone are extremely high.[75] According to the Office of Technology Assessment, reducing VOC emissions by 35 percent (in 1989 dollars) from their 1990 levels will cost between $6.6 billion and $10 billion annually by 2004.[76]

Gasoline Standards as Trade Barriers

Although EPA's mandatory commingling of ethanol with gasoline was halted (at least for the time being) by a court order in April 1995, oil refineries had already begun to retool, at considerable expense, to produce reformulated gasoline, including ethanol-based fuel. Thus a legacy of the mandate, as well as of the fuel's long-standing differential tax treatment, was to saddle refineries with a sunk cost that they would soon try to offset. One way to do so would be by seeking relief from foreign competition.

On December 15, 1993, the EPA issued regulations implementing the reformulated gasoline provisions of the Clean Air Act of 1990. These rules required the sale of cleaner-burning gasoline in the nation's smoggiest areas beginning January 1, 1995.[77] Gasoline sales in a number of cities, including New York, Philadelphia, Washington, Hartford, Baltimore, Chicago, Houston, Los Angeles, and San Diego, were covered by this requirement. To avoid disrupting the fuel market and to provide refiners with enough time to adjust their production, the EPA decided to issue a five-year interim standard rather than a fixed one. During 1995, 1996, and 1997, refiners were required to reduce the amount of olefins (a chemical that leads to emissions of nitrogen oxide, which in turn contributes to ground-level concentrations of ozone). The reductions would be made on a percentage basis, using 1990 as the base year.

However, although American refiners were allowed to use their actual 1990 production as their baseline, foreign refiners were required to measure their improvement by using the U.S. average or statutory baseline. In addition, to prevent refiners from dumping high-emission RFG by-products into conventional gasolines, all non-RFG gasoline sold in the United States was required to be at least as clean in 1995 through 1997 as it was in 1990. Once again, the 1990 base was calculated differently for foreign and domestic refiners.

The EPA recognized from the outset that this rule would make it more difficult for gasoline produced by foreign refiners to be sold in the United States. In fact, EPA Assistant Administrator Nichols "told a Senate committee that she was motivated by a desire to lean in the direction of doing something that would favor the competitiveness of U.S. petroleum companies vis-à-vis Venezuelan companies."[78] Publicly, however, the agency claimed that it would be impossible to hold foreign producers to the same standard as the domestic firms because very few importers collected the data in 1990 needed to set their own baselines.[79] Accordingly, the EPA stated it had little choice but to employ a more "objective" standard, the 1990 domestic average. In practice, this meant that the standards applied to imported gasoline would in some cases be stricter and in other cases more lax than those for domestic producers.

Venezuela, one of the primary suppliers of imported gasoline to the United States, immediately filed a formal complaint with GATT on the grounds that the U.S. rule violated the trade agreement's national treatment clause, article III, by holding a like product to different standards, depending on its country of origin. Not eager to risk losing a trade dispute in the midst of the Uruguay Round negotiations, the Office of the U.S. Trade Representative pressured the EPA to modify its rule. Prudently, the office considered it "essential to try to make our country's environmental objectives and trade objectives compatible where possible."[80]

In exchange for convincing Venezuela to drop its complaint, the EPA proposed a corrective rule that would allow foreign refiners to establish their own baseline.[81] The agency stated it would approve the use of baselines for any foreign refinery that could supply it with the necessary data. This rule in effect exempted Venezuela because only its national oil company, Petroleos de Venezuela S.A. (PDSVA), appeared to have the data. At the same time, to ensure no significant deterioration in U.S. air quality, the new rule provided that any increase in the volume of gasoline imports from their 1990 levels would have to meet the statutory baseline as well.

This compromise outraged both environmentalists and the U.S. refining industry. The environmentalists chastised the EPA for sacrificing American environmental standards to gratify the State Department and the U.S. Trade Representative. EPA's amended rule appeared to confirm their fears that trade liberalization would compromise domestic regulatory standards.[82] Members of Congress also criticized the agency for bowing to pressures from the White House, claiming that the administration had been hoodwinked by Venezuela. For their part, the interests of the domestic refineries, mostly owned by the integrated oil companies, were straightforward: having been forced by the 1990 Clean Air Act amendments to invest billions of dollars in new technologies for refining gasoline, they now wanted federal regulations that would at least protect them from less expensive gasoline imports.[83] Industry representatives accused the EPA of tampering with the rules, claiming that its decision created "uncertainty" about the government's standards for reformulated gasoline, thus making it more difficult to deliver on schedule the new clean fuels required by law.[84]

Led by Sun Oil, a major marketer and refiner in the Northeast, where virtually all gasoline from Venezuela is sold, a coalition that included the National Petroleum Refiners Association, the American Petroleum Institute, and several major American oil companies lobbied to have Congress overturn the EPA's revised rule. The effort was strongly supported by environmental groups.[85] The alliance was effective. In August 1994 the Senate passed an amendment to the EPA's appropriations bill that prohibited the agency from implementing the new regulations. The amendment was later passed by the House. The EPA was compelled to reinstate its original rule. In effect, the domestic refiners had treated independent distributors and foreign refiners more or less the same way that corn farmers and ethanol producers had dealt with the refiners: each coalition had successfully lobbied in defense of an environmental regulation that would maintain its market share. The result was a regulatory apparatus that did little to improve environmental quality and also served as a trade barrier.

The World Trade Organization Dispute

Venezuela responded by resubmitting its complaint, first with GATT and then with the newly established World Trade Organization. The WTO convened its first dispute settlement panel to hear the case.[86] Subsequently, the panel agreed to examine a similar complaint from Brazil. Venezuela's financial stakes in the outcome of this dispute were considerable. Petroleos de Venezuela S.A. (PDVSA) had already embarked on a $1 billion refinery upgrading program, most of which was contracted to U.S. engineering and construction firms, to meet U.S. reformulated gasoline requirements and enable it to double its gasoline exports to the United States. Unless the rule was changed, Venezuela's U.S. exports would decrease by 50,000 barrels a day, costing it $150 million a year in sales through 1997.[87] PDVSA would be faced with the choice of either modifying its refineries to produce gasoline that satisfied the U.S. statutory baseline or finding an importer that would blend Venezuelan gas with other gas to meet the U.S. standard. The first option would be extremely costly and would undermine Venezuela's ability to compete with U.S. refineries, which would not have to make similar modifications until 1998. The second option would also probably diminish the cost competitiveness of Venezuelan fuel.[88] All these difficulties would be avoided if, like its U.S. competitors, PDVSA were permitted to use an individual rather than a statutory baseline.

The environmental stakes in this trade dispute ranged from modest to nonexistent. The average olefins content of Venezuelan gasoline is two times higher than the Clean Air Act baseline. According to a federal report, "RFG produced to Venezuela's 1990 baseline would have as much as 13.9% greater NOx emissions than U.S. average RFG."[89] This in turn could significantly increase ozone levels in the Northeast, where nitrous oxide plays a major role in ozone formation.

However, in congressional testimony it was also reported that fifty-nine of eighty-eight domestic refiners had olefin levels higher than the statutory baseline to which foreign refineries were being held.[90] Only sixteen domestic refineries were able to meet the parameters of the statutory baseline. Indeed, in an internal memo, an EPA official admitted that "some domestic refiners have some individual gasoline baseline parameters that are as dirty or dirtier than PDVSA's," adding that the overall NOx increase from permitting PDVSA to use its 1990 baseline would be much less than 1 percent.[91]

Venezuelan gasoline is comparatively clean in other respects. PDVSA's planning manager for refining emphasized, for example, that "Venezuela exports only unleaded regular gasoline to the U.S. and, when compared with U.S. regular gasoline with which it competes, it has the same or lower sulfur and olefins content."[92]

Like the debate over the EPA's ethanol content mandate, the dispute over the health effects of Venezuelan gasoline appeared to have less to do with environmental protection than with the use of environmental rules to allocate market shares, internationally as well as domestically. Not surprisingly, PDVSA's demand that it be permitted to use its own baseline was strongly endorsed by the Society of Independent Gasoline Marketers of America. SIGMA represents 250 independent gasoline marketers and chain retailers throughout the United States, and its members account for 20 percent of domestic motor fuel retail sales. For these independent marketers, maintaining a diversity of supply sources, domestic as well as foreign, is essential to remain competitive with the fully integrated oil companies. According to a spokesman for CITGO, a major domestic marketing and oil transportation company owned by PDVSA, in overturning the EPA's revised rule, "Congress was duped by a few domestic refiners who saw an opportunity to unfairly seize a larger share of the government-mandated Reformulated Gasoline (RFG) market." The domestics, he continued, "were not worried about the environmental impact of foreign gasoline, they merely saw an opportunity to have Congress squeeze the supply of RFG thus causing a price increase and a shift of market share."[93]

A significant reduction in gasoline imports not only damages the interests of independent distributors, but also hurts American consumers. Only 3 to 7 percent of the gasoline used in the United States is imported, and of this about 50 percent comes from Venezuela, amounting to approximately 70,000 barrels a day.[94] However, gasoline markets are regional, and foreign refiners have supplied about 16 percent of the gasoline sold on the East Coast and 20 percent of the gasoline sold in the Northeast.[95] Restricting gasoline imports would limit competition and raise prices to consumers there.

In fact, this already has occurred. Because reformulated gasoline is less fuel efficient, more of it must be produced. By 1995 domestic refineries were operating at close to capacity. At the same time, thanks in part to the EPA rule, during January and February 1995 gasoline imports were 45 percent lower than during the comparable period in 1994. In June 1995 the price for a gallon of regular unleaded conventional gasoline in New York Harbor had increased by 19 percent from the previous year, while the price for super unleaded conventional gasoline had gone up 14 percent. The increase in prices for reformulated gasoline was equally significant: regular unleaded RFG was up 23 percent, while the price of super unleaded climbed by 16 percent.[96] So consumers in the region are paying considerably more for gasoline in return for little improvement in their air quality.

The WTO Decides

On January 17, 1996, the WTO dispute panel issued its decision. The panel began by noting that the U.S. standard clearly accorded imported gasoline less favorable treatment. It observed:

> According to the United States, as of August 1995, approximately 100 US refiners, representing 98.5 percent of gasoline produced in 1990, had received EPA approval of their individual baselines. Only three of the refiners met the statutory baseline

for all parameters. Thus, while 97 percent of US refiners did not and were not required to meet the statutory baseline, the statutory baseline was required of importers of gasoline.[97]

The panel then addressed the question of whether this difference in treatment was necessary for the United States to achieve the legitimate objective of cleaner air. It concluded that there was no such justification. The United States had not demonstrated that the nation's air quality would suffer if foreign refiners were allowed to use their individual baselines rather than the U.S. statutory average. Moreover, if doing so did result in adverse environmental impacts, then the appropriate policy for the United States was to impose slightly stricter requirements on both imported and domestic gasoline, not to hold them to different standards.

The panel concluded that holding gasoline produced by domestic and imported refineries to different standards violated American obligations under GATT's national treatment article. U.S. Trade Representative Mickey Kantor responded by stating, "Nothing related to this matter will undermine fulfilling the objectives of the Clean Air Act."[98] Environmentalists were incensed with the WTO: the panel's decision affirmed the "'right' of foreign oil companies to make profits in the U.S. market by selling dirty gasoline . . . over our right as citizens to pass laws protecting the quality of the air we are forced to breathe."[99]

The United States appealed the decision to a newly established WTO internal review board, which in April 1996 affirmed the panel's ruling. Under WTO rules, Venezuela and Brazil could either impose tariffs on U.S. imports equivalent to their losses from the disputed rule, estimated at $150 million, or demand the equivalent in compensation. However, on June 19, 1996, the Clinton administration announced it would propose changes in the application of clean air rules to imported gasoline to bring the United States into compliance.[100]

THE COMMUNITY REINVESTMENT ACT

The two cases discussed in detail in this chapter are somewhat unusual. In each, U.S. social regulations were formally challenged through dispute settlement proceedings of GATT-WTO. But these two prominent stories do not exhaust the list of government rules that have been questioned by America's trading partners. Obviously, not all the criticisms are well founded. Just because a regulation imposes disproportionate strains on importers does not automatically make it protectionist. There are many legitimate reasons why it is often easier for domestic producers to comply with a particular national regulatory standard. Many regulations do make both domestic producers and consumers better off, even if they vex foreign firms.[101] But what is striking is that more than a few regulations deemed abrasive by U.S. trading partners are also questionable as domestic policies. Consider another example, namely, the Community Reinvestment Act.

Best Intentions

The Community Reinvestment Act was passed in 1977 to address redlining, the practice in which banks draw lines around particular geographic areas, usually in central cities and populated by poor minorities, and deny financing to borrowers because they reside in these areas rather than because their credit histories are inadequate. Apart from violating people's civil rights, the alleged lending discrimination may accelerate urban decay.

The Community Reinvestment Act obligates commercial banks and savings and loan institutions to "meet the credit needs of the local communities in which they are chartered, consistent with the safe and sound operation of such institutions."[102] The law was, of course, broadly worded and did not aim specifically to allocate credit, create affirmative action in lending, or require depository institutions to support local charities.[103] It was based on the idea that depository institutions could make a profit in their local communities and thus help preserve them. This logic applied to institutions in low-income urban areas as well as those in wealthy suburbs.

Depository institutions were not automatically punished by regulators for noncompliance with the law. Although CRA compliance assessments were made at regular bank examinations, compliance was largely enforced at the point when an institution filed an application for acquiring another bank, merging with another bank, or establishing a new branch. Before 1989 both types of CRA assessments were confidential, but that year Congress amended the law, requiring regulators to prepare a public evaluation of an applicant's CRA record. These resulted in stricter CRA enforcement, mainly because the evaluations could be used by urban community activists to put political or legal pressure on regulators, indirectly exacting concessions from lending institutions. With the 1989 amendments it became easier for regulators and local advocacy groups to obtain funds and services (for example, pledges to offer more checking services, pledges of loans to specific neighborhoods, or changes in terms of credit).

Problems

There has been considerable criticism of the CRA. First, direct compliance costs are high. Bankers claim that this latest regulatory venture requires massive paperwork, an especially onerous burden for small community banks. Two surveys by banking associations found the law to be the most costly of all regulatory burdens imposed on banks.[104] Second, it is claimed that the CRA conflicts with the soundness of depository institutions by forcing loans on terms that would not be normally available, thus heightening risk. Being required to hold such loans also reduces the ability of an institution to diversify its loan portfolio, adding systemic risk for the institution. Third, by effectively raising the costs of doing business in low-income neighborhoods, the law may chase away as much capital as it obtains for such areas. Fourth, by enforcing the law at the time of an application for expansion, merger, or branching, the CRA places a tax on the banking industry's restructuring and consolidation. This complication has resulted at times in delays of proposed mergers and consolidations and the abandonment of acquisitions altogether. Finally, because the CRA affects only banks, it places them at a relative disadvantage vis-à-vis credit unions, pension funds, life insurance companies, and the fast-growing mutual fund industry.

Behind all these doubts is the proposition that the banks can ill afford added regulatory baggage.[105] Implicit in the logic of the CRA is that banks can use high profits from other areas of business to subsidize the riskier loans. But in an era of increasing international competition in financial services, the banks' capability for such cross-subsidization is weakening.[106]

For years the Community Reinvestment Act was solely a domestic matter. With the passage of the Riegle-Neal Interstate Banking and Branching Act in 1994, however, the CRA began to assume an international dimension.

The CRA applies only to insured retail banks. Because the European banking presence in the United States largely consists of uninsured, wholesale banks that are not covered by the Federal Deposit Insurance Corporation, the European banks at first were mostly exempt from the law's requirements. As federally insured institutions, however, U.S. wholesale banks were required to comply with it.

The relaxation of interstate banking restrictions opened new opportunities to branch across the United States. Because the branches of foreign wholesale banks would seldom be bound by the CRA, the United States feared a growing inequity: that European bankers might develop a competitive advantage in the U.S. market. The concern found sympathy in the Senate, where legislation was introduced requiring foreign banks to use a U.S. subsidiary to take advantage of the new interstate branching authority. The House version, however, allowed foreign banks to branch freely, without the U.S. subsidiary proviso. In conference the final bill generally followed the House's rendition, but to assuage the concerns raised by senators, several compromises were made. Most notable was a stipulation that a foreign wholesale bank acquiring a retail bank and then converting it into an uninsured branch must keep its branches in compliance with the CRA.[107] The difficulty here is that national treatment standards are violated because foreign wholesale banks are not FDIC insured but are being asked to assume some additional credit risks when branching across state lines by acquiring U.S. banks.[108]

CONCLUSIONS

These three cases illustrate situations in which the imposition of new regulations on a domestic industry has led to policies that create new and sometimes unequal burdens for foreign competitors.

Thus significant additional rules imposed on the U.S. automobile industry that were aimed at furthering energy conservation were also structured to protect U.S. producers. Wholly intended or not, the protective components of CAFE were a necessary price for its passage. CAFE's domestic deficiencies and its protectionist consequences are directly linked to one another. A better energy conservation policy – for example, a straightforward tax on automotive fuel – would not discriminate against vehicles on the basis of where they were manufactured or on the range of a manufacturer's product lines. In effect, CAFE has been a disappointment onshore as well as off: it has not conserved energy efficiently, and it has managed to antagonize producers from America's largest trading partner, the European Union.

A similar irony pervades U.S. policy regarding reformulated gasoline. As in the case of CAFE, serious doubts have been raised as to whether the reformulated gasoline requirement in general and the subsidization of ethanol in particular have been effective means of improving public health by restricting pollutants produced by motor vehicles. Yet once again, when faced with significant compliance costs, a major U.S. industry reached for an import restriction. And in the end, American motorists in the Northeast are paying higher prices for gasoline with no discernible improvement in air quality.

In this instance, the protection of both domestic ethanol producers and domestic refineries has been paid for not by manufacturers of luxury products in advanced countries but by the producers and workers from less developed nations in the Caribbean and Latin America. The manufacturers of expensive European automobiles have experienced some marginal reduction in sales in the United States as a result of CAFE. But the effect of U.S. trade restrictions on the exports of Caribbean nations, Venezuela, and Brazil have carried a much more significant economic penalty relative to the developmental needs of their economies. Although the trade disagreement with Venezuela and Brazil may have attracted little public attention in the United States, in the Latin American countries the matter was serious. Venezuela in particular depends on petroleum exports to the United States to service its massive foreign debt. The European Union and Norway also watched the dispute closely.

Both the domestic and international implications of the Community Reinvestment Act are far less dramatic. But here, too, a regulation is imposing substantial costs on a U.S. industry, costs that are not clearly offset by social benefits, and the rule has become the subject of international criticism.

Finally, it is important to note that in each of these cases the efforts to shift some of the costs of regulatory requirements from domestic firms to their foreign competitors was supported by public interest groups. CAFE has always been enthusiastically applauded by consumer and environmental organizations; they have spearheaded every effort to raise the fuel economy requirements. These same organizations also strongly criticized the European Union's challenge to CAFE through GATT. Environmental advocates did not promote the ethanol mandate, but they have been vigorous proponents of the quest for rules mandating clean fuel at almost any cost. And they have worked closely with the domestic oil industry to secure different standards for gasoline refined in Venezuela. Likewise, both the Community Reinvestment Act and the decision to extend its provision indirectly to foreign banks were backed by community groups.

If there is a lesson in all this it is that trade liberalization and regulatory reform can be mutually reinforcing. At least in the case studies examined in this chapter, the interests of the American public would have been better served had the United States chosen to accomplish its legitimate policy objectives by adopting the least trade-restrictive alternative. In the cases of both CAFE and reformulated gasoline, the interests of foreign producers and of American consumers actually complemented one another. Thus the complaints of America's trading partners about the discriminatory effects of some U.S. regulatory policies warrant serious reflection. Trade agreements can help improve domestic regulatory policies because they can highlight rent seeking that is masquerading as consumer or environmental protection. Just as U.S. efforts to pressure Japan to open its markets have frequently reinforced internal Japanese efforts to reform that country's economy, so might America's trading partners become equally constructive in bettering some U.S. regulatory practices. What may be good for them is sometimes also better for us.

COMMENT BY I. M. DESTLER

David Vogel has written an interesting and informative paper. It is impressive how the U.S. government tied itself in knots by trying to promote fuel economy without a gasoline tax. It is dismaying, but hardly surprising, that the case for cleaner fuel became transmuted into a battle over economic rents among regional economic interests and between them and foreign economic interests. In any case, it is hard to retain much enthusiasm for CAFE as even a second- or third-best measure for fuel conservation or as a venture into the regulation and subsidization of motor fuel content.

The author needs to highlight the constructive tension between the paper and the apparent premise (and provocative title) of the conference. "Comparative *dis*advantage" is a label reinforcing the common perception that U.S. regulations are a burden on U.S. producers, cutting into their capacity to compete. That hypothesis also requires, of course, that analysts find disproportional impact on a particular industry – otherwise regulation will not affect *comparative* advantage, though it may reduce overall national welfare.

In any case, Vogel's stories do not conform to the hypothesis, for these regulations were certainly not burdens borne atypically by U.S. producers alone; they applied, not always equally, to all major players in the U.S. market. One major reason is that unlike many environmental laws they were not regulations of the production process but of the product going into the U.S. market. In intent, and in some respects in their specific language, these regulatory programs were closer to the opposite: burdens on foreign producers. In effect, CAFE – the more interesting case – was mixed, as Vogel notes. This highlights the enormous difficulty of crafting indirect protectionist measures in a world where Robert Reich's question "Who is us?" remains a vexing one, implying a tension between the interests of companies and the interests of favoring home production.

The treatment of CAFE in Vogel's chapter is powerful, even devastating, but sometimes the heat of the argument impedes the shedding of light. As Vogel catalogues the nefarious effects of this unusual law, I find myself repeatedly asking "Compared to what?" or "Was CAFE the *only* reason?" or "What is the balance here?" Let me offer a few examples.

Early in the chapter the reader learns that with a gas tax out of political reach, Congress decided to shift the burdens of reducing gasoline consumption onto the manufacturers of motor vehicles. One might infer that manufacturers responded by supporting a gas tax because it would shift the burdens onto consumers. But wait. A gas tax surely burdens the manufacturers as well and would likely have had the same effects as a tax on low-efficiency cars in increasing the market share of Japanese models. There was no way to deal with the issue without burdening the U.S. manufacturers, and on a comparative basis, CAFE was probably better for them than in gasoline tax.

Similarly, Vogel then stresses – no doubt accurately – that CAFE standards drove the Big Three to reduce the weight of their motor vehicles, increasing occupants' vulnerability in case of accidents. But wouldn't a raising of gasoline prices to European levels have had a similar impact? Which route, comparatively, was better for auto safety then? The chapter doesn't even ask the question, much less address it.

Instead, the argument against CAFE takes on the character of piling on. One is told, on one page, that CAFE, together with other new-vehicle regulatory standards, is entirely responsible for an increase of two full years in the average age of cars on the American road. Nothing is said about quality improvement as a possible cause, or income stagnation among American auto buyers, or price rises with causes other than those cited.

Subsequently, the author notes that CAFE drove Detroit to shift gas-guzzler production overseas, because the fleet average for imports allowed it. But he does not balance this result against the earlier-noted effect (and intention) of concentrating economy car production in the United States because the fleet average for domestic production demanded it. Thus the assertion that it "costs American jobs" is dubious, since no comparison is made of the two opposite effects.

My point is not to question the conclusion that CAFE standards and the requirements for reformulated gasoline were an inefficient means of reducing energy consumption or of improving air quality. My purpose is only to urge greater restraint and proportionality in the argument. I, too, favor the gas tax alternative, but there is no sense pretending that it would not have had some of the same negative impacts that Vogel attributes to CAFE. As often as possible, therefore, he needs to show that the means he is critiquing do more damage than other plausible means.

Vogel also makes a persuasive case on trade policy: CAFE did discriminate against foreign firms, and in some respects, against foreign-owned production. It would have been better, in my view, had the GATT panel also found the fleet-averaging requirement inconsistent with U.S. trade obligations, though I can sympathize with throwing this bone to the largest GATT member – given the efficacy of CAFE as a protectionist instrument, which the chapter documents. But let me close my comments with broader reflections on how to define protectionism and how one would like the necessary future debate on U.S. trade policy to proceed.

I start with a suspicion I have: the Ways and Means Committee members who drafted CAFE would vigorously deny that they were protectionists. They had no plan to block imports; they just wanted to keep Toyota and other companies from gaining additional advantage – and General Motors and other companies from further injury – by way of gasoline conservation measures. But by one simple and logical standard Congress was undoubtedly protectionist, just as it is when it enacts antidumping (AD) laws or countervailing duty laws that "offset" subsidies granted by Canadian provinces but not subsidies granted by American states. The logical definition of protectionism is: *any* law that treats goods produced abroad – and by extension, production by foreign-owned companies – less favorably than goods produced within the fifty states. Since the United States does not have a domestic antidumping law, the law for foreign trade is protectionist.

This definition is different from the question of GATT consistency. The main provisions of the AD law are GATT consistent, though Mickey Kantor and Congress may have stepped over the line in certain provisions of the 1994 Uruguay Round implementing legislation. The definition is also different from the view of the broad liberal-trade consensus in the United States that tolerates or even endorses numerous measures that in fact discriminate against non-U.S. production. But it seems to me that we need a clear intellectual delineation of free trade, a principle that advocates can argue with conviction, not that pragmatism, even if it will not always prevail. In today's politics, the Office of the U.S. Trade Representative cannot take this line, and perhaps it will never be able to.

Finally, in some cases, what is protectionist by this standard will also be GATT-inconsistent. Venezuela should probably win its World Trade Organization case on the merits, as the initial panel finding suggests it will. In others, the standard put forward here will clearly go beyond current international trade agreements but might help the United States in framing future ones. It may help, therefore, to curb or limit domestic regulations that apply different roles to domestic and foreign producers.

COMMENT BY SHARYN O'HALLORAN

David Vogel's essay addresses the use of nontariff barriers, disguised as social and economic regulations, to limit imports into the United States. The paper presents three examples in which environmental regulations serve to hinder free trade, principally through CAFE standards on fuel economy for cars and the provisions of the 1990 Clean Air Act dealing with ethanol-based fuels and with reformulated gasoline.

Vogel argues that while the intent of these regulations may have been well meaning, the end result has been to hurt American consumers and the public by raising domestic prices and limiting imports. Furthermore, these measures have proved rather ineffective in achieving their original intent of improving overall environmental quality. The explanation for these policies, according to Vogel, is that they are the result of special interest groups wielding undue influence in the political process. To overcome the natural tendency for law-makers to misuse social policies to protect well-organized domestic producers, Vogel suggests that following the rule of "least restrictive trade" when setting environmental regulations would lead to a more efficient and effective regulatory setting.

However, if these policies are so inefficient and run counter to American consumers and the public interest at large, how did they get enacted in the first place? In my comments, I want to offer the following explanation of how we got here and where a policy of strict adherence to "least restrictive trade" might lead us. In the American system of government, passing broad regulatory policies

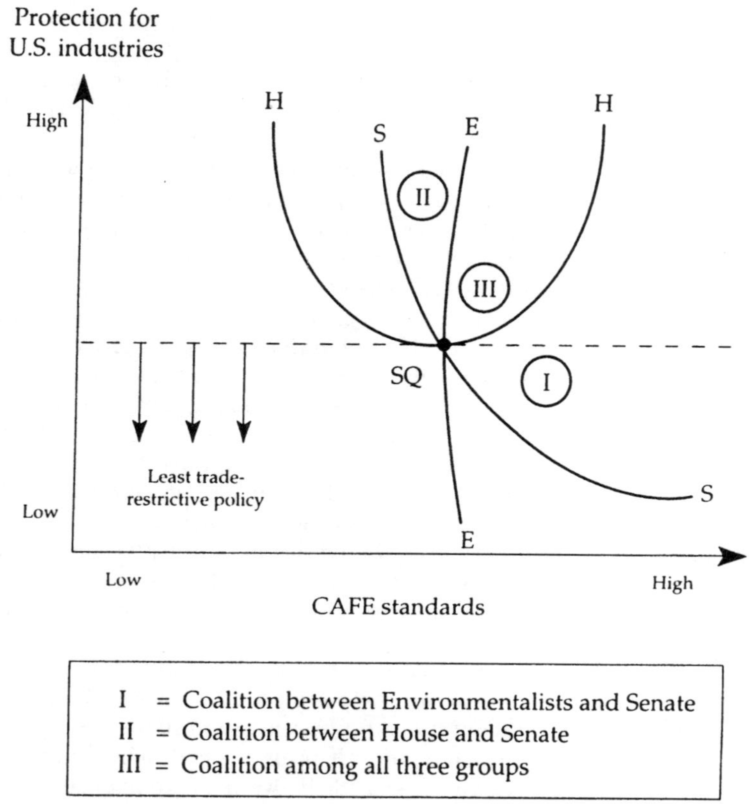

FIGURE 3.1 1990 Clean Air Act CAFE Standards.

requires broad-based social coalitions. Often, attracting the support of different groups requires concessions that are not in themselves efficient. However, given political constraints, these concessions may be necessary to achieve *second best* policy outcomes. Furthermore, these outcomes may improve overall social welfare even though they do not follow the course of least restrictive trade. In the end, a policy of least restrictive trade may lead to a reinforcement of status quo policies by eliminating the possibility of coalition building among key political actors.

In the following paragraphs, I briefly review the three cases analyzed by Vogel and offer an explanation of why trade restrictions were implemented hand-in-hand with environmental reforms. In each case, a persuasive argument can be made that the real choice was not between social regulation that was trade restrictive and social regulation that was less restrictive, but rather between social regulation with trade concessions or no regulation at all.

CAFE Standards

The first case is corporate average fuel economy standards. To examine the politics of CAFE standards, figure 3-1 shows two policy dimensions: the level of CAFE standards and the degree of protection afforded U.S. industries. In this policy space, the status quo CAFE standard as of the late 1980s was set at 27.5 mpg. That is, every car maker had to achieve an average of 27.5 mpg for the entire fleet. Vogel notes that this policy was slightly protectionist in favor of U.S. auto producers, owing to the requirement that each producer meet the CAFE standard for its domestic and imported fleets separately.

There are three major actors to consider in passing higher CAFE standards: the House, the Senate, and environmentalist groups. Figure 3-1 shows indifference curves running through the status quo policy for all three players. Here I assume that the environmentalists care only about increasing CAFE standards and are unconcerned about protecting U.S. industries. The House answers to more local concerns and would thus be expected to react strongly to U.S. auto makers' demands for protection. In particular, the chair of the House Commerce Committee during this time was Representative John Dingell from Detroit, making it unlikely that any legislation that did not confer some protection on the auto industry would pass through the House. The Senate, having broader constituencies and therefore being better equipped to supply public goods than the House, shared both environmental and protectionist concerns. These competing demands are represented in the indifference curves by the relative willingness of each actor to trade off some protection for higher CAFE levels.

Under this particular configuration of preferences and status quo policy, what are the possible coalitions that could form in favor of a new policy? In the figure, region I represents deals that could be made between environmentalists and the Senate. Note that this includes areas with higher CAFE standards and disadvantages for U.S. car makers in the form of lower protection. Region II represents House-Senate deals, all of which give higher protection for car makers. And region III represents the intersection of all three groups; this area represents the set of policies that environmentalists would endorse and Congress would enact. Note that all points in region III have both higher CAFE standards and higher protection for U.S. car makers. In fact, throughout the discussions of raising CAFE standards in the late 1980s, automakers suggested options like the percentage approach and antibacksliding provisions, both of which would discriminate against foreign producers.

Vogel's policy prescription suggests that the United States should adhere to the policy of least restrictive trade. If this condition is added to the figure, then the constraint is that no regulations can further disadvantage foreign importers, meaning that any policy enacted must lie below the dotted line. Note, however, that this would also cut out any possibility of policy movement, as the intersection of all four sets is empty.

The implication of the preceding analysis is that the price of any policy movement in this area – improvement in environmental standards – is higher protection. To put it another way, given the current political configuration, the requirement of least restrictive trade policy will end up enforcing the status quo. It may be that this is the best outcome for all concerned. But there may be some welfare-improving policy options (like those represented in area III) that cannot be achieved under the policy of least restrictive trade.

Ethanol

The second big case discussed in the chapter refers to fuel standards that favor the use of ethanol as a gasoline additive to create what are called clean fuels. Whereas CAFE standards do have some redeeming public policy merits, I do agree with Vogel's assessment that it is hard to justify the ethanol program on good policy grounds. However, this raises the question of why these pro-ethanol standards were ever adopted.

Again Vogel's response relies on the privileged position of powerful interests groups in the political process. But as figure 3–2 shows, the number of groups who stood to gain from ethanol mandates – farmers and corporations like Archer Daniels Midland – were certainly outnumbered by the forces arrayed against ethanol – the auto industry, the oil industry, and essentially the rest of the nation. If we take the size of these humps as an indication of the relative size of the two groups, the pro-ethanol forces were clearly in the minority. Thus a median voter argument would predict that the antiethanol forces would prevail and ethanol would remain unprotected.

So why were pro-ethanol standards adopted? This is an issue that cannot be studied in a vacuum, as the ethanol standards were implemented as part of the 1990 Clean Air Act. By examining the larger picture, literally as well as figuratively, the following scenario emerges.

In the bottom half of figure 3-2, the dimensions are pro-or anti-ethanol, as above, and overall levels of environmental reform. The status quo represents the current level of environmental standards and a slightly pro-ethanol policy. The two ovals represent the set of ideal points of the antiethanol and pro-ethanol legislators, who are assumed to represent antiethanol and pro-ethanol groups, respectively.

The politics surrounding the enactment of the Clean Air Act produced three distinct groups. The opponents of ethanol were divided into group A, who favored stronger environmental standards, and group B, who favored weaker environmental standards or the status quo. The ethanol promoters are labeled group C and, as the diagram shows, they were more on the pro-environment side of the debate.

The key to the politics of the Clean Air Act is that passing any policy required two out of the three groups; no group alone had a clear majority. As in figure 3-1, I have drawn indifference curves through the status quo for each group. Groups A and B are indeed antiethanol, but they care relatively little about this dimension compared with larger environmental issues. By contrast, the indifference curve of group C opens up and to the right, indicating their pro-environment and pro-ethanol stance.

What were the possible coalitions? As usual with spatial diagrams, the set of points that beat the status quo are represented in the petals that are the intersection of any two win sets. So one coalition that could have formed would be

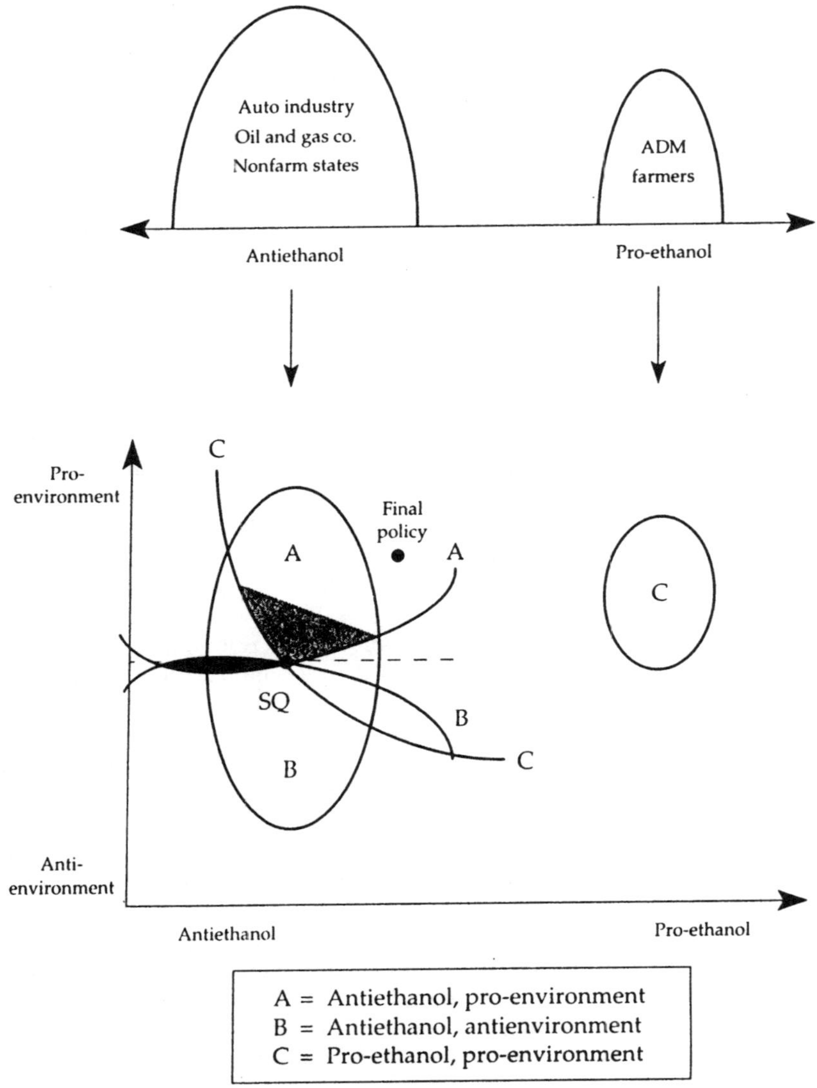

FIGURE 3.2 1990 Clean Air Act Clean Fuels: Ethanol.

the purely anti-ethanol forces, groups A and B, represented by the shaded area. But then not much would happen for the ethanol forces by the antienvironmentalists, a coalition between B and C, as shown in the area with vertical lines.

In the end, the coalition that formed, after a marathon series of negotiations, was between the pro-environmentalists and the ethanol supporters, groups A and C, indicated by horizontal lines. This probably resulted because the pro-ethanol forces included a number of legislators close to the chamber median,

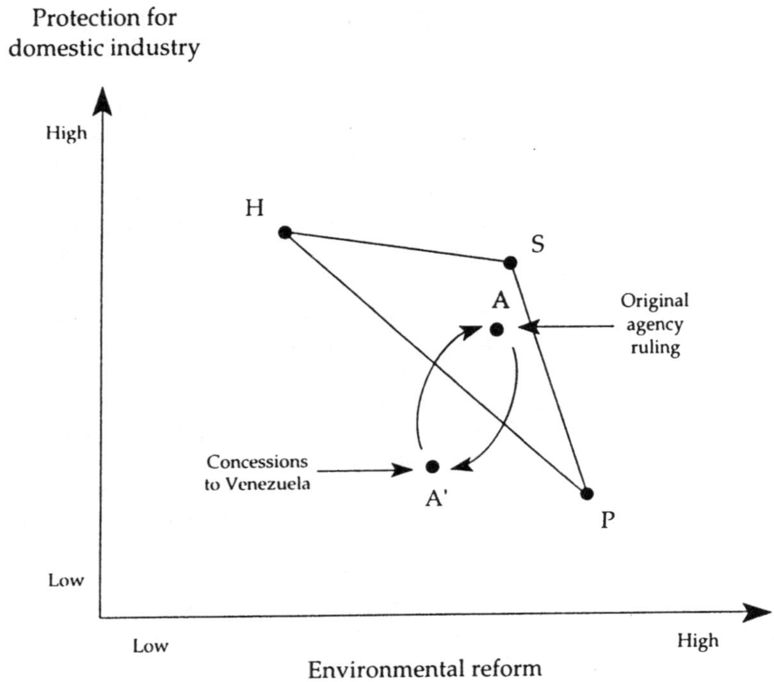

FIGURE 3.3 1990 Clean Air Act Reformulated Gasoline.

such as Senators Robert J. Dole from Kansas and Charles E. Grassley from Iowa. The final bill thus contained the pro-ethanol provision. But it also included a number of important environmental gains: acid rain provisions, phase-out of chloroflurocarbons (CFCs), limits on motor vehicle emissions, regulation of toxic air pollutants, and a reduction of urban smog.

Thus the overall policy gains made in the 1990 Clean Air Act were not inconsequential, even though the act did include provisions to appease the ethanol producers. Again, the bottom line of the story is that given political realities, concessions had to be made to special interests in order to achieve broader policy goals. The policy that resulted may not have been "first best," but the alternatives were either the environmental bill that was passed or no bill at all.

Reformulated Gasoline

Finally, let us take a look at the other side of the fuel standards issue, which is the reformulated gasoline debate. The 1990 Clean Air Act left a number of questions open for future determination by the Environmental Protection Agency (EPA). One of these was the phase-in requirements for reformulated gas in nine major cities. In 1994 the EPA issued regulations that strengthened gas standards but required foreign producers to improve their standards more quickly than domestic producers.

I represent the EPA ruling graphically in figure 3-3 by again considering a policy space with two dimensions – environmental reform and protection for domestic industry. The ideal points of the House, Senate, and President are shown, with the House preferring the highest level of protection and the President preferring the most reform for the environment. Again this story is consistent with the size of the constituencies of the three branches. Note that passing new policy requires the assent of all three actors. Thus it is only points inside the shaded triangle that cannot be overturned by any viable condition. However, policies outside this triangle can be overturned by a coalition of all three branches. The policy originally promulgated by the EPA is shown as point A, inside the Pareto triangle – cleaner gas but some protection.

After Venezuela protested that the new regulations were discriminatory, the EPA responded by exempting Venezuela from the faster phase-in requirements, thereby shifting policy to point A' in the figure. While this policy was less discriminatory, it also weakened the environmental component of the regulation, as Venezuela, one of the major suppliers to the United States, produced somewhat dirtier gas than American reformulated fuels. These concessions, however, moved policy outside the Pareto triangle, breaking the coalition necessary to sustain environmental reform. This action, in turn, provoked a congressional response overturning the EPA's ruling and returning policy to point A.

The moral of this story is that even when policy is made by apparently neutral administrators, who may try to promote freer trade, outcomes may still be trade restrictive. Regulatory policy is ultimately made by the elected branches of government, and any regulations that stray too far away from their preferences will merely be overturned. Again, there are political limits to what can be obtained from social regulations.

Conclusions

The political reality in all three cases is that domestic regulations are made by domestic politics. This implies, first of all, that certain policy instruments will not be feasible, even if they are economically desirable. For instance, David Vogel correctly notes that significantly higher gas taxes or a carbon tax may be more efficient than CAFE standards, but such taxes would have no realistic chance of passing. (Note the current debate over eliminating the 4.3 cents a gallon gas tax.) It also implies, given the American system of separate powers, that enacting broad social regulations requires a broad-based coalition of interests. In some cases, this may mean that domestic industries will receive policy concessions in the form of phase-in periods or relief from foreign competition. But the requirement of "least trade restrictive" policies that do not disadvantage foreign producers may eliminate the possibility of policy movement altogether. Thus the original CAFE standards bill and the 1990 Clean Air Act could not have been passed without some degree of policy concessions. In the world of second best, where political constraints effectively prevent states from adopting the most efficient policy solution, the price of two steps forward on environmental issues may be one step back on trade.

NOTES

1 The most comprehensive analysis of CAFE is Pietro S. Nivola and Robert W. Crandall, *The Extra Mile:Rethinking Energy Policy for Automotive Transportation* (Brookings, 1995). See esp. pp. 22–42.
2 For an overview of the politics of clean air legislation through 1981, see David Vogel, "A Case Study of Clean Air Legislation 1967–1981," in Betty Bock and others, eds, *The Impact of the Modern Corporation* (Columbia University Press, 1984), pp. 309–86. For the 1990 amendments, see Gary C. Bryner, *Blue Skies, Green Politics: The Clean Air Act of 1990* (Washington: Congressional Quarterly Press, 1993).
3 See, for example, Lester B. Lave and Gilbert S. Omenn, *Clearing the Air: Reforming the Clean Air Act* (Brookings, 1981).
4 John D. Graham "Saving Gasoline and Lines,' in John D. Graham and Jonathan Baert Wiener, eds, *Risk versus Risk: Tradeoffs in Protecting Health and the Environment* (Harvard University Press, 1995), pp. 88–89.
5 "Ford Ends Stalemate, Signs Energy Bill," *1975 Congressional Quarterly Almanac* (1975), pp. 220–43.
6 Nivola and Crandall, *Extra Mile*, p. 23.
7 Quoted in Daniel C. Esty, *Greening the GATT: Trade, Environment, and the Future* (Washington: Institute for International Economics, 1994), p. 45.
8 Matthew L. Wald, "How America Perpetuates Its Gas Crisis," *New York Times*, May 5, 1996, p. E4.
9 Agis Salpukas, "What's Next, Tail Fins: Fast Speeds and Big Cars Send Gas Consumption Up?" *New York Times*, February 15, 1996, p. C1.
10 Graham, "Saving Gasoline and Lives," p. 90.
11 Ibid.
12 Robert W. Crandall, "The Changing Rationale for Motor Vehicle Fuel-Economy Regulation," *Regulation* (Fall 1990), p. 11.
13 Nivola and Crandall, *Extra Mile*, p. 23.
14 William K. Stevens, "Trying to Stem Emissions, U.S. Sees Its Goal Fading," *New York Times*, November 28, 1995, p. B8.
15 Wald, "How America Perpetuates Its Gas Crisis," p. E4.
16 Nivola and Crandall, *Extra Mile*, p. 8. This figure has remained relatively stable through 1995. See Stevens, "Trying," pp. A1, B8.
17 Quoted in Nivola and Crandall, *Extra Mile*, p. 33.
18 Ibid., pp. 33–34.
19 Ibid., pp. 49–50.
20 See, for instance, Thomas Gale Moore, "A Hidden Culprit in Auto Imports," *Wall Street Journal*, January 14, 1992, p. A14.
21 Paul A. Eisenstein, "Automakers Are Being Pushed toward Fuel Economy," *Christian Science Monitor*, March 23, 1989, p. 9.
22 Nivola and Crandall, *Extra Mile*, p. 11.
23 Wald, "How America Perpetuates Its Gas Crisis," p. E4.
24 Nivola and Crandall, *Extra Mile*, p. 5.
25 Sam Kazman, "Death by Regulation," *Regulation* (Fall 1991), p. 20.
26 Graham, "Saving Gasoline and Lives," p. 95.
27 Kazman, "Death by Regulation," p. 20.

28 Ibid., p. 21.
29 Nivola and Crandall, *Extra Mile*, p. 41; and see also Kazman, "Death by Regulation," p. 21.
30 Kazman, "Death by Regulation," p. 21.
31 See David P. Baron, *Business and Its Environment* (Prentice-Hall, 1996), pp. 221–27. See also Neal Templin, "Fuel Economy Law That Would Stymie Japanese is Sought by U.S. Auto Makers," *Wall Street Journal*, December 5, 1989, p. A11.
32 Templin, "Fuel Economy Law," p. A11.
33 "Fuel-Efficiency Effort Defeated in Senate," *1990 Congressional Quarterly Almanac*, vol. 46 (1991), p. 280.
34 Crandall, "Changing Rationale," p. 12.
35 Frances Williams, "Brussels Wins U.S. Car Tax Probe," *Financial Times*, May 13, 1993, p. 6; and Nancy Dunne, "EC Challenge over U.S. Fuel Economy Tax," *Financial Times*, May 11, 1993, p. 5.
36 Reginal Stuart, "Car Makers Are Getting Back in the Driver's Seat," *New York Times*, July 21, 1985, p. E2.
37 "GATT Rules against CAFE, Opens Door to Conservation Exception," *Inside U.S. Trade* (October 4, 1994), p. S-4.
38 John Griffiths, "Fuel Economy Rule May Hit Jaguar," *Financial Times*, February 28, 1983, p. 1; and David Vogel, *Trading Up: Consumer and Environmental Regulation in a Global Economy* (Harvard University Press, 1995), p. 132.
39 Dunne, "EC Challenge," p. 5.
40 "EC Seeks GATT Panel on U.S. 'Gas Guzzling' Taxes," *Reuter European Business Report*, May 11, 1993.
41 "EC Threatens Formal Action against U.S. Car Taxes," *Reuter European Community Report*, February 11, 1993.
42 "U.S. Blocks EC Bid for GATT Dispute Panel on Car Tax," *Reuter European Business Report* (March 24, 1993).
43 See, for example, Doron P. Levin, "Detroit's Assault on Mileage Bill," *New York Times*, May 11, 1991, p. L35.
44 Quoted in Dunne, "EC Challenges," p. 5.
45 Quoted in Peter Behr, "Trade Case Could Endanger Environmental Law, GATT: Europeans Contend That Gasoline Consumption Standard Is Unfair to Their Auto," *Washington Post*, June 10, 1994, p. F1.
46 "GATT Rules against CAFE," p. S-5.
47 Ibid.
48 Ibid., pp. S-5, S-6.
49 Ibid., p. S-1.
50 Ibid., p. S-7.
51 Ibid., p. S-7.
52 Bryner, *Blue Skies, Green Politics*, p. 134.
53 Dan Carney, "Dwayne's World," *Mother Jones*, July–August 1995, pp. 44–47.
54 James Bovard, "Corporate Welfare Fueled by Political Contributions," *Business and Society Review*, no. 94 (Summer 1995), pp. 24, 26.
55 Ibid., p. 26.
56 Ibid., p. 28.
57 Quoted in ibid., p. 26.
58 Quoted in ibid., pp. 26–27.
59 Jonathan H. Adler, "Clean Fuels, Dirty Air: How a (Bad) Bill Became Law," *Public Interest*, no. 108 (Summer 1992), pp. 128–29.
60 "Fuel Efficiency Effort," p. 229.
61 Testimony of Charles J. DiBona, "Clean Air Act Amendments," Hearing before the

House Subcommittee on Oversight and Investigations of the Committee on Commerce, 104 Cong. 1 sess. (Government Printing Office, 1995), p. 42.
62 Jeffrey L. Katz, "Home State Interests Prevail as Ethanol Rule Squeaks By," *Congressional Quarterly Weekly Report*, August 6, 1994, p. 2259.
63 Bovard, "Corporate Welfare," p. 28.
64 Quoted in Margaret Kriz, "Fight over Clean Fuels Gets Dirty," *National Journal* (April 16, 1994), p. 898.
65 "EPA's Ethanol Additive Proposal Draws Fire," *Oil and Gas Journal* (May 23, 1994), p. 31.
66 Quoted in James Bovard, "Dole, Gingrich and the Big Ethanol Boondoggle," *Wall Street Journal*, November 2, 1995, p. A18.
67 Bovard, "Corporate Welfare," p. 27.
68 "Corn Growers Preserve Energy Rule," *Congressional Quarterly Weekly Report*, August 6, 1994, p. 2260; and Bob Williams, "MTBE, Ethanol Advocates' Squabble May Complicate RFG Implementation," *Oil and Gas Journal* (February 13, 1995), p. 22.
69 Quoted in Bovard, "Dole," p. A18.
70 Senator Malcolm Wallop quoted in "EPA's Ethanol Additive Proposal Draws Fire," *Oil and Gas Journal*, May 23, 1994, p. 30.
71 Bovard, "Corporate Welfare," pp. 28–29.
72 Ibid., p. 29.
73 Kenneth Chilton and Anne Scholt, "A Primer on Smog Control," *Regulation* (Winter 1990), pp. 31–40.
74 Ed Rubenstein, "Clearing the Air," *National Review* (March 5, 1990), p. 15.
75 See, for example, Chilton and Sholtz, "Primer on Smog Control," pp. 31–40; and Kenneth Chilton and Christopher Boerner, "Smog in America: The High Cost of Hysteria," Center for the Study of American Business, Policy Study 128 (Washington University, January 1996), pp. 1–28.
76 Chilton and Boerner, "Smog in America," p. 20.
77 Steve Charnovitz, "The WTO Panel Decision on U.S. Clean Air Act Regulations," *International Trade Reporter*, vol. 13 (March 13, 1996), p. 459.
78 Ibid.
79 "U.S. Defends Gas Rules in WTO against Charges of Discrimination," *Inside U.S. Trade*, vol. 13 (July 7, 1995), p. 8.
80 Testimony of Ira Shapiro, "Reformulated Gasoline," Hearing before the House Subcommittee on Oversight and Investigations of the Committee on Energy and Commerce, 103 Cong. 2 sess. (GPO, 1995), p. 67.
81 Letter to Office of General Counsel, Office of U.S. Trade Representative, from Steven R. Berlin, CITGO Corporation, May 12, 1995.
82 Steve Charnovitz, "The Environment v. Trade Rules: Defogging the Debate," *Environmental Law*, vol. 23 (April 1993), pp. 475–517.
83 David E. Sanger, "World Trade Group Orders U.S. to Alter Clean Air Act," *New York Times*, January 18, 1996, p. C5.
84 "Venezuela Defends Its EPA Exemption for RFG," *Oil and Gas Journal*, vol. 92 (May 30, 1994), p. 30.
85 Caleb Solomon, "Venezuela's Pressure on Clean Air Act Stirs Environmental, Trade Controversy," *Wall Street Journal*, November 9, 1993, p. A5.
86 Frances Williams, "WTO Sets Up First Disputes Panel," *Financial Times*, April 11, 1995, p. 6.
87 "RFG Exemption for Venezuela Gasoline Comes under Fire," *Oil and Gas Journal*, vol. 92 (May 2, 1994), p. 54; and Guy de Jonquierres, "WTO Receives First Calls to Settle Disputes," *Financial Times*, February 11, 1995, p. 3.
88 "U.S. Defends Gas Rules in WTO against Charges of Discrimination," *Inside U.S. Trade* (July 7, 1995), p. 8.

89 Summary of NEC meeting on PDVSA reprinted in "Reformulated Gasoline," Hearing, p. 116.
90 Letter to Office of General Counsel from Berlin, May 12, 1995.
91 Meeting with Petroleos de Venezuela, S.A., "Reformulated Gasoline," Hearing, p. 163.
92 "Venezuela Defends Its EPA Examination," p. 30.
93 Letter to Office of the General Counsel from Berlin, May 12, 1995.
94 Solomon, "Venezuela," p. A5.
95 John Gilardi, "Drivers in Northeast May Face Soaring Gasoline Prices," *Reuter European Business Report*, September 13, 1994, pp. 10–11.
96 Prepared Statement of the Society of Independent Gasoline Marketers of America, "Clean Air Act Amendments," Hearing, June 7, 1995, p. 58.
97 "WTO Panel Report on US–Venezuela Gasoline Dispute," January 17, 1996, p. 8.
98 Alan Tonelson and Lori Wallach, "Overruled by the World Trade Organization," *Washington Post National Weekly Edition*, May 13–19, 1996, p. 23.
99 Kevin Danaher and Rick Rowden, "Trade vs. Our Environment," *San Francisco Chronicle*, February 21, 1996, p. A17. See also Tonelson and Wallach, "Overruled," p. 23.
100 Richard W. Stevenson, "U.S. to Honor Trade Ruling against It on Foreign Fuel," *New York Times*, June 20, 1996, p. C3.
101 This theme is developed in Vogel, *Trading Up*.
102 Quoted in Lawrence J. White, "The Community Reinvestment Act: Good Intentions Headed in the Wrong Direction," *Fordham Urban Law Journal*, vol. 20 (Fall 1993), pp. 281–92.
103 For a description and history of the CRA see Jonathan R. Macey and Geoffrey P. Miller, "The Community Reinvestment Act: An Economic Analysis," *Virginia Law Review*, vol. 79 (March 1993), pp. 291–348.
104 Grant Thornton, *Regulatory Burden: The Cost to Community Banks* (New York: Independent Bankers Association of America, January 1993); and Barbara A. Rehm, "ABA: Cost of Compliance Equals 59% of Bank Profits," *American Banker* (June 18, 1992), p. 1, cited in Macey and Miller, *Community Reinvestment Act*, p. 325.
105 This argument should not be taken lightly. Revenue growth in the banking industry has stalled and profits have thinned as nonbank rivals apply new competitive heat and costs increase. Since 1987 Congress has imposed some forty major regulatory measures on banks and thrifts. The ultimate cost of the paperwork and red tape has been estimated to be perhaps as much as $14 billion annually. See Toby Roth, "Perfect Time for a New Banking Era," *Wall Street Journal*, January 16, 1996, p. A14; and Kelley Holland with Zachary Schiller, "Bankers' Hours Don't Look So Good: Slowing Profit Growth Is Forcing Banks to Pass Out Pink Slips," *Business Week*, December 19, 1994, pp. 102–03.
106 For this and the above argument see Macey and Miller, *Community Reinvestment Act*.
107 For a basic layout of the debate and compromises reached see Andrew Taylor, "Interstate Banking Law," *Congressional Quarterly* (December 3, 1994), p. 3462–63; and *International Banking Focus*, col. 16 (August 4, 1994) and vol. 16 (September 23, 1994).
108 See European Commission, *1995 Report on US Barriers to Trade and Investment* (Brussels: Services of the European Commission, May 1995), p. 55.

15. Globalization, Labor Markets and Policy Backlash in the Past

J. G. Williamson

Two important features of the world economy since 1970 also characterized the economy in the late 19th century. First, the earlier period was one of rapid globalization: capital and labor flowed across national frontiers in unprecedented quantities, and commodity trade boomed as transport costs dropped sharply. Second, the late 19th century underwent an impressive convergence in living standards, at least within most of what we would now call the OECD club, but what historians call the Atlantic economy. Poor countries at the European periphery tended to grow faster than the rich industrial leaders at the European center, and often even faster than the richer countries overseas in the New World. This club excluded, of course, most of the third world and eastern Europe, and even around this limited periphery there were some who failed to catch up.

A recent literature has developed which argues that most of the convergence between 1850 and 1914 was due to the open economy forces of trade and mass migration. By inference, it also suggests that convergence stopped between 1914 and 1950 because of de-globalization and implosion into autarchy. These facts are directly relevant to debates over globalization today.[1] The new historical research shows that these forces of globalization had a significant distributional impact within participating countries. It also suggests that these distributional events helped create a globalization backlash which caused a drift towards more restrictive immigration and tariff policy prior to World War I.

This essay starts with a brief review of the convergence evidence. It focuses on factor prices — like real wages — rather than GDP per capita or GDP per worker, since factor prices provide a more revealing way of discussing the connections between economic forces and political reactions than do GDP aggregates. It then documents inequality trends around the Atlantic economy, a systematic rise in the labor-scarce economies and a systematic decline in the labor-abundant economies. The essay then turns to immigration policy responses in the labor-scarce New World, since it was mass migration which was doing most of the work driving convergence, and observers then thought it was also mass migration which was doing most of the work driving inequality. Next, the essay explores tariff responses in land-scarce Europe to the invasion of foodstuffs from the New World. The impact of these globalizing price shocks on land rents and landed wealth appear to have been the central ingredients of rising tariffs. I conclude with some reasons why these powerful lessons of history need to be qualified.

LATE 19TH CENTURY CONVERGENCE

Convergence of What?

Most economists who have written about the comparative growth of nations have used GDP per capita or per worker-hour to measure catching up and convergence.[2] This essay favors instead real wage rates – purchasing-power-parity adjusted, and typically for urban unskilled workers. I can think of at least four good reasons why it is a mistake for the convergence debate to have ignored wages and other factor prices.

First, the pre-World War II real wage data are probably of better quality than the GDP data, and they are certainly available for a wider sample of 19th century economies. The bigger sample reduces the risk of selection bias identified by De Long (1988) and others. Second, income distribution matters, and wage rates with other factor prices offer a window to look in on distribution issues. Real people earn wages or profits or rents, not that statistical aircraft known as GDP per capita. GDP per worker-hour is a sound measure of aggregate productivity, but I would argue that the living standards of ordinary workers as captured by real wages are a better indicator of the economic well-being of a society. By averaging all incomes, we throw away valuable information. Third, factor price movements help in understanding the sources of convergence. For example, rapid technological catch-up in a poor country is more likely to increase all factor prices equally than is mass emigration or an export boom in labor-intensive manufactures. The open economy mechanisms which were important in driving late 19th century convergence – trade, migration and capital flows – operated directly on factor prices, and thus only indirectly on GDP per capita. A focus on GDP per capita misses a large part of this story. Fourth, and possibly most important, economic change nearly always involves winners and losers, a fact which is crucial in accounting for the evolution of policy. Changes that would increase GDP per capita but would also cause losses to some politically powerful are often successfully resisted, and examining the behavior of factor prices is the first step in understanding such political resistance.

Divergence Shocks and Convergence Responses: 1830–1870

The Atlantic economy in the first half of the 19th century was characterized by high tariffs (even in Britain where the Corn Laws were repealed only in 1846), modest commodity trade, very little mass migration (the famine-induced Irish flood was not released until the late 1840s), and an underdeveloped global capital market. Two profound shocks occurred in this environment still hostile to liberal globalization policy: early industrialization in Britain which then spread to a few countries on the European continent; and resource "discovery" in the New World, set in motion by sharply declining transport costs linking overseas suppliers to European markets, so much so that real freight rates fell by 1.5 percent per annum between 1840 and 1910 (O'Rourke and Williamson, 1998, ch. 3). These two shocks triggered a divergence in wages across countries that can be documented as starting at least as early as 1830 and lasting until the middle of the century.

Source: Williamson (1995, Table A2.1; revised in O'Rourke and Williamson, 1997).

FIGURE 1 International Real Wage Dispersion, 1830–1869.

Figure 1 documents real wage dispersion between 1830 and 1869. The summary statistic plotted there, C(N), is the variance divided by the square of the mean for a sample size, N, of either eight (line with diamonds) or 13 (line with squares) countries.[3] Based on the eight Atlantic countries for which data are available in the early part of this period – Brazil, France, Great Britain, Ireland, the Netherlands, Spain, Sweden and the United States, C rises from 0.143 in 1830 to 0.402 in 1846, a near-tripling in the dispersion of real wages, and, presumably, in the dispersion of living standards. While we do not have similar real wage data this early in the century for, say, Canada or Australia, the U.S. evidence suggests that the global labor market disequilibrium was being driven primarily by rising wage gaps between Europe and the English-speaking New World. Does it follow that there were no industrial-leader and latecomer-follower dynamics which served first to augment wage gaps in Europe before catching up eroded them? No. We must remember an inherent selectivity bias underlying this small sample, which includes only six European economies. Since the sample excludes many poorly-documented latecomers, real wage dispersion within Europe is likely to have risen even more than these figures suggest.

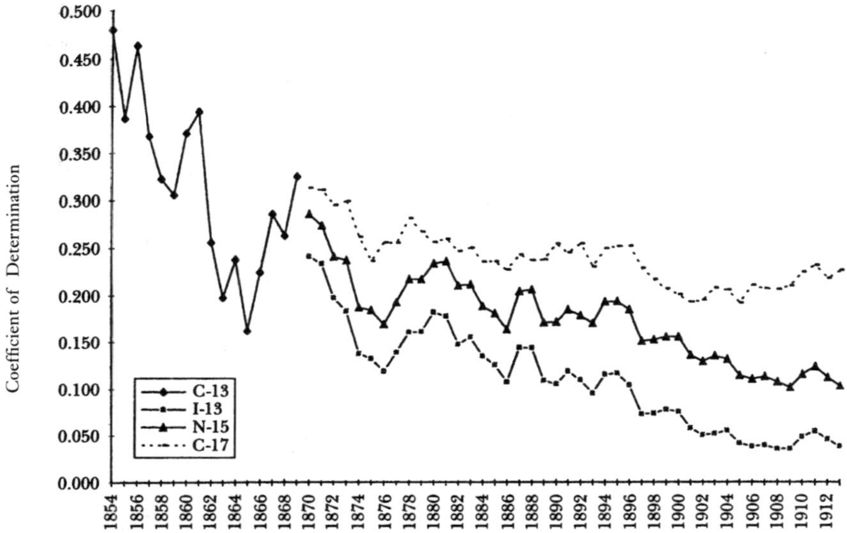

Source: Williamson (1995, Table A2.1; revised in O'Rourke and Williamson, 1997).

FIGURE 2 International Real Wage Dispersion, 1854–1913.

Late 19th Century Convergence

According to Figure 1, the years between 1846 and 1854 denote a secular turning point toward convergence of real wages. This convergence appears in both the eight-country sample (line with diamonds) and an expanded 13-country sample (line with squares). The five countries added to the broader sample are Australia, Belgium, Germany, Norway and Portugal. Figure 2 shows that the striking convergence which started in mid-century continued up to 1913. The line on the upper left of Figure 2 is a continuation of the 13-country sample from Figure 1. The dashed line in Figure 2 shows an expanded 17-country sample, now including in addition Argentina, Canada, Denmark and Italy. This measure shows the convergence tide ebbing around 1900. If we exclude Canada and the United States, two "exceptional" rich countries which bucked the convergence tide, convergence continues rapidly up to 1913. If we exclude in addition Portugal and Spain, two countries that failed to play the globalization game, convergence up to 1913 is faster still. In the full sample of 17 countries, the measure of wage divergence drops by more than a third over the three decades 1870–1900 (falling from 0.313 to 0.200), and divergence drops by perhaps two-thirds over the half-century following 1854.

The wage dispersion evidence suggests that the middle of the 19th century is an appropriate date for the start of modern convergence in the Atlantic economy. One might view this convergence as one of transition toward globally integrated Atlantic factor markets. The convergence in wages from about 1854 to the end of the 19th century was the most extensive that the Atlantic economy has seen since 1830, including the better-known convergence of the post-World War II era, although the "speed" per decade wasn't as fast as during the spectacular post-World War II epoch (Crafts and Toniolo, 1996). Most of the convergence was complete by the turn of the century.

Convergence wasn't limited to real wages and living standards of the working poor: GDP per capita converged as well (O'Rourke and Williamson, 1998, ch. 2). However, real wage convergence was much faster than convergence of GDP per capita, and the globalization arguments which follow offer some reasons why.

Our measure of Atlantic economy wage dispersion can be decomposed into three additive parts: wage dispersion within the New World; wage dispersion within the Old World; and the wage gap between the Old World and the New (Williamson, 1996). On average, the wage gap between the New World and the Old accounted for about 60 percent of the real wage variance across these 17 countries over the four decades prior to 1913. The remaining 40 percent of the real wage variance was explained equally by the variance within Europe and within the New World. Thus, real wage variance among the European countries in our sample was a modest part of real wage variance in the Atlantic economy as a whole (although as already confessed, the absence of poor east European nations from the sample probably accounts for much of this result). Finally, about 60 percent of the convergence between 1870 and 1900 is explained by the collapse in the wage gap between Europe and the New World, although that gap did not disappear altogether.

In the late 19th century, wage convergence was mostly a story about Europe catching up with the New World, and of Argentina and Canada catching up with Australia and the United States. It was less a story about European late-comers catching up to European leaders. Convergence *did* take place within Europe, but it was a modest affair in the aggregate since the spectacular catching-up successes on the continent were offset by some equally spectacular failures. This European experience deserves a closer look.

Given the great debate about Britain's loss of industrial leadership (Crafts, 1998), there is a tendency to seek evidence of convergence by looking at German or U.S. catching up on (and overtaking of) Britain. But that's the wrong place to look for general lessons, since it deals only with who was at the top among the rich countries. What mattered far more for convergence was whether the really poor agrarian countries in Europe were catching up on the rich industrial ones. The well-to-do European economies of that time included the Netherlands, Belgium, France and Germany, as well as Britain. In contrast, the nine members of the European periphery at this time were Austria, Denmark, Finland, Ireland, Italy, Norway, Portugal, Spain and Sweden. (Austria and Denmark can be viewed as straddling the margin between core and periphery.) The industrial core countries had levels of GDP per head 67 percent higher than the poor European periphery (O'Rourke and Williamson, 1997, Table 1.1), and their real wages were 86 percent higher than the periphery. Note again that the sample excludes east and southeast Europe simply because the late 19th century data are inadequate for those regions. We do know, however, that these countries were relatively poor even compared with our sample European periphery of nine countries. Bairoch's

(1976, Table 6, p. 286) rough estimates suggest that Bulgaria, Greece, Romania, Russia, and Serbia all had levels of GDP per head that were just 40–50 percent of the core. Thus, this essay ignores the poorest parts of Europe, with the exception of Portugal. As better historical data emerge from east and southeast Europe they can be used to test the same assertions which follow.

The narrative begins with a spectacular Scandinavian catch-up to the leaders. The first column of Table 1 shows comparatively rapid growth of wages in Sweden, Denmark, Norway and Finland. Real wages in Scandinavia grew at rates almost three times those prevailing in the European core. In fact, no other country in Europe underwent real wage growth even close to that of Sweden, Denmark or Norway.

Table 1 (column 2) also documents trends in the wage/rental ratio. These relative factor price movements are an important analytical component of the open economy impact and policy response. While the ratio of wage rates per worker to farm land values per acre fell everywhere in the New World by an average rate of about 3 percent per year over the period 1870–1910, it rose everywhere in Europe (with the exception of Spain). These events reflect the invasion of grains from the New World (and Russia) which lowered farm rents and land values in Europe and raised them in the American Midwest, the Australian outback, the Argentine pampas, and the Ukraine. Note that this relative factor price index converges fast too, just like real wages and absolute factor prices. For example, the Scandinavian wage/rental ratio rose half again faster than that of the European core (2.65 percent versus 1.74 percent per annum).

Aggregate measures using gross domestic product per worker also confirm the impressive Scandinavian catch-up, as shown in columns 3 and 4 of Table 1, although the differences are less spectacular than those for relative or absolute factor prices. Consistent with the fact that Scandinavian emigrants were economically active, leaving behind young and old dependents, the superiority of Scandinavian GDP per capita growth over that of the industrial core (1.45 versus 1.2 percent per annum) is even smaller than that of GDP per worker-hour, but it is still superior.

Scandinavia outperformed the rest of Europe (and probably the rest of the world) in the late 19th century, of that there can be little doubt. They were over-achievers even by catching-up standards,[4] and we know the reasons why: three-quarters of the Swedish catch-up on the U.S. wage was due to mass migration and capital inflows, a tenth to trade, and the small remainder to schooling and to other as yet unidentified "new growth theory" forces (O'Rourke and Williamson, 1997, Table 10). What about the rest of the periphery? Based on Maddison's (1994, 1995) data, Austria seems to have done about as well as Scandinavia: GDP per capita and GDP per worker-hour grew almost exactly as fast (1.46 versus 1.45 and 1.76 versus 1.77). In contrast, while Ireland obeyed the laws of convergence, it was no over-achiever. Irish real wages grew twice as fast as they did in the industrial core (1.79 versus 0.90 per annum), but they grew about as fast as the periphery average, and they recorded only three-quarters of the Scandinavia growth rate. On the other hand, the Irish wage/rental ratio rose faster.

The western Mediterranean basin did very badly. Spain and Portugal fell far behind the growth rates recorded in the rest of the periphery. Real wages crawled

TABLE 1 *Relative Economic Performance of the European Periphery in the Late 19th Century: Growth Per Annum (percent)*

Country	*(1) Real Wage per Urban Worker 1870–1913*	*(2) Wage/Rental Ratio 1870–1910*	*(3) Real GDP Per Capita 1870–1913*	*(4) Real GDP Per Worker Hour 1870–1913*	*(5) Impact of Migration 1870–1910 on 1910 Labor Force (%)*
The European Periphery					
Denmark	2.63	2.85	1.57	1.90	–14
Finland	na	na	1.44	1.80	na
Norway	2.43	na	1.31	1.65	–24
Sweden	2.73	2.45	1.46	1.74	–20
Scandinavia	2.60	2.65	1.45	1.77	–19
Italy	1.74	na	1.28	1.33	–39
Portugal	0.37	na	0.69	1.10	–5
Spain	0.44	–0.43	1.11	1.52	–6
Austria	na	na	1.46	1.76	na
Ireland	1.79	4.39	na	na	–45
Periphery	1.73	2.32	1.29	1.60	0022
The European Industrial Core					
Belgium	0.92	na	1.05	1.24	9
France	0.91	1.80	1.30	1.58	–1
Germany	1.02	0.87	1.63	1.88	–4
Great Britain	1.03	2.54	1.01	1.23	–11
The Netherlands	0.64	na	1.01	1.34	–3
Switzerland	na	na	1.20	1.46	–2
Industrial Core	0.09	1.74	1.20	1.46	–2
Europe	1.39	2.10	1.25	1.54	–13
The New World					
Argentina	1.74	–4.06	na	na	86
Australia	0.14	–3.30	0.87	1.08	42
Canada	1.65	na	2.29	2.31	44
USA	1.04	–1.72	1.81	1.93	24
New World	1.14	–3.03	1.66	1.77	49

Notes and Sources: All averages are unweighted. Columns 1–4 from O'Rourke and Williamson (1997b, Table 2). Column (5) from Taylor and Williamson (1997, Table 1). See appendix for description of the data.

upwards at only about 0.4 percent a year in those countries. Thus, Spain and Portugal missed out on the first great globalization boom – with small emigration rates and big trade restrictions, as did Egypt, Turkey and Serbia at the other end of the Mediterranean Basin (Williamson, 1998).[5] While the wage/rental ratio soared at 3.23 percent a year elsewhere around the periphery, it *fell* by 0.43 percent a year in Spain. The same wide gap appears for GDP per capita growth, which averaged 0.9 percent per annum for Spain and Portugal and 1.42 percent per annum elsewhere around the periphery. Maddison's real GDP per worker-hour data also confirm the poor performance for Spain and Portugal, but the gap is not quite so great. Italy does somewhat better, but even she – except for real wages – falls below the average for the periphery. The importance of the Iberian failure to overall Atlantic economy convergence has already been seen in Figure 2; remember, convergence after 1854 was steeper for the line where Spain and Portugal are removed.

Four countries can be used to illustrate the convergence process best: Ireland and Sweden (with heavy emigrations from the late 1840s onwards); the United States (with heavy immigrations from the late 1840s onwards); and Britain (the industrial leader, but losing its leadership). In 1856, unskilled real wages in urban Sweden were only 49 percent of Britain, while in 1913 they were at parity, an impressive doubling in Sweden's wage relative over 57 years. Relative to the United States, Sweden's real wages rose from 24 percent to 58 percent over the same period. In 1852, and shortly after the famine, unskilled real wages in urban Ireland were only 61 percent of Britain. Real wages in Ireland started a dramatic convergence with Britain during the 1850s (and did so largely in the absence of Irish industrialization) so that they were 73 percent of British levels by 1870, and 92 percent by 1913. Irish convergence with the booming U.S. economy was less dramatic, but Irish real wages did increase from 43 percent to 53 percent of U.S. real wages between 1855 and 1913.

What a Difference Factor Prices Make

The forces of convergence which seem to be so pronounced in the real wage data, adjusted for purchasing power parity, lead to different conclusions from those often reached by prominent studies that have focused on GDP per capita or per worker-hour. For example, in the words of Moses Ambramovitz (1986, pp. 385, 395): "the rate of convergence . . . showed marked strength only during the first quarter-century following World War II"; and "in the years of relative peace before 1913 . . . the process [of convergence] left a weak mark on the record." We have already seen how the convergence behavior of these measures differed in the past, with real wages and other factor prices converging far faster than the GDP aggregates. Now consider three reasons why this was so.

First, GDP per worker can be thought of as a sum of per unit factor returns weighted by factor endowments per worker. Factor price convergence does not imply that all factor prices in the rich country fall relative to the poor. Some may rise. Suppose the initially rich countries are land-abundant and labor-scarce, while the initially poor countries are land-scarce and labor-abundant. While factor price convergence implies that low wages in poor countries catch up to high wages in rich countries, it also implies that low land rents in the rich catch up to high land rents in the poor. A similar argument applies to skill premia. Thus, wage convergence is likely to be more dramatic than convergence in GDP per worker, and relative factor price convergence, as measured here by the wage/rental ratio, should be most dramatic. This was typically the case.

Second, the GDP and wage deflators differ. In a world of very incomplete commodity price equalization, the difference may matter, especially since laborers heavily consume wage goods which are expensive to move internationally like dwelling space and foodstuffs. The truth of this statement is especially easy to defend for the previous century, when declining transport costs edged the global economy closer to commodity price equalization, especially in the grain market, but also for butter, cheese and meats. Thus, the price of food, relative to the implicit GDP price deflator, fell in much of Europe, but rose in North America.

Third, there may be a wedge between per capita and per worker indices, created partly by differences in labor force participation rates across countries over time, combined with different migration environments and differential rates of population growth. If the forces of demographic transition (higher fertility and lower infant mortality) are strongest for richer countries, causing population growth to exceed labor force growth, then per capita convergence will be faster than per worker convergence. If the forces of mass migration dominate instead, then the opposite would be true, since migrants were disproportionately young adult males. It turns out that the latter dominated the Atlantic economy during the age of mass migration (Williamson, 1997b).

In short, factor prices like wages, and aggregate productivity measured through GDP, *should* exhibit different convergence properties. However, factor prices will be far more helpful in identifying winners and losers, and thus in understanding policy responses.

GLOBALIZATION AND INEQUALITY

Eli Heckscher and Bertil Ohlin (translated in Flam and Flanders, 1991) argued that integration of global commodity markets would lead to convergence of international factor prices, as countries everywhere expanded the production and export of commodities which used their abundant (and cheap) factor intensively. Table 1 is consistent with Heckscher and Ohlin: the trade boom led to rising wage/rental ratios in Europe, and falling wage/rental ratios in the New World; as a consequence, conditions improved for the poor unskilled worker relative to the rich landlord in much of Europe, while the opposite was true of the New World.

Migration helped the process of factor convergence along. The poorest European countries tended to have the highest emigration rates while the richest New World countries tended to have the highest immigration rates. The correlation wasn't perfect, since potential emigrants from poor countries often found the cost of the move too high, and some New World countries restricted the inflow from certain countries along the poor European periphery (and Asia). But the correlation is still very strong (Hatton and Williamson, 1998, ch. 3). Furthermore, the last column of Table 1 shows that the labor force impact was very big: mass migration after 1870 had augmented the 1910 New World labor force (in the four countries listed) by 49 percent, reduced the 1910 labor force in the emigrant countries around the European periphery (in the eight countries listed) by 22 percent, and reduced the 1910 labor force in the European industrial core (in the five countries listed) by 2 percent. Mass migration by itself may explain about 70 percent of the real wage convergence in the late 19th century Atlantic economy (Williamson, 1996; Taylor and Williamson, 1997; O'Rourke and Williamson, 1998, ch. 8).

Since the migrants tended to be unskilled, and became increasingly so as the late 19th century unfolded (much like the U.S. experience in recent decades), they tended to flood labor markets at the bottom in destination countries, thus lowering the unskilled wage relative to the skilled wage, as well as relative to white collar incomes, entrepreneurial returns and land rents. Mass migration implied rising inequality in labor-scarce, resource rich countries. Emigration implied falling inequality in labor-abundant, resource poor countries.

Complete income distributions at various benchmarks between the mid-19th century and World War II are available only for a few countries and dates,[6] but even if fuller data were available, it is not obvious that they would be the best way to explore the underlying causes and impact of globalization. Our interest here is factor prices: wages, rents and the structure of pay. How did the typical unskilled worker near the bottom of the distribution do relative to the typical landowner or capitalist near the top, or even relative to the typical skilled blue collar worker or educated white collar employee near the middle of the distribution? The modern debate over inequality has a fixation on wages, but since land and landed interests were far more important to late 19th century inequality trends, we need to add them to our distribution inquiry.[7] In any case, we have two kinds of evidence available to document late 19th century inequality trends: changes in the ratio of the unskilled wage to farm land values per acre, and changes in the ratio of the unskilled wage to GDP per worker-hour.

Recall from Table 1 that relative factor price convergence *did* characterize the four decades prior to World War I. The wage/rental ratio plunged in the New World, where it had been initially high. One study has it that the Australian ratio had fallen to one-quarter of its 1870 level by 1913, the Argentine ratio had fallen to one-fifth of its mid-1880 level, and the U.S. ratio had fallen to less than half of its 1870 level (O'Rourke, Taylor and Williamson, 1996). In Europe, the (initially low) wage/rental ratio surged up to World War I. The British ratio increased by a factor of 2.7 over its 1870 level, while the Irish ratio increased by even more. The Swedish and Danish ratios both increased by a factor of 2.3. Not surprisingly, the surge was more pronounced in free trade than in protectionist countries. As examples of protectionist countries, the ratio increased by a factor of 1.8 in France, 1.4 in Germany, and not at all in Spain.

Landowners tended to be near the top of the distribution, although this was certainly more true of Europe, Argentina and the American South, and less true for the American Midwest and Canada, where the family farm dominated. The evidence that the wage/rental ratio was dropping in the rich, labor-scarce New World is consistent with the hypothesis that inequality was falling in poor, labor-abundant Europe. There is also some evidence that globalization mattered:

European countries staying open to trade absorbed the biggest distributional hit; European countries retreating behind tariff walls absorbed the smallest distributional hit (Williamson, 1997a)

What about the ratio of the unskilled worker's wage (w) to the returns on *all* factors per laborer as measured by Maddison's (1995) estimates of GDP per worker-hour (y)? Changes in this ratio measure changes in the economic distance between the working poor near the bottom of the distribution and the average citizen in the middle of the distribution. It turns out that this statistic is highly correlated with more comprehensive inequality measures in the few cases where both are available.[8]

The 14 countries in our sample (all mentioned in this paragraph) exhibited *very* different inequality trends over the four decades prior to the Great War. When the index of unskilled wages/GDP per worker is normalized to 100 in 1870, we get the following for 1913: the index is at about 153 for Denmark and Sweden, and at 53 or 58 for Australia and the United States. An alternative way to standardize these distributional trends up to 1913 is to compute the annual percentage change in the index for each country relative to its 1870 base: the per annum rates range from +0.97 and +0.98 for Denmark and Sweden, to –1.22 and –1.45 for Australia and the United States. This measure of inequality change is plotted against the 1870 real wage in Figure 3, and it offers strong confirmation of the globalization hypothesis: between 1870 and 1913, inequality rose dramatically in rich, land-abundant, labor-scarce New World countries like Australia, Canada and the United States; inequality fell dramatically in poor, land-scarce, labor-abundant, newly industrializing countries like Norway, Sweden, Denmark and Italy; inequality was more stable in the European industrial economies like Belgium, France, Germany, the Netherlands and the United Kingdom; and inequality was also more stable in the poor European economies which failed to play the globalization game, like Portugal and Spain.

GLOBALIZATION BACKLASH: IMMIGRATION RESTRICTIONS

Measuring Immigration Policy

The American doors did not suddenly and without warning slam shut on European emigrants when the U.S. Congress overrode President Wilson's veto of the immigrant literacy test in February 1917, or when it passed the Emergency Quota Act of May 1921. Over the half-century prior to the Literacy Act, the United States had been imposing restrictions on what had been free immigration – including contract labor laws, Chinese exclusion acts, excludable classes, head taxes, and so on – and had long been debating more severe restrictions. The Quota Act of 1921 was preceded by 25 years of active Congressional debate, and the first vote in 1897 had 86 percent of the Congressmen favoring more restriction in the form of a literacy requirement (Goldin, 1994, Table 7.1). The United States was hardly alone in this trend. Argentina, Australia, Brazil, and Canada enacted similar measures, although the timing was sometimes different, and the policies in these countries more often took the form of an enormous drop in or

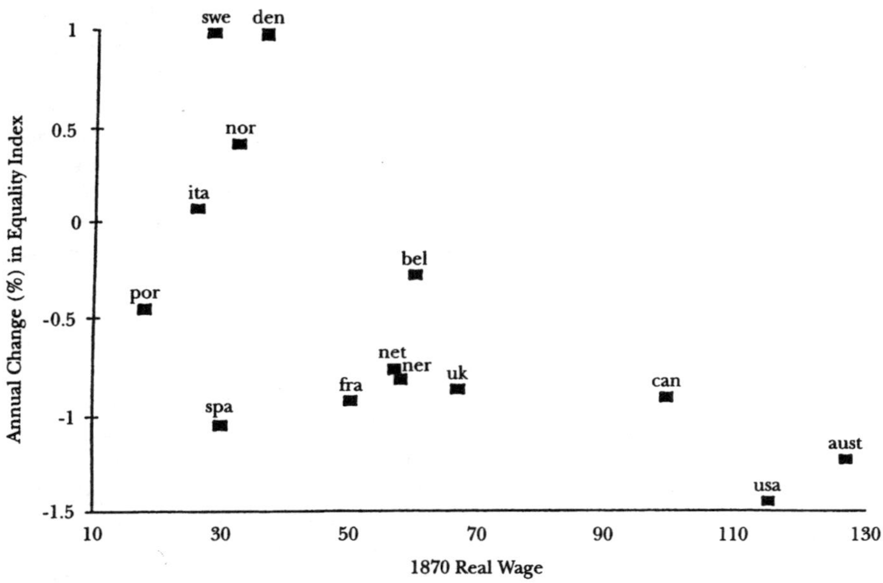

FIGURE 3 Initial Real Wage vs Equality Trends, 1870–1913.

even disappearance of immigrant subsidies, rather than of outright exclusion. Contrary to the conventional wisdom, therefore, the United States did not make an abrupt regime switch around World War I away from free immigration to quotas, but rather evolved toward a more restrictive immigration policy. One important goal of these policies was to segment the international labor market into two parts, what we would now call North and South (Lewis, 1978, ch. 3).

In two recent papers, Timmer and Williamson (1996, 1997) constructed an immigration policy index which ranges over a scale of +5 to –5. A positive score denotes a pro-immigration or open policy, typically including comprehensive subsidies for passage and support upon arrival. A negative score denotes anti-immigration policy, typically an outright ban on some groups, quotas, head taxes, literacy tests and discriminatory treatment upon arrival. A zero denotes policy neutrality.[9] The immigration policy indices constructed for Argentina, Australia, Brazil, Canada and the United States reveal that despite universal openness to immigration in the 1860s, the New World doors were effectively closed by 1930. With some exceptions, immigration policy was typically slow to change, sometimes remaining constant over a decade or more, even though there was almost always intensive political debate underlying that apparent quiescence. The best examples of this stability are Brazil over the three decades from 1890 to 1920, a period which ended in 1921 when tough immigration restrictions were imposed, and the United States from 1888 to 1916, a period which ended with the override of President Wilson's veto in 1917 and the quotas in 1921. However, the policy evolution varied widely over those seven decades: Argentina and the United States exhibited a relatively steady drift away from free immigration;

Brazil remained open much longer, suddenly slamming the door shut in the 1920s; and Canada actually reversed the trend in the 1920s, while Australia did it more than once over the period.

Immigration Policy: Searching for Hypotheses

There is a general consensus in the historical literature that immigration policy has been sensitive to labor market conditions, and also that immigration flows have been sensitive to wage and unemployment differentials between countries. For example, Goldin (1994) notes that there was a strong push for immigration restrictions in the United States in the late 1890s, a time of economic recession and high unemployment. At that time, however, the rate of immigration slowed dramatically, reaching a secular low in 1897, the same year that the first vote on immigration restriction was taken in the House of Representatives. Similarly, Australian inflows dropped sharply in the recession of the 1890s, even as attitudes towards immigrant subsidies hardened (Pope and Withers, 1994). These events suggest that the political impetus to restrict immigration was far more sensitive to labor market conditions than to immigration levels. Inequality is one manifestation of these labor market conditions, and the living standard of the working poor is another.

Presumably, the policy response to immigration should take a far-sighted view. That is, immigration may induce falling wages for unskilled workers and greater inequality in the short run, but the key question for some voters might be whether it augments or inhibits economic growth in the longer run. The traditional Smithian view had it that the rising inequality would place relatively more income in the hands of those who save, thus raising the investment rate and growth. Modern political economists tend to take a different view, arguing that if a country lets its poorest voters become too poor, richer voters might join poorer voters to pass distortionary redistributive policies that can slow growth (Alesina and Perotti, 1994; Perotti, 1996). Economists do not yet have a clear answer to this question, especially for a century ago when government redistributive intervention was modest. But citizens might also vote for immigration restriction for other reasons: they may simply dislike seeing a deterioration in the living standards of their unskilled neighbors, or they may fear that these events might provoke some sort of political rebellion from below. Furthermore, since the stronger economic position of unskilled labor was manifested by a stronger political voice in the labor-scarce immigration countries, their economic condition was more likely to be translated into a restrictive policy response.

Immigration Policy: Some Evidence

The empirical literature on the determinants of immigration policy is very new, so that much of what follows is still speculative. But some outlines are beginning to emerge (Timmer and Williamson, 1996, 1997).

The most consistent pattern is that immigration policy has been slow to change. This was especially true of Brazil and the United States, but it is worth noting that these two countries with the strongest historical persistence also exhibited the biggest policy switch at the end of the period of quiescence, from wide open to tightly closed. Big policy switches usually required long periods of debate. Thus, measures of current macroeconomic conditions – like unemployment rates – are unlikely to help account for long-run policy changes.

Labor market conditions have also had a consistent influence on immigration policy, and it appears that both the absolute and relative income performance of unskilled workers mattered. Poor wage performance was associated with more restrictive policy in Australia, Brazil and the United States. However, the most consistently significant variable reported by Timmer and Williamson (1996, 1997) is the ratio of the unskilled wage to per capita GDP, or of income near the bottom of the distribution to income in the middle. Rising inequality was associated with increasingly restrictive immigration policy. It is well known that (new) immigrants were unskilled and tended to cluster at the bottom of the distribution, at least initially, and that this was increasingly true as the late 19th century unfolded (Hatton and Williamson, 1998, ch. 7). Regardless of what else is included in the regression, this measure of unskilled labor's relative economic performance stands out as an important influence on immigration policy. Rising relative unskilled labor scarcity encouraged more open immigration policies; declining relative unskilled labor scarcity encouraged more restrictive immigration policies.[10]

The evidence just summarized speaks to the indirect impact of immigration on policy by looking at absolute and relative wage performance in labor markets. What about the direct impact of immigration on policy? To measure these direct immigration effects, one might use some proxy for the quality, or human-capital content, of the immigrants and the change in that quality proxy; one such proxy that has been effective is the real wage of unskilled urban workers in the source countries. Alternatively, one might measure immigrant quantity by the foreign-born population share. It does appear that low and falling immigrant quality precipitated more restrictive immigrant policy, even after controlling for other forces. To some extent, therefore, New World policy anticipated the impact of low quality immigrants on unskilled wages and moved to shut it down. The other measure of immigration's attributes – the difference in ethnic composition between the current immigration flow and the foreign population stock – seems to have had little bearing on policy.

To what extent was a change in a country's policy in part a reaction to changes in immigration policy elsewhere? The United States – the immigrant leader of the New World – was completely unresponsive to competitors' policies. For most other countries, policy elsewhere mattered a great deal. For Argentina, it was the combined impact of Australian, Canadian and Brazilian policy that mattered, with more restrictive policy abroad including more restrictive policy at home. Brazil tended to mimic the policies followed by Argentina and the United States. Australia tended to favor open immigration policies when the United Kingdom offered more generous subsidies to its emigrants, and also, to some extent, when Canada adopted more open policies.

To summarize, while the absolute size of the immigrant flow did not seem to have any consistent impact on New World policy up to 1930, its low and declining quality certainly did, provoking restriction. Policies adopted by one's global competitors mattered even more. Labor market conditions mattered most, with deteriorating conditions provoking a restrictive policy reaction, as New World countries acted to defend the economic interests of unskilled labor.

GLOBALIZATION BACKLASH: EUROPEAN TARIFFS

Land-abundant New World economies became increasingly integrated with labor-abundant European countries in the late 19th century. While the distributional impact of this shock varied from country to country, there is broad support for the Heckscher-Ohlin prediction that European land and American labor suffered. Not surprisingly, European agricultural interests lobbied for protection. Landowners were successful in some countries, such as France and Germany, and tariffs were introduced. These tariffs can be viewed as the precursors of today's European Common Agricultural Policy (Tracy, 1989). Other countries, like Britain, Ireland and Denmark, stuck to their free trade guns, forcing agriculture to adapt or decline.

What explains the differing European political responses to the grain invasion? While this question has become canonical in the comparative political economy literature, only recently has it been decomposed into the relevant component parts: the size of globalization shock experienced by each country, the distributional impact within each country, and, only then, the policy response (O'Rourke, 1997; O'Rourke and Williamson, 1998, ch. 5).

O'Rourke (1997) explores these issues by looking primarily at the grain market. He finds that where tariffs were raised, they were high enough to insulate continental Europe from the globalizing impact of steamships, railroads and international canals: German grain prices did not converge on American prices at all; French and Swedish prices converged only modestly; but British and Danish prices converged dramatically. The contrast between free-trading Europe (Britain and Denmark) and protectionist Europe (Germany, France and Sweden) is also born out when European prices are compared with those of the Ukraine. There is no evidence of grain market integration on the continent during the 40 years prior to World War I. An era when Europe and the New World became globally integrated was also one when grain markets *within* Europe became more balkanized. In this sense, globalization was not a universal phenomenon, even during the comparatively liberal late 19th century.

The literature which seeks to explain tariff responses to grain invasions begins with Charles Kindleberger (1951) and Ronald Rogowski (1989). Oddly enough, Rogowski the political scientist uses a conventional Heckscher-Ohlin model to sort the problem out, while Kindleberger the economist uses sociology and political science. Yet, both authors implicitly assume that the grain invasion generated the same shock to all economies, and that identical price shocks had the same impact on income distribution! O'Rourke (1997) shows that neither assumption held.

Consider the assumption that the grain invasion generated the same shock to all economies. Denmark was a free trader, but while real cereal prices fell by 29 percent in Britain between 1870 and 1913, they fell by only 10 percent in Denmark (O'Rourke, 1997, app. 5). Without protection, French and German cereal prices would have declined by an estimated 34 percent under free trade, and Swedish prices would have declined by 27 percent. If the grain invasion lowered cereal prices by less in Denmark than in the rest of Europe, then the grain invasion lowered Danish rents by less as well. If the elasticity of land prices with respect to grain prices was around 0.5, as O'Rourke estimates, then the cost to French, German and Swedish landowners of maintaining free trade in the face of the grain invasion would have been a 12 to 18 percent reduction in land values, while cheap grain lowered Danish land values by only 4 or 5 percent. Moreover, globalization raised the prices of Danish animal products exported to British markets. Armed with this new evidence, the Danish decision not to protect agriculture seems less surprising.

The second assumption was that identical price shocks had the same effects on income distribution, but depending on the structure of production, the effects could have been very different. Agriculture was a relatively small sector in capital-abundant Britain, an early industrial leader. Therefore, the 29 percent decline in real grain prices that Britain absorbed *increased* real wages in free trade Britain, while in the absence of tariffs a similar price shock would have *reduced* real wages in more agriculture-dependent France, and in the absence of tariffs it would have lowered real wages only modestly in Sweden, according to computable general equilibrium calculations (O'Rourke, 1997). These differences can be easily interpreted in the context of the sector-specific factors model: cheap grain lowered workers' costs of living economy-wide, but reduced the demand for agricultural labor. Where agriculture was a big employer, nominal wages fell economy-wide. Where agriculture was a small employer, nominal wages did not fall economy-wide. Only 23 percent of the British labor force worked in agriculture in 1871, while the corresponding figure for France was 51 percent. Thus, a negative shock to agricultural labor demand had a much bigger impact on French nominal wages, while the impact on workers' cost of living was about the same. One key reason why Britain maintained free trade while the continent protected agriculture was that agriculture was a lot less important to Britain than to the continental economies. Not only did this imply that cheap grain was better for British than for continental workers, but it also meant that the assets of the landowning rich declined by less (land was a smaller share of total assets), and that agricultural interests had less political clout.

THE LESSONS OF HISTORY

Factor prices converged in the Atlantic economy up to 1914. This was true of absolutes, like real wages and farm rents, and it was true of relatives, like wage/rental ratios. The post-World War II decades have exhibited the same convergence, although economists have tended to measure it by use of aggregates like GDP per capita and GDP per worker. Convergence of relative factor prices implies something about inequality trends too. Where unskilled wages rise relative to farm rents and skilled wages, inequality falls; where unskilled wages fall relative to farm rents and skilled wages, inequality rises. The evidence from the late 19th century confirms that prediction, since inequality was on the rise in labor-scarce New World countries, while it was on the decline in labor-abundant Old World countries. The United States, and to some extent Europe as well, has exhibited the same inequality rise since the early 1970s.

Recent work by economic historians suggests that a large share of these trends in factor prices and inequality everywhere around the late 19th century Atlantic economy can be explained by globalization forces. Not all, but a large share. Is the same likely to be true of the late 20th century? Probably not. After all, it looks like mass immigration played the central globalization role a century ago, not the indirect effects of trade, and migration has never returned to "mass" levels since the quotas were imposed after World War I.

There was a de-globalization implosion after 1914, coinciding with two world wars, two periods of fragile peace, a great depression and a cold war. The last few decades of the 20th century have marked a successful struggle to reconstruct that pre-World War I global economy. The standard view of history has treated these spectacular changes in global policy largely as switches in regime that were pretty much independent of economic events and thus can be taken as exogenous (Sachs and Warner, 1995).

This view ignores the evidence of factor price convergence and trends in income distribution cited a moment ago. It also ignores the fact that immigration policy in labor-scarce parts of the global economy became increasingly less generous and more restrictive prior to 1914, and that much of this retreat from open immigration policies was driven by a defense of the deteriorating relative economic position of the working poor. In addition, it fails to note the fact that liberal attitudes towards trade were brief, and that protection rose sharply almost everywhere on the European continent from the 1870s onwards. Much of this retreat from free trade was manifested by protection of domestic agriculture from the negative price shocks associated with globalization. And most of this retreat from free trade was driven by a defense of the trade-induced deterioration in the relative economic position of both the landed rich and the landless poor.

Thus, a more accurate narrative of globalization experience in the decades prior to World War I would read like this: A spreading technology revolution and a transportation breakthrough led first to a divergence of real wages and living standards between countries. The evolution of well-functioning global markets in goods and labor eventually brought about a convergence between nations. This factor price convergence planted, however, seeds for its own destruction since it created rising inequality in labor-scarce economies (like the United States) and falling inequality in labor-abundant economies (like those around the poor European periphery). Obviously, most gained by the globalization process, but the improved economic conditions of now-less-abundant European stayers and of the recently-moved new immigrants were not relevant to restrictionist debates in destination countries, nor were the improved economic conditions of labor and capital in growing export sectors well represented in protectionist debates on the European continent. The voices of powerful interest groups who were hit hard by these globalization events *were* heard, however, and these were in particular the ordinary worker in labor-scarce economies and the landlord in the labor-abundant economies. These interest groups generated a political backlash against immigration and trade, and this backlash, which had been building up for decades, was brought to a head by events around World War I.

A late 19th century globalization backlash made a powerful contribution to interwar de-globalization. Is this history likely to repeat? Maybe not. After all, wealth and employment are not nearly as concentrated in the tradable sector today as they were a century ago, thus insulating OECD economies from the kind of trade backlash seen in the past. And while restrictions on farm imports are still prominent in Europe today, OECD farm sectors are far too small to matter economy-wide to the extent that they did a century ago. Furthermore, the migrations from poor to rich countries today are pretty trivial affairs compared with the mass migrations up to World War I. Today, only the U.S. has across-the-border migration rates anything like those recorded *all over* the converging Atlantic economy prior to the quotas. And governments today have far more sophisticated ways to compensate losers than they had a century ago.

All of these qualifications may suggest that a move towards de-globalization is unlikely to repeat. Yet history does supply that warning: if a globalization backlash can be found in our past, it may reappear in our future.

DATA APPENDIX

Real Wages: These are urban male unskilled wage rates, typically weekly and for construction work. They are deflated by cost of living indices. These real wage time series are projected from purchasing-power-parity benchmarks constructed for the period 1905–1914 by the author. Sources, methods and the data are elaborated in Williamson (1995), but the data have been revised in O'Rourke and Williamson (1997). This revised "Atlantic economy" data base will be made available on diskette upon request from the author at <jwilliam@kuznets.fas.harvard.edu>, along with a detailed appendix describing its construction and sources.

Wage/Rental Ratio: The nominal wage rates under "real wages" above are divided by nominal per unit farm land values, and indexed 1901=100. The data are described and defended at length in O'Rourke, Taylor and Williamson (1996, pp. 521–4).

Equality Index: The nominal wage rates under "real wages" above are divided by nominal GDP per worker-hour, the latter taken from Maddison (1995). The ratio (w/y) is indexed 1870=100. The data are described and defended at length in Williamson (1997a).

GDP per capita and per worker: These data, nominal and real, are mainly from Maddison (1994, 1995) as revised and augmented in O'Rourke and Williamson (1997).

Policy: The New World immigration policy index described in the text ranges from – 5 (restrictive) to +5 (open with subsidies) and it measures political message rather than impact. The index is described at length in Timmer and Williamson (1996).

Net migration impact: Net migration between 1870 and 1910 is converted from population to labor force equivalents, and then expressed as a share of the sending or receiving 1910 labor force. The figures are taken from Taylor and Williamson (1997, Table 1).

NOTES

This paper has been supported by NSF grant SBR-9505656, and it has benefited enormously by collaborations with Kevin O'Rourke of University College Dublin and Ashley Timmer of Harvard University. I want to thank both of them for allowing me to draw freely on our as yet unpublished work. Bill Collins and Asim Khwaja were also helpful in solving some technical problems. In addition, I would like to thank Alan Krueger, Brad De Long, Dani Rodrik and Timothy Taylor for comments that improved the paper.

1 For an overview of the rapidly expanding literature which argues that open economy forces were central in driving convergence prior to 1914, see Williamson (1996), Hatton and Williamson (1998), and O'Rourke and Williamson (1997a).

2 The literature is enormous, but it has been led by Abramovitz (196), Barro (1991, 1996, 1997), Barro and Sala-i-Matin (1992, 1995), Baumol (1986), Bloom and Williamson (1997), Mankiw, Romer and Weil (1992), Sachs, Radelet and Lee (1997) and Sachs and Warner (1995). See also the recent surveys in this journal by Pritchett (1997) and Jones (1997).

3 Dispersion statistics like C have been used extensively in the convergence debate, and it is our measure of what has come to be called (σ)-convergence. C is equivalent to the coefficient of variation, but easier to decompose.

4 All of the assertions here and in the next paragraph have been successfully tested with conditional convergence models (O'Rourke and Williamson 1997; 1998, ch. 1).

5 The appendix indicates that an "Atlantic economy" real wage data base for 17 countries between 1820 and 1940 is available upon request. The author will also have available a similar data base for Latin America and Asia, like that for the Mediterranean Basin cited in the text (for example, Williamson, 1998).

6 Some evidence on late 19th century inequality trends has been collected by economic historians since Simon Kuznets published his presidential address to the American Economic Association in 1955. For a recent survey, see Lindert (1997). These data seem to offer support for the view that inequality was on the rise in the United States before World War I while it had been falling in Britain since the 1860s. But the Atlantic economy coverage is not sufficiently comprehensive to be used in the pre-1914 discussion which follows.

7 Recent studies of the impact of globalization on inequality in the third world also tend to focus on wage inequality, and sometimes even only *urban* wage inequality. This is a big mistake for countries where rural wage employment is significant and where landed interests are powerful. Surely, the economic positions of the landlord and the rural laborer matter in economies where agriculture is one-fifth, one-quarter or even one-third of the economy.

8 Some countries do have time for more comprehensive inequality indicators. Between 1870 and 1929, we have both the top 10 percent income share and w/y for Denmark, Germany, the Netherlands, Norway, Sweden and the United Kingdom: for these, $R^2 = -.944$ (Williamson, 1997b). The w/y data are reported at length in Williamson (1997a).

9 It takes some doing to summarize these policies with a score for each year, but applied economists struggle with the same problem when trying to summarize just how open a country's trade policy is at any point in time (Anderson, Neary, 1994; Sachs and Warner, 1995).

10 Furthermore, this effect is likely to be biased downwards since open immigration policy implies more immigrants and lower ratio of unskilled wages to per capita GDP, as I argued above.

REFERENCES

Abramovitz, M., "Catching Up, Forging Ahead, and Falling Behind," *Journal of Economic History*, June 1986, *46*, 385–406.

Alesina, A. and R. Perotti, "The Political Economy of Growth: A Critical Survey of the Recent Literature," *World Bank Economic Review*, September 1994, *8*, 351–71.

Anderson, J. E. and J. P. Neary, "Measuring the Restrictiveness of Trade Policy," *World Bank Economic Review*, May 1994, *8*, 151–69.

Barioch, P., "Europe's Gross National Product: 1800–1975," *Journal of European Economic History*, May–August 1976, *5*, 273–340.

Barro, R. J., "Economic Growth in a Cross Section of Countries," *Journal of Political Economy*, May 1991, *106*, 406–43.

Barro, R. J., "The Determinants of Economic Growth," *Lionel Robbins Lecture*, London School of Economics, February 20–22, 1996.

Barro, R. J., *Determinants of Economic Growth*, Cambridge, Mass.: MIT Press, 1997.

Barro, R. J., and X. Sala-i-Martin, "Convergence," *Journal of Political Economy*, April 1992, *100*, 223–52.

Barro, R. J. and X. Sala-i-Martin, *Economic Growth*, New York: McGraw-Hill, 1995.

Baumol, W., "Productivity Growth, Convergence and Welfare: What the Long-Run Data Show," *American Economic Review*, December 1986, *76*, 1072–85.

Bloom, D. and J. G. Williamson, "Demographic Transitions and Economic Miracles in Emerging Asia," NBER Working Paper 6268, National Bureau of Economic Research, Cambridge, MA, November 1997.

Crafts, N. F. R., "Forging Ahead and Falling Behind: The Rise and Relative Decline of the First Industrial Nation," *Journal of Economic Perspectives*, Spring 1998, *12:2*, 193–211.

Crafts, N. F. R. and G. Toniolo, *Economic Growth in Europe Since 1945*. Cambridge: Cambridge University Press, 1996.

De Long, J. B., "Productivity Growth, Convergence and Welfare: Comment," *American Economic Review*, December 1988, *78*, 1138–54.

Flam, H. and M. J. Flanders, *Heckscher-Ohlin Trade Theory*. Cambridge, MA: MIT Press, 1991.

Goldin, C., "The Political Economy of Immigration Restriction in the United States, 1890 to 1921." In C. Goldin and G. D. Libecap, eds, *The Regulated Economy: A Historical Approach to Political Economy*. Chicago: University of Chicago Press, 1994.

Hatton, T. J. and J. G. Williamson, *The Age of Mass Migration: An Economic Analysis*, New York: Oxford University Press, 1998.

Jones, C., "On the Evolution of the World Income Distribution," *Journal of Economic Perspectives*, Summer 1997, *11*, 19–36.

Kindleberger, C. P., "Group Behavior and International Trade," *Journal of Political Economy*, February 1951, *59*, 30–46.

Lewis, W. A., *The Evolution of International Economic Order*. Princeton, NJ: Princeton University Press, 1978.

Lindert, P. H., "Three Centuries of Inequality in Britain and America." In A. B. Atkinson and F. Bourguignon, eds, *Handbook of Income Distribution*, Amsterdam: North-Holland, 1997.

Maddison, A., *Phases of Capitalist Development*. Oxford: Oxford University Press, 1982.
Maddison, A., "Explaining the Economic Performance of Nations." In W. J. Baumol, R. Nelson, and E. N. Wolff, eds, *Convergence of Productivity: Cross-National Studies and Historical Evidence*. New York: Oxford University Press, 1994.
Maddison, A., *Monitoring the World Economy 1820–1992*, Paris: OECD Development Centre Studies, 1995.
Mankiw, N. G., D. Romer, and D. N. Weil, "A Contribution to the Empirics of Economic Growth," *Quarterly Journal of Economics*, May 1992, *107*, 407–37.
O'Rourke, K. H., "The European Grain Invasion, 1870–1913," *Journal of Economic History*, December 1997, *57*, 775–801.
O'Rourke, K. H., A. M. Taylor and J. G. Williamson, "Factor Price Convergence in the Late Nineteenth Century," *International Economic Review*, August 1996, *37*, 499–530.
O'Rourke, K. H. and J. G. Williamson, "Around the European Periphery 1870–1913: Globalization, Schooling and growth," *European Review of Economic History*, August 1997, *1*, 153–90.
O'Rourke, K. H. and J. G. Williamson, *Globalization and History: The Evolution of a 19th Century Atlantic Economy*. Cambridge, MA: MIT Press, 1998, forthcoming.
Perotti, R., "Growth, Income Distribution and Democracy," *Journal of Economic Growth*, June 1996, *1*, 149–87.
Pope, D. and G. Withers, "Wage Effects of Immigration in Late-Nineteenth-Century Australia." In Timothy J. Hatton and Jeffrey G. Williamson, eds, *Migration and the International Labor Market, 1850–1939*. London: Routledge, 1994.
Pritchett, L., 'Divergence, Big Time," *Journal of Economic Perspectives*, Spring 1997, *11*, 3–17.
Rogowski, R., *Commerce and Coalitions: How Trade Affects Domestic Political Arrangements*. Princeton, NJ: Princeton University Press, 1989.
Sachs, J. D., S. Radelet, and J-W Lee, "Economic Growth in Asia," ch. 2 in *Emerging Asia*. Manila: Asian Development Bank, 1997.
Sachs, J. D., and A. Warner, "Economic Reform and the Process of Global Integration," *Brookings Papers on Economic Activity*, Washington, D.C.: Brookings Institution, 1995.
Taylor, A. M. and J. G. Williamson, "Convergence in the Age of Mass Migration," *European Review of Economic History*, April 1997, *1*, 27–63.
Timmer, A. and J. G. Williamson, "Racism, Xenophobia or Markets? The Political Economy of Immigration Policy Prior to the Thirties," NBER Working Paper 5867, National Bureau of Economic Research, Cambridge, MA, December 1996.
Timmer, A. and J. G. Williamson, "Immigration Policy Prior to the Thirties: Labor Markets, Policy Interactions and Globalization Backlash," Department of Economics, Harvard University, March 1997.
Tracy, M., *Government and Agriculture in Western Europe 1880–1988*, 3rd ed., New York: Harvester Wheatsheaf, 1989.
Williamson, J. G., "The Evolution of Global Labor Markets Since 1830: Background Evidence and Hypotheses," *Explanations in Economic History*, April 1995, *32*, 141–96.
Williamson, J. G., "Globalization, Convergence and History," *Journal of Economic History*, June 1996, *56*, 1–30.
Williamson, J. G., "Globalization and Inequality, Past and Present," *World Bank Research Observer*, August 1997a, *12*, 117–35.
Williamson, J. G., "Growth, Distribution and Demography: Some Lessons From History," NBER Working Paper 6244, National Bureau of Economic Research, Cambridge, MA, October 1997b.
Williamson, J. G., "Real Wages and Relative Factor Prices Around the Mediterranean Basin 1500–1940," paper presented to the *Conference on Long Run Economic Change in the Mediterranean Basin*, Istanbul, Turkey, June 4–6, 1998.